DIGITAL PREPRESS
COMPLETE

Donnie O'Quinn and Matt LeClair

with Steve Furth and Tim Plumer

Hayden
Books

Hayden Books

President
Richard Swadley

Associate Publisher
John Pierce

Publishing Manager
Laurie Petrycki

Managing Editor
Lisa Wilson

Marketing Manager
Stacey Oldham

Acquisitions Editor
Robyn Holtzman

Development Editor
Bront Davis

Copy/Production Editor
Michael Brumitt

Technical Editor
Richard Romano

Publishing Coordinator
Karen Flowers

Cover Designer
Jay Corpus

Cover Illustration
Eric Lindley

Book Designer
Ann Jones

Manufacturing Coordinator
Brook Farling

Production Team Supervisor
Laurie Casey

Production Team
Dan Caparo
Kim Cofer
Terrie Deemer
Jason Hand
Aleata Howard
Linda Knose
Beth Rago
Erich Richter

Indexer
Ben Slen

Digital Prepress Complete

Library of Congress Catalog Number: 96-78103
ISBN: 1-56830-328-9

Printed in the United States of America 1 2 3 4 5 6 7 8 9 0

Warning and Disclaimer

TRADEMARK ACKNOWLEDGMENTS

ABOUT THE AUTHORS

Donnie O'Quinn and Matt LeClair met as English majors at the University of Maine and are now partners in a graphic arts consulting group based in Portland, Maine. They've worked in digital prepress as designers, production specialists, and educators for over eight years.

They welcome your comments and suggestions. E-mail them at OQLeC@gwi.net.

DEDICATION

To our families:

Don, Lois, & Sharon O'Quinn

Henry, Ethel, Stephen & Jeff LeClair, Caritha Curti

ACKNOWLEDGMENTS

Thanks to the many people without whom this book would not have been possible: Steve Kurth and Tim Plumer for their invaluable contributions; Dave Rogelberg and Studio B for keeping things in perspective; Michael Brumitt and Bront Davis for all the laughter and tears; Colleen Caron for wine, support, and hand massages every 10,000 words; Rachael Dyer for her infinite patience and understanding; Lynda Weinmann for getting us on the right track; Laurie House, for believing in us; Adam Cassel and Fred K. Gildred III for their sage advice; Mike Johnson and Kerry Scammell of Maine Printing Exchange; Christine Morgan for her encouragement and combat stories; and finally, all the purveyors of fine coffee and micro-brewed beer in Portland's scenic Old Port.

HAYDEN BOOKS

The staff of Hayden Books is committed to bringing you the best computer books. What our readers think of Hayden is important to our ability to serve our customers. If you have any comments, no matter how great or how small, we'd appreciate your taking the time to send us a note.

You can reach Hayden Books at the following:

Hayden Books
201 West 103rd Street
Indianapolis, IN 46290
317-581-3833

Email addresses:

America Online:	Hayden Bks
Internet:	hayden@hayden.com

Visit the Hayden Books Web site at `http://www.hayden.com`

CONTENTS AT A GLANCE

TABLE OF CONTENTS

Chapter **1**

INTRODUCTION: DIGITAL PREPRESS COMPLETE

Prepress refers to every step involved in moving a publication from its initial concept to its final form on paper. If you are responsible for any single stage of that process, whether you are a print broker, an artist, a designer, an output technician, or a printer, you are a prepress professional.

Your success and your profitability depend on understanding the entire prepress process, not just your specific responsibilities. If you work in print publishing, you're part of a chain. The choices you make affect every other link of that chain. An error made by an artist can result in a file that cannot be output to film. An incorrect command made by a scanner operator can cause problems that aren't noticed until the publication is on press. Mistakes in any stage of the process cause missed deadlines and cost overruns, the bane of any graphic arts professional.

The introduction of the computer into the prepress process has increased the need for understanding the entire process. Digital prepress is transforming the entire print industry. It has increased capabilities and reduced costs and turn-around times. At the same time, however, digital prepress makes the entire prepress process even more integrated. The professionals are more interdependent than ever before.

CONVENTIONAL PREPRESS

To understand digital prepress, we must first discuss conventional prepress. Despite all the changes computers have wrought, we're still doing the same thing we have been for centuries: putting ink on paper. The methods may have changed, but the responsibilities have not.

In the conventional prepress process, the publication goes through a complex lifecycle involving many professionals responsible for a specific stage or task.

Conceptualizing and Designing

At this stage, an individual or a group decides what the project is, how it will look, the number of pages, and the publication's budget. This information is then handed to the designer, who creates a series of *roughs*—rough sketches made by hand, giving a general idea of the placement of the text and graphics. The roughs may be crudely drawn, but they have to be accurate in all measurements and specifications.

Typesetting and Image Acquisition

Creation, design, and typesetting were originally done by the same person: a monk who hand-lettered every page.

Guttenburg's invention of movable type considerably improved things. Letters were dipped in ink and pressed onto paper. The process was still laborious, requiring hand placement of every letter of every word of every sentence and so on, but after they were in place, multiple copies of the page could be printed. When you think about it, things really didn't change for the next 500 years. Although inventions, such as film and electronics, have made things a little faster and easier, until the introduction of the computer, things were completely hands-on. Lines of type still had to be put into place by hand, whether those lines were made of wood, metal, or photographic film.

Working with images also has changed very little. From woodcuts to metallic engraving to photographic images, the size of the images in print must still be planned in advance and hand placed in the proper position.

Paste-Up, Stripping, and Impositioning

The use of film for printing created jobs for new types of prepress professionals. The designer would give the text and the type specifications to the typesetter, who was responsible for the font, style, weight, and spacing of the type. The type had to be specified and output precisely in order to fit within its designated spaces.

The typesetter would finally composite the type using a linotyper, or some other device. This type was given to a paste-up professional, where the type was fixed to its proper place on the paste-up board with sticky wax. The paste-up person also was responsible for placing black FPO (for placement only) boxes where the images would be. The pages were shot with a camera and the negatives made were given to the stripper, the person responsible for preparing and arranging plate films.

Images, acquired with a camera, were then enlarged or reduced through photographic processes to the proportions of the FPO boxes. Negatives were made and given again to the stripper, who was relied upon for checking and correcting everything, from cropping and dimensions to register and cut marks. All films were taped into place on sheets of plastic or paper.

These assembled sheets, called *flats*, were then *imposed*, or taped, to larger sheets exactly as they were to be printed, ensuring the accuracy of page numbers after these sheets were folded and trimmed. These were made into lithographic plates, which would be used to apply ink to paper on-press.

Proofing and Revising

Proofing at one time required that a few pages be printed and carefully examined. If there were errors, new negatives were created and then stripped in *very* carefully into the problem areas so that they lined up perfectly with the existing text and images. They were made into plates once again and reprinted, and the process was repeated until everything was perfect.

An entire print project could easily take months to complete. There were many responsibilities and the entire process was tightly integrated. A mistake made by one person was felt all the way down the line. If the designer didn't specify type properly, the typesetter would output type that the paste-up person couldn't use. If the person photographing and scaling the images scaled the image too large, the stripper might unknowingly crop the image to fit the FPO, and the mistake would not be discovered until pages were printed.

Though the methods have changed, this interconnection and level of responsibility remain the same with digital prepress.

DIGITAL PREPRESS

Digital technology has blurred the lines distinguishing the various prepress tasks. The laws of physics defining the needs of a printing press have not changed, however; the goals and issues of a digital prepress are the same as any traditional process.

Conceptualizing

An individual or a group decides what the project is, how it will look, how many pages it is going to be, and what the budget for the publication will be.

This information is then given to the designer. The designer makes a series of roughs, pages created on the computer using generic dummy text and FPO clip art images, and outputs them on a laser printer. The roughs provide a fairly accurate representation of what the final piece is going to look like. The dummy text in the digital rough draft can be swapped out and replaced with the true copy. The FPO images can be replaced by the actual images and the rough is transformed into the final document. Everything can be quickly and easily edited and changed.

Designing

In digital publishing, many of the disciplines formerly requiring seasoned professionals—typesetting, design, acquisition, color correcting—are often performed by the same person.

The designer receives text in digital form. She can freely change the font, the size, the style, the position of the text on the page. In this sense, she is both the typesetter and paste-up person. She can scan in photographs, crop them, scale them, color correct them, and put them into position on the page. In this sense, she is both the image acquisition person and the stripper.

The biggest difference in digital prepress is that she can continually change and edit her pages and images right up to the final output. If there is a problem with the text, she can enter the change with a click of the mouse and a few taps on the keyboard, rather than involving typesetting, paste-up, and stripping in the process.

Proofing and Revising

Even with digital prepress, the only way to truly see what the project will look like is to run a job on-press. With digital proofing systems, however, you can come very close. By examining printouts from laser printers and color inkjet printers, which can be output quickly and inexpensively, you can identify and eliminate most, if not all, problems before costly films, plates, and prints are made. With digital proofing systems, you get almost instantaneous feedback (see Chapter 18, "Proofing"). Changes can be made to the digital file by the designer without the need to involve an entire team of people.

Printing

Printing is the one thing that has remained relatively constant throughout the change from conventional to digital prepress, yet it is changing rapidly. In the final stages of the process, films are made and used to create plates (see Chapter 19, "Output"). When digital prepress began 10 years ago, files were output on a laser printer or other printer, and then shot to film, just as paste-ups were shot to film in conventional prepress. Then that film was used to make plates. Now, the digital file is output directly to film and systems that image directly to plate are becoming increasingly common.

Making the Transformation

Digital prepress has simplified the process of getting things into print, but it has not reduced the responsibilities. It has changed the roles and the expectations. As stated earlier, what was once the domain of highly-trained experts, now often falls squarely onto the shoulders of one person. If you are reading this book, that person is probably you.

Despite the power of digital prepress, you have a lot working against you. There are no experts. Ten years is not enough time to produce experts, especially not in a field that changes as rapidly as this one. It takes decades to produce an expert typesetter, and theirs is a field that has changed relatively little in the 500 years since it began.

Fortunately, there is hope. You are not working in isolation. Many people are involved in the process of bringing a publication into physical existence. You need only look as far as your service bureau or printer. It's in the best interest of all of them to see that you succeed.

Also, you can feel safe with the knowledge that nearly everything that can go wrong during the development of an electronic file is predictable and avoidable. First, you have to abandon some misconceptions spawned by the incestuous coupling of marketing hype and wish-fulfillment fantasies.

Computers Are Not Magic

For the majority of people living in this country, computers are still new. They are an alien invasion sweeping over the land, transforming our society, our culture, and our way of life. People have found themselves completely surrounded by computers almost overnight, with little or no choice in the matter, and little or no preparation or education. Never before in the history of human civilization have such sweeping, transformative, technological changes happened to so many in so short a time, and these changes are accelerating. Because of this, people's expectations have not caught up with the reality of computer technology. Generally speaking, people expect far more of you than is realistically possible because you are using a computer; and we tend to expect more of ourselves than is possible, too. How many times have you said, "I'll have this done in 10 minutes," only to find that you are still working on it two hours later.

It is up to you to know what the computer can and can't do, and what you are personally capable of. Being able to communicate this information to your client or your employer goes a long way toward avoiding misconceptions and false expectations.

Computers Will Not Do Your Work For You

Many people are frustrated and disappointed because they invested thousands of dollars into technology, only to discover that there is no single "Make Art" command. A common scenario just happened to a friend of ours. Her boss plopped a computer down on her desk, expecting her to suddenly be able to produce the company newsletter. She protested and her boss replied, "What? You have a computer now, don't you?"

The computer is just a tool. It will do nothing for you that you don't instruct it to do. In the digital prepress arena, it means that you need to be aware of the requirements of every stage of the process and to make sure those requirements are met.

No One Works in a Vacuum

It is the rare person indeed who accomplishes every task from design to print. Digital prepress is a complex chain involving many different people and you are part of that chain. Your actions affect others and their actions affect you. It is up to you to understand what your role is in that chain, and how the choices you make affect every other part of the process. Communication is of utmost importance in assuring that a project makes it into print on time and as you envisioned it.

The initial concept of the project is directly tied to the final printing and to every step along the way. Every job must begin with a call to the printer and work backward from there. Here is just one example of what can happen otherwise. A designer at a printing company pitched a brochure to a client. Without consulting with the company's printer, she unwittingly included a complicated seven-fold. When the printer got the job, he came to the designer, absolutely livid. The requested fold was nearly impossible to do in-house. "Look at it this way," he said. He picked up a piece of paper and folded it in half. "Five hundred dollars," he said. He folded the paper again. "A thousand dollars." He folded the paper a third time. "Fifteen hundred." He kept going until the seventh fold, each one adding another $500 to the total cost of the project. The cost of the folding was not included in the estimate, and because the special fold was promised to the client, the company had to eat the cost. All problems could have been easily avoided if only the designer had spoken to the printer first.

You Cannot Be Passive

Unless you're independently wealthy and working in the digital graphic arts strictly for the fun of it, you're in it for the money. You are either a freelancer or you are working for someone else. Either way, your income depends upon getting your job done. Getting it done right results in more money. This means reducing the amount of deadline-induced stress. Getting the job done right means that you have to *make it happen*.

Troubleshooting is NOT a Solution

Finding output-oriented problems and fixing them is a great idea. So is an emergency tracheotomy performed by a paramedic, but the damage has already been done. By the time you've found out what the problem is and fixed it, you've already spent time and money. This is unacceptable. The only true troubleshooting is doing it right in the first place. This can only happen if you understand the steps in the process.

THE GOAL OF THE DIGITAL PREPRESS PROFESSIONAL

Our goals are simple: to produce work on time, under budget, and with the highest quality possible. But this is a tricky industry. It's difficult and counter-intuitive. There are many steps and many things that go wrong along the way.

You can, however, take control. At every step of the process, you can ensure that things happen flawlessly. You can optimize our computer to avoid crashes and corrupted files. You can prepare your files to ensure that the person outputting to film will be able to output them properly, without problems.

It takes time, effort and commitment, but the rewards are many: decreased frustration, lower costs, faster turn-around, and the respect and admiration of colleagues, supervisors, and clients.

Most important, if you meet the challenges of digital prepress, you become more profitable.

THE GOALS OF THIS BOOK

The goal of this book is to increase your productivity and profitability. It does this by providing you with an understanding of the complete digital prepress process and where you fit into it. It demonstrates how everything you do affects every subsequent step of the process. It teaches not just the steps, but the *reasons* for the steps involved in the process. By understanding why things are done the way they are, you can intuitively know the right way to do things and how to avoid the mistakes that cause missed deadlines, wasted money, and lost clients.

Chapter 2

CREATING THE WORK ENVIRONMENT

The horror of the situation sunk in slowly. The technology manager swept his arm around the room at the six Performa 630s with 13-inch monitors, 230MB hard drives, and no external storage devices.

"...and I got this all set up." he said proudly.

The newly formed digital design group was in trouble. They knew it, but they didn't know how much trouble the were really in. But they would, soon enough. That's why we were there. If only they'd called us sooner. Now they had less than a month to design the packaging, manuals, and marketing materials for the company's most important product launch in years on pathetically inadequate machines.

It was almost a worst-case scenario.

In this section, we are going to go through all of the elements necessary to create a productive work environment. A productive environment is one in which the digital graphic artist works quickly and efficiently. This doesn't just mean that the trash cans are empty and the coworkers are happy. It means that all aspects of the environment, from the furniture to the lighting to the computer to the files on the computer itself, are arranged in such a way that the digital graphic artist can work as safely, as comfortably, as quickly, and as efficiently as possible.

ONE: THE HARDWARE YOU NEED

Most people responsible for purchasing digital prepress systems fail to realize that print publishing uses the computer more intensively than just about anything else. Applications use up all of the processor speed, hard drive space, and memory you can throw at them and still want more. Most computer vendors and people responsible for setting up and maintaining computers in the workplace are not used to this. Their experience is mostly with word processing, spreadsheets, and other applications that only use a fraction of most computer's resources—even wimpy ones. Logically, they make their purchasing decisions on their past experiences which, unfortunately, do not apply to the world of print. Digital prepress has demands that are different from other computer uses. Failure to meet these demands results in lost productivity and wasted time.

Digital prepress has one thing in common with other computer-based industries. You need a computer. This seems obvious, but obvious doesn't mean easy. Thousands of choices can be made when it comes to purchasing computer hardware, and all of them affect productivity in some way.

Tip

When it comes to purchasing the hardware, one general rule of thumb is: the more you spend, the more productive you can be if you make educated spending decisions.

Five key parts to a computer affect your ability to work more than anything else. These are the operating system, the central processing unit (CPU), the monitor, the keyboard, and the pointing device.

The Operating System

The first choice to make is which operating system to run on your computer. You have many operating systems to choose from, such as Macintosh OS,

Windows 95, Windows NT, OS/2, and UNIX. For digital prepress purposes, your choice is between the Macintosh OS, Windows 95 (or Windows, as it is most commonly referred to), Windows NT, or a combination of the three. Deciding which to use is a source of interminable debates, heated arguments, and sometimes, political battles.

The Macintosh OS

If you have the option, you should be doing digital prepress on a Macintosh-based computer. This is not out of any sort of personal bias or misguided product loyalty. We are business people. We enjoy our work, but, in all honesty, we are really in it for the money. If there were another computer that would make our work easier, help us to produce more efficiently, save us time or money, we would switch in an instant. There really isn't any other choice when it comes to digital prepress. If you are serious about creating for print, your only choice is a Macintosh. The Macintosh platform is the industry standard for digital prepress. Eighty percent of all digital prepress takes place on the Macintosh.

There are many reasons for this. The Macintosh was created to be a graphics machine. The PC was created to be a number cruncher. When the PC was created, it could only display text. No graphics. And the text could only be displayed at one size. The Mac, however, supported graphics, fonts, and font sizes from the very beginning. Everything that makes digital prepress possible became commercially viable on the Macintosh first, including graphics and the linchpin of the computer industry, PostScript. The Macintosh was designed from the start to be able to handle these things, whereas all of these were added as an afterthought to the PC.

What this means to you is that although the major digital prepress applications are available for both PCs and Macs, making them work for you is much easier and cost effective on the Mac. You will have more reliable and consistent output from a Macintosh. Service bureaus have a more difficult time outputting PC files. This is probably a combination of the inability to predict how the PC is going to handle the PostScript code, and lack of operator knowledge of the PC. People responsible for outputting the files are much more experienced with Macintoshes than PCs since it has been a standard for so much longer. Whatever the reasons, PC files take longer to print at the service bureaus, which makes them more expensive to use. Files created on the PC can cost 50 to 100 percent more to output.

This will change, of course. Historically, service bureaus have been able to charge more for, or turn away, PC files, but as more and more people demand that their PC files be output, service bureaus must adapt or die.

Adobe, the creator of PostScript and one of the major players on the digital prepress field, is working very hard to make digital prepress viable on the PC. The release of Adobe PageMaker 6.5 occurred first for Windows 95. This is, perhaps, the first time in the history of the industry that a major prepress application has come out for Windows before the Macintosh. On the other hand, Microsoft, the maker of Windows and current controller of the destiny of the PC, sees the future as being multimedia and the Internet, not print, and their support of the platform as a print solution is not what many people would wish it to be. We need to keep an eye towards the future, but we really must be making money right here, right now, today. Today, and most likely tomorrow as well, the Macintosh platform is where that is happening. The day after that, we'll see about.

Windows 3.1 and 95

Given that the majority of all computers in the world are Windows-based, you may have little choice in the matter of operating systems. You may be working for a business that is Windows-based, or you may have already invested years in learning the Windows operating system and invested thousands into the hardware. Don't fret. Yes, you can do prepress on Windows machines. The information we are presenting to you is even more vital to you than it is to Mac OS users. You have far less margin for error when it comes to setting up your system and preparing files. You are going to be sending files to service bureaus and printers who are far more experienced with Macintoshes than they are with PCs. They are more familiar with the problems on the Mac and how to fix them. Sure, they are going to charge for the time spent fixing a Mac file just as they would a PC file, so it is vitally important to do things right on the Mac as well. It is essential that you do things right on the PC because you are going to pay a premium for your mistakes if you don't.

Don't consider using anything less than Windows 95. Windows 3.1 is not suitable for prepress production for many reasons. Windows 95 manages memory better and crashes less often. It allows for longer file names, which greatly facilitates workflow and file management (see Chapter 5, "File Management"). Windows 95 prints faster than 3.1, and networking is also faster. Running Windows 95 may require upgrading your hardware with more RAM, a faster hard drive and a faster processor, but if you are serious about prepress, you should have all of these things anyway.

Windows NT 4.0

To be honest, though, if you are serious about doing digital prepress, you should be working under Windows NT 4.0. If you are doing prepress on a Windows machine, consider upgrading to Windows NT. Not only is Windows NT faster, but it operates with a stability that makes even the most hard-core Mac fanatics envious. It is also necessary to be running NT to take advantage of the full power of the new Pentium Pro and multi-processor systems.

The speed of Windows NT is primarily because of its lack of 16-bit code. Windows 95 was written so that users could make the transition from the 16-bit Window 3.1, so there is a lot of leftover 16-bit code in the operating system. 16-bit code runs far less efficiently than 32-bit. On a Pentium Pro processor, 16-bit code runs more slowly than on a slower Pentium processor, because the code has to go through another step, called thunking, which converts the 16-bit code into code that the 32-bit processor can use. Windows NT was designed from the ground up to be native 32-bit, so it runs much faster and more efficiently than Windows 95.

Windows NT has other advantages that are greatly important in the production environment. Pre-emptive multitasking allows the processor to be shared simultaneously by multiple applications. While both the Mac and Windows 95 operating systems enable you to have multiple applications open, they don't allow for true multi-tasking. You can't copy a file, format a drive, and be working on an image in Photoshop at the same time. While there are certain applications and utilities that enable you to do this, it is not without a significant performance decrease in all of the applications involved. This is not the case in Windows NT.

Windows NT also uses protected memory. Programs open in their own area of memory. If they crash, they don't affect any other open applications. If you crash in the Windows 95 or Mac OS, chances are you lose everything that hasn't been saved in any open application. This rarely happens with Windows NT.

The big drawback to Windows NT is that hardware and software must be precisely configured in order to work. All communication between software and hardware goes through NT, as opposed to the hardware/software combination with Windows 95 and the Mac OS. This means that hardware must be specifically designed with Windows NT in mind. Software also needs to be written to run native in 32-bit. The advantages of the NT system far outweigh these drawbacks, though.

Tip

If you want the advantages of NT but still need to run Windows 95 or even Windows 3.1, you can easily create a double-boot or even a triple-booting system by installing all of these operating systems on your computer. You need to decide which system you need to be operating with at startup. You can't change operating systems without restarting the computer. Consult the manual that came with your system software for more information.

Developers are hard at work creating the CHRP, or common hardware reference platform, and new PowerPC processors, which will run both the Windows and Mac operating systems, so you will be able to run as many different operating systems as you want to without needing to purchase separate machines. Perhaps this will finally end the annoying Mac versus PC debates.

THE CENTRAL PROCESSING UNIT

The CPU is what most people think of when it comes to computers. The CPU is an information storage, retrieval, and manipulation unit. It is the brain of the computer, if you will. The monitor, keyboard, and pointing device enable you to interact with the computer, but the CPU is where all the action happens. When people talk about the type of computer, it is the CPU and the operating system that the CPU is capable of running which determines this. This combination is also known as the platform.

You need to take into account several things when deciding which CPU to buy. The CPU consists of the processor, the motherboard, the internal hard drive, the RAM, the ROM, the VRAM, the buses, and, on the Power Macs and Pentiums, the level 2 Cache. Everything affects the performance of the computer, but you should never compromise on three elements: the processor, the RAM, and the hard drive.

The Processor

If we think of the CPU as a brain, the processor is the cerebral cortex. This is where all the thinking is done, or in computer terms, where the data is processed. The faster the CPU, the faster the data is processed. The way the processor is made also affects the speed. This is where things get tricky. Currently, all new Macintosh computers are being made with either a 603 processor or a 604 processor. Those numbers really don't mean anything. They're just unimaginative names to differentiate between types of chips and are not measures of performance. Both the 603 and the 604 are PowerPC RISC chips, but the 604 processor works far more efficiently than the 603. A 603 processor and a 604 processor can have the same clock speed, but the 604 processor is able to carry out instructions at roughly twice the speed of a 603 processor. The 604 processor uses more power, runs hotter, and costs more than the 603, so it is used primarily in high-end systems. The 603 is used primarily in Performas and Powerbooks.

The rule here is not to be deceived by numbers. You want to get the fastest computer you can, but you need to look at overall speed, not just the MHz. Retail ads scream out the clock speed of the computers they sell as if they actually were the definitive measure of speed. But a computer with a 120 MHz 603 processor will run slower than one with an 80 MHz 604. When comparing CPU speeds, do so in a relative sense. Only compare clock speeds within processor families, whether it is the 68040, 601, 604, Pentium or other processor.

What Processor Should You Get?

Get the fastest processor you can afford. You really can't afford to get anything less. While there are many things that affect the speed of the computer, the speed of the processor ultimately controls how fast your computer runs, and its speed is set in stone. Don't consider getting anything less than a higher-end Power Mac or Pentium. If you are using an older computer, one with a 486 or 68040 processor or lower, it is time to think about donating your computer to a school. The increase in performance between the 604 processor and the 68040 processor is so great that if you haven't yet upgraded, you are throwing away time and money. The same is true for Windows systems running 486 or lower processors.

Remember, however, that a Pentium Pro running non-native 32-bit applications will run them slower than a regular Pentium, thereby defeating the purpose of having a faster processor. Don't purchase a Pentium Pro if you aren't going to make the commitment of running fully 32-bit native applications, and this includes the operating system. Similarly, applications that are not written to run native on PowerMacs will run faster on non-PowerMac processors.

The Price of Slow Processors

The most important reason for getting the fastest processor you can is a truth that people have known for a very long time: time is money. This is the most important thing to realize. If you take one thing away from this book let it be that. The faster the computer, the less time it will take to get the job done. The faster the computer, the less time you will spend doing nothing while you wait for the computer to do what you want it to.

To the technology manager who bought cheap computers that were never meant for anything more than non-professional home use, we might have asked, "How cheap is it to have employees sitting around doing nothing?," which is exactly what he was condemning them to do. Businesses can't afford to get their employees anything less than the best. Anything less is just going to be wasting money.

The situation for freelancers is slightly different. If a freelancer is billing by the job, every second longer that the job takes is a second for which you're not getting paid. If you are billing by the hour it is slightly different. You can still be making money while you sit around waiting for the computer. This is very risky in the highly competitive and fickle graphic design market. What happens when someone comes along who can give their clients the same quality work as you at half the price, since they are able do the same amount of work you are in half the time?

Multiple Processors

Of course, as with everything in computers, there are no hard-and-fast rules. Computers now have more than one processor, such as the Daystar Genesis machines, which have four. It stands to reason that if machines with the fastest processors are the most cost-effective, then machines with more processors would be even more cost-effective, right? Yes and no. In an ideal world, this would be the case. Unfortunately only applications which are multi-threaded, written to take advantage of multiple processors, benefit from having them. If the software you need to run isn't written this way, not only will you receive no benefit, but you might even receive speed penalties. Even if you are using multi-threaded applications, having two processors won't make things run twice as fast. Many other factors dictate the speed of the computers. Adding another processor might only give you a 50 percent speed boost.

Thanks to its pre-emptive multitasking capabilities, Windows NT is in a position to take advantage of multiple processors in ways that Windows 95 or the Mac OS can't. Even applications that are not multi-threaded can benefit when running on a multi-processor NT system, since NT can allocate a separate processor to each application.

More and more applications are being written to use multiple processors and the cost of these machines is dropping steadily. Be sure, however, to check that the applications you need are multi-threaded before you invest the extra money in multiple processors. Photoshop is one program that is multi-threaded. If the majority of your time is spent doing high-end photo retouching in PhotoShop, or if you are running Windows NT, you may want to consider purchasing a multi-processor system. Otherwise, your money is better spent elsewhere.

Upgradable Processors

When you buy a CPU, the processor will come in one of three ways. It will either be soldered to the motherboard, on a card, or in a removable socket. If the processor is soldered to the motherboard, then it can only be upgraded by replacing the entire motherboard. Upgrade cards are available, but these usually provide only some of the benefits of a complete processor upgrade. If the processor is in a socket or on a card, then it can be upgraded cheaply, easily, and with a high degree of compatibility with your existing hardware and software.

Socketed processors have been fairly standard on the Windows side for some time now, but currently only the higher-end PowerMacs come with their processors on cards. It is worth the extra expense of purchasing a computer with an upgradable processor as it will extend the useful life of your computer and help you get the most from your investment.

Random Access Memory

The RAM, or Random Access Memory would be roughly equivalent to a human's short term memory. When people talk about how much memory a computer has, this is what they are referring to. The processor controls how fast the computer can *think*, and the RAM controls how much the computer can think *about* at one time. Picture the last time someone told you an important phone number and you repeated it over and over to yourself so that you wouldn't forget it. After you wrote it down, you forgot it completely. As long as you make the effort to keep that thought you can remember it long enough to write it down, unless something interrupts or distracts you. RAM is *volatile,* just like short-term memory, which means that unless energy is spent maintaining it, it disappears.

When you launch a program on a computer, all or part of it loads into RAM. Things happen in RAM far faster than they do on the hard drive, because RAM has no moving parts. The activity in RAM is a pure dance of electricity through silicon. Most programs load themselves into RAM entirely if there is enough available. There, the program can execute commands at an incredibly fast speed. If there is not enough RAM for the entire program to load, then the program will load only the part of itself that is currently being used, while the rest stays on the hard drive. If there is too much going on in RAM when the program tries to access the part that is still on the hard drive, then you will get a message like "Insufficient memory to complete command."

Note that if something is on the hard drive it remains on the hard drive even when it is loaded into RAM. When you launch a program, the program makes a copy of itself in RAM while the program itself remains on the hard drive unaffected.

Just like programs, the part of the file you are working on also loads. The rest of the file is read from the hard drive when it needs to be. Changes made to this file stay in RAM until it gets re-written to the hard drive when the file is saved.

Get Enough RAM!

The most common mistake people make when getting a new computer is not getting enough RAM. Too many times we have seen people buy the top of the line computer only to be incredibly frustrated when they find that they can't do anything because they haven't installed enough memory. Digital prepress takes a lot of memory. As well as being among the most processor-intensive programs, digital prepress programs are also the among the biggest memory hogs. Most people who are familiar with computers but haven't done prepress before are completely unprepared for the amount of memory it is going to take. They are used to word processing, spreadsheet, or simple graphics applications, which only use a fraction of the memory. The unfortunate technology manager at the beginning of the chapter provided the Performas with 32MB of RAM, which seemed like an incredible amount to him. This paltry sum borders on uselessness for the jobs that they were planning to do.

Here is an example. The same technology manager planning on creating magazine ads with graphics with full-page bleeds. The magazines that these were going to be printed in required an image 11.25 inches by 8.75 inches. The images needed to be in CMYK and at 300 ppi. Aside from basic RAM requirements, the image size alone, was 33.8 megabytes! We already know that the processor speed of the Performas was inadequate for the job at hand. The problem was compounded by insufficient memory. Every byte of the image that was being worked on that didn't fit into RAM had to be written to the hard drive every single time even a slight change was made. Every brush stroke, every copy and paste, every time one element was retouched. Slow? It was torture! Things that could have been done in minutes on a proper machine took hours!

Open files are just one thing that eats up your precious memory. The applications themselves require a certain amount of memory just to be open. We'll be getting more into specific memory needs of programs in Chapter 3. The minimum amount of memory that Adobe recommends for Photoshop is 10.3MB. We've found that minimum recommended amounts are all but useless recommendations. They are just the smallest amounts you can have and still open the program, but if you try to actually do anything, the computer will crash or you will get insufficient memory messages. A little more useful are the suggested memory sizes. The suggested memory for Photoshop running on a Power Mac is 13.4MB. This is still low, but it will do in a pinch, if that is all you have to give to it, or if you have a lot of other applications you need to have running at the same time. Here is where we immediately see how useless a Power Mac with 16MB of RAM is, which is how much the 9500s originally shipped with. The System alone will use up 8MB or more of RAM. At the absolute minimum, Photoshop needs 10MB just to open. Photoshop can't even open on this machine, even though it has one of the fastest processors on the market! If you don't have enough RAM your computer is useless as far as prepress goes.

How Much Is Enough?

As much as you can afford, and then some. In all honesty, unless you are doing very specific things that don't require a lot of RAM, you will never have enough RAM. But you can get enough to get the job done.

It largely depends on what kind of prepress work you are doing:

◆ Will you be working in color or black and white? If you know for a fact that you will never be working in color, your RAM needs are significantly reduced. That 33.8MB full-bleed, full-page graphic that we talked about previously becomes a mere 8MB when it is in black and white. Typically, black-and-white graphics are a fourth to a third of the size of color graphics.

◆ Will you be creating 11×17 full page bleeds?

◆ Are you going to be doing a lot of image compositing, where you will need to have many graphics open at once?

◆ Are you going to be working on poster-size images?

◆ Are you going to be working on images for billboards?

The answers to these questions affect how much minimum RAM you will need.

The next question is how efficiently do you want to work? Producing a publication typically requires three programs: a page layout program, such as Quark or PageMaker; a drawing program, such as Illustrator or FreeHand; and a paint program, such as Photoshop. We will go into depth about these different programs and why you need them in this chapter's software section. To work most efficiently, you should be able to have these three types of programs open simultaneously. Even if you're a graphic designer at the end of the chain, assembling the text and graphics that others have created to make a document in a page layout program, you still need to do a certain amount of graphics manipulation. With enough memory, you can jump effortlessly between page layout, drawing, and painting programs. Otherwise, if you need to change a graphic, you will have to save your publication, quit your page layout program, open up the graphic in the graphics program, modify the graphic, save it, quit the program, and re-open your publication in the page layout program. Hopefully, you got the graphic right, because if you didn't you have to go through the whole thing again. Every time you have to quit out of an application and launch another you are wasting valuable minutes.

The absolute minimum of RAM required to do digital prepress is 48MB. This may sound like an intimidating amount, but RAM will pay for itself quickly. If you must, start with the minimum amount, but add more as soon as you can. You'll be glad you did.

Purchasing RAM

Computers are configured with a standard amount of RAM, usually 8, 16, or 32MB, so you will have to add more when you buy a new computer. Either have your vendor install the RAM, or order it through a third-party mail order company and install it yourself. Both ways have their advantages. You can often find great deals on RAM through mail order. Installing RAM is fairly safe and simple if you follow the instructions the mail order company provides. If they don't provide instructions, take your business elsewhere.

The advantage to having the vendor install the RAM when you buy your computer is that, although you might have to pay a little more, the work is guaranteed. If a stray static spark happens to fry the motherboard, your vendor will have to replace it, whereas if you fry it yourself, you are out of luck. Vendors often give discounts on RAM if you purchase it with your computer as well. Bargain with them. It never hurts to ask, and it can save you money.

Here are a few key RAM issues to keep in mind when you buy a new computer:

◆ How much RAM comes installed on the computer? Most computers from Apple, with the exception of the high-end Macs come with memory permanently soldered to the motherboard. This is a practice that is virtually non-existent on the Windows side. High-end Macs and most Windows computers come with a certain amount of RAM installed in Simmers or DIMMs. This is one instance when less is best. Computer manufacturers charge a premium for the memory they install. You can save yourself a lot of money by purchasing a computer with the minimum amount of RAM installed and purchasing the RAM from a third-party vendor.

◆ How much RAM will the computer support? All computers have an upper limit as to how much RAM they can hold. The limit for the Performa 630s that our much maligned technology manager bought was 32MB. Had everything else about the computer been adequate, this limit would have prevented it from ever becoming a useful computer.

◆ How many RAM slots does the computer have? RAM comes on cards that can be snapped into slots on the motherboard of the computer. The more slots you have the better off you are. If you can only afford just enough RAM to start with, you can add more RAM later on, when you can afford it, but only if you have enough slots. Those Performa 630s only had two slots for RAM. This means that even if the computer could handle more RAM, the 32MB it already had would have to be taken out in order to make room for the new memory. The old chips would have to be sold, given away, or moved to another machine. Any option would have resulted in a loss. You want to be able to add more memory in the future without losing what you already have. If possible, buy machines that have eight memory slots.

◆ What memory configurations does the computer support? Do memory modules need to be in matched sets? The first generation of PowerMacs, the 6100, 7100, and 8100 needed to have the memory installed in matched pairs. This makes upgrading memory a hassle, because you always have to do things in twos. If a friend gave you a 16MB SIMM that she happened to have lying around, you would need to buy another 16MB SIMM in order to be able to use it. This isn't quite as bad as the old Macintosh II Fx, which needed the memory installed in sets of four identical Simmers. Currently, most Pentium computers require that RAM be installed in matched pairs. The Pentium will run with mismatched pairs, but it will use the memory according to the lowest denominator. If you used a 8MB DIMM and a 4MB DIMM, then your total usable RAM would be 8MBs instead of 12.

More recent incarnations of the Power Mac, such as the 7600, 8500, and 9500, can accommodate DIMMs in any configuration. You can start with a pair of 32MB DIMMs, throw in an 8MB and a 16MB DIMM later on, and a 64MB DIMM after that. This provides you with tremendous flexibility and the maximizes the value of your purchases.

Some of the newer Power Macs, such as the 7600, 8500 and 9500 again, take advantage of memory interleaving. If you install your memory in pairs, the computer will access the pair at the same time, giving you a speed increase. This is great because you still have the flexibility to add memory as you please. You aren't required to install the memory in pairs. It won't hurt if you don't, and it will give you a slight speed advantage if you do.

Level 2 Cache

Most of the newer Power Macs and Pentium computers support a Level 2 Cache. Level 2 Cache is a special type of RAM that stores recently used, frequently used, or predictably used data where the processor can access it instantly instead of reading this information from the hard drive every time. The computer is using this type of information constantly whether you are aware of it or not. The addition of a Level 2 Cache enhances the performance of your computer 20 percent to 50 percent. Caches come in 256k, 512k, and 1 MB sizes, but 256k is sufficient for digital prepress purposes. A 256k cache can be purchased for under $100. In light of the performance increase and the inexpensiveness of the cache, it is a wonder that they aren't standard on all computers. Make sure the computer you buy supports a Level 2 Cache, and make sure you have one installed if it does.

The Hard Drive

If RAM is like a human's short-term memory, then the hard drive is like long-term memory. Information on the hard drive is non-volatile, unlike information in RAM. When something is put on the hard drive, it stays there until it is removed to make room for other things to be stored (unless something tragic happens and you lose everything, that is. But we'll cover that in Chapter 6).

The hard drive is a spinning platter of oxidized, magnetized metal. There is a head on a movable arm resting just above the surface of the platter that reads and writes the magnetic charges on the platter. Since it has moving mechanical parts, accessing the information on the hard drive takes longer than information in RAM. RAM speeds are measured in nanoseconds, while hard drive speeds are measured in milliseconds.

As with the processor and RAM, spending the extra cash on a larger, faster hard drive enables you to work more quickly and efficiently, and make you more profitable. Working on the computer involves a constant exchange of information between the hard drive and the RAM. The faster the hard drive, the faster this can take place.

How Big Is Big Enough? How Fast Is Fast Enough?

Get the biggest, fastest hard drive you can afford, of course! Getting it right the first time is not as important as it is with the processor and the RAM, since adding external hard drives is quite easy, whereas processor upgrades are costly, if they are possible at all, and computers can only hold a limited amount of RAM. You can hook up external hard drives as your needs grow, however. Still, you need enough to get started. Insufficient disk space will bring you to a screeching halt.

As with RAM, how much is enough depends on the work you are doing. If you are not working with color bitmapped graphics, then your graphics file storage requirements decrease by 60 percent or more. If you are doing large, full-color catalogs with lots of high-resolution graphics, then your storage needs are going to be tremendous. A general rule of thumb is to estimate the largest amount of hard drive space you could ever conceive of using, double it, and buy that size drive. We'd add another 250 to 500 megs on top of that if you are planning on using Photoshop, and, if you are doing digital prepress, that is a given.

Photoshop is a very demanding program. Not only does it demand all the RAM it can get, it also requires that a certain amount of the hard drive be empty of files just to open and work with images. It is easy to generate hundreds of megabytes of Photoshop files without even realizing you are doing it. Unfortunately, most people don't have hundreds of megabytes of RAM. Fortunately, Photoshop is able to use hard drive space as though it were slow RAM. Hard drive space is much cheaper than RAM, and most people have much more hard drive space than they do RAM space. In order for Photoshop to utilize this space, though, it must be empty. If the empty space isn't there, Photoshop will give you a very frustrating, "Primary scratch disk is full" message, and it will not let you do anything you want to do, except for saving the image and quitting the program you can search the hard drive for things to throw away.

We recommend at the barest minimum a hard drive that has enough space to hold the applications you use regularly, the current projects you are working on, and enough space to keep Photoshop happy. If you are working on the Windows platform, we highly recommend a hard drive with enough additional space that you can create the double-booting Windows 95 and Windows NT system we mentioned earlier in this chapter. This means you will need at the absolute minimum a two gigabit hard drive for either platform.

How fast is fast enough? The faster the better, of course! But to be honest, we have found that even the slower models

The Rest of the Stuff in That Box

The computer needs several things in order to run. These do affect performance, but not in the controllable ways that things like RAM, processors, and hard drives do.

Read Only Memory (ROM)

The ROM is kind of like the human brain stem, which contains the essential information necessary to keep the body alive, like hunger and sex drive. ROM stands for Read Only Memory. It holds information that is only read. It can't be written to or changed. It is a vital part of the computer, but is generally not one that affects performance or needs to be changed.

Flash ROM

Some newer Pentiums contain Flash ROM, which can be written to (it makes us wonder why it is still called Read Only). Updating the ROM provides increased compatibility with future software updates. The ultimate in upgradability would be a computer with both a socketed processor and Flash ROM.

The Motherboard

The motherboard is the central nervous system and the bones of the CPU.

continues

> The motherboard is a large card that holds everything and wires it all together. It contains the slots that hold the RAM and the ROM, the cards, and the connectors for the various drives.

of the current crop of hard drives from the major manufacturers such as Seagate or Quantum to be fast enough for most prepress purposes. The exception is, again, Photoshop. If you are doing extensive editing of large Photoshop files, then you should consider upgrading to a high-performance hard drive. Check the manufacturers recommended uses for the drive to find a drive to suit your needs.

EXPANSION

The Processor, the RAM, and the hard drive all control how fast and how efficiently you will be able to work, but this is only part of what you need to consider when you are setting up your prepress system. The next issue is the expandability of the computer. You will be adding many things to your computer, such as a keyboard, a mouse, internal and external hard drives, scanners, monitors, and other things. How many things you can add and how easily it is depends on three things: expansion bays, expansion slots, and ports.

Expansion Bays

Expansion bays enable you to add additional drives to the inside of the CPU. Typically, Windows systems have far more expansion bays than Macintosh systems. This is largely because SCSI ports (see below) are standard on the Macintosh. SCSI ports make it very easy to add external drives to the computer, reducing the need for internal drives.

In the past, we always tried to buy computers with the most expansion bays as possible so that we could have the greatest amount of expandability. We found, however, that we rarely used these expansion bays. External drives are much more versatile because they are much easier to change or move around, whereas any time you need to change an internal drive you have to ground yourself, crack open the case, and muck around inside your computer with a screwdriver.

The advantage to internal drives is that they are cheaper than external drives since they don't need cases or power supplies. We've found that the extra $20 to $80 dollars for an external drive to be well worth it.

We've found two expansion bays to be quite adequate on any system with an external SCSI port. One expansion bay can be used for an internal CD-ROM drive, and another for a secondary hard drive. Sure, it is always nice to have more room for expansion in the future, even if you aren't using it. It gives one a secure feeling, but not enough of a secure feeling to be worth spending a lot of extra money for.

Expansion Slots

Expansion slots greatly enhance the usefulness of your computer, especially on the Windows platform. Expansion slots hold cards that add specific functionality to the computer. They can be anything from modems to video cards to 3-D rendering accelerators to just about anything else.

Expansion slots, also called busses, enhance the functionality of Windows computers more than Macintoshes because traditionally more things come built into the Mac, which are just options on the PC. It is often necessary to add extra cards to a PC in order to get things like sound, video, and SCSI ports, all of which come built into nearly all Macs. On a Mac, it is possible to go through life never needing to add another extra card to your computer. This is rarely an option on Windows machines.

Determining your expansion slot requirements is much easier for the Macintosh. There are only two choices: NuBus and PCI, and NuBus is no longer being used. Two slot types are currently in common use on the PC: ISA and PCI. It is necessary to have a mixture of slot types.

Macintosh: NuBus and PCI

NuBus is an architecture used exclusively on Macintoshes up until the first generation of Power Macs. New Macs are being sold with PCI busses, so there really is no choice to make unless you are considering buying an older Mac. Before you do, though, there are some things to consider. Availability of NuBus cards is very limited now that manufacturers have stopped making computers with NuBus busses. NuBus cards, when you can find them, are slower and more expensive than their PCI counterparts. In other words, get a PCI-based Mac.

PCI cards are used in Macs, PCs, SGIs and others. Manufacturers are now able to make one card for many computers, changing only the software so that it will work with the system it is sold for, which makes PCI cards much cheaper than NuBus cards. PCI cards are also faster than NuBus cards. It is well to your advantage to buy computers that use PCI slots.

In terms of digital prepress on the Macintosh, you will be filling your expansion slots with one of two things: video cards and SCSI-2 or Ultra SCSI cards, all of which we will be talking about later in this chapter. Since newer Macintoshes come with support for fast video displays and support for high resolutions at millions of colors, it is only necessary to install a video card if you are doing high-end color correcting, or if you wish to add a second monitor. It is only necessary to install SCSI-2 or Ultra SCSI cards if you work extensively with very large files (over 50MB).

It is quite possible that you will never need to use your expansion slots on your Macintosh. On the other hand, if you do need them and don't have them, you are totally out of luck. The number and type of expansion slots are not things that can be upgraded. If you can't fit the card you need into your computer, your only options are to do without or to buy a new computer.

For an example again of what *not* to buy, let's turn to the Performa 630 the technology manager was so proud of. The Performa 630 only has one slot for an expansion card, which was bad enough. To make matters worse, the slot was a half-height NuBus card, an obscure variation of the NuBus card, which was even less common than the NuBus card. Having only one slot is limiting enough. Having that one slot be able to only take a very limited supply of cards is even worse. When a 21-inch monitor is needed to be added to one of the stations, there is only one card to choose from. This card occupies the one slot the computer has, thereby eliminating all hope that this computer could ever be upgraded.

You need a computer that will be able to do everything you want it to today, and to have room to grow in the future. A Macintosh with three PCI slots will provide you with that.

Windows: ISA and PCI

Your expansion slot requirements are higher on the Windows side than on the Mac side, since so much less comes standard. Networking, sound, and video support come built into most Macs, while these are things you will need to add on the PC. While you might never need to add a card to a Macintosh, you are going to need to add several to the PC. These will include a SCSI controller, a sound card, a video card, and a network card, if the computer will be part of a work group.

The two main flavors of slots on the PC are ISA and PCI. ISA, like NuBus on the Mac, is slower than PCI. Since ISA cards are much more common than NuBus cards, however, they are much more inexpensive. Not all card uses require top speeds, either. A sound card is a nice option to have, since many applications will provide you with certain auditory cues as to their functioning, but since you will not actually be working with sound, you don't need the speed. PCI cards provide more speed than networks can use, so ISA cards are also fine for networks. PCI cards are vital, however, for video and for SCSI cards, where speed is of utmost importance.

For the highest degree of compatibility to meet your needs now and in the future, get a computer which has a minimum of three ISA slots and four PCI slots.

Ports

Ports enable you to attach peripheral devices to your computer. Unless you want to add SCSI-2 or Ultra SCSI to your Mac, there really aren't any choices to make when it comes to configuring ports on the Macintosh. The SCSI port is standard on the Macintosh. If you buy a peripheral that the manufacturer specifies as being compatible with the Macintosh, you are virtually guaranteed that you will be able to attach the device to one of the ports on your computer and have it work with a minimum of effort.

On the PC, this is much more problematic, because PCs often use less expensive EIDE ports instead of SCSI ports. EIDE is inferior to SCSI in many ways, which makes it unacceptable in the production environment. EIDE controllers can only support two devices, whereas SCSI controllers can support up to seven daisy-chainable devices. This is vital due to the large number of peripheral devices used in digital prepress. EIDE controllers use the computer's processor to handle information, while SCSI controllers use their own built-in hardware. This means that EIDE will decrease the overall performance of the computer by using up valuable processor time in ways which SCSI controllers don't.

By adding a SCSI controller to your PC, you will greatly increase the ease with which you add and remove peripheral devices to and from your Windows computer, as well as the performance of the computer when using external devices. The SCSI controller and the port come on a card that can be added easily into one of the PCI expansion ports.

An additional benefit is that if you are using computers in a mixed Windows and Macintosh environment, you will be able to share drives between the computers with relative ease.

SCSI-2 and Ultra SCSI

SCSI-2 and Ultra SCSI are two types of ports that can be added to your computer by adding cards in the aforementioned expansion slots. SCSI-2 and Ultra SCSI are faster versions of SCSI. SCSI-2 can support speeds up to 20MB/sec, more than twice what standard SCSI is capable of. Ultra SCSI can support speeds of up to 40MB/sec.

Since we've insisted on getting the fastest of everything at every point along the way, why aren't we jumping up and down about SCSI-2 and Ultra SCSI? SCSI-2 and Ultra SCSI are great things, but you pay a premium for their speed. Not only will you need to pay hundreds of dollars more for SCSI-2 and Ultra SCSI drives, you will also need to spend an additional $200 to $500 for an adapter card in order to use them. The speed of a SCSI chain is only as fast as the slowest device on that chain, therefore, if you use a SCSI device on a SCSI-2 chain, or a SCSI or SCSI-2 device on an Ultra SCSI chain, you will lose all the speed benefits.

SCSI-2 and Ultra SCSI are definitely a blessing, often a necessity, if you are working with very large PhotoShop files. Speed is always a great thing to have. Faster is always better, but if you have a limited budget and aren't doing high-end image editing, then your money would be more effectively spent elsewhere. We have found that ordinary high-performance external SCSI hard drives are sufficient for nearly all digital prepress purposes.

Peripheral Devices

Peripheral devices encompass any hardware that can be attached to your CPU, adding essential functionality to your machine. These include keyboards, mice, trackballs, monitors, and so on. Often, these define our interaction with the machine, so be certain to choose your peripheral devices carefully, based on your specific needs.

Keyboard

You've spent thousands on the CPU, don't scrimp on the keyboard. The keyboard and the pointing device are two of the most important parts of the computer, since most of your interaction with the computer will be through them. The nicest keyboards rarely cost more than $130. You'll need a keyboard that has function keys across the top. Many software programs enable you to assign your own functions to these keys. It is a great time saver when you can hit a single key instead of going through pull-down menus to find a command, especially when you have to repeat the same command again and again on a project. Find a keyboard with a lively feel to it when you are typing. If you are going to be typing a lot, you should try out a split ergonomic keyboard. Your hands are your wage-earners. Protect them at all costs.

Pointing Devices

Pointing devices must be able to perform two functions: positioning the cursor and clicking. You can choose from several devices: mice, touchpads, trackballs, and pressure sensitive tablets.

A mouse comes bundled with nearly every computer sold. The mice from both Apple and Microsoft are both excellent . Contoured to fit comfortably in most hands, they have a big responsive button that invites clicking. The only drawback to these mice is that it forces you to hold your hand in an awkward hovering position while you use it, which causes strain after a while. Many users also find themselves limited by having only one button on the mouse. The mouse is sufficient for most digital prepress tasks, but there are many options for those who the mouse fails to meet their needs.

◆ **Trackballs.** The most popular alternative to the mouse is the trackball. The trackball is stationary, which eliminates the need to have your arm hovering above it in order to be able to move it. Trackballs are excellent alternatives for those who have suffered from mouse-strain.

◆ **Touchpads.** Touchpads have been adopted from Powerbooks and are now available as separate pointing devices for desktop computers. Touchpads sense the position of your finger on a square sensing surface. They work great on Powerbooks, but they don't translate as well to the desktop. One advantage they have is that they have no moving parts to break or get dirty, but that is about the only advantage. Your hand will still need to hover above the surface as you would with a mouse, and the learning curve is greater with a touchpad than with a mouse or a trackball.

◆ **Pressure-Sensitive Tablets.** Some people approach pressure-sensitive tablets as alternatives to mice, but really, pressure-sensitive tablets are created to be complementary to other pointing devices. Pressure-sensitive tablets were designed to emulate "traditional" methods of recording information, such as pens or pencils. They use a stylus to send position and pressure information on a tablet. Programs like Painter, Photoshop, and Illustrator can use pressure-sensitive tablets to recreate paint brushes, chalk, ink pens, and so on with surprising realism. The harder you press with the stylus, the greater the effect it will have, just as if you were using a real drawing or painting tool.

Tablets are indispensable tools for anyone creating original artwork on the computer, and especially for those who are schooled in the traditional visual arts and are incorporating the computer into their artistic toolbox. Pressure-sensitive tablets are vital for high-end, precision photo-retouching. The big advantage over the mouse is the pressure-sensitivity. Mice and other pointing devices have two levels of sensitivity: 100 percent or None. The mouse is either clicked or it isn't. Pressure-sensitive tablets, on the other hand, let you have 100 percent, None, and everything in between. For adding shadows and matching subtlety changing tones, pressure-sensitive tablets are indispensable. In fact, they can make creating almost any artwork far more enjoyable and natural on the computer. It is what they were designed for. What they were not designed for, however, is point-and-click and menu oriented functions; they will be a hindrance for such things. Get a pressure-sensitive tablet to increase your range of creative capabilities, not to replace your mouse.

Keyboards and pointing devices on the Macintosh side are daisy-chainable, which means you can hook several of them together in a row, so you don't need to limit yourself to just one. You can have a mouse, a trackball, and pressure-sensitive tablet all hooked up to the same work station. This can be an excellent solution. On the PC side, this can be more problematic, since every device needs its own port. Most PCs come with a port for the mouse, a port for the keyboard, and two serials that can be used to attach a wide variety of pointing devices to your computer.

Monitors and Color Cards

You have a huge range of options when it comes to monitors, ranging from 12-inch black-and-white monitors to 21-inch full-color monitors, ranging in cost from hundreds to thousands of dollars. For digital prepress, however, your choices are severely narrowed. If you are doing high-end color correcting and image editing, you must have a 21-inch color monitor with an accelerated graphics card. If not, then you might get away with spending thousands less and getting a 17-inch multisync monitor.

Note

You stare at the monitor the whole time you are working. Get something that is comfortable to look at for extended periods of time. Don't buy a black-and-white monitor, even if you are only going to be working in black and white. Why? The human eye is used to perceiving things in color. Black-and-white monitors put more strain on the eye than color monitors, making your eyes grow tired faster.

Multisync Monitors

All new color monitors being made now are multisync, meaning that a monitor can emulate monitors of different sizes. Provided with enough VRAM, a 13-inch monitor can display all the information that a 21-inch monitor can, only at a much smaller scale. We really don't recommend that you try to do digital prepress on a 13-inch monitor, although they do have a place in digital prepress. 13-inch monitors on their own are just too small to be useful. They will cause you great eye strain if you have them displaying things that really should be viewed on a 21-inch monitor. For page layout purposes, you really want a monitor that can display in their entirety two 8 1/2 by 11 inch pages side by side at a size that will let you see what they really look like. A 21-inch monitor will let you see two 8 1/2 by 11 pages at a size that is very close to their printed size. This enables you to compose your pages as they were meant to be composed, as whole integrated pieces, which is very hard to do if your monitor is so small that you have to keep scrolling around the page in order to see it. A 21-inch multisync can display as though it were a smaller monitor. This really is only useful when playing computer games, most of which have fixed dimensions of 640x480 (the native resolution of a 13-inch monitor).

Computer games can be quite stunning when played full-screen on a 21-inch monitor. Of course, we would never advocate playing games on your workstation!

A monitor displays images using a grid of squares of light called pixels, which is short for picture element. Pixels are the most basic element of picture. A screen pixel is always the same size, usually 1/72 of an inch, and it can only display one color at a time. When a multisync monitor changes resolution, what is really happening is an illusion. The monitor is emulating other sizes through a process of interpolation. One screen pixel emulates two or more pixels to create the effect that the monitor is larger than it really is. While this is fine for most desktop publishing purposes, it isn't suitable for color correcting, because interpolated monitor resolutions will not give an accurate representation of the color of the monitor. Every monitor will have one native resolution where one screen pixel truly equals one screen pixel, and this is where "true" colors will be displayed. Of course, there is more to getting true colors from your monitor. For more on this, turn to Chapter 14: "Color Management and Proofing Systems."

When Do You Need a 21-inch Monitor?

Don't mess around. If you are serious about color correcting, get a 21-inch monitor and a video card to drive it. Digital prepress requires the use of high-resolution image files. Images can contain 300 pixels per inch or even more. The only way to accurately color-correct an image is when the ratio between the pixels and the monitor is one-to-one. This is when one pixel onscreen represents one pixel in the image. At any other proportion, the screen is interpolating the information. It is either dropping information or creating information to display the image. If your monitor is at 72 pixels per inch, then the image you are correcting needs to be displayed at 72 pixels per inch. If your image is three inches by three inches at 288 ppi, you will need to view it at four times its size on the screen (288 divided by 4 is 72) in order for one screen pixel to represent one pixel in the image. This means that the image will be very large when it is onscreen. Frequently, it will be larger than even a 21-inch monitor can display, but the more the monitor can display of your image, the more efficiently you will be able to work, and the more accurately you will be able to do color correction.

If your work is primarily color correcting or image editing, you need a 21-inch monitor. Anything less and you are working against yourself.

If your work is doing page layout for full-color magazines and catalogs exclusively, you also should get a 21-inch monitor. Only on a 21-inch monitor can you display two 8 1/2×11 page spreads at full size, and this is the only way you can truly get an accurate representation of how the printed piece is going to look without printing it.

You will never get a totally accurate representation of the printed piece until you print it out. If it is absolutely essential that your display is as close to what will be printed as possible, you will have to invest in monitor designed specifically for digital prepress, such as the Radius PressView 21SR. These types of monitors come at a premium, usually $1000 to $2000 more than an ordinary monitor of the same size. For the extra cash, you get absolutely the best quality display money can buy, as well as a host of hardware and software to ensure that the displayed color is accurate and stays accurate.

Most digital prepress work, however, doesn't require such super-critical color representation. Even when it does, proper color calibration and color proofing can go a long way to eliminating the need for a very expensive monitor. (See Chapter 14, "Color Management and Profiling" and Chapter 18, "Proofing.")

When Is a 17-inch Monitor OK?

A 17-inch monitor is acceptable, even preferable, if you will not be doing any high-end color correcting and don't need to see full pages at their actual sizes. A 17-inch monitor will cost you $500 to $1000 less than a 21-inch monitor. Some people actually prefer a 17-inch monitor to a 21-inch because a 17-inch monitor causes less eye strain. This can be a great solution if the work you are doing has that flexibility. Since a multisync monitor can change resolutions without needing to restart the computer, you can work in your monitor's native resolution and change to higher resolutions when you want to get a better idea of what the entire composed page looks like.

When Do You Need a Video Card?

Your Macintosh or PC will come with video, either on a card or on the motherboard. If you can drive a monitor at millions of colors with what you already have in your computer, you may not need to add a video card. You need to be able to display millions of colors if you are working in color. Only a display running millions of colors will display color accurately.

If you are doing high-end color correcting or other image editing, then you need an accelerated video card, also known as an accelerated graphics card. When you are working with bitmapped images, the monitor needs to draw every single pixel it displays, and redraw them every time you move the image onscreen. The higher the resolution of the image, the longer it will take to draw onscreen. Images destined for print are at higher resolutions than images created for any other purpose. Without an accelerated graphics card, working on these images will be a slow process, even if you have a very fast processor. You may be able to process the data fast, but it will only display as fast as the graphics card allows it to.

Recent Power Macs let you add enough video RAM to drive a 21-inch color monitor at 16.7 million colors at speeds that are adequate for page layout. Page layout applications enable you to display images at lower resolutions, thus reducing drawing times (see Chapter 15, "Page Layout Issues"). If you are not doing extensive image editing on your computer, the need for an accelerated graphics card is less critical. It speeds things up when you are doing page layout or working in a vector-based graphics program, but it doesn't make nearly as much difference as it does with image editing.

On the other hand, an accelerated graphics card is a powerful addition even if you aren't doing extensive photo retouching, since they speed up the screen redrawing rate for everything, not just for Photoshop graphics. The same principles that apply to the CPU also apply here. How long can you afford to sit around waiting for things to happen? How long can you wait for the computer to draw every pixel in an image? If you have 20 88MB images that need to be color corrected and retouched for a catalog that goes out next week, you can't wait. An accelerated graphics card will help you make those tight deadlines.

Graphics cards can be purchased for fairly little, between $300 and $500. These would be fine for smaller monitors and for work with a light to medium amount of image editing. A high-end image editing station needs a high-end accelerated graphics card, such as the TwinTurbo 128M8 from Integrated Micro Solutions, or the ThunderPower 30/1920 from Radius.

Note

Add a Second Monitor!

Not many people realize it, but the Macintosh computer is capable of supporting as many monitors as you have graphics cards in your computer. When you add an accelerated graphics card to your Mac, use the computer's built-in video to drive a second monitor. Graphics applications all use many floating pallets. These provide handy access to the tools and commands of the application, but they also obscure your work, forcing you to be forever opening, closing, and repositioning palettes. If you have a second monitor, you can position all palettes on the smaller monitor and have an unobscured view of what you are working on on the larger monitor. Leave all your palettes open so that they are always there when you need them, instantly accessible at all times. Since all you will be using it for is palettes, speed and color fidelity are not critical, so you can use the cheapest of color monitors as your second monitor. Imagine working without ever having to open, close, or reposition another palette! Now stop imagining, go get an accelerated graphics card and a cheap monitor, and make it happen on your computer right now. The few hundred dollars that this costs will be made back in short order by the increased efficiency with which you will be able to work.

Unfortunately, this option is only available on Macintosh-based computers, but it should be available on all computers. Write your person of Congress today!

Removable Media

One absolutely must-have, can't-live-without-it item is a removable storage device. Floppies don't cut it. You must be able to get your work to the service bureau. You must be able to receive work from clients. At least one type of removable media is a must, be it tape, CD-ROM burner, or cartridge type. What media you choose is largely a matter of what your service bureau will support. Check with your service bureau to find out what types of storage they support before you invest in something useless. We'll be going extensively into removable storage in Chapter 6, "Transport and Storage: Media Dexterity."

Printers

The ability to see the work you are doing in a printed proof is vital. No matter how good the monitor is, things always look different in print. When you buy a printer you need to weigh the cost of the printer, maintenance, and supplies against the costs, both monetary and timewise, of going to a service bureau. For proofing purposes we recommend getting a 600 dpi 8 1/2 by 11 or 11 by 17 inch grayscale laser printer with level 2 PostScript. This gives you a fairly good idea of what the printed piece is going to look like at an affordable price.

We are big fans of using service bureaus for our color proofs. There are many advantages to this, but the biggest advantage is that we can get better quality proofs for less money than it would cost us than to own and maintain a color printer. For a modest fee (which you can pass on to your client), you can get output from a precision-calibrated high end color proofing system such as an IRIS printer which could cost you $40,000 to over $100,000 if you bought it yourself.

On your own, you are going to have to spend a lot of money to get a printer that is slow and doesn't give accurate color. You would have to buy a lot of high-end color proofs from a service bureau to equal the cost of a good color printer. If you do find yourself buying a lot of color proofing from your service bureau, it might be worthwhile to investigate purchasing your own color proofing device.

On the other hand, if all you need is a rough idea of what your printed piece is going to look like, then an affordable color ink jet might suit your needs. For under $400, the Epson Stylus Color Pro gives astoundingly good quality color printing. This gives you a much better idea of what the final, printed piece is going to look like than seeing it onscreen. Unfortunately, the Stylus Color Pro is a very slow printer. We've heard reports of pages taking half an hour or more to print out at the highest quality. Still, if you schedule your time wisely and send things to print while you are at lunch or gone for the night, the Epson Stylus Color printers could be an excellent solution for you.

For more on information on printers, printing, and proofing, turn to Chapter 18, "Proofing."

TWO: THE SOFTWARE YOU NEED

Compared to configuring hardware for digital prepress, getting set up with the necessary software is easy. You will need six basic types of software:

- A word processing program

- A vector-based illustration program

- A painting program

- A page layout program

- A font management utility

- System/disk maintenance programs

Word Processing Programs

Word processing programs enable us to easily enter and edit text before it is imported into the page layout program. Files created by word processors are small and easily transportable between different brands of word processors, and even across different platforms, virtues which page layout programs often lack. Don't do word processing in a page layout program. Don't do page layout in a word processing program. This might seem obvious, yet people waste their time trying to do it with alarming frequency. We have the software manufacturers to blame for this. In the never-ending battle to create a word processor that will dominate all others, software manufacturers add more and more features to their word processors. And so you get 22MB monstrosities like Microsoft Word 6, which will do everything but write the document for you when what we really need is a program that is small, fast, and works right.

We prefer WordPerfect, but we use Word 6 because it is what everyone else uses. For reasons that have more to do with marketing and tradition than with the quality of the program, Word 6 is the dominant word processing program on both the Mac and PC platform. Other word processors are faster, more reliable, and take up fewer resources than Word 6. Sadly, in this industry, doing what everyone else is doing is often the key to profitability. Using applications that everyone else uses ensures that the files you create or receive can be easily and transparently opened and worked with by everyone involved in the process.

Tip

Even when other applications are clearly superior, it is almost always wiser to use what everyone else is using, even if it seems clearly wrong. If you need to make a moral stand, stop eating meat, start a campaign to ban clearcutting in the few remaining forests in your region, and make sure that your female employees are paid just as much as your male employees for the same work. Don't fool yourself into thinking that because you've made a stand over inanimate objects such as computer hardware and software you've actually contributed in some significant way to life on this planet. Use what everyone else is using. You will prevent hassle and save yourself time and money.

If you don't use Microsoft Word 6, make sure the word processor you are using can open and save Word 6 files in their native format. Fortunately, since Word 6 is such an industry standard that many other word processors can open and save Word 6 files.

Vector-Based Illustration Software

Illustration programs such as Illustrator and FreeHand are vector-based, which means that the image information is mathematically defined, scaleable, and geared for high-resolution output. Illustration software has several key advantages:

◆ A production-level illustration program writes true level 2 PostScript code which can be output on any PostScript imagesetter at the highest resolution the imagesetter is capable of.

◆ Mathematically defined artwork means that images created with illustration software can be scaled to any degree, from pin-hole size to billboard size, and it always prints at the highest possible resolution.

◆ Illustrations are infinitely editable. You can make as many changes to them as you want without losing image quality.

The drawing program you choose is not just a matter of what you prefer. It is also a matter of what your service bureau supports and what they can output most reliably. Call them to find out. Corel Paint and Deneba Canvas both are fun programs to use and you can create fine pieces of artwork in them, but if these programs are not supported by your service bureau you are taking a risk every time you create something. Before investing time and money into buying and learning a drawing program, call your service bureau and ask them what drawing program they are able to get the most consistently reliable output from.

Pixel-Based Graphics Software

The other primary method of creating computer graphics is through pixel-based graphics software, also called paint programs. Paint programs create images using squares of color called pixels. Pixel-based images have several differences and advantages over vector-based images:

◆ They are less scaleable than vector-based images, since image quality is based on pixel size. The more pixels in an area, the more "realistic" it will look.

◆ They are better for more "organic" type images than vector-based images.

◆ Vector-based drawing programs have many advantages, but they fall short when it comes to recreating realistic or highly detailed images. Since vector-based programs define images mathematically, they come short with subtle tone differences, shading and such. The difference would be rather like trying to paint the Mona Lisa using nothing but stencils. You could do it, but it would be a big hassle and wouldn't look very good. Every single pixel in an image can have one of 16.7 million colors, and defining color differences isn't a problem.

In this book, we try to avoid specific hardware and software recommendations, but when it comes to paint programs for digital prepress there really is only one choice, and that is Adobe Photoshop. Although there are plenty of other paint programs, none comes close to matching Photocopy's industry support and reliability when it comes to quality color separations. There is wide third-party developer support, nearly unlimited training opportunities, and hundreds of instructional books available. It is also just a very good program.

Page Layout Software

Page layout programs are what tie word processing files, vector based images and pixel-based images all together. These should be the end point of all your creations. While page layout programs may have word-processing capabilities and even image editing capabilities, refrain from using them. You may have a saw on your Swiss Army Knife, but it is no substitute for a real saw. You waste both time and effort doing so and may even be creating files that cannot output properly.

Here again we recommend going with the industry standards when it comes to page layout programs. These are QuarkXPress and Adobe PageMaker. There are many other page layout programs, but none of them have the industry support that these programs have. Before you use any other program, check with your service bureau to find out what page layout program gives the most consistently reliable separations.

Font Management Utilities

Over time you will be building up a library of hundreds, even thousands of fonts. You must have a consistent and reliable way to handle all of these fonts or you will run into nightmarish situations. Proper font management ensures that you can get your work done and that the service bureau will be able to open and print your files. A font management utility, such as Symantec's Suitcase or Alsoft's Master Juggler, is indispensable for this task.

System Maintenance Utilities

After you have our operating system, utilities, and applications running, we need to keep them running smoothly. System Maintenance utilities aid in these tasks:

◆ We talked earlier about how files could be written to the hard drive in pieces. This happens all the time, but it really isn't the most efficient way of doing things. Defragmentation software fixes this problem.

◆ Reduces crashes, and locate the cause of crashes

◆ Makes things run more quickly

◆ Automates repetitive tasks

These are good things for everyone who works on computers to do, but few things place more demands on the entire system than digital prepress. System maintenance is vital. Remember: time is the most valuable thing you have. Do everything you can to prevent your time being wasted. For a more thorough look at ways in which you can save time by optimizing your system, turn to Chapter 3, "Optimizing the Work Environment."

THREE: THE KNOWLEDGE YOU NEED

Getting the right hardware and software is the easy part. Now comes the task of actually doing something with it. If only it were as easy as buying the stuff! If it was, then businesses would have saved millions in improperly printed material just last year alone. Putting the hardware and software all together and making it work for you is an ongoing task. Getting it right is a game of strategy, skill, and a certain amount of blind luck. There are many things, however, that you can do to tilt the odds in your favor. You will not be an expert for a long time. You will still make mistakes, but the more you know, the less costly those mistakes will be, and the easier it will be to recover from them.

Basic Software Rules

If there is a single word of advice to give when it comes to digital prepress software it is this: don't be a pioneer. Being a pioneer is fun and exciting. Succeeding at doing something no one has done before can win you the respect and admiration of friends and colleagues. But failure is costly. Can you afford to lose your clients or your job? Can you afford to waste time creating files which may or may not print, no matter how lovely they are? If you can, then by all means, do whatever you feel like, using whatever untried, untested method you want. Someone has to. If you want to do your best to guarantee that your files are output right the first time, you should stick with industry standards.

Training

You can spend an infinite amount of money on hardware and software, and it will not equal the value of good training. There is nothing more valuable than proper training. The most expensive software and hardware is worthless if the person using it does not know what they are doing. A year from now the hardware you buy will be worth a fraction of what you paid for it, while training increases in value. If proper training prevents you from making one mistake then it pays for itself instantly. If training teaches you a more efficient way of doing things then it pays for itself again and again.

Training is expensive, and there is an awful lot of bad training out there. Even good training is not always relevant to what you are trying to do. Finding the training you need takes effort on your part, but it is worth it to be sure before you invest hundreds, thousands, or even tens of thousands into training, not counting the cost of the time investment.

How do you find the right training?

◆   Assess your needs.

◆   Before you or your employees sign up for a class, call the training facility. Explain to them where you are with your skills and technology, and tell them what you want to be doing. This is a highly technical field with nothing intuitive about it, yet people make the mistake not asking for help all the time. This can be a very costly error. One business that we worked with had just started to incorporate digital printing technology into their work flow. Their primary business was creating print advertisements. They sent their employees to Macromedia FreeHand classes. The business is to be applauded for knowing that they needed training, and for being wise enough to pay for training for their employees. However, by not making a single phone call they spent a lot of money in a misguided direction— a creatively oriented graphics class—when what they really needed was a production-oriented page layout class. The employees learned how to create graphics but did not learn how to incorporate these graphics into their advertising, or how to get them to output. The benefits of the training were lost because they could not put the knowledge to use in their production environment.

The training facility should be able to recommend a course for you. If they can't then you should seriously consider seeking out a different training facility. Some training facilities even offer free, on-site consultation, where they will send a representative to your work site to assess your needs and come up with a plan of action.

◆   Request a course outline. A good training facility will be able to provide you with a course outline on request so that you can see what the goals of the class are before you sign up for it, and what skills you can expect to come away with. They will also be able to provide you with references of people who have attended the class so you can call them up and find out how satisfied they were with their experience.

◆ Look for hands-on training. Does the training facility offer hands-on classes, or is it strictly lecture? Lecture style classes are of limited value. Chances are you'd be better off buying a book. Humans are experiential beings. We learn far more by doing than by watching. Unless you are able to sit in front of the computer and test for yourself what the trainer is telling you, you will learn far less than you could be. If the training facility does not offer hands-on training consider finding one that does.

◆ Look for a class format that best fits your needs. Some classes are intensive, day-long workshops. Some meet once a night for several weeks in a row. Some classes meet all day for a week. You have to consider what works best with your learning style and your schedule. Day- and week-long intensive courses may seem like a good idea, but can you absorb all the information that they will be throwing at you? Night courses can be good, but can you afford the time commitment for an extended period of time?

◆ What kind of follow-up can the training facility provide? With any training course, you want to have the ability to follow up whatever class you take with additional training and consulting. After you return to work after taking the class, you start applying the skills and concepts you've learned from the class. If you discover that something you learned was incomplete or unclear, will you be able to call the training facility with questions? Training facilities that are connected to service bureaus are often the best with this kind of follow-up since, after you and your clients, service bureaus are the ones who benefit the most from making sure you know what you need to.

◆ Are the classes ongoing? You will want to be able to go back to the training facility for additional courses after you have had a chance to put what you learned to practice. Does the facility offer their classes in an integrated series?

Simply put, you need training. You can't afford to be without it. Training is costly and it will cut into your valuable time. Be smart about it and you will maximize your efforts and your training will pay for itself in short order. Be stupid about it and you will stand a better chance of benefiting from opening a window and throwing your money out of it.

Reference Material

Books, training on CD-ROM, videos, magazines and the Internet are all worthwhile investments of time, but they have their limitations. Anything you can do to make yourself more familiar with any aspect of digital prepress, from the creative to the technical, is worthwhile. The biggest trouble is time. Time is a limited resource you can't afford to waste. The biggest problem you will face when you start to learn digital prepress is making the distinction between what information is directly relevant to you and what is merely interesting. When we started learning digital prepress, everything pretty much carried equal weight. A cool type trick in Photoshop seemed as valuable, if not more so, than knowing the difference between RGB and CMYK files. Examine carefully what you are doing, what you know how to do, what you are having problems with, and what you want to be able to do, and judge all information accordingly.

Books

Books? Who has time for books? No one reads those things! Honestly, though, books can be your most valuable resources when used properly. Books can contain the largest amount of useful information of any resource, and they are relatively inexpensive. Knowledge is worth money. Even if you only get one good technique or idea from a book then the book has paid for itself. Read through the back of the book, the table of contents, and the chapter summaries to see if there is anything substantive, and if there is, buy it. If you can, charge it to your employer. If you can't, declare it as a tax write-off. At the very least, having the books on the shelf near your computer make you look like you know what you are doing even if you don't ever read the things.

Training on Video

Studies have shown that information that is both seen and heard is retained better than information that is just seen or just heard. Video training has the drawback of being dependent on the television and VCR. If the video provides hands on, follow-along demos (which it should), then you will have to move the TV near your computer or vice-versa. Good video training can provide you with a way of learning things that is interesting and effective. Bad video training is a big waste of time and money. Read the description on the box carefully to see how it applies to what you want to be doing, and make sure you can return it for a full refund if it is unsatisfactory.

Training on CD-ROM

Training on CD-ROM often consists of many sets of QuickTime movies that walk you through various techniques of using a program, pretty much like training on video does, only the movies are much smaller in scale and have lower sound quality. Training on CD-ROM has an advantage over training on video in that it takes place on the very instrument you are supposed to be learning about. You can watch the movie, then switch to the application and try the techniques for yourself right then and there. CD-ROMs have another advantage over video in that they are generally longer than video tapes. Training on video is generally under 90 minutes, whereas a CD can hold hours of movies. We have seen some that have from five to seven hours on a single CD! In that amount of time surely there must be something worth knowing in there!

Magazines

Magazines are also great resources. Unlike books, CD-ROMs and videos, magazines can come out monthly or even weekly, so the information can stay much more current and timely. Magazines also have advertising and design that can serve as inspiration for your own print projects. Any bookstore worth its salt will have a wide variety of prepress-related magazines. The best ones will not be found in the computer section, however, but in the art and design sections. *Step-by-Step Design* and *How* are two examples. Computer technology has become so all-pervasive that it is hard to find any magazine without some sort of computer content these days. Browse for an hour or so, then take the subscription cards and subscribe to as many magazines as you can afford. You'll be glad you did.

The Internet

Many valuable resources are on the Internet. The problem is finding them. Information on the Internet comes from two sources: user groups and the World Wide Web. Once you get past the hype, you'll find that the entire World Wide Web is pretty much the same as someone learning digital prepress for the first time, only worse. Everything carries equal weight. Searching for a subject such as "digital prepress" can give you hundreds of responses, but sorting through what sites are merely advertisements for goods and services and what contains relevant information can be a difficult task. Once you have found a useful site, though, it can make the time and frustration of finding it worthwhile. The Internet is unique in that the information can be updated moment-to-moment, making it possible for the information to be most current. Sadly, though, the Internet is not yet living up to its promise as a provider of useful information. Too much of it is pure marketing hype. The potential is there, though, and some vendors are starting to tap into it. The Adobe site, for example, is shaping up into a site that can be visited and revisited. It has the potential of becoming a service that adds value to all of Adobe's products by providing not only software updates and plug-ins for Adobe products, but interviews, articles, and tips and tricks for using their software. The site is still predominantly an advertisement for Adobe products, but it is getting better. Hopefully they and other vendors will start using the Web as a way of enhancing their products, rather than simply trying to sell them. Added value after the sale such as this could do more to boost sales than any amount of advertising on a Web site.

The other source of information on the Internet are newsgroups. There are more than ten thousand newsgroups on the Internet covering every subject imaginable and a few that aren't. Newsgroups are totally driven by the people who use them. On a newsgroup you can post a question, get an answer to it, and browse through other people's questions. The answers may or may not be right, but it is good to know that there are many more people out there seeking knowledge than just you.

Learning digital prepress is one of the most complicated things you can do on the computer. You can't afford to overlook any potential source of knowledge. Ironically, getting the knowledge consumes your most valuable resource: your time. You need to find out everything you can, but you can't afford to waste time. You can avoid wasting time by approaching every potential source of information with the same questions: where are you now in terms of your digital prepress abilities? Where do you want to be? How will this source of information help you get there?

FOUR: THE RIGHT PEOPLE

Being successful in digital prepress requires that you establish a series of connections from the original concept of the documents you create to the final publication, not just on the computer, but with the world. It means surrounding yourself with people who are willing and capable of helping you attain the goal of getting from the concept to the publication without problems. The digital prepress process does not happen in a vacuum. You need the right people.

Employees/Coworkers

In the digital prepress industry, your employees or coworkers are generally going to be one of two types of people: Those who have been working in traditional prepress and are making the transition to digital prepress, and those who have been involved with computers and have discovered that they can make money applying their computer skills to prepress. These are, of course, the extreme ends of the spectrum. The ones in the middle do all right. It is the extremes you have to watch out for.

The fastest growing number of people getting involved in digital prepress are those who have been working in traditional prepress and are now being forced to relearn their trade to adapt to a rapidly changing world. "Rapid change" and "prepress" are two concepts which never came near each other until the advent of digital prepress. Thanks to computer technology, there have been more changes in the past ten years in the print industry than in the previous four hundred years.

Those who are making the change from traditional to digital methods find themselves in an awkward position. After many years of stability, they find themselves forced to change, to learn entirely new ways of doing things. After working for years at a job known for its consistency and predictability and tradition, they find themselves faced with the prospect of adapting or looking for a new career. Some will welcome the change with excitement and enthusiasm. Some will try their hardest but will find that the traditional methods are so ingrained that they can't change. Some will view it with hostility as an unwelcome hassle and a threat to what they thought were their secure jobs. Those who are making the change will either be your greatest asset or your biggest liability.

On the flip side are those who have tremendous computer skills but don't necessarily have any other real abilities. These types were most prominent during the advent of desktop publishing who were primarily computer users and not designers or prepress professionals. Hallmarks of this time were inch marks instead of quotation marks, 17 different type faces and sizes on a single page, and many really, really bad designs. Fortunately, most of these people now work at *Wired* Magazine.

How Do You Utilize Them?

If you are an employee, you can learn a tremendous amount from both the seasoned prepress veteran and the young computer jockey. The question is, will you be able to? We've heard seasoned prepress professionals say, "I'm not going to let some punk kid tell me what to do!" Unfortunately, the seasoned professional's job depends on what that punk kid has to teach him. We've seen others who think they know everything about prepress because they've memorized all the keyboard shortcuts in QuarkXPress. They won't listen to a single thing anyone has to tell them.

Success in this business requires an ability to learn from others and to share that knowledge. There is no room for proprietary attitudes over one's knowledge. There is no room for inflexibility and unwillingness to change or learn. If you are an employee, it is up to you to learn everything you can from your coworkers and to be willing to help them learn. Proprietary attitudes towards one's knowledge are pointless in an industry which changes as rapidly as ours. If you aren't continually revising and updating your knowledge and skills then you will rapidly become as obsolete as the knowledge you have hoarded. If you feel that you are putting yourself in jeopardy by teaching another what you know, then you must have very little confidence in your own ability to learn new things, or you are in an incredibly hostile work environment. Either way, it is time to seek a new line of work.

If you are an employer or a manager, pay attention to the two types of employees working together. Are they working together to get the most from their respective experience? The transition from traditional prepress to digital prepress can be a very difficult one. The change can be met with fear and loathing or with enthusiasm. As an employer or manager, you may be forced with the difficult problem of the long-time employee who can't or won't make the change. Be prepared.

Print Brokers

A print broker can be a wonderful thing. Like a stockbroker, they advise you how to spend your money in ways that make you most profitable. The role of the print broker can range from finding you the cheapest printer to completely managing the print job, taking your files to have proofs made, going over those proofs with you, having films made, and bringing them to the printer. Generally, the print broker is someone who knows all the ins-and-outs of the industry, but this is not always the case. Print brokers can also be sales representatives who only know what the output looks like and what it costs. Either person can help you, provided they are willing to work with you to understand your needs, and can communicate them to others.

Chances are your print broker is not going to be an expert in digital prepress. Digital prepress has only become viable during the past 10 years. Only recently has it reached a point where prepress professionals are receiving the message to adapt or die and print shops are incorporating digital technology *en masse*. There are very few experts, even among those who use the technology every day. It is unlikely that your customer service rep will be as technically savvy as you are. This does not mean that they can't be valuable to you. What it does mean is that you will both need to make an extra effort to communicate. As long as the print broker is clear and honest about what they know and can communicate your needs to the service bureau and printer and vice versa, the print broker can be a vital player in the equation.

Without communication, print brokers become a liability. On one job the printer assumed that a vital piece of information about file preparation had been communicated by the print broker to the designers. The designers were expecting the print broker to give them the information they needed, so they hadn't talked to the printer. The error wasn't discovered until 100,000 boxes had been improperly printed. Words flew, fingers were pointed, accusations were made. The printer had to eat the cost of the misprinted boxes. The business having the boxes printed missed the first shipping date of their new product—which was to have shipped in time for the holiday season. Needless to say, the print broker lost a major client. Simple communication would have prevented all of these problems.

How Do You Utilize Them?

Your relationship with your print broker is one that will increase in value over time. Digital technology changes a playing field that has remained constant for decades. It is in a state of finding and redefining itself. Both you and your print broker need to be aware of this and work with each other through this process. If you don't feel comfortable working with your print broker, find another.

Keeping a few things in mind when you are working with your print broker will make your relationship most profitable:

- ◆ **Define your relationship from the start.** The role of the print broker can vary widely. At the minimum, the broker is just finding you a printer. At the other end of the spectrum, the print broker handles all aspects of the job once it leaves your hands. Knowing up front what to expect from each other improves everything.

- ◆ **Make your needs clear.** The print broker lives to find you the best deal in printing. Unfortunately, the best deal in printing does not always mean the best quality. Let your print broker know how important quality is. You can often get great bargains if you aren't too concerned with quality. On the other hand, if you demand the cheapest printing without specifying that you need quality as well, chances are you will not get the quality of printing you need.

- ◆ **Make no assumptions.** If you assume that your print broker is going to provide you with the printer's specific file requirements, and your print broker assumes that you are speaking with the printer, you are all headed for trouble.

Service Bureaus

Service bureaus made digital prepress possible. From the start, the technology has been expensive and has changed so rapidly that it is difficult for individuals and small businesses to keep up with it. With the help of a service bureau, it isn't necessary to own the latest and greatest of every piece of equipment. That responsibility is left up to the service bureau. A good service bureau is a partner who enhances your abilities and compensates for any areas in which you are lacking.

Need a color scan? A good service bureau can provide you with scans sized to your exact specifications and perfectly color corrected. Color proofs? The service bureau should be able to provide you with a wide variety of options. It should also be able to provide you with everything that would not be cost-effective to do in-house.

A bad service bureau is like an auto repair shop out to exploit your lack of knowledge. As in any industry where there are people with knowledge that others don't have, people take advantage of those who don't know that they are being taken advantage of. Telling the difference between the two is not always easy. In the corporate environment, it is even easier for bad service bureaus to take advantage of their clients, since often the bill for the service gets sent to the purchasing department and the person who requested the service never sees the bill. It is always a good idea to go over the bill very carefully, even when you are not the person paying it.

How Do You Utilize Them?

Finding the service bureau is the tricky part. Bad service bureaus are not too common, but they can cost you a lot of money. Here are some things to look for in a good service bureau:

- ◆ **Price lists.** The service bureau should be able to tell you before-hand how much the service is going to cost. There is no good reason why the service bureau should not be able to do this. If they can't, then they are probably leaving it open so they can extort as much money from you as possible.

- ◆ **References.** A good service bureau can provide you with the names of satisfied customers you can check with to get feedback on the quality of work the service bureau does.

- ◆ **Samples.** The service bureau should be able to provide you with samples of the work that they do.

- ◆ **Tour the facility.** The service bureau should be happy to show you around the facility, to see the technology and personnel at work.

Once you have found your service bureau, your life and your capabilities improve dramatically. Whatever technological capabilities you lack, your service bureau can provide you with. Your relationship with your service bureau, like your relationship with your print broker, becomes more valuable as it matures. Invest the time to find one you like. It is an investment that will pay you back many times over.

Tip

Before you create any files on your computer, find out the capabilities of the service bureau who will be outputting your files. You might spend hours creating the perfect document, only to find out that the service bureau can't output that type of file. You are stuck with the stress of creating new files in a program they support, or with finding a new printer. Either way you've blown your deadline.

For information on what to do once you've found your service bureau, turn to Chapter 7, "Project Planning."

Printers

The printer uses the plates made from your digital files to print your documents. This much is obvious. What isn't as obvious is the wide variety of options that are available to you at the printer. Digital prepress and new printing technologies have opened up a wide variety of printing options, from the vibrant colors of high-fidelity printing to highly-automated form printing.

Emerging print technologies are continually transforming the way we do business. Take the simple matter of printing forms. Until recently, businesses would have forms printed at the printer, and then take those forms back to the business where the individual client information was printed from the database. Digital printing allows printers to take the form *and* the data from the database and print them together. At the same time, the forms can be collated, sorted, and mailed out from the printing plant, saving a tremendous amount of time and eliminating the need for transportation and storage of the forms.

Printers range from small mom and pop shops who offer limited services and limited quality at really cheap prices, to giant printing plants who rarely do print runs under a million. Some printers have the ability to make films from your digital files, while others expect you to provide them with films.

How Do You Utilize Them?

Communication again is key. You need to be able to work closely with your printer to ensure that your files are printed the way you envisioned them. This can mean going to the plant and sitting and watching while the printer runs your job when quality is critical. Your printer wants to see you succeed. A good printer will work with you to make sure your files are prepared so they print properly the first time.

- **Begin the prepress process with a call to the printer**. Different types of printing, different inks, and different papers can require that files be prepared differently. Your printer will be able to tell you how to do this to ensure the best possible quality of print.

- **Know the requirements of your printer.** If the printer will be outputting your digital files, you need to know what programs and what versions they support, as well as what media types they accept. Find this out BEFORE you start creating files on your computer. Failure to do this can lead to scrambling to recreate files or finding another printer who can still meet your deadline.

- **Know the capabilities of the printer.** Different printers often have reputations for excelling in one specific type of printing. One printer may be great at full color printing, while another may excel in duotones. You may want to use several different printers to meet all of your print needs. These are considerations your print broker can help you find the answers to.

Above all, you need a printer you can feel comfortable communicating with. Meet the printer who is doing your work. As with a service bureau, take a tour of the plant and get samples of their work. Invest time into your relationship with your printer. The success of your print projects depends on your partnership with your printer.

Freelancers

Freelancers can also enhance your abilities. Freelancers can help you get the job done in three ways:

- ◆ **Deadlines.** By employing freelancers, you can make deadlines you wouldn't be able to by yourself or with your current staff.

- ◆ **Abilities.** You may not be an artist, but that shouldn't prevent you from having original artwork in your publications. Hire a freelance graphic artist! You can't be expected to know absolutely everything about everything.

- ◆ **Cost-effectiveness.** Freelancers reduce the need for permanent staff in environments with inconsistent workflow. You can bring a freelancer on for a project and send her away when the project is done.

Freelancers are one of four types of people. Those who want to work for themselves, those who can't find permanent work, those who have wealthy spouses or a trust fund and can afford to live without a steady income, and those who have jobs and wish to supplement their incomes. Whatever their reasons, it really doesn't matter to you, so long as they can make your deadlines with the quality of work you need.

How Do You Utilize Them?

Finding a freelancer is the tricky part. Once you get the word out that you are looking for a freelancer, however, you can expect to receive many calls. Freelancers are an aggressive, self-promoting lot who will actively seek you out if they know you are looking for them. You can get the word out through advertising and through business associates who use or know freelancers.

Once you find a freelancer, you need to assess how well they will work for you. Many people approach hiring a freelancer just as they would a regular employee. They ask for a résumé, a portfolio, and references. In some ways, it is even more important to thoroughly evaluate a freelancer before you hire one than it is with a regular employee. Unless the freelancer will be working on-site, you will not be supervising them. You need to have a high level of communication and trust with your freelancers.

Once you hire a freelancer, there are several steps you need to take in order to ensure that things go smoothly:

◆ **Use a written contract.** Spelling things out beforehand eliminates problems in the future. Be clear about who owns the rights to the work the freelancer does, and pay attention to usage rights.

◆ **Clearly specify acceptable programs.** The freelancer is creating files that will be usable by you and your company. Therefore, the freelancer is responsible for providing you with files created in the same programs that you use at your company. You are responsible for making it clear to the freelancer exactly what programs and what versions of those programs you support. This information can be included in your contract.

◆ **Clearly specify acceptable media types.** The freelancer needs to provide you with digital files on media that you can use. Provide the freelancer with a list of the media that you accept.

◆ **Clearly state your policy for font usage.** There are tens of thousands of different fonts in existence, and more are created every day. To further confuse matters, there is no way to tell what version of a font you are using. Different versions of the same font can have different font metrics. If your freelancer uses one version of a font and you have another on your systems, the work your freelancer provides to you will not print properly. Create a policy whereby you provide your freelancer with the fonts you use or vice versa.

◆ **Specify naming conventions.** In Chapter 5, "File Management", we suggest strategies for file naming conventions. If your freelancer uses your naming conventions, their work can be easily incorporated into your workflow and file management systems.

As with every other player in the digital prepress chain, the more your relationships with your freelancers grow, the more profitable you will become.

You

Finally, it all comes back to you. You are but a small part in this great chain of being called the Prepress Process, but you are the most important part. If you take a proactive role in ensuring that your employees, print broker, service bureau, printer, and freelancers are all working together and communicating. This may seem like a daunting task, but you have one advantage that few people in any industry can boast: your success is in the best interest of everyone involved in the process.

In terms of the technology, you are also your most important tool. You can spend tens of thousands of dollars on the technology and be no more productive than someone who spent a tenth of what you spent if you don't know how to use the equipment properly. The computer is nothing but a paperweight without a knowledgeable operator. It is up to you to be continually updating your skills, learning better and more efficient ways of doing things, and adapting to this ever-changing world. If you are a manager or employer, it is up to you to create a working environment where the employees are excited about doing this. Investments of time into yourself, your employees, and everyone else involved in the process will pay off many times over.

Chapter 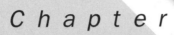 3

OPTIMIZING THE WORK ENVIRONMENT

In the last chapter we talked about the things you need to create the work envirinment. Now the fun begins. Buying the stuff is the easy part. Putting it all together and making it work is the tricky part. Creating the optimized work station means that every element in the environment, the software on the machine, the peripherals attached to it, the desk, and the lights in the room, work together to make you productive, healthy, and happy.

The ideally optimized workstation is subliminal. You should notice it only if you are making a point to. There should be nothing between you and the work you are doing. If you notice it, there is something wrong. If your computer crashes, or is slower than you should be, you notice it. You don't notice when your computer runs at the speed it should and doesn't crash. Generally speaking, you don't notice you have wrists. You don't need to. But if your wrists hurt, then you notice them. Generally, if something in your work environment comes to your attention, it is because there is something wrong with it. Our goal for this chapter is to make your work environment something you don't notice, which will be accomplished in three ways:

- ◆ **By optimizing your physical work environment.** This includes everything that doesn't happen on the computer, from the chair you are sitting in, to your desk, to the lights in the room.

- ◆ **By optimizing your computer.** How you set up the computer can greatly affect how productive you are and how comfortable it is to use.

- ◆ **By maintaining the System.** It is the third law of thermodynamics and it happens on your computer as it does everywhere else in the universe. Things go from order to chaos and ultimately total entropy unless we work to prevent it. Deliberately paying attention to your computer on a regular basis prevents it from *demanding* your attention during a tight deadline.

OPTIMIZING THROUGH ERGONOMICS

It may seem odd to you to be talking about ergonomics in a book so devoted to computer hardware and software. We would be negligent if we didn't though. Ergonomics are perhaps the most important part of the prepress process. Throughout this book we talk about maximizing profits by doing things right, increasing efficiency, and eliminating wasted production time. Proper ergonimics maximizes the functionality and preserves the usefulness of your most valuable piece of equipment: you. Ignoring proper ergonomics can result in discomfort, pain, and loss of productivity that can last into months. More than any other area, you can't afford to make mistakes when it comes to ergonomics.

Repetitive Stress Injuries

Computers have transformed our society in more ways than one. One of the more unfortunate transformations is that where once people moved around when they worked and did different things, people now spend much of their time sitting in the same position, doing the same things over and over again. This is such a recent development the medical industry has not had time to respond. As more and more people find themselves spending an increasing number of hours in front of the computer, America faces a medical crisis of epidemic proportions. Fortunately, it is a crisis with obvious causes that are easily preventable. Unfortunately, employee health and industry profits usually are not added up on the same line, so that the money needed to prevent the crisis usually does not get spent until it is too late.

The medical problems caused by spending eight hours a day repeating the same actions over and over again are many. One is that Americans are getting fatter and fatter. We would have to look too closely at ourselves and our increasing waistlines if we were to address this issue. We'll leave this one for the dieticians and physical fitness experts. The more alarming issue is the increase of RSIs, or Repetitive Stress Injuries. Repetitive stress injuries now account for nearly two-thirds of all workplace illnesses. Working with computers seems so *safe*. Who would have thought that it would be the most dangerous job of all!

Carpal Tunnel Syndrome

The most famous RST is *carpal tunnel syndrome*. In carpal tunnel syndrome, the nerve that travels from the arm to parts of the hand gets trapped within the carpal tunnel. The carpal tunnel consists of ligaments and tendons that surround the median nerve as it passes through the wrist and palm area. This median nerve gets compressed due, in part, to a repetitive stress, such as typing, or using the mouse extensively. Nerve tissue is one of the most sensitive tissues in the body. It is also one of the most easily damaged. Carpal tunnel causes pain in the wrist that radiates into the hand; numbness and tingling in the thumb, index, and middle fingers; and weakness in the hand. Fixing the damage of carpal tunnel syndrome can require a cessation of the activities that caused it, physical therapy, splinting the wrist in a neutral position, steriod injections, and in some cases, surgery. The surgery is particularly unpleasant, requiring the removal of tendons in an effort to widen the carpal tunnel, and a two to three month rehabilitation period.

In 1995, the U.S. National Center for Health Statistics estimated there were over 1.89 million cases of carpal tunnel syndrome in the U.S. This is only one form of RSI. Other debilitating forms of RSI are even more prevalent. They include upper limb disorders, tendonitis, DeQuervain's Syndrome, Thoracic Outlet Syndrome, Tenosynovitis, back and neck strain, and many other nasty strains and syndromes. All of them cause you pain or discomfort and all of them can cause you to loose work time. Can you afford this? Can you afford to loose employee time due to completely preventable injuries?

Warning

Our advice is based on the best available research and advice from physicians and occupational therapists, but it is just that: advice. It should not replace the personal guidance of a trained physician or therapist, nor should it substitute for medical help.

If you are in pain, damage is already being done. Get professional help now. Pause just long enough to go to the Human Resources Director's office to fill out an incident/accident report. Properly documenting your syndrome facilitates worker's comp claims. This is a work-related injury, so call a physician.

But first, another word of warning, in case you weren't sufficiently paranoid. Computer-related injuries are so new to the medical world they may not be diagnosed or treated properly. Many RSI are diagnosed as carpal tunnel syndrome. Doctors are familiar with carpal tunnel syndrome because it occurs in carpenters, warehouse workers, and others who repeat the same motions over and over all day long. There are big differences in computer-related injuries and other injuries. Other computer-related RSIs are frequently misdiagnosed as carpal tunnel syndrome.

As with any diagnosis, don't hesitate to get a second or third opinion, especially if surgery or any other costly or uncomfortable treatment is involved.

Prevention

Momma always said, an ounce of prevention is worth a pound of cure. A few dollars up front and a few minutes a day will save you thousands of dollars in lost productivity, prevent costly and painful surgery, and avoid months of rehab time. Preventing RSIs is a simple combination of optimizing your workstation and changing your work habits.

Posture

Piano teachers have the right idea. So do typing instructors. Unfortunately for many of us, typing lessons and piano lessons were traumatic events forced on us by our parents and teachers, painful memories we try to forget. Unfortunately, there was one thing we should have remembered: posture posture posture!

Sit bolt upright in your chair, your back at a 90° angle to the floor. Head up, face forward comfortably, as it naturally is when you are walking or having a conversation. Your shoulders should be relaxed but don't hunch or slouch. Your upper arms should dropped, making a 90° with your forearms, which should be parallel to the floor. Your thighs should also be parallel to the floor. Your upper leg and lower leg should also meet at 90° and your feet should be flat on the floor (see Figure 3.1). Your hands should make a straight line with your forearms. They should not be tilted up or down (see Figure 3.2). They should also not be turned to either side (see Figure 3.3a) but make a straight line with your forearm (see Figure 3.3b).

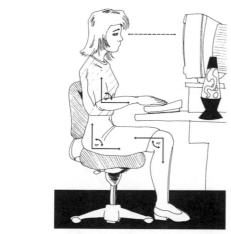

Figure 3.1

When you sit, everything should be at comfortable 90° angles, and the top of the monitor screen at eye level. Also note the comfortable, diffuse lighting provided by the lava lamp.

Figure 3.2

The nerves, ligaments and tendons in your hands and wrists can be damaged if you aren't careful. Keep your wrists in a neutral position above your keyboard.

Figure 3.3a

Don't turn your wrist to the side.

Figure 3.3b

Keep it in a straight line with your forearm.

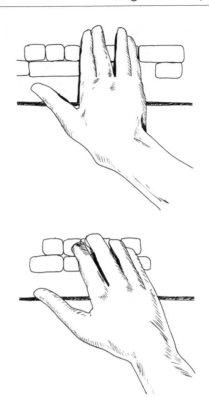

Sitting with this posture should feel comfortable and natural to you. If any part of you is strained or tires quickly when you are in this position, don't blame yourself. It could be your furniture.

The Furniture

Many people try to fit themselves to their furniture. This is a big mistake. You can't make yourself "fit" to anything. Your bones are a fixed length and, barring growth spurts or unfortunate injuries or diseases, they will remain that length until you die. If you sit in the proper position described above, your arms will be at a certain height, as will your knees, your eyes, and every other part of your body. Why anyone would try to force themselve to fit into desks and chair that don't fit them is beyond us and we've all tried it. You wouldn't buy shoes that are half your size and expect your feet to miraculously transform to fit them.

Why should our furniture be any different? In fact, we should demand that our furniture fit us better than our clothes, because using badly fitting furniture can, over time, result in injury.

The Desk

When you sit in the recommended posture, with your arms at 90°, you should be able to access the keyboard with your wrists in the neutral position. It's okay if your elbows bend slightly away from the 90° in order to do this, just so long as your wrists are not bent, and your neck and shoulders don't feel any strain. Elbows are rarely damaged by computer-related RSI, but pay attention how your wrists, neck, and shoulders feel. This requires, or course, that your desk be at a fairly exact height, which will be different for every person.

This correct posture requires a desk that is easily adjustable. The design of the desk should facilitate and encourage adjusting by the user. The best desks are ones that have an easily usable crank, which enables you to adjust the height of the table while the table is fully loaded. You can sit down at the table and adjust it to the exact height that feels comfortable to you at any time. Many adjustable desks force you to remove everything from the surface, then crawl underneath it to pull the pins while two friends lift the top of the desk for you. You won't find out if this is the right height until after you've got everything back on and start working again. If it isn't, you'll have to go through the hassle of doing it all over again until you get it right. What is more likely is that you'll give up before this and settle for a desk that doesn't fit. Ideally, get a desk which is as adjustable as a good adjustable chair. Unfortunately, this means spending a little extra money up front. Doing so will keep you from spending far more later, in lost work, doctor's bills, or worker's comp claims.

The Chair

Your chair is the single most important computer equipment you can own. Think about it. Unless you work standing up, your chair is the one piece of equipment you spend the most time interacting with. You use the chair more than the computer you are sitting at! More than anything else, your chair affects your physical well-being because it determines the shape your spine for the eight hours or so that you are sitting in it. Your spine is the center of your entire physical existence. All of your limbs connect back to the spine, and where your nerves radiate from once they leave your brain.

Ideally, when you are sitting, your spine, as well as your shoulders, head, and neck, should be as they are when you are standing. Unfortunately, many chairs twist the spine into all sorts of weird positions (see Figure 3.4).

Figure 3.4

Many chairs force your spine to bend when you are sitting, putting great strain upon your nerves and muscles.

If your back feels tired after sitting all day, or if your neck or shoulders hurt, your chair is not fitting you properly. Another way to tell is if sitting in the proper position described earlier feels uncomfortable, awkward, or is hard to maintain for any length of time. In a good chair, your body goes into this position naturally.

A chair needs to be fully adjustable, not just in the height of the seat, but the angle of the seat as well, the height of the arms, the height of the lumbar support, the angle and amount of recline. Your back should be curving the same way when you are sitting as it does when you are standing. The more adjustable the chair is, the more you will be able to tailor it to your body, rather than forcing your body into positions it is never meant to be in.

Adjustability also comes with a price. The chairs we are sitting in cost $1200, which seems a painfully high price. Ironically, we'd spend the same amount on a scanner or another piece of equipment without batting an eyelash. Once we finally convinced ourselves to spend the money for new chairs, we realized how well that money was spent. After many days of spending 14 hours at a stretch without experiencing a backache, sore neck, or sore shoulders, the price seemed a bargain.

It is unfortunate that comfort carries such a high price, but the price is far lower than the price of discomfort, pain, lost work, and potential injury.

Input Devices and Accessories

Keyboards and pointing devices, though essential for computing, can cause pain and occassionally permanent damage if used improperly or for long periods of time. Gloves and wrist rests are a way to improve the ergonomics of these devices, but can, in themselves, pose health problems. There are no guaranteed fixes, but some of these tips can help you stay productive.

Keyboards

Many styles of keyboards can be chosen from, many of which advertisers claim to be more ergonomic than standard keyboards. Currently, no conclusive studies show that such keyboards reduce RSI in any way or prove the connection between keyboarding and RSI. Don't worry, though, soon there will be many such studies. Once people start sueing keyboard manufacturers for not putting warning labels on their products, you better believe the research dollars are going to start pouring in. For now, though, all we have to go on is annecdotal information, which says that many people who have experienced keyboarding injuries have found their pain reduced or eliminated when they switched to different keyboard designs.

A remarkable and exotic array of keyboards are available, from keyboards that follow the standard 101-key layout yet are curved and angled to better match human hands, to keyboards that break into several pieces and can be angled to any degree. Other keyboards abandon the 105 key approach altogether in favor of five or seven key stenographer-style pads.

Two of the more interesting ideas are the Comfort Keyboard System and the Datahand. The Comfort Keyboard System is based on the standard 101-key keyboard, but it is sliced into three sections (see Figure 3.5). Each section is on a "custom telescoping universal mount." Each section independently adjusts to an infinite number of positions. This enables the typist to adjust the keyboard completely to find the most natural position.

Figure 3.5

The Comfort Keyboard System is a standard keyboard with an incredible amount of adjustability.

A solution like the Comfort Keyboard System provides the user with the minimum amount of learning time since it is just a modification of the same keyboard that the user already used to. It may not be the best, though. A solution like the Datahand (see Figure 3.6) requires that one learn a new way of typing. The Datahand uses two "pods", one for each hand. The four main fingers have five switches apiece: forward, back, left, right, and down. The thumbs have a numerous switches, as well as a built-in pointing device. In spite of the odd appearance, the key layout closely resembles QWERTY and is reported to be easy to adapt to. The idea is that the hands never have to move the whole time that the computer is being used, aside from a twitching of the fingers to click the switches. The idea has merit. How can repetitive stress injuries occur if there is no motion to cause them? We especially like the fact that the mouse is also incorporated into the datahand, since, as we shall see, the mouse is capable of doing much more damage to you than the keyboard.

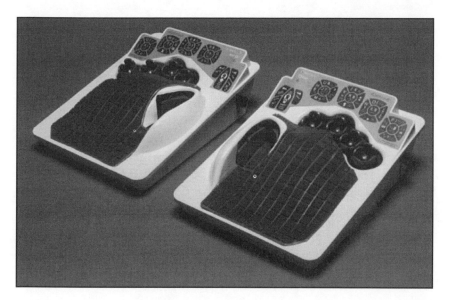

Figure 3.6

The Datahand takes a radically different approach. All keystrokes and mouse movements can be accomplished by wriggling the fingers.

Because no scientific evidence supports the idea that alternative keyboards make a difference, save for the claims of thousands who say that their careers have been saved by them, we really can't recommend one over the other. Our own experience has been with the simple, inexpensive split-style keyboard, which, once we got used to the unusual feel of the keyboard, we found to provide a much more comfortable keyboarding experience and our fingers didn't tire as fast.

You shouldn't hesitate to experiment until you find the perfect fit. Keep in mind, however, that good posture, a chair, and a desk that fit you properly can do far more to prevent RSI than any keyboard ever can.

Pointing Devices

To the graphic designer and computer artist, the pointing device is far more of a threat. It goes without saying that repetitive stress injuries happen because of repeated stresses to the bodily tissues. The more a specific stress is repeated, the more damage it can do. During keyboarding, the stresses are divided between ten fingers and two hands. Using a mouse, all of the stress is focused on one hand and one or two fingers. Graphic designers and computer artists are usually at highest risks of mouse injuries because they use the mouse almost exclusively, using the keyboard only for limited text entry and naming files.

Unfortunately, pointing devices are pretty much inescapable in our line of work. Our advice here is to get a variety of them. Dozens of input devices can be chosen from, and most of them are available for under $100. On the Macintosh, these devices are daisy-chainable. You can have as many as seven input devices hooked up together, all of them usable without problem. The configuration we like is a trackball for one hand, a mouse for the other, and a drawing tablet for the third, or for when we do any sort of painting, freehand drawing, or photo-retouching. Change the devices around frequently. If you start feeling strain in one hand, remove the device on that side completely until the pain goes away. If the pain doesn't go away in a day or two, call a health practitioner.

Wrist Wrests

Once touted as a way to make keyboarding more comfortable and prevent strain, wrist wrests are now viewed as quite the opposite. In fact, a new trauma is being talked about which is called *wrist resting syndrome*, which feels and looks like carpal tunnel syndrome. It is also frequently diagnosed and treated as such, but it is different. If you rest your wrists on the table while you type, this concentrates the weight of the arms and hands directly on the highly vulnerable two square inches at the wrist over the unprotected median nerve. With wrist resting syndrome, the damage comes from the force of external contact pressure, and not from swelling in the carpal tunnel.

This doesn't necesarily mean you should avoid wrist wrests but should avoid resting your wrists while you are typing. Your wrists should only be rested when you aren't typing. A padded wrist rest can help prevent damage if you absent-mindedly rest your wrists. It is better than the cold, hard desk. If the wrist rest is more of a temptation to injure yourself than the bare desk is, then you should get rid of it.

Gloves

Several manufacturers offer gloves designed to be worn while working at the computer as a way to prevent or help heal injuries, and to protect the vulnerable median nerve. Again, according to anecdotal evidence, these help greatly. One thing that is certain is that they help keep your hands warm and this is of great benefit. Any athelete can tell you that you need to warm up before engaging in physical activity in order to avoid injury. Typing is no exception.

The big problem with the gloves is that they are really, really ugly. Everyone could benefit from wearing such gloves, but medicinal blue doesn't look good with anything. Since most people would rather look good than feel good, especially when they are at the office, they are unlikely to wear ugly gloves at work. Now if those gloves were, say, made of ever-fashionable black leather, it might be a different story. The manufacturer of a typing glove that was both functional *and* fashionable would not only become very rich, but they would be performing a great service to typists everywhere.

Experiment and Prioritize

An almost infinite variety of keyboards, pointing devices, gloves and other accessories exist to make your life more comfortable while you are working on the computer. We recommend experimenting with as many things as possible to find out what works best for you. The very act of experimenting itself puts your hands into a wide variety of positions, which is very healthy. Most manufacturers offer at least a 30-day money back guarantee on their products, so you really have nothing to loose.

What is far more important than any sort of device, though, is that your chair and your desk fit you. Make this your priority. This may contradict tradition in a large office environment, where rank is reflected by the quality of the desk and chair the person sits in. This attitude is destructive both to health and productivity and it must be exterminated.

TAKE BREAKS!

What is far more important than anything you can buy, however, is that you take frequent breaks. Get up, walk around, stretch, stare out of the window at the beautiful day you are missing because you are stuck in front a computer all day, say hi to the cute new office temp in the third cubicle on the left, downstairs, all the way to the back. RSI is caused by doing the same things over and over. When you take a break, you give your body a chance to undo the damage. We don't mean take the two fifteen-minute breaks mandated by federal law. That is pathetic. We're talking about taking breaks hourly, or even half-hourly. Yes, this goes against the corporate philosophy that you should have your head down and be working all the time. Such an attitude is unhealthy and counter-productive in the long-run. A good manager sees to it that her charges take frequent breaks. If you are lucky enough to work for yourself, treat yourself right and you will be rewarded for a lifetime.

Eye Strain

After spending hours on the computer, your eyes may start to feel tired, your vision might start getting blurred, and your abilty to focus on things at a distance might be lost, along with your night vision. Don't worry, you are probably just experiencing eye strain. Your eyes are tired and they need a rest. If these symptoms don't subside when you are away from the computer, then it *is* time to start worrying. Go see your optometrist right away.

Currently, no scientific evidence proves eye strain causes permanent damage. Be that as it may, eye strain is unpleasant and debilitating enough in the short term to be worth avoiding. Preventing eye strain is easy:

◆ Take frequent brakes. Just as with RSI, frequent breaks give your eyes a chance to recuperate. Get away from the computer and stare into the distance.

◆ Make sure your monitor is at the right height and the right distance away. The top of the screen should be level with your eyes when you are sitting in the proper position, and twenty to thirty inches away.

◆ Blink. Studies have shown that people blink far less when they are working at the computer than when they are doing just about anything else. Sometimes, as infrequently as three times a minute! If you don't blink, your eyes dry out and you will be miserable.

◆ Use a good, color monitor. On a good monitor everything is crisp and in focus with no perceptible flickering. A monitor should be a pleasure to look at.

◆ Use proper lighting. Banish florescent and overhead linting from your work environment. Also get rid of any lights that glare on your screen. Every work station should have its own adjustable lighting. Use low-key, diffused lighting. If you are doing color-critical work, use a color balanced light, available from photography and art supply stores.

◆ Visit your optometrist. If you frequently experience eye strain, your optometrist may have additional methods for reducing the strain, such as a different perscription or tinted lenses. Chronic eye strain may be indicative of other problems as well, which should be attended to.

OPTIMIZING THE SYSTEM

After you've got everything out of the packages and hooked up, you should take one step before you install any software. Do a low-level reformat of the hard drive using the formatting utilities which come with the system, or with a formatting utility such as FWB's Hard Disk Toolkit. This gives you two benefits. Some manufacturers have an interesting habit of formatting hard drives to the exact size they say it is and this number is rounded down from the actual capacity of the hard drive. If they advertise a drive as being 1000 megs, that is the size it will be formatted to, even though it might actually hold 1050MB. The second benefit is that you are reassured that the formatting has been done properly. An improperly formatted hard drive can cause you no end of grief.

Formatting

A low-level format defines the sectors on the hard drive that information can be written to, the read and write specifications, and other basic information. Basically, a low-level format completely rewrites all of the information that defines the disk and replaces it with new information. An initialization, which takes much less time, simply erases stored files and replaces the information that makes the drive readable by the computer. Some people claim that initialization is sufficient, and that low-level formatting is overkill. When it comes to protecting your productivity, there is no such thing as overkill. Drive manufacturers do a low-level format of their drives before they ship them to you, but before they get to you, those drives have been subjected to heat, cold, magnetic fields, shocks, and vibrations during the shipping process. Why take chances? Do a low-level reformat every time you get a new hard drive. The disk then needs to be re-initialized. Follow the instructions included with your system software, or with your formatting utility.

Partitioning

After you have formatted the hard drive, partitioning the drive into several partitions is a good idea. The computer treats each partition on the hard drive as though it were a separate hard drive. This gives you several advantages:

◆ More efficient storage: Files take up more space on drives over 250MB. This size difference is only a few k per file, but if you have hundreds of fonts or Web Browser cache files, this amount adds up rapidly.

◆ More efficient operation. Files can be found faster.

◆ Organization. Files can be separated by function.

◆ Optimum performance of Photoshop's scratch disk. As Photoshop operates, it writes anything that it can't hold in RAM to whatever space it can find on the hard drive. Files can be written to the hard drive in several parts, like a magazine article broken across many pages, where you reach the end of a column to find "continued on page 46," so you flip to page 46 to finish the article. Photoshop does this with whatever it can't hold in RAM, writing its files into whatever non-contiguous space it can find. Of course, if it has a contiguous space to write files to, it works much faster. A disk partition specifically designated for this purpose and kept clear of all other files allows Photoshop to work as its fastest possible speed. For more information, see Chapter 9, "Fundamentals of Digital Imaging".

A recommended partitioning scheme is to divide the drive up into four partitions or more, depending on the size of the drive. Each partition has a specific purpose:

I. The System Partition. This contains the operating system and elements related to its operation, such as fonts, and utilities such as Suitcase. This will need 100 to 200MB.

2. The Applications Partition. This contains all of your applications. For Prepress, this partition needs to be between 200 and 300MB.

3. The Photoshop Scratch Disk Partition. Described above, this area is also useful as an area to render movies, 3-D renderings, and batch-processed files to.

4. The Work Partition(s). Here is where you store all the files you are working on. The remainder of the drive can be used for this. If you have a very large drive, you may want to use several partitions. Remember: files are stored most efficiently in partitions of 250MB and under.

Installing the System

After you've reformatted the drive and set up your partitions, you're ready to start creating a clean, efficient digital prepress machine. For inspiration, turn to the writings of Japan's greatest poet, playwright and novelist, Yukio Mishima. His writing possesses an elegant simplicity. He uses exactly the words he needs to get his point across—no more, no less. Every word is in its place and every word is exactly the right one. This is an ideal you should strive for when you are setting up your system and installing software. Have exactly what you need and no more. Have everything where it should be.

Note

The Windows operating systems do not use Extensions and Control Panels, as the Mac OS does. Instead, they use drivers that applications load dynamically when they need them. The Mac OS loads the Extensions and Control Panels into memory when the computer is started, and they remain there unless you turn them off and restart the computer. This is not the case on the Windows side. On the Mac side, it is vitally important to thoroughly manage your Control Panels and Extentions, since they are loaded whether you are using applications that need them or not. On the Windows side, drivers are only loaded as needed. For this reason, driver management is not something that really needs to be paid attention to. If you work exclusively on the Window platform, please skip ahead to "Installing Applications," later in this chapter.

What You Don't Need

When you do a complete install of your operating system software, a wide variety of things are installed, which range from the indispensable to the superfluous. What you don't need, get rid of. Back it up onto a removable if you are uncertain, but get rid of it. What gets installed during a complete install generally is fairly benign. It won't make you crash excessively or use up excessive system resources, but then again, everything counts. Every control panel and extension uses a little amount of RAM. Every control panel and extension adds a little bit more instability to the system. It is one more thing that could possibly conflict with something else. Anything that doesn't help get your job done, that uses up system resources, and increases the chances of conflicts is worth getting rid of.

The trick is figuring out what to keep and what to get rid of. This is going to take practice and a certain amount of trial and error. Fortunately, mistakes at this level are easy to recover from. When you install the System software, you have two choices: doing a complete install or a custom install, which lets you decide what gets installed. We recommend doing a complete install. You can turn off what you don't need using the Extensions Manager control panel. If this causes important things to stop working, turn them back on.

Once you've determined something is of no use to you, you can delete it if you need the extra space. Extensions and control panels take up little storage space, however, and won't interfere with anything once they are turned off. You may need to re-install it at a later date. Once you are familiar with what you need and don't need, you can do a custom install when you re-install the System and install only what you need.

Certain control panels and extensions are often found to be useless:

- **Printer drivers for printers you don't have.** A complete install installs drivers for all the printers Apple makes. You only need drivers for the printers you have.

- **Networking software.** You only need this if you are networking. If you are using a stand-alone computer, then you generally won't need networking software. This includes:

EtherTalk, if you aren't using ethertalk for anything.

File Sharing Extension, if you are not sharing files on your computer with anyone over a network.

TCP/IP, if you are not connecting to the Internet.

◆ **AppleScript** is a powerful tool if you choose to learn the scripting language. If you are not using scripts, this is just taking up space and RAM.

◆ **ColorSync** If you are not using programs and input and output devices that support ColorSync profiles, or if you are not doing anything that requires specific color, there is no point in using ColorSync.

◆ **Text-to-Speech** This reads to you what you've written in SimpleText, WordPerfect, or CyberDog in a funny, emotionless voice of your choice. The effect is quite surreal. Amuse yourself with it and then throw it away when the novelty wears off.

◆ **Macintosh Easy Open** Throw this away immediately. If you try to open a file from a program you don't have on your computer, this enables you to specify an alternate program that may or may not convert the file and open it. When it encounters a file of that type, it automatically opens it up to that. This is not something you want occurring in the prepress production environment. You should either have the program or know what program you want the file opened into before hand.

◆ **PC Exchange** A very handy thing to have if you receive files from PC users. This lets you mount and use PC formatted disks on your Mac without needing to reformat them. If you don't need to use PC disks, you don't need this.

Fonts

Remove all fonts from the Fonts folder in the System folder, except for Chicago, Courier, Geneva, Monaco, New York, Palatino, Symbol, and Times. You really only need Chicago, Geneva, and Monaco. The other fonts come with every Macintosh and are so commonly used that it's a hassle if you don't have them installed. Having them in the Fonts folder in the System instead of the Type Library folder ensures that they are always available. We recommend, however, that you replace all TrueType fonts except for Chicago, Geneva, and Monaco with their Type 1 PostScript equivalents. Please see Chapter 4, "Font Management," for more information on fonts.

If you are using Adobe Acrobat, you should also keep the fonts Adobe Sans and Adobe Serif in the Fonts folder as well. Acrobat works fine if you use a font management utility to open these fonts, but ATM warns you every time you start your computer that font substitution can't take place without these fonts if it doesn't locate them in the Fonts folder.

Apple Menu Items

The Apple Menu is a quick and efficient way to access certain functions on your computer. If many things are on the Apple Menu, the quickness and efficiency are compromised.

- **Graphing Calculator.** This was only useful to demonstrate the power of the PowerPC when it first came out, but it is no longer useful or impressive.

- **Jigsaw Puzzle.** This serves no purpose and takes up space. There are other fun games to waste your time with. If you have an extra minute, though, you really should get away from the computer altogether.

- **Scrapbook.** This once had a purpose. Back before the MultiFinder, you had to copy things to the Scrapbook first before you could paste them into another file. The Scrapbook still remains, but we aren't sure why. It has no use in Digital Prepress.

- **Stickies.** Digital Post-It notes. These are unnecessary since they are really the Note Pad in a different form. You might find them useful, though. If not, get rid of them

- **Shut Down.** AppleScript lets you write scripts that cause certain things to happen when you shut down the computer. Shutting down from Shut Down in the Apple Menu works without executing the shut down scripts. If you haven't written any of these, then this is just more clutter.

Control Panels

◆ **File Sharing Monitor.** This is a handy way of seeing what kind of activity is going on with your shared computer, such as who is connected to you and how much they are using your files. If you aren't sharing files, or if you don't need this information, then you don't need this control panel.

◆ **Launcher.** A nice idea, poorly executed. It lets you organize aliases for easy access to files and folders. Unfortunately, it takes up too much memory and quits in low memory situations. It also takes up too much space on the monitor.

◆ **Map.** Pinpoint almost any city on a tiny all-black map of the Earth. What is the point to this?

◆ **Users and Groups.** Vital if you are on a network. Useless if you aren't.

Getting rid of everything you don't need helps simplify your life and lets you work more quickly and efficiently. In addition, keeping things to a minimum enables things like disk optimizations and desktop rebuilds to work faster. After a little practice, telling the difference between what is useful and what isn't becomes second nature. Things have a way of creeping into your system folder, especially when you install new software. Routinely checking through your Control Panels and Extensions folders keeps things running smoothly.

INSTALLING APPLICATIONS

Always do a Custom Install when installing applications. Applications install a slew of things you don't need when you do a complete install, such as:

◆ **Sample Files.** These things are created by in the application in an attempt to teach you how to use the program. If you already know the basics of the program, you don't need these.

- ◆ **Tutorial Files.** Another attempt to teach you the basics of the program, often using the samples in the sample file. These are only helpful if you know nothing about the program.

- ◆ **Control Panels and Extensions (on Macs).** Check to make sure you don't already have more recent versions of whatever the program wants to install. The Install program is supposed to be "intelligent;" it detects an extenuation, and if it is already installed or if there is a more recent version installed, it does not install over it. Unfortunately, we have had newer versions of Extensions overwritten by install programs more than once. This, of course, causes a real hassle.

- ◆ **Product Demos.** Third-party vendors make deals with other software vendors to include demos of their products on the install disks of other products. These are sometimes installed automatically, which is quite rude. You've got better things to do, obviously, or else you wouldn't be installing the program in the first place.

- ◆ **Clip Art** comes free with many word processing and other pro-grams. It's useful only in letters to friends and family but has no place in the production environment. It was free for a reason.

Everything else probably serves some vital purpose to the functioning of the program and you should install it. If you don't, you really run little risk, though. Most programs tell you it doesn't have the files it needs to run. If this happens, you can just install them from the install disks.

RAM ALLOCATION

Unfortunately, the amount of RAM you have is finite. No matter how much you have, you will always be wanting more. You don't need to have an infinite amount of RAM, however, if you meet the base requirements. (See Chapter 2, "Creating the Work Environment") Managing the amount of RAM you have wisely compensates for having a limited amount of RAM. Before you use an application, you have to allocate a certain amount of RAM to it. This determines how much RAM the program has available to it. Allocating RAM is a simple yet tricky juggling game. You want each application to have as much RAM as it can. At the same time, you run into problems if you use up all of your available RAM. If you've allocated the majority of your RAM to one application and open up another application that has more than the available RAM allotted to it, it opens with all of the remaining RAM. This can cause headaches when certain functions are unavailable within the programs, and when certain features of the system also cease to function.

The key is to always change your memory allocations depending on the work you are doing. If you are going to be working solely in Photoshop, give it all the memory you have, leaving a few megs left over for stability's sake. This is easy, but what if you are creating a publication totally on your own? You are responsible for the images, the illustrations, and the layout, and this requires you to have Photoshop, Illustrator, and PageMaker open at the same time. All you have is 80MB of RAM and you need to allocate this memory to all three programs in a way that lets you operate most effectively.

From the Finder, go to the Apple menu and go to About This Macintosh (see Figure 3.7).

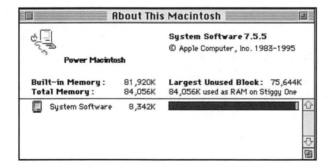

Figure 3.7

The About This Macintosh window.

This shows you how much memory the System is using and how much you have left to allocate to applications. Locate the applications and, with the applications closed, select the application by clicking it once. Go to File: Get Info for each application (see Figure 3.8).

Figure 3.8

The Get Info windows enables you to allocate memory to applications.

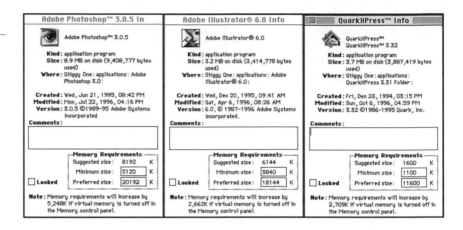

In the lower right hand corner of the info windows is a sub-section called Memory Requirements. There are three numbers: Suggested size, Minimum size, and Preferred size.

- **Suggested Size.** This is the *minimum* amount the manufacturer recommends that you assign to the program to have all the functionality of the program. Certain things the program does requires different amounts of memory. The program might be able to open with less memory than the suggested size, but not all functions of that program are available.

  Note: The Suggested Size just covers what the manufacturer provides with the program. Additions to the program from third-party vendors such as plug-ins can increase this amount without providing any warning. It is always a good idea to allocate more than the suggested size.

- **Minimum Size.** This is the minimum amount of space the program tries to open with. The program checks the amount of remaining RAM before it tries to open. If it has less than the Minimum size, it won't even bother trying. Increasing this amount can be a time saver if you know for a fact that an application won't do what you need it to do without a certain amount of RAM.

◆ **Preferred Size.** You will use this size specification the most. This is where you tell the program how much memory to open with if the memory is available. The higher the number, the better the application runs. Up to a point, that is. A mail program generally does not run any better with 100MB assigned to it than it will with three, but most programs you use for prepress are very memory intensive, especially when you are working with color graphics.

Now, your System is taking up 10MB. Leave 5MB free, as a buffer. Certain actions change the amount of RAM being used, so it is good to leave some extra space to prevent problems. This leaves you with 66MB of RAM to distribute between three applications.

You could just divide the remaining memory up into thirds and give each application 22MB each. This would not be the wisest use of your resources though. Photoshop is a real memory hog. It operates best when the most memory is assigned to it. If Illustrator is only going to be used for line art, it doesn't need as much RAM as it would if you were going to be working with placed images in it. The Page Layout application can go either way. If you need WYSIWYG high-res previews of images, then you need more memory than if you are just working with grayscale images, or if you are just working with FPO images with image previews turned off.

Give 10MB to Illustrator. This is still 1.2MB above the suggested size, so you should be fine. Give 20MB to PageMaker. This is where you will be doing most of our work, but PageMaker is far less memory intensive than Photoshop. We'll give the remaining 36MB of RAM to Photoshop. It would be nice to give Photoshop more, but that is all you have. This compromise enables you to work fairly efficiently until you can afford to get more RAM. If you find yourself working more extensively in one program, you can quit out of the applications and re-allocate the memory.

Get into the habit of changing the memory allocation regularly. Memory allocation should reflect what you are doing. If you are working exclusively in one program, give all your memory to that program. If you are working in several programs, redistribute the memory so that you can have them all open without encountering system conflicts. With a little practice, you will soon get an instinctive feel for the amount of RAM to allocate to each program.

SYSTEM SETTINGS

The Mac OS and, to a far lesser extent, the Windows 95 and NT 4.0 operating systems enable you to customize and personalize your system. The choices you make here can leave you with a powerful digital prepress system, or a quaint, interesting novelty item. All of the system settings are handled through various Control Panels on the Macintosh, and through the Properties dialog boxes of Windows 95 or NT 4.0.

Optimizing the settings for the Windows platform is a far simpler task than on the Mac. Far fewer settings on the Windows side affect your performance in the digital prepress setting than on the Mac OS. Nearly all of the settings that affect performance are automatically set to their optimum settings by Windows 95 or NT 4.0, while on the Mac many require tweaking. The exception to this is Background. We recommend that you read this section, then skip ahead to Necessary Extras.

Additionally, many other Control Panels are necessary in the Mac OS, but we choose not to talk about here because they have no effect on your performance in terms of digital prepress. Here we are focusing on the settings that directly affect your ability to work efficiently in the prepress environment.

Memory

Memory settings can make or break a good system. How you allocate memory determines the way applications run and can prevent disastrous system crashes (see Figure 3.9).

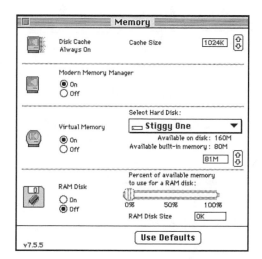

Figure 3.9

All the settings within the Memory Control Panel can have a substantial effect on the overall performance of your computer.

Disk Cache

Disk Cache is something of a misnomer, since the caching is really happening in RAM. Disk Cache sets aside a space to store repetitive calculations, which enables the system to run faster. The general rule of thumb is to give 32KB for every meg of RAM, up to 512KB. Over that amount, test it, (if you've got time on your hands) to see if it makes a difference in the speed.

Modern Memory Manager

Always leave this set to "On," even though certain older programs won't run with Modern Memory Manager turned on. It causes a significant decrease in performance when it's turned off, so leave Modern Memory Manager turned on, and ditch or upgrade those shoddy programs.

Virtual Memory

Virtual Memory uses part of the hard drive as RAM. It should be turned on and allotted at least 1MB.

Virtual Memory provides three benefits for Macintosh OS users:

1. The Macintosh OS has been optimized to work with Virtual Memory turned on. With Virtual Memory turned on, it can work more cleanly and efficiently, leaving parts of the System that aren't being used on the hard drive.

2. With Virtual Memory turned on, file mapping can occur. Applications only load pieces they need by priority. This allows applications to use memory much more efficiently.

3. On Power Macs, applications require less RAM.

We *used* to advise leaving Virtual Memory turned off, but this has changed. Virtual Memory used to make things run much more slowly, but with recent improvements to the System, Virtual Memory no longer gives the same performance hit. Virtual Memory also used to conflict with Photoshop, but this has been fixed.

Virtual memory can degrade performance if used improperly. Remember two things and you will be fine:

1. True RAM runs much faster than the hard drive. Your total RAM allocation to your applications should not exceed the installed RAM on your computer. You should only exceed the built-in memory when you absolutely have to because you don't have enough RAM for the specific task at hand.

2. The memory you allot in Virtual Memory is hard drive space that will not be available to you for the whole time that that memory is allotted.

RAM Disk

RAM Disk should be left off, unless you have hundreds of megabytes of RAM. RAM Disk is the opposite of Virtual Memory. It makes a portion of RAM behave as though it were a hard drive. Applications copied onto a RAM Disk run very fast, because all commands are accessed from RAM.

Typically, this is not a good idea, however. The RAM Disk is volatile. Things left in it vanish when the computer is turned off. Also, it uses up valuable RAM that would be better used allocated to applications.

Views

The Views Control Palette controls how the computer presents information about files to you. Many different choices can be made, but we have found one set of settings that enables us to work most efficiently.

Font for Views

We have experimented with many different fonts and font sizes to try to find which works best and have finally decided that the default, 9 point Geneva, works best. Other fonts may be more "friendly" but none of them provides the same level of readability. This is what Geneva was created for, so it is no surprise that it would work best.

Icon Views and List Views

List Views and Icon Views control how files appear in open windows. Go to the Desktop, click and hold on Views, and you are given a choice of six views. The first two views are called Icon views because they use just the Icon and the name of the file to represent the file. The Icons are free-floating and can appear anywhere in the window. The List views present file information in a designated hierarchical order.

Icon Views

If you check the "Always Snap to Grid" function, when you move a file in a window that has been set to View by Icon, it moves the icon to a space on an imaginary grid, which is either Staggered or Straight, depending on which radio button is selected. We have found that this invariably puts the icon in the wrong place. Leave this button checked off. If you want your icons to snap to a grid, you can hold down the Command or Alt key while dragging the icon and it snaps it in place. This is all a moot point if you use the List Views instead of viewing windows by Icons, which is recommended.

List Views

List Views is something of a misnomer because they also include icons. We prefer List Views to Icon Views because it provides so much more information.

Choose the middle icon size from List Views, because it displays the icons large enough for them to provide the instant file recognition that icons provide, while being small enough that the information can be displayed efficiently in the window (see Figure 3.10).

Figure 3.10

The Views Control Panel affects the way information about files is displayed onscreen, a necessary thing for file management.

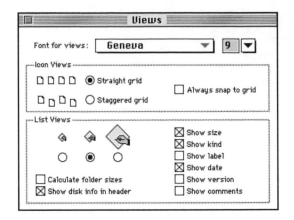

Leave Calculate Folder Sizes checked off. It calculates folder sizes too slowly to be useful and serves as more of a distraction. On slower computers, it can actually slow window redraw time. If you need to know the size of the contents of a folder, select the folder and go to File: Get Info. This is much faster.

Turn Show Disk Info in Header on. This lets you know how much space you have left on any mounted storage device, and how much is stored on it.

Turn Show Size on. Individual file size is very useful information.

Show Kind is useful to a beginner, but it doesn't provide any information than the icons do when you know what to look for. When you learn how to read icons, turn this off.

Show Label is only useful if you use labels. Turn it on if you do, leave it off if you don't.

Show Date provides useful information for revision control if you fail to include the date and time in the title when you save files. It will also tell you when an application was created, as well as when a control panel's settings were last changed.

Show Version shows you the version number of applications. It's not all that useful since most applications give their version number in their titles.

Show Comments shows you the comments that you can leave when you do a File: Get Info on a folder or file. Until very recently, comments left in info windows would be deleted when you rebuilt the desktop, so no one really uses them. If you can find any use for this whatsoever, you probably have too much time on your hands and really should be getting out more.

Desktop Pattern/Background

The Macs Desktop Pattern Control Panel, and Windows 95's Display Properties dialog box lets you import any image or color to become a tiled pattern. Don't do this. Choose the neutral, boring, featureless gray pattern and leave it at that. If you don't have a neutral, boring gray pattern, create one in Windows 95's pattern editor, or copy one from Photoshop. This gives you several benefits:

◆ The neutral gray causes the least eye strain of any color or pattern (see Figure 3.11).

◆ It also makes it easiest to find things on the desktop. Patterns make it harder for the eye to pick out objects on the desktop.

◆ Color of any sort affects the way we perceive other colors. Blue makes orange colors appear more orange. Neutral gray affects the way eyes perceive other colors less than any other color. This is important if you are doing any color work.

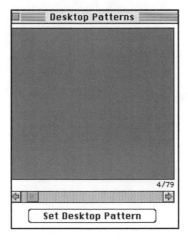

Figure 3.11

A neutral, gray background may be boring, but it benefits you in many ways.

Extensions Manager

Extensions Manager is a handy utility to manage all of those control panels and extensions (see Figure 2.12). Without Extensions Manager, Control Panels and Extensions can be turned off easily since they only work when they are in the Extensions or Control Panels folder. Drag them out of their respective folders and they won't load. Extensions Manager does this for you by creating Extensions (Disabled) and Control Panels (Disabled) folders and moving the things you turn off into them (see Figure 3.12).

Figure 3.12

The Extensions Manager provides you with ways to take control of your Extensions and Control Panels.

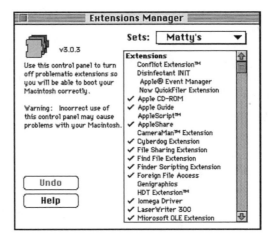

The big advantage to the Extensions Manager is that it saves sets. Depending on what you are doing, you will need different extensions. The fewer extensions you have turned on, the more stable your system is. Things run faster, more memory is available, and you crash less. If all you are doing is photo-retouching in Photoshop, you don't need any text-related extensions, such as Type Reunion, ATM, or Suitcase. If you are only working with text, you don't need QuickTime.

Get in the habit of creating sets of extensions for the specific tasks you are doing. When you start the computer, hold down the space bar while the computer is starting. Extensions Manager launches, allowing you to choose which set to use.

General Controls

Two specific settings in the General Controls panel are relevant to our discussion (see Figure 3.13). The first is the "Warn Me if the Computer Was Shut Down Improperly" check box. Always leave this box unchecked. Few things are more annoying than this warning after you've just crashed and restarted. It's like getting hit by a car, and, as you are lying on the pavement, crumpled and bleeding, having someone come up to you and say, "Hey, you just got hit by a car!"

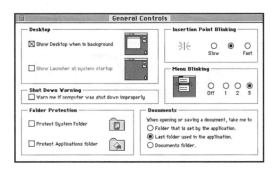

Figure 3.13

Everything that didn't quite fit anywhere else is put into the General Controls Control Panel.

The second thing to do in the General Controls panel is select Last folder used in application. This makes file management much easier, because usually you are saving things to the same folder over and over again.

Necessary Extras

No operating system is perfect or does everything it should. Fortunately, other people work to do everything they can to fix the system and improve upon it. These fixes are available from the company or from third party vendors. Sometimes the fixes created by third parties become part of the System. Extensions Manager is a good example of this. Certain third party control panels and utilities you really can't do without.

Font Utilities

Adobe Type Manager(ATM). Years ago there was a sad and pathetic battle between Adobe and Apple, both of whom wanted their font types to be the standard. Adobe's Type 1 PostScript fonts became the standard, while

Apple's TrueType fonts were generally shunned by the prepress industry (see Figure 3.14). This may have something to do with why industry standard fonts today won't display properly on the Mac OS or on Windows unless you have Adobe Type Manager installed. Without ATM, PostScript fonts appear jagged at larger sizes (see Figure 3.15).

Figure 3.14

With ATM turned on, type appears at its highest quality.

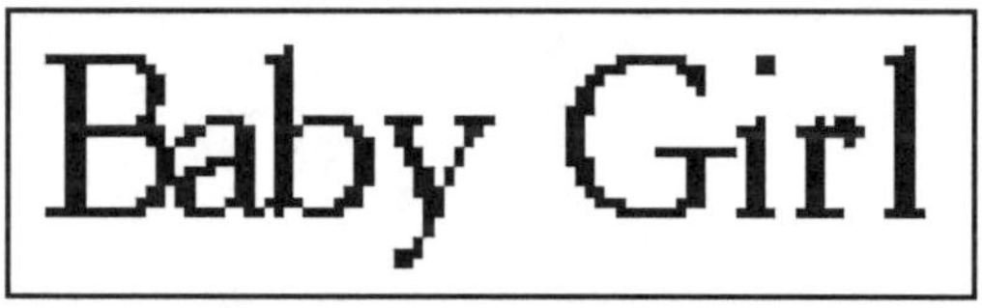

Figure 3.15

Without ATM, type is a blocky mess.

Adobe Type Reunion. The Mac had only a handful of fonts originally, so there was no real need for font organization. Now a single font family such as Futura has more members in it than all the fonts on the original Mac (the original PC only had one font). Without some sort of organization, you will have an unusably long list of fonts, even if you have just a few font families installed. Adobe Type Reunion organizes fonts by family, with flyout sub-menus for individual fonts within a family. Using fonts is almost unbearable without it.

With Type Reunion and Without

Type Management Utilities. Always use a type management utility such as Suitcase or Master Juggler to open and close fonts, rather than using the Fonts folder in the System folder. There are dozens of advantages of this, which Chapter 4, "Font Management," goes into in depth.

KEEPING THINGS OPTIMIZED

Once you have things all set up, your work is not done. You need to keep things running smoothly. This requires a combination of software and maintenance. Fortunately, many things can help you do the job.

AN EMERGENCY BACKUP DISK

An emergency startup disk is essential for system maintenance. This is a removable drive, such as a Zip disk or a SyQuest disk, which has several things on it:

◆ **A system.** Use your system install disks to create a system on the removable disk. This enables you to boot the computer from the removable disk in case the System on the hard drive gets corrupted and needs to be reinstalled.

◆ **System Install Files.** It's much faster and easier to re-install the operating system if all of your files are in one place. Installations from floppies and CDs are much slower than from removable hard drives.

◆ **System and Driver Updates.** System and device driver updates are released regularly. Make sure you have the latest ones and keep them on the Emergency Startup Disk. You will need to reinstall them when you reinstall the system.

◆ **Hard Drive Diagnostic Programs.** These programs, such as Norton Disk Doctor, help to diagnose and repair damaged drives.

◆ **Disk Optimization Software.** It is often necessary for disk optimization utilities to boot off an external System in order to fully optimize the hard drive.

◆ **File Recovery Software.** When you delete a file, you are not really removing it from the drive. You are really just telling the computer the space that file occupies is available to be written over. If you accidentally delete something, you might be able to recover it. The trick is that if you attempt to recover it to the same drive that it is on, you risk writing it over completely. Recover it to the Emergency Startup Disk and you stand a far better chance of restoring what you have lost.

◆ **Disk Formatting Tools.** You also need to boot an Emergency Startup Disk in order to reformat the hard drive.

Every computer should have its own emergency backup disk. This goes a very long way to making System maintenance a breeze.

Software

Many applications help you keep things running smoothly and make you more productive. Many of them are available as downloadable demos so you can try before you buy, which is a great thing. Several applications we have found to be indispensable—you should not be without them.

Antiviral Utilities

Prepress professionals are among the most digitally promiscuous people around, taking in files from anyone who comes along. Remember, when you put that cartridge into your SyQuest drive, you are linking up to every computer that SyQuest has ever been connected to. Catching a virus can be uncomfortable and can result in lost productivity. Giving someone a virus is not only embarrassing, but it can almost guarantee a lost client. Always use protection when you mount any media or receive any file from an outside source.

As damaging as viruses can be, you don't need to be excessively paranoid. Simply have a virus detection program running at all times that alerts you if it detects suspicious activity and can fix it for you. We recommend Disinfectant, which can be downloaded from many locations on the Internet (see Figure 3.16). It works, it is unobtrusive and automatic, it is regularly updated, and it is free.

Figure 3.16

Disinfectant offers effective protection from viruses.

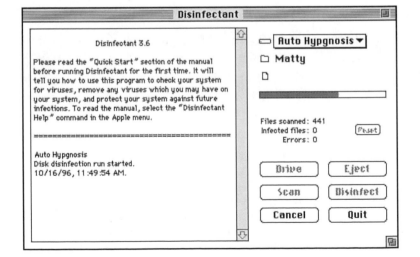

If you want to be excessively paranoid, several heavy-duty commercial programs do virus protection. These can be set to automatically scan every removable that is mounted on your computer and every file that is down-loaded from the Internet automatically, as well as regularly scanning your hard drives for viruses that might have gotten by the first time. These certainly would provide the highest level of protection, but it might be at the cost of productivity if you have to wait every time you try to move a file onto your computer. We like the fact that Disinfectant works behind the scenes, doesn't interfere with workflow, and still prevents damage from viruses.

Disk Optimizing Utilities

Files are written to the hard drive pretty much to wherever the read/write head on the hard drive finds the first available space. If that space isn't big enough, it will break the file up into several pieces until the whole file is written. This may sound pretty dumb, but the hard drive is intelligent enough to read files back completely, even if they are in hundreds of places around the hard drive. Of course, this isn't the most efficient way of doing things. Files that are stored contiguously open much more efficiently (see Figure 3.17).

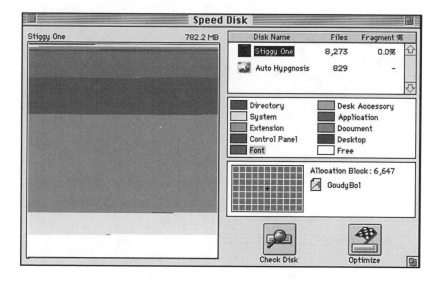

Figure 3.17

Disk optimization utilities reorder the files on your disk enabling efficient access to the information.

Defragmenting software brings files back together so they are stored contiguously on the hard drive. Optimizing software moves all of the files on the hard drive to the inside or the outside of the drive, leaving an empty space for files to be written to. This makes future defragmentation/optimization go faster, because files are more likely to be written contiguously to wide open spaces. Also, if you haven't provided a separate space for Photoshop and Virtual Memory to use as a scratch disk, this wide open space enables both of those things to operate much more effectively.

Disk optimization software called Disk Defragmenter is included with Windows 95, but you will need to purchase it from a third-party vendor if you are using the Mac OS. Third-party defragmenters are also available for Windows. We recommend Norton Speed Disk, which comes as part of Norton Utilities, a must-have software package for both the Windows and the Mac OS (see Figure 3.18).

Figure 3.18

Norton Speed Disk gives a graphic representation of the fragmentation of files on a disk.

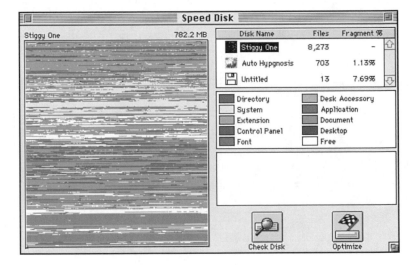

Conflict Catching

A large number of crashes on the Mac OS happen because of conflicts between extensions. This is the main reason why we recommend using as few of them as you possibly can. What happens when you are running with minimum extensions and you are still crashing?

If you are crashing, it is easy to determine if you are crashing because of extension conflicts. Hold down the Shift key while you restart to restart with all extensions turned off. Repeat what you were doing when the crash occurred. If the crash doesn't happen, then you have an extension problem. If the crash does happen, then it wasn't an extension problem. Extensions can't cause crashes if they aren't loaded!

Figuring out that you are crashing because of extensions is the easy part. The hard part is figuring out which extension is causing the problem.

Conflict Catcher from Cassiday and Greene will help (see Figure 3.19). Conflict Catcher is a powerful version of the Extensions Manager. It has diagnostic tools that help determine which extension or extensions are the source of your problems. Conflicts can also occur simply because of the order the extensions are loaded. Unlike Extensions Manager, Conflict Catcher lets you change the order in which extensions load. Conflict Catcher does many amazing things, too numerous to mention here. Suffice it to say, if you need complete control over your extensions, Conflict Catcher is must-have software.

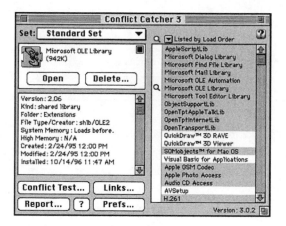

Figure 3.19

Eliminating conflicts is a vital part of managing problems.

Repairing Damage

Bad things happen to the files on your computer, especially when the computer crashes. When these things happen to the files you've been working on, it means lost productivity. When it happens to system files, it can mean a degradation of performance and an ever greater loss of productivity. It is not a matter of if it is going to happen. It *will* happen. Be prepared. Keep disk diagnostic utilities on your emergency startup disk.

Both the Mac OS and Windows 95 come with diagnostic programs, Disk First Aid and ScanDisk, respectively. Diagnostic programs by third parties, such as Norton Disk Doctor for the Mac or the PC, are much more robust (see Figure 3.20). Disk First Aid and ScanDisk can often help you, but we strongly recommend using third party diagnostic utilities additionally. It is not overkill to have several disk diagnostic utilities on hand. Many things can go wrong with the files on a hard drive, and disk diagnostic utilities can sometimes create new problems when they repair the original problems.

Figure 3.20

Diagnostic utilities, such as Norton Disk Doctor, find and repair problems on disks.

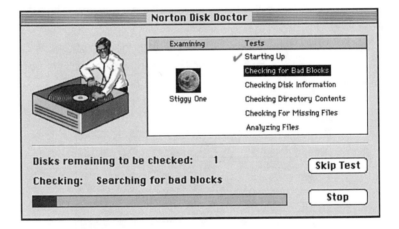

Norton Disk Doctor also comes as part of the Norton Utilities package. The entire package is a suite of tools that range from the essential to the redundant to the annoying. Norton Disk Doctor, however, is worth the price of the package on its own. We have found it to be the most reliable tool we've used to repair damaged files. From corrupted files to drives that wouldn't mount, Norton Disk Doctor has saved our butts many times over and enabled us to return to full productivity with a minimum of lost time.

Whatever disk diagnostic utilities you choose, if you diagnose and repair a disk, you should always do it again, to be sure. Repeat the diagnose and repair cycle until the utility reports that it found no problem. Remember: there is no such thing as overkill when it comes to ensuring productivity.

Maintenance

Make maintaining your system part of your weekly routine. It is a good way to begin or end the week. Run a virus check, optimize your drives, and run Norton Disk Doctor. Preventative medicine goes a long way to keeping you productive.

There are two more things you will want to do on a regular basis: rebuilding the desktop and zapping the PRAM.

Rebuilding the Desktop

Whenever you bring a file onto your computer that has an icon the computer hasn't seen before, it stores a copy of that icon in the Desktop file. Over time, this file can become so bloated that problems occur. Windows are slow to open, the computer can take a long time to reboot, and overall performance can degrade. Hold down the Shift key, the Command key, and the Option or Alt key while you restart. The Shift key prevents extensions from loading that might interfere with the rebuild. The Command and the Option or Alt key force the desktop to rebuild, which clears out all of the unneeded icons and slims down the desktop file.

Zapping the PRAM

Hold down the Command key, the Option or Alt key, the P and the R. When done with one hand, this maneuver is identical to the Vulcan nerve pinch, with which you can send your coworkers into a harmless coma. The computer starts, then restarts a second time. Let go of the keys when it starts a second time. This purges the PRAM and restores it to its pristine original condition.

RECOVERY

Taking a pro-active stance by maintaining your system carries you far, but accidents still happen. Furthermore, accidents always happen when we can least afford them to. Just as animals can sense fear, computers can sense stress. With a tight deadline, stress is at its highest. Your computer knows this and will crash as often as possible, especially after all the tech support people have gone home and you are on your own. How you react in this situation makes the difference between making the deadline and blowing it. Fortunately, there are simple steps you can take.

◆ **Do a little research.** With the incredible complexity of today's programs, bugs and conflicts are inevitable. Most of them are known things and are reported. There are several Web sites devoted to System maintenance and bug reports, with information on how to fix problems. Bulletin boards and discussion groups are also good ways to find out if other people are experiencing the same problems you are, and what they did about it. If you are getting error messages then finding out the meaning of the error message is a good place to begin investigating. If you are having problems in one specific program, go to the Web site of the manufacturer of that program to see if the problem is documented there. If you have time, you should also mail the tech support of the manufacturer and describe the problem as precisely as you can.

You should also call tech support. You can expect to spend a lot of time listening to cheesy music while you wait on hold, so you should do what you can to narrow down who to talk to about your problem. If you are experiencing problems with everything you try to do on your computer, call the manufacturer of your computer first. They might direct you to call the manufacturer of the system software you are running (Microsoft or Apple). If you are having problems with one specific application but not others, or if you first started experiencing problems with your computer when you installed an application, call the manufacturer of that application. If you are experiencing problems with a peripheral device, or if the problems you are experincing on your computer began when you attached that device, call the manufacturer of that device.

Unfortunately, crashes tend to happen when there is no one around to turn to for help. You are on your own. You can either pack up and go home, resign yourself to dealing with an irate client when you explain to them why the deadline was missed, or you can try to solve the problem yourself.

◆ **Check the extensions.** Most crashes are caused by extensions. Restart with extension off. Does the problem go away? Is so, then you have an extension problem. Start turning off extensions, starting with the last extensions you remember installing. Restart with the remaining extensions on. Does the problem go away? If it does, then you've located the problem. Now you have another problem if the extension was vital to the work you were doing. Chances are, though, that if you were having problems, other people were too, and the manufacturer knows about it. Go to the Web site of the manufacturer of the program and see if there is an update for the extension. In our experience, there has almost always been an update for the problem extension. If that doesn't work, try:

◆ **Rebuilding the Desktop.** You should rebuild the desktop on a regular basis, before problems start, but it is easy to forget. If you are experiencing problems, try rebuilding the desktop. We have found that this will often improve the situation. If you are still having problems, though:

◆ **Throw away the Preferences.** If you are experiencing problems in just one program and not across-the-board, you could have a corrupt preferences file. Located in the System folder is the Preferences folder. Any application, when it is first opened, creates a file in the Preferences folder. This file holds the information about the settings of the application. If this file gets corrupted, it can cause the application to act bizarre and to crash. With the application closed, throw away its Preferences file. A new one is recreated when the application is reopened. You will have to go back to reset all of your default settings in the application. If this doesn't work, try:

◆ **Zap the PRAM.** The PRAM is a tiny cache of memory which stores such settings as Time and Date. This can become corrupted and make the computer act funny. Restart the computer and hold down the Command key, the Alt/Option key, the P and the R. The computer restarts, then restarts a second time.

◆ **Disconnect the SCSI chain.** This eliminates the possibility that the problems are being caused by a SCSI conflict.

- ◆ **Run Norton Disk Doctor.** Running Norton, or other diagnostic programs, eliminates the possibility that the problems are being caused by corrupt files or damaged files. If this doesn't work, it is time to get serious:

- ◆ **Reinstall the Application.** If you are still experiencing crashes in one application, then the application itself might have become corrupted. Reinstall the application from the original disks and throw away the old application.

- ◆ **Do a clean reinstall of the system software.** If you are experiencing problems, you need to do a clean reinstall. Doing an install is not enough. This merely updates the system. If there are problems there, then these may not be affected. Boot up your computer from your emergency startup disk, or from your System Install disk. Under the Mac OS, launch the Installer. Instead of clicking Install, hit Command-Shift K. This opens up a dialog window, which asks you what kind of install you wish to do. Select Install New System Folder and click OK. This renames your old System Folder, preserving its contents, and installs a new System Folder. You will need to copy all of your extra extensions from the old folder to the new one. Once you have everything out of the old System Folder that you need, trash it. Before you start re-installing extensions, though, check to make sure that this solved the problem.

  Under Windows 95, you can use the Windows 95 uninstall option to remove all traces of Windows 95 from your computer, then use the Windows 95 install application to re-install the software. If this failed, then it is time to start from scratch:

- ◆ **Do a low-level reformat of the drive.** You've wasted enough time already. It is time to stop fooling around. A simple re-initialization of the drive might do the trick, but you'd still have to take the time to reinstall everything anyway, only to have to do it all over again after you've reformatted. Use Apple's Disk Tools or FWB's HDT Primer to completely reformat the disk. Take a break, go get some coffee, take a walk around the block. Reinstall the System and all your applications from the original system disks.

By this time you have already lost several hours of production time, but that is still better than the days you might have lost if you had to take the thing into the shop. If, after trying all of these steps, you are still having problems, there is one thing left to try:

◆ **Get professional help.** A good therapist can help you overcome the grief of lost work and wasted time associated with a sick computer. A good computer shop can help your computer.

SUMMARY

You are the most important part of your work environment. Optimizing that environment should begin with you and end with you. Do whatever it takes to make yourself comfortable, enable yourself to work efficiently, and keep yourself healthy.

Too often we focus completely on our computers and on the projects we need to do on them. Creating and maintaining the work environment takes an investment of both money and time. With tight budgets and tight deadlines, optimizing and maintaining the environment often gets neglected. This is a huge mistake. An optimized environment enables you to be more productive and to avoid work lost to computer crashes, personal illness, and injury. While optimizing your environment is an intitial investment of time and money, it is an investment that will pay many dividends.

FONT MANAGEMENT

If you mention fonts to a designer or prepress professional, the likely result is what many soldiers call "The Thousand Yard Stare," an expression worn only by seasoned veterans of combat. It evokes the image of peering just beyond the horizon, knowing that the enemy lurks somewhere out there, mindless of your humanity, waiting only to carve the next notch on his rifle stock.

Yeah. Fonts are like that.

The term "font" originally pertained to a single point size of a single style of a single typeface (such as 10-point Garamond Italic or 14-point Futura Bold). Even back in the earliest days of print, fonts posed some ponderous and time-consuming problems. Crafting a font required precision tools to cut each character by hand, and it could take months or years to ready a high-quality family of typefaces for general release.

Fonts, digitally speaking, are the small files that contain the information required both to display the typeface on your monitor and to print the typeface on an output device. Fonts can easily cause the most headaches in your production environment. Many of us have experienced at least one of the following problems:

- The default font Courier appearing where your carefully selected faces should have appeared

- Fonts you need are not available in your applications

- Applications taking forever to load

- Fonts not included when a client drops off a file

- Output resulting in fouled-up tracking or kerning

- Printed text reflowing

- Boldfaced or italicized words losing their type style during output

- Naming or number conflicts appearing

For the purposes of this chapter, let's not confuse "fonts" with "type." Type refers to letter characters as they are arranged on our digital and physical pages. It is type that we adjust for style, tracking, kerning, color, and anything else that controls how the type looks. This chapter will familiarize the user with what fonts are, how they work, and what can go wrong when using them. Most importantly, this chapter shows how to establish an efficient, trouble-free system of working with large type libraries and client fonts. Although many of the problems you may have encountered are discussed, rest assured that most of them can be (and should be) avoided altogether.

Let's face it—fonts *are* tricky. Questions always arise: why are there two separate font files? Why do I have to send my fonts to the service bureau when I know they have the same fonts? Why do I have to request so many fonts from our clients? Do I need to use a font management utility? And how do I get these stupid things to work consistently? In fact, fonts are possibly the most counter-intuitive weapons in our production arsenals (thank goodness they're not explosive). As you'll see, our guiding font philosophy is very simple: *You can never be too careful when it comes to fonts!* Handling all of these auxiliary files often seems like a questionable expenditure of time and effort, especially at the end of a project when deadlines loom as tall as angry giants. Remember that fonts (and type) are one of the most essential components of any print-destined file—and if your fonts don't output properly, no one's happy. This chapter presents guidelines that ensure as much proactive safety as possible, just like your mother making you wear boots to ward off pneumonia.

In this chapter, you will:

- Learn how fonts do what they do

- Understand the convoluted history of fonts and how it impacts our daily work

- Learn to create an organized type library

- Understand the use of Expert sets and Multiple Master typefaces

- Learn to use a font management utility to maximize the efficiency of your workstation and workflow

- Understand preflight font requirements

- Establish a system of requesting fonts reliably from your client base, or delivering fonts to your service bureau

- Understand the applicable licensing issues surrounding the use of fonts

- Learn the best methods of creating a type catalog to display fonts for staff and clients

THE NATURE OF FONTS

Before we get too far into the specifics of fonts, let's cover some general terms. Fonts consist of up to 256 individual characters, ranging from a lowercase b to a bullet, a trademark symbol, or special decorative shapes (see Figure 4.1). When entire sets of letter, number, and symbol characters are grouped together with very similar design characteristics, it's called a *typeface design* (see Figure 4.2). Futura, Helvetica, and Times are examples of typeface designs. Different versions of a typeface design are called *typestyles,* which include Italic, Bold, Heavy, Extra Bold, Light, and other variations (see Figure 4.3). All of a font's variations combine to form a *typeface family,* in essence making each typestyle *members* of that family (see Figure 4.4).

Figure 4.1

Individual character shapes.

Figure 4.2

Typeface design: characters sharing characteristics.

ABCDEFghijklm1234

Figure 4.3

Typestyle: variations on a theme.

Light

Regular

Oblique

Bold

Figure 4.4

Typeface family: all typestyles combined.

Futura Light
Futura Light Oblique
Futura Book
Futura Book Oblique
Futura Regular
Futura Regular Oblique

Futura Heavy
Futura Heavy Oblique
Futura Bold
Futura Bold Oblique
Futura Extra Bold
Futura Extra Bold Oblique

On the Mac platform, each font consists of screen and printer fonts (see Figure 4.5). Screen fonts should always appear in a suitcase file, which enables them to be accessed directly by the operating system. Adobe Type 1 fonts—by far, the most popular font platform—always have accompanying printer font files. These do not go in the suitcase file. In fact, if you try to put them there, you are denied. This combination of screen and printer font information is at the heart of all font technology. Add to the mix a font utility called Adobe Type Manager, and you have the basis of all font usage on both the Windows and Macintosh platforms.

Printer Fonts

Printer fonts have little to do with what appears on your monitor. Rather, they contain the scaleable, vector-based information that's sent to a high-res PostScript output device when a file is sent to print.

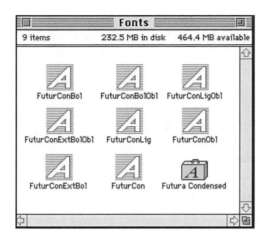

Figure 4.5

Printer fonts with suitcase file for screen fonts.

Regardless of what size type may be in your document, the printer automatically calculates what those character shapes look like at that particular size. If you've ever worked with Beziér curves in a program such as Adobe Illustrator or Macromedia FreeHand, you've already worked directly with this type of information. They're sometimes called *outline* fonts, in reference to the resolution-independent, vector-based character outlines (see Figure 4.6). This information is what allows PostScript fonts to output smoothly at any size.

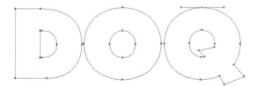

Figure 4.6

Vector-based outlines contained in a printer font.

Screen Fonts

Screen fonts contain the information that appears on your monitor. They're sometimes called "bitmap" fonts because they contain 72-dpi renderings of every character of a typeface at a particular point size (see Figure 4.7). If you double-click a font suitcase, you'll see what we mean: each screen font has a number in its title, such as 10, 12, or 14. These are the point sizes of the bitmapped characters contained in each file. When we first began using digital fonts, the vast majority of us didn't have access to PostScript output devices. We used ImageWriters, or other devices of its ilk: 72-dpi, screeching dot-matrix printers. We could only display and print type that we had the appropriate screen font for, so if we needed our Avant Garde headline to print at 52 or 13.5 points, we were outta luck.

Figure 4.7

Bitmap character shapes contained in a screen font.

Adobe Type Manager

The final piece of the digital type puzzle appeared in the form of Adobe Type Manager, a system file that finally enabled us to work typographically on our computers. ATM effectively combines screen and printer font information. By taking a peek into the printer font information, ATM determines what your type should look like. It then renders your bitmap type as smoothly as possible onscreen, regardless of point size, zoom factors, rotation, or scaling (see Figure 4.8). The best part is, it all happens automatically with no necessary interaction on your part. All ATM needs to accomplish this is one screen font (regardless of its point size) and the printer font. Theoretically, you could go into all your font suitcases and discard all but one screen font for every member of every family—but don't bother. You'll spend a lot of time, risk throwing out something important, and not save that much room on your hard drive.

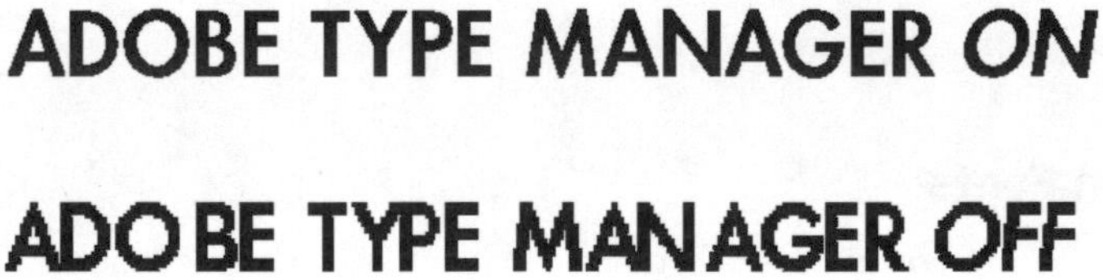

Figure 4.8

Type onscreen before and after using Adobe Type Manager.

ADOBE TYPE MANAGER ON

ADOBE TYPE MANAGER OFF

ATM also lets you print Type 1 fonts (the most commonly encountered font architecture) smoothly to non-PostScript printers, like StyleWriters, DeskWriters, and low-end personal laser printers. If you've ever purchased Adobe fonts or other Adobe software, ATM came bundled with it.

If you're working in Windows, ATM works without screen fonts being present, creating onscreen bitmaps from existing .pfb files, or the outline fonts used on the Windows platform.

So you have three pieces of software working together to give us type that looks and prints as smoothly and accurately as possible. The only thing you need to do is follow these guidelines:

◆ Keep a font's suitcase file and printer fonts in the same folder. Separating them prevents proper output.

◆ Never remove screen fonts from their suitcases. Consider screen fonts in a suitcase as one file, even though the suitcase contains many different files.

◆ Never combine screen fonts from different families in the same suitcase. Doing so makes it more difficult for both designers and output professionals to keep track of which fonts are available.

◆ Never change the names of suitcases or printer fonts. Your type library may be huge and organization is the key.

DEVIATION FROM THE NORM: EXPERT SETS AND MULTIPLE MASTER FONTS

Expert collections and extra fonts that accompany certain typefaces are a way of compensating for the limited number of characters each font can offer (the highest number of possible characters in a single font is 256). Expert sets generally contain special characters, such as fractions, numerals with descenders, and other symbols not contained in standard fonts. Adobe fonts often have additional Small Caps and Old Style Figures (abbreviated "SC&OSF") font sets as well. These font sets broaden the range of possible letter shapes (see Figure 4.9).

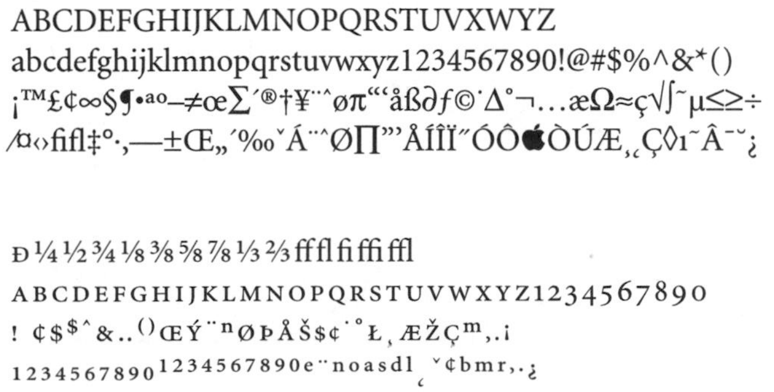

ABCDEFGHIJKLMNOPQRSTUVXWYZ
abcdefghijklmnopqrstuvwxyz1234567890!@#$%^&*()
¡™£¢∞§¶•ªº–≠œ∑´®†¥¨ˆøπ“‘åß∂ƒ©˙∆˚¬…æΩ≈ç√∫˜µ≤≥÷
/¤◊fifl‡°·‚—±Œ„´‰ˇÁ¨ˆØ∏”’ÅÍÎÏ˝ÓÔ◉ÒÚÆ¸Ç◊ı˜Â˜¿

Ð ¼ ½ ¾ ⅛ ⅜ ⅝ ⅞ ⅓ ⅔ ff fl fi ffi ffl
ABCDEFGHIJKLMNOPQRSTUVWXYZ1234567890
! ¢$$^&..()ŒÝ¨ⁿØÞÅŠ$¢˙˚Ł¸ÆŽÇᵐ,.¡
1234567890¹²³⁴⁵⁶⁷⁸⁹⁰eˀnoasdl ˅¢bmr,.¿

Figure 4.9

Minion Regular and Minion Expert character sets.

Multiple Master Typefaces give the user a unique possibility. Have you ever been setting type and felt that Futura Heavy is just a touch too light, but Futura Bold (the next step up) is way too fat?

Multiple master technology enables you to literally create variations of a typeface from extremely light to extremely bold, very condensed to very expanded, and any combination therein (see Figure 4.10). Use them sparingly. Some older laser printers and imagesetter software may be incompatible with Multiple Master fonts. Also, many service bureaus have found that many people do not supply the necessary Multiple Master font files when a job is dropped off for output. Again, the purpose of this book is to lower the margin for error as much as possible. Limiting your use of this font platform will do just that. If you do use these fonts, contact your service bureau to ensure that they can handle them, and make sure that you include the appropriate font files with your job.

Figure 4.10

Multiple Master fonts.

A BRIEF AND SORDID HISTORY

If it wasn't for the advent of PostScript fonts back in 1984, who knows *what* would have happened to all of us. The graphics revolution would have stalled. Conventional prepress techniques would still dominate the industry and you'd be reading something else right now, like a month-old *Newsweek* or maybe an issue of *Pravda*. For the first time ever, digital typefaces enabled us to assume personal and exacting control over the visual nuances of the words so vital in our communication. So we don't hate fonts for being beautiful—rather, we just get frustrated by their inherent complexity that hasn't changed since day one.

Three forms of font files circulate throughout the graphics industry: Adobe Type 1, Adobe Type 3, and Apple's TrueType. To Mac-based professionals, the industry standard is Adobe Type 1. The vast majority of fonts in the marketplace—at last count, over 45,000 different faces—are Type 1. If you've purchased fonts from a credible vendor in the last six years, the chances are very good that you bought Type 1 fonts. These fonts exist in much the same form as the first versions of Helvetica or Times that Adobe released: a combination of screen and printer fonts that enable you to manipulate type and send that information to a high-res output device.

Remember, Adobe introduced PostScript, the revolutionary page description language that gave the digital graphics industry its initial kick in the butt. Also, remember that PostScript-driven outlines, the vector-based character renderings that allow type to be output at high resolutions at different sizes, lies at the heart of font technology. Back in the mid-80s, the rights to PostScript font technology was a hot commodity indeed. So hot that Adobe decided not to divulge all its secrets to third-party developers. Early in the game, Adobe mastered the art of the effective font format, called it Type 1, and said "ch-ching!" while dollar signs appeared in their eyes. For years, Adobe had all the Type 1 cards held securely to their vests and, frankly, who could blame them. This font format had—and still has—all the qualities we've come to appreciate most in our type libraries, namely, predictable system behavior and reliable output.

Third-party font developers, meanwhile, were left with *most*, but not *all*, of the Type 1 information to work with. The result? Adobe Type 3 fonts. Most notably, Type 3 fonts were unhinted, or did not contain the information needed to print to lower-resolution output devices while maintaining print quality. Type 3 fonts also were not compatible with Adobe Type Manager or non-PostScript printers.

Throughout the 80s, Type 3 fonts abounded. Before too long, anyone with a little patience could produce these fonts in their living room and release them to the world through bulletin board services and usenet groups. The differences between Type 1 and Type 3 fonts were subtle, but important. They looked the same onscreen, they both had suitcase files and outline fonts, and they both referenced Adobe. They both essentially *smelled* the same. The primary difference was manifest during output: Type 3 fonts printed *far* more unreliably than Type 1. By unreliable output, we mean that there were more instances of random misprinting, unaccountable text reflow, and awkward tracking and kerning results, just to name a few.

Things changed in 1989, however, when Apple was preparing to release the first version of System 7. Hungry for a piece of Adobe's pie, they developed what they hoped would be a font format as revolutionary as Type 1, called TrueType. It was quite a departure from what we already knew about Type 1 and Type 3 fonts. For one thing, each font consisted of only a suitcase file— no outline fonts. The Mac-based graphics industry was in the midst of taking off and Apple had big plans for its new font platform. Until, of course, Adobe caught wind of the whole thing and decided to make a proactive strike of its own.

To succeed, Apple would have to convince all those developers to stop wasting time on the inferior Type 3 fonts and give TrueType the attention it deserved. Being an unproved platform, TrueType could only survive with plenty of developer support. Adobe, however, made the developers an offer they couldn't refuse. Faced with a competing font platform, they released *all* the Type 1 font creation secrets to any developer who wanted them. As any sane person would do, the developers went with the proven product, while TrueType fonts languished for years before resurfacing, ironically, in the Windows-based graphics market. Without the support it needed so badly, TrueType fonts never evolved to the same reliable form as Type 1 and never found a niche in the Mac-based graphics market. Adobe Type 1, after all these years, still wears the crown.

Now for the big question: "What does all of this have to do with me and my work?" The short answer is "Use only Adobe Type 1 fonts," but it's not always that easy.

Millions of individual Type 3 fonts are still swimming around the marketplace (a friend of ours still has over 800 of them stashed away on floppies). When you think about it, a lot of people out there have been using the same fonts for 10 years or more, transferring them from system to system. It's absolutely possible for these same people to unwittingly use those Type 3 fonts today in a design project, bring them into the service bureau, and get surprisingly inaccurate results. The only way to determine if your old fonts are Type 3 is to examine the printer font icon (look for a number three) or take a look at the Read Me file that might have accompanied the font. Type 3 fonts were required to identify themselves one way or another (see Figure 4.11). Today's new, improved hardware and software does nothing to rectify the potential hassles built into every Type 3 font. The best solution is always going to be throwing them away. Peruse your library, choose the fonts you need, and purchase the Type 1 versions. Discard the rest. Your work is worth it. And if you are receiving Type 3 fonts from your client base, kindly but firmly recommend that they do the same.

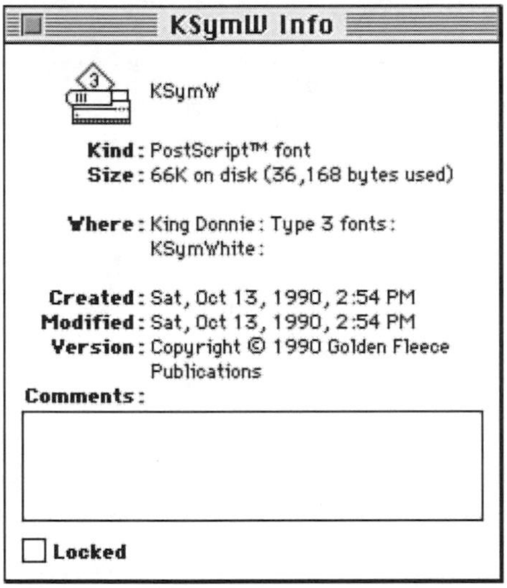

Figure 4.11

Type 3 fonts are recognizable by their icon or by a descriptor under "kind."

Similarly, sneaky appearances are made by TrueType fonts. Every Macintosh computer ships with a bevy of TrueType faces pre-installed in the System's Fonts folder. Also, everytime you purchase an Apple LaserWriter and run the software installation program from the accompanying diskettes, TrueType fonts are often automatically installed again in the Fonts folder. All the user sees are new typefaces spontaneously appearing in the Fonts menu. If your only use for fonts is to output to a relatively low-resolution laser printer, TrueType fonts work just fine. If you need to output your fonts to an imagesetter or a digital press, they should be sought out and destroyed.

The best bet is to periodically check your Fonts folder for any new and unwanted fonts. There are also utilities available that perform similar missions. Our favorite is "theFONDler," from Rascal software. It searches for different font platforms, regroups misplaced outline fonts with their associated suitcases, and eliminates potentially troublesome duplicate fonts, among other tasks.

TrueType works relatively well on Windows-based systems. On a Macintosh workstation, you should look for two things when identifying TrueType fonts. First, look for any font consisting of only a suitcase with no printer fonts to be found. Second, open the suitcase. If the icon for the file or files within has the "triple-A" TrueType mark, then discard the font immediately (see Figure 4.12). When using Windows, look for the .FOT filename extension.

Figure 4.12

TrueType fonts are recognizable by their tell-tale "Triple A" icon.

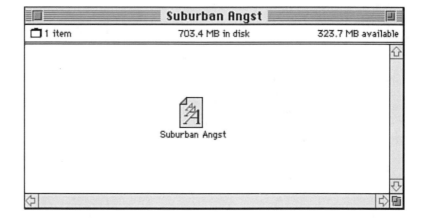

The key here is not succumbing to the notion that you're deleting important and valuable software. On the contrary, using only Type 1 fonts is hands-down the safest bet in the industry and that should be reason enough. As far as new fonts are concerned, the playing field is pretty safe. As we've said, nearly all fonts sold today are available in Type 1 form and almost all fonts available for free downloading are in both Type 1 and TrueType form. If you must use TrueType fonts, understand the disadvantages are unpredictable output and incompatibility with new technologies, such as digital presses.

If you have no means of replacing your fonts with new versions, another option is to use font creation programs, such as Fontographer and Font Monger, to convert your Type 3 and TrueType fonts to Type 1. This is not the panacea it seems; however, the most delicate font information is not guaranteed to translate accurately and reading a proof is the wrong time to find that out. New, honest Adobe Type 1 fonts are always the winning choice.

USING FONTS, PART ONE: THE FONTS FOLDER

You can "turn on fonts," letting you access them in your programs, in two ways. You can use the Fonts folder, a feature built into every Macintosh operating system, or a font management utility, such as Symantec Suitcase or the latest version of ATM. Although we absolutely recommend using a management utility in nearly every production environment, let's talk about the Fonts folder: what it does, what it's good for, and its limitations.

The Fonts folder is like a big Go button. Drop a suitcase and printer fonts into it and the font title appears in the type menu of all your applications. Tired of using that font? Take them out of the Fonts folder (see Figure 4.13). It seems simple, and in the right circumstances, it is. Using the Fonts folder is adequate if the following is true:

◆ You own fewer than 50 fonts. If you use more than that regularly, you're a perfect candidate for font management.

◆ All of your printing is done in-house and from your computer.

◆ You seldom, if ever, need to transport or copy fonts to other locations.

◆ You seldom, if ever, receive fonts from outside clients.

Managing Fonts with ATM

Adobe is finally building a feature into ATM that should have been there years ago: font management.

ATM DeLuxe, released in Winter 1996, contains a built-in interface that allows the construction and use of font sets. Just as with Suitcase, you can delineate sets for different projects and uses, as well as standard sets for everyday use. It also ships with an upgraded Type Reunion, which takes font management one step further by enabling you to create custom font menus from within your applications. Imagine being able to organize your font menu by projects and clients, rather than just alphabetically.

Also like Suitcase, it has the capability to quickly load and unload font information, as on an output workstation.

From what we've seen, the major advantage ATM DeLuxe has over Suitcase is that almost everyone on the planet already uses ATM. Many people are sure to start using it to manage their fonts, and since it's from Adobe, you can be sure the product will improve over time. We still give the nod to Suitcase, whose interface is more sublime, and allows a few options that ATM does not, like sets that

continues

don't have to be manually deactivated to be kept from loading on startup.

Windows 95 and Fonts

Unfortunately, there is no Windows-based font management utility we can safely recommend. At best, management on this platform will most closely resemble using the Macintosh's Fonts folder.

All fonts on this platform must be installed using the Fonts Control Panel, similar to the Mac's Font/DA Mover of years past. Or, you can use the Windows Explorer to drag-and-drop font files from a disk into the Fonts Folder (although this will not always register properly; print a test page to make sure).

Once installed, a Registry is generated in the Control Panel, listing all fonts alphabetically. Additional fonts are added by using the Files: Install dialog.

Fonts are easily removed from the Registry by using Windows Explorer to drag-and-drop them into the Recycle bin.

Be certain to delete client fonts as soon as a file has been output. Otherwise, they remain permanently added to the font Registry.

Some workstations have hundreds of fonts installed in the fonts folder. Many designers like the idea of having *all* their fonts available to them, and the Fonts folder is an easy way to make this happen. However, some risks are inherent in this technique:

◆ Large numbers of continually activally fonts radically slow down system and application startups.

◆ At last count, a 128-suitcase limit was in the Fonts folder. So either you'll only have access to the first 128 suitcases in your font library (appearing alphabetically), or you'll be compelled to combine suitcases to squeak past the limit. The latter technique wreaks havoc on organizing a coherent library, especially if the new suitcases are given names like "Fonts," "A-D," or "Type Suitcase 2."

◆ You have no easy way to deal with naming or numbering conflicts.

Note

The only fonts that should remain in the Fonts folder are Chicago, Geneva, Monaco, and Symbol (see Figure 4.14). These fonts are never used for high-res output. They're system fonts and leaving them in the Fonts folder ensures that they are available to your operating system all the time. Beyond that, we'll never use the Fonts folder again.

The Fonts folder is where you put fonts and then forget about them. It has nothing to do with font *management,* an efficient and flexible workflow system. The only time you should manually handle your fonts is when copying them to or from transport media. The more you move these files back and forth on your hard drive, the more likely it is that fonts will be misplaced, deleted, duplicated, and generally disorganized. It's not that we think you're incapable of handling all your fonts—we think you shouldn't have to. You're busy enough as it is, without tempting human error.

And that's exactly what font management will help us avoid.

Figure 4.13

Using the Fonts folder.

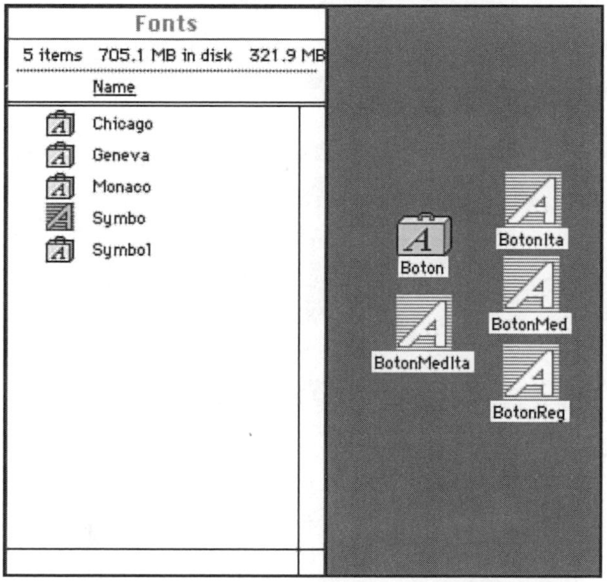

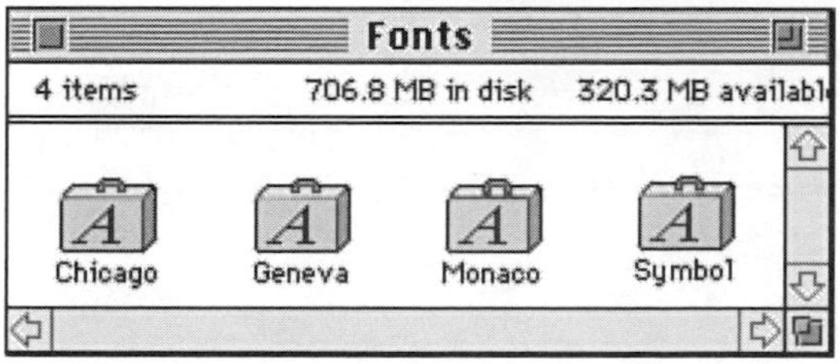

Figure 4.14

Leave only Chicago, Geneva, Monaco, and Symbol in the Fonts folder.

USING FONTS, PART TWO: SETTING UP A FONT LIBRARY

An organized library is the first step toward true font management. In it, you will have separate folders for your legally-owned fonts, another for your temporarily held client fonts, and another for permanently-held client fonts. Of course, you'll find it's easy to add new folders, depending on the classification of fonts that works best with your environment.

Setting up a basic library is easy:

1. Create a folder called "Type Library." Don't call it "Fonts." The System Folder already has dibs on that one (see Figure 4.15).

Figure 4.15

Create a folder called "Type Library."

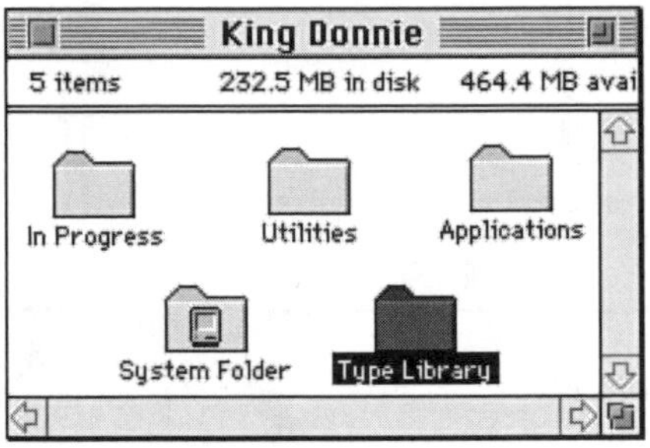

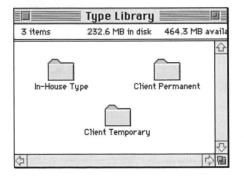

2. Don't keep your library in your System Folder—keep it in plain sight on your main volume with your System Folder, applications folder, utilities, and so on.

3. In "Type Library," create three folders: "In-House Type," "Client Temporary," and "Client Permanent" (see Figure 4.16).

Figure 4.16

Create three additional folders to complete a basic library set-up.

4. Place all of your legally owned fonts into "In-House Type." Often, this involves dragging the contents of the Fonts folder into the new folder. Whenever possible, don't store different sections of your in-house type library in separate folders—keep them all in the same volume (see Figure 4.17).

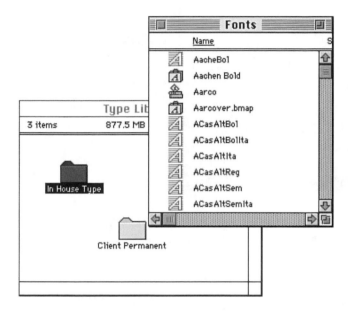

Figure 4.17

Store all legally-owned fonts in "In-House Type" folder.

5. If you are holding type for client work (read: if you have type that's not legally yours), place it in the "Client Permanent." Feel free to keep individual client folders within the Client Permanent folder (see Figure 4.18).

6. The "Client Temporary" folder will be used for type that comes and goes on a day-to-day basis.

Figure 4.18

Store client type in "Client Permanent" folder.

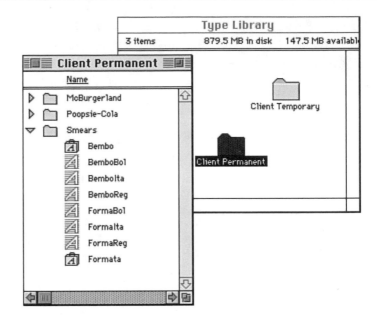

7. Open each folder and select "By Name" from the Finder's View menu. This displays all of the font files in alphabetical order. Notice that suitcases appear in immediate proximity to the necessary printer fonts. This makes things very simple when it comes time to locate specific fonts and copy them onto another disk (see Figure 4.19).

Figure 4.19

Apply the "By Names" view to all font folder windows.

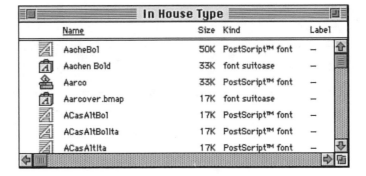

Your type library is now organized. Whenever you purchase new fonts, copy them directly into your "In-House Type" folder. Even if you have hundreds of fonts in one folder, that's OK. After you begin using a management utility, you'll find that it makes things easier. If your fonts number in the thousands, you may want to divide your folders: "In-House Type A-M," "In-House Type N-Z," and so on. But unless you have that many different fonts, there is no immediate need to do this.

USING FONTS, PART THREE: FONT MANAGEMENT

Your library may be organized, but now that the fonts are out of the Fonts folder, you'll find they can't be accessed in any of your programs. They must be turned on, or recognized by your operating system. This is where your font management utility comes in. The essence of font management is this: you can turn on and off fonts as you need them. That sounds overly simple, but think about it. Accessing only the fonts you need solves many problems:

◆ Font naming and numbering conflicts are avoided.

◆ Sluggish system and application startups are prevented.

◆ You can access only the fonts supplied by a client for outputting a job.

◆ Accidental duplication and misplacement of fonts are prevented because a font will not have to be moved to be turned on.

The circumstances in which you'll be accessing your fonts will differ according to your responsibilities, but it all revolves around your basic library set-up. As we cover methods of using our font management utility, we'll discuss techniques specific to both designers and output specialists, including:

◆ Establishing permanent startup fonts

◆ Establishing easy-to-access font groupings

◆ Workflow systems for working with client type most effectively

Symantec Suitcase

The venerable Suitcase is the most widely used font management utility, and until its recent upgrade to Version 3, it was one of the most frustrating. Gone now are the random crashes, corrupt extension files, and damaged font suitcases. All that has been replaced with a sleeker, more intuitive interface, higher reliability, and compatibility with PCI Macs to boot. If you're still using Suitcase 2.1.3 or 2.1.4, upgrade to 3.0 (or higher) right away.

The first thing you see when you select Suitcase from the Apple Menu is a window titled "Sets." This will be our primary font management tool. In this window, we're going to establish sets, or little groups of font names, that we can turn on and off with wanton abandon.

The first set you see is one called "Startup Set." If you want certain fonts—your favorite or your most commonly used—to be available to your system everytime you start your workstation, this is the set in which they belong. And no, don't add your entire library to the Startup Set. This defeats the entire purpose of font management and you'll have wasted the fifty bucks you spent on the utility in the first place. Plus, trying to open huge libraries all at once can freeze your system on startup. Try to keep the number under 30.

I. Select the set (see Figure 4.20).

Figure 4.20

Select the set by clicking.

2. Click the Add button (see Figure 4.21).

Figure 4.21

Click Add to access fonts.

3. Find your In-House Type folder in the navigation window that appears (see Figure 4.22).

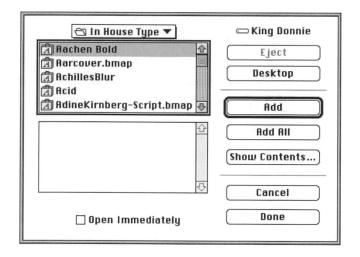

Figure 4.22

Locate the In-House Type folder.

4. One by one, add the names of the suitcases you want as startup items (see Figure 4.23).

Figure 4.23

Add startup fonts.

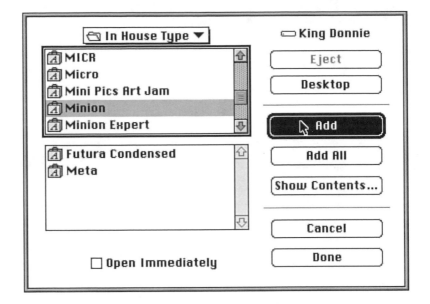

5. Click Done (see Figure 4.24).

Figure 4.24

Click Done to complete process.

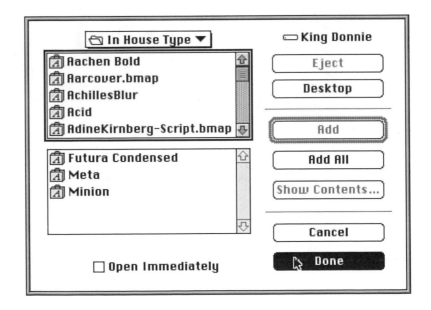

Review the Sets window. Unless we tell Suitcase to open the font, no connection is made between the font and the operating system. That's exactly what happens with Suitcase—it forces the system to recognize the fonts you have "opened." *Your fonts have not been moved on the hard drive.* After you select the Startup Set, you can choose either the Open or the Close button underneath.

Establishing Your In-House Set

Here's where Suitcase is most useful, but it gets a little tricky. By creating additional sets in the Sets window, you create groups of font suitcases that you can access quickly. Unless you point out to Suitcase that a particular font exists (by either listing it in a set or manually navigating through the Add function everytime), you can't turn it on or off on the fly. So you make additional sets, depending on your needs, that let us work most efficiently. These sets are called Temporary because unlike the Startup Set, these fonts are not be turned on whenever your workstation starts. You'll have to open an entire set or a font within a set to use it in an application.

Our first temporary set contains all of our in-house fonts:

1. Click New Set. Name it "In-House Type," the same as your primary type library folder (see Figure 4.25).

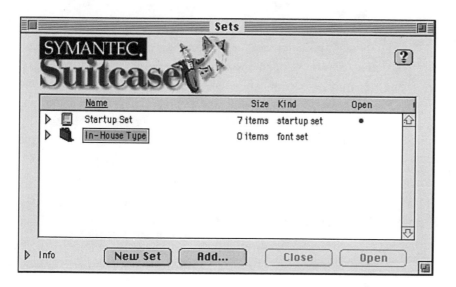

Figure 4.25

Create In-House Type set.

2. Click Add and navigate to your In-House Type folder.

3. Click Add All to add every suitcase to the set. *Make certain that "Open Immediately" is NOT checked.* You don't want all these fonts open at the same time, remember? (See Figure 4.26.)

Figure 4.26

Add every in-house font to set by clicking Add All.

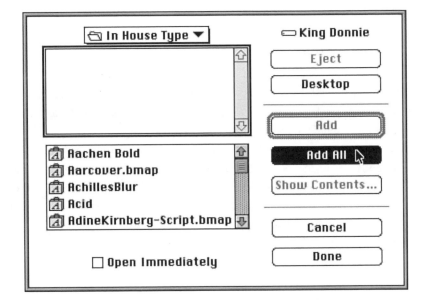

4. Click Done.

All of your in-house fonts have been added to a temporary set in Suitcase. Whenever you want to open or close a font, you launch Suitcase from the Apple Menu, go to your In-House set, leave the little side arrow in the down position to have this list visible at all times (see Figure 4.27), and select the fonts you want to open or close. There's no need to move things around and no extra navigating through the Add window. For designers, this offers the quickest access to type libraries. For output specialists, this method also provides the surest way to deal with come-and-go client type.

Establishing Job and Client Sets

Additional sets can be created for job- or client-specific font groupings. The same font can be added to multiple sets, so you can be as organized as you need to be. Here are a couple examples.

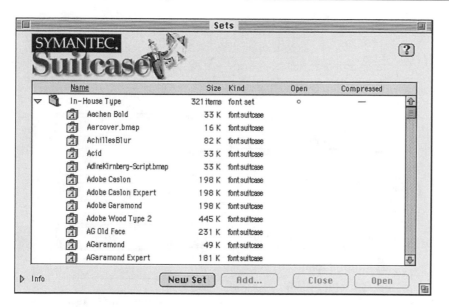

Figure 4.27

All fonts are immediately accessible.

Job-Specific Sets

Let's say you're designing a full-color brochure. Your fonts are Adobe Caslon, Franklin Gothic, and Viking. These fonts are part of your large in-house library, but you don't need to go hunting through your in-house set everytime you want to open them up. Make a set dedicated to the project:

1. Create a new set called "Brochure Fonts" (see Figure 4.28).

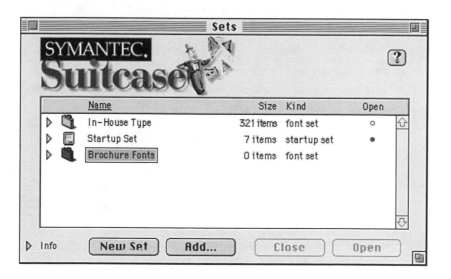

Figure 4.28

Create a set for project-specific fonts.

2. Add Adobe Caslon, Franklin Gothic, and Viking to the set. It doesn't matter if they already appear in another set. If you prefer, you can drag-and-drop suitcases from one set to another and avoid the whole navigational process (see Figure 4.29).

Figure 4.29

Add appropriate fonts to set.

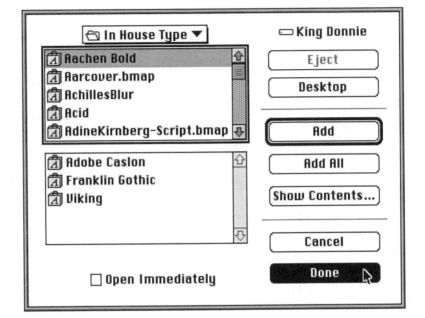

3. Whenever you need to open these fonts to work on the project, select the Brochure Fonts set, click Open, and work away (see Figure 4.30).

4. When you're done with the fonts, close them. When done with the entire set, select it and choose "Remove Selected Items…" from the Edit menu (see Figure 4.31).

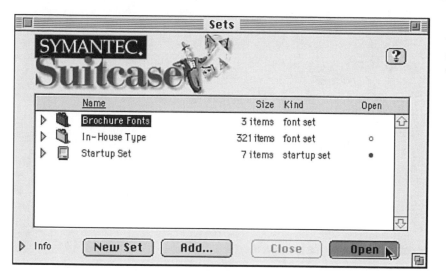

Figure 4.30

Open the fonts by selecting Set and clicking Open.

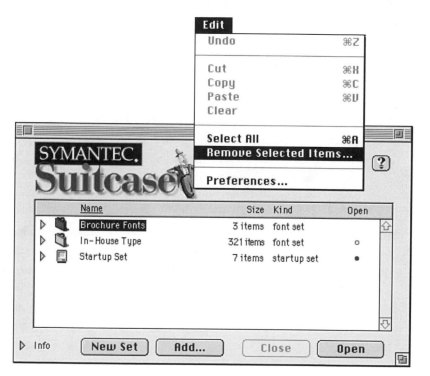

Figure 4.31

Remove unneeded sets.

Client-Specific Sets

Most designers have clients who they work with over and over again. Many of these clients are companies with "Corporate Fonts" or typefaces used in any collateral materials based on their corporate identity. Making a client set gives you quick access to their fonts next time you work on one of their projects. To do so:

1. Create a new set named after the client.

2. Add the client's fonts to the set.

3. Open and close the set whenever necessary.

Preflight Font Requirements

Everything we've talked about so far revolves around a trouble-free system for using fonts. The important part of that system is ensuring the most accurate output possible. Again, our advice is simple: whenever a job is sent to a service bureau or printer for output, *all of the fonts that were used during the creation of that job must be supplied by the client.* There are no exceptions to this rule. Even if the font in question is Helvetica, it is a font *everyone* must have.

Fonts, like any other software, are upgraded as well. The only thing is, you aren't notified about it. No version numbers exist, but if you Get Info on a printer font file (single-click the file and then select ⌘+I), you'll see creation and modification dates (see Figure 4.32). The changes in the upgrades are very minimal: a micron less thickness in the descender of the lower-case *p*, or a fraction more space in the kern pair of *t* and *h*. Adobe has released maybe seven or eight versions of Helvetica that do not include any third-party variations. If you create a file using the 1987 version of Helvetica, send the file to a service bureau, and output the file using their 1994 version, *you are using a different font to output your file!* This can easily cause text reflow, unexpected bad kerning, and generally unsatisfactory results. The only way to avoid this is for service bureaus to refuse to accept files with no fonts included.

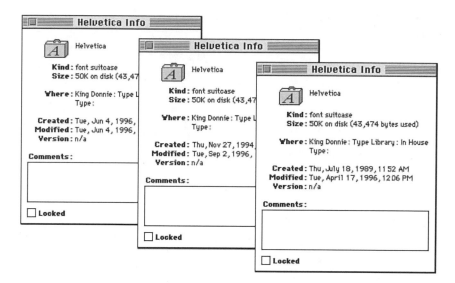

Figure 4.32

Note the different creation dates on these font files.

Including the appropriate fonts is a breeze:

1. In your page layout program, use the font utility to determine which fonts need to be supplied. In Quark, it's "Font Usage" under the Utilities menu (see Figure 4.33). In PageMaker, it's "Pub Info" under the Utilities menu/Plug-Ins (see Figure 4.34).

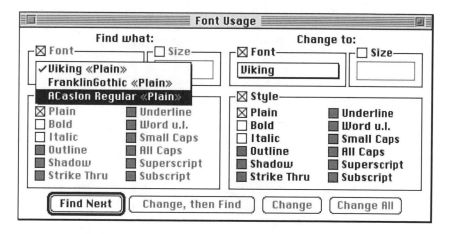

Figure 4.33

Quark's Font Usage window.

Figure 4.34

PageMaker's Pub Info window.

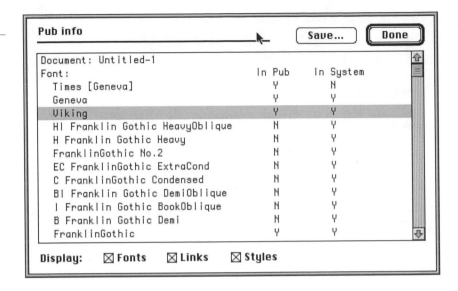

2. In Suitcase, select your In-House Type set and click Close (open fonts cannot be copied to another disk).

3. Open the In-House Type folder in your type library. Select the suitcases and printer fonts for the entire font family of each font used in the publication and copy them to your transport media (see Figure 4.35).

Figure 4.35

Selecting font families is simpler because of View By Name command.

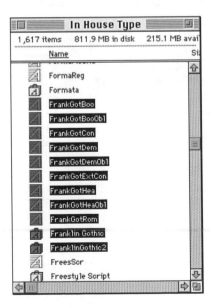

Another important reason to supply entire font families has to do with the Type Style features in many applications. In days past, if you highlighted text and applied an Italic or Bold style tag, the application would force the type to look italic or bold. That way, one only had to supply the Plain version of the font. Today, applications automatically apply a command that substitutes those style tags with the proper font. This means that if you have strategically italicized key words throughout the text of your document, the italic version of the font must be supplied as well. If it's not present, none of the type will be italicized (see Figure 4.36). Unfortunately, if you just use those style buttons, the application does not warn you if the font is missing during output. Including entire font families eliminates that problem. Some people go one step further and use their application's Find and Replace command to swap enforced typestyles with true Italic or Bold text.

Feeling *dusted,* shoes like *mustard,*	Feeling dusted, shoes like mustard,	**Figure 4.36**
Haven't got a *clue*	Haven't got a clue	
Sensing *reeling,* pigs all *squealing,*	Sensing reeling, pigs all squealing,	*One sample had the entire font family supplied (left), the other didn't (right).*
Everything turns *blue*	Everything turns blue	
Mythic *poems,* Leonard *Cohen*	Mythic poems, Leonard Cohen	
Touching my *tattoo*	Touching my tattoo	
Tears and *heartache* at the *clambake,*	Tears and heartache at the clambake,	
Someone ate my *food.*	Someone ate my food.	

Now you can output the file while avoiding as many troublesome areas as possible. With the preceding font system in place, the process for loading, outputting, and unloading fonts is as follows:

1. On the output workstation, use Suitcase to close *all* open fonts. This is critical—it virtually eliminates naming and numbering conflicts (see Figure 4.37).

Figure 4.37

Close all open fonts.

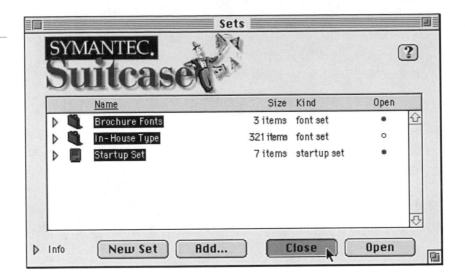

2. Create a temporary set and use Suitcase to open only the fonts that the client provided. If any fonts have not been supplied, it will be apparent when the document is opened (see Figure 4.38).

Figure 4.38

Open only client fonts.

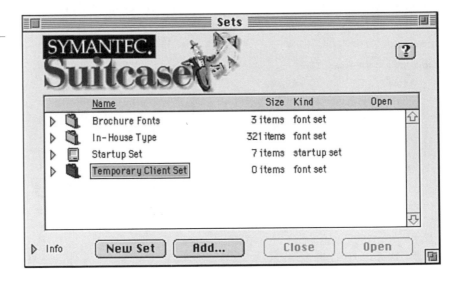

3. Output the file.

4. In Symantec's Suitcase, close all the client fonts and remove any temporary sets (see Figure 4.39).

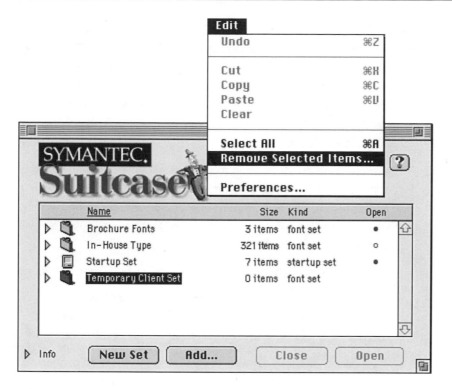

Figure 4.39

Removing the temporary sets from the Suitcase.

5. Decide what needs to happen next: if you have another job to output, go back to step two and repeat the process. If you are finished, you can turn your original fonts back on.

FONTS, SERVERS, AND NETWORKS

Many companies store font libraries on central servers and enable system-wide users common access to the font information. Suitcase even enables users to share the same font at the same time. Our advice is simple: *do not do this*.

We learned this the hard way and we're not the kind of guys who get any satisfaction out of watching people make the same mistakes we did. You see, when you open a font and use it in an application, your operating system makes a constantly active connection with that font. Networks were not intended for that kind of activity. Data transfer? Fine. Font connection? No way. If your font connection is interrupted, it causes your computer to freeze. If someone is sharing the same font as you, they'll freeze, too. And if the server from which everyone is sharing fonts crashes, everybody freezes.

It seems like a good idea, sharing fonts. Some people appreciate the space it frees on their hard drives; after all, our 500-font library takes up 120MB. Others have libraries so large (or hard drives so small) there's no way to store all the type on individual hard drives. Others simply mistake a program feature for something that can be automatically trusted. Consider first how much time, work, and money is lost every time a computer crashes. Then consider the following simple guideline.

The safest method, hands down, is to install identical type libraries on every workstation. If necessary, configure the type library (as described earlier) on one workstation, copy it to a SyQuest, Zip, or other transport medium, and copy it to all workstations. Large numbers of fonts don't copy well over networks, either, which is another hard lesson.

If your type library is too large to fit on a workstation, here are two options:

◆ Purchase an external hard drive for each workstation's type library. Connecting to fonts on an external drive is far safer than over a network and IGB drives can be purchased for under $300.

◆ If you store your fonts on a server, do not use Suitcase to connect to them. Instead, figure out which fonts you need, copy them from the server to your workstation, and then use Suitcase. It's a little extra effort, but it beats re-creating work lost to a system freeze.

FONTS DURING PRINTING

Whenever you send a document to print, it goes through a process of searching for the necessary font information. Because the documents and support files in our industry are so transient—jobs and fonts can be shuffled from workstation to workstation countless times—we recommend manually installing fonts on your hard drive, as we've discussed in this chapter. The font information is then be downloaded to your output device during printing. But for the record, this is the sequence of locations your document will search:

1. Font information manually sent to the printer's RAM

2. Fonts stored in printer ROM

3. Fonts stored on a hard drive connected to the printer

4. Fonts stored in your workstation's operating system and downloaded by the printer driver

If none of these locations contains the information needed to output a font, Courier will be used instead.

LICENSING ISSUES

A bit of confusion exists over the licensing of font technology, or your legal rights when using a font you have purchased. We have been frustrated by clients who refused to give us their fonts out of fear of prosecution and we have seen the Software Police threaten a local business with $10,000 fines if they didn't purchase legal versions of their software. The rights pertinent to the production environment are:

◆ When you buy a font, you may install that font on all your company's workstations. You do not have to buy one-per-computer, like other graphics software.

◆ When you buy a font, you buy the right to use that font to create an ultimately printed product. This means it is perfectly legal to supply a font to anyone involved in the process of printing or reproducing the font, like freelance designers, service bureaus, or print shops.

◆ It is also legal to hold client fonts, provided you do not use them for any other work but the client's. This is the difference between *copying* and *pirating*. It's pirating if you make money by using a font that doesn't belong to you.

◆ It is legal to change or edit fonts using programs such as FontMonger or Fontographer. Legally, typefaces cannot be copyrighted; only the coded information used in creating that particular font are

Creating a Font Catalog

Designers and service providers alike will find it convenient to keep a catalog of their available type. Usually, this entails a sampling of all the characters of each typeface arranged on an appropriately titled page (see Figure 4.40). Creating something like this by hand is needlessly time consuming, especially if you have a large type library. Fortunately, a great utility called "The TypeBook," also from Rascal Software, is available. For $40, you can automatically inventory, view, catalog, and print your entire font library. It's handy, efficient, and cheap, even counting the couple of bucks you'll spend on the three-ring binder.

copyrighted. So, if you make a couple of microscopic changes in a typeface, you have a font you can use freely, or even sell. Unfortunately, everytime a font is converted to another platform, certain information is lost. This eventually impacts how well the font will output, if at all.

Figure 4.40

One page of a type catalog created with The TypeBook.

Avenir-Heavy

FONT: R Avenir Roman   Style: Bold   ID: 14680   Type: PS

6 pt. ABCDEFGHIJKLMNOPQRSTUVWXYZabcdefghijklmnopqrstuvwxyz0123456789!?,"¢$&%{}*
7 pt. ABCDEFGHIJKLMNOPQRSTUVWXYZabcdefghijklmnopqrstuvwxyz0123456789!?,"¢$&%{}*
8 pt. ABCDEFGHIJKLMNOPQRSTUVWXYZabcdefghijklmnopqrstuvwxyz0123456789!?,"¢$&%{}*
9 pt. ABCDEFGHIJKLMNOPQRSTUVWXYZabcdefghijklmnopqrstuvwxyz0123456789!?,"¢$&%{}*
10 pt. ABCDEFGHIJKLMNOPQRSTUVWXYZabcdefghijklmnopqrstuvwxyz0123456789!?,"¢$&%{}*
12 pt. ABCDEFGHIJKLMNOPQRSTUVWXYZabcdefghijklmnopqrstuvwxyz0123456789!?,
14 pt. ABCDEFGHIJKLMNOPQRSTUVWXYZabcdefghijklmnopqrstuvwxyz012
18 pt. ABCDEFGHIJKLMNOPQRSTUVWXYZabcdefghijklmno

48 pt.
ABCDEFGHIJKLMN OPQRSTUVWXYZab cdefghijklmnopqrst uvwxyz0123456789! ?,"¢$&%{}*

9/10
This page was generated by "theTypeBook", a power tool by Jim Lewis and published by Rascal Software. This is just one of many of the built in layouts. Each with its own set of configurable options. Both this copy and the page footer printed at the bottom of each page may also be customized, all easily accomplished through the Edit Menu. For technical support, or other information regarding products by Jim Lewis contact Rascal Software at (805) 255-6823. Or you can Fax them at (805) 255-9291.

10/11
This page was generated by "theTypeBook", a power tool by Jim Lewis and published by Rascal Software. This is just one of many of the built in layouts. Each with its own set of configurable options. Both this copy and the page footer printed at the bottom of each page may also be customized, all easily accomplished through the Edit Menu. For technical support, or other information regarding products by Jim Lewis contact Rascal Software at (805) 25

11/12
This page was generated by "theTypeBook", a power tool by Jim Lewis and published by Rascal Software. This is just one of many of the built in layouts. Each with its own set of configurable options. Both this copy and the page footer printed at the bottom of each page may also be customized, all easily accomplished through the Edit Menu. For technical support, or other informatio

Point size:	6	7	8	9	10	11	12	13	18	20	24	36
Chars/Pica:	4.2	3.6	3.15	2.8	2.52	2.29	2.1	1.94	1.4	1.26	1.05	0.7

Cap Height:	0.25"	0.5"	0.75"	1"	1.25"	1.5"	1.75"	2"	2.25"	2.5"	2.75"	3"
Approx. pt. size:	23.81	47.63	71.44	95.26	119.07	142.88	166.7	190.51	214.33	238.14	261.95	285.77

theTypeBook
A Power Tool from Jim Lewis

Brought to you by **Rascal** SOFTWARE

Chapter

5

FILE MANAGEMENT

File management and workflow design have been strategies of successful prepress professionals for as long as print has existed. The very language of type reflects this. "Uppercase" and "lower case" refer to the cases that type was stored in during the days of movable type. Lowercase letters were used much more frequently, so they were stored within easier reach than the less-frequently used "uppercase" letters. Early typesetters knew they needed workflow systems to make their work run more smoothly and efficiently. Although you may not be pulling type from cases to create printed material, the need for an organized approach to the collective aspects of your work is no less important.

YOU AND YOUR SYSTEM

The message is a simple one: To succeed, you need to develop a file management system and workflow methodology. This will:

◆ Help you replicate your successes and eliminate problems in your system

◆ Make it possible for other people to work on the same project without problems

◆ Make it possible to adjust to anything, from sudden emergencies to the rapidly changing world of computer technology

Competition is always growing in the prepress industry. Your ability to respond to client needs makes the difference between growth and stagnation for you and your company.

If you want to set yourself apart from the growing crowd, you need to do something to make sure that your product has an advantage over the products created by the increasing number of competitors.

More and more people are putting the money into desktop systems and adding their documents to the ever growing tide of paper. You need to set yourself apart from them. With file management and workflow systems, you can increase your level of quality while reducing the time you spend. Here are some examples of what can happen when emphasis is placed on getting things done, rather than getting them done right.

From a design standpoint, this means:

◆ The use of inch (') marks and foot ('') marks instead of true quotation marks, ''like these''

◆ Baselines creeping up and down among columns and pages

◆ Inconsistent column widths among pages

◆ Spelling mistakes in the final copy

◆ Indents drifting back and forth

In terms of prepress, this means:

- Type that defaults to Courier because the fonts weren't properly sent with the file

- White fringes around colored elements because of bad trapping

- Visible pixels in a scanned graphic

- Halftones with about three levels of gray in them—white, black, and very black

- Fine details disappearing in line art

If you want to set yourself apart from the growing crowd, do something to make sure that your product has an advantage over the products created by the increasing number of competitors.

For designers, it means making sure that the product is tight, consistent, and professionally composed. For prepress professionals, it means increasing both the speed and quality, while also increasing the number of solutions offered to clients. It comes down to adaptability. If you take advantage of opportunities for growth and change, you'll succeed.

"Yes," you may say, "but I have to get my files out, films made, proofs signed…." If you want to stay in the pattern of just-in-time production, you can. Do nothing. If you want to succeed, you need to know where you are now in the scheme of things. What is your methodology? Where are your files? What stages of the workflow create bottlenecking? How do you avoid the things that prevent you from going home to see your family and friends?

ESTABLISHING YOUR BASELINE

Finding a baseline means knowing how you work now. From that, you'll begin establishing a workflow and file management scheme. Without the baseline, you'll never find the answers. Without a workflow system, you'll never be able to take advantage of the answers you find. Answers that could even get you home early some nights. It most likely doesn't mean starting from scratch and developing a whole new way of working, but it might.

The first tools we recommend are surprisingly analog:

- **Notebooks.** Become an aggressive note taker. As we said, the more you know about where you are, the more you'll know about where to go. Even if you discover you do each job differently, you'll know more about your workflow than before.

- **A dry erase board.** Visualize your workflow and file management schemes and show them to others.

- **A file cabinet.** There is nothing like a well organized filing system, even if it is an "analog" one.

- **Time.** Invest the time now and it will pay off later.

Your goals are:

- To create a system where any file, anywhere in the process can be located at a moments notice with a minimum of information.

- To use that system to separate those files that are active from those files that are inactive. This facilitates both good housekeeping and efficient, fast, back-up strategies.

- Enable anyone filling in for you to sit at your workstation, work on your projects, and save the files comprising those projects in such a way that you can find them upon your return.

How you achieve these goals is a matter of using an effective file management system. Although we will present some specific recommendations for such a system, it has to meet your needs. This means our suggestions are nothing more than that and you'll need to make appropriate changes to our recommendations to make sure they are useful to you.

HOUSEKEEPING: CLEANSING THE SYSTEM

Start by cleaning house. Any file that doesn't somehow help you do your work should be archived and/or deleted from the System Folder to your individual job folders. Reducing the clutter on your hard drives grants many immediate benefits:

◆ There are fewer chances for files to pile up or get lost. It is surprisingly easy to have a bunch of files collect whose purpose is a mystery. Fear of the unknown can make you reluctant to trash them.

◆ The added disk space you'll have after you sort through your various folders and dispense with unnecessary items.

◆ The entire system will run more efficiently. Functions such as Find File will not have to look through unnecessary files to find things. Disk optimization software will not have to optimize unneeded files.

◆ You will be able to work more efficiently, as you will not have to hunt through extra files to find what you are looking for.

Some specific files to hunt down and banish:

◆ **Extra copies of SimpleText, WordPad, and NotePad.** Simple Text comes with most Macintosh applications, but you only need one to read all of the 90 million Read Me files you'll get in your lifetime (see Figure 5.1). Windows comes with the WordPad and the NotePad applications that are used for the Read Me files.

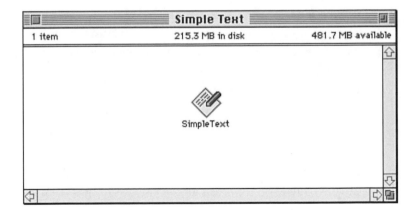

Figure 5.1

SimpleText.

◆ **Read Me (Mac) README (Windows) files.** These are loaded with good information. Read them. If you think you'll refer to them later, print them and save them in a folder in your file cabinet (see Figure 5.2).

Figure 5.2

Read Me file.

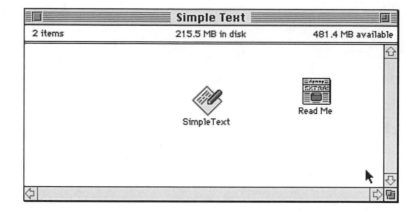

◆ **Sample files.** Most applications install samples of the kind of files they can create. These are often associated with tutorials or descriptions of processes found in the manual. In any case, they often provide no real benefit to you in your production role. Although we really do enjoy the Cowden Dinosaur sample file FreeHand has been providing since FreeHand 4.0, the 700 to 800 KB it takes to store it could be put to much better use.

◆ **Tutorial files.** Tutorials are often included when you install a program. They can provide an excellent way to learn the basics of the program, but once you know the program they are just wasting your valuable space. Delete them. You can always re-install them from the installation disks if you need to.

◆ **Extra plug-ins for applications.** Most software comes with a host of useful and not-so-useful plug-ins. They might also be called filters, XTensions (QuarkXPress), XTras (FreeHand), or Additions (PageMaker) (see Figure 5.3). Refer to your manual to determine their uses. If they add unneeded functionality to an application, send them packing. Removing these not only cleans your drive, but it enables the application to run more efficiently. Each plug-in adds to the amount of time the application takes to load, the amount of RAM the application uses, and the CPU time needed by the application. They also increase the chances that the application will come into conflict with some other piece of software. If after removing one you later decide that you want it back, you can selectively load it from the application source disks.

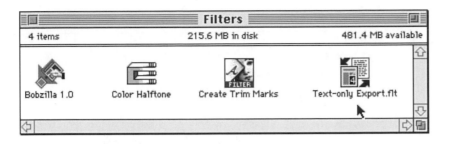

Figure 5.3

XTension, Plug-in, Illustrator Filter, PageMaker Filter.

- **Orphaned/lost files.** Many applications, when you launch them for the first time, default to their own enclosing folder as the place to save new files. It doesn't take long to build a collection of lost files inside the application folders on your drive.

- **Revisions.** As you update files during the creation or production of a job, it is easy—perhaps desirable—to create several duplicates. Make sure you dispense with them. We like keep a separate folder in each job folder that holds these revisions. Before dumping a file into the folder, we'll add the date on which we're dropping it into the revisions folder. That way, we have record of the file's history, a backup of the job, and folder you can toss entirely when the job is complete.

- **Recovered/rescued files.** When your machine crashes, some applications attempt to give you recovery capabilities by creating recovery files that update periodically. PageMaker, for instance, does a mini-save every time you change the page. If you crash, you'll end up with a temporary file that PageMaker can use to re-build files. These temporary files and any like them should be deleted. They tend hide in one of three places: the trash (Mac) or recycling bin (Windows), the System Folder (Mac), or the application's folder or directory.

This is more than just a problem of clutter. If you are losing files into the document folder, you are losing files. It is better to prevent this problem than to correct it. Some applications allow you to set, as a preference, the default folder to which it wants to save documents. Those that don't, automatically use their own folder first. Make sure you tell the application to use the folder you want it to use when you save a file. Get in the habit of saving files to the correct place—even if it means tying a string to your finger to remember.

There are software packages that can automate this, such as File Buddy, but we don't like to supplant good habits with automation. If you want to use software to enhance file management habits, but not as a replacement for them.

◆ **Auto-save files.** Some applications, such as QuarkXPress, have auto-save functions that release you from having to save all the time. This seems fine until you find that your hard drive filled with auto-save files. These are usually stored in the same folder or directory as the original document.

Frankly, we're not big fans of any auto-save feature. They tend to save the document right as you decide to launch some complex command. The results can be disastrous when the computer hangs as a file is being auto-saved or the file is irretrievably corrupted. At the very least, it's annoying to wait for the computer to finish saving so you can continue your work.

Don't leave this up to the computer. You know better than the computer does when you need to save your files. Develop the habit of saving. We save every time we sit back to think and after every correction to a file. If you can't develop a good saving habit, use an alarm clock that beeps every 15 minutes to remind you. Whatever it takes, save early and save often.

◆ **Personal files.** Doing your personal work on your workstation is one fringe benefit you can't do without. We are not so cruel as to insist that workstations have no personal files. Keep personal items down to a reasonable few. You may well want to keep personal files on a removable of some sort.

Warning

In many states, it is perfectly legal for an employer to view the contents of an employee's hard drive without warning and to use that information against him or her in a court of law. If you have sensitive files (love letters from the secretary, pornography, pirated software, and so forth) that you don't want others to see, don't leave them on your office workstation. Not that we are recommending adultery, pornography, or theft, of course! These are just a few things that can get you into very uncomfortable situations at work). Never take stupid chances.

◆ **Printer descriptions (Mac).** The Extensions folder of your System Folder contains a Printer Descriptions folder. Open it and locate the file that relates to your particular printer or printers. The rest can go; you don't need them. It is a good idea, however, to keep the General file. It may enable you to print if the file for your printer becomes corrupted.

◆ **De-installing a printer (Windows).** Windows installs printers through the use of the printer wizard. Once installed, a printer appears in the printer window as an icon with a particular printer name. Simply select it and choose File, Delete. It's gone.

Now you have a hard drive with much less clutter and a bit more room. Now what?

A FILING SYSTEM

Use folders or directories the way folders were made to be used—to collect files in logical groups. The groups we recommend are (see also Figure 5.4):

◆ **Applications.** A folder containing all the application folders you have makes it easy to locate an application and its various components. For our purposes, we call any software used to produce work an application.

◆ **Type.** All type should be kept in one place: in a Type Library on your hard drive.

◆ **Utilities.** Software designed to help keep things running smoothly should be gathered together.

◆ **System Folder (Mac).** The System Folder needs to contain only files used by the Macintosh operating system. We've heard of people hiding files there. Don't do that.

◆ **Jobs.** All your work, whether its been started, is in progress, or is completed, should be here.

◆ **Artwork.** If you keep artwork on your local hard drive (as opposed to keeping it on some networked server device, a topic for later in this chapter), create a folder to hold it.

◆ **Personal.** If you and your colleagues work on personal projects, get email, or use the computer for any other personal work, keep it separate from job files.

◆ **Pre-trash (Mac) or Pre-recycling bin (Windows).** Create a folder on the desktop with this name. That way, if you are squeamish about emptying the trash or bin, you can root through the Pre-trash folder and toss files that you are sure you can live without. Empty the Trash as soon as you transfer files into the Trash.

Warning

You may think of trying to use a couple of places for storage, from which we'd like to steer you away:

◆ *__The Desktop__. You may not think of this as a folder, but the computer does. Connect to another Macintosh via AppleTalk and you'll see that the desktop is folder. Don't keep much on your desktop. You'll end up tossing it in frustration later and then regretting that you did so.*

◆ *__Trash__. We've actually known people who used the Trash folder as a storage option. Hey, it is on the desktop after all. Don't do this!*

◆ *__Diskettes__. We don't know how many of these things we've had die on us. With an unbelievably high failure rate, floppies are really only good for moving files via sneakernet, installing very small pieces of software, or keeping hot mugs from leaving a water stain on a nice desk.*

◆ *__A Temporary Items Folder__. The system creates these folders for its own special purposes and items left in them will be deleted automatically when you restart.*

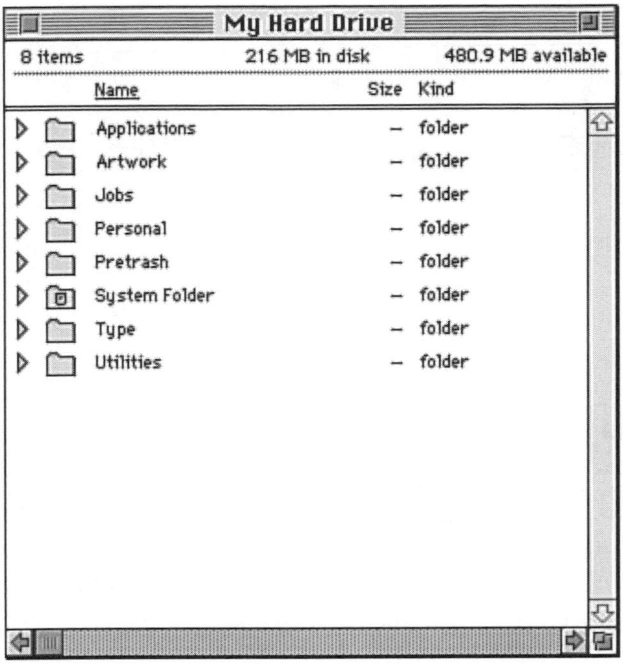

```
╔═══════════════════ My Hard Drive ═══════════════════╗
║  8 items          216 MB in disk      480.9 MB available  ║
║ ·············································································· ║
║       Name                          Size  Kind               ║
║  ▷ 📁  Applications                  —   folder              ║
║  ▷ 📁  Artwork                       —   folder              ║
║  ▷ 📁  Jobs                          —   folder              ║
║  ▷ 📁  Personal                      —   folder              ║
║  ▷ 📁  Pretrash                      —   folder              ║
║  ▷ 📁  System Folder                 —   folder              ║
║  ▷ 📁  Type                          —   folder              ║
║  ▷ 📁  Utilities                     —   folder              ║
╚══════════════════════════════════════════════════════╝
```

Figure 5.4

The organized drive.

ORGANIZING YOUR WORK

Each project you work on should be stored in its own folder. The folder will eventually contain all of the pieces needed for completing the job. Depending on the number of files in a project, you may need to create folders within this folder for the following (see also Figure 5.5):

♦ **Graphics**

♦ **Fonts**

♦ **Text files**

♦ **Reports or other electronic information**

♦ **Electronic estimate file** (if you use an electronic estimation process)

- **Time sheet file** (if you use electronic time sheets)

- **SimpleText files** (with notes from the client)

Figure 5.5

An opened jobs folder.

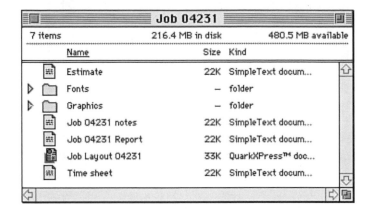

Name	Size	Kind
Estimate	22K	SimpleText docum...
▷ Fonts	—	folder
▷ Graphics	—	folder
Job 04231 notes	22K	SimpleText docum...
Job 04231 Report	22K	SimpleText docum...
Job Layout 04231	33K	QuarkXPress™ doc...
Time sheet	22K	SimpleText docum...

Job 04231 — 7 items — 216.4 MB in disk — 480.5 MB available

As a container for the project, this folder is also your way of organizing a project within the workflow. That workflow can also be organized with the use of folders…

The Jobs Folder

After you have organized the overall contents of your hard drive and collected the pieces of a job into its own folder, it's time to organize the Jobs folder. This folder should not be a loose pile of the work you are engaged in over a few months or years. Break it up in such a way that you know what stage a job is at by looking at it. As a project moves through its stages of completion, move its job folder into the folders that describe its current stage (see Figure 5.6).

- **Gathering folder.** This holds the job as you pull the many pieces you'll use together. Keep these here until you actually begin adding the sweat from your brow to the mix.

- **In progress folder.** Once a job is in progress, meaning you are actually working on it in some fashion, move it to this folder.

- **On hold Folder.** If a job gets stuck for some reason, put it in a waiting area until whatever held it up can be addressed.

- **Being proofed Folder.** Whatever kind of files you create, you'll want to proof them somehow. While you do, keep it in this folder until the proofs are complete.

- ◆ **In the Queue Folder.** As you wait for the job to be printed, keep it in a folder until it comes back from the printer or print room.

- ◆ **Completed Jobs Folder.** After you see the printed piece, you'll want to pack up the files that go into the job and ready them for archiving or trashing.

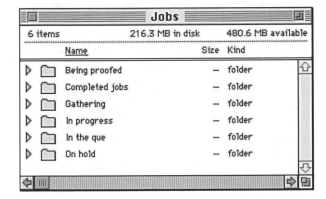

Figure 5.6

An organized jobs folder.

At this point, we could go deeper into your folders and tell you how to break them up. We'll spare you this tedium as long as you promise to consider, create, and use further groupings within your folders.

Examine the Files You Have

Examining the types of files you work with helps you understand the management needs you have. You also will be better able to make storage, archiving, and back-up decisions. This mostly relates to a file's size. If you are working with files that, on average, use one MB of disk space, then your storage and archiving needs require smaller drives and removables than if your average file size is 50MB.

The best place to see that information is in an opened folder's window. With any of the list views (Name, Kind, Label, or Date from the finder's View menu) selected, the window gives you some useful information (see Figure 5.7). For those who don't like the list views, the Get Info command from the finder's File menu will give you similar information about a single file.

Figure 5.7

List views give quite a bit of information.

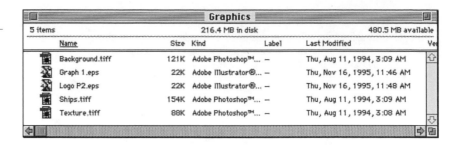

5 items			216.4 MB in disk		480.5 MB available	
Name		Size	Kind	Label	Last Modified	Ve
Background.tiff		121K	Adobe Photoshop™...	—	Thu, Aug 11, 1994, 3:09 AM	
Graph 1.eps		22K	Adobe Illustrator®...	—	Thu, Nov 16, 1995, 11:46 AM	
Logo P2.eps		22K	Adobe Illustrator®...	—	Thu, Nov 16, 1995, 11:48 AM	
Ships.tiff		154K	Adobe Photoshop™...	—	Thu, Aug 11, 1994, 3:09 AM	
Texture.tiff		88K	Adobe Photoshop™...	—	Thu, Aug 11, 1994, 3:08 AM	

Let's break this down a bit. There are five pieces of information about your files you should know :

♦ **File size.** The amount of room used on disk also clues you into the amount of RAM you'll need to work with the file.

♦ **File contents.** Scans, illustrations, layout files, and text files all use different amounts of space, have different compression capabilities, and require different management strategies.

♦ **File creator.** What application made it? Familiarity with this aspect of files in general adds to your understanding of the abilities you have for translating or using files from unfamiliar software.

♦ **The file's place in the project.** Knowing how the file fits into the larger scheme of things gives it context. It also determines where it should be kept, how accessible it needs to be, and when it will be used.

♦ **File format.** Most applications enable you to store the files in a format other than their native format. This allows the file to be useful in a variety of situations. Plus, you'll need to choose from a small few when it comes time to print the job. For example, Adobe Illustrator can save files in an Illustrator format or an Encapsulated PostScript (EPS) format (see Figure 5.8). This enables you to work on the file in the native format and then package it for printing in the EPS format.

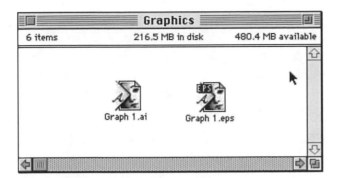

Figure 5.8

Saving Illustrator files.

Gather Statistics

Examine your files and gather statistics. Not complicated, average variations from the mean, median, and midpoint, but useful data you can collect and track, as in the following:

◆ File types you work with

◆ The most common file types you accept from clients/vendors

◆ Average file sizes

◆ The age of the files on your drive

◆ The kinds of files that go into most common projects

You'll be surprised at how useful this information can be. Knowing your averages helps you make a variety of decisions when you are optimizing the workstation. Plus, you can better focus your efforts. At the very least, you'll be able to describe your projects with respect to the files they require, enabling you to make better purchasing decisions.

File Formats

Keep in mind that you'll be storing all files in one of three file formats. Each has its own file management requirements.

◆ **TIFF.** Because this is a raw pixel storage format, it is the most compact way to store pixel-based files. Pixel-based files, however, can be large, especially if they are full-color scans. When you save a file as a TIFF, you are offered the choice of LZW compression. This can save you a dramatic amount of file space if you are working with bitmapped data. The savings are less when it comes to grayscale and color files. You should avoid LZW compression for files destined to go to an imagesetter because some imagesetters can't understand files stored with this type of compression.

◆ **EPS.** This is a PostScript format that includes a PICT preview built into the file. Pixel-based EPS files are larger than the same Pixel-based file saved as a TIFF. Unless you need the Pixel-based file saved as an EPS for some reason (clipping paths, duotones, built-in screens, and so on) use TIFFs. Vector-based EPS files tend to be smaller than Pixel-based anything.

◆ **Native Layout.** Your layout application, either QuarkXPress or Adobe PageMaker, uses its own file format for the layout file. These can vary wildly in size, depending on the number of pages, amount of text, and use of style sheets. The only way to keep the file size down is to reduce the number of blank pages or unnecessary items in the document.

◆ **PostScript File.** Here, an entire document is written into a single, non-editable file. Often, documents created on the Windows platform are turned into PostScript files and downloaded to an imagesetter via a Macintosh workstation. Also, programs such as Adobe Trapwise require PostScript files to execute their commands.

Tip

Save your graphics files in their native formats, but be sure to change before you send them to the printer. If you're going to have to change them for printing anyway, why save them as native? Most native application formats give you functionality not supported by the printing format. Consider Photoshop's layering, which can't be stored in a TIFF file. Layered files have to be sorted as Photoshop files until you wipe out the layers and store them for printing. Often, the native format is easier for the application to understand and use, and in some cases, the application can't open or edit its own files saved in the non-native format.

File Conversion

Whether you are a Macintosh or a Windows user, you will undoubtedly come across a host of other file format options. All told there are more than 150 file format options out there. Avoid all of them when creating files for print except for EPS, TIFF, and the native page layout format, unless specifically instructed to do otherwise by your printer or service bureau. Unfortunately, this might mean that you have to refuse files from clients or freelancers unless you can convert them into useful formats.

For those of you who really want to help your fellow human, you can try a couple of file conversion utilities:

◆ Photoshop is amazing with any pixel-based files. It will try to open just about anything, from just about any platform. Launch Photoshop and select Open. Locate your mystery file and have at it.

◆ DeBabelizer can convert just about every graphics file format, be it from Mac, Windows, SGI, Sun, Amiga, Atari and others.

◆ DataViz offers MacLink Plus and Connections Plus, which offer a wide variety of file conversion.

Tip

There are some formats that simply shouldn't be converted because they will not provide you with the quality of output necessary for high-resolution printing. With the explosion of publishing on the World Wide Web, JPEG and GIF files are becoming much more prevalent. Neither of these formats are suitable for printing. Both are designed to compress for faster delivery over the Internet. JPEG is lossy compression, which means that valuable image detail is lost during the compression process. GIF images must first be converted to Index Color before being saved in the GIF format. When this happens, the color range is changed from 16.7 million colors to 256 or fewer colors, again resulting in the degradation of the image. This is totally unacceptable for printing purposes. If you receive files in these formats, you are fully justified in requesting that they be sent to you as TIFFs or another acceptable format.

It does no good to have as many file management strategies as you have computers. This completely defeats the purposes of file management and workflow systems. If you are in an environment with several workflow systems, bring people together and develop a unified system.

We are not advocating the complete rubber-stamping of every workstation in the digital prepress world. This would be counter-productive. We urge you to at least develop a system for storing your work files that everyone can use consistently. A "personal computer" must be more than that. It must be an efficient, money-making system.

Keep in mind that your attempts to help your client may back you into a corner of expectation. If you attempt to help, but fail to make your client understand the reality that a file may *never* be convertable into a usable form, you'll find yourself in the hot seat if the file can't be converted.

Internal Job Tickets

Keep a record of what you do as you do it. An internal job ticket including the name and location of companion graphics will go a long way toward keeping track of things. Most people wait until the preflight phase of the project to make lists of the various files needed for a job. A simple form for jotting down filenames, types, and locations eases the burden of the task. You should also include the following items:

◆ Name, address, and phone number of the client

◆ Name and application of the layout file

◆ A list of the typefaces used in the document

◆ Any notes made by the client or vendor(s) on the job

◆ Estimates for output, printing, and any other service used by the job

In addition to a manual ticket, remember the Collect for output function in Quark or Display Pub Info in PageMaker. Each will list the companion files for you.

NAMING CONVENTIONS

You are allowed up to 31 characters and spaces on a Macintosh and up to 128 on a Windows 95 workstation in a folder or filename—use them (Windows 3.x limits you to eight characters, no spaces, and a three letter extension). If you are working in an environment where Windows 3.x stations are still in use, you may need to modify the naming structure for your Windows 95 and Mac computers so that files will be understandable to that pathetic system. Develop a set of naming conventions that help you locate a file you know exists but can't seem to find. Some suggestions for your naming conventions scheme include:

◆ Job start date.

◆ Enough of the job ticket or account number to identify the job.

◆ Part or all of the client's name.

◆ In the Mac OS and Windows 95, name extensions such as .tif for TIFF files, .qxp for Quark files, and so on. Windows 3.x already uses extensions to identify the file type to the system, so don't change them.

◆ A letter or number in front of the rest of the name to force the file into a particular order in a list view (Mac) or list view with details (Windows). You can also use special characters for this, such as an * (asterisk) to force files/folders to the top of an alphabetized list, or the ~ (tilde character) to force them to the bottom.

You have plenty of latitude here and you'll undoubtedly create your own conventions. However, here are some things to avoid:

◆ Don't develop your conventions as you are working on a job. If you do, they will be too specific to that job and you'll end up starting all over again on the next job.

◆ Don't try keep track of anything in your head. Write the convention down somewhere. That way, if you need to change it, share it with others, or use it again, you will be able to.

◆ Don't be afraid to let your conventions evolve and grow. Let them change with your needs, but keep notes about changes you make.

◆ Do not use the same or extremely similar names for individual files in a project.

◆ Avoid jargon or secret codes. You'll forget them and others won't know them at all. Try to be descriptive.

◆ Don't depend too much on the file and folder names to identify individual files. This creates a confusing mess.

◆ Don't neglect your convention. If you invest time in creating, documenting, and evaluating a system for yourself, use it.

You'll discover many reasons to be glad about your naming conventions. Develop and use them.

GRAPHICS FILES

Most of your work involves graphics. Since both of the major page-layout applications, QuarkXPress and Adobe PageMaker, support the use of linking with graphics files, you'll need to gather these files together when it comes time to print. Managing them is an important step in game. The first part of that step is to know what files you need. Management in advance will save you when you've spent three 16 hour days spent working on a project and can't remember how to spell your first name, let alone remember what you've done with all the graphics.

Storing Graphics Files

Develop good habits with file storage. In many projects, several parts come together into a whole only at the end of the creation phase. If more than one person is working on the job, it is crucial to gather the graphics files in a specific place with consistent naming conventions so that all of the players know where they are supposed to run when the play starts. Start by keeping the graphics in the same enclosing folder as the layout file. It is dangerous to keep companion files all over the place on the computer's hard drives. If that happens, it's guaranteed you'll miss something when it's time to pack up the files for their final journey to an output device.

Image Libraries and Archives

If you have a series of graphics files you refer to regularly, it is better to have multiple copies of a graphic than to have a graphic file missing. Copy the image file into the job folder when you decide to use it. Linking to files all over your drive, even if you know exactly where each one is, means copying those files eventually. Copy graphics when you need them.

If you have large image libraries of 20 or more files, create a catalog of them by printing them and stapling the pages together. You can also purchase software such as Adobe Fetch, a cataloging application that allows easy browsing and selecting in your image libraries that helps with this task.

Large image libraries of 100-plus files may require the use of external storage resources. Removables are excellent for this. A good cataloging scheme with a library of removable cartridges is a good, cheap way of storing multiple image files. Here are some considerations you should factor into the equation:

◆ All magnetic media is subject to damage from magnetic fields. They also degrade over time no matter how well you treat them, so factor a life span into any storage library using them.

◆ Pre-formatted media is risky. If you don't know what software was used to format the storage device, reformat it with reliable software before you begin storing images on it. We recommend FWB Hard Drive Toolkit software, which formats far more than just hard drives. It's easy to use, thorough, and reliable.

◆ Magneto-optical (MO) discs are slow, but better than straight magnetic media. MO is not permanent. Over time they will degrade, and they are also subject to damage from magnetic fields.

◆ Write Once, Read Many (WORM) drives can burn a CD-ROM that is as permanent as it gets. Many allow you to write multiple sessions, so you don't have to fill them up the first time you use them. Prices on CD-ROM burners are dropping daily, and if you have large file storage needs, the cost is worth it. A CD can hold 650MB of uncompressed data.

◆ Use Digital Audio Tape (DAT) for routine backup of the entire network, or for large, long-term archiving. DATs are extremely slow, and recent studies suggest that DAT has failure rates of up to 25 percent. For these reasons they are not suitable for storage of frequently needed files. On the plus side, DATs are cheap and they hold a tremendous amount of information, which makes them acceptable for backup purposes with lots of redundancy.

Budget, ease, and frequency of use are all pieces of this puzzle. For an in-depth study of these issues, turn to Chapter 6, "Transport and Storage: Media Dexterity." As you develop a library of images, plan for the future and imagine the most room you'd ever need. Quadruple that amount and you have a good place to start. Take a lesson from computer history. When Steve Jobs at Apple Computer first designed the Macintosh, he doubled the amount of on-board RAM to 128KB, figuring that would be all the RAM anyone could possibly need in a personal computer!

Compression and File Storage

File compression might seem like a good idea in terms of file management. Compression programs rearrange the data in files stored on the hard drive so that they take up less space. This would give you the effects of a larger hard drive without the expense, right? Unfortunately, no. File compression has drawbacks. Compressed files need to be expanded before they can be used. Expanding takes time. That time is lost production time. You would be better off with the one-time expense of an additional hard drive rather than the repeated expense of compressing and expanding files. From a file management standpoint, compression should be considered carefully and weighed against the cost of extra removables and hard drives.

At some point, however, you will need to compress files. Maybe you'll need to rush a forgotten image file over the Internet to a service bureau. Maybe a miscommunication to the purchasing department means that you are down to your last 100MB Zip cartridge and you have 120MB worth of files that need to go to the printer. Your only choice is to compress files.

Compression works one of two ways: lossless and lossy.

Lossless Compression

The compression choice you make, usually a software package of some sort, reads the file and looks for large strings of characters that repeat. It then replaces those strings with a single character or two characters. The file becomes encoded and is useless until it is expanded by the software. The savings in file size depend on the nature of the file, but they can be dramatic (see Figure 5.9).

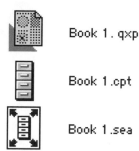

Book 1.qxp

Book 1.cpt

Book 1.sea

Figure 5.9

A Quark file uncompressed, compressed, and compressed as a self-extracting archive.

Some choices include:

◆ Stuffit, from Aladdin Systems Inc., is a robust compression program that can expand compressed files in just about every format. It comes in both commercial and shareware versions, so you can try before you buy.

◆ Disk Doubler from Symantec—another old reliable

◆ Compact Pro, which is shareware. It also works well.

If you are sending files from these applications to clients who don't own them, you can send them as self-extracting archives that automatically expand when you double-click them. These are compacted files with a tiny expander built into them. The self-extractor adds some, but not much, to the compacted file's size. That way you don't have to depend on everyone to own the same software you do.

If you receive a compressed file you can't seem to open with anything you own, go to Aladdin's home page and download StuffIt Expander. It's freeware that can decompress just about anything. In fact, if you're using Netscape, you really shouldn't be without this utility, because it can also translate binary and hexadecimal files, like those that the Internet delivers when you download a file.

LZW Compression

The LZW compression scheme is built into Photoshop. It automatically compresses TIFF files when you ask it. The Save As TIFF dialog box offers it as a choice (see Figure 5.10). Should you use it? Well, this is a sticky issue. Since it builds the compression into the file without telling you it has been done, you have to trust that anything referring to the file can read and understand LZW compression. We've had problems on this front including:

◆ Lower-end imagesetters being unable to recognize LZW-compressed files

◆ Quark and PageMaker failing to print them

◆ Transparent pixels in line art appearing as white, opaque pixels

Figure 5.10

Photoshop's Save As TIFF dialog box.

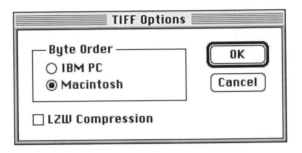

If you need to compress Photoshop files, use an application mentioned above, so the output operator knows they have been compressed and can decompress them. Most service bureaus prefer that you send decompressed data, since it saves time on their end. Talk to your service bureau if you use one. If you are one, talk to your clients about your needs.

It's good practice to leave your files uncompressed anyway. There is always the chance that the compression software will make a mistake. When you expand the file, it will either fail to expand completely or be so riddled with garbage information it can't be used. Times will occur when you'll want to compress things. If you do:

1. Duplicate the file.

2. Compress the copy of the file.

3. Copy the compressed file.

4. Decompress the copied compressed file.

5. Open it in its native software to test it.

As you might sense from this description, it doesn't make sense to approach compression from a catch-as-catch-can point of view. Do it deliberately as a part of file management, and you'll be successful. Otherwise, it will end up costing more in rework than you'll save in disk space.

Lossy Compression

This is a whole different scheme for compressing information. It's at the heart of the JPEG compression philosophy. Lossy compression decides what detail is important to your image, and discards the rest. The result is a loss of data, which you can never get back (see Figure 5.11) This is a bad way to compress data for print. The detail in the image is what you will spend a good chunk of time creating, so why toss it after you're done? Lossy compression is a necessary evil when dealing with publishing on the World Wide Web. For print, it doesn't work. Avoid it.

Figure 5.11

A Photoshop file before and after JPEG compression.

File Servers

At some point, the image library idea becomes too clunky a system to use. Although an increased frustration level and a bottleneck at the library will be good indications of the need for a better system, it's better to plan ahead for the more complete solution than depending on a pile of removables to store images.

The next step is to use a dedicated file server. This is usually a computer, sitting by itself doing nothing but holding files that are used, sometimes by several people, for a variety of projects.

If any of the following are, or are likely to be true of your working situation, you will want to consider using a dedicated file server:

◆ **Many files kept on hand.** If you keep an extensive library of files, you should not keep them on local hard drives. Keeping them on larger hard drives rather than keeping them on several removables allows much faster access to a given file.

◆ **Large files kept on hand.** If the files you keep and use frequently are large files, such as color scans, it makes more sense to keep those on a big hard drive, rather than to squeeze them onto removable cartridges, or to clutter the valuable space on your local hard drive with them.

◆ **Many people needing access to the same files.** You will run into problems whenever more than one person needs to use the same files, unless you make a duplicate copy of everything in the library for every person, or unless you use a file server.

You'll also reduce the wait at the media dexterity station—the station connected to the various removable media options you support—or reduce the costs of adding removable drives to a large number of workstations, by adding one overall file serving station. Although, with prices on ZIP, SyQuest EZ, and other removables dropping, it is a good idea to get a removable for workstations anyway. See Chapter 6, "Transport and Storage: Media Dexterity" for more on creating a media dexterity station.

◆ **Many frequently-used files.** Digging out the same library cartridge day after day, week after week, month after month, year after year, is silly. Keep the file somewhere easier to reach. A file server is one such place.

Any of these make the use of a file server a more efficient method of accessing files than swapping removables or filling up your internal drive. As we said, it is far better to plan ahead for this need, building it into the file management scheme overall than, to try and add it in later.

Creating a File Server

File servers can be expensive, dedicated, mean, ugly machines that use strange computer stuff like A/UX to make them go. You can use more familiar equipment to set up your system at a much reduced cost. We don't mean to completely disregard some larger serving solutions; they have uses, but most small to medium sized shops can save money and reduce complexity by setting up a file server of their own.

Some aspects of a typical file server are:

◆ **A computer using the same operating system.** A server that uses the same system that you know is automatically a more familiar server.

◆ **A station that isn't used for production.** Anything that taxes the serving computer, also taxes the server. It is too easy to treat a server like a workstation, unless you completely avoid the temptation to do so.

◆ **A fast CPU.** The faster the computer can think, the faster it can locate and serve the files you request.

◆ **A wide, fast hard drive.** The standard SCSI that comes with most computers out of the box is not the fastest available. Of course, you pay extra for the fastest, but for those with large files, the cost is worth it. The size of the drive is a function of the size and number of files you want to store.

◆ **Asanté NetDoubler** (or other network optimizing utilities). This speeds up copying by more efficiently using RAM during the process.

169

The Macintosh copies a file into RAM from the hard drive before it gets sent out, but this is limited to 128KB segments. Optimizing utilities raise this limit, enabling files to copy much faster.

- **Fast network connections** No matter how much you spend on a dedicated server, data can only be moved as fast as the connections allow it. AppleTalk is the cheapest form of connection, and it comes built in on most Macs, but it is too slow for sending anything but the smallest of files. Ethernet is much faster, and comes built in on most new Macs. Ethernet cards are fairly inexpensive if your Mac doesn't have ethernet built-in, and worth the price for the speed increase over AppleTalk. Fast Ethernet (100 Base-T), which is a new and faster form of Ethernet, without getting into the extremely high costs of fiber optics and other high-end networking options.

- **A network with a hub.** A hub will control the amount of cross talk by directing traffic from your workstation to the server and back without interfering with other network traffic. Plus many calls to the server will also be managed, reducing the frequency and severity of crashes.

- **A lean operating system.** The operating system of the server can be stripped to basics, since the only programs running on it will be backup utilities. It will not need print drivers, Adobe Type Manager, QuickTime, or anything else that is not directly related to net-working.

You may be able use an older workstation rather than a new machine. Whatever you use, don't defeat the server idea by skimping so much that it can't meet your needs. A good file server is an investment that pays off.

Hiring Network Service Providers

As with any investment, before you lay down a lot of cash, it may be wise to hire a consultant. There are many people who specialize in setting up networks for businesses. They will help you make the most of your investment.

When you speak with a network service provider or consultant, make sure they understand the magnitude of what the network server will be used for. Most network technicians are used to dealing with businesses that use text files primarily, which are a few kilobytes in size. Graphics files are typically measured in megabytes. A single person moving graphics over the network can use as much of the server's resources in an hour as a dozen non-graphics people use in a week. We saw one company bring its network of over 200 people to its knees when they added the design group, a mere five people, to the network. Be sure you communicate your needs very clearly when investing the money in dedicated servers.

Integrating the Server

Once the server is built, integrating it is easy.

♦ Connecting it to the network is a matter of adding node. This requires the computer to use the same cabling as the network you use for the rest of the computers in house.

♦ Sharing files should be as easy as possible. This means turning on sharing and sharing all of the contents of the server freely. Avoid passwords and hidden folders. They only make it harder for you to access files on the server.

Generally, the server should look pretty much like all the other computers on the network. For more information about networking, see Chapter 6, "Transport and Storage: Media Dexterity."

Using a File Server

If you use a file server to store files, make sure that you copy the file to your local drive before you open it. This includes graphics, fonts, text, or any other files you intend to store on a server. Unless you own some very expensive, dedicated software and hardware designed specifically to handle files over a network, you risk crashing your system, corrupting the file, and bringing the network to a crawl if you open the file from the server.

Dedicated Server Systems

If you have more to spend, you can buy a pre-fab dedicated file server. Apple computer makes the Workgroup server line, which can use a combination of the Macintosh Operating System and A/UX, Apples implementation of UNIX, a very powerful operating system. These are optimized for the purpose of serving and come with network management software.

Beyond Apple's Workgroup Servers are Windows NT and UNIX-based systems created for the sole purpose of moving and storing vast amounts of information very quickly. These are often expensive, complex, and powerful systems that can require dedicated personnel to operate. If you feel you need that kind of power, consult with a network service provider that deals with large systems.

Windows and Mac Stations in the Same Shop

There are a variety of methods for integrating a Macintosh and PC into the same network. Most involve treating a Macintosh like a PC, and fooling the network into believing it is. However, a good solution is to allow the two computers to see each other in a peer-to-peer connection. MacLAN, a hardware and software combination available for Windows 95, allows a Windows station to connect to both Macintosh computers and printers directly.

Publishing Systems

In addition to hardware, you should consider the use of software designed to manage your files. With such a system, several people can collaborate on a single project. The main problem with collaboration is keeping updated. If two people pull the same file from a server, make changes, and copy it back, one of the changes will be overwritten. You may not notice this until the proofing stage. It may take too long to fix the problem on the deadline for the job.

The Quark Publishing software can solve such problems. It operates from a file server, allowing users to act as clients. Each user signs out files to edit, checks them in, and indicates the status of the job. The system offers other benefits such as copy fitting by line counting. If your managing needs warrant the expense, investigate this system.

Your Own System

If you are not looking to spend the kind of cash a system like this costs, some habits can emulate such systems nicely:

- ◆ Add a letter to the filename indicating whether the file has been checked out. Add a second letter to indicate who has it (see Figure 5.12).

◆ When you log on to the server and pull a copy of the file, change those letters in the filename before you copy it to your local drive.

◆ When you put it back, change the check in/out letter to indicate that you have put it back. Leave the letter for your name in place, so that you can answer any questions about the step you have completed.

 Chapter 10.Complete

Chapter 10.Copy 3

Chapter 10.NotComplete

Chapter 10.Ver12/23/96

Figure 5.12

Filenames can be used to indicate a file's status.

OFF-SITE STORAGE AND THE FPO

If you don't want to keep large files on-site, consider off-site storage of the high-resolution data. This typically means color scans, which are good to out-source anyway. Many color separation or film output houses offer file storage at reasonable rates. They'll give you a For Position Only (FPO) file, which is a low-resolution, 72 ppi copy of the scan in a PICT or TIFF format. You place it when you compose the job; they replace it with the high-res file when they output the films and you both win. FPO files are easy to create and offer a great way to represent large files with minimum storage requirements.

In fact, FPO PICT files tend to look a bit better onscreen than their high-res TIFF parents (see Figures 5.13 and 5.14). This is because Quark and PageMaker have to create a 72 ppi PICT file when you place a graphics file in the layout. It's this PICT preview of the file that you move around the page. The problem is that it has to build the preview file each time you re-open a page containing that graphic file. This forces you to set the application's preferences to use low-quality representations of any TIFF files if you want the screen to redraw with any reasonable speed. The high-quality option can really bog a computer down when you flip to a page with more than a couple of color scans. However, down-sampling in Photoshop, the master of all pixel data everywhere, allows it to do its magic. The resulting FPO file looks excellent and can be more easily represented onscreen by the page layout application. Of course, none of this affects the printed piece but helps speed workflow a bit. Plus, your presentation people can use this information if you ever need to re-purpose a graphics file.

Figure 5.13

A down-sampled Photoshop FPO.

Figure 5.14

PageMaker's PICT preview (on low-quality).

Even if you keep the large files on-site, you may want to create FPO files to use for layout, replacing them with the high-res files later in the process. It's easy to do:

1. Open the original file.

2. Select Image Size from the Image menu.

3. De-select the Constrain Proportions option at the bottom.

4. Drag-select over the value in the Resolution field and type 72.

5. Choose OK in the Image Size dialog box.

6. Choose RGB from the Mode menu (unless it is a greyscale file, in which case you'd ignore this step).

7. Save the file with a similar name and some indication that it's an FPO. Consider using (filename).FPO.

EPS files already have a PICT preview file built into them and they deliver it directly to the page layout application. Since vector-based EPS files tend to be small enough to keep on-site, you have no reason to store them off-site. Pixel-based EPS files also have the preview built-in. In fact, the EPS format in Photoshop has the capability to automatically peel off the PICT preview as an FPO file.

File Swapping

The only drawback to the FPO game is the necessity of file swapping that comes with the process. You need to establish practices that completely, without a shadow of a doubt, prevent the FPO file from ever being printed. The file, being a 72 ppi PICT file, is completely useless when it comes to printing. We recommend that you use an FPO folder when you link the graphics in the first place. Tag the filenames from the original with an .FPO designation. Using the layout software, re-link the graphics to the non-FPO versions as the last step before proofing the document and trash the FPOs (you can keep them if you think you need them later). After re-linking all the files, save the document and close it. Move the FPO files into another folder or the trash. Re-open the file to see if it asks for any missing graphics. Moving the FPO files prevents the application from finding any leftover links to FPO files. If the layout application complains about missing files, jot their names down and re-link those to the high-res versions.

If you use a service bureau that offers scanning and file storage, consult with them about naming conventions and practices they use (and want you to use) with FPO files.

Desktop Color Separation

Desktop Color Separation (DCS) has two purposes, one for file management, the other for the color separation house. The file management use of the DCS file is to have Photoshop automatically create the FPO. Color separation, the process of breaking a graphic into its cyan, magenta, yellow, and black components, is normally done by the layout application upon output. Using DCS with color scans has Photoshop separate the files in advance. The FPO file is used during composition and the C, M, Y, K files are used for printing.

You can create a five-part DCS file yourself.

1. Save a CMYK Photoshop file in the EPS format.

2. In the Save As EPS dialog box, choose Macintosh/IBM PC 8-bit Color under the Desktop Color Separation (DCS) pop-up menu (see Figure 5.15).

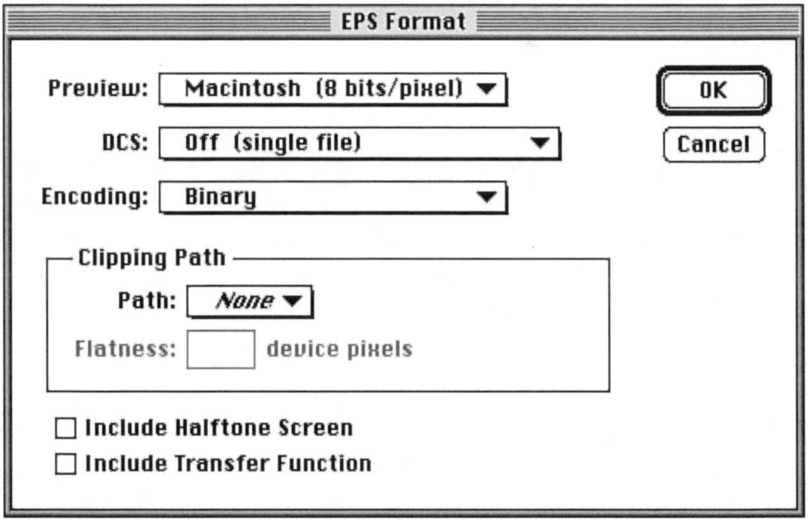

Figure 5.15

Photoshop's Save As EPS dialog box.

3. Save the file by clicking OK.

The result is five files: one is the FPO, called the master file, and the other four are the color file, pre-separated into their cyan, magenta, yellow, and black plates. The names for the files change by the addition of a .C, .M, .Y, and .K respectively (see Figure 5.16). The master file's name does not change. Most service bureaus that offer FPOs use this method because the file swapping problem vanishes. The master file knows to look for the color plate files. As long as they are in the same folder as the master file when the job prints, the layout will have no problem locating it.

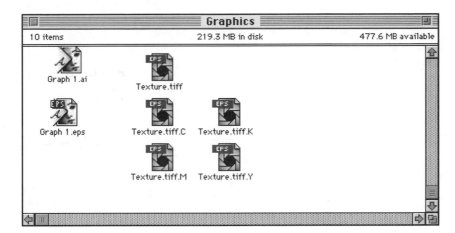

Figure 5.16

A five-part EPS DCS file.

Vector-Based FPO

Sometimes you will have very complicated vector-based graphics files that redraw slowly. You can turn these into FPO's also. Here are some methods to try:

1. Open the file in its native application, and take a screen shot (press Command-Option-3, or use a utility such as Capture or Flash! It). Open the screen shot in Photoshop to crop it and save it as a PICT file.

2. For applications that support it, clippings work well. Select all of the pieces of the illustration that you want an FPO of and drag them out of the window onto the desktop. If a clipping file appears, you have a file that is a PICT representation of the vector-based file (see Figure 5.17). Open it in Photoshop, save it as a PICT file. If not, your application doesn't support the use of clipping or your operating system is too old.

3. If you have created the file in the latest versions of FreeHand or Illustrator, you can export it as a PICT file.

Figure 5.17

Clipping file.

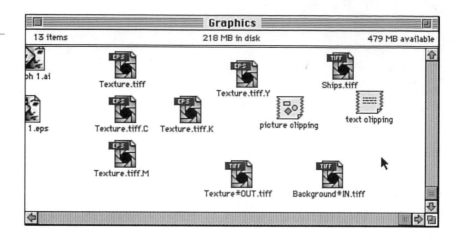

BACKUPS

If you have been in production long enough (a day), you've experienced a crash or two. It's a necessary evil in this day and age of high-level, user-friendly operating systems combined with all-powerful, killer applications. Get used to them. Save early and save often.

However, occasionally you'll corrupt a file you're working on. This happens when the file is in the process of being written to the drive from RAM when the crash occurs. It also happens when some drastic event wrecks the hard drive the file is on. Either way, the file is history, so you'll need to start over, from scratch unless you've made a backup.

Too often people make backing up a long and complex affair, so they stop after a while. It's easy to lull yourself into believing that your computer won't do you wrong after it hasn't for a while. That's when it will. Oh, believe us, it will. Don't make that mistake. Protect your work from the perils of crashes.

Your backup scheme needn't be a work of bureaucratic wonder, requiring a 200-page manual to describe. It should be as simple as copying the work you do in a day onto a removable cartridge and taking it home, or sticking into a fireproof safe and breathing a little easier. If you crave redundancy, make a backup at lunch and one at the end of the day. If you are a little more brave, you can choose to backup every other day. You will want to keep at least a week's worth of backup media around so that you'll have a backup of an entire week on hand. This is as easy as naming a removable for each day of the week and using it on its day.

Automatic Back-Ups

There are utilities that automatically back up your files, but these should enhance rather than replace your own backup routine. By taking the time to do it yourself, you ensure that your important files are backed up, rather than relying on a mindless automaton to save your files for you.

On the other hand, an automatic back-up system only needs to save just one important file to pay for itself. As an additional level of protection, they are worth having. Consider backup utilities, such as Dantz's industry standard Retrospect Remote, which can automate the backup procedure. Operating from a file server, it can be used to perform nightly backups of everything on every computer on the network.

If you have such a system in place, don't neglect to perform backups of your important files on your own. Locating a single file amongst the thousands of files in a remote backup can be a very time-consuming process, and there are no guarantees that your files actually did get backed up.

If you have broken the Jobs folder into stages as we recommended previously, you'll be able to target your backup easily.

♦ **The Gathering folder** only contains data that you got from another source anyway. You don't need copies of this.

♦ **The In-progress folder** contains files that you have worked on. Back this up.

♦ **The On Hold folder** contains the project in a varying degree of completion. Since that degree may be different from the last time the project was backed up, back it up.

♦ **The Proofing folder** holds the completed copy of the project. Back it up.

♦ **The Completed Jobs folder** will be broken up and archived or trashed. Backups shouldn't be necessary.

♦ **All of your Applications, System files**, Utilities, and Type will only need one backup with periodic updates. Don't bother backing these up every day.

This back-up system requires that you keep your jobs in the right place. When you finish a job, move it into one of the finished folders. Make sure do this before you make your back up, so you can easily find the job in the event of a crash.

For those liking automation, there are software packages that handle this function automatically. Retrospect offers such automation. Use these packages as a way to automate the actual copy step only, though. Don't get lazy and just back up everything all the time. Aside from being unnecessary, it eats up back-up media, time, and increases the chances of a crash during back-up. Efficiency is still a key issue with automated software.

SUMMARY

All the information presented here will be an exercise in futility if you don't remember to use it. This means developing new habits and probably breaking old ones too, so prepare yourself for a little change. If you attempt to remember the whole thing without help, you'll forget what you want to do. Notes about your system go a long toward keeping you on track. Plus, you'll have a method for evaluating your system—remember, you can't know where to go if you don't know where you are. Granted, this will be a living document for a long time. You'll make changes to it as you accept new and different jobs, but at least you won't overhaul the whole thing every time you forget what you had decided to do. Plus, you'll have a way to create documents describing your specs to others. This contributes toward creating the kind of internal consistency that saves money and time.

If you are not solely responsible for the systems everyone uses, become a champion for the cause, put on a diplomat's hat, and hammer out a system among colleagues. The effort you put into it will pay big dividends later.

Chapter

TRANSPORT AND STORAGE: MEDIA DEXTERITY

Media dexterity encompasses many functions for transportation and storage. It includes the capability to send your files from your station to the service bureau, to the printer, or to other stations in your office quickly and flawlessly. It also enables you to receive files from clients and freelancers, having immediate access to them. With media dexterity, you can store vast amounts of data and still find the files you need immediately, without spending hours searching. Ultimately, your use of removable storage media should be transparent, a process so automatic it's a natural process that doesn't need a second thought.

In short, you need to have media dexterity. The price of not having it is, of course, lost work, missed deadlines, and wasted money. Days of production time can be lost without it. If you send files to a service bureau via FedEx overnight and the service bureau can't read the media, you've lost a day. By the time you've re-sent the file on appropriate media, another day has passed. At best, this is a two day delay. Two days, however, is enough time for the print window to have closed and your job will have to be pushed back days or weeks. Archiving a job on unreliable media also means you have to recreate a job from scratch when it comes time to update it.

Sending large graphics files over the Internet can take many hours. Sent improperly, they will be unreadable to the recipient, which results in more wasted time.

Media dexterity not only saves time and money, it can help you transcend the physical limitations of the computer. Personal computers are *finite*. Hard drives can only hold a fixed amount of information. That information can only exist on the computer and nowhere else without using something external to the computer. Scanners can let you turn solid objects into data your computer can understand. Printers can let you bring that data back out of the computer in a form that you can understand. It takes media dexterity, however, to bring the data beyond the confines of one computer to another. This is made possible by removable storage media, networks, and the Internet.

Until recently, media dexterity was completely dependent on removable storage media, which is still the major component of media dexterity. Removable storage media come in a wide variety of sizes, shapes, and costs. Floppy disks, CD-ROMs, removable hard drives, and Digital Audio Tape (DAT) are just a few examples. Which one will best enhance your media dexterity depends on the work that you do.

Removable storage media serve several purposes such as the following:

- **Backing up files.** Our ability to produce files inevitably surpasses the hard drive's storage capacity, leaving us with a hard drive too full to work. When you throw away files, you risk losing work that took hours to create. Backing up files onto removable storage media enables you to clear the hard drive so that you can work again. Additionally, hard drives can become corrupted, destroying all the data stored on them. If the information is backed up this is a hassle, not a tragedy.

- **Archiving files.** Completed projects should never be thrown away. A client could want the same ad again next year with minor modifications. Parts of files can always be recycled for other jobs. Creating files requires an investment of time, effort, and money. Don't throw away that investment—archive everything.

- **Transporting files.** Files need to have a way to move from one workstation to another. Outsourced scans need to get from the service bureau to you. You need a way to get work to and from coworkers, as well as getting finished files to the service bureau or the printer. All of this was once done entirely on removables. Now networks and the Internet provide additional options for file transportation. However, most files are still transported on removables.

◆ **Maintaining workstation configurations.** Creating a working system on a workstation is a lengthy process involving many applications, system extensions, and other elements. Sometimes it's necessary to reformat the hard drive and restore everything. Most removable storage media can be made into a bootable System disk, containing everything you need to recreate the working computer.

NEW OPTIONS FOR MEDIA DEXTERITY: LANS AND THE INTERNET

Originally, all media dexterity was handled through removables. Currently two other options are replacing significant use of removables: Local Area Networks and the Internet. Local Area Networks (LANs) have all but replaced the use of removables for moving files between computers in a small area, such as within companies. Due to the slow speeds of networks, removables are still preferable for moving large files, but this is changing as network speeds increase. For smaller files, networks enable files to move from one computer to another with greater ease and efficiency than removables. The Internet has the potential to do for the entire world what LANs did for businesses. In the near future, getting files to the service bureau will require as much effort as it takes to copy them to a removable. In some instances, as we shall see, this is already the case.

An old saying goes something like "You can never have too much money or be too beautiful." Computer graphics professionals have a similar saying. "You can never have too much RAM or too much hard drive space." Both sayings are true. Right now, though, we are just dealing with the finite capacities of the hard drive and how to extend it toward the infinite through media dexterity.

Through media dexterity, you can:

◆ Increase the file storage capacities of your computer.

◆ Increase the file transportation capabilities of your computer.

◆ Receive files from anyone, anywhere, and have no trouble opening and using them.

◆ Send files to anyone, anywhere, and be immediately usable.

◆ Avoid losing important data.

◆ Move files over a Network.

◆ Utilize the Internet to move your data.

What Prevents Media Dexterity?

Too many options. Usually, having many options is a good thing. When it comes to media dexterity, however, the number of options can be a problem. New forms of removable media are introduced almost daily. Some, like CD-ROMs, become indispensable. Others, like the Floptical are all but forgotten a few months after they are introduced. The problem is that the different options are not always compatible.

Industry standards change incredibly fast. Last year SyQuest cartridges were the prepress standard for removable storage media. This year it is the Zip cartridge. Next year it will be something else.

Standards can be area-specific. The service bureaus in our area report that roughly 80 percent of the files they receive are on Zip cartridges. A service bureau in another part of the country reported the same of the SyQuest EZ cartridges and claimed to get very few Zip cartridges.

Commitment to outdated technology. It can be hard to let go of the past, especially when you've invested so much money into it. Newer removable storage media are cheaper and faster, but problems arrive when you send it to someone who only has a 44MB SyQuest drive.

A BRIEF HISTORY OF STORAGE

One of the most significant developments in the history of digital prepress actually happened more than a decade before digital prepress became an option on the computer. It was a development without which digital prepress would never have become an option. In the early 1970s, IBM changed the world of computing forever by creating a technology called Winchester.

The Winchester featured two spinning, magnetized, 14" metal platters. A lightweight head floated just above the surface of the platter, held by an actuator arm, which could move the head to where the information was stored on the disk. The head could read the magnetic charges, which the computer could understand as data, and write different charges to the disk. This device had advantages over other storage devices. It had a faster rate of data transfer and, unlike tape, the information was randomly accessible. On tape, information is stored linearly. To retrieve information at the beginning of the tape, the tape must be rewound to the beginning. The Winchester could access information on any part of the platter at any time. The Winchester got its name from the 30/30 Winchester repeater rifle. Each of the platters held 30MB of data.

The Winchester mechanism was the predecessor to the modern hard drive. Although modern hard drives are smaller, faster, and hold more data, the technology is the same. In fact, they are still called Winchester hard drives. All hard drives in personal computers today are Winchester drives. The majority of removable storage media today are also based on the Winchester mechanism.

Shortly after the Winchester drive was created, a creation made it possible for computers to become "personal," rather than the sole domain of institutions large enough to support the gigantic mainframe computers the Winchester drives were created for. This creation was the floppy drive. Before the floppy drive, programs needed to be written into the computer by hand every time the computer was started, unless one was fortunate enough to have a tape system that could record the program and read it back into the computer. The floppy changed all that by allowing programs and files to be read to and written from memory dynamically. The creation of the floppy for the personal computer was equivalent to the invention of the written word for the development of the human mind. In both cases, information no longer needed to be information lost and re-created when it was needed. It could be remembered, stored, accessed, used, copied, and passed along. Unlike the original Winchester drive, floppies were inexpensive and transportable.

From its very beginning, the digital graphic arts have pushed computers to their very limits and still wanted more. When we first started in this industry nine years ago, bitmapped graphics took too long to print to be cost-effective to use on a job, even on a fairly expensive laser printer. Of course, back then all laser printers were expensive. We also had to scan in graphics, then trace them in Illustrator to create files small enough to print in any reasonable amount of time. Graphics files were larger than other types of files and they needed more storage space. Hard drives made it possible to create large files, but this left the problem of getting them off the computer. One final element was needed.

In 1983, the fledgling SyQuest Technology came up with a brilliant idea. They took a Winchester platter and separated it from the rest of the drive mechanism, encased it in a dust-free plastic cartridge, and created the first "infinite hard drive." It was a Winchester hard drive with infinite storage capacity since the platter, which held the data, could be swapped out when full and replaced with an empty platter.

To a large extent, the SyQuest drive made digital prepress possible. Desktop publishing made it possible for anyone with a little cash and a modicum of ability to create documents that could have only been created by trained profession-als on systems costing tens or hundreds of thousands of dollars. Creating documents on the computer is only half the battle, however. Getting them into print was another challenge altogether. What truly put professional publishing power in the hands of the masses was the creation of the service bureau. Eight years ago, a 600 dpi grayscale PostScript printer with reasonable print quality cost around $20,000. Even this could not produce the quality needed for professional publications. High-resolution image setters were needed, which cost into hundreds of thousands of dollars. Although the act of creating the digital file may have been affordable to average people, the act of printing the file was not. To meet this need, service bureaus arose.

Service bureaus focused on high-end scans and output. They could afford the expensive equipment because they used it around the clock. Service bureaus made the products of these devices available to anyone who could get files to and from them. Since high-resolution printing requires large graphics files, floppies, the only other removable media at the time, were inadequate. The files were moved on SyQuest cartridges. Without SyQuest cartridges, the digital revolution would not have been possible.

Ever since the creation of the removable hard drive, manufacturers have constantly increased the speed and capacity of removables to keep pace with the increased capabilities of the personal computer. Every increase in processor speed makes it possible to create larger files faster, which fills the hard drive faster and creates an ever greater need for more removable storage.

CHOOSING THE RIGHT MEDIA

Today a staggering array of removable storage options exist; most of which are variations of the Winchester mechanism. Others use widely varying options, from tape media and CD-ROM to magneto-optical and hot swappable hard drives. How do you choose which ones are right for you? There are several criteria, each of which will be discussed in detail below:

- **Manufacturer Reputation.** If the manufacturer has a good reputation, chances are that you are going to get a good product from them.

- **Product Performance.** Compare the storage device against others. Is it faster? Can it store more information? What is the cost per megabyte of storing information on the removable media?

- **Market Penetration.** The more people using a form of storage media, the more useful it is to you in terms of file transportation.

- **Intended Use.** How you use it will determine how useful a specific product is to you.

Manufacturer Reputation

Reputation is everything. Although reputable companies have made bad products in the past, this is rare. Any company that gets a reputation for making bad products is doomed. Cheaper versions of the same product may be made by a no-name company from Tahiti, but if it fails you in a moment of crisis, any amount you have saved will be lost 10 times over.

Things to look for in a company before you buy products from it:

◆ Does the company have a toll-free tech support number?

◆ Does the company have a Web site?

◆ Are drivers and software updates available on the Web site? Many removable storage drives require special software to run. New System software can conflict with these, as will drivers for other storage devices. Drivers are constantly being updated to make them compatible. If these are available on a Web site, it will be quick and easy to update your drivers.

◆ Does the company have technical and troubleshooting information on their Web site? Due to the incredible number of variables involved in computer technology, every single problem might not be found before a new drive ships and will not be documented in the material that comes with the drive. Often, these problems can be solved easily if you know how. A troubleshooting section on a Web site can give you the answers.

◆ Does the company provide online tech support? Toll-free tech support is a very important thing. Often, especially during business hours, you can wait for a long time before someone is available to help you. Unless the problem with the drive has brought you to a standstill, you could be doing something more useful with your time than listening to the mantra, "All our technical support representatives are busy. Please stay on the line." Instead, send email detailing your problem as specifically and completely as possible. You won't have to wait for more than a day to get a response. For simple problems, this is a far more efficient way of getting help than waiting on the phone.

◆ Have you heard of the company before? Can you find reviews of their products in major magazines? What do the reviews say?

◆ Is the product warranted? Does it come with a money-back guarantee?

All of these recommendations are true no matter what piece of computer hardware or software you buy. A little research up front will save you tremendous time and headaches in the future.

Product Performance

In an ideal world, product performance would be easy criteria for selecting anything. Product performance should be a matter of simple mathematics. Unfortunately, things are not that simple. While product specifications are easy to find, determining what specifications are relevant is a tricky business. Then there is the question of whether the manufacturers are using the same standards in measuring their specifications.

How expensive is it to purchase and use? How fast is it? How long will it last? These are all important issues, but they should not be used as the sole criteria for your decisions. Performance, as we shall see, does not necessarily measure how useful a device is, but how useful the device *might* be.

Many resellers use just one measure of performance, such as RPM or seek time when promoting their products. A more useful indication of performance, however, takes into account many aspects. No performance estimate is completely accurate, however, because true performance is also dependent on the computer system the drive is attached to.

Since the majority of removable media is based on the Winchester mechanism or a variation thereof, measuring performance uses most of the same criteria as hard drives. Since non-removable hard drives are the fastest and most widely used form of storage media, we will be using them as the standard for comparing removable storage media.

Storage Capacity

Measured in megabytes, how much information can the media hold? The amount of usable space will be slightly less than the total storage space, since the formatting of the disk uses up some of that space (see Figure 6.1).

Figure 6.1

Storage capacity of removable media. Longer bars are better.

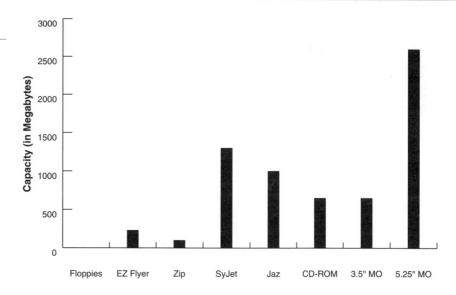

Seek Time

With the exception of tape media, all removable media stores its data in thousands of concentric circles called *tracks,* which go from the outermost edge of the disk to the innermost. The amount of time it takes for the actuator arm to move the read/write head to the track where the desired data is stored is called the *seek time*. This time is measured in milliseconds (ms). If the attenuator arm is seeking data on adjacent tracks, then the time it takes to move can be as short as 2 ms. If it has to move from the outermost edge to the innermost edge, it might take 20 ms or more. Seek time is an average of many random information requests.

Put another way, seek time is the amount of time it takes to locate the data on the hard drive.

Milliseconds may seem like an irrelevantly minuscule amount of time, but remember that drives are random-access devices. Data can be stored on the disk in any location and in any order. To read a single piece of requested information, the actuator arm may have to move the read/write head hundreds or thousands of times. The milliseconds start adding up fast! The seek times for today's hard drives average from 8 to 14 seconds (see Figure 6.2). In terms of seek time, lower numbers are better.

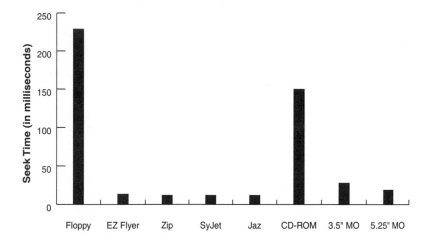

Figure 6.2

Average seek times of removable media. Shorter times are better.

Note

Tape media are sequential access, not random-access. Instead of moving the read/write head to the desired track, the media itself must be moved. Seek time in terms of tape is the amount of time it takes the tape to be fast-forwarded or rewound to the point at which the data is stored.

Rotational Speed

Disk media must spin at very high speeds to work. Data in tracks is divided even further into sectors. Once the read/write head is in position over the proper track, it must wait for the sector containing the desired data to spin around. This waiting period is called *rotational latency*. The higher the rotational speed, measured in RPM, the lower the rotational latency.

Rotational speed is an important factor in the performance of a drive. Unfortunately, it is only relevant when comparing drives of the same type. When comparing hard drives, for example, the higher the rotational speed is, the better. It is not really that useful when comparing different media types such as Zip drives and CD-ROM drives. We include it here, however, because you will often see it listed in product specifications.

Note

Herein lies the rub: Data access time is really a combination of seek time and rotational latency. Unfortunately, most product specifications omit rotational latency or combine it with seek time. Combining that information it is not a bad thing, provided that everyone is doing it. The problem is, how do you know? One can only hope that the major manufacturers use the same system!

Originally, hard drives started spinning the moment the computer was turned on and didn't stop until the computer was shut down. In an effort to reduce wear and to lower power consumption, modern drives sense the amount at which they are being accessed and stop spinning, or "go to sleep," if they have not been used for a length of time. Nearly all removable storage media also have this feature. This adds two more items to the list of product specifications: Time until sleep and stop/start time. Preferably, time until sleep is user definable. For stop/start time, the faster the better, but this is less relevant than other performance measures. The drive only sleeps when it senses inactivity and this feature can often be turned off completely if it causes too many delays.

Transfer Rates

Once the read/write head is in position, the drive can read data from the disk or write data to it. This involves a transfer of data between the disk and the CPU. The faster the data transfer rate, the faster the computer will be able to open up files, launch programs, and copy or move files (see Figure 6.3). Transfer rate is measured in megabytes per second (MB/s).

Often, you will see *cache buffer* listed among product specifications. This is a more recent development to improve transfer rates. Often, the CPU processes things much faster than the much slower drive can provide them. The CPU has to wait for the drive to catch up. At other times the drive pushes out the data faster the CPU can respond. A cache buffer, built into the drive, compensates for these discrepancies. Information can be read into the disk buffer before the CPU needs it. It can also store information that is waiting to be written to the disk. This can boost transfer rates substantially.

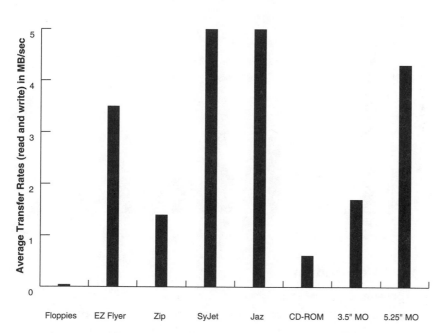

Figure 6.3

Average transfer rates for removable media. Longer bars are better.

Cost per Megabyte

The cost per megabyte tells you how much it is going to cost you to own (see Figure 6.4). Usually, this price just considers the cost of the removable media, but we recommend that you break it down into two costs: initial cost and use cost. The initial cost is the cost of the drive with one removable, divided by the number of megabytes the removable holds. The use cost is the cost of the removable divided by the number of megabytes. Cost per megabyte is measured in dollars per meg ($/MB).

The cost per megabyte is not the bottom line. You must also consider how efficiently you will be able to use the media. If a cheap storage media is so slow that it hinders production, then the money you saved will be eaten up quickly by wasted time.

Media Life

The life of the media is an estimate of how long data will last without becoming unreadable on a cartridge sitting on a shelf in a protective storage case. These are only estimates since most media have a life span far in excess of the length of time they have been in existence.

Figure 6.4

Removable Media's cost per megabyte.

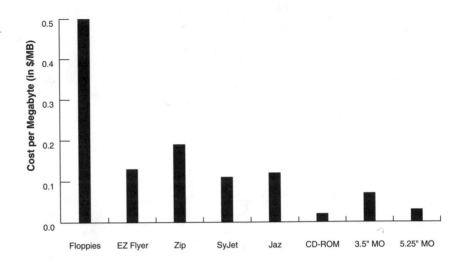

Market Penetration

For better or for worse, a measure of how useful a storage device is dependent on how widely it is used. Usually, the market penetration of a device has more to do with timing and marketing than with the performance of the device.

A Tale of Two Standards

The first standard for removable storage for digital prepress was the 44MB SyQuest drive. It was the first, so everyone bought it. Shortly after the SyQuest drive came out, Iomega introduced its Bernoulli drive. Iomega knew that to draw people away from the SyQuest drive they would have to come out with a superior product (or so they thought). The Bernoulli drive was superior to the SyQuest drive in construction and performance in both the drive mechanism and the removable cartridge. The reliability of SyQuest drives was compromised by the fact that the cooling fans sucked dust into the drive, which could interfere with the read/write head. The Bernoulli drives didn't have this problem. The drives were faster. They had handles so that they could be carried easily. The cartridges could be tossed against the wall and still work fine. The Bernoulli drive was almost a complete flop. The Bernoulli had the tremendous misfortune of coming out a short time after the SyQuest. Today you are lucky if you can find cartridges for Bernoulli drives, while an estimated 98.9 percent of all service bureaus are able to read 44MB SyQuest cartridges. It was all a matter of timing.

Perhaps Iomega learned something from this. In 1995, Iomega introduced the Zip drive. A few months later, SyQuest released the technologically superior EZ drive. The cost-cutting that was done on the Zip drive was shameless. It was so light that the weight of SCSI cables could drag it off the table. It had no on/off switch, so you had to unplug it if you wanted to turn it off. The SCSI ID could only toggle between two settings, 5 and 6, and the SCSI connectors were 25 pin instead of the more widely usable 50 pin. The EZ drive, on the other hand, was made of heavy-duty components and had an on/off switch. The SCSI ID switch could be set to any ID and it used 50 SCSI connectors. The disks held more than a third more data and they had faster seek and file transfer times as well. Because the Zip came out a few months earlier, however, everyone bought them. Today, the Zip has all but replaced the original SyQuest drive as the digital prepress industry standard for removable storage and the SyquestEZ drive is being discontinued.

The point of this all is to drive home the fact that while technical specifications tell you a lot about the quality of the product you are buying, they don't always relate to how many units of the product are going to sell. How useful a product will be as a transport medium is directly related to market penetration. We have SyQuest and Bernoulli drives in our office, as well as Zip and EZ drives. Whenever we send files out of house we send them on SyQuest or Zip cartridges, while the Bernoulli and the EZ drives are used for strictly in-house purposes, such as backups and sneaker net.

When in doubt, call. If you plan to send and receive files using removable storage media, talk to the people you are going to be doing this with. Find out what they use. Call your service bureau and ask them what media they can accept. Also, ask them what media the majority of files they receive come on. This is a good indicator of what people in your area are using and what will be most useful to you.

Intended Use

Finally, you have to determine how you are going to be using the removable storage media. Each use of removable media has special requirements:

◆ **Transporting files.** Compatibility is of utmost importance. The media is worthless if it can't be read by other people.

- **Backing up files.** Here compatibility is not an issue because the media only needs to be read by one computer. Speed is a plus, because backing up should be done frequently.

- **Emergency startup disk.** The disk must be bootable. The faster the drive, the sooner you'll be up and running.

- **Archiving.** Storage capacity and media life are most important. Speed isn't, unless you plan to access archived files frequently.

- **Alternate Hard Drive.** If you are going to be using the media as a secondary hard drive, then speed and storage capacity are of utmost importance, but compatibility isn't.

TYPES OF MEDIA

The number of options for removable storage media is dizzying. Choosing the right media can be further complicated by the fact that most removable media today is pretty good and all of them have their virtues.

Storage media falls into four basic categories:

- **Magnetic.** This includes floppy disks, hard drives, and removable hard drives, such as the Zip and EZ. This is the most common of all media.

- **Optical.** Optical drives use a laser to read discs. The most common of these is the CD-ROM, which is the only optical drive format at the consumer-level and the only one we will concern ourselves with.

- **Magneto Optical.** As you might guess, this is a hybrid between magnetic and optical. MO drives use a combination of lasers and magnetics to read and write to disks.

- **Tape.** Tape is a throwback to the dark ages before hard drives existed. Data is recorded onto DAT (digital audio tape) or DLT (digital linear tape).

> **Note**
>
> *All prices and speeds are estimates based on the best available data and are given for comparison purposes only. The true performance of any device is dependent on the computer it is hooked up to. Costs per megabyte are based on single cartridge prices. Prices are significantly lower when buying in bulk.*

Magnetic Media

Diskettes

Storage capacity: 720KB to 1.4MB

Average read/write: 39 kilobytes/second

Average seek time: 229 ms

Approximate cost per megabyte: $.50

Media life span: under five years

At one point in time, the diskette was all. A single diskette held the operating system and the application program with enough room left over to save files to the same diskette. Then life on earth adapted to live on dry land. Diskettes are the last relics of a time when hard drives and other options were too expensive for all but the largest of institutions, when there was no other choice of media. The only reason they exist now is that everyone has one. This is perhaps the one instance where we do not recommend going with what everyone else has.

Pros

Everyone has one. Per unit price is very cheap. Floppy disks can usually be found for under $.50, with boxes of 100 available for between $20 to $50.

Cons

Diskettes are the worst possible removable storage media you can use for the following reasons.

- They are slow.

- They are unreliable. Remember, media life span estimates are based on media that is sitting on a shelf in a protective case, not on real use.

If you actually are using the diskette, expect a life of a few days to perhaps several years.

◆ Diskettes hold very little. If you have more than 1.4MB, you will need to compress the file or break it up to fit on several diskettes, both of which will waste your time and increase the chances of file corruption.

◆ They are marginally supported technology. Now that hard drives and other storage media are available, no research is going into improving drive or disk performance at this writing. Computer manufacturers are also using cheaper diskette drives in their computers, further reducing the reliability and performance of the media.

◆ They are expensive. While cost per disk may be low, the cost per megabyte is more than most other media options. Add to this the cost of waiting for the disk to write, then rewriting the file when the write fails, reformatting the disk, throwing it away when the initialization fails, formatting another floppy, and finally copying the file. You have a prohibitively expensive media storage option that should be avoided at all cost.

Uses

Diskettes are okay for transporting small files in non-critical situations. They are also good for giving files to people who have a reputation for not returning things, because diskettes are so cheap you won't get upset if they don't come back. They also make good coasters.

Hard Drives

Storage capacity: up to 9.1 GB

Average read/write: 4 to 6 megabytes/second

Average seek time: 7 to 12 ms

Approximate cost per megabyte: $.18 to $.27 (external)

Media life span: 5 to 10 years

We have, on rare occasions due to circumstances beyond our control, been forced to copy files to an external hard drive, power down the computer, disconnect the hard drive, and carry the thing, SCSI cables and power cord draped around our necks, to the service bureau. The service bureau technician received it with a long-suffering humorless smile and a look that said on no uncertain terms, "You should know better." We did and you should, too. Never use external hard drives as removable media.

External hard drives were created to remain stationary. With a few specific exceptions, they are not built with the shock absorbing capabilities that most removable media have. Moving it risks damaging it. Hard drives are too valuable to be treated that way. You are also required to shut down the computer when removing or attaching the drive, which causes hassle for everyone involved.

Pros

Hard drives are very fast and have a fairly low cost per megabyte.

Cons

They are not easily transportable.

Uses

Hard drives, of course, are best used for what they are meant to be used for: as a space to work and to store the files you are currently working on. They are not meant to transport files, nor are they meant for archiving files.

RAIDs

RAID currently stands for Redundant Array of Independent Disks. It used to stand for Redundant Array of *Inexpensive* Disks. Unfortunately, RAIDs are far from inexpensive. The CPU can work much faster than the hard drive. RAIDs help to overcome these speed differences.

Redundancy is the key. All RAIDs use a minimum of two drives. RAIDs either write copies of the same information across multiple disks or write the information to several disks at once. In the first case, the data is very secure because multiple copies of it are being written simultaneously. In the second case, speed bottlenecks are eliminated. Certain RAIDs can read/write at 200 MB/sec!

RAIDs are excellent for digital video and for editing large images. RAIDs are now available as docking systems. Drives can be pulled out and swapped with empty drives. Drives are *hot-swappable*, which means the computer does not need to be powered down to remove a drive, much like other removable storage media. Unlike other removable storage media, however, there is no consistency among docking systems. If a remote location does not have the same system that you do, then your drives are useless to them. If having absolute speed is worth any price to you, then hook a removable RAID array up to every workstation. There is no faster way to work with, or transport, data.

Docking Stations

A permanent dock leaves the wiring and power supply in place, while the drive mechanism itself is removable. Docking stations can hold removable hard drives, RAIDs, removable cartridge drives, and DAT decks. The drive mechanism is hot-swappable so that you can change to whatever storage medium you need.

A system like this has both drawbacks and advantages. If all the machines within a work group are standardized on this system, it reduces the need for redundant drives because not everyone needs to use all of their drives at all times. In terms of media transportation, swapping removable hard drives is much faster than copying them to and from removable cartridge media. The drawbacks are that drives can't function without their docking station. Either you have a dock or the drives are useless to you. Docking stations do not come in standard configurations. Drives from LaCie's docking system are not compatible with those of MicroNet's. Still, docking stations are an interesting solution for making the widest range of media available to as many computers within your workgroup as possible without buying a separate drive for each media of each station.

5.25 Inch Media

Storage capacity: 44MB, 88MB, 200MB

Approximate cost per megabyte: $.95/$.47/$.31

Media life span: 5 to 10 years

SyQuest pioneered the removable hard drive. SyQuest was both the creator of the technology and the name of the technology itself. Many different manufacturers have made SyQuest drives and SyQuest cartridges.

The SyQuest 44MB removable hard drive was the first standard for removable storage media for digital prepress after the diskette. It was very popular, yet the very popularity of the 44MB drive thwarted SyQuest when they introduced the 88MB drive. The original 88MB drive could not read and write 44MB cartridges. People were reluctant to invest money into technology that couldn't use the media they had already invested so much money into. Responding to this, SyQuest came out with the 88c, which could use the 44MB cartridges as well as the 88MB cartridges. This was followed by the 200MB SyQuest drive, which could read and write 44, 88, and 200MB SyQuest cartridges. This drive was briefly popular, because the higher capacity cartridges better served the ever-increasing needs of digital prepress, while providing backwards compatibility with the abundant 44 and 88MB cartridges.

Pros

After floppy drives and CD-ROMs, SyQuest drives are the most ubiquitous of removable media. Nearly every service bureau has one, as does everyone involved in the digital graphic arts for over a year.

Cons

They are slow and the media is expensive. They are rapidly being made extinct by more modern media such as the Zip drive.

Uses

We can only recommend investing in this media if you need the compatibility. Aside from that, SyQuest 4.25" technology has run its course. For about the cost of three 44MB SyQuest cartridges, you could buy an EZ drive with a 135 meg cartridge. You'd have a faster drive and be 15 megs up on the deal. Still, a lot of people out there only have SyQuest 4.25" drives. They are reluctant to give them up because they have invested a lot of money into the technology and don't want to let go of that investment. This is understandable, but 5.25 inch SyQuests are simply no longer cost-effective. Old SyQuests are still fine for backups and emergency startup disks though.

3.5 Inch Media (First Generation)

Storage capacity: 105MB, 270MB, 540MB

Average read/write: NA, NA, 3 Megabytes/second

Average seek time: NA, NA, 9.9 ms

Approximate cost per megabyte: $.51/$.17/$.11

Media life span: 5 to 10 years

Somewhere between the 88 and 200MB drives, SyQuest came out with a drive that read 105MB 3.5" cartridges. The drives weren't compatible with anything else and they weren't significantly larger than the 88MB drives. They got a reputation early on as being unreliable. Whether this was true or not is irrelevant. People believed them to be unreliable, so they didn't buy them. They disappeared fairly quickly. Then SyQuest came out with a 270MB drive, which more people bought than the 105. Still, the user base for SyQuest 4.25" media was so great it worked against SyQuest yet again. The 270 never gained wide acceptance. Most recent is the 540MB 3.5" drive, which can also read 270MB cartridges.

Pros

They are faster and hold more data than SyQuest's 4.25" media. The 540 has speeds approaching those of a slow hard drive and the cost per megabyte of the 540 media is fairly low.

Cons

They are dead-end technology that never had wide acceptance. The 540 is a decent, fast drive, but it is eclipsed by Iomega's Jaz drive and SyQuest's own SyJet drive.

Uses

Due to the low acceptance factor, these drives are only recommended for backup and archiving.

3.5 Inch Media (Second Generation)

Storage capacity: 135MB, 230MB

Average read/write: 1.4 to 2.4 megabytes/second, 3.5 megabytes/second

Average seek time: 13.5 ms

Initial cost per megabyte: $.88/$1.3

Approximate cost per megabyte: $.19, $.13

Media life span: 5 to 10 years

We already talked about the sad fate of the EZ 135. It was superior technology that lost out to the Zip largely due to timing. SyQuest lowered the price of the EZ to the point where the company was losing money on every sale of the EZ drive to try to break the strangle hold of the Zip. It didn't work. The EZ is being discontinued to make way for the EZ Flyer, which uses 230MB cartridges but can read and write the 135 cartridges.

Pros

Fast, cheap.

Cons

The EZ Flyer costs about $100 more than the Zip drive. Even though the initial cost per megabyte is lower than the Zip, that $100 will be enough to make most people choose the Zip over the EZ Flyer. You will encounter far fewer clients and freelancers who use EZ cartridges than you will find using Zip cartridges.

Uses

EZ drives are cheap enough that many service bureaus buy them and they are useful as transport media to service bureaus. They are also fine for local transportation of media, as well as backups, archiving, and emergency startup disks.

SyJet 1.3 GB

Storage capacity: 1.3 GB

Average read/write: 5 megabytes/second

Average seek time: 12 ms

If history is any indication, the SyJet is an excellent drive doomed to failure. Why? Because, once again, Iomega was able to get their similar product, the Jaz drive, out months before the SyJet. People who needed to have gigabytes of removable storage already bought the Jaz and they aren't about to switch.

Pros

The SyJet is really fast. Fast enough to use as a hard drive. Cartridges hold a huge amount of data at a low cost per megabyte.

Cons

Not in as widespread use as the Jaz drive, which limits its usefulness as transportation media.

Uses

Its large storage capacity and speed makes the SyJet excellent for anything but transportation to remote sites.

Bernoulli

Iomega created the Bernoulli drive, a high-performance removable storage drive. They never caught on and we are not going to get into individual specs for the drives. They are no longer sold and media is all but impossible to find.

Pros

Fast, reliable, built to take abuse.

Cons

Nobody uses them. Media is expensive if you can find it.

Uses

Backup, archive, emergency startup disks.

ZIP

Storage capacity: 100MB

Average read/write: up to 1.4 megabytes/second

Average seek time: 12 ms

Initial cost per megabyte: $2.00

Approximate cost per megabyte: $.19

Media life span: 5 years

SyQuest 5.25" media reigned for years as the digital prepress standard for removable storage media. This changed almost overnight with the introduction of the Zip. The Zip drive is the semi-disposable Swiss furniture of the removable media kingdom. Iomega challenged conventional thinking by making a drive that was, well, *cheap*: It could have backfired on Iomega completely, but instead it paid off. They were able to make a drive that cost less than anything anyone else had to offer. The public loved it.

Making the drive so cheap contains a certain wisdom, other than the fact that people like inexpensive things. Our Bernoulli drives are so well made they'll function for many years to come, but so what? The technology is already obsolete! Conventional wisdom says that you should build things to last as long as they can. This flies in the face of computer reality. Computers are not cars or blue jeans. They become obsolete far faster than they wear out. They can become worthless in terms of usefulness although they function perfectly. The Zip drive was designed to be functional for about five years. By that time, something far faster and with more storage will make the Zip obsolete. Because it's such an inexpensive drive, we are not going to be too upset about that because we will have gotten our money's worth.

Pros

It is cheap and nearly everyone has one.

Cons

It is cheaply made and fairly slow. It's so lightweight it needs to be held in place when inserting disks and can be dragged to the floor by the weight of its own SCSI cables. No on/off switch, limited SCSI ID capabilities, 25-pin SCSI connectors instead of the standard 50 pin.

Uses

In spite of the cheapness of the drive's construction, we love the Zip drive. If there is one "must have" drive, this is it. Its affordability, combined with its widespread acceptance, make it ideal for transporting files. We wish it were faster, but for most purposes it functions excellently.

JAZ

Storage capacity: 1 GB

Average read/write: up to 5.5 megabytes/second

Average seek time: 12 ms

Initial cost per megabyte: $.5

Approximate cost per megabyte: $.10 to $.12

Media life span: 5 years

The Jaz is the beefed up big brother of the Zip. It is five times faster and holds ten times as much.

Pros

It is very fast and has a low cost per megabyte.

Cons

It has a high *perceived* cost. Even though the cost per megabyte is less than most other media, the cost of the drive is around $500 and the cost per cartridge is around $100. These prices keep many people away from the drives and prevent as high a market penetration as the Zip.

Uses

The Jaz is a great solution for those who need large, fast, removable storage. Its speed and high storage capacity make it excellent for just about any purpose. Its usefulness as a transportation medium remains to be seen, however. Call before sending someone a Jaz cartridge.

Optical Media

The most familiar optical media is the CD. There are other types of optical media, such as the video disc and the rewritable compact disc, but these are fairly obscure and unused in the digital prepress world, so we will not talk about them here. What we will talk about is the CD-ROM, the most commonly used form of removable media after the floppy.

When optical media is written to, a laser is used to burn pits into the disk, creating spirals of "pits" and "lands" to encode the binary information. Optical media is incredibly reliable because it is non-magnetic. Information stored on magnetic media can be corrupted by any magnetic field of enough strength, be it a magnet, static charge, or other source. Because data is written physically to the optical disk rather than electromagnetically, data can't be lost or corrupted by magnetic fields. It could take an electromagnetic pulse (EMP) from a nuclear warhead without corruption of data. Of course, the optical drives themselves would be useless at this point and people have things on their minds other than their CD-ROMs, but it is comforting to know that something will survive of all that we've created.

Speeds of CD-ROMs are defined in terms of the first CD-ROM player, which spun between 200 and 530 RPM. The double speed, or 2x, spins twice as fast. Speeds go all the way up to 10x. Most CD-ROM readers are 4x or 8x and most consumer-level writers are 2x or 4x.

CD-ROM Writers

Storage capacity: up to 650MB

Average read/write: 352 kilobytes/second (2x), 614 kilobytes/second (4x)

Average seek time: 150 to 300 ms

Initial cost per megabyte: $.92(2x), $1.69 (4x)

Approximate cost per megabyte: $.02

Media life span: 100 years

Once very slow and very expensive, CD-ROM writers are quickly becoming a great option for transporting and archiving. CD-ROM burners use WORM (write once, read many) media. CD-ROMs can only be written to once.

Pros

Very low cost per megabyte. CD-ROMs are almost invulnerable. You have to really try hard to corrupt the data on a CD. They have an estimated shelf life of at least 100 years. Everyone in the digital graphic arts has a CD-ROM reader.

Cons

Once a WORM is burned, that's it. The data is unchangeable. Fortunately, most CD-ROM burners support multi-session writing. Only a portion of the disk is written to, leaving the rest available for more data at a later date. CD-ROM readers are also very slow, with speeds closer to floppy disks than hard drives, and CD-ROM writers are even slower. Finally, they require a large amount of hard drive space. CDs are written to in sessions. Before this session can begin, all the data to be written to a special file, called an image, is a specially formatted copy of all the data you want to burn on the CD. This requires that an area be set aside that is the size of the all the data to be written. Older CD writers had a big drawback in that they needed a constant rate of data flow from the hard drive. If the data flow fell below a certain speed, the session would fail and that part of the CD would be useless. Write caching on the CD-ROM burner mechanism and faster hard drives have mostly eliminated this problem. CD-ROM writers are also very slow. A 2x CD-ROM burner can take half an hour to write 650MB of data.

Uses

The inexpensiveness and durability of the media and the market penetration make CD-ROMs an excellent choice for transporting files. Their reliability and longevity make them perfect for archiving as well. Their slow speed and the fact that they can only be written to once make them less suitable for backup purposes, however.

Magneto Optical

Magneto optical disks are the coolest of removable media technologies. An MO disk is made from materials that cause it to be highly resistant to magnetic fields at room temperature. The MO drive uses a laser to heat the MO disk to the Curie point, the temperature at which magnetic particles on the disk's surface can be realigned by the magnetic field generated by the read/write head. This has two advantages over other media. A laser can be focused in a much tighter field than traditional magnetic read/write heads are capable of, so data can be written much more densely than on ordinary magnetic media. Since the data can only be changed when the disk is heated to high temperatures, information stored on MO cartridges is incredibly stable.

Traditionally, MO drives have required two passes to write data. Even though rotational speeds of MO disks are comparable to those of magnetic media, until recently they could only function at half the speed of magnetic media. More recently, however, manufacturers have developed MO drives that write in one pass, doubling their speed.

3.5 Inch MO Drives

Storage capacity: 128, 230, 650

Average read/write: 1.7 megabytes/second

Average seek time: 27 ms

Initial cost per megabyte: $1.50 (230), $.93 (640)

Approximate cost per megabyte: $.12/$.09/$.07

Media life span: 30 years

3.5 inch MO drives have been around for several years, but they haven't caught on until recently. Optical drives were once slow and expensive, but recent improvements in the way the drive writes to the disk have increased speeds substantially. Prices have also come down considerably. 128MB drives are no longer available, but 230MB drives can read 128MB cartridges. 640MB drives can read both the 128 and 230MB cartridges.

Pros

Magneto-optical is a technology whose time is almost here. It has the advantages of both magnetic and optical media, without the disadvantages. Unlike magnetic media, they have a high resistance to magnetic fields and are ultra-stable. Unlike optical, they can be rewritten. Newer MO drives have speeds rivaling that of magnetic media. MO media has a very low cost per megabyte.

Cons

MO technology has yet to receive the industry-wide acceptance that magnetic media has, making it problematic as a transport media.

Uses

If the person you are sending files to can read your MO cartridges, their stability makes them excellent for file transportation. Their longevity and low cost per megabyte makes them great for archiving. Older drives might be too slow for backups and purposes other than archiving, but newer drives are good all-around storage media.

5.25 Inch MO Drives

Storage capacity: 650 MB, 1.3 GB, 2.6 GB

Average read/write: 3.1 megabytes/second (650 MB), 4.3 megabytes/second (2.6 GB)

Average seek time: 35 ms (650 MB), 19 megabytes/second (2.6 GB)

Initial cost per megabyte: $.94/$ (650 MB) $.76 (2.6 GB)

Approximate cost per megabyte: $.07/$.04/$.03

Media life span: 30 years

5.25 inch MO media has all the advantages of 3.5 inch MO drives with much higher capacities and faster speeds.

Pros

Among the lowest cost per megabyte of any removable storage media. Highest storage capacity of any removable media other than tape. Fast, reliable.

Cons

The 5.25 inch media size is old-fashioned. 3.5 inch is easier to store and transport and nearly all of the new removable media drives are using the 3.5" form factor. 5.25" cartridges are written on both sides, so the cartridge has to be flipped over to write on the other side. High cost of drives, around $2,000 for 2.5 GB models, prevent them from having the wide acceptance of other media.

Uses

An excellent choice for archiving and backup. MO jukeboxes are now available, which can hold up to 2.5 Terabytes! Not as useful as a transport media.

Magnetic Tape

Magnetic tape was one of the first computer storage technologies. It was commonly used on mainframe computers. Remember the wheels full of tape spinning round and round in the old sci-fi movies? That's the stuff. Fortunately, the tape drives of today are much more compact and the media can fit into a pocket. Unfortunately, tape technology still has the same major problem it always did. It is linear access, rather than random access like disk drives. This means the tape must be fast forwarded and rewound to find data, just like locating your favorite song on an audio tape. Tape is also subject to more traumas than other media. How many of your favorite tapes were eaten by the tape player before you finally switched to CDs forever?

Thanks to modern technology, magnetic tape has become a much faster and safer storage medium than it was just a few years ago. Still, we can only recommend it for archiving purposes. Truthfully, modern magnetic tape storage media was not intended for anything else but archiving, though some service bureaus accept files on tape.

Due to the limited nature of tape and the lack of any standards when it comes to tape, we won't go into depth with tape here but will give you a brief review of the media.

The two major types of tape media are DAT (digital audio tape) and DLT (digital linear tape). DAT is slower and generally holds 8 GB, which is less than DLT. On the other hand, DLT is fairly speedy, compared to other tape media, and can hold up to a whopping 40 GB on a single tape!

Media costs for tape are incredibly low: $.002/MB to $.006/MB, with initial costs varying from $.12/MB to $.17/MB. DLT will probably become the archiving medium of choice. For under $5,000, a DLT drive can write 40 GB to a tape, which costs under $100. This kind of storage was once only available to the largest of companies who could afford to pay for it. Now it is affordable for small companies.

Archiving is like insurance. You do it, but you hope that you never have to use it. It should not take the place of backing up files on your own. Ideally, every machine on the network should be routinely backed up entirely every day in case something happens to a workstation. The workstation can be rebuilt from the archive and all the hard work that has been done that day will not be lost. This security is worth the cost of an archiving system. As a way of retrieving a single lost file, however, a tape backup can be problematic. Finding a single file amongst 40 GB or even 8 GB can be a real hassle, often involving the network administrator.

Final Recommendations

As we have seen, you have many excellent choices for removable storage media. There are valid reasons for choosing just about every media we talked about. Ultimately though, we have to recommend using what everyone else is using. This will save you the most frustration when dealing with clients, freelancers, and service bureaus. This week, everyone is using Zip cartridges for their transportation media. Zips are affordable, reliable, and easy to use. We recommend them without reservation. SyQuest 5.25 inch media will remain viable for a few more years, however, due to its industry prevalence.

For personal backup and for emergency startup disks, nearly any of the preceding options will do (except for magnetic tape), since speed and compatibility are not as important.

For archiving, we recommend burning your work to CDs because of their reliability and low cost. Due to their slow speed, however, they may not be suitable if you have a large volume of archiving. If your archiving needs are high and money is no object, consider a magneto-optical jukebox for its speed and reliability. For high-volume archiving on a budget, 30 and 40 GB DLT is the way to go.

STRATEGIES FOR MEDIA DEXTERITY

In order to fully develop your media's adroitness, plans should be made for standardization and the creation of media dexterity situations.

Standardize

In an environment with several workstations, choose a media and make sure every station has a drive that can support those stations. Do this even if you have a high-speed Ethernet network in place. The time you save by doing this will pay for the drives in no time.

There are many advantages to standardizing:

◆ Digital prepress involves large files that take a long time to copy over a network. Copying over a network means that the sending station is tied up (unless you are using a copy optimizing utility, such as Speed Double). The network and the receiving station are also slowed down causing everyone's productivity to be decreased. Using removable media to transport files between stations ensures that everyone will be able to work at top speed while files are being copied and transported.

◆ It makes the life of the system administrator easier. They can create an emergency startup disk for every station and distribute new software more easily.

◆ It speeds up the gathering of files to be sent out-of-house. Instead of being copied to one station that has the drive, everyone can copy their files onto the media from their own station.

◆ It is much easier to receive and use client media if everyone has a station that can use the most common media. Make sure the client knows which media you prefer.

Determining which media to standardize on requires an analysis of both internal workflow issues and the marketplace in which you work. We highly recommend the Zip drive, but if you frequently create files that are over 100 MB, the Zip is too slow and will not have enough storage capacity. The Jaz, the SyJet, or higher-capacity MO will better serve your purposes. The drawback to this is that although you gain speed and storage capacity, you lose compatibility with clients. If you need both speed, capacity, *and* compatibility, you may need more than one type of drive per station. Conduct an informal survey of your clients, as well as the service bureaus and printers you use, to find out what they are using. This will help determine what media is right for you.

Media Dexterity Stations

If you frequently receive media from a wide variety of clients, you need to set up a media dexterity station. Rarely is it cost-effective for every workstation to have every type of storage device attached to it, but having one or more workstations dedicated to receiving media can save time and money. It will also keep your clients happy.

Your media agility station works best for you if you keep a few key things in mind:

◆ The wider the variety of media you support, the more dexterous you will be.

◆ Newer, higher capacity versions of drives can often support older media. The SyQuest 200 can read 88 and 44MB cartridges, for example.

- You are limited to seven devices (including the computer) on a SCSI chain. If you have more drives than this, you will need to add another SCSI card to your computer. A SCSI-2 card can increase the performance of many external drives.

- Do not put DAT drives on the media dexterity station. Optimally, you should have two DAT drives on two separate stations, one for archiving and retrieving in-house files, and one for unloading, archiving, and retrieving client files. DATs are slow and they will create bottlenecks if they are placed on the media dexterity station. No one can use the station until the DAT is finished.

- Monitor the station. If people are waiting to use it, you are losing productivity. Create a second station. Redundancy ensures productivity.

- Never spend time swapping drives back and forth. If you need a drive to use on a second machine, buy another drive. Consider the costs of swapping drives back and forth. Two computers need to be shut down, removing them from the productivity loop. Cables need to be disconnected and connected. SCSI IDs and termination issues need to be resolved.

- Always have your client's device. Never make the client wait needlessly. Never make your client bring in her own device to be hooked up to your equipment. This requires communication with your client beforehand. It might require investing money on a new drive. Remember, a satisfied client will repay the cost of the drive many times over.

NETWORKS

If you have more than one computer in your workplace, you should have a network in place. Although networks are not as useful for large (over 2.5MB) files, they are much more efficient than removables for copying small files between computers (see Figure 6.5). To transport a file using a removable, you must first copy the file from the hard drive to the removable, then from the removable to the hard drive of the destination computer. Even though networks copy things more slowly, they only need to do it once because they can copy directly from hard drive to hard drive.

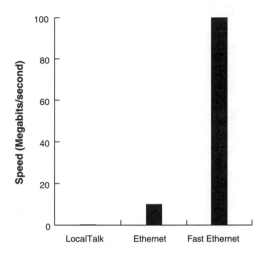

Figure 6.5

Relative speed of networks operating under optimum conditions. Longer bars are better.

LocalTalk

A local talk network is the simplest and cheapest kind of network to set up. It is also the slowest. Local Talk requires only a transceiver for each computer on the network and ordinary telephone cord to connect things together. With a little shopping around, you can get all you need to connect two computers together for under $30.

Local talk, however, is *slow*. It runs at about 230*kbits*/sec. This is too slow for anything but text files and small vector graphics files. Still, it is better than no network at all.

Ethernet

It is well worth the cost to spend a little extra and set up an Ethernet network. Ethernet is still quite slow, but at 10 megabits per second, it is much faster than LocalTalk. If you have a newer Mac or Mac clone, Ethernet is still fairly inexpensive, because Ethernet comes built-in on most new Macs. Two computers can be connected via Ethernet for under $100. If Ethernet is not built into your computer, you will need an additional Ethernet card for your computer, which is available for under $75.

Fast Ethernet

Fast Ethernet runs at 10 times the speed of Ethernet, or 100Mbps. Unfortunately, you have to pay for that extra speed. Fast Ethernet currently does not come standard on any computer yet. Fast Ethernet requires an additional card for each computer on the network. The cost of a fast Ethernet can be two to three times the cost of ordinary Ethernet, but if you use your network extensively, this is money well spent.

Ethernet Hubs

Networks do not necessarily need hubs, but the larger and more complex a network is, the more it will benefit from a hub. Hubs can increase the speed and performance of the network. Hubs manage the flow of data between computers and help ensure that data travels between computers intact. Without a hub, data can get lost or corrupted and the entire network can freeze. These things are less likely to happen with a hub.

Network Media Dexterity

A few simple steps will ensure that you are working as efficiently as possible when you are using the network to transport files. These steps apply primarily to Macintosh-based systems and not necessarily to Windows-based systems. This is because Windows systems handle network traffic much more efficiently than Macs do. Although it is vitally important to take steps to ensure you are working as efficiently as possible when you are using a Mac on a network, it simply isn't as much of an issue with a Windows machine.

Connect and Disconnect

Connect to the server or other computer, copy the files you need to, then disconnect. Macs are notoriously "chatty." On a network, they are constantly sending information to each other, even when you are not actively copying files over the network. This steals processor time away from both computers that are connected and it also slows down the network. Always disconnect when you are not actively using the network.

Share Just a Folder, Not the Whole Computer

Create a folder. Select it, then go to File:Sharing, select Share this item and its contents, and also select Make all currently enclosed folders like this one. Close this window. After a moment, you will see cables grow out of the folder. This indicates that this folder is actively being shared. Now, if you haven't done it already, go to the control panel Users and Groups, double-click Guests. Select "allow guest to connect" and close the control panel. Disable sharing for the rest of your computer if it is active.

This will give you several immediate benefits:

◆ It decreases network traffic because only one folder needs to be addressed, rather than all the folders on all the hard drives on your computer.

◆ It provides more security for you because only one folder on your computer can be accessed by outsiders.

◆ It allows guests to connect to that folder without needing to waste time entering a password.

Use Aliases

Using aliases enables you to work much more efficiently, especially if you follow the previous advice. When you connect to a shared folder, make an alias of it. Next time you need to copy a file to that folder, simply drop it onto that alias. Your computer automatically connects to the computer that folder is on and copies the file to that folder, eliminating the need to go to the chooser completely. If guest access has been enabled for that folder, copying things over the network using aliases is as easy as copying them to drives on your own station. Unfortunately, copying files this way does not automatically disconnect you as well. Remember to disconnect afterward.

NEVER Work Over a Network

This is absolutely essential whether you are using a Windows or a Macintosh machine! Copy the file you need to work with to your hard drive and disconnect from the network. DO NOT open the file up over the network and try to work on it from your station. Doing this slows you down almost to a complete standstill. Ethernet moves data at about one-twentieth of the speed of a slow hard drive. Working on even small text files is slow if you try to do it over a network.

To make matters worse, the increased network traffic bogs down the entire network. Not only will you decrease your own productivity, but everyone else's as well.

This is one of the most common mistakes made by people who are new to networks and it is also the worst. It is an easy one to make. Once you have connected to another computer, the folders and files on that computer appear exactly as they do when they are on your own computer. There is nothing to differentiate them from what is local. Always remember to copy the files you need to copy and then disconnect. This will keep you out of trouble.

MODEMS

The final way to move files from your computer to others is via modem. Traditionally, modems have been too slow and unreliable for routine use of moving files that are more than a few kilobytes. As with any other computer technology, however, modems are getting faster and better. It will still be a few years before modems replace removable storage media, but it will happen. If you start using the technology now, however, you will be in a position to take advantage of them in the future.

How useful modems are to you right now depends largely on who you are sending files to. Many businesses are relying more and more on modems to receive files from remote clients. Modems transcend distances. A file can be sent from Tokyo to New York faster and cheaper than it could be sent on a removable.

Larger print shops are taking advantage of modems and digital printing technology. A bulk mailing company in the Midwest has found that the cheapest printing rates are in the Northeast. The company mails advertising to the entire US. They send files via modem to the printer. The ad copy comes from Missouri while the graphics come from Ohio. Both are recieved and composed on the same machine, then printed, sorted, and mailed directly from the plant. Utilizing the modem provides faster turn around time and eliminates the need to use local printers, copywriters, and artists. Granted, all of this could have been done over the phone and through express mail services, but with smaller files, the modem is faster and cheaper than any other option.

Modems come in a variety of speeds (see Figure 6.6) and styles, but the majority of them fall into one of three categories: POTS, ISDN, and T1.

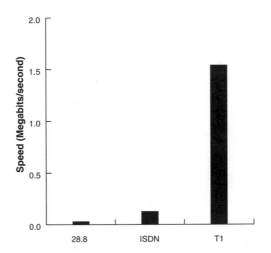

Figure 6.6

Relative speeds of modem connections. Longer bars are faster.

POTS Modems

POTS modems use the "plain old telephone system." They are the most common and most inexpensive modems. They are also the slowest and least reliable. This is because they use the plain old telephone system, a system which was put in place decades ago, when such things as modems only existed in the dreams of science fiction writers. Everyone has experienced noise on the telephone line. Static, other voices, bad connections. Although this is an annoyance to us, to the modem it means slowed or lost connections and corrupted data.

POTS modems are primarily for recreational use, but if you want to try out a modem before you invest in faster ISDN or T1 connections, get at least a 28.8 baud modem. Under ideal circumstances (which are rare) a 28.8 baud modem can transfer data at a rate of 28.8 kilobits per second. The speed of a 28.8 baud modem hovers just above the frustration level. If you use a slower modem, you will go mad waiting for things to happen if you use it for anything other than email.

ISDN

ISDN (Integrated Services Digital Network) provides higher speed access with a price. ISDN requires that a special digital phone line be installed on your premises. Depending on where you live, this can be as inexpensive as standard phone line, unless you live in places like Maine, where you can expect to pay several times as much. ISDN modems are available for under $400.

For the price, ISDN delivers far greater performance than POTS modems. At 128 kbps it delivers almost five times the speed of the fastest POTS modems. Digital phone lines are far more reliable than standard phone lines. There is virtually no noise on a digital line, which means that slowdowns or errors associated with POTS modems are eliminated.

The performance increase is so great with ISDN lines over standard modems it is well worth the price if you frequently send or receive files via modem.

T1

For businesses that rely on the Internet for transferring files, a T1 line offers the highest performance available. The cost of using a T1 line can run into thousands of dollars a month, so it is used primarily by larger businesses. Unlike POTS and ISDN lines, T1 lines are generally used to connect entire companies to the Internet, not just one computer.

A T1 line uses 24 64 kbps ISDN lines for a total throughput of 1.544 megabits per second. The throughput is divided amongst the people using the line. Twelve people could be connected at 128 kbps, or two people at 772 kbps.

If your business requires all of your employees have fast connections to the Internet, or if you are an international magazine publisher receiving advertisements, articles, and images from all over the world, then T1 is the only way to go.

Media Dexterity with a Modem

You have two ways to send and receive information over via modem. One is to go through the Internet. The other is to dial in directly to a computer at the place you want to send information to. The first way is cheaper; the second is faster and more reliable.

Connecting through the Internet

Sending files over the Internet is often cheaper than dialing directly because, if you have a local dial-in, you only have to pay for a local call. If you dial directly, you have to pay the long distance charges to that location. Sending files via modem is very slow, but if you are using a local dialup and have unlimited access time, this can be an acceptable solution. File transfers this way may be slow, but they can be done in the background, enabling you to work on your computer while the files are being transferred. Be aware, though, that if a transfer is interrupted, you will have to upload the entire file again from the start, even if you were a few kilobytes away from finishing.

There are two ways to send files over the Internet: as an email attachment (see Figure 6.7) and via FTP.

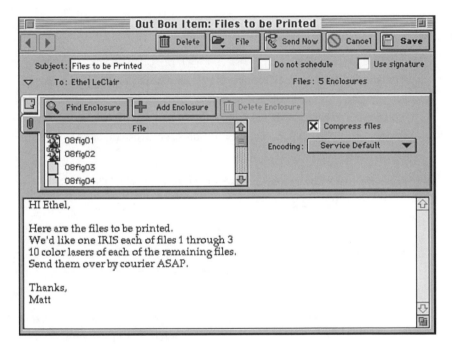

Figure 6.7

Files as an enclosure in Claris Emailer.

Sending files as an email attachment can be a problematic solution. Problems will be minimized if you pay attention to certain things:

◆ If you are sending them from a business that has email as part of its network services, check with your network manager first. Businesses often have strict size limits to the size of attachments that can be sent with email. Exceeding these size limitations can bring down the entire network. Check with your network manager before sending files.

◆ If you use an Internet service provider, your service provider may have restrictions on file sizes that can be transferred via email. Call or email them to be sure. Tell them exactly how large the files you want to send are. Don't just tell them "large files" because, if they are not in the digital graphics industry, they have no idea how large the files can be.

◆ Always check with the person to whom you are sending files to make sure it is acceptable to him. It's very bad form to send someone large files that they will have to download at their own expense without asking first.

FTP Transfers

FTP (File Transfer Protocol) transfers are a more professional way to transfer files over the Internet than sending them as mail attachments (see Figure 6.8). On a hard drive of a computer belonging either to the service provider or to a business, a space is set aside for the express purpose of transferring files. This space is usually divided up into several folders, which can be open to the public or can require passwords.

FTP has several advantages over sending files as email attachments:

◆ It uses a designated space, so you know the file is where it should be and that it is welcome there.

◆ FTP programs monitor the transfer and alert you if there is a problem with the transfer. They also prompt you to resend the file. Email often does not do this.

◆ Typically, file size has no limits, though the larger the file, the more likely the transfer is to be interrupted, forcing you to resend the file.

◆ It does not interfere with regular email messaging.

Check with the person to whom you want to send files in order to find out if she has FTP capabilities. If she does, she will be able to provide you with an address and a password.

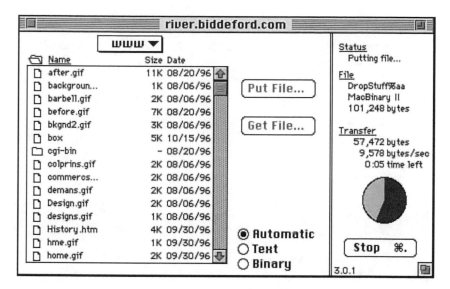

Figure 6.8

FTPing files.

If you want to receive files via FTP, you have two options. If you have an Internet account through a local access provider, chances are you already have space on their computers to use as an FTP site. Call your access provider to ask them how utilize this space.

An FTP site at your access provider does have one drawback; you must download the files to your own computer to work with them. To eliminate this extra step, you can set up a computer of your own to enable people to upload files directly to you. Using a program like FTP, you can allow people to connect to your computer and download or upload files to you. People will still need to go through the Internet to get to you, and your computer will need to be constantly connected to your Internet access provider constantly. This is pricey unless you have unlimited access.

Direct Connections

Using special software, a computer can be set up to receive files just like an answering machine can receive incoming calls. This requires the receiving computer be left on at all times to receive calls. The advantages to this are speed and reliability. Files transferred directly between computers travel much faster because they have far fewer steps to take to get there. This also results in greater reliability in the transfer. The fewer steps, the less likely the data is to get corrupted.

Several software packages enable you to do this. FreePrint, for example, was designed specifically for the print industry. It allows you to set up your computer to receive calls with the click of a button (see Figure 6.9). It also enables you to create special client copies of the program to give to your clients. The client copy contains all the information necessary for your clients to send files to your computer with just the click of a button. FreePrint also lets you include a complete job ticket and an email message with the attached files. It is an ideal tool for sending and receiving files directly, but it can also send files to locations on the Internet as well.

Figure 6.9

FreePrint, software designed for the print industry to exchange files via direct modem connection.

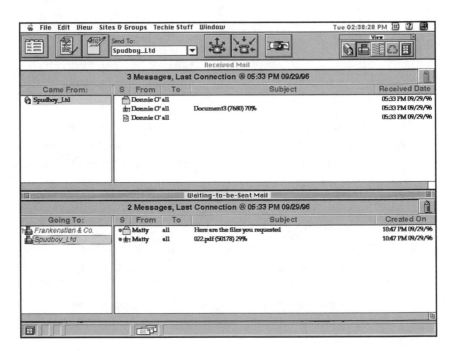

If you wish to dial in to your service bureau or clients directly, give them a call. If this is a service they provide, they will give you the software and instructions you need to connect to them.

If you plan to transfer files this way frequently, you should get an ISDN line and modem. Remember, though, connections between two modems can only take place at the speed of the slowest modem in the connection.

MEDIA DEXTERITY AND YOU

Digital prepress requires communication throughout all aspects of the process, and media dexterity is no exception. You need to communicate with everyone with whom you exchange files. Doing so will prevent hassles, save both time and money, and help to ensure that files are output on time.

Chapter

PROJECT PLANNING

The digital graphic arts industry resonates with two very dangerous myths.

Myth Number One is that digital color publishing, being computer-based, is a simple, automated process. The work we are responsible for today is subject to all the same planning, attention, and laws of physics as work produced using conventional techniques. In a perfect world, we could stand in front of a stainless steel box, type in some basic parameters like page size and paper type, press a few buttons, and watch perfect printed results roll out the other side on a conveyor belt. In real life, however, the computer is just another tool used in the process, like rubylith tape or a Heidelberg press. It's powerful, but it's no miracle cure.

The capabilities granted to us by digital technology lead us straight to Myth Number Two: all the tasks of a project can be handled by one person.

All the different tasks of prepress—stripping, color, design, typesetting, and so on—used to be areas of craft, requiring years of disciplined training and experience to master. Today, most people believe these prepress areas have become sciences, meaning the craft can be broken down into steps anyone can follow. To a certain degree, this is true. The hardware is inexpensive, the software is fairly easy to learn, and more "How-To" documentation is being written than ever before.

However, the context for these tools—producing quality ink on paper—hasn't changed in 100 years. The issues are just as complex and demanding as they ever were. How could we expect only one person to handle all prepress and publishing responsibilities?

Planning a project before design and production is just as important now as it ever was. Unfortunately, good project planning is one of the first tasks cut in the interests of saving time (a tip of the hat to what's quickly becoming Dangerous Myth Number Three: computers enable us to slash already outrageous deadlines in half). Deluded by the sweet-tasting marketing fable that computers actually do the work for us, many of us simply open our page layout program, turn on a few fonts, and tear right into the project, figuring we can take care of any other details as soon as the need arises.

Any commercial printing project consists of a dizzying array of variables, and project planning is like laying the foundation for all the design and prepress tasks that wait ahead. The earlier we consider and plan for these variables, the more control we have over quality, cost, and time.

At the start of any project, the first thing we must do is evaluate our own skills. Can we honestly handle a six-color annual report with custom folds and die-cuts if our most intensive experience is with two-color business cards and letterhead? Can our equipment come through under the same circumstances? Chances are, probably not. Few things can overwhelm designers like biting off more than they can chew. If you're bidding on work involving new, more complex, and more expensive techniques, consult with your service providers, printers, and colleagues before accepting the job. Get an honest assessment of the time and know-how required.

The remaining variables fall under two categories: Project Requirements and Project Tasks.

PROJECT REQUIREMENTS

Every printed project is a combination of budget, schedule, and quality. Although these issues don't apply to personnel or project content, working through each one of the following items ensures that your printed result takes advantage of the money available, the time allocated, and the ultimate printing process.

Determining Job Requirements

In this industry, there are two basic rules concerning project cost:

◆ Everything costs something.

◆ No one likes being surprised by the final cost of a project.

Budget is by far the most defining influence on design and production today. As much as everyone would like four-color logos, brochures, and catalogs, it is just too expensive. Therefore, we must keep the project parameters within the limits of what we are able to spend.

The final cost of a project is the total of:

◆ **Design hours** (content, page layout, and illustrations)

◆ **Production/prepress hours** (scanning, color, trapping, imposition, proofing, and output)

◆ **Materials** (film, paper, plates, and ink)

◆ **Press run** (setup, inking, printing, and cleaning)

◆ **Finishing** (binding, cutting, and folding)

◆ **Distribution**

When estimating a job, all of these issues must be considered. For designers, this process is as simple as describing the nature of your project as clearly as possible and getting estimates from different service bureaus and printers.

Most people, however, get burned in one of two places. First, make sure you include enough design hours in your estimates. At the end of a project, it feels good to receive, say, $3000 for design time (based on an estimate of 40 hours at $75 per hour). If you actually put in two weeks of 12-hour days, the realization that your hourly rate has dipped to under $20 will be a sad one indeed. If you're unsure of how long a specific project may take, turn to the graphic arts community for council. Ask your service bureau for advice. Consult other graphic designers you've met. Join an on-line graphic arts newsgroup. You'll find that the vast majority industry professionals are willing to share their knowledge, or at least their opinions.

Second, don't allow the parameters of a job to change without re-evaluating your project estimate. Sometimes it's too easy to let a persistent supervisor or client make "just one more tiny change." Even the smallest deviation from your original estimate can make a big difference in cost. In terms of physical design, the final cost of a typical project is increased by the following:

◆ Increasing the number of colors.

◆ Increasing the number of pages.

◆ Larger page sizes.

◆ Bleeds and crossovers.

◆ Multiple folds.

◆ Custom die-cuts.

◆ Graphics requiring trapping.

◆ Using higher-quality paper.

◆ Critical color.

◆ Short deadlines and rush charges.

◆ Last-minute changes or corrections.

◆ Last-minute file repair or "massaging."

Every publication must be discussed with your service bureau and printer. All of your vendors should be involved in even the most preliminary decisions. They are the only ones who can tell you exactly what the costs are, what the potential printing problems are, and ultimately who the best people are to handle specific prepress tasks.

Determining Quality Requirements

Aside from content and design—which for the time being, we gladly leave in your able hands—the perceived quality of your final project is very much affected by the printing process. Sure, everyone wants the finest stochastically-screened Hexachrome color on the best paper, but the trick is finding the most appropriate degree of quality for the specific project at hand. Doing so is vital for both the designer creating the project and the printer preparing to reproduce it.

The following issues affect our quality requirements:

- **Market longevity.** How long will the publication remain viable and useful? Is it promoting an event that happens on a certain date? Or is it an item that will be used again and again?

- **The intended audience.** This determines how the publication must present itself. Newsletters, for example, often have an audience already. Some printed pieces compete with similar items for audience attention. Other pieces must live up to an audience's discerning standards, whereas others must communicate a company's solidity, worth, and well-being.

- **Image clarity.** How important are the fine details and colors in your scanned images to the final printed result? A textbook of screen shots requires little attention to image clarity, whereas a furniture catalog might require detailed reproduction of woodgrains, fabrics, and textures.

- **Color accuracy.** This usually comes down to a choice between color matching or color balance. Clothing and furniture catalogs often require pinpoint color matching, so customers know exactly the color of the items they desire. On the other hand, images of food usually just need to be balanced, or made to appear pleasing instead of matching the original objects.

Examples of Quality Expectations

Below, we've listed some examples of different publications to illustrate how quality expectations change from project to project. Although these descriptions are not carved in stone, they give some insight into the issues that determine our expected printed results: paper stock, the discerning nature of our audience, shelf-life, and color.

One-Color Newsletter

Here, the product is short-lived, intended for one or two readings before being replaced or discarded. The paper is usually inexpensive "photocopier" stock. Images are reproduced only fairly and fine details (often highlights) are lost. Quick-printed or quick-copied publications fit into this category as well.

Two-Color Newsletter

The product may be a one-shot deal but may be intended to be used for a few months. These jobs are typically run on presses that hold up to a 150 linescreen. Halftones reproduce well, holding more detail. Newsletters may continue to use cheaper paper, but two-color corporate identity pieces—business cards, brochures, and similar pieces—require better stock.

Computer Wholesaler Catalog

This item is in full-color and printed on materials kept in stock by most printers. Color fidelity is not an issue because customers are not using color as criterion for purchasing something. Image reproduction is clear and registration is usually to within .5 pts. The expected lifespan of this item ranges from a week to a couple of months.

Furniture or Clothing Catalog

The color in this catalog must match the actual items so customers can make informed and accurate decisions. Although the lifespan of these publications may be short (three to four months), premium paper and inks are used to make an impression of quality. The publication is fully trapped and the press registers to within .3 pts.

The No-Holds-Barred Annual Report

Often the design adventure of a lifetime, this one-shot publication has the responsibility of communicating the company's entire image through design and print. Color matching may not be required, but color reproduction is of the highest quality. Images are crisp, often screened at 175 or 200 ppi, with no apparent flaws.

ASSIGNING PREPRESS RESPONSIBILITIES

You can handle a prepress task in three ways:

◆ Do it yourself, digitally.

◆ Assign it to someone else to do digitally.

◆ Have it done conventionally.

If you are new to commercial printing, it's wisest to turn the majority of prepress tasks over to a professional. The ability to take this work in-house takes time and experience to perform successfully. Assume new responsibilities one at a time, allowing yourself enough time to absorb the last aspect of the prepress process before launching into the next. As you gain experience and make contacts in the industry, consider investing in classes and new equipment that better enable you to handle these tasks.

If you're new to prepress, we ask you to wait before taking control of prepress responsibilities because of the major downside of doing it yourself: accountability. The overriding reason to do your own prepress work is to save money, but it can cost more to repair a bad file than it would have to farm out the work in the first place.

You may already be at the point where you perform all of your own prepress tasks, delivering a ready-to-output electronic document to your service provider. Even so, communication with your printer and service provider is paramount in making your decisions.

The tasks most frequently farmed out to specialists are:

♦ **Scanning/Color Correcting.** It's uncommon for most facilities to have the scanners and rigidly calibrated systems needed to acquire and correct critical color. Even if your color isn't critical, scanning and correcting is time-consuming and most flatbed scanners, which many designers possess, don't really generate a high-enough quality color scan for good reproduction. Service providers can also provide FPO images rather than complete scans, holding the high-res information in-house until it's time to output films.

♦ **Trapping.** Some service providers use dedicated trapping software to take care of this task and others just manipulate the tools found in QuarkXPress and PageMaker. Often, the specialists are most familiar with the issues involved in creating a successful trap.

♦ **Stripping.** Here the printer uses conventional techniques to arrange and impose the page films before shooting the job to plates. Most printers prefer setting the job up this way, rather than imposing a file digitally.

CHOOSING A SERVICE PROVIDER AND PRINTER

Most print shops and service providers are happy to offer a tour, samples of their work, and lists of customer references. To better help designers in their continual searches for facilities, we have included a list of questions to ask each one. Their answers should determine whether or not they possess the level of commitment and expertise your work requires.

Questions for a Digital Prepress Service Provider

1. **What formats and platforms do you accept for digital work?** Ask about their supported software and transport media. See Chapter 6 for more information on transport media.

2. **What are your rates?** Many service bureaus are cross-platform but may increase their processing fees for Windows-based files by 50 to 100 percent, while keeping their Macintosh margins razor-thin to remain competitive.

3. **Do you offer any training or technical support?** Some service bureaus have their own in-house training facility and offer clients free or reduced-rate training.

4. **What type and size imagesetters do you use?** Some facilities can only output letter- and tabloid-sized page films. If your work is larger than this, you'll have to look elsewhere. See Chapter 19 for more information on imagesetting and screening.

5. **How often are your imagesetters calibrated?** Look for a service bureau that calibrates at least every day, as well as whenever the film is changed. Calibration consists of checking emulsion density and halftone dot consistency. Someone on staff should also be checking the film processing chemicals to ensure they are not depleted or diluted.

6. **What screening options are available?** More and more establishments are offering stochastic screening and other types of custom screening. Ask for samples and a description of the steps involved in getting the most out of such technologies.

7. **Do you offer scanning and color correcting services?** Ask to see samples of their work, as well as their scanning equipment. Be leery of any facility offering critical color if their only device is a flatbed scanner. Also inquire about using Desktop Color Separation files. See Chapters 10, 11, and 12 for more information on scanning issues and requirements.

8. **What color proofing systems are available?** Viable systems include laminate systems, IRIS ink-jet, calibrated Fiery (or another color laserprinter), and bluelines. See Chapter 18 for more information on proofing.

9. **What trapping services are available?** Some service bureaus use dedicated trapping software but charge considerably more for the service. Others use a combination of dedicated software and manual techniques. Others still include a certain amount of trapping in the overall cost of output. See Chapter 16 for more information on trapping.

10. **Who will be the primary contact?** Will you only communicate with a salesperson? Or are you encouraged to contact the people responsible for processing your file? Choose a system that makes you most comfortable.

Questions for a Commercial Printer

1. **Do you accept digital files?** If so, see "Questions for a Service Provider" above. No one should feel obliged to hand over files to a printer for processing if you don't feel comfortable with their level of digital experience. Also note that some printers, under the auspices of providing digital services, merely farm out the work to a service bureau and mark up the cost.

2. **What are your rates?** If possible, ask about cost breakdowns for representative samples of your work to get a better idea.

3. **Do you offer any training or technical support?** Most printers encourage designers to call with even the tiniest inquiries. Find out the proper people to contact with such questions.

4. **What prepress services do you offer?** Ask for their input on what prepress services might be more cost-effective if performed conventionally.

5. **Are both sheet- and web-fed presses available?** By describing the nature of your projects with your printer, you can determine how these best suit the needs of your work. See Chapter 1 for more information about different printing presses.

6. **How many colors can be printed in a single run?** Many print shops run four-color jobs on two-color presses. This makes press-checks almost impossible without using a densitometer. Stochastically-screened images and five or six color-jobs are also more difficult to print successfully and take more time to complete.

7. **Do you offer high-fidelity color printing?** Typically, only shops possessing six-color presses offer this service. Ask for samples printed on their presses.

8. **What is your average turnaround time?** Also ask for rush rates.

SUMMARY

For today's designer, good project planning means meeting your deadlines, getting the highest quality for your budgeted dollars, and ensuring that you make a profit—all without driving yourself crazy. This takes more than learning how to write a good project estimate. It means:

◆ **We understand that the responsibilities of producing a color publication are vast and complex,** and we're encouraged to turn to outside resources—freelancers, service bureaus, and printers—for assistance.

◆ **We recognize new, unaccounted-for changes in our project** and how they affect final deadlines and cost.

◆ **We know the issues that determine the final printed quality of our publications,** which range from paper stock to target audience to color requirements.

◆ **We have an objective, global view of our project at all times.** It's easy to get caught up in the smaller details, like scanning images or physically designing a page layout, while other issues are ignored until the last minute.

Call it greasing the skids, laying the groundwork, or pounding the beach with artillery before the invasion. All the strategies that lead to a successful project are born before the actual project begins.

VECTOR-BASED GRAPHICS

Vector-based graphics programs, along with page layout programs and pixel-based graphics programs, form an unrivaled trinity of prepress power. Vector-based graphics programs are vital to the prepress process. They are among the most powerful and useful of graphics programs, but they are also the most misunderstood and misused.

Vector-based graphics programs, also known as PostScript drawing programs or simply as drawing programs, have their origin in the early days of the Mac. The early Macs came with three programs, MacWrite, MacPaint, and MacDraw. MacWrite was the predecessor to modern word processing programs and the uncle to page layout programs. MacPaint was the origin of pixel-based graphics programs, whereas MacDraw was the starting point for vector-based graphics programs. Today bitmapped graphics programs are commonly known as paint programs while vector-based graphics programs are called draw programs.

The basic distinction between a paint program and a draw program is the same now as it was then. Paint programs use pixels to define images. A pixel, short for picture element, is a square of color. Everything in a bitmapped image is defined by these squares of color arranged in a grid like a Georges Seurat painting, who painted as if he were restricted to using graph paper and couldn't paint outside the lines (see Figure 8.1). A draw program uses points connected with curved or straight lines, like a connect-the-dots (see Figure 8.2). The spaces defined by the lines can be empty or filled with color.

Figure 8.1

Bitmaps define shapes with squares of color on a fixed grid.

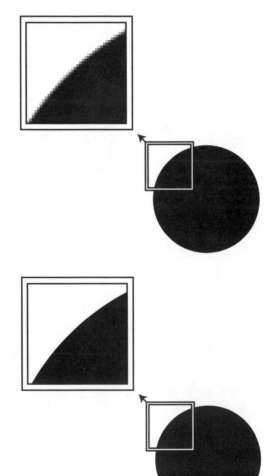

Figure 8.2

Vectors define shapes with lines, which create areas that can be filled with color.

Put another way, people like to say that vector-based programs define images mathematically. This isn't really saying all that much, because everything on the computer is defined mathematically. To put it differently, when you use a vector-based graphics program, you are writing code. The fact that you are doing this is far removed from you, so you don't need to know any coding to use vector-based graphics programs. In the case of programs like FreeHand and Illustrator, that code is PostScript code. Although both programs provide a graphical interface, the fact remains that you are writing lines of code. These files can even be opened as text in a word processor.

Part of the code for a black box looks like this:

```
0 g
0 i
0 J 0 j 1 w 4 M []0 d
%%Note:
283.5 487.5 m
283.5 616.5 L
154.5 616.5 L
154.5 487.5 L
283.5 487.5 L
f
```

This really doesn't mean a lot to anyone who can't read PostScript code. Basically, it is a set of XY coordinates that tell the program where to set the location of the square. Other commands instruct lines to be drawn between the points and black to fill the defined space. The key element to remember here is that it is all done with text. Herein lies the magic of PostScript drawing programs. If you were to increase the size of a bitmapped object, you would either need to add more pixels to it or make the pixels bigger, which means that new data needs to be created or the resolution of the image lowered. If you increase the size of an object in a vector-based graphics program, the code is changed to move the XY coordinates farther apart. The quality of the image and the file size stay the same, no matter how much bigger you make it. This magic gives all vector-based drawing programs the following qualities:

♦ **Objects are infinitely editable.** When you create an object in a drawing program, you can change it as much as you want, just as you would with text in a word processing file. Nothing needs to be permanent until it is on the printed page.

♦ **Objects do not degrade.** Just about everything you do to a bitmapped image causes the image to degrade. If you rotate the image or scale it, it needs to re-create every pixel in the image, always at a loss of some information. Ultimately, after enough manipulation, the image degrades to the point where it is only useful as abstract art. You can do all of these things to a vector image with no loss of quality (unless you deliberately set out to do so).

◆ **Objects are infinitely scaleable.** A vector-based image can be increased or decreased in size to any degree and it will still appear and print at the highest quality.

◆ **Objects print at the highest possible resolution.** The mathematics of a vector-based graphic enable it to be printed on any PostScript printer at the highest resolution that printer is capable of. Pixel-based graphics are at a fixed resolution and can't print at any higher resolution than the graphic has.

◆ **Objects create very small files.** Sizes of vector-based graphics files are usually measured in kilobytes, whereas pixel-based files that have a high enough resolution to produce printable quality are measured in megabytes. Very complex vector-based illustrations can be as large as bitmapped files, but this is rare.

Uses of Vector-Based Programs

The unique qualities of PostScript drawing programs make them excellent for certain uses:

◆ **Logos**. Logos need to be highly scaleable, portable, and consistent— all of which PostScript artwork provides.

◆ **Stylized Type.** PostScript drawing programs use the same language in which fonts are written. This makes them perfect for editing and enhancing type.

◆ **Scaleable Artwork.** You only need to create the artwork once. It appears at its best whether it is billboard-sized or postage stamp sized.

◆ **Traced Images.** With vector-based graphics programs you can trace bitmapped images and turn them into stylized (and stylish) PostScript artwork.

Vector-based programs are not good for anything else. This doesn't mean that you *can't* use vector-based graphics programs to do other things, but your time would be much better spent in other ways:

- **"Natural" Images.** In a bitmapped graphic, every single pixel can have a different color. In a high-resolution graphic with hundreds of pixels per inch, this can reproduce the subtle shading and tone changes we find in nature. In a vector-based graphic, each different color needs to be defined as a separate area (except for gradients and patterns which offer limited functionality). Imagine creating a photo-realistic portrait using stencils. You might be able to do it, but it would take so many stencils that you would go insane trying.

- **Complex Images.** Everything needs to be defined mathematically in a vector-based graphics program. This doesn't mean that you can't create complex images in one, but it will take a long time to do so.

- **Drawing.** In spite of the fact that vector-based graphics programs are called *drawing* programs, they really aren't good for the free and natural style of artistic expression, which we associate with the concept of drawing. Although the graphical interface separates you from the knowledge that you are writing PostScript code, PostScript has strict parameters that the program won't (or shouldn't) let you violate. This prohibits you from being freely expressive, which is a must when you are drawing. We have seen many artists open FreeHand or Illustrator and try to do the same kind of work that they do when they draw a freehand illustration. Despite the names, this isn't what the programs are good for.

- **Page Layout.** More page layout features are added to FreeHand and Illustrator with every new version. The programs now have support for tab settings, spellcheckers, and many more functions usually associated with page layout programs. We strongly advise against using vector-based graphics programs as page layout programs. It is not what they were created for. Your Swiss army knife may have a can-opening blade on it, but an actual can opener will serve you much better for opening cans. Page layout programs offer you many more features to help you create pages easily and efficiently. It is self-abusive to try to do page layout in a drawing program.

PARTS OF A VECTOR-BASED GRAPHIC

Let's take a closer look at what makes a vector-based graphic. As we know, a PostScript drawing program is a graphic interface for writing PostScript code. This should make it much simpler and easier to understand than manually writing the code would be. Unfortunately, vector-based graphics programs are neither intuitive or easy. Of all the programs in the digital prepress process, these are the least intuitive and have the sharpest learning curve, but they do use a consistent logic. Once you adapt your mind to their way of thinking, you will be able to use them with ease.

Points

The smallest unit of a vector-based graphics is a point, the point being an XY coordinate that defines the shape and dimension of an object. Points are invisible, but they are there and they control everything. You need at least two points to create anything. Corner points and curved points are the two types of points. The type of point matters when there is a line attached to the point. To modify anything in a vector-based graphics program, a point must be selected. If there is no point selected, nothing can happen to the graphic. This provides tremendous control over graphics because you can modify them one point at a time.

An unselected point is invisible, but it is still there and contains information (see Figure 8.3). There are dozens of unselected points on this page. Selected points, on the other hand, are visible and can be edited or modified (see Figure 8.4)

Note

Points that are not connected (called strays) contain information, even though they are invisible. Any information, visible or invisible, requires processing time. It is a good idea to remove them before you save a file. In Illustrator, go to Filter: Select: Select Stray Points and press Delete.

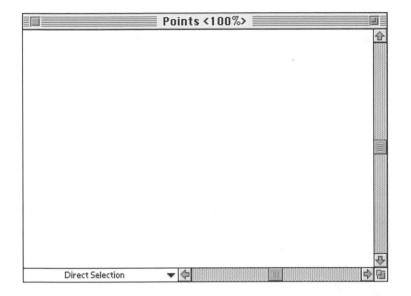

Figure 8.3

An unselected point.

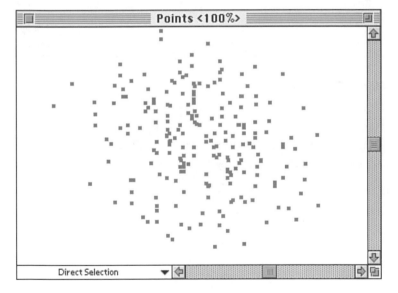

Figure 8.4

A copious amount of visible, selected points.

Segments

Two points joined together with a line are called a *segment*. Segments are either curved or straight. The type of points in the segment dictates whether it will be curved or straight. In a curved line, at least one point will have a Bézier control attached to it. A straight line either has no Bézier controls or the controls are set such that the line appears straight. The shape of anything created in a vector-based graphics program is defined by straight lines and curved lines (see Figure 8.5).

Figure 8.5

A straight and curved line created by a vector-based program.

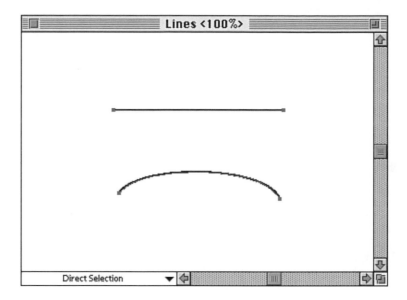

Bézier Controls

Bézier controls are manipulated by BCPs (Bézier Control Points). These controls extend from points. A point can have up to two Bézier controls extending from it. These controls not only dictate the shape of a line, but the behavior of two lines when they meet (see Figure 8.6).

Corner points don't need to have Bézier controls (see Figure 8.7). At a corner point which has Bézier controls, the controls act independently from each other (see Figure 8.8).

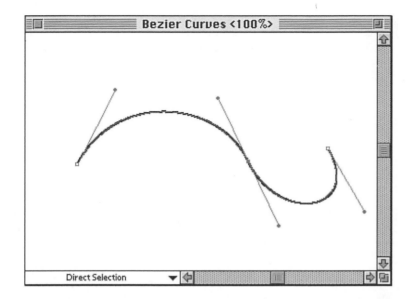

Figure 8.6

Bezier controls in action.

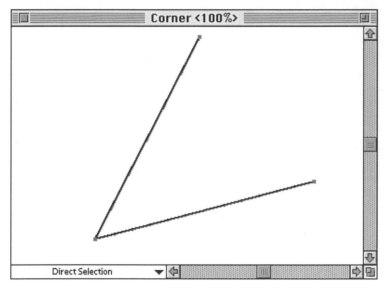

Figure 8.7

An example of corner points.

Figure 8.8

Independent controls.

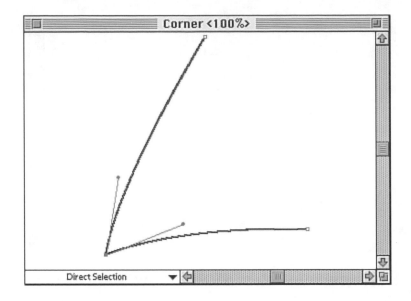

At a smooth point, the Bézier controls are connected (see Figure 8.9).

Figure 8.9

Connected Bezier controls.

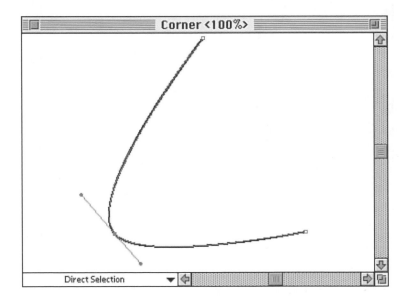

The trickiest part of learning vector-based graphics programs is understanding how Bézier controls affect the lines they are associated with. The distance a Bézier control point is from its originating point controls how much of an effect it will have upon the line. Also, the degree of the angle formed by the line connecting the Bézier control point to the point, and the line drawn from that point, affects that line (see Figures 8.10 through 8.13).

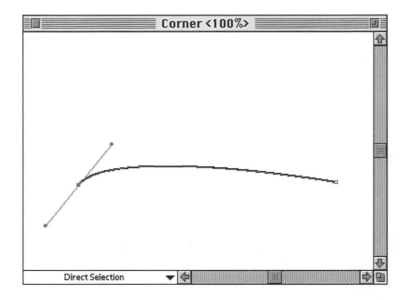

Figure 8.10

A short BC curves the line a little.

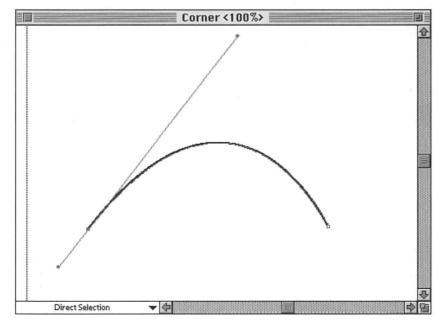

Figure 8.11

A long BC makes the line very curved.

Figure 8.12

A slight angle barely curves the line.

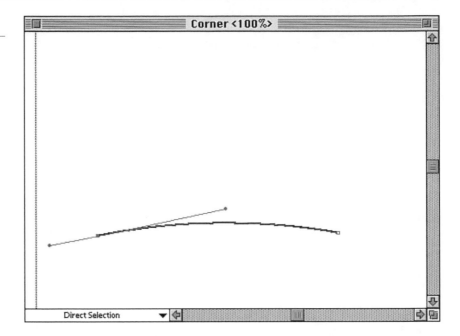

Figure 8.13

A sharp angle makes the line more curved.

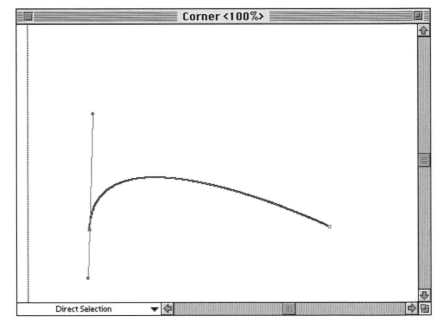

Two Bézier controls give you a more rounded line. This is the best way for defining a curved line, because it gives you the most control over the line (see Figure 8.14).

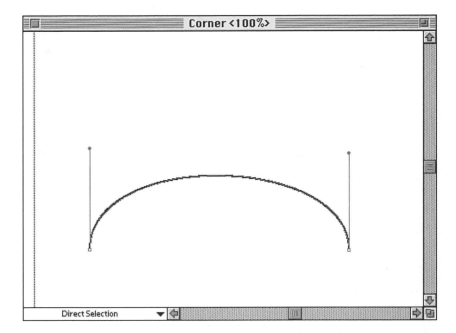

Figure 8.14

A Bézier control tag team.

Understanding lines and how points and Bézier controls affect them is everything to creating in FreeHand and Illustrator. Everything else is just variations on this theme. They are also the most difficult thing to learn in both programs. Devote all your time to learning how to use them until you know instinctively how to create with them.

Path

One or more connected segments are considered to be a path. Everything that is connected is in the same path. Paths can be opened or closed. In an open path, the first and last point are separate (see Figure 8.15). In a closed path, the first point and the last point of the path are the same (see Figure 8.16). Generally, you always want to use a closed path because the fill is more predictable.

Figure 8.15

Open path.

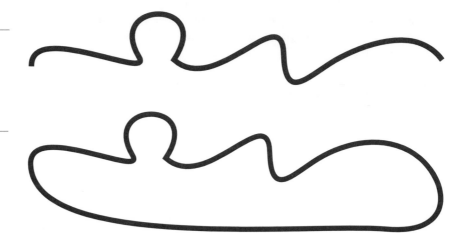

Figure 8.16

Closed path.

Fill

Any path or curved segment can have a fill. A straight line can also have a fill designated, but you won't see it. A fill needs an area to contain it. In an open path, an invisible line is drawn from the first point in the path to the last point (see Figure 8.17). In a closed path, the fill is in the area within that closed path (see Figure 8.18). The areas along the path that the line closes off are filled. The results of the fill will be much more predictable if you use a closed path. A fill can be a process, a spot color, a gradient, a pattern, or nothing at all.

Figure 8.17

An open path filled.

Figure 8.18

A closed path filled.

Stroke

Fill defines what is contained within the lines of a path. Stroke defines the lines themselves. Stroke can have color and thickness, which is called *weight*. It can also have no color and no stroke at all, in which case the path merely defines the area to be filled.

Compound Paths and Masks

Compound paths and masks use two or more paths to create certain special effects. In a compound path, the point at which two selected paths overlap each other drops out, leaving an empty space revealing whatever is behind the objects (see Figure 8.19). Non-compound paths are just the opposite (see Figure 8.20).

Figure **8.19**

Compound paths.

Figure **8.20**

Non-compound paths.

With a mask, the topmost path crops out the paths it is selected with. The topmost path becomes invisible when this happens (see Figure 8.21). Unmasked paths, however, are visible (see Figure 8.22).

Figure 8.21

Masked paths.

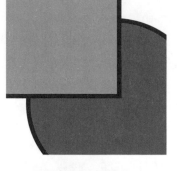

Figure 8.22

Unmasked paths.

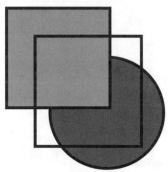

An important thing to remember is that with compound and masked paths, nothing actually is gone; it has just been redefined. This definition can be changed back by releasing the mask or the path.

TEXT AND TYPE

Eighty-seven percent of everything you do in Illustrator or FreeHand, if you are using the programs as they were truly meant to be used, is done using variations of paths, compound paths, and masks. The other 13 percent is done working with text and type.

Working with text and type in FreeHand and Illustrator is a lot of fun if you remember one thing: you are in a vector-based graphics program to manipulate the text, not to do page layout. If you are not going to manipulate the text, you should be working in a page layout program. Even if you are going to be working with text and vector-based graphics, create the graphic in Illustrator or FreeHand, import it into your page layout program, and work with the text there.

The following are several reasons why you should never do text layout in a drawing program when you don't have to:

◆ **Editability.** If you do text layout in an drawing program, and then import it into your page layout program as an EPS graphic, editing that text becomes a huge pain. You will have to open the graphic file, make your changes there, save it, and re-import it into the page layout program. If you did the text layout in the page layout program, you would simply select it and change it.

◆ **Font Usage.** When you use text in an vector-based graphics program and import it into a page layout document, the page layout program is *supposed* to keep track of the fonts used in EPS files, tell you what you've used, and warn you if it can't find those fonts when it opens the document. Unfortunately, we have found that this is often not the case. It is easy to lose track of those fonts and forget to include them with the file when you send it to be output at the service bureau.

◆ **Utility.** Page layout programs were created to make handling large amounts of text as easy as possible. There are many features in those programs created for that purpose, which drawing programs simply do not have.

Tip

FreeHand makes an especially big deal of its text editing capabilities. In fact, the default setting for the text tool seems to exist solely so that the program can shout, "Look at me! I am a page layout program, too!" It causes a text ruler bar to appear above your text along a white text window, completely destroying the possibilities of doing any WYSIWYG text editing. Disable this feature in Preferences before you do anything in FreeHand.

We don't want to belabor the point, but we've seen too many people make the mistake of trying to do page layout in their drawing program—don't! Spend the money and apply the effort to a true page layout program instead. It is an investment that will pay for itself in the first job you do.

So, What *Do* You Do with Type, Anyway?

Get creative! PostScript drawing programs give you *total control* over type, right down to each point and every curve that defines each letter. You can do many things with type in a PostScript drawing program that you simply cannot do anywhere else.

Type within an Area

First, create your area to be filled with text. In FreeHand, choose your Text tool, click anywhere on the page, and enter your text. Then choose Type: Flow Inside Path. The text instantly jumps to the inside of the object. In Illustrator, choose either the Text tool or the Text Inside a Path tool, then click the object and type away (see Figure 8.23).

Figure 8.23

Any path can be filled with text.

All of them were a little twisted in one way or another, except for the one son that died in the war. They had another son that we used to chum with. He was OK. We just didn't like him very much, but he was an OK person. We used to go over to their house. They always had dolls and doll clothes. That was something we didn't have. We used to think that was just marvelous, those dolls clothes. The only reason we ever played over there was so that we could play with those doll clothes. Then we'd accuse the mother of trying to poison us. The mother, Altera Lizzie, would try to do us a favor. She'd give us bisquits and molasses. We'd eat them, and we loved them. She was a real good cook,

Type Along a Path

In FreeHand, create your path and your text separately. Select them both, and choose Type: Bind to Path. The text will jump to the path and flow along the outside of the path (see Figure 8.24). You can change where the text flows on the path within the Inspector window. In Illustrator, create the path. If the path is open, choose the Type or the Type on Path tool. If it is a closed path, choose the Type on Path tool. Click the path where you want the text to begin. You can change where the text flows along the path using the Direct Selection tool.

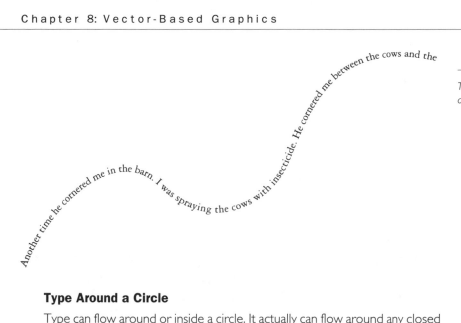

Figure 8.24

Type can flow along a path of any shape.

Type Around a Circle

Type can flow around or inside a circle. It actually can flow around any closed path, but circles are popular for flowing text around (see Figure 8.25).

Figure 8.25

A circular type pattern.

In FreeHand, create the circle and the text separately. Select them both, then choose Type: Bind to Path. The text instantly will center itself over the top of the circle. You can change the position of the text by using the Inspector. In Illustrator, create the circle. Choose the Text on Path tool, and click the circle. Enter your text. You can change the position of the text around the circle by using the Direct Selection tool.

Tip

When you add type inside or around a path in Illustrator, that path and its fill become invisible. If text is flowing around an object that you need to remain visible, make a copy of that object, flow the text around the copy, then drag the text into place over the object. FreeHand gives you the option of having the path visible or invisible when you add text to it. You access this option in the Inspector.

Working with Type

Working with type can be tricky at first. You need at least two tools to work with type. The Type tool can edit the type, but it can't move the type. The Selection tool can move the type, but it can't edit it.

Illustrator and FreeHand handle type in different ways. Each one is equally annoying. Illustrator makes it too difficult to select type; FreeHand makes it too easy.

Type in Illustrator needs to have an origin point. This point contains the coordinates the type is linked to. Unless the type is selected, this point is invisible. Unless you select the point, you will not be able to move the type, and if you don't know where the point is, it can be tricky to select (see Figure 8.26).

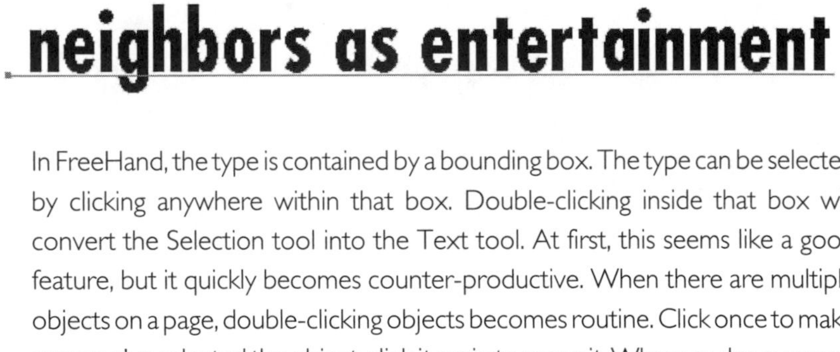

Figure 8.26

Selecting the type's point.

neighbors as entertainment

In FreeHand, the type is contained by a bounding box. The type can be selected by clicking anywhere within that box. Double-clicking inside that box will convert the Selection tool into the Text tool. At first, this seems like a good feature, but it quickly becomes counter-productive. When there are multiple objects on a page, double-clicking objects becomes routine. Click once to make sure you've selected the object, click it again to move it. When you have several objects on the page, you don't know until you see the control point highlight that you have selected the desired object. Double-clicking an object that you want to move and having the Selection tool change to the Text Tool is annoying. You can't move anything with the Text tool. You have to choose the Select tool from the tool palette all over again. This is not a feature, but a bug!

Tip

To facilitate the selection of text or any other object in complex illustrations in Illustrator or FreeHand, always use layers. Keep your text separate from other objects in a layer. Lock layers that you are not working with. Because objects in locked layers can't be selected, it is much easier to select the objects you want from unlocked layers.

Converting Text to Paths

In Illustrator or FreeHand, you can convert text into paths. In Illustrator, select the text using Selection tool. Then go to Type: Create Outlines. In FreeHand, select the type with the Select tool or the Type tool, then go to Type: Convert to Paths. This changes the text into graphic elements that are based on the actual PostScript code contained within the fonts. When you do this, your text becomes a graphic. It can no longer be edited as text.

Text as paths has three advantages:

◆ **Infinite Editability**. Every point and every line can be changed. Different colors can be added to the line and fill of the text (see Figure 8.27).

◆ **File Integrity**. Once text has been converted to paths, the fonts are no longer needed and do not need to be included with the file when it gets sent to the service bureau. The file will print consistently.

◆ **Simplicity.** One level of complexity is removed. With no links to fonts, it is one less thing to worry about, one less thing that could go wrong.

Tip

Text that has been converted to paths loses its capability to be edited as text. If you have to make a change to the contents of text, you are going to have to retype the whole thing. Before you convert text to paths, make a copy of the text and set it aside or save it as a different file. That way you can avoid retyping it if changes need to be made.

Figure 8.27

Editing the text as a graphic.

DEFINING AND APPLYING COLOR

Applying color is easy to do in a vector-based graphics program. All you need to do is select the path you want to apply color to, then choose the color from the Paint Style or the Color List pallette. You can define colors for both the fill and the line, or you can make either the fill or the line invisible by choosing none.

Defining the color is a little more tricky. Vector-based graphics program enable you to do all kinds of things you shouldn't when it comes to building a file that will output the way you want. This has a lot to do with defining colors that won't print the way they are shown onscreen.

Destroy All Colors

Remove all the colors from the Paint palette. Why? Because they are useless. You don't know what they are or what they are going to look like. You don't know if they have been properly defined, or if they have just been created to look good onscreen with no eye toward print (see Figure 8.28).

The first thing to do is eliminate all the colors and gradients from the Paint style palette (see Figure 8.29). Click the first color of the second row of colors in the Paint Style palette holding the Command and Option keys down. Now drag down to the large square in the lower right-hand corner of the palette. All the colors vanish, leaving just the top row of colors, which are Black, White, and None. In FreeHand, you don't have to worry about this, because the Color List only contains Black, White, Registration, and None for colors by default.

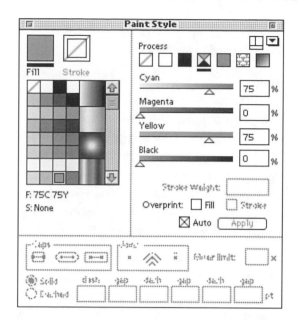

Figure 8.28

These colors are lovely onscreen, but how will they print? To ensure that you get the colors you want, get rid of these colors and define your own.

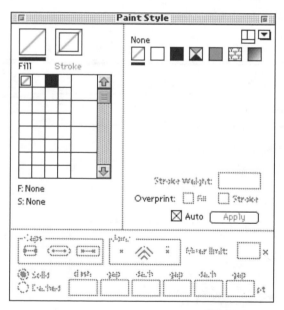

Figure 8.29

This clean palette is far more useful to you than the default palette filled with unusable colors.

To ensure that the colors separate and print as you want them to, define them yourself, swatchbook in hand. A swatchbook is the only thing that gives you an accurate representation of the printed color. We recommend two swatch books: the TruMatch swatch book for process colors, and the PANTONE Spot Color swatch book for spot colors.

Defining Color

Both the TruMatch and the Pantone color libraries are included with the Illustrator and FreeHand. To use them, in Illustrator, go to File: Import Styles. Illustrator prompts you to select a file to import. Go to the folder the Illustrator application is in and then to Utilities. Within that folder is another folder called Color Systems. Choose the color system you want. If you are working with process colors, choose the TruMatch file. If you are working in spot color, then choose the Pantone Coated colors. Illustrator annoyingly imports the entire color library into the Custom Colors section of the Paint Styles.

Defining colors from color libraries is easier in FreeHand. On the Color List, click and hold Options. Scroll down to the color library you desire. The Library window pops up, where you can select the colors you desire. Shift-click to select more than one color. Only these colors are imported into the color list, not the entire palette (see Figure 8.30).

Figure 8.30

FreeHand lets you import just the colors you are going to use.

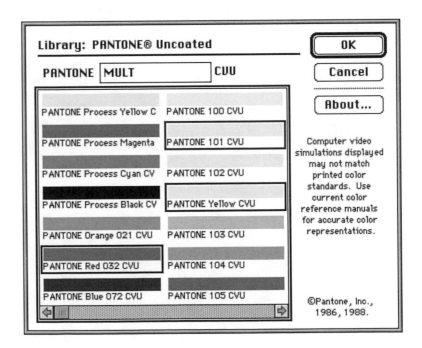

Build your color palette by choosing your colors first from your swatch book, and then match them up to the name in your color palette. In Illustrator, you can facilitate the use of your desired colors by dragging them from the list into the color squares to the left. This isn't necessary in FreeHand, because the colors appear exactly where they should be.

Tints and Spot Colors

Both Illustrator and FreeHand enable you to do tints of any designated color. A color can be printed at any percentage, but this is not always a good thing. Spot colors are designed to be tinted. Spot color defines color with one solid color. If you use a percentage of that color, you get predictable and consistent colors. A process color, on the other hand, mixes percentages of four colors: cyan, magenta, yellow, and black to define a color. These percentages are specific to a certain color. If you use a tint of this color, it scales back all percentages equally. This might seem like it will give you the color you desire, but it won't. The physics of process color just don't work that way. Don't tint a process color. Instead, find the color you seek in the TruMatch swatch book, or a similar book that shows process color mixes, and use that color. This gives you more accurate colors.

When it comes to spot colors, however, tint away! This is what spot colors were made for. It is still a good idea, though, to find a swatch booklet that shows tint values of spot colors. Colors onscreen never match how they appear in print, especially with spot colors.

Naming Colors

What's in a name? When it comes to output, names are everything. When you define spot colors in your vector-based graphic and import the graphic into your page layout document, all the colors you use come with it exactly as they are named. Different applications may name the same colors differently, even though those colors are exactly the same. FreeHand will name PANTONE 185 as PANTONE 185 CVC or PANTONE 185 CVU, whereas in PageMaker the name will be PANTONE 185 CV. The color itself is exactly the same, but even though there is only one letter difference between the three names, a separate plate will print out for each different name (see Figure 8.31).

Figure 8.31

Watch out! These three PANTONE 185 colors are identical in spite of the slight differences in their names. One letter difference is all it takes to make an image setter print a separate plate for that color.

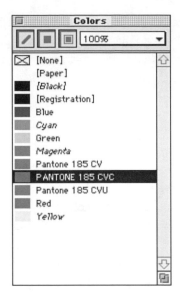

Furthermore, you will not be able to remove or delete the name of this color from the list of colors in the page layout program because the color will register as being in use.

You should always make sure that the names of the spot colors in your vector-based graphic match those in the page layout program. Spot colors can be renamed. This won't affect their color or the way they are printed, but it will ensure that the same colors get separated to the same plate during output.

In Illustrator, go to Object: Custom Color (see Figure 8.32). Select the color from the list and re-title it to the color name your page layout program uses.

In FreeHand, simply double-click the name of the color in the Color List palette. The name will highlight and you can enter the new name.

Deleting Colors

When you import a vector-based graphic into a page layout program, the page layout program should recognize which defined colors are actually used in the graphic and which are just defined on the pallette. The page layout program *should* only import colors used in the graphic. Our experience has been that this is not always the case. Sometimes the page layout program imports all the defined colors. Just as the same color with different names prints a separate plate for each name, the page layout program also prints a plate for every color it thinks it is using, even if there is nothing on those plates. This results in a great waste of film and time. It doesn't always happen, but it is worth taking measures to avoid, since it only takes a second.

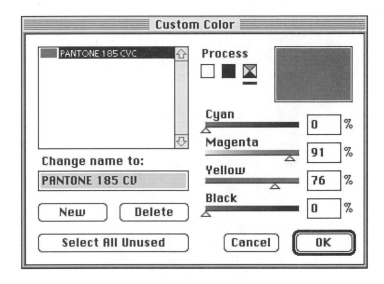

Figure 8.32

Re-titling a spot color.

In Illustrator, go to Objects: Custom Colors. At the Custom Color window, choose Select All Unused and press Delete. Click OK (see Figure 8.33).

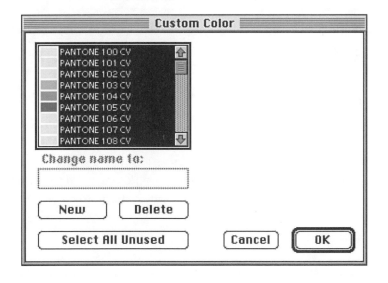

Figure 8.33

Deleting the unused colors in Illustrator.

In FreeHand, click the first color in the list in the Color List (see Figure 8.34). Hold down the Shift key and click the last color in the list. Scroll down to see all the colors if you need to. With the colors still selected, click Options in the Color List and choose Remove.

Figure 8.34

Removing colors in Freehand.

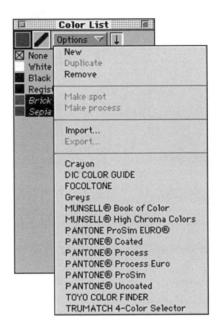

FreeHand informs you some colors were in use and could not be deleted (see Figure 8.35). This is as it should be. The files you weren't using are deleted. Click OK.

White and None

In traditional printing, the word for none is white. The designation of white in CMYK printing means, "use no ink in this area." The white of the paper provides the white for the graphic. This is mostly true in Illustrator and FreeHand as well, but with a few differences. White exists within Illustrator and FreeHand as a color. Objects with a fill of white obscure other objects (see Figure 8.36).

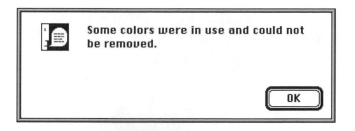

Figure 8.35

Computers often protect us from ourselves. Deleting the colors we were using would prevent us from printing.

Figure 8.36

The circle has a white fill.

Objects with a fill of None reveal the images behind them (see Figure 8.37).

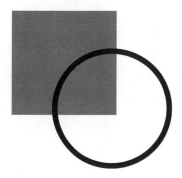

Figure 8.37

The circle has a fill of None.

A stroke with a color of None has no width whatsoever, whereas a white stroke is just that (see Figure 8.38).

Figure 8.38

The small square has a stroke of none, whereas the circle has a white stroke.

For printing purposes, however, the designation of white or None still results in no ink printed for anything with that designation. The difference is that the designation of white also prevents any colors beneath the white from being printed, whereas None enables them to be printed. Think of White as a knockout command. Anything behind the white is not printed.

Black

Black is black. This may sound obvious, but in this industry, things rarely are. Black is 100 percent process black (K) ink. This is different from the black of images, which uses a mixture of CMYK to define the blacks. If you are using black vector-based graphics with images, know that the black may look washed out in comparison. To compensate for this, you may want to add other process colors to the black. For more information on this, see Chapter 16, "Trapping."

Knockouts and Overprinting

When colors overlap, they must do one of two things: knockout or overprint. When colors knock out, only the topmost color is printed. When colors overprint, ink is laid down for all the colors.

Colors knockout by default in FreeHand and Illustrator. The only thing that does not knockout by default in these programs is text, which overprints.

This can be changed. In FreeHand, select the object you want to overprint. Go to the Inspector. Click the Colors Inspector and put a check in the Overprint box (see Figure 8.39). In Illustrator, go to the Paint Styles palette and check the Overprint box. To learn more about when and why to use knockouts and overprints, see Chapter 16.

Figure 8.39

Only black and text overprint by default. Other colors need to be defined separately when you need them to overprint.

Blends, Gradients, and Patterns

One of the fastest ways to destroy the quality and printability of an illustration is to use any of the predefined gradients or patterns in Illustrator. All the problems you had with predefined colors are here, but they are compounded by the fact that there are now multiple colors.

The problems with patterns are the worst because the pre-defined patterns that come with the program can also be PICT images, which were never meant to be printed. In addition, you have no easy way to find out which colors the predefined gradients or patterns contain to see if they match up to the colors in your swatch book, so there is no way to predict how they are going to look in the final printed piece.

Finally, even if you can get the gradients or patterns to print, you really don't want to. Nothing says cheesiness like an instantly recognizable default pattern or gradient. Using them makes it painfully obvious that you have no talent, no creativity, and are only capable of recycling someone else's ideas.

After you have deleted all the predefined colors, the next thing you should do is delete all the predefined patterns and gradients from the application. In Illustrator, go to the Object: Pattern. In the Pattern Window, choose Select All Unused, and press Delete. Next go to Object: Gradient. Unfortunately, there is no Select All Unused command here. Select the first gradient in the Gradient list and scroll down to the last gradient. Hold down the Shift key and click the last gradient in the list. Press Delete.

A Word of Caution About Gradients

You may think that because you deleted all the patterns and gradients you eliminated their potential to do harm. Think again. Gradients and patterns are stylistic flourishes that may look cool, but really should be avoided unless they are absolutely integral to the artwork:

◆ Gradients and patterns are very complex pieces of PostScript code that may or may not output properly on the imagesetter.

◆ Even if they do output properly, the processing time will be great, increasing the overall cost of the job.

◆ You have no way to accurately predict which colors result from a gradient as well.

◆ Gradients should not extend over eight inches. Banding is inevitable if they are longer than this.

If you want to continue after these warnings, go ahead. At least define your own patterns and gradients carefully using swatchbooks. Your chances of succeeding are greater if you do.

Blends

Object blends increase your chances of success even further. They define each color within a gradient as simple, separate paths for each color in the gradient, which imagesetters have a much easier time interpreting. This greatly simplifies the code and reduces processing time. After you've made a blend in Illustrator, go to Object: Expand to convert the gradient into separate objects. This also works on a pattern.

SAVING AND EXPORTING

Illustrator allows you to save files in many different formats. FreeHand only enables you to save files in its native format, but it allows you to export files in many different formats. This means you will be creating a second file whenever you need a FreeHand illustration to be imported into a page layout application or other program. FreeHand and Illustrator provide you with many options for saving and exporting into different file formats; however, we are only interested in two of them: native and EPS.

Native

As with any other program, while you are working on files, you want to save them in the program's native file format. This ensures all the functions of the program will continue to work on that file. Saving in formats other than the native format may convert certain elements to forms that the other format can use. While you are working, it is much more efficient to work in the native format.

EPS

If the Illustrator or FreeHand graphic is going to be used in a page layout, it needs to be in EPS, or Encapsulated PostScript format. The EPS format contains the pure PostScript code, as well as a PICT preview so that you can see the image onscreen and work with it in your page layout program. This is the only format that can be imported into page layout documents and still retain all of its valuable PostScript characteristics. Illustrator lets you save, open, and edit EPS files freely, whereas FreeHand makes you export the FreeHand file as an EPS. FreeHand can't edit an EPS file. If you want to edit a FreeHand file after exporting it, you need to include the FreeHand document in the EPS. You do this by checking the option in the Export dialog box.

Warning

FreeHand's exporting options enable you to export the file without including the FreeHand document. This is extremely bad. After you do this, the EPS is set in stone. It can't be modified in any way without first jumping through a lot of hoops, such as turning on "Convert editable bitmaps" in the preferences, creating a new document, and placing the FreeHand EPS into the new document. This is so bad it is amazing that it is an option. If there is something wrong with the file, the service bureau can't open or change it. If someone needs to update the page layout document and they don't have the original FreeHand document, they are going to have to re-create it.

Ironically, an EPS exported from FreeHand without including the FreeHand document *can* be opened in Illustrator easily. The results are not always consistent and should not be relied upon, however. *Always* include the FreeHand document in the EPS.

If you are working in Illustrator, this is not a problem. You can save a file as an EPS and open and modify that EPS document freely.

IMPORTING

FreeHand and Illustrator can import bitmapped graphics files in dozens of different formats. This is actually seen as a virtue to some. If you are in a position where you don't have to deal with your own mistakes, it could be a good thing because you don't have to pay attention to a thing you're doing. If you are reading this book, though, it's because you care about doing things right. If you care that your file is printable, you will only import TIFF files or EPS files. If you are going out to print, use absolutely no other formats than these. TIFF and EPS are formats specifically created for printing. Anything else is not worth the risk.

EPS

Use EPS format when your graphic needs to contain extra PostScript information, such as clipping paths, DCS, or duotone information.

TIFF

Use TIFF format for everything else, since it is the most widely used, most consistent, and most reliable bitmapped graphic format for printing.

Follow the Page Layout Rules

Your vector-based graphics program is not a page layout program, but when it comes to place bitmapped graphics, the same rules apply. Following these rules ensures that you get quality output when working with imported bitmapped graphics in FreeHand or Illustrator. You need to obey all the same rules you would in a page layout program:

◆ Use graphics of a high enough resolution to print at optimum quality at the linescreen you are printing. Don't scale the graphics more than 10 percent in any direction.

◆ Do not embed graphics. Choose No if the application asks you if you want to include placed graphics. Once a graphic is embedded, it can no longer be worked with. This can be a problem if the person responsible for outputting the file needs to edit it at the last minute.

◆ Be sure to include the files of the placed graphics with the Illustrator or FreeHand file when you send them to the service bureau.

ENSURING SUCCESSFUL OUTPUT

When you place a bitmapped graphic into a Illustrator or FreeHand file and then place that graphic into your page layout program, it should output fine if you've followed the rules. Whatever you do, simplify, simplify, simplify. Everything you do to the file adds a level of complexity to it. The more complex the file, the more likely you are to have problems when outputting. Unfortunately, programs do nothing to prevent you from creating documents that are totally unprintable. The trick is to learn to recognize when you are creating unnecessary complexity.

Avoid Complex and Unnecessary Scaling

Take scaling for example. Let's say you have a bitmapped graphic you need to incorporate into a logo. You've created your vector graphics in Illustrator and your bitmapped graphics in Photoshop. You save the Photoshop file as a TIFF and import it into your Illustrator file (see Figure 8.40).

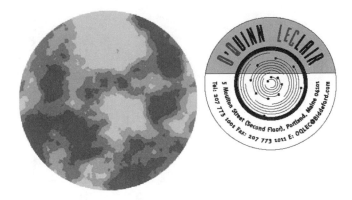

Figure 8.40

A bitmapped graphic and vector graphic.

The TIFF is way too big to fit where you want it to in the logo, so you shrink it down and make it fit (see Figure 8.41).

Figure 8.41

Shrinking the TIFF file enables it to fit into the logo.

Save this as an EPS and bring it into your page layout program (see Figure 8.42). The graphic is the wrong size, so you scale it again to make it fit.

Figure 8.42

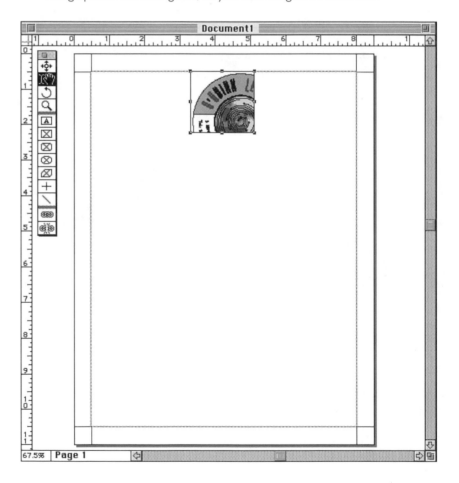

Now the piece looks perfect, just the way you want it to (see Figure 8.43).

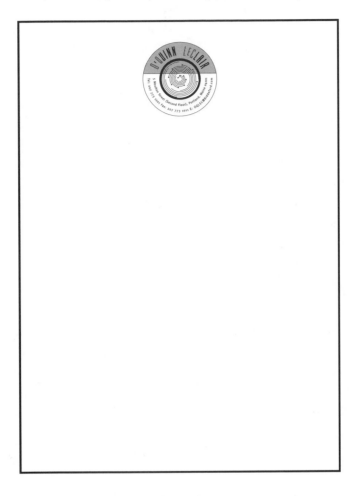

Figure 8.43

The finished file.

You send it to the service bureau to have films made and can't believe it when they can't do it. It serves you right, though. You can blame the service bureau if you need to cover your butt, but think about it for a moment. When you place a graphic, you aren't actually physically putting that file in the document. You are creating a link to that file. When you scale that file, you are adding code that instructs the program to display and print the file at that size. You've placed that file into your page layout program and scaled it again, adding even more information to the file. It might print; it might not. Since it takes no more time to do it right, why take chances?

The proper way to handle it is to start with the destination. Figure out how big the completed logo needs to be when it is in the page layout program. Base the size of the bitmap on the size it needs to be in the page layout program. Adjust the size in Photoshop. This changes the actual physical dimensions of the image, eliminating the need for the image setter to mathematically re-interpret the size as it does when you scale it in the drawing program or the page layout program. When you import the graphic into the drawing program, scale the vector graphics, not the bitmapped graphics. When you scale the vector graphics within the drawing program, it re-writes the PostScript code, so it does not need to be re-interpreted as it would if you scaled it in the page layout program.

A little thinking ahead prevents costly mistakes. Start with the destination and think how you can simplify things at all steps of the process.

Avoid Matryoshka

A Matryoshka is a beautiful Russian toy. An ornately painted figurine opens up to reveal a smaller figurine, which opens to reveal a smaller figurine and so on. This is an interesting novelty, but it has no place in printing. A bitmapped image placed inside a vector graphic placed inside a page layout program should print properly when it is prepared properly. A Photoshop graphic placed inside a FreeHand file placed inside an Illustrator file placed inside another Illustrator file placed inside a PageMaker document will most likely crash the computer if you try to print it, but there is nothing in the programs that prevents you from doing this.

Every time you place a file inside another, you add a level of complexity. You increase the processing time at best and create an unprintable file at worst. There is rarely ever a reason to place a vector graphic inside another vector graphic. Instead of placing the graphic, open both files, then copy and paste the graphic. This produces a single, unlinked file that will print faster and is less likely to have problems.

SUMMARY

As with every other aspect of digital prepress, choose wisely and work thoughtfully. Deciding *when* to use vector-based graphics programs can be the trickiest part of using vector-based graphics programs. Since vector-based graphics programs fall in a middle-ground between paint programs and page layout programs, it is easy to make the mistake of using them for one or the other. Don't fall into this trap.

Vector-based graphics programs serve you best when you use them to create simple pieces of art, such as logos, or when you use them for creative type manipulations. These functions best utilize the full power of drawing programs: infinite scaling, infinite editability, and highest-quality PostScript output.

Attempting to use vector-based graphics programs for more painterly purposes, such as creating images with subtle shading or for highly detailed images, is counter-productive. A paint program such as PhotoShop or Painter will serve you much better. Using a drawing program for page layout will also cause you more trouble than it is worth.

You will be most successful creating files that can be printed quickly and consistently if you always strive for simplicity when creating your vector graphics. Never create a link if you don't have to. This means never place a vector graphic inside another. Instead, open both files, copy, and paste the graphic into the destination graphic. It also means converting type into paths to eliminate links to fonts outside the graphic file.

When you create a simple, solid vector graphic, you are creating a file that not only prints quickly, consistently, and with utmost quality, you are also creating a highly portable file, which can easily imported into your page layout application, or rasterized into your bitmapped graphics program.

Chapter 9

THE FUNDAMENTALS OF DIGITAL IMAGING

Brian just couldn't understand it. He knew that he had done everything right, but every time he tried to print his piece, he got an unpleasant, jagged ridge along the sides of his art and all the colors were breaking into little squares. The first page looked bad, but the other 75 photos were probably fine. This was probably one of those computer viruses he had heard about.

But the next one wasn't fine either or the one after that. In fact, the entire magazine looked bad. The virus must have spread. We were called in to visit Brian, the new nighttime production manager of a small monthly magazine to troubleshoot this virus. We asked to see the problem files first. Looking at them, we confirmed what we had suspected: the files had each been scaled up between 350 percent and 600 percent in QuarkXPress. We pointed this out to Brian but he threw it back in our faces: "Of course I scaled them up, they're EPS files!" If this doesn't seem funny to you right now, keep reading.

THE DIGITAL IMAGING PROCESS

In the world of desktop publishing, photographs are re-expressed as digital information for the purpose of printing. In this chapter, we'll look at the process of turning photos, and any other artwork that wasn't created entirely within a computer environment, into this digital information so that they can be printed. Any printing, traditional or digital, is a difficult undertaking to get correct. Literally thousands of things can conspire against your images printing correctly, not the least of which is user error. It's important to understand the core concepts behind imaging and printing. If you disregard any facet of the process, you're bound to end up with either inferior, unprofessional results or hours of costly reworking.

To understand the complicated issues on digital imaging, you should start where you intend to end: on paper. Here's a rough synopsis of the process of preparing a photograph digitally for printing (see Figure 9.1).

Images are converted to squares called pixels by a scanner or digital camera. The pixels, which only exist inside the computer, make a map of the image that is used to print film, like a mosaic or a needlepoint sampler. The image, made up of all those pixels, is placed inside a layout document created in an application, such as QuarkXPress or PageMaker. When the document is printed, the page layout program translates the pixel information into PostScript code, which describes the space the pixels represent in a way the printer can understand. Upon printing, the square pixels are substituted with dots. The dots usually are round, take the place of several pixels, and have neither the color of the pixel nor do they cover the entire area the way the pixels did.

Figure 9.1

A typical model for digital workflow.

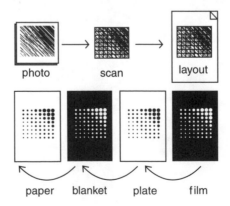

The dots create an optical illusion by changing their size so that the tone appears continuous when viewed from a distance. They are able to do this because pixels described the space.

The dots are printed on film as a negative of the original layout. The film makes a plate, which prints to a blanket on the press that prints to paper. The image flip flops negative to positive to negative to positive again, so you see the image correctly when it comes off the press.

Let's look at what happens in action. In this scan (see Figure 9.2a), the section outlined by a square gets converted by the scanner into the grid of pixels we see in Figure 9.2b. When it's time for the figure to printed, the pixels get translated into the corresponding halftone dots (see Figure 9.2c). The halftone dots themselves are made out of smaller printer dots (see Figure 9.2d).

Figure **9.2a**

Small section of scan to be converted into grid of pixels.

Figure 9.2b

A grid of pixels

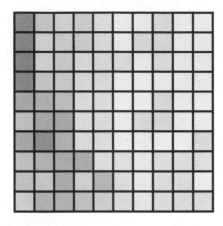

Figure 9.2c

Pixels translated into corresponding halftone dots.

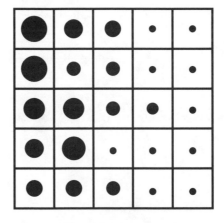

Figure 9.2d

Printer dots.

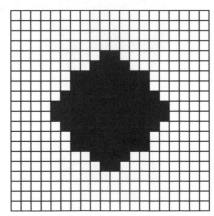

This model is a typical one, but not the only one. Instead of a scanner, a digital camera might be used. Perhaps the job is being printed to a digital press, which doesn't use film, or to an Iris inkjet, which doesn't make a halftone screen. Whatever variables change, the constant in the process of representing photographic information in printing digitally is the pixel.

Pixels

Pixels are tiny square building blocks and, unlike vectors, the building blocks for shapes in drawing applications, such as FreeHand and Illustrator, have no comprehension of the big picture. They don't know what the pixels around them look like, and they don't know what sort of picture they're building. It is much harder to select and manipulate objects in Photoshop than it is in a vector-based drawing program because there are no "objects," only pixels (see Figure 9.3). That's because in Illustrator or FreeHand, for example, objects think of themselves as objects. They realize that they are squares, for example. In Photoshop, the pixels are much more independent. They are little guys living in a grid, and they refuse to associate themselves with others easily.

TIFFs and EPSs

You need to understand only two file formats to correctly print out pixel based information, TIFF's and EPS's. We'll go into detail about them in the next chapter. You should be aware, though, that vector data from FreeHand or Illustrator is stored in the EPS format.

Pixel-based information also can be stored in the EPS format. This, however, doesn't mean that because the pixel information is encoded in the same format as that of vector data that all EPS files share the same properties. Although you can freely scale a vector-based EPS file up or down, you cannot do so with a pixel-based EPS. We told you that opening paragraph would be funny.

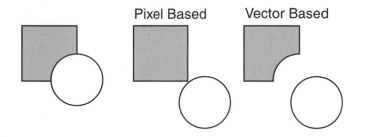

Pixel Based   Vector Based

Figure 9.3

Object-oriented versus pixel-based graphics.

Pixels, as a result of their nature, are good at one thing: describing complicated tonal space.

All of the minuscule changes in color and texture in the natural world can be replicated with pixels. Vectors can't do that. Vectors are joiners; they like sharp edges and big areas of flat color. Don't get us wrong: pixels are also very useful

Pixel Etymology

"Pixel" is a coined phrase that comes from the words PIcture and ELement. Slap an "x" in there, and you've got it. The "x" is supposed to evoke the image of a Cartesian grid, which has an x and y axis. If another letter had been chosen, though, we might be talking about pikels per inch. Imagine how happy the folks at Vlassic would be. On the other hand, it could almost have been pimpels per inch, and nobody would be happy about that.

The Unsquare Pixel

There's an exception for every rule and this is the one for pixel shape. Most pixels are perfectly square, but some are not. Pixels in some systems, like Amigas, use rectangular pixels for video work. If you're importing these pixels into your system for some reason, you'll have to compensate for this disparity. Amiga format files have a pixel aspect ratio of 1.45 x 1. If you downsampled the file 80 percent vertically, you would be fine.

for describing black-and-white line drawings and other things as well. Essentially anything that isn't produced entirely inside the computer becomes an arrangement of pixels at one time or another. A leaf, a crayon drawing, a piece of stationary, black-and-white photographs, a bra: anything that starts in the real world becomes pixels before it can go anywhere else.

Pixel Size and Printing

Pixels have two things. They have size and they have depth. The size of the pixels is important because of their use in informing the printing process. If there aren't enough pixels, detail could fall out or worse, the image can look blocky like Brian's files in our introduction to this chapter. On the other hand, the more pixels you have in an image, the larger your file size will be. The challenge then is to set your number of pixels large enough so that you capture all the information required for printing and still keep your files optimally efficient. The industry standard for the minimum number of pixels per inch (ppi) to maintain image quality is 1.5 to 2 times as many pixels per inch as you intend to print lines of halftone dots.

Because pixel size has a very specific relationship, with how pixels are printed, you don't get a lot of leeway once they're generated. You've already seen what happens when you try to scale up a file in a page layout program. You get fat, blocky edges that look bad. This is in stark contrast to a vector-based file, which you can scale up or down all day long with impunity.

If you scale up a pixel-based file up in Photoshop, you'll have better luck than you did in the page layout program, but it still won't be exactly what you want, especially when there aren't many pixels there to begin with. You're asking Photoshop to look at the image and guess what it would look like at a larger size. Your best bet is to scan the image to the size at which you want it to print.

It all gets down to knowing what you intend to do with the pixels once you have them. What purpose will your image serve? Make these decisions before the image is scanned.

Bit Depth

Pixels also possess depth. When we talk about a pixel's depth, we're describing the color potential each pixel has. What range of colors (black counts as a color), could that pixel have? The more memory associated with each pixel, the greater number of colors each pixel can have.

The memory we're talking about in the case of pixels is bits. Bits are on and off switches. They have two states: on and off. If you have two bits you could have them both off, the first one on and the other off, the first one off and the other one on, or both off them on. The more bits you have, the more combinations you can make. The more potential mathematical combinations you can make, the more potential colors you can assign to the pixel.

How does bit depth relate to color potential? It's exponential. The number of states in a bit (2) to the power of the number of bits equals the total number of potential combinations, or tones. See the following chart.

Bit Depth	Associated Mode	Possible Colors
1	Line art	2 (2 to the first power is 2)
8	Grayscale	256 (2 to the eighth power is 256)
24	RGB	16.7 million (2 to the twenty fourth power is 16.7 million)

Because the CMYK color space has 32 bits, you might think that CMYK will give you 4,294,967,296 potential colors (2 to the 32nd power). Oh, if only that were true. The impurities of the inks involved limit our potentials. We'll talk at greater length about that later.

Halftones

So you have this arrangement of pixels at a certain size with each pixel assigned a certain value. How and why do they turn into dots when you print them? The why part of that question might be answered glibly: because dots are what printers print. But we'll take it a little deeper because it begins to illustrate an important concept we'd like to elaborate on. The reason printers make dots, or more precisely *halftone* dots, has to do with the nature of the dots themselves, the material involved, and money.

Each dot in a traditional printing scenario sits on an imaginary grid with each dot's center spaced equidistantly (see Figure 9.4). The number of lines of dots in this arrangement is referred to as the line screening. You also hear it called screen frequency, or lines per inch (lpi). The reason for the "screen" term dates back to the traditional, analog method of creating a halftone, which involved using a physical screen. The more lines of dots you have in an inch, the smaller and less visible the dots are.

Figure 9.4

Halftone dots sit on an imaginary grid.

150 lines per inch

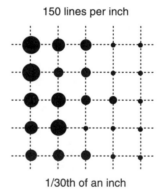

1/30th of an inch

The dots are a solid color and vary in size. The size of the dots and the spaces around them create the illusion of a continuous tone when viewed from a distance. Bigger dots look darker and smaller dots look lighter (see Figure 9.5).

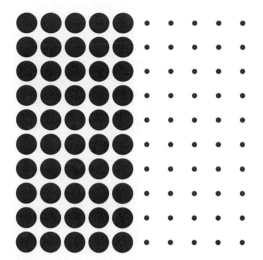

Figure 9.5

The combination of dot size and white space makes tone.

Printing this way is beneficial because it does the most with the least and opens up the process to more materials. You can't print continuous ink on newsprint. The substrate just can't support it. Not to mention that the way the printing press works simply doesn't allow for that to happen. Printing halftone dots, although not the only way to print, is the widest spread for commercial uses because of its utility and efficiency.

So now you have pixels that want to become dots. Typically, you have twice as many pixels as you will have dots. So if your intention is to print 150 lines per inch on press, you usually have 300 pixels per inch. When we talk about resolution this way, we're talking about *linear* resolution. That is, how much of a thing is in a line. So, although we commonly say the linear pixel resolution of a file is 300 pixels per inch, the file actual is composed of 300 pixels horizontally by 300 pixels vertically, a total of 90,000 pixels inside a square inch.

Halftone cells are also specified in a linear fashion. When there are twice as many pixels as there are halftone dots, four pixels inform the creation of each halftone dot. The raster image processor averages the values of the four pixels to arrive at an aggregate tonal value for that specific geographic location in the image (see Figure 9.6). A halftone dot is then generated to match the size specified by the values of the pixels.

Figure 9.6

*Pixels values are averaged to
determine spot size.*

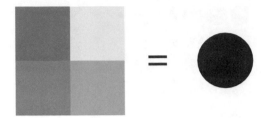

Halftone Creation

How are these halftone cells created? This gets a little tricky. An output device, like a laser printer or an imagesetter only prints dots in one size. The size of the dots they produce is expressed as their resolution: dots per inch. The printer dots are also called machine dots. The size of the dots is essentially their resolution as a fraction over one. A 600 dpi printer makes dots that are 1/600th of an inch.

When you're printing solid objects like text, the printer dots need to be small enough so that you don't see them. If you see them, edges look staggered, like a staircase. When you print photographic information create halftone spots—larger, circular dots of varying sizes. Square printer dots need to be small enough so that you can build a large variety of circular halftone spots sizes out of them. Think about it this way. If you had four floppy disks in your hands and were asked to arrange them on a page to make as many shapes as you could, you really couldn't make too many shapes. Now imagine you've got a handful of scrabble tiles. How many shapes could you make?

The size of dots in your output device is fixed, and therefore, so is the amount of dots your printer or imagesetter can produce in an inch. When you print photographic information, you divide that large grid of total dots on the page into another grid. The second grid of printer dots is where halftone spots will be built (see Figure 9.7). The size of the smaller grid is determined by the line screen of the printing press where the job will go. Let's say your press can hold a 150- line screening. The halftone cells (the size of the space the halftone dots lives) are 1/150th of an inch.

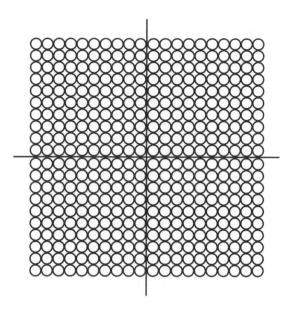

Figure 9.7

*Line screen divides total dpi into
a smaller grid.*

You find the number of printer dots in a halftone cell by dividing printer resolution by line screen. So if you print 150 lines on a 2400 dpi imagesetter, the individual halftone cells will be built out of a 16x16 grid of printer dots (2400 dots in the output device divided by 150 lines equals 16 printer dots on each side of the matrix). Square that number and you have the total number of printer dots in the matrix. 16x16 = 256 and that's the number of different sized dots you can make with that grid (see Figure 9.8).

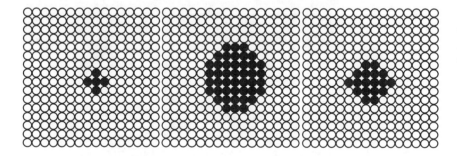

Figure 9.8

*Smaller printer dots combine to
create a halftone spot.*

Embedded Line Screens

Usually, the line screen you print to is a function of the best your device can offer you. You dial in the line screen in your page layout app when you print the file. There are some rare times, however, when you'll want to ensure your Photoshop file prints at a specific line screen, even if the rest of your document prints at a different one.

To do this, open the Page Setup dialog box that lives under the File menu. Click the screen button and go crazy. You'll need to save the file as an EPS. Unless you're doing this for a good reason, like creating a duotone, consult your output specialist first.

Think of the Scrabble tiles. The more dots you have to build a halftone, the greater possible variations of tone—ergo 256 shades of gray (including the one for no dots at all). The more printer dots you have to build your halftone spot from, the more possible size dots you can create.

To explore this relationship for yourself, try this simple test. Place a grayscale graphic into a page layout program and then print it to your laser printer. Once you've printed it, reset the line screen to 300 lines per inch. Print it again. The laser printer, like an imagesetter can only print so many dots. The dots are 1/600th of an inch on a 600m dpi laser printer. A 300 line screen would divide those printer dots into 2×2 squares for the purposes of halftone creation. It's like the four floppy disks. You can only fill those squares a few ways. Result: an image with only five tones (see Figure 9.9). Trouble.

Figure 9.9

The relationship between printer resolution and screening determines the number of tones available for printing.

Screen Angles

The halftone dot grid is typically printed at a 45 percent angle to make the dots less visible. In the case of color images, however, things get a little more complicated.

Typically, full-color images are replicated on press by overlapping a series of four halftone grids of different colors. The four famous printing colors are cyan, yellow, magenta and black. This model is called process color and it can produce a wide array of color with only a few inks. In print it works the same as a simple halftone with each ink printing an array of dots just as the halftone does. In the case of process color, each ink is placed at a different angle from each other.

The 45° angle is considered the best to print at because it is the least visible. For this reason, the darkest color on press (black) typically prints at 45°. The worst angle to print at is 0° because it's the most visible. Generally, the lightest color on press (yellow) resides at 0°. The other angles used place the inks at 15° (or 165°) and 60° (or 105°) (see Figure 9.10).

It's important to angle the screens away from each other because the grid patterns can interfere with each other and cause a visible, unpleasantly distracting interference pattern onscreen. The pattern is called moiré and it's bad news on press.

Frequency Modulation Printing

What we've just gone over is the traditional method of printing. It's not the only method. The traditional method is sometimes called Amplitude Modulation or AM printing. It's possible, and more and more common, to print with a Frequency Modulation structure instead. In this scenario, instead of printing dots of differing sizes (the amplitude) on a screen grid, you print dots of all the same size in a random pattern. You vary tone by printing more dots (frequency). This is sometimes called a *stochastic* dot. The term comes from the Greek word for random.

This method of printing still relies on pixels to inform, but because there is no screen involved, it avoids some of the problems a traditional screening can engender.

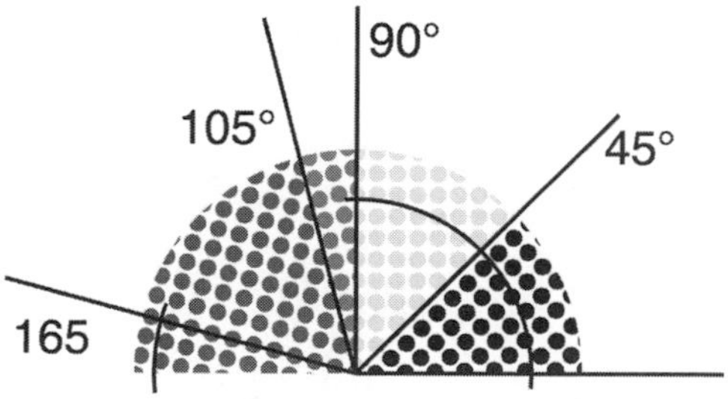

Figure 9.10

Typical screen angles for printing.

Spot Shape

The final variable in halftone creation is the shape of the spots. The standard shape of a PostScript halftone spot is typically round in the highlights, square at 50 percent, and a reversed white dot on black in the shadows (see Figure 9.11). Depending on the specifics of your output device, you may find changing the dot shape gives you better results on press. The ability to control this also lives in the Page Setup dialog box under the File menu. An experiment or two and a conversation with your press operator is in order before undertaking a spot function change.

Figure 9.11

The typical shape of PostScript halftone dots.

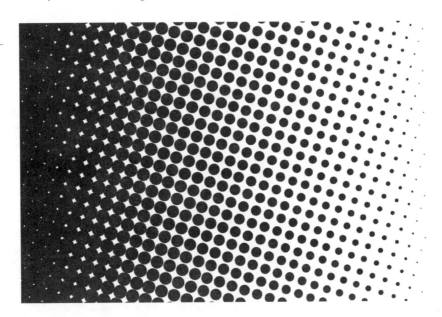

Resolution

All the different elements discussed so far are measured and expressed as resolution. Resolution is the measurement of quantity over a given area. You may hear the word "dot" substituted for "pixel", but that's imprecise and confusing. Each step along the image's path is followed by the resolution measurement term associated with it and typical values. It is intended for perspective only; your values may well vary.

Scanner: Samples Per Inch (1.5 - 2x line screen)

Samples per inch refers to how many times a scanner looks at an image in an inch when it scans it? This number may not necessarily be the same as pixels per inch. For more information on scanner resolution, see the following.

File: Pixels Per Inch (1.5–2x line screen):

The samples become pixels per inch. This refers to how many pixels are in a digital file? This number should be set in relationship to the amount of halftone dots you intend to print in the final printed piece. You want enough pixels to accurately represent what's really in your image, but not so many that your file becomes inefficiently large. The typical scenario when scanning photographic material is to have 1.5 to 2 times as many pixels as you intend to print lines of spots (see below). Any more and file size increases without increasing quality; any less and image quality may suffer. Line art is a special case and should be handled differently. For more information on scanning line art see below.

Monitor Resolution: Pixels Per Inch (72 ppi)

How many spots of light are there in an inch of my monitor? Monitors produce images by shooting light at you. Although this number can vary, most monitors shoot 72 beams of light at you in every inch.

Because of this, your monitor may have one monitor spot hold the place of several pixels or one pixel represented by many monitor spots. This can cause some confusion among novice users who expect to see their files at some percentage of their actual size, the way you view files in other applications. In image editing programs, you see them as ratios of monitor pixels to image pixels.

Film: Dots Per Inch (1200–3200 dpi)

How big are the dots your output device or imagesetter creates? Printers make dots in a fixed, constant size. Their resolution describes that size. More resolution means smaller dots. Smaller dots means smoother lines and greater flexibility. An imagesetter also uses these dots when it builds the larger halftone spots the printing press needs. Because the size of halftone spots relates directly to their tones, printing film from your imagesetter with smaller dots is beneficial.

Printing Press: Lines Per Inch (100–225 lpi)

How many halftone spots will your printing press make in an inch? Halftones are optical illusions created by printing dots of different sizes whose centers fall evenly distant from each other. From a distance, the combination of dot and its corresponding white space appear to be a continuous tone. The size of the dot and the white space around it determine how light or dark it appears when viewed. The dot and space around it are sometimes thought of as a cell. Full-color printing is made with the same strategy by printing transparent inks on top of each other and at different angles. Combinations of cyan, yellow, magenta, and black halftones produce the wide range of colors you're accustomed to seeing in print.

Use Your Illusion

We said before that halftones were optical illusions. Given that, you must be aware of the following to correctly pull one off.

Final Destination

Is this scan being printed? What type of paper are you printing on and how will it be printed? A job that is scanned for newsprint needs different treatment than a job printed on coated stock. The nature of your press will affect how you scan. Scans for the World Wide Web or multimedia need even different treatment. Knowing what you're going to do with a scan will inform all your decisions along the way.

Mechanical Limits

Printing presses are great things. Understanding what they can and can't do makes them even more useful to you. There are some measurable mechanical limits to what a press can do and it's your responsibility to work around them. A little communication and testing will make everything run right the first time, saving costly reworks, finger pointing, and grief.

See what your printer knows about the following things. If he doesn't know the answer, ask to arrange a test or ask to speak with other clients who have run similar jobs. Typically, printers will know some of these things, but when it gets into the world of color separation, most don't know very much. See Chapter 11 for a run down on the color issues you'll face and sensible things to do about them.

End Points

Your imagesetter can make some tiny dots. Very small dots may not show up when a plate is burned. Even if they make it to the plate, they may not print predictably (read: at all) on press. By the same token, your press may not be able to resolve the differences between the darkest darks in your image. A 95 percent gray may look exactly the same as a 98 percent gray. Detail in those shadows would be lost completely.

When tones print with no discernible difference between them, they are said to be "posterized." You see this in newsprint a lot. People's faces will be half-black shadow and half-empty paper (see Figure 9.12).

Figure 9.12

An example of posturized tones.

Blown Out Highlights and Posterized Shadows

Posterization can happen in input as well as output. If your scanner knocks light tones down to zero percent, you've blown your highlights and you can't get that detail back in Photoshop. The thing to recognize when thinking about highlight end points is that there are two kinds. A specular highlight is paper, lighter than light. A diffuse highlight is the lightest point in an image that holds detail. If you burn this to zero, you've got trouble. The trick is going to be in correctly imaging your diffuse highlight and then taking action to ensure that on press it does not become a specular highlight. This is no mean feat and one that can introduce new problems.

Dot Gain

Even if you nail your end points, the tones in between can meet with trouble. Absorbent paper, high printing speeds, and malicious goblins can conspire to darken your image on paper. Imagine the Bounty commercial at the end where it picks up the Kool Aid. The Kool Aid spreads out across the paper towel like a dilating pupil. The same thing happens on a smaller scale when ink hits paper on the press. Some of the ink is absorbed into the paper causing the dot to expand in shape (see Figure 9.13). Because dot size is directly related to tone, this will have the affect of darkening your image overall.

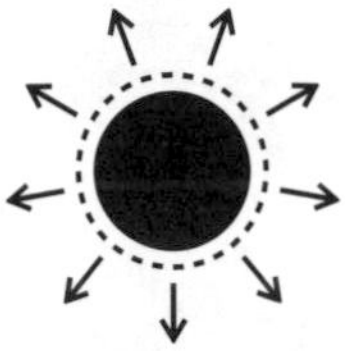

Figure 9.13

Dot gain changes dot size unwantedly, making the image darker.

Different presses and paper qualities experience different dot gain. Also, different tones in the image are affected by dot gain to varying degrees. When printing colors, Photoshop will do some things to automatically compensate for dot gain if you tell it to, but it's certainly not an issue you should ignore completely.

Total Ink

When printing in CMYK, you can end up with a lot of ink on paper in your shadows. Different substrate material can hold ink differently. Newsprint, for example, can hold nowhere near the amount of ink a high-quality coated stock can. If you don't take measures to control how much ink you put down, shadows become clogged and gummy, ink drips from press sheets, and your clients will look at you like you don't know what you're doing.

Special Inks

Not everyone is printing with the convenient CMYK colors. It's not terrifically uncommon for one of the four process inks, typically magenta, to be swapped for a spot ink. Typically this is done by newspapers who want a denser red for text and rules. To save money, they print with the same darker red in the place of magenta in their separations.

Other Problems

A scan is just a mosaic grid of colored tiles. When printed, it creates an optical illusion that tricks people into thinking it's a continuously toned image. If you don't build enough information into your scan, no one will be fooled. If you try to double the size of the scan in a page layout program, you'll just spread the pixels out, reducing your effective resolution. If you try to add size in Photoshop, you'll just increase the amount of information you're using to describe the same thing. Scaling up in Photoshop is like writing 20 new pages to say what you've already said in two.

Isn't there anything you can do to scale my image up without rescanning? Well, maybe. We declared that you should have 1.5 to 2 times as many pixels in you image per inch as you want to print halftone spots. If you scanned your image at two times as many pixels, you can use the extra pixels as scaling. How big can you make it? To save the worrisome calculations, open the file in Photoshop (Image: Image Size). Lock file size and change the resolution to the minimum you can use (1.5 times the line screen) (see Figure 9.14). Your image dimensions will jump up. That's how much bigger you can make your image.

Rotating

This is another thing that's a snap to do in your page layout application. Of course, PageMaker or Quark isn't doing the work; it passes that buck along to the RIP, which has to do the math to figure out where to put what. If you know your image is going to be at a certain angle when you print it, rotate it in Photoshop before you save it.

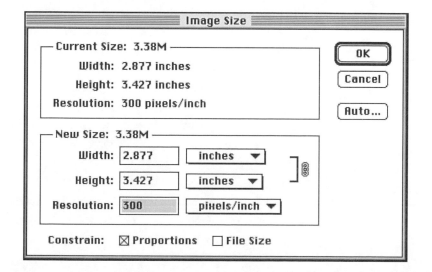

Figure 9.14

You can sneak some scaling out of "extra" resolution.

Why Bother Cropping?

There once was a client who wanted to make a booklet for her high school reunion. She got the big group photo from her yearbook and scanned it. With her 40MB EPS scan in hand, she set up her file in PageMaker and placed her scan into the file. Aha. Then she cropped out everything except Jimmy Football Star's head and set some text around it. Then she imported the same file again and cropped out everything except for Kevin McDillan's head. And so on and so on 30 more times until she had everyone's face inside her file.

One quick look over the document and it's off to the prepress house! What the client didn't realize is that the RIP, or Raster Image Processor, at the prepress house (the thing that translates PostScript code into dots), does exactly what she did to her scan. It looks at all of it, and then disregards the part that's cropped out. That is to say, it processes the entire file and then only prints part of it. So it processed, or tied to process, 40MB each of the 30 or 40 times the file was placed in PageMaker. The RIP, being a reasonable machine, quit and refused to print her preposterous file. The client had to pull apart her document and her scan, costing her days and dollars, learning the hard way to crop your images in Photoshop, not a page layout program.

Cropping

There's no sense taking more than you need. It's important to make your crops as efficient as possible. Additionally, asking a scanner to look at only the part of the image you're concerned with may actually improve your scanners chances of correctly resolving the tones in your image. Do it in Photoshop if you must, but do it. See *Why Bother Cropping?* for anecdotal evidence.

Sharpness

The scanning techs have two mottos. One is "garbage in, garbage out." The other is "It only gets worse." While this may be overstating the case slightly, it does raise the important point that scanning is a damaging act both to tone and to content. Almost everything that gets scanned needs to be assisted in some way. Some more than others. Scanning tends to soften the edges of the things being digitized. Almost every scan needs some level of sharpening. The amount of sharpening required depends on the how the image is being printed, the final size of the printed piece, and the composition of the image.

Touch Up and Tonal Correction

One of the other things that happens to scans is that they receive some level of retouching to remove flaws caused in the scanning process. Defects can be introduced by dirt and scratches on the scanner bed, fingerprints on photographs, random noise from the scanner, and any number of other internal or external sources. You'll have to remove these to realize professional level printing. Almost all scans also need tonal correction. This could just be lightening the image overall, or removing color casts caused by the weathering of the original. Whatever the cause, scans are seldom perfect right off the scanner. Service bureaus have professionals whose job it is to correct images for this very reason. Even the most expensive scanners will produce results that need your attention. Scanners are like idiot savants. They can do great things, but they have identifiable weak points and they need your help to shine.

So this is what it comes down to. Because photographic imagery is essentially an optical illusion created by a grid of colored squares, the squares are important. You can't scale them up without problems; you need to have the right amount of them, and each one will be accounted for. Even if you crop them out in your layout program, they get counted and processed. The pixels have size and depth. No matter what you do with images later, ones that weren't created in the computer have to get in there somehow, and doing that means turning them into pixels.

Chapter **10**

SCANNING LINE ART AND HALFTONES

We were touring the production house of a weekly newspaper as part of a workflow evaluation. When the subject of photographs and halftones came up, the Production Chief, who was a traditional prepress veteran, phrased her sentences carefully. "We have Photoshop and a scanner," she said, "but the images we get from the scanner are typically so dark and clogged that we don't use it." The implication was that the entire paper was composed digitally except for the photographs, which had to be inserted later. Additional steps and hours of work were being added and several thousands dollars worth of viable technology were laying fallow because someone hadn't learned to use them. When we offered that learning to produce halftones digitally wasn't that hard and would save hours, empower her onscreen layout, and open up design possibilities, the Chief stood firm. She declared that she simply didn't have the time to learn the technology and that it probably wouldn't work anyway. There was time to work around the problem but never time to learn to save time.

INTRODUCTION TO PHOTOSHOP

Unfortunately, the fear of Photoshop is not an isolated incident. Photoshop is big and can do a lot of things. The conceptual gap between printer and monitor doesn't help matters much, either. It's frustrating to spend hours adjusting an image just so and then see it look bad on press. Too often Photoshop ends up a $600 toy with prepress professionals making random adjustments to a file in hopes of a lucky accident. Or worse, a misunderstood distraction that actually acts as an impediment to the prepress process.

There's no reason for either of these things to happen. Photoshop is not a mystery and, with a little systematic exploration, the printing process doesn't have to be either. Understanding a few simple tools and issues will help you take real control of your image acquisition, editing, and output issues.

In the course of this chapter, we'll discuss Photoshop's use strictly as a production tool. Our plan is to use Photoshop to acquire and adjust images for printing as quickly and painlessly as possible. Get in, get it correct, and get out.

Specifically this chapter addresses the following:

◆ Setting up Photoshop correctly for production uses.

◆ Correctly scanning and adjusting line art and halftones for specific press conditions.

◆ Strategies for tackling difficult and crooked line art.

◆ Building fail-safes and backdoors into the process.

◆ Basic, functional methods of selecting specific areas to correct.

◆ File saving and compression strategies.

Photoshop's RAM Requirements

There's a price to pay for Photoshop's power and it's RAM. If you don't know how to set RAM for your applications, go back to Chapter 1. Set your RAM for Photoshop as high as you can. Make it a few megabytes less than the "available" RAM number from the Finder's "About this Macintosh" (under the Apple menu). Set both the minimum and the preferred RAM allotments at the same amount (see Figure 10.1). You always want to use as much as you can. You should have at least 20MB of RAM for Photoshop if you're going to do any real work in it. At the time of this writing, RAM is at an all-time cost low and the efficiency return on this investment is a good one.

Note

If you don't know how to set RAM for your application, see Chapter 1.

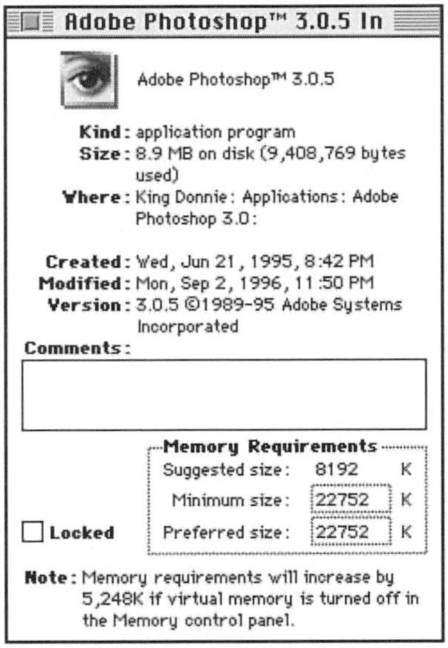

Figure 10.1

RAM settings for Photoshop.

So why does Photoshop need all this RAM? When you open a file in Photoshop, you're actually opening three files. One, the file you're working on, and two, a file just like that one only without the last change you just made. This gives you the opportunity to undo what you just did. Photoshop simply swaps the version of your file with the error in it with the earlier version before the error came along. You can also go all the way back to the saved version of your file by choosing Revert from the File menu. In all, that's three versions of your file that Photoshop has in its memory. That means the optimal size to run Photoshop is three times the size of the file you want to work plus about 5MB for Photoshop itself.

Photoshop's Hard Disk Requirements

Photoshop also requires a lot of hard disk space. For one thing, Photoshop files take up space quickly. For another, Photoshop has a built-in virtual memory

Scratch Disks

Ever wonder how much of your hard disk Photoshop is using? Finding out can be useful because it's a measure of how efficiently Photoshop is running at any given session. Look at the lower left-hand corner of any open Photoshop window (see Figure 10.2). A memory pop up window is there. If you set it to Scratch Sizes, it will show you a ratio of the RAM used by all open windows (the number on the left) to the amount of RAM available to Photoshop (the number on the right). If that ratio divides out to more than one, your hard disk is being used for virtual memory.

scheme that uses your hard disk space as RAM to do some of its calculating. It's called a *scratch disk*. Photoshop requires hard disk space to be at least equal to the amount of RAM you have allocated to Photoshop. Photoshop also prefers that this disk space be contiguous, that is, space that is available as a single block. If you're going to do a lot of Photoshop work, consider dedicating a partition of your drive to Photoshop. For more information on contiguous disk space and partitioning a drive, refer to Chapter 3.

Figure 10.2

File Sizes, Scratch Sizes, and Efficiency.

Photoshop Preferences

Set some basic Preferences and settings for production work in Photoshop (see Figure 10.3). You should know that the choices you make here get written off into a nice little file called Photoshop Preferences, which lives in the Preferences folder inside your System Folder. On an IBM system, the Preferences are written off to an .ini file, which makes it inconvenient to transfer. After your Preferences are set, it's a good idea to copy the file and put it someplace safe. If Photoshop starts acting funny, it might be because the Preferences file has become corrupted and needs to be thrown away. We keep a folder with copies of things that we worry might become corrupted for just such occasions.

If you've trashed your Preferences file, Photoshop builds a new one with the default settings the next time you launch the application. From there you can set your Preferences back the way you want them. Having a copy of your Preferences saves you from the drudgery of this step. When we were freelancing, we also kept a copy of our Preferences on a floppy disk we took with us when we were working on client's stations. We'd pull their copy of their Preferences out and insert ours, and everything would be how we expected it to be. When we were done, we'd reinsert the original Preferences file and be done.

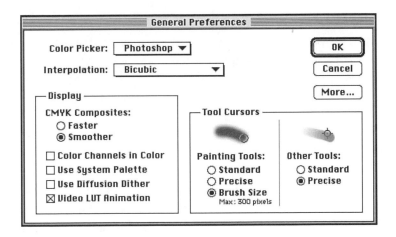

Figure 10.3

General Preferences (File: Preferences: General).

Interpolation: Bicubic

When Photoshop resizes an image up or down, or adds or subtracts pixels, it is interpolating data. In other words, Photoshop guesses what the image would look like if changed. The three methods available to you are listed in order of decreasing speed and increasing quality:

◆ Nearest Neighbor

◆ Bilinear

◆ Bicubic (slowest but highest quality)

As Photoshop interpolates data, it compares pixels' values to get an educated guess about what to do. Nearest Neighbor and Bilinear look at fewer pixels when it does that. Setting this to Bicubic gives you stronger data results.

CMYK Composites: Smoother

Just as you choose better quality interpolation, you also choose better quality CMYK previews over quicker ones. This means that when you're working in CMYK, Photoshop translates that color information into RGB, the color monitors work in. Do you want it to do this quickly or well? Since color accuracy on the monitor is so important, we prefer the more accurate, albeit slower, setting.

Video LUT Animation: On

Video LUT, or Look Up Table, lets you see adjustments to tone and color more quickly by changing the appearance of the entire screen rather than calculating individual pixels. This is handy. Plus, when you're doing important detail work, you can ask Photoshop to give you the real pixel display by clicking the preview box.

Tool Cursors

Set Painting tools to brush size and other tools to Precise. You get much more accurate cursors with these settings. The icon-based Standard tools show you what tool you're using but make it difficult to tell exactly where the effect will occur. When you're doing detailed work, you'll appreciate the accuaracy of the precise settings.

Next, click the More button in the General preferences (see Figure 10.4) and make sure you've chosen these settings:

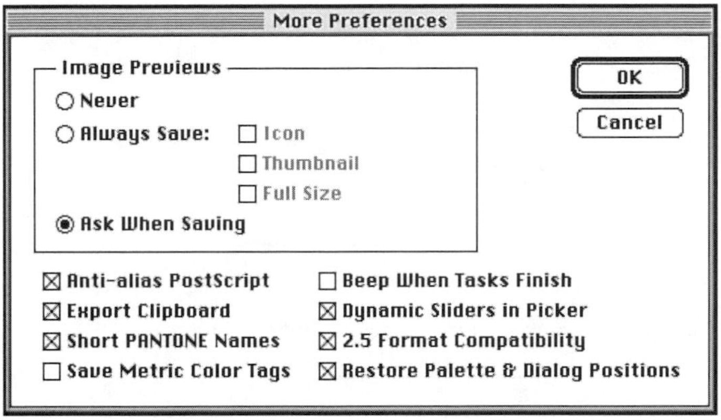

Figure 10.4

More Preferences...

◆ Image Previews: Ask When Saving.
Do you want a PICT preview of your file? Maybe you do, maybe you don't. They can be handy little buggers or they can slow things down. It's nice to have the option to go either way.

◆ Anti-Alias PostScript: On.
Turn it on and leave it on. It smooths out jagged edges and makes life easier when you're turning vector-based graphics like the ones made in Adobe Illustrator into pixels.

◆ Export Clipboard: On.
Photoshop has its own internal clipboard. If you ever want to paste something you've copied from a Photoshop file into another applica-tion, turn this on. Photoshop exports the contents of its clipboard to the system clipboard. Otherwise, you'll only be able to paste things copied in Photoshop inside Photoshop documents.

◆ The Eyedropper.
This is a tool, not a preference. It samples the color of anything you put it on, whether it's the active window, inactive window, color swatch window, picker window, or swatch. Double-click the Eyedrop-per to bring up its tool options (see Figure 10.5). Set the sample size

here to 3 by 3 or 5 by 5. These methods average the values of a group of pixels (a 3 by 3 or 5 by 5 group) and provide a more accurate assessment of color than the Point Sample option, which looks at only one pixel. Point Sample is faster, but you run the risk of hitting a misrepresentative pixel.

Figure 10.5

Eyedropper Options.

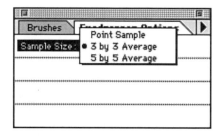

Other important preferences can make or break your color output. Since how you set them varies from job to job, we'll discuss those in much greater detail in Chapter 11.

Photoshop Toolbox and Command Shortcuts

All of the tools in Photoshop also have options associated with them. The first thing to notice is that all of Photoshop's tools have keyboard shortcuts (see Figure 10.6). Click the keyboard button that goes with the tool and Photoshop switches to the tool. Consult Figure 10.6 for the tools and their shortcuts. Keep in mind that some of the tools are nested. Hitting the keyboard shortcut a second time will toggle you through the series. You also could Alt/Option-click the tool with the mouse to switch tools, but that would be defeating the purpose of the keyboard shortcuts.

Tip

Double-clicking any tool from the toolbox in Photoshop brings up that tool's options.

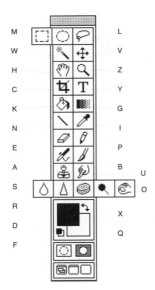

Figure 10.6

The keyboard shortcuts (Mac and PC) for Photoshop's tools.

In addition to those shortcuts, Photoshop lets you write your own shortcuts for frequently used functions. Choose Window: Palettes: Show Commands to bring up this set. The palette can be used as a control panel; click the command to launch it, more efficiently, simply use the keyboard shortcuts. With a little practice, you'll easily remember the shortcuts and have no need to clutter up your monitor with extra palettes. If you want to keep the palette open though, you can color code the commands and arrange them by groups.

To change the commands around, choose Edit from the pop up menu for this palette under the black triangle in the upper-right corner (see Figure 10.7). To reorder them in the list, just click and drag the command from the list in the Edit Commands window. A black line appears below the command's new position. From this menu, you can edit the existing set of commands, delete unwanted commands, add to your set, or save the commands as a discrete file. This is handy *and* dandy. Editing the commands is easy work. The palettes tell you exactly what to do. You can also Shift- or Control-select the Command from its palette to call up the Edit box.

Figure 10.7

Editing Commands.

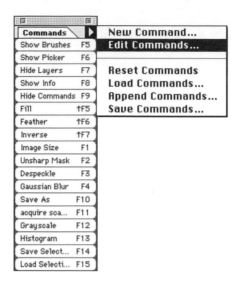

Photoshop's default Command settings are a little odd and you ought to trash some right away. There's little sense wasting command space on commands you know anyway like Cut, Copy, Paste, and Undo. Replace them with things you use frequently (see Figure 10.8). Don't forget that you also can change the name of the macros. That may make it less likely that you might confuse Inverse and Invert. You also can save this set as a separate file, which you can then load back in. If more than one person works on your station or you do freelance on location, this is a major plus.

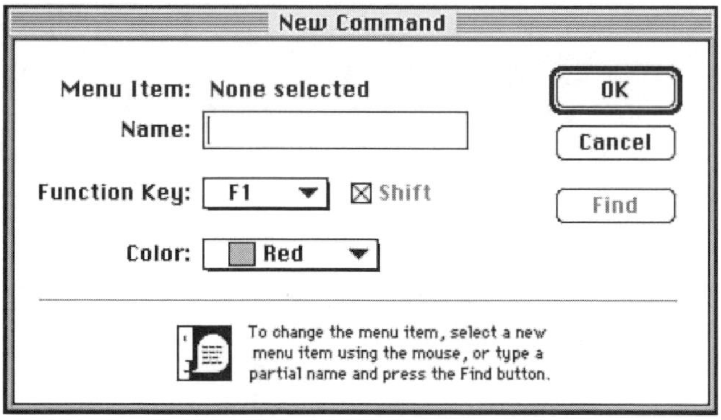

Figure 10.8

Adding new Commands is easy.

USING A FLATBED SCANNER

Scanners are an example of a SAD system. SAD stands for Source, Attenuator, and Detector. In a SAD system something is changed and then measured. In the case of scanners, light is the subject we're interested in; it is the *source*. The nature of the light's wavelength changes as it encounters the object being scanned. The light is said to be *attenuated* by the item. Then the light is measured, or *detected,* in some way by the scanner.

Two basic types of scanners exist in the world today. They're de-

> ### Nesting Menus
>
> Another monitor geography saver is Photoshop's capability to nest menus by dragging and dropping them from window to window. You can customize how PS's palettes are displayed by clicking the title section of the palette, and dragging it either out by itself as a free-floating palette, or dropping it into another palette. This is a charmer and we hope that Adobe institutes this feature on other applications.

fined by the technology that informs their detection. Some scanners use Charged Couple Devices (CCDs) some use Photo Multiplier Tubes (PMTs). Flatbed scanners use CCDs. Drum scanners use PMTs. Flatbed scanners look like desktop photocopiers. Drum scanners actually have a Plexiglas tube inside them that originals are mounted to, which spins around during scanning. Drum scanners tend to be larger than desktop scanners and have historically been the quality leader of the two. Both scanners beam light at or through the object (or "copy") being scanned. CCD scanners compare the electrical charge of light before and after it hits the copy. The change is translated into a tone and a pixel is born. In color scanning, colored gels are used to filter part of the light wavelength and the changes in light can be determined for Red, Green, and Blue light.

Drum scanners behave differently. When light bounces off or through copy (depending on whether the original is transparent like a slide, or reflective like a cocktail napkin) in a drum scanner, the resulting attenuated light hits a Photo

Multiplier Tube, which becomes electrically excited. The dynamic range of this excitation is more analogous to an organic response than it is in the case of CCD scanners. What this means is that because PMT behave more like the human eye, they tend to do a better job of noticing the differences between shadows. Does this mean that all drum scanners are better than all CCD scanners? Yes and no. Drum scanners have long been the industry standard for high-end scanning and clearly have a mechanical advantage, but CCD scanning software has made great strides in recent years. Plus, they're good and inexpensive.

Under the Scanner's Hood

In addition to the basic types of scanners to consider, other features should affect your decision to purchase a scanner. Here's a quick summary:

Dynamic Range. How dark *are* your darks? The relative "darkness" of things is measured in terms of their light stopping power. Machines like densitometers (another SAD system) are used to measure how opaque things are. Since the numbers used to express these ideas are so small that they aren't useful for description, some complicated math is applied to the measure of this opacity to re-express it more intuitively. The result is a scale of relative darkness, which runs from 0.0 to 4.0. Four is the theoretical density of carbon black; 0.0 is pure light. It's important to note that this scale is an algorithmic one, with each step toward 4.0 twice as dense as the one before it.

Let's put this into context:

Copy	Typical Density
Photographic transparencies	3.0
Photographic print	2.8 - 2.0
Coated, high quality paper	2.0
Newsprint	1.8

Scanners are rated by their capability to correctly capture tonal range by this same scale. Your scanner should have a density range higher than the range of the copy it's trying to realize (see Figure 10.9). So, if your scanner has a density range of 2.2 and you're trying to scan chrome transparencies, good luck to you and the Red Sox. No amount of post-scan correction will *ever* replace tone that was missed at the time of the scan. An inadequate density range is a sure way to lose shadow detail. How much is enough? A density of 3.2 can get most of your work done. Flatbed scanners tend by nature to have a dynamic range of 1.8 to 2.0, while desktop drum scanners have a dynamic range of about 3.2 to 3.8. High-end drum (PMT) scanners can manage a dynamic range of about 4.0.

3.0

2.8

2.0

1.8

Figure 10.9

Density ranges of various materials.

Optical Resolution: How many samples does the scanner take in every inch? Scanner manufacturers may boast how many *pixels* in an inch their scanner can generate, but that's not the same as how many samples it takes in an inch. The two numbers could be quite different. Scanners make guesses about what pixels should look like if you ask them to. A scanner may produce a file with 4,800 pixels per inch, but the scanner may have only actually consulted the image 300 times per inch. That's a lot of invented pixels and that's the difference between native and interpolated resolution. Interpolation may or may not produce useful results. It's really a matter of how good the scanners internal interpolation is. We've seen remarkable quality differences, especially in slide scanners, when using native, rather than interpolated, resolution.

Scaling is another reason why optical resolution is so important. Keep in mind that scanners can only "see" so many samples in a given space. It's a fixed constant. As you scale an object up, the scanner concentrates its pixels on a smaller area. So as scaling goes up, relative resolution goes down.

Bit Depth: How much information does your scanner gather when looking at color? This is related to density range. The question is how much information does my scanner gather about the nature of the color of each sample? In PostScript level 2, color is limited to 256 tones each for Red, Green, and Blue. Many scanners, however, can take in more than that and then reduce the steps to 256 for output. Scanners may be 10-, 12-, or even 16-bit depth in variety per channel, instead of merely eight. Multiply by three and you've got 30-, 32-, and 48-bit scanners. This corresponds to 1,024, 4,096 or 65,536 steps per channel. Scanners that gather more information than required do a better job. Again, the bigger, the better.

Speed and Interface: How fast can my scanner preview and process my scans, and how long do I have to spend to get the scans the way I want them? Of the two, we prefer a smooth, full-featured interface to a nimble clock time. Of course, speed is important too and this is a good reason to get a test drive of your scanner before you buy. Trade shows and associates are often the only way to test scanners.

Scanner Plug-Ins

You might have inferred from the above that scanners have their own controlling software. That's true. Typically, scanners come with several important pieces of software. A plug-in, which should go in Photoshop's Acquire/Export folder, is inside the Plug-Ins folder as well as some sort of system level software, like an extension and a control panel. It wouldn't be the worst idea you've ever had to copy those files off and stick them in that emergency folder we were talking about earlier. We found this out the hard way when we were looking at 75 scans that absolutely, positively had to be done yesterday and our scanner refused to function due to a corrupted plug-in. Imagine our chagrin when we were unable to locate the source disks. If we didn't happen to have a chum who had the same scanner and, hence, same scanning software, it would have cost us a client.

Recommended Features in an RGB scanner

Onscreen densitometer—a must (see Figure 10.10).

Multiple scan modes—every scanner should be able to see more than just RGB. A negative setting can come in very handy as well.

A transparency adapter—this may be extra money and pointless on cheaper machines but very handy and well worth considering.

Intuitive tonal correction—tonal correction should be easy to do and not produce hard tonal jumps.

Option to manually place end points—your scanner may need help finding the lights and darks. It's nice to be able to have a manual override switch.

Sharpening features—scanners with sharpening features that let you set how and when scanners sharpen are much nicer than ones with one-touch settings.

Tonal, sharpness settings by channel—scanners may not give you analogous results on all three channels. The capability to compensate for that, and fine tune images by channel, is a must.

Savable settings—You've just spent all day perfecting your scan for a specific film type. Do you want to go back and do it again tomorrow?

OCR—Optical Character Recognition. This is the capability to scan text and have it come out as editable ASCII characters and not pixels arranged like letters. This would be great if it really worked. Usually the results you get need so much editing anyway that it's faster and cheaper to hire some college kid to retype it for you.

Descreening functions—images that have been printed are said to be "screened." They can produce a special problem when you try to scan them called moiré. A descreening function will help defeat that problem. For more on moiré, see Chapter 13.

Batch scanning—the capability to set up and scan several scans at once, relieving you of having to baby-sit the scanner.

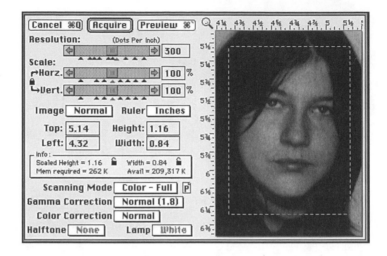

Testing Your Scanner

Flatbed scanners don't always work perfectly. They tend to image differently in different areas. Light leaks and the imperfections of the mechanics can introduce variances that can adversely affect image quality. The more you know about what your scanner does and where, the more tools you'll have to get your scans right the first time.

One of the best things you can do to help yourself is to acquire a scanning target. GATF makes some nice ones, but you can get a perfectly fine one at your local photographic supply store. You can get these for different emulsion types and in both reflective and transparent varieties. They typically feature a neutral gray strip; intensity scales for the cyan, magenta, yellow and black; tints of those colors; and the combinations that produce reds, greens, and blues. There will usually also be a variety of other likely test swatches, such as flesh tones. A photograph of a figure may be included to test for sharpness.

Whether the target is elaborate or a simple gray ramp, you can compare the results your scanner gave you yesterday with the ones it gives you today. You need to be able to predict what your scanner will do and a test target will let you compare apples to apples. Additionally, the test should enable you to identify trouble areas in your scan so that you can correct around it. Keep in mind that scanners of the same make and model may not be exactly the same.

What was correct for one scanner may not be true of its brother. You need to test *your* scanner. If you don't, you'll never know.

Here's an example of testing in action. When you scan your gray ramp, do so with the knowledge that in the RGB world, like amounts of red, green, and blue add up to gray. Scan your test strip and inspect the values all along the ramp by setting the info box (Window: Palettes: Show Info) to RGB. You find similar amounts of red, green, and blue all along your curve except for the highlight end. There you see equal amounts of green and blue but too much red (see Figure 10.11). Knowing this, you can compensate for the inadequacy before you scan. The idea is to use constants to establish a profile for the scanner. If no consistent profile emerges, your scanner is probably too unstable for color work.

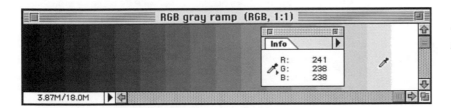

Figure 10.11

A highlight color cast.

Establish Base Settings

The idea is that if you can find out what your scanner does everyday, you can get an idea which of its software settings produce the most effective results for each scan type. For example, given a reasonably clean piece of line art, which settings will most effectively capture it? Frontloading your work here saves you time down the road and makes you more productive.

If you don't have a test target already, go to the prepress house and ask them to make a positive of their test film. Prepress houses and other businesses with imagesetters around frequently print test strips to gauge and calibrate their device's performance. Most test sheets feature resolution testers. They are starbursts made of micron-thin lines (see Figure 10.12). The delicacy of these makes them nice for a line art scanning target. Try out different settings on your scanner and see how well you can do realizing those thin lines. Print out lasers to see how you did and save your settings. Record everything in a notebook somewhere.

Figure 10.12

A resolution tester.

Make a Map

We said before that your scanner bed probably wasn't uniform. To test this, get a large sheet of uniformly colored paper. A piece of RC paper would be good. Scan the sheet in RGB with all your software settings at their defaults. After you've done that, have a look at the scan in Photoshop. To exaggerate the differences in the tones try Image: Map: Equalize (see Figure 10.13). The dark, splotchy areas that result tell you where not to scan. The clean, consistent areas show where your scanner is processing things correctly. Typically, the edges of the scanner bed will be the worst. You could even print out your test, cut out the cleaner areas for scanning, and create a mask for your scanner bed.

Figure 10.13

Equalizing a test scan emphasizes trouble spots.

Cleaning Your Scanner

Nothing destroys detail faster than dirt. You should clean your scanner at least once everyday (probably more like five or six times a day). Better machines, which are more sensitive, need more cleaning, but all scanners need some. Make yourself a cleaning kit. It should include the following items:

◆ An anti-static brush

◆ Glass cleaner (some scanners call for non-ammonia glass cleaner)

◆ Scanner wipes

◆ Photo wipes

◆ Film clean

◆ Can of compressed air

Most of these items are available at your local photographic supply store. Use the brush, glass cleaner, and scanner wipes to clean the scanner plate. The photo wipes and film clean will get rid of fingerprints and gunk on the face of your photographic originals. If the scanner or the originals get too funky, spray them down with your compressed air.

SCANNING LINE ART

Line art is the term that describes art with a one-bit pixel depth. Its pixels can therefore have one of two states: on (black) or off (no ink) (see Figure 10.14). The following are the basic steps for scanning line art.

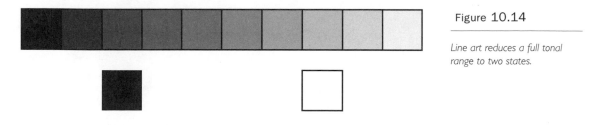

Figure 10.14

Line art reduces a full tonal range to two states.

1. Set your mode in your scanner to line art.

2. Set your resolution. An industry standard for line art is 1200 pixels. Much more than that and you'll increase your file size without increasing image quality. Scan it for as many samples as you have dots in your output device or no fewer than 800. Your file size will be small anyway compared with 8-bit information and having a file with more pixels in it makes it more flexible. We'll also compress the file when we're done. What's more, some imagesetters actually print line art faster at certain higher resolutions.

3. Preview the image. This is your big chance to check for trouble spots. Your scanner looks at the tones in your image. If it detects a sample is more dark than light, it will make it 100 percent black. Otherwise, it will make it zero percent black. Tough choices. It means that if your image has detail in it that's less than 50 percent gray, like lightly applied pencil work, you can kiss it good-bye.

   Make any scanner level corrections you think are appropriate. CCD scanners have a hard time seeing the difference between darker tones. As a result, many scanners have a default tonal adjustment, usually called gamma, which lightens the image overall. If you're scanning line art, you probably don't need this correction. Most flatbed scanners we've tested have done a good job with line art when we turn our base gamma to 1.0 (no adjustment) and brighten the image slightly.

4. Acquire your scan.

5. Touch up your scan. Review your scan quickly. Did you lose too much detail? Go back and rescan it if you did. If not, you're ready to proceed.

   The first step is to get a firm look at what's in your image. The only way to do this is to set your pan in on your image until you're at a 1:1 view. That number is the ratio of monitor pixels to pixels in your image, and it appears in the title bar of your scan's window (see

Figure 10.15). There are a number of ways to change your view ratio in Photoshop. The fastest and easiest is to use the keyboard shortcuts. Command-plus and Command-minus zooms you in and out, respectively. Double-clicking the magnifying glass also snaps you to a 1:1 ratio. If you want a more exact area enlarged, the Command Spacebar combination snaps whatever tool you're using to the magnifying glass. Command + Option + Spacebar is the demagifying glass. Remember that the magnifying glass can be used to drag an enlargement marquee as well.

Our First Line Art Scan

The first time we scanned a piece of line art, we didn't really understand the pixels to monitor pixel ratio. When we looked at the scan, we tried to pan in and out until it looked like the actual size we wanted to print at. It looked fine at that depth so we saved it to disk (see Figure 10.16). Imagine our horror and embarrassment to discover the thousands of minuscule spots in the image caused by dirt on the scanner (see Figure 10.17). They were completely invisible at a 2:1 ratio, but the client noticed them on his printed piece right away. In fact, he called us some names. We learned the hard way to inspect our images closely.

Mickey/Hanging (1:2)

Figure 10.15

The title bar shows a ratio of monitor dots to pixels.

321

Figure 10.16

Our scan at 1:2 ratio: things look great!

Figure 10.17

At a 1:1 ratio, however, we've got defects.

The Pencil Tool

After you're at a viewing depth where you can see what's in your image, you need to inspect all of it for errant pixels and defects. The best way to do this is to move though your image screen by screen from top to bottom. The pencil tool works well to retouch line art. This is because it features the handy Auto Erase option, located in the Pencil Tool Options box you get when you double-click the Pencil tool (see Figure 10.18). The Auto Eraser works like this: click any point with the pencil and draw. You get a hard-edged line of the foreground color. If, however, the first point you click is the same color as the foreground color, the pencil writes in the background color until you release the mouse. This is handy because it enables you to wipe out black pixels on the white background and fill in white pixels in the solid blacks. No swapping foreground and background color. Keep in mind that the pencil's size is driven by brush size as well.

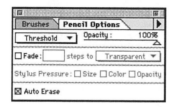

Figure 10.18

The Pencil Tool Options features the handy Auto Erase.

Two Wrongs Made Right

When you're working in Photoshop, you have to be aware that you can only undo one step and plan around it. You do have the opportunity to "undo" more than one step, but you still need to think ahead. If you're doing anything especially provocative to your file, like converting it to CMYK, it might be a smart play to build a backdoor into your work. Choose Save As from the File menu and give your file a new, descriptive name. Doing this gives you the opportunity to recall your work at exactly the stage you want it, avoiding the need to repeat a lot of tedious work.

Try taking a snapshot (Edit: Take Snapshot) (see Figure 10.19). This writes another version of your file into RAM and gives you more options for reworking. Your snapshot can be of the entire image or any part of it that you have selected. It includes any layers that are visible, treating them as one layer. The penalty you pay for this luxury is that your file size spooled to RAM increases, making everything go slower.

Figure 10.19

Snapshots add more Undoing options.

What should you do with your snapshot after you've taken it? Choose Edit: Fill: Contents: Snapshot to fill a selection or layer or entire image with your snapshot.

The Rubber Stamp

Use the Rubber Stamp to selectively paint parts of your snapshot exactly where you want them. Double-click the rubber stamp tool to get the Rubber Stamp Options palette up. Double-clicking any tool from the toolbox in Photoshop brings up that tool's options. From the Option pop up menu, choose From Snapshot (see Figure 10.20). Your rubber stamp will now paint pixels from the snapshot version of the file wherever you choose.

Figure 10.20

The Rubber Stamp.

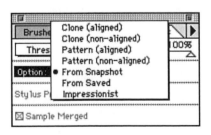

It's easy when looking at line art at a 1:1 ratio to go crazy and try to fix every minor defect along the edges of lines to make them all perfectly straight. Keep in mind, though, the depth you're seeing things at. Now, we're not saying that you should do a half-baked job of correcting your line art; we're just saying keep in mind how long things are taking and what level of quality you're getting back. *We're in this for the money.* If you ever have any questions about the quality of your lines, print a laser. It's probably not as bad as you think.

Working with Difficult Line Art

No matter how good a job you do exploring your scanner's controls for line art, some line art will simply refuse to be scanned correctly. This is a time when you have to step in and take some decisions out of your scanner's hands.

Lost Detail

When your scanner is in line art mode, it is looking at each sample it takes and deciding whether to make that sample black or not. If the sample is 50 percent gray or more, it makes it black. Otherwise, it makes it white. When lines are lighter, they simply don't show up in the scan. The first thing to do is to scan the line art in grayscale mode. Scan it at the resolution you intend to print the line art at, 1200 pixels. This results initially in a very large file. Each of the pixels,

> ### Selective Reverting to Saved
>
> It's worth mentioning here that the Rubber Stamp also can stamp from the saved version of your file as well. Just choose From Saved in that same Rubber Stamp option palette. If reverting to saved will ruin a lot of good work, consider just stamping part of the old file into place.
>
> The Eraser tool also does this quite nicely. As you might be able to deduce, double-clicking the Eraser tool brings up the Eraser tool options, which contains the Erase to Saved button. Keep in mind that the Eraser Tool's area of effect is driven by brush size. That's the palette behind the Tool options palette for both the Paintbrush and Eraser tools. Choose a diffuse one that's not too big when you're working on anything but line art.

however, has gray values associated with them. This is invaluable. Every time Photoshop makes an adjustment, it's actually doing math. In a one-bit environment, no matter what math you do, the answers always have to be zero or one. Scanning as grayscale opens up many of Photoshop's tools that are unavailable in line art mode.

Threshold

The first option to try is the Threshold (Image: Map: Threshold). This does exactly what the scanner was trying to do in line art mode (make the darks black and the lights white), only you get to set the centerpoint wherever you want. Sliding the center point back and forth sets the break between black and white. This also affects the thickness and thinness of the lines in the image. If you find you've gone too far, the Option button turns the Cancel button into a Reset key. On the whole, we've found Threshold useful but not terribly full-featured.

Unsharp Mask

Another handy little nugget is the Unsharp Mask filter. This filter's use is explained in full detail below. For the time being though, try applying the filter with settings around 300/1/3.

Measure and Adjust

Find the values of the pixels that you don't want burned out and adjust them specifically using Image: Adjust: Curves to make them greater than 50 percent. Doing this work in gamma also gives you the option to write your curve in such a way that our shadow details don't fill in too dramatically.

Crooked Originals and Logo Stat Sheets

Back in the days before vector art, logos were usually scaled to a variety of sizes and scattered out on a sheet, which would be reshot with a stat camera. It's not uncommon to receive logos for scanning that have been cut out of these sheets. Usually these logos scan fine, but since they've been cut out, there's no easy way to place them on the scanner bed so that they line up straight. You have to preview and then lift the scanner lid to readjust.

To avoid this problem, scan the logo as grayscale, giving yourself plenty of room around the original and the resolution you'll want for a line art scan. This gives you the opportunity to rotate the scan in Photoshop. The fastest way to do that is to use the Cropping tool. Set up your crop by dragging out a rectangle around the logo. Once you have it, hold down the Option key and click one of the corners of the crop marquee. Dragging the mouse now freely rotates the crop so that you can line it up with the baseline of the logo (see Figure 10.21). Once the rotation of the crop is parallel to the baseline in the image, expand the crop marquee so that you don't lose any image area, and crop. The logo snaps to a perfect 90° (see Figure 10.22).

Figure 10.21

In grayscale, you can rotate crops...

Figure 10.22

...and straighten things out.

Note

Important: Converting Back to Line Art

Once you've done the work you needed to do in grayscale mode, it's a good idea to convert your file back to line art. That way there won't be any unpleasant extra pixels knocking things out behind them when you place the file into a page layout program (see Figure 10.23). Doing it is a snap. Choose Mode: Bitmap from the menu. Make sure you keep your resolution high and choose 50 percent threshold in your bitmap options.

Figure 10.23

*Line art is transparent;
grayscale isn't.*

Redraw It

If the line art you're working on is something you intend to use frequently, at different sizes or with variations, consider taking the time to redraw it in a vector-based application like Adobe Illustrator. You'll get cleaner lines, more professional results, and a much more flexible file. Most logos aren't really that hard to redraw and the time spent doing it will be made up in the time you spend futzing around, trying to get good pixels out of bad copy. Usually, you can use the initial scan as a guide. Place the scan in your drawing application, lock it into place and then redraw around it. When you're done, unlock the scan and delete it.

Image File Formats: TIFF and EPS

You need to think about only two options here: TIFF or EPS (see Figure 10.24). TIFF is the Tagged Image File Format and EPS is an Encapsulated PostScript file format. In the case of pixel-based information, such as Photoshop files, the information it's saving is exactly the same. Just a lot of zeros and ones. The rule of thumb for most Photoshop files is that unless you're doing something special to your file, save it as a TIFF. Pixel-based EPS files tend to be larger than TIFFs. That's true here, too.

EPS

The special thing you might do with an EPS here would be to save the line art with opaque whites. Remember that the "white" pixels in the line art scan are actually transparent. If you are compositing the image in your page layout program on top of another object, the bottom object shows through. If you wanted to incur the file size penalty for that effect, go for it. Otherwise, save it as a TIFF. For a full run down of times when you need to use an EPS file, see Chapter 5, "File Management."

Tip

If you're sick of looking at all those file formats when you save things, pull the plug-ins of the formats you don't want to see anymore out of Photoshop's File Formats folder. Put them in a different folder entirely, like your Utilities Folder, or Photoshop will track them down.

Figure 10.24

File Formats.

```
Photoshop 3.0
Photoshop 2.0
Amiga IFF
BMP
CompuServe GIF
EPS
Filmstrip
JPEG
MacPaint
PCX
PICT File
PICT Resource
Pixar
PixelPaint
Raw
Scitex CT
Targa
✓TIFF
```

TIFF Options

When you save TIFFs you get the TIFF Options box (see Figure 10.25). It will ask you if you want IBM or MAC byte order. It's the same information whichever one you choose. The data is just structured differently within the file. Choose whichever one is more convenient for you. You also have the option of compressing your file using LZW (Lempel, Ziv, Welch) compression. This is what's called a lossless compression scheme (as opposed to a "lossy" scheme). That means that unlike some file formats that save space, such as JPEG for example, no pixels are ever thrown away. Instead, the crafty LZW compression scheme looks for patterns of similarity among the pixels and groups the information differently to save space. So, in files that have large areas of pixels that are the same, like line art, you can experience a large savings in file size. Because of this, the scheme works less well in grayscale or full color, because they have fewer areas of similarity.

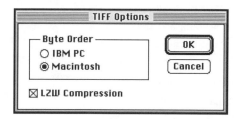

Figure 10.25

TIFF Options box.

Almost everyone supports LZW now, but it is a good idea to double-check with your service bureau before sending files this way. Also, you probably shouldn't bother using another compression scheme, such as Disk Doubler, on top of the LZW.

Here are two things to think about when you're saving your files.

◆ Build a backdoor. When you scan something directly into Photoshop, it comes in as an untitled file. That means there is no saved copy of it anywhere. If you mess up, you have to re-scan. Consider saving it in the native Photoshop 3.0 format. Because most page layout programs do not support that format, your raw, unrefined scan will have no danger of accidentally being placed into your page layout program instead of your finished piece. This eliminates the possibility of printing the wrong version of your file.

◆ Name things descriptively. If you're using a Mac, include some indicator of what file format it is. Choose a name that will make sense two years from now. For sequential versions of the same file, consider a numbering system. We know a gent that saves his full color files and adds codes to them to let him know which version of the file it is. "Scan A.tif" for the raw scan, "Scan B .tif" for the retouched RGB file and "Scan C.tif" for the converted CMYK version. Subsequent

What's In a Name?

A desktop publishing cooperative produced a weekly events calendar for several years. All the scans they used went into one folder. The scanning tech used the memory technique that associates ideas with rooms of a familiar house. When he scanned a picture of a woman holding flowers he named the file "pantry picture" because the pantry in his imagination had a picture on the wall of flowers like the ones the woman was holding. It worked fine until the tech was fired by the cooperative's insane, tyrannical administrator. The remaining employees were left with over one hundred and fifty scans and no possible way of identifying them other than to inspect each one individually. The next problem came when the 150 newly renamed files were taken over to the cooperative's IBM system. All the line art scans had been named with a ".la" at the end to differentiate them from the ".ht" halftone files. But IBM machines use the dot character in a name to introduce the file type code. So while the IBM would have known that "flowers.tif" was a TIF file, it had no idea what "flowers.la" was. Once again all the files had to be renamed. Choose your names wisely.

versions of each type receive numbers like "Scan B 02.tif" and so on. Files sorted by name are alphabetical and you can include special characters (like asterisks and tildes) to affect that order. Asterisks come first in the alphabet and tildes come last. You could also consider sorting the individual folder that your scans live in by date. That way the latest, or most current version of the file, will come first in order. Another handsomely underused option is the Mac's Labels feature. Use the Labels Control Panel to establish names for the various states your scans will be in and apply them accordingly.

SCANNING AND ADJUSTING HALFTONES

In Chapter 9, we talked about what a halftone is and all the unsavory things that can go wrong with it. In this section, we're going to discuss how to set those things aright and make our images sing. Here you'll learn about why images often come out on press too dark, how to correct that without making our image look dull and lifeless, and a host of other common problems that plague scans. This is the down and dirty business of image correction. This isn't art and it's certainly not a black art. It's craft and it's simple if you take control of it. Understanding tonal correction is also the key to understanding the more complicated color corrections you'll be doing in Chapter 12.

Press Conditions

Much of the troubles people have when printing halftones stem from a lack of information about the printing process. Printing presses aren't the same as computer monitors and much of your work involves adjusting our beautiful halftones so that they can printed correctly on press. Like any adjustment in Photoshop, the act of doing this throws away information. The trick here is to make your image look better and print right, even with less information.

The Plan

Most scanned images need the same sorts of things done to them before they're ready to go to press. Whether or not you follow every one of these steps depends on the image you're working with. You should consider each of the following areas closely.

1. Assess the Image, Learn its Purpose

2. Preview, Measure, and Adjust Your Image

3. Scan

4. Assess Your Scan, Rescan if Necessary and Save

5. Fix Any Glaring Problems

6. Sharpen Your Image

7. Check/Adjust Endpoints for Press

8. Adjust Tones

9. Retouch

10. Review, Massage, and Save (As)

1. Assess the Image, Learn Its Purpose

This is a vital, often overlooked part of the scanning process. Making an appraisal of your image assists you in identifying trouble spots, prevents you from wasting your time scanning dirty originals, helps inform your decision-making and grounds your corrections in reality. If the object you're scanning has no information in the highlights, you'd be wasting your time trying to pull some out in the scan. Get to know your original.

When you look at your original, there are several things to notice. The location and distribution of tones throughout your image. Where are the highlights; where are the shadows? What is the overall composition of the image? Try and guess what values you'll see when you measure the image onscreen. What part of the image is apt to give you trouble? Deep, impenetrable shadows? Diffuse lighting which renders the image flat? Don't wait until the image is scanned to start correcting it. And lastly, what's really important about the image? Scanning is a trade-off. You may have to sacrifice something to get what you want. Identify the thing that is most important about the image you're scanning and fight to protect it.

The scan also has the purpose of being printed at a certain size on a certain machine. You need to know the size of the scan and the line screen the device you're printing to can support. You need to do this so you can set the resolution of your scanner to sample the image correctly. Recall that you need 1.5 to 2 times as many pixels in your image as you intend to print lines of spots on press. If you're printing on a 150 line screen device, scan your image at 300 samples per inch. Most laser printers can't print past 80 lines. If the final destination of your scan is a laser printer, you don't need 300 pixels an inch.

The red flag here, of course, is a low line screen. Coarse line screens, like 65–85, often signal that your image will experience other troubles, such as a fat dot gain and very restricted tonal range. Find these things out before you scan. These issues are even more important when you move into full color, so get used to thinking about them now.

2. Preview, Measure, and Adjust Your Image

Scanners typically have a preview mode that gives you an overview of the scanner bed. Additionally, there also might be a Prescan function that enables you to get a better look at your image. On many scanners, the prescan also gives the scanner a better look at your image. It rechecks for the lights and darks in the image within the area you're interested in, resulting in a better scan.

Finesse your settings to make initial tonal corrections. We talked earlier about testing your settings out on a constant image and then measuring and recording the results. That's good advice here, too. Adjusting your scan and measuring the results with your onscreen densitometer, instead of running on default settings and making adjustments in Photoshop, is good for several reasons. One, you'll save time and grief if you sample correctly. Two, tonal correction in Photoshop throws information away. The more work you do in Photoshop, the farther you move away from your scan data. Better to have good information to begin with. Three, detail may be lost irrecoverably. No amount of adjusting in Photoshop can recover detail that's not there.

3. Scan and Save

Frequently, it's beneficial to make several scans of the same image with different settings. If you have batch scanning (the capability to set up multiple scans at once), this is easy. Having more than one scan may seem like a waste of process time, but it lets you choose which scan to correct and forces you to make quality decisions immediately. With grayscale scans, you should be able to get pretty close to the original with some practice. Having two scans, however, can be a handy tool to have when you want some options.

4. Assess Your Scan, Rescan if Necessary

After you've got your scan, you need to decide if you can work with it. A quick review of the scan and the original should give you the answer to this. Pan in on shadows and run your cursor across the areas to check the tonal values there. Does the value change as you move around? If it does, there are tonal differences. Difference is detail and detail is good.

If it doesn't change, you've got trouble. If there was detail in the original that didn't come through on the scan, you've got to go back and rescan. Do the same thing on the highlights. Aren't you glad you looked the original over thoroughly, so you know where to look for the highlights?

As you're looking at your scan for detail loss, you should also look for defects introduced in scanning. If there is an inordinate amount of dust, clean the scanner bed and scan it again. It'll probably be take less time and produce better results than manually removing all the defects.

Save your scan as soon as you've acquired it. This prevents you from having to rescan in the event of a crash or multiple mistakes.

Finally, make a list of the problems the image has and where they are. This will be a checklist to review after we've adjusted our image for press conditions.

5. Fix Any Glaring Problems

The order we've listed for correcting files follows a logical procedure. Since each step you take affects the choices you will make in the next step, order is important. In the real world, however, you need to see what's in your image before you can make intelligent choices about it. Fixing the big problem first lets you know if you have a scan you can actually work with. Typically, fixing the big problem fixes some smaller problems as well. We'll discuss the tools you'll use to fix the problems in a second. For now, just keep in mind that it's a good policy overall to take first things first. If this means disregarding the color correction order for a time, that's fine.

6. Sharpen Your Image

Just about everything that is scanned needs some sharpening. The act of scanning tends to smooth some of the crisp edges in an original, which is one reason to sharpen. Another is the final destination of the scan. Some varieties of output, newsprint specifically, are less forgiving than others. Sharpen your image with the original and the printed piece in mind.

The plan is to use a Photoshop filter to create greater contrast where two edges in the image meet. This is a tonal adjustment, which is why you're doing this first. After you apply this filter, the tonal value of many pixels in the image changes, moving them away from their initial values. This can subvert subtle tonal corrections you may have made and push pixel values into the unprintable ranges.

The premier filter in Photoshop for sharpening is the Unsharp Mask (Filter: Sharpen: Unsharp Mask.) This filter offers the greatest level of control of any of the other Sharpening filters Photoshop includes. The other filters for sharpening don't allow any user input at all. This makes it impossible to control what the filter does and fine tune the results for your specific image.

The Unsharp Mask filter goes through the image and looks for places where two tones adjoin. We'll call the line between them the terminator. An Unsharp Mask darkens or lightens the pixels on either side of the terminator incrementally as they approach it (see Figure 10.26). The lights get lighter as they approach the line; the darks get darker. The result is greater contrast between the tones at the terminator line. Our goal is to sharpen the image so that it looks realistic without creating so much contrast that things look unnatural. The Unsharp Mask has three settings to be aware of (see Figure 10.27).

Figure 10.26

Sharpening changes the values of pixels as they approach an edge.

Figure 10.27

Unsharp Mask.

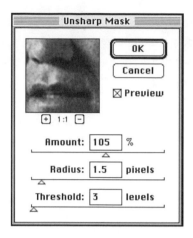

Amount: how much lighter and darker will the pixels get? A larger number results in greater contrast, with some pixels eventually being knocked to black and white. A smaller number produces a less dramatic effect. This doesn't affect the size of the sharpening halo, just the content of it.

Sharpness is also related to size and content. As images get larger, detail becomes more apparent and needs less enhancement. As images get larger, try decreasing the Amount. Likewise, images with crisper edges require less sharpening than diffuse ones. They need a smaller Amount value in their Unsharp Masks. In addition to that, images that have less tonal contrast might need more sharpening than images with a normal amount of contrast. The only way to find out is through trial and error. It's impossible to really see what the effects of the filter are on your monitor. A pretty good rule of thumb is, if it looks like you've sharpened it just *that much too much*, it's probably just about right.

Radius: over how large an area will pixel values be changed? Keep in mind that though the size of the sharpening halo is measured in pixels, it is not a literal measurement and the actual halo will be slightly larger than the number you enter.

Radius is important to the appearance of a natural, realistic-looking sharpening. It's also related to output. Recall that these pixels will end up as halftone spots. The size of the sharpening halo you build here is important. If you're printing to a coarse line screen, a too-small halo may well disappear when the pixels are translated into spots. In general, with 300 pixel per inch images, a Radius of 1.5 is a pretty good place to start.

Threshold: how much difference does there have to be between the pixels before any sharpening happens at all? A higher number means there has to be a lot of difference to be considered an edge, a low number means less tonal variation is required. A Threshold of zero sharpens everything; a Threshold of 255 won't sharpen a thing.

Undoing Filter Effects

At the top of the Filter menu is the name of whatever filter you used last, complete with a keyboard shortcut (see Figure 10.28). If you want to use it again with the same settings you used last time, just press „+ F. Typically though, we find that we apply a filter, are unhappy with the results, and want to change them. Just undo the filter you didn't like and press „ + Alt/Option + F. This calls up the filter box you used, complete with the settings you chose last time. Make them right and off you go.

This can be a handy tool to help you protect tones that you don't want sharpened. A higher Threshold means that only more marked differences are considered edges. When you scale up 35mm slides past a certain point, you can actually see film grain. If your Threshold is too low, Photoshop assumes that the grain is detail and sharpens it. That's not what you want. Likewise, when you have subtle tonal changes, like in flesh tones, you don't want those sharpened either. Threshold is your friend in this matter. Test it out to find numbers that suit your purposes exactly. Remember to let realism be your guide and the printing press be your goal.

Figure 10.28

Command F repeats the last Filter you used.

Identifying Endpoints with Levels

If you open up the Levels box, you are presented with a graph called a Histogram. It's essentially a bar chart of the tonal composition of the image. Each tone from white to black is displayed by way of a gray ramp along the bottom of the histogram. The higher the bar over each tone, the more pixels of that tone are in the image.

If you turned on Video LUT (refer to Chapter 8) and you turn off preview in your Levels, you can get an idea where the lightest and darkest points in your image are. This only works in grayscale, RGB, Duotone, or multichannel. Hold the Alt/Option key down and click either end point slider. You'll see which pixels in your image are either all white or black (see Figure 10.29). If you don't want that to happen, you need to adjust those particular pixels with your endpoint eyedroppers.

7. Check and Adjust Endpoints for Press

Endpoints are simply the lightest and darkest points in the image you're working on. In the case of the lighter end point, we make a further distinction. A dot with no information, pure white paper, is said to be a *specular highlight*. The lightest dot in an image that carries detail, or that has information in it, is said to be the *diffuse highlight*. Both kinds of highlight are important.

The plan here is to identify the diffuse highlight and shadow points in your image and check to see if they are within the printable range of your press. If they are and things look fine, you're done here; move on to Step 8. If they aren't, you need to intelligently change their values so that they can be printed. You don't want to dramatically affect the rest of your image data. Controls like Brightness and Contrast lighten or darken *all* of the pixels in your image. That's not what you want.

You want the pixels that need more lightening or darkening to get more and the pixels that need less change to get less.

Endpoint Targeting

The best way to set your endpoints for printing is with the highlight and shadow eyedroppers. You can find them in both the Levels (Image: Adjust: Levels) and Curves (Image: Adjust: Curves) boxes. Of the two, we prefer the Curves. Curves offers a wider range of controls than Levels and simply makes more intuitive sense to us. Additionally, to do professional color work in Photoshop, you really have to use Curves, so you might as well get used to it. The only feature that Level gives you that Curves doesn't is rendered moot if you assessed your image well before you scanned it. In all actuality, Curves are really simpler and more effective than Levels.

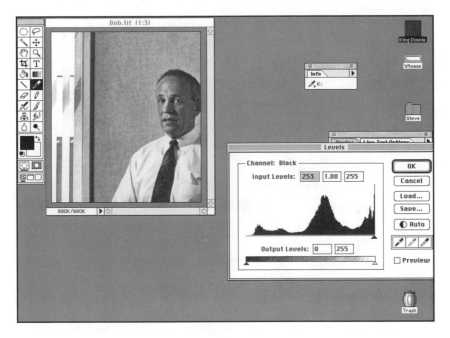

Figure 10.29

Endpoint clipping offers a quick way to locate extreme pixel values.

Curves, Gamma, and the Rest of Your Life

The Curves control is also called gamma and you'll use it to do the bulk of your tonal correction forever. Gamma, which you'll see in several other places as well, is simply an expression of change, a ratio of input to output. That relationship can be expressed as a chart like the Curves box (see Figure 10.30) or as a number. Your scanner probably has a gamma setting on it somewhere, which is something like 1.8. Again, it's a ratio of input to output. If you changed a 50 percent gray pixel to a 27 percent pixel, the ratio of input (the starting number) to output (the finishing number) would be 50/27 or 1.8. The image is lightened. A gamma number of 1 would be no change. Fifty percent input to 50 percent output would be 50/50 or one. A gamma of less than one darkens an image. Fifty percent input and 62 percent output would be 50/62 or .8, a darker image.

Figure 10.30

The Curves box is an invaluable tool.

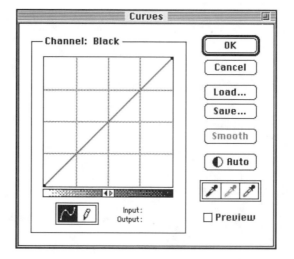

But how does this relate to the Curves dialog box and setting your endpoints to match press conditions? The Curves control lets you do a number of things. One of them is to load numbers you know press can hold into Photoshop's eyedroppers. Armed with that information, you can adjust the pixels in your image so that they match what can be held on press. You're using the eyedroppers for this because it affects the image overall and is less damaging than other forms of (linear) correction.

Double-click the highlight eyedropper and you'll get the white target color picker (see Figure 10.31). This is where you'll load in the highlight value you know our press can hold. Let's say it's five percent gray, not an uncommon number for coated stock printed at a reasonably high line screen. If you don't know what these numbers are, talk to your pressman. If he doesn't know, ask to set up a test or take your business elsewhere. Load the value into the K box in the CMYK section. If you happened to know the RGB values of five percent gray, you could have loaded those instead. Click OK to close this window and load your settings. Do the same thing with your shadow eyedropper, but only load in the shadow endpoint settings.

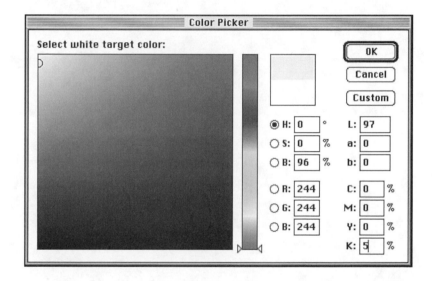

Figure 10.31

Set your target endpoint to one you know your press can hold.

Now get out your highlight eyedropper and find your diffuse highlight (see Figure 10.32). If you don't have your Info box set to grayscale or actual color, say OK to the Curves box without making any changes and go back and get that window open. After you've located your highlight, click it with the highlight eyedropper. You should see two numbers separated by a slash in your Info palette (see Figure 10.33). These are your before and after correction values. Before is on the left. Now your diffuse highlight can print correctly and you haven't affected your midtones or shadows at all. Track down your shadow endpoint if you need to and click it with the shadow eyedropper.

Figure 10.32

Inspect your image for the location of endpoints.

Figure 10.33

Target your endpoints to values your press can hold.

Keep in mind that you're after the diffuse highlight here, not the specular one. If you have pure white highlights that are important to your image, don't force them to gray. The image that results will be too flat. You'll find yourself going after the highlight much more frequently than the shadow point. Also recall that if you have a 2:1 ration of pixels to line screen, the value of four pixels is averaged to produce the halftone spot, so a single zero percent pixel may not burn out.

When you're doing this work, don't pay too much attention to what the Curves graph is displaying. The math that's going on is more subtle than it can easily show you and certainly don't replicate the curve you see on another scan without using the eyedroppers. The results will not be the same at all.

After you've set your endpoints, or really made any provocative change in Photoshop, it's a good idea to take a quick before-and-after look at your handiwork. Undo and redo, my friend. You'll quickly see if the choices you made were correct. You can also see the changes directly in the Curves box. If you have the preview box unchecked and are using Video LUT, clicking the title bar shows you the file before your correction. If you feel you've erred in your selection of end points, hold down the Alt/Option key and the Cancel button becomes a Reset one. Pip! Pip!

8. Adjust Tones

You probably noticed that if you reset your endpoints to meet press requirements, your image begins to look noticeably flatter. The differences between your lights and darks are simply not as great. The image loses some of its contrast as a result. You'll need to address that issue by making another correction. You should also get out your mental notes from the Prescan Assessment and a copy of the original to compare with the scan and start making some critical decisions.

Curves is the tool you'll use here and it should therefore receive a little more attention. We said Curves was a graph of change. The chart shows input along the horizontal axis and output along the vertical one. Make sure the gray ramp along the bottom of the graph has the dark side on the right. This displays values as percentages of ink, rather than levels of brightness. It's typically more intuitive to think this way. If your darks are on the right, just click the gray ramp itself and it switches positions and readout styles.

The dotted lines divide the Curve up into highlights, quartertones, midtones, three-quarter tones, and shadows. If you prefer, Alt/Option-click anywhere on the graph and it the four-by-four grid is swapped for a more descriptive ten by ten grid.

Changing the shape of the curve changes the values of the pixels in the image. You can change the shape of the curve by clicking and dragging. Notice as you move part of the curve, the whole curve changes. Output values change throughout your image to match the values your new curve is describing.

To better describe how Curves work, let's use them to compensate for the flatness we introduced back in step 7 (see Figure 10.34). As you may recall, you constricted the tonal range of your image to match press conditions. The curve below (see Figure 10.35) is a classic contrast curve. The first thing you did was to darken our shadows. You moved the cursor over the 75 percent input line and then you went straight up until you found the point where 75 percent input was about 80 percent output. By clicking the mouse you automatically add a point that the curve snaps to. Then you went to the 25 percent input line and moved down it until you found the point where 25 percent input was 20 percent output. Click. Snap. OK. The lights get brighter and the darks get darker. My mud tone stays put. These values are just guides; you should let the content of the image dictate your actual behavior. Your image may require more or less adjustment in your quarter tones than in your three-quarter tones. You may also need to add a second pint in the shadow curve to open up extreme darks a little. Whatever the case, you won't know until you inspect your image.

Figure 10.34

Constricting the tonal range of an image means that darks and lights are closer together; the result is a flat image.

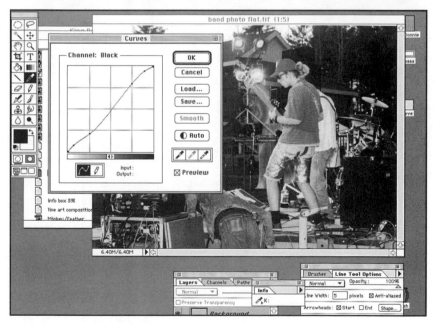

Figure 10.35

A contrast curve helps our image quality while keeping it printable.

Recalling Curves

When you apply a Curve to an image and then go back to the Curves box, you see a straight line again. That's because Curves is a reflection of change. The pixels have new values now and the straight line in curves is asking you if you want to change them again. Sometimes though, it's useful to know what Curve you applied last time, especially if it wasn't quite right and needed some fine tuning. Hold the Alt/Option key down when you call up the box („-Option M). All your old values appear. This also works on the Levels box as well.

The plan here is to consult the Info box to confirm what your eyes are telling you about the content of your image and then correct the part of the tonal range that needs help. If you need further visual information about any given pixel's tonal value, move the cursor over it with the Curves box up and hold down the mouse. A little ball appears over the point's position on the curve and the input/output readout tells you everything you need to know (see Figure 10.36).

Figure 10.36

Hold your mouse down in your image to find the tone's value on your Curve's readout.

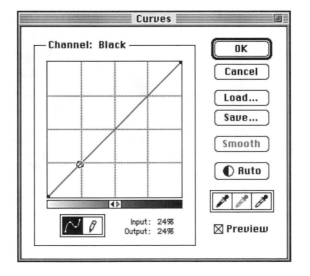

9. Retouch

Just as you inspected your line art for defects, you need to inspect grayscale images as well. Since there are more values involved than in line art, correcting 8-bit images is more challenging but also more fun. This is one area where it's very easy to see the creative uses of Photoshop and you can begin to enjoy the application simply on its own merits.

Earlier this chapter, we talked about cloning from saved or snapshot versions of our files. This works fine to correct mistakes you've made, but what about mistakes that were already there? The Rubber Stamp is the tool for the job. It's power, fun, and simplicity combined, making it our favorite Photoshop tool.

The Rubber Stamp copies one part of our image (or any open file) and pastes it into another part of our image. This means that if part of the background in your image has some defect, like a scratch, some dirt, or your ex-boyfriend, you can simply copy a part of your background with no boyfriends in it and paste into the part with the problem.

To do this, you first indicate from where you want to copy. Alt/Option-click on a point near the defect that looks similar to the area you want to copy to. Your cursor switches to the target scope. Once you've established that point, move to the area you need to copy to, and Rubber Stamp away. The source point maintains its distance and direction from you as you paint (see Figure 10.37). The sizes of both the area you copy to and the one you copy from are driven by brush size. Choose one that's the right size for the job and diffuse.

Figure 10.37

Keep your eye on the source point as you're cloning.

The best way to keep your retouching a secret is to sample from several different places. Taking a zipper pattern by sampling from either side of the area around the defect is a fine strategy (see Figure 10.38). If you only select one source point and drag along, you create a noticeable visual streaking. Take a piece from here and a piece from there and dab them into place. Be careful also not to get your source point fouled up in areas you've already pasted to. You create a pattern that everyone will see. While we're wrapping up Rubber Stamp odds and ends, the Sample Merged check box lets you clone from layers if you find yourself working with them.

Figure 10.38

The Zipper Method.

Photoshop comes with a filter that can remove dust and scratches. We've gathered this from the fact that it's named "Dust and Scratches." It lives in the Noise filter set (Filter: Noise: Dust and Scratches). The filter's effect can best be described as a reverse Unsharp Mask. It can blend differently colored pixels based on the disposition of the pixels around them. Doing this can really destroy detail in an image fast. If you're going to use it, be sure to very carefully select only the exact area where the defects are located and a few pixels around them.

10. Review, Massage, and Save

Once you've done your tonal correction, sit back and review your work. Are there areas that could use a little more help? How did you do on your mental correction checklist? You need to compare the original with the scan and critically assess your work with the printing press in the back of your mind. Go back and make adjustments as necessary. Once you've done everything you feel you need to do, you need to do something else.

Dot Gain

When ink hits paper on the press, the size of the halftone dots we worked so hard on can change shape. This is caused by the absorbency of the paper and the speed of the press. The resulting is a darkening of the image overall. The place where dot gain is the worst is in the midtones. On that part of the curve, the relationship between dot size and white space is the most delicate. In the darker dots what you're actually seeing is the space between the dots. While it is a problem there as well, it is still more pronounced in the midtones.

Visual Guide to Gain

Photoshop can change its monitor display of grayscale information if you want to get a visual idea of what may happen to your image on press. Go to your Preferences under the file menu and choose Printing Inks Set Up. From the pop up list there, choose the type of inks you anticipate printing with. SWOP is the Specifications for Web Offset Printing, and you'll probably want one of those three. Choose the type that matches your printing substrate: coated, uncoated or newsprint. With each ink type, the Dot Gain number changes. You can also dial in your number directly. Click the Use Dot Gain for Grayscale button. This won't change the information in your grayscale file, but it gives you some idea what it may look like on press. You need a well calibrated monitor to use this setting effectively and should definitely consult the numbers anyway, but this may help.

You have several options for handling the dot gain problem. They all involve writing a curve that reduces the size of the 50 percent dot, and the other tones as well. The idea is that if you make the dot smaller in proportion to the dot gain, the tones should fall neatly into place on press. Because other sized dots experience gain to differing degrees, they should be adjusted to differing degrees.

How much to change the curve is a function of the press and paper. Running a test will let you know exactly, but this chart may give you some idea about where to start. Keep in mind that if you separate into CMYK correctly, and you'll learn how soon, you won't need to make this adjustment.

PRESS	DOT GAIN	SIZE OF 50% DOT
Web/coated stock	15 - 25%	36 - 30%
Sheetfed press/coated stock	10 - 15%	41 - 36%
Sheetfed press/uncoated stock	18 - 25%	35 - 30%
Newsprint	30 - 40%	28 - 25%

This is saying that if you expect a 10 percent dot gain on press, a 41 percent mid tone dot will produce roughly a 50 percent dot. At 15 percent gain, you need a 36 percent dot to get a midtone on press. These numbers may vary. With time, you should be able to get a very accurate description of where your tones gain and how much.

What you can do to compensate for gain is a matter of preference. The quickest and easiest way is to simply change the data in the image with a Curve correction (see Figure 10.39). If you're going to do this, you might be happy if you save the file under a different name like "scan w/10% gain.tif." This gives you the option of going back and repurposing your scan for other functions if you need to.

Figure 10.39

Correcting for dot gain.

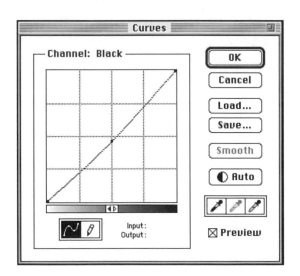

The other option for compensation involves saving the curve as an EPS and making the correction at the time of printing. To do this, choose Page Set Up from the File menu. Choose the Transfer Function button. Slap the number you want right in the 50 percent box (see Figure 10.40), save it as an EPS, and hit "Include Transfer Function." Your image information is unharmed. You could do the same thing by making the image a Monotone, but this method seems simple enough. The price to pay for the flexibility of your transfer function is increased file size.

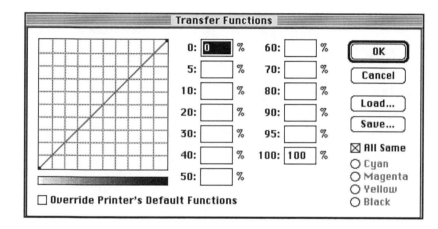

Figure 10.40

Transfer Functions work like Curves.

Grayscale RGB

Just as scanning a piece of line art as grayscale has advantages, so does scanning grayscale images as RGB. Scanning in RGB and converting to grayscale may increase process time and add an additional step to your work flow, but it has its advantages. For one, your scanner may do a better job of capturing detail if it's looking three times instead of once. For another, more information means more choices for you.

You can convert your image to grayscale directly from RGB and get a great image. You may also consider taking a quick look through your channels. Command 1, 2, and 3 takes you to Red, Green, and Blue. Command 0 brings you back to RGB. You could also click the desired channel by opening up the Channels palette (Window: Palettes: Show Channels). Lurking among those channels may be the gray scale file you want to correct. You can also begin experimenting by combining the channels. For more information on channels, see Chapter 13.

REQUISITE SELECTION TECHNIQUES

So far, all the correction techniques we've talked about have been global corrections. They affect the entire image. Granted, with Curves you are only altering a specific part of the image tonally, but Photoshop looked at the entire image when it made its adjustments. In this section, you'll limit the areas Photoshop considers when it makes changes geographically. In other words, you'll decide exactly which parts of your images need to be changed and change only those parts. Every tool Photoshop has is subject to the whims of your selections. Doing this greatly advances the ability and precision with which we correct files. We'll talk about the basic tools here and then raise the bar in Chapter 11.

What Is Selection?

When pixels are selected, they are the only pixels that can be changed in any way. Anything that's not selected can't be changed (see Figure 10.41). Because pixels are squares that form a grid, this can lead to problems. If the selection you're making isn't perfectly horizontal and vertical, some of the edge along the selection can be a staggered staircase. Photoshop has to select one pixel or the other and the result can be an unwanted hard edge.

Figure 10.41

Selection enables you to only affect specific pixels.

The solution is to tell Photoshop you want to smooth that hard edge out. Each of the Selection tool's option boxes (except the rectangular marquee) has the anti-alias check box. Photoshop selects not only the pixels you wanted initially but also the pixels on either side of the selection line. Those pixels each change tonally, creating the illusion of a smooth edge (see Figure 10.42). You should go through your tools and turn this option on now, before you start making selections.

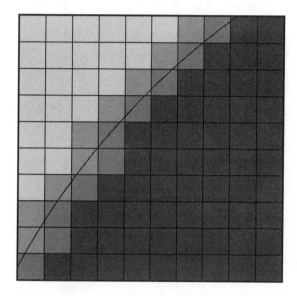

Figure 10.42

A close up of an anti-aliased selection shows the blending.

Feathering

Feathering is similar to anti-aliasing, but it takes the principle to its logical extreme. Anti-aliasing only selects a one pixel-width edge around our selection. Feathering affects as many as you want (see Figure 10.43). This makes it a nice choice for creating vignettes or special effects, but anything much more than a two pixel feather is too much for day-to-day production work.

Figure 10.43

Feathering a selection.

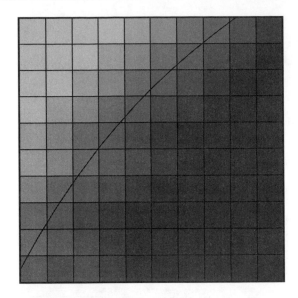

Altering Your Selection

It's uncommon to nail your selection perfectly the first time. You may want to add to or subtract from a selection. To add to an existing selection, hold the Shift key down as you select. To subtract from a selection, use the Command key. Don't forget that just because you started your work in one tool, you aren't bound to using only that tool. Switch selection tools around to suit your needs.

Filling and Moving Selected Pixels

We talked earlier about filling a selection with a snapshot or a saved version of a file. You can also fill it with the Foreground or Background color you have selected in your tool box. Deleting is simply filling pixels with the background color. Option deleting fills the pixels with the foreground color. For even more options for filling pixels up, look at Fill under the Edit menu. From there you can create a number of effects, including the popular ghosting effect. Just select white as the color you want to fill with and then change the opacity up or down depending on the kind of effect you want.

You'll notice that if you position any of the basic selection tools over an existing selection, it becomes the familiar pointer arrow. If you click and drag now, you'll take the pixels you have selected with you, leaving the background color in the place of the pixels (see Figure 10.44). To lift a copy of the selected pixels off of the original ones, choose Float from the Select menu or just hold down the Option key as you drag (see Figure 10.45). You get a cloud of selected pixels hovering above the face of the scan. Move it where you want. Drag it off into another file or off onto the desktop, we don't care.

Figure 10.44

Dragging a selection leaves the background color behind.

Perhaps you'd like to move the selection without moving the pixels? Option command drags the selection. This has gotten us out of tight spots a few times where reselecting an entire area would be too time-consuming, but nudging it a bit to the left worked just fine.

Figure 10.45

*Option dragging drags a copy of
the selection.*

Three Basic Tools: The Magic Wand, The Marquee, and The Lasso

Photoshop has three basic tools for making selections: the Marquee, the Lasso and the Magic Wand. Other, more precise tools are available for selection and we'll get to those in Chapter 13. These tools are the basics, however, and can often do the job just fine. At the very least, you need to at least understand their function before you can move onto other techniques. We'll look at the basic three in order of usefulness for prepress work from least to most useful.

The Magic Wand

Nothing is terribly magical about the Magic Wand. It has about one functional use in prepress and that's about it. The idea behind it, however is an attractive one. The idea is, you click a point in your image and the Magic Wand examines all the pixels around that initial point. If the pixel it examines is suitably similar to the initial pixel, it becomes selected. Then the pixels around *it* get examined and so on, until all the pixels that are like that initial one and are geographically contiguous to one another become selected. So if your scan was of a word on a white background and you clicked a letter, you'd select only that letter and not the rest of the word. The other letters are similar to the initial point, but separated by white space, which is not very similar.

How similar is similar? You decide. Photoshop assigns a relative brightness to every pixel and thinks of how light or dark it is on a scale of, surprise!, Zero to 255. In the Magic Wand's option box, there is a setting for Tolerance (see Figure 10.46). This literally means how many levels of brightness greater or lesser than the initial pixel can each adjacent pixel be and still get selected. If your initial pixel has a brightness of 100 and your tolerance is set to 20, adjacent pixels with values as bright as 120 and dark as 80 become selected. You may have deduced from this that because the Wand is looking at the values of pixels, this doesn't work for line art.

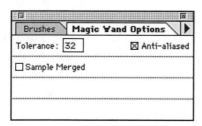

Figure 10.46

More Tolerance means more difference is accepted. Now isn't that sweet?

Reversing the Selection

About the only thing the Magic Wand is really efficient at is quickly selecting objects on flatly colored backgrounds. Once you've selected the background or everything you don't want selected, choose Inverse from the Select menu. Photoshop selects everything that wasn't selected before and deselects everything that was selected. The flat background becomes deselected and the foreground object becomes selected.

The Marquee Tools

Actually two tools are here, the rectangular and elliptical marquees. You can get to them from the Tool options box pop up menu, by Alt/Option-clicking the tool, or by pressing the M key until you get what you want.

Click and drag either of these tools to make a rectangle or ellipse whose upper-left corner (or lower-right corner depending on which way you drag) is the first point you starting dragging from. To start dragging from the center, rather than the corner, hold down the Option key as you drag. This is particularly handy in the case of the oval marquee. Who knows where the upper-left hand corner of a circle is going to fall? To drag out a perfect circle or square, hold down the Shift key.

If you are making selections that need to be a specific size, the Marquee tool options let you set that as well. This way you can select identically sized areas from multiple files. Or you could constrain the size ration of the marquee. We've used both of these when we needed to ghost specifically sized rectangles so that type could be placed over it.

The Lasso

If you've ever used the Lasso, you know it's like drawing with a bowling pin. Why, then, did we list it as the most useful selection tool of the three? Because of the Option key. Before we go much further, let us take a step back and elaborate. The Lasso lets you make a selection by drawing it freehand. You have to go back to the place you started drawing from or the tool will connect the end of your selection with the beginning. It's a messy tool.

But with the Option key down, it becomes much more pleasant. Alt/Option-click to start your selection and let go of the mouse. Don't drag. Just move your cursor. A straight line selection follows you. A few Alt/Option-clicks later and you've got a dandy polygon. Well done old snout!

BASIC MONITOR CALIBRATION

Even if all you're ever going to do in Photoshop is correct grayscale images, you should still do something about monitor calibration. We spoke earlier about the importance of establishing predictable results from a scanner. Getting predictable results from your monitor is equally important if you intend to make any judgments based on the information it's giving you.

You'll notice we said "predictable" results and not "100 percent accurate" results. This is because even with the best of calibrations, it's extremely difficult to reproduce printed materials with transmitted light. Calibration should be used to establish consistency, not to completely predict color. If you can get your monitor looking the same all the time, whether it's right or not, with experience you'll learn to know exactly what you'll see on press. Regardless of what you see on the monitor, your onscreen densitometer, or info box, is your link to the printed world. If you monitor looks purple but your values read 45C, you can bet it will print 45 percent cyan.

The two types of calibration are software calibration and hardware calibration. Software calibration involves adjusting your monitor by making visual choices and using the Gamma Control Panel, which ships with Photoshop (see Figure 10.47). It is difficult, painstaking work, which typically produces mediocre results. Hardware calibration involves sticking a device with a suction cup onto your monitor to measure a light stream. The stream is produced by calibration software, which compares the light the suction cup measured to an internal constant that it generates. It's more expensive, but less work and more accurate.

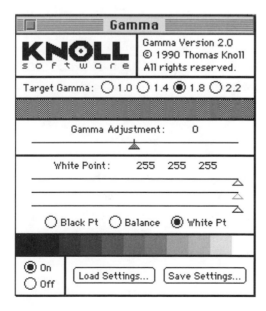

Figure 10.47

Better than nothing? The Gamma Control Panel.

Whichever calibration you want to use, keep a couple of things in mind. One is that having a consistent production environment is vital. If you spend all morning calibrating your system and then the sun comes up shining right on your monitor so you can't see anything, you've wasted your time. The printing industry has established a standard of lighting that defines what sort of lights you should view things under. Having a light box with a standard lighting source eliminates a lot of variables and lets you communicate intelligently with other professionals viewing the same image elsewhere. Keep in mind that the human eye is extremely adaptable and that makes it susceptible to influence by other colors. If your pink walls are tinting the way you see things, get them painted a standardized, neutral color.

The other is that you need to calibrate every couple of days. Your monitor is an unstable thing. That's why you should never calibrate for at least a half hour after you've started up in the morning. Your monitor's colors change quite a bit initially from boot up and then stabilize. Once it has stabilized and is producing a relative constant, you have to assess whether the colors it's producing today are the same as the ones it produced yesterday. Often, they won't be, and you'll need to re-calibrate.

Hardware calibration systems are much more efficient and predictable than software systems. Unfortunately, they are an investment. If you intend to do serious work with color, strongly consider hardware calibration. SuperMatch and Daystar both make fine devices for this purpose. Even if you do buy one, still attend to step one below.

If you want to calibrate with the Gamma Control Panel, here's how to do it.

1. Set your Monitor Set Up Preference in Photoshop. The pop up list of monitor names plugs in numbers for the other values. If your monitor isn't there, find out the information Photoshop requires about your monitor and plug those values in there. The information should be in the literature that came with your monitor. Under Ambient Light, choose what seems appropriate to you. If you are using a hardware calibration, set this to high. It lets the calibration hardware do its job better.

2. Open up a file you have access to all the time. Preferably one with good lights and darks and a range of color. Make sure your desktop pattern is set to a neutral gray. If you want to compare it to a specific gray, make a one pixel by one pixel new file in Photoshop. Dial in the gray value in the color picker that you want to compare (typically a photographic 18 percent neutral swatch), select all and Option-delete the color into place. Copy the pixel and paste it into the desktop patterns control panel.

3. Set your monitor's brightness and contrast where you think it is appropriate. Tape the knobs down so your buddy doesn't come along and prank you. Alternately, turn the brightness and contrast up as far as it will go.

4. Set a base gamma correction. Typically 1.8. Then tweak the gamma by sliding the Gamma Adjustment knob back and forth until the gray bars over it appear the same color if you squint.

5. Get some RC paper and hold it up to your monitor. Select the White Point radio button and slide the red, green, and blue balance sliders until the white in your monitor looks like the white RC paper.

6. Adjust the balance sliders for the Balance to eliminate any cast the monitor may have. Here it will be very helpful to have a real life neutral wedge to compare to. You should have one anyway. Go buy one.

Save your settings and include the date in the name. Check it again in a couple of days.

SUMMARY

Scanning line art and halftones for printing may seem a daunting enterprise at first, but it's really not that complicated. The keys to good reproduction on press lie in solid information about the final purpose of the scan up front and a clear plan of the steps to get there. Keep notes of the steps you took and the tools you used. Focus on the printability of your image, and maintaining a reproductive connection to the original piece. Tone, detail, and sharpness are the key elements by which to judge your halftones.

The more complicated world of color reproduction is grounded in the same core issues that govern halftone reproduction. The notes that you made during your work with halftones will help inform your understanding of a four-color environment. Keep these issues at hand as we explore color during the next two chapters.

COLOR SPACES AND PRINTING

The junior art director was livid. He had worked for days specifying exactly how everything should look at the annual exhibition invitation and this just wasn't it. It was his first major piece for the company and it would be under a lot of scrutiny. He was looking at a proof that bore little or no resemblance to what he saw on the monitor and he was running out of time. The subtle grace of the cover photograph was running three steps toward neon and the impressionists all looked like fauves. He had relied on his monitor to tell him how things would print and he had gotten burned. Now the proofing tech at the prepress house was getting an earful of grief that he owned no part of.

The problem of color on press is endemic to the industry. The equation is further complicated by digital technology. Color, as we'll see, isn't *just* color. It's a physical phenomenon and, as such, is very dependent on the circumstances in which it occurs. Color on a monitor is made differently than color on a printed page. Therefore, it behaves differently and we need to treat it differently as well.

To make matters worse, everyone sees color differently and nobody sees it the way a computer does. The same swatch of ink can also look different under different lighting conditions and even more different when it's next to other colors. Clearly, the issue of color imaging is geometrically more complicated than the issues associated with halftones.

In this section, we'll look at the following:

- The different ways Photoshop has to think about color

- The relationship between the RGB and CMYK color spaces

- How to separate for specific press conditions

- The variables that interfere with our reproduction of color

- Why the same color looks different under different lights

UNDERSTANDING COLOR

The first thing to think about is color itself. Color, simply put, is a form of light energy that comes in waves. The vibrations of the waves can be measured and the size of the wavelength is related to its appearance. Some wavelengths can't be seen by the human eye. Some, like infrared light, are too long to be detected. Others, like X rays, are too short to be seen. The rest make up the visual spectrum we all learned about in ninth grade physics. The visual spectrum is a continuous one, but for convenience, it is divided into red, orange, yellow, green, blue, indigo, and violet. The most dominant colors in the spectrum are red, green, and blue.

Color as Physical Phenomenon

Different colors are created when light waves combine. Wavelengths of certain frequencies combine and create the experience we view as color. White light is a combination of all the colors we can see. Non-luminous objects, like paper or ink, have no actual color but appear to when light hits them. Part of the light wavelength is absorbed by the material, changing the wave, and the rest bounces off. In the case of transparent materials, like slides, light is filtered rather than absorbed. In both cases though, the change in the combination of the wavelengths results in the color experience. Given this, differences in the light that strike the attenuating object can strongly impact the resulting color wave and hence, our experience of the object's color. If two waves of light (with different wavelengths) strike the same color swatch, a constant wave portion is absorbed, but since the waves were different to begin with, the resulting color is different. This is why the same image can appear very different under different lighting conditions (see Figure 11.1).

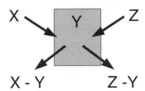

Figure 11.1

The content of light affects what we see.

Try this for yourself. Look at a box of Wheaties carefully in the shopping center and then inspect it again when you take it home. The light in the supermarket and the light at your home are comprised of different combinations of light energy. The cereal box remains constant but appears differently in each circumstance because the light has changed. Light X minus Y is different from Light Z minus Y.

For the purposes of eliminating such variables, you can measure the temperature of light to obtain a standardized constant. The temperature of light is measured in a scale whose units are called degrees Kelvin. This temperature scale is much broader in scope than the ones we're used to dealing with. Zero degrees Kelvin (-273° C) is thought to be absolute zero, the point at which molecules stop moving. The temperature of light ranges between 1900K for candle flames and 7500K for bright daylight. The standard lighting for viewing color is 5000K. You sometimes hear people referring to 50K lighting conditions—this is what they mean. Ideally, everyone involved in making decisions about color should be viewing things under these same lighting conditions. This way the color correction pro at the prepress house and the designer in his studio can look at the same proof with fewer variables impeding their communication and understanding of color.

If light is so important to color, why not proof printing jobs under the conditions the materials will be viewed in? Why not proof materials destined for the supermarket under yellow florescent lights or magazine covers under daylight? The problem is one of standard. Would the lighting standard for supermarkets take into account different light bulbs? What about ceiling height? What about when the Wheaties come home? The task of reproducing lighting conditions for every possible viewing scenario would be monumental and counter productive. Better to rely on an industry standard that is optimal for viewing what's actually in the image and adjusting as situations warrant.

Our understanding of color is contextual not only with regard to the lighting environment it's placed in, but also the colors that surround it (see Figure 11.2). The perception of color and its values are influenced by the colors surrounding it. This further complicates the problem of color correction and should be accounted for when the job is prepared. This is one of the reasons to proof entire pages rather than simply the images appearing on them. Their appearance may be affected by other design elements on the page.

Figure 11.2

Colors affect our perception of other colors around them (see color insert).

The human eye's physiological structure is geared toward red, green, and blue. Different types of cones inside your eye are more receptive to either red, green, or blue light. Light hits the cones, which triggers an neural response understood in the brain as color. Slight, genetic differences in these microscopic cones explain why two people can look at the same color and each see it differently.

Color as Experience

People also understand color differently for any number of psychological reasons. Color information is a strong part of our emotional association fields. We all tie ideas and subconscious feelings to a variety of resonant touchstones. Studies show that people's overall mood and perception of events can be affected by the colors of their surroundings. People are soothed by some colors and jarred by others. If you ask most people their favorite color, they'll tell you it's a shade of blue. Blue is peace, wisdom, and depth, but the intonation we apply to blue affects its perception. Blue can denote beatitude, but it can also suggest depression. The soft values we associate with colors temper our perception of them.

Because color plays such a strong role in memory, the memory of color itself is also important. When you view colors you've seen before, you tend to accept the color as a proxy for the color in your brain and mentally fill in the blank spaces. You "see" the color by remembering a different color. If color isn't reasonably close to what you expect of it, though, it can completely wreck the illusion of photography. If the sky doesn't look like the sky, everything about the image is wrong and the job will surely be rejected. These colors are called memory colors and they'll be important ones to attend to when you get down to the business of color correction.

The human eye can detect an amazing amount of light energy, but what happens to it from there is a matter of physio-psychology and not necessarily color science. Societal pressures influence your understanding of color as well. Different countries have different cultural references and expectations of color than we do in the US. Different locations have different sets of printing inks to work with that shape the range of colors they produce. Other countries even use a different type of light as a standard for viewing proofs and photographs. Color is very much a personal experience, complicating the task of assessing and correcting it.

Color in the Digital Workflow

Another inevitable variable in the digital color process is the monitor. In the case of most monitors, a cathode ray tube is used to beam light at glass that has been coated with fluorescent phosphors. Different colors are produced when the charged electrons the CRT shoots out hit the phosphors at different speeds. The impact excites the phosphors and they happily vibrate and glow. The speed of their vibrations determines the color of the glow they produce. This sounds neat but has some inherent flaws.

- ◆ The mechanics and content of the phosphors create inherent color flaws.

- ◆ The high color temperature of the monitor is near the blue end of the color spectrum and tends to give things a bluish cast.

- The curve of the monitor glass tends to create viewing and color abnormalities.

- The differing charges of the electrons involved can lead to monitor misregistration and an overall lack of sharpness.

- The instability of the system overall creates unwanted color shifts during both the working day and life of a monitor.

It should be noted that this description applies to CRT monitors, the kind that are used almost exclusively in production environments. Other monitors, which use the flatter LED technology, are on the way as well. This may spell change for the industry.

TWO VITAL COLOR MODES

Color, light, and what happens when light energy hits inks have been discussed. We've alluded to a fundamental difference between two forms of color: color that is transmitted, like light from a monitor, and color that is reflected, like light bouncing off paper. The two types are different and at the same time related. You need to understand them both to work correctly with scans (transmitted light) to produce images for press (reflected light).

Tone

To understand both types, another issue needs to be elaborated on: tone. When we talked about grayscale, we talked about the tones that composed the image. What we mean is the lights and darks of the image. A grayscale environment is made up of only one color, which has areas that are relatively lighter and darker from each other. Grayscale images, essentially, only have tone (for more on grayscale images and halftones, see Chapter 10).

Color has tone, too. Regardless of what the actual color looks like, it has relative lightness or darkness associated with it (see Figure 11.3). Two colors that appear very different can still register with the same tonal value. Tone gives color shape and definition.

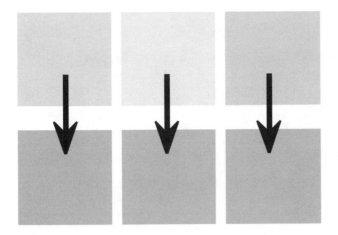

Figure 11.3

Very different colors can have the same tone (see color insert).

Brightness

The difference between the lightest and the darkest areas of the image are its tonal range. In PostScript, the language that describes all this to an output device, you are limited to 256 tonal steps for any given color. These 256 steps correspond to eight bits of color. Each step is given a numerical value that measures the amount of brightness the pixel has. A value of zero, or no brightness, is black. A value of 255 is extremely bright, or white (see Figure 11.4). The lower the number, the darker the tone of the pixel. When you add more light, the pixel becomes lighter.

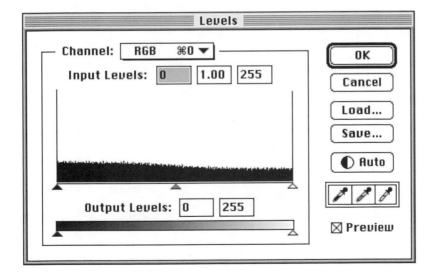

Figure 11.4

Brightness is measured on a scale of 256 step scale.

Ink

This is exactly the opposite of what happens when you add ink. When we talk about what a pixel will look like printed, we often think in terms of ink percentages. Ink is typically measured on a scale of 0 percent (no ink) to 100 percent (complete coverage). As you add ink, the image becomes darker (see Figure 11.5)

Figure 11.5

Ink is measured in percentages from 0 percent to 100 percent.

Brightness and RGB

When we think about transmitted light, we think about red, green, and blue. Since this is the same combination your eyes are built to see, red, green, and blue can produce almost all visible colors. It would be possible by introducing another base color to the RGB system to produce even more color combinations, but the gains would be slight compared to the cost expenditure that would be required.

RGB light is measured using the 256 step tonal scale. Each of the three channels is assigned a value to describe its tone. A value of zero would still correspond to no light, but a value of 255 for any given channel would refer to pure red, green, or blue light. Levels of 255 for all three would combine to make white light. A value of 255 for red and zero for green and blue emulates pure red light.

Because in the RGB world we're combining light, it's thought of as an additive color model. Adding light produces color. We're building up from black, or no light, to some color, which is measured in the units of light it took to produce it. Scanners measure images in RGB, monitors display images in RGB.

Ink and CMYK

When we think about printing colors, though, we focus on the combination of inks used to produce the color on press. The combinations of red, green, and blue produce the greatest combination of colors from the fewest base colors in the world of transmitted light. In photographs, another trichromatic system is used. This time cyan, magenta, and yellow dyes are used on film. Controlling the intensities of each produces new colors. On press, however, a fourth color is required. The combination of cyan, magenta, yellow, and black is used. Without the additional black plate, colors look muddy and insubstantial. Black increases the density, contrast, and tonal range of the image, producing a much more pleasing result on press.

Keep in mind that when you're talking about printed color, all sorts of real-world logistics enter the equation. Even though you've added a printing plate and helped your density, you still have considerably smaller total color possibilities in this model. You simply can't print all the colors in the visible spectrum with the four process colors.

Reflected light is measured in terms of the inks that are required to produce a color. Typically this is cyan, magenta, yellow, and black or CMYK. K stands for black in this acronym. A given pixel has a value expressed as a percentage of ink for each of the four inks. The scale for CMYK is 0 percent to 100 percent rather than 255 to 0.

The RGB and CMYK Relationship

In the case of printing, you start with the white, transmitted light and subtract part of its wavelength, which is absorbed into the dyes. The more ink you have, the more light is absorbed and the darker the resulting reflected color becomes. This is thought of as a subtractive color model. You start with white light and subtract out parts by adding inks.

The two color models appear to be very different from each other but are actually the inverse of each other. When you view them keeping in mind what you know about how light produces color, it all makes perfect sense. Light, which can be described as a combination of red, green, and blue, strikes a swatch of color, which can be described as a combination of the inks it took to print it. Part of the wavelength is absorbed and you see it in reflection (see Figure 11.6).

Figure 11.6

Red, green, and blue light combine to form light. CMYK inks subtract light.

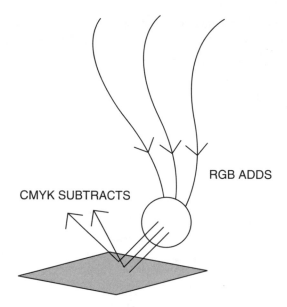

CMYK SUBTRACTS

RGB ADDS

Because the two color models are the opposite of each other, they have a relationship. The relationship isn't perfectly inverse, but it's close enough to be informative. When you combine any two RGB colors, you get a CMY color. When you combine any two CMY colors, you get an RGB color. The relationship is described by an informative color wheel (see Figure 11.7). On the wheel, color is arranged as RGB color, CMY color, RGB color, and CMY color. Each color on the wheel can be described in the opposing model as a combination of the colors on either side of it. So, for example, red can be described in a CMY model by combining yellow and magenta. Magenta can be built in RGB by combining red and blue, the colors on either side of it.

Figure 11.7

The color wheel describes the relationship between RGB and CMYK.

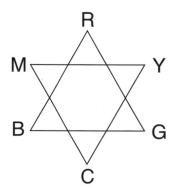

Complementary Colors

The color that does not contribute to the creation of a color is that color's opposite. In the case of red, both yellow and magenta contribute to create red. The remaining CMY color, cyan, is the opposite of red. Opposing colors are arranged opposite each other on the color wheel and are referred to as *complementary colors* (see Figure 11.8).

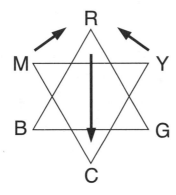

Figure 11.8

Yellow and magenta combine to form red. Cyan is not used and is therefore the complement of red.

Knowing a color's complement can be useful in the scanning of an object. Let's say you're scanning an element that is too yellow. You'd like to use your scanning software to push the yellow back. Unfortunately, no yellow color controls are on an RGB scanner, only red, green, and blue. What should you do? You have two choices. Yellow is a combination of red and green. Decreasing them is the same as decreasing yellow. On the other hand, the opposite of yellow, its complementary color, is blue. If you increase blue in the image, you're also decreasing yellow. Of these two choices, it may be smarter to try to pull out color before you push in color. Complementary colors are important to the tone and sharpness of an image.

COLORS, COMPONENTS, AND COMPLEMENTS

Color	Components	Complement
Red	Yellow + Magenta	Cyan
Blue	Magenta + Cyan	Yellow
Green	Cyan + Yellow	Magenta
Magenta	Red + Blue	Green
Cyan	Blue + Green	Red
Yellow	Green + Red	Blue

Keep in mind that this model doesn't address the black printer in the CMYK model. It also assumes a four-color printing model. It is increasingly common to print with more than four colors. Special, additional colors can be added to create specific, richer visual effects. This could take the form of printing the black plate twice to add depth or printing with a combination of spot and process inks. The technology also exists, although not widely in use, to convert files from RGB into six colors rather than the traditional four. As exciting as these processes are, understanding the basics of the RGB and CMYK models is vital to working professionally with color.

Transiting Color Spaces

When you move from RGB to CMYK, a number of things happen. If you don't take control of them, they'll be decided for you. This can result in disappointing results on press.

Gamut Differences

The RGB spectrum is broader than the CMYK spectrum. Simply more colors are in the RGB space than can be expressed with the CMYK inks. In Photoshop's densitometers (in the Color Picker and Info palette), you will be warned with an exclamation point if the color you are requesting in an RGB format is unavailable in CMYK (see Figure 11.9). If you are working in RGB, you can also select Gamut Warning from the Mode menu. This doesn't change the color information but warns you of unprintable RGB combinations by coloring pixels that contain those colors with a warning color. The Gamut Warning color is a preference you set by choosing File: Preferences: Gamut Warning (see Figure 11.10).

Figure 11.9

The gamut alarm warns you with an exclamation point when you're measuring a color that can't be reproduced in CMYK.

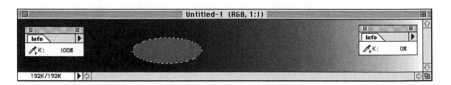

```
Mode
  Bitmap
  Grayscale
  Duotone
  Indexed Color...
✓ RGB Color
  CMYK Color
  Lab Color
  Multichannel

  Color Table...

  CMYK Preview
✓ Gamut Warning
```

Figure 11.10

The Gamut Warning paints out of gamut RGB colors with an odd display.

The sad fact that the RGB spectrum is larger than the CMYK spectrum means you really only get one chance to move between color spaces. When you convert from RGB to CMYK, you ask Photoshop to describe the former RGB pixels with a combination of CMYK information based on information you give Photoshop about what you'll do with this file. Doing so tosses out information. Converting back won't give the pixels the RGB colors they once had. It simply asks Photoshop to describe the new CMYK-colored pixels with RGB information. The change has happened and you can't get it back (see Figure 11.11).

Vital Separation Preferences

Making the actual change to CMYK color is as easy as choosing it from the Mode menu. However, you need to take a series of steps before you do that and failing to do so may result in unexpected printed results. Basically, you need to address three areas to convert to CMYK correctly for a specific purpose: which colors Photoshop references when it refers to RGB, which inks Photoshop is trying to describe when it refers to CMYK, and how the CMYK piece will be printed. All of these concepts are controlled by Preferences, located under the File menu, which you need to set before you convert from RGB to CMYK. All three preferences are important to the correct generation of color. Careful attention should be paid them.

The Island of Lost Colors

What happens to the colors that CMYK can't describe? The answer is an unfortunate one. The colors are clipped. That is to say, Photoshop converts the intense RGB colors to the closest CMYK color it can. It just takes all the colors that fall outside of its range and pushes them to the borderline. This means two different RGB colors can translate to the same CMYK color. All the difference is gone.

Figure 11.11

Converting to CMYK destroys information you can't get back.

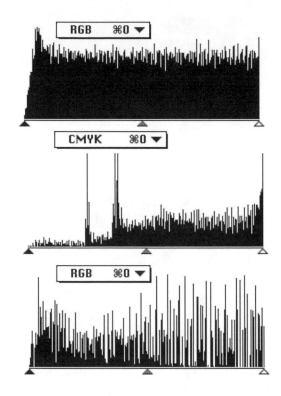

The Conversion Question

Before you push those buttons, the question of when to convert to CMYK should be given a little attention. We've said the RGB spectrum is larger than CMYK. From this, you might infer that doing all your corrections in RGB gives you greater flexibility. This is true. It's also true that working in CMYK is a little slower than working in RGB. Every time Photoshop shows you a CMYK color, it first has to translate that into RGB because that's

Monitor Setup

The preference that controls which colors Photoshop references when it refers to RGB is Monitor Setup (see Figure 11.12). You need to set this preference once and then leave it alone. As long as you don't change monitors, you don't need to change Monitor Setup. Monitor Setup establishes a reference basis to inform Photoshop about the RGB you're looking at on your monitor and what happens to color when you change modes. This preference doesn't change how RGB information is displayed, but it does change how CMYK (and Lab color) are displayed on your RGB monitor. It also changes the values generated when you move from an RGB to a CMYK color space. The idea is that Photoshop is trying to determine what colors you're looking at and, hence, what colors you're trying to reproduce in a CMYK space. Try it yourself by building an RGB file and filling it with some colors. Then duplicate the file by choosing Image: Duplicate. Convert the first one to CMYK, change the Monitor Setup values, and then convert the duplicate file to CMYK. The RGB information you saw stays the same when you changed the Monitor Setup values, but the CMYK information generated is different.

To set your Monitor Setup, first look at the Monitor pop up list. This list has preset values for the three Monitor Parameters settings. If your monitor is on the list, choose it. It will load the preset values. If your monitor isn't listed but one that's similar is, choose that one. If you still don't have one listed, the values for the Monitor Parameters settings are probably listed in the literature that came with your monitor.

The values for Monitor Parameters from the Monitor Setup Preference are Gamma, White Point, and Phosphors. Gamma is , essentially, an overall correction to the monitors contrast. If you're doing print work, set it at 1.8. If you're doing multimedia, a higher correction value, say 2.0 or 2.2, may be appropriate. The Ambient Light setting, also in the Monitor Setup preference, makes a slight adjustment to this value. The idea is to enable you to compensate for environmental changes without changing your entire Monitor Setup. Setting this to High causes no change at all. Setting this to Low lightens your image slightly upon conversion compared to the High setting. Generally, we set it to High and then calibrate our monitors without Photoshop's interference. If you're using a hardware calibration, you definitely want to do this.

all your monitor can show you. That translation process slows things down a bit. Both are valid reasons to work in RGB.

In practice, however, people tend to correct in CMYK. No disappointment is greater than color correcting your file to perfection, then converting to CMYK, and having all your colors shift, typically becoming duller. Almost as validly, it's much harder to think in RGB. If we asked for a color that was 45 percent cyan and 10 percent black, most people would know what we meant. On the other hand, 124 red, 193 green, and 220 blue doesn't exactly sing to the masses. In our work, we like to split the difference. We make our bulk corrections and adjustments in RGB. Then we fine tune and target for printing in CMYK. We get the speed and color depth of RGB and aren't often unpleasantly surprised by what we see in CMYK.

Earlier we talked about the Kelvin scale used to measure the temperature of light. The values you see under White Point are also in that scale. The White Point value setting essentially says, "what do the whites in your monitor look like?" If you're working with standard lighting, dial the temperature of the lights you're working under into that field. Typically, the standard in the US is 5000K.

The Phosphors setting asks what kind of chemicals coat your monitor glass. It's important because it determines what the most saturated red, green, and blues look like. Set this to the kind your monitor uses and let it be.

Figure 11.12

Photoshop's Monitor Setup preference.

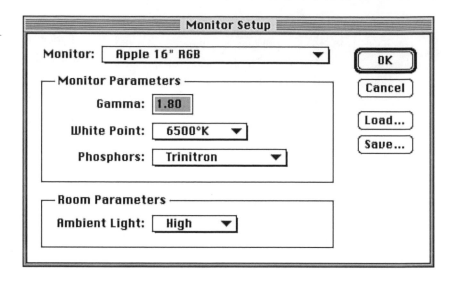

Printing Inks Setup

The Preference that establishes a description of the CMYK colors Photoshop generates is the Printing Inks Setup preference (see Figure 11.13). This affects the values that are generated when a conversion from RGB to CMYK is made. It also plays a hand in how CMYK images are displayed. Recall that regardless of what type of file you're working on, your monitors display things in RGB. When a CMYK image is displayed on an RGB monitor, Photoshop first consults the Printing Inks Setup box to see what kind of inks the CMYK values refer to and then looks at the Monitor Setup preference to figure out how to display those images.

Ink Colors

The first field to be set in Printing Inks Setup is the Ink Colors pop up menu. This gives Photoshop a model of what the inks you intend to print with look like. In all likelihood, you'll be using one of the SWOP (Specifications for Web Offset Printing) sets. It's the most common set of inks in the US. Choose the one that matches how you intend to be printing: coated, uncoated, or newsprint. The Toyo set is Japanese and the Eurostandard is European. You should find out if your printer is using one of these sets. If this is the case, you also need to be careful about where your proofs are generated.

Correcting from a proof based on the SWOP set and then printing in Toyo is mostly just guesswork. The preparation just can't anticipate the reality of the situation.

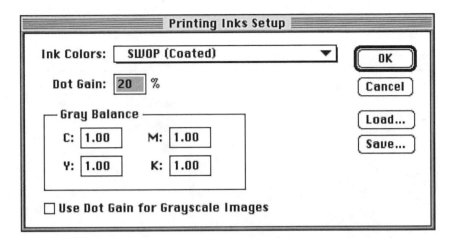

Figure 11.13

The Printing Inks Setup preference.

Nonstandard Printing Inks

A more likely but equally disruptive possibility is the case of printers not printing with the standard process inks. The last time we saw this was a case in which a newspaper was printing with a spot red color instead of magenta in its separations. The red gave them a richer, snappier look than magenta would have if it alone were used for headlines or rules. It was economical and expedient for them to continue to use that red in their separations. The problem, of course, is that separations made for CMYK will print like who-knows-what without CMYK inks.

If this is happening, you need to let Photoshop know ahead of time. The best way to do this is to print some test bars without changing your Separation Setup. Measure the swatches you get with a colorimeter. Choose Custom from the Ink Colors pop up list and then enter the Yxy values for the substituted ink that you got from your densitometer.

If the substitute ink you're working with is a PANTONE color, you could also do one of the following things. Find out the Yxy values for the color. Pantone's color driver software has this information as do several other sources. You could also open the color in Photoshop's Color Picker (see Figure 11.14). Simply go to the Color Picker, select custom and then dial in the PANTONE number you want. From there, choose Picker (see Figure 11.15). This gives you the Lab values for the PANTONE color in question. Write those numbers down. (Lab color is also explained in more detail later in this chapter).

Figure 11.14

Photoshop's Custom colors from the Color Picker.

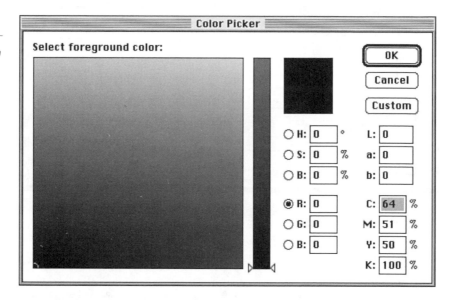

After you have the Lab colors of the PANTONE color, go back to the Printing Inks Setup preference. Click the swatch of the color you intend to replace. There's the Color Picker again. Enter the Lab numbers of the replacement color for the old process color. Save the Preference so that you don't have to do this work again. Make new separations and print the result.

Gray Balance Defined

If you are printing with a nonstandard ink, you'll also have to make some adjustment to the Gray Balance of your inks. Conveniently, this is also located in the Printing Inks Setup.

The first, essential question to ask is what actually is Gray Balance? It refers to the combinations of colors that produce gray. When you mix red, green, and blue colors in like amounts, the resulting color is a gray (see Figure 11.16). Brightness values of 200 red, 200 green, and 200 blue are the same as 25 percent gray. Remember that the brightness and ink percentages are on inverse scales. Grays are referred to as neutrals. The implication is that they are uninfluenced by any one color more than another. If you mix 210 red, 200 green, and 200 blue, the result is a warmer gray. It still looks gray, but it is no longer a neutral. It has become influenced more strongly by a given color and is said to have a color cast.

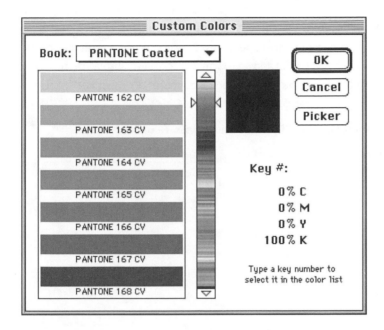

Figure 11.15

Selecting Picker from the Custom Colors displays the associated Lab colors.

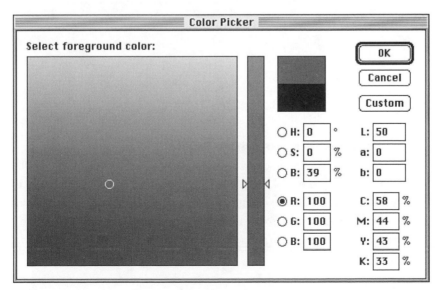

Figure 11.16

Equal amounts of red, green, and blue make gray.

When you move into the printed world of CMYK, things don't work so neatly. Equal amounts of cyan, yellow, and magenta don't result in a neutral. They produce a lighter, muddier gray than a true neutral. This is caused by the impurities of the inks involved. To get a solid neutral in the CMYK space, you need to increase the cyan component of the color. In the same way that blue flecks in detergent make it appear cleaner and whiter, extra cyan helps the other two colors become cleaner and crisper. Twenty-five percent cyan, 16 percent magenta, and 16 percent yellow adds up to a neutral 25 percent gray. The CMY values that add up to gray are constants and can be charted (see the table below). Photoshop understands this relationship and behaves accordingly when it transfers RGB color into CMYK color.

COMBINATIONS OF CMY INK PERCENTAGES THAT EQUAL GRAY

Cyan +	Magenta +	Yellow =	Black
5	3	3	5
10	6	6	10
20	13	13	20
25	16	16	25
30	21	21	30
40	29	29	40
50	37	37	50
60	46	46	60
75	63	63	75
80	71	71	80
90	82	82	90
95	87	87	95

Nonstandard (process) Inks and Gray Balance

This brings us back to the case of what to do if you're not printing with the standard inks. Different inks combine in different ways and there's nothing to say that a PANTONE color mixes to form gray in the same way a process color does. The Gray Balance boxes in the Printing Inks Setup preference let us adjust how this happens. First, you need information about what your inks actually do.

Build a file like the one in Figure 11.17 and print it with your nonstandard inks. In the boxes, cyan remains constant in the swatches although yellow and magenta vary in small amounts across each row and column. Compare the CMY swatches with the black swatches and find the CMY swatch that matches it. This gives you the value combinations that produce a neutral with your nonstandard inks.

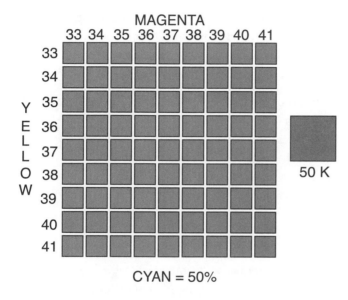

Figure 11.17

Printing test swatches isolates the correct combination of colors that produce a neutral (see color insert).

Go back into Photoshop and create an RGB file with neutral swatches of the same values as the ones in the test. Set your info palette to display RGB and CMYK color values. The CMYK values you see are the ones you'd get if you converted to CMYK with your current Printing Inks Setup. Increasing the value of an individual ink in the Gray Balance box from the Printing Inks Setup increases the amount of that ink created in the conversion process. Decreasing that number decreases the generation. The idea is to nudge these numbers up or down as needed until the swatch, which you know is neutral, converts to a CMYK combination that prints a neutral with your nonstandard inks. For instance, if you know that on your press 25 percent cyan, 18 percent magenta, and 16 percent yellow produce a neutral, rather than the typical 25 cyan, 16 magenta, and 16 yellow, you should increase the magenta number until you see those numbers for CMYK when you measure your neutral swatch. Save your results so that you never have to do this again.

Using Gray Balance to compensate for nonstandard inks is really the only use for this setting. The only other case where it may be required is if your imagesetter is producing a consistent, identifiable cast that isn't being caused by anything you can correct any other way, which is almost never.

Printing Inks and Dot Gain

The remaining field in Printing Inks Setup is Dot Gain. We talked about dot gain in some detail in Chapter 10. It's the propensity of ink spots to increase in size on press as ink is absorbed into paper. Other things cause dot gain as well, but absorbency is the most common. Because the size of the dot is really its tone, larger dots than you requested means a darker image than you wanted.

Dot gain is the biggest problem in the midtones. There the balance between the dot's size and the white space around it is the most delicate. The values Photoshop gives for dot gain, refer directly to the midtone dot. The value it's giving you is the strict additive value of what it expects will happen to the midtone dot on press. A 20-percent dot gain means that a midtone dot will print at 70 percent. A 10-percent gain means that a 50-percent dot will print at 60 percent. Photoshop automatically adjusts for this gain when it separates, but you need to find out what sort of gain is anticipated on press and set this value into the Preference before you convert to CMYK. It won't do anything to existing CMYK information. It's important that when you talk to your printer you're talking about the same thing. Make sure that the dot gain the printer's talking about is what happens to the 50 percent dot between film and press, not between proof and press.

Dot Gain and Grayscale

The final setting in the Printing Inks Setup preference is the Use Dot Gain for Grayscale Images. Checking this only changes how grayscale files are displayed, not how they're printed. The image information stays exactly the same. The idea is that if you're using a calibrated monitor to make your correcting decisions, selecting this gives you a better idea what your image will look like on press. Knowing this gives you a better opportunity to correct it visually. The problem with this preference, though, is that the results tend to be unpredictable. Depending on how your other Preferences are set, it may actually lighten the image rather than darken it. This can be confusing. We've found it useful in cases where we're printing to newsprint and are experiencing large dot gains. Even then, it should be thought of only as a reference guide, not as gospel.

Separation Setup

The final preference for color separation is a big one. Separation Setup controls not only how much ink is printed on press, but also how black is created (see Figure 11.18). Setting this correctly is vital to getting good color on press. It's also a setting that may require some real world testing and evaluation to fine tune its use. We'll go over the concepts involved here and include some typical settings. Keep in mind the principles involved as you put them into practice and let the printing conditions you work under be your guide.

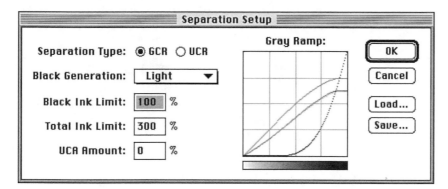

The first issue you have to address here is ink coverage. Certain printing conditions can only support so much ink on paper. If too much ink is placed, it causes problems. Ink doesn't dry correctly as it's being printed. It can cause paper to stick together or it can fly off the cylinder and make a mess. Total ink coverage is measured on a scale of 0 percent to 400 percent. One hundred percent of all four printing inks would be 400 percent. This presupposes a four-color print job. The amount of ink that can be held is a factor of the speed, the kind of the press, and the quality of the printing substrate. In almost no case are presses capable of holding a full 400-percent ink coverage. Usually, the numbers tend to run from around 260 percent for newsprint to 350 percent for high-quality sheet fed presses.

So the problem we have is getting rich, vivid colors on press while limiting the amount of ink we print with. Black to the rescue. Back when we were talking about the Printing Inks Setup, we introduced the concept of Gray Balance and here it is again. The idea is that certain combinations of ink together produce gray. Given this, you can print with black instead of those colors. If you have an area colored with 50 percent cyan, 37 percent yellow, and 37 percent magenta, in principle, it's the same as printing with 50 percent black (see Figure 11.19). Instead of putting down 124 percent total ink (50 percent + 37 percent + 37 percent), we just put down 50 percent.

Take that idea a step further and you can remove the elements of a color that add up to black and leave the rest behind. If your color were 60 percent cyan, 37 percent yellow, and 40 percent magenta, you could print 10 percent cyan, 3 percent magenta, and 50 percent black (see Figure 11.20). The elements of the color that were black (50 percent cyan, 37 percent yellow and 37 percent magenta) are replaced by the black plate and the remaining color parts would print on their own plates.

Figure 11.19

Combinations of ink that produce neutrals can be substituted with black ink.

Figure 11.20

The black portion of a color may also be substituted with black ink.

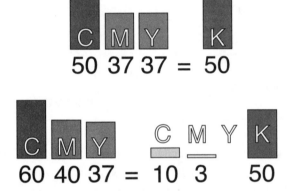

The downside is that the more color you replace with black, the less color you have to work with. Shadows can look flat and lifeless while images with little color components are harder to color correct. Fortunately, you're given some choices about how and when you swap color for black.

UCR

The first choice controls the circumstances under which you generate black. The two options for this are GCR (Gray Component Replacement) and UCR (Under Color Removal). The reason that UCR is called under color *removal* is that color is literally being removed from under a gray area. In an under color removal scheme, cyan, yellow, and magenta are only replaced with black in neutral areas. Places that are already a shade of gray are now just printed with a gray ink. This mostly removes a lot of ink in the shadows but keeps the rest of the image full of CMY color. Because of this, UCR schemes are sometimes thought of as harder to control on press.

GCR

Gray Component Replacement, on the other hand, replaces color with black everywhere it can. It's a more powerful and more destructive tool. Because of this, Photoshop gives you some controls to limit and mitigate its effects. The first of these is Black Generation, which enables you to limit tonally which pixels are allowed to have black substitution take place in them. The human eye, being designed to work mostly in the daytime, is much better at seeing things between the 0 percent and 50 percent tonal range. It's beneficial to have the lighter colors in this tonal range less corrupted with black. Black Generation gives you the power to control that.

Black Generation

The settings for this Black Generation determine where tonally black generation can begin. Along with the other fields in this box, it determines the shape of the black generation curve. A light setting sets the start point for black, sometimes called the black highlight, at 40 percent. This means that values tonally below 40 percent don't experience black substitution. To get a more intuitive idea of what is actually happening to color where, build yourself a little test.

1. Make a new, rectangular RGB Photoshop file.

2. Set the foreground and background colors black and white by clicking the default colors icon.

3. Use the Gradient tool to drag a gray wedge from one side of the file to the other. Holding the Shift key down constrains the wedge to a 90° angle.

4. Set your Info palette to display CMYK values.

Running your cursor along the wedge shows what you'd get if you converted to CMYK with your current Separation Setup. Notice that with a Light Generation Setup, you don't begin to see black in the separation until about 40 percent (see Figure 11.21). If you choose Medium, Heavy, or Maximum from the pop-up list, you'll begin to generate black more and more liberally.

Figure 11.21

Using a Light Separation Setup prevents black from being substituted for color in the light part of the tonal range. No black is generated until the 40 percent tones.

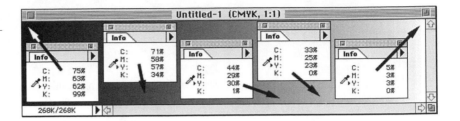

The black highlights for each setting are:

None...	No black is created, resulting in a CMY image.
Light	40%
Medium	20%
Heavy	10%
Maximum	0% Black is substituted for color everywhere.

Customizing a Black Generation Curve

Photoshop also offers you the option of writing your own black generation curve. Choose Custom from the Black Generation pop up list. The chart's current settings are the ones from the last setting you chose. Be careful here, black plays a strong role in how your image looks on press. The Custom Black curve works the same as the Curves box when it's set for ink. Changing the shape of the curve affects which tones and to what extent black can be substituted for color. It's essentially gamma. Input is charted against output, in this case black generation along the vertical axis. The horizontal input axis refers to tone. Typically, this will be driven by cyan.

You can use this curve effectively for several uses. If your printer asks for a skeleton black (a very light black plate), you can write a curve that produces even less black than the light setting. More commonly, though, you can use black generation to assist high or low key images. Problems in photographing or image content may produce images that are extremely light or dark. Very light images overall, the polar bear in a snowstorm, are said to be high key while very dark ones, the black cat at night, are said to be low key. These images, in addition to being difficult to scan correctly, also create problems with black generation. Low key images tend to generate a lot of black, further darkening their tones. High key images, with very little color, tend to produce very little color. These sorts of originals can be assisted by customizing black generation.

In the case of low key images, the black highlight may start higher along the curve, perhaps at 50–55 percent (see Figure 11.22). Extremely low key images may also want an adjustment made to the black midtone. Pulling 10 percent out assists in normalizing very dark images. The high key images, on the other hand, could stand to have a little more black buoying them up. Try starting with a medium generation curve (black highlight = 20 percent) and nudging it up from there to a 30 percent highlight. Very high key images may also need an increase in the black midtone size (see Figure 11.23).

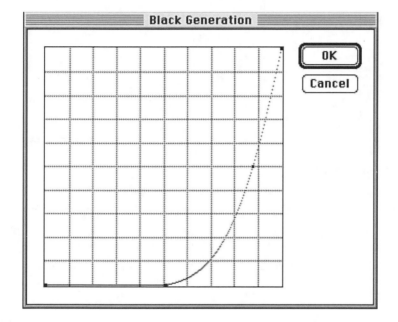

Figure 11.22

Adjusting the black highlight of a low key image.

Black Ink Limit

The next field that influences the shape of the black generation curve is Black Ink Limit. Simply put, it's the darkest black value of black you'll allow in the shadows. Just as Black Generation established the highlight dot for black, Black Ink Limit sets the shadow dot for the black printer. In cases where you'll be limiting the Total Ink, you may also want to reduce the black end point. Your options here should be driven by the limits your printer has for the black plate. If they don't know, try setting it conservatively at, for instance, 85 percent and then nudging it up. To keep your options open, leave the limit at 100 percent. You can always reduce black in color correction. Typical separation values are listed in the *Typical RGB to CMYK Separation Setups by Printing Type* table below.

Figure 11.23

Adjusting the black highlight of a high key image.

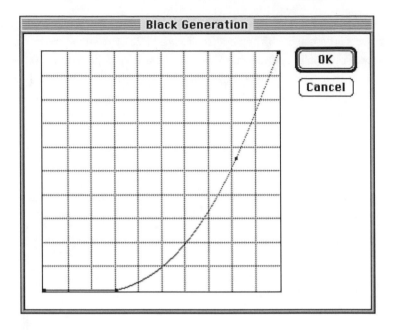

Total Ink Limit

Total Ink Limit sets, as you might expect, the upper limit of all the ink that can be laid down on press. This is determined by the kind of printer you intend to print with and the substrate you'll be working with. In principle, more ink yields a better image. More ink also has problems associated with it. Ink trapping and drying can be a problem and can show through. Most printers know how much ink their press can hold. If you're not sure where and how an image will be printed, try dialing in an average, utilitarian setting, like 280 percent total ink. In cases like this where you're limiting total ink, it might be smart to limit the black to 90 percent or so.

Under Color Addition

The final setting from the Separation Setup preference is UCA (under color addition). Like Black Generation, it's only available for GCR schemes. When you substitute lots of black for color, you run the risk of flattening out your shadows and losing detail. Under Color Addition puts some color back under the neutral shadow areas to help compensate for this. UCA only adds a little color, so you still keep the benefits of reduced ink overall. UCA only affects neutrals and even at the maximum setting only affects the darker half of the gray ramp. Typically, a small amount of UCA is all that is required, perhaps 10 percent.

Printing Inks Setup and Separation Setup should be set every time a new output source is considered. Photoshop enables you to bundle these two preferences together into a Separation Table. Simply set the two preferences for a given printing scenario and then choose Separation Table from the Preferences subset under the File menu. Selecting Save writes the two preferences together into their own file that you can then load back in when you need to. Recall that Monitor Setup should be set once and left alone.

Your printer might be able to help you set the values you need to know to separate correctly. Some printers can be right on the ball with this whereas others haven't even heard of ink limits, let alone gray balance. This is a roundabout way of cautioning you that although you should definitely ask as much as you can of your printer, be prepared for the fact that he may not be very knowledgeable. In a case like that, the best thing to do short of moving on to another printer is to try and partner with your printer to set up a test. This also may not happen. If that's the case, try starting with the values below. Evaluate the results you get on press carefully and then adjust your settings accordingly. Keep a record of the choices that you make and the results you get. Doing a little hard work in the beginning will save a lot of tears down the road.

TYPICAL RGB TO CMYK SEPARATION SETUPS BY PRINTING TYPE

Coated Stock

Separation Type:	GCR
Black Generation:	Light
Black Limit:	90%–100%
Total Ink:	290%–340% (less for Web Press, more for Sheetfed)
UCA:	0–10% (typically 0%)
Ink Colors:	SWOP Coated
Dot Gain:	12%–25%

Uncoated Stock

Separation Type:	GCR
Black Generation:	Light

continues

TYPICAL RGB TO CMYK SEPARATION SETUPS BY PRINTING TYPE, CONTINUED

Uncoated Stock

Black Limit:	90%–100%
Total Ink:	270%–300% (less for Web Press, more for Sheetfed)
UCA:	0–10% (typically 0%)
Ink Colors:	SWOP Uncoated
Dot Gain:	18%–29%

Newsprint

Separation Type:	GCR
Black Generation:	Medium
Black Limit:	90%–100%
Total Ink:	290%–340% (less for Web Press, more for Sheetfed)
UCA:	0–10% (typically 0%)
Ink Colors:	SWOP Newsprint
Dot Gain:	30%–35%

Newsprint (alternate method)

Separation Type:	UCR
Black Limit:	70%–80%
Total Ink:	290%–340% (less for Web Press, more for Sheetfed)
Ink Colors:	SWOP Newsprint
Dot Gain:	30%–35%

OTHER COLOR MODELS

The relationship between RGB, CMY, and CMYK is a complex one at the heart of PostScript color imaging. Understanding this relationship is crucial to correctly separating and printing your images. There are more ways to think about color, however, and an awareness of these will expand understanding of color and your ability to correct it.

HSB Model

The first of these alternate color description models is Hue Saturation, and Brightness. Using this model, you can describe any color with three criterion. The Apple Color Picker (see Figure 11.24) uses this model. If you've ever painted, HSB will make intuitive sense to you.

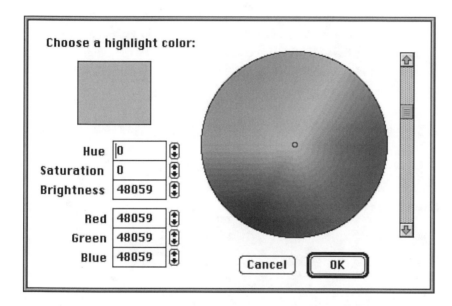

Figure 11.24

The Apple Color Picker uses an HSB model.

Hue refers to the general type of color in question: its pigmentation. Is it a red or a blue? Hue indicates this and describes the colors as spread around a circle in 360°. Each color in the spectrum is assigned an angle. Red is at 0° and the rest of the colors are spread out exactly the same as they are in the color wheel we described earlier. So cyan, the compliment of red, rests at 180°. Yellow is at 60°, between red at 0° and green at 120°. Blue is at 240° and magenta is at 300°.

Saturation refers to the intensity, or purity of the color. If you've painted with watercolors, what happens as you add more water to the color? The color's intensity fades and becomes more pastel. It becomes desaturated. Use more paint and less water, and you increase the purity or saturation of the color. A saturation of zero is gray. All of the neutrals have a zero saturation. Saturation runs on a scale of zero to 100. One hundred is the full, pure version of the color.

Brightness is the relative tone of the color. How light or dark is it? A brightness of 100 percent has a full complement of light falling on it. It appears at its lightest. As brightness decreases, the color becomes darker. In painting, it would be said to be a shade of itself.

When you're trying to get an idea of how these color models work intuitively, open Photoshop's Color Picker by clicking the Foreground or Background Color swatch. Clicking the radio buttons for any of the RGB or HSB values changes the large color graph at right. When you select one, you see a slider representing the values for that color or attribute. The remaining two values are graphed horizontally and vertically across the color field graph (see Figure 11.25). So if you select brightness, you get a slider for brightness and the graph changes to show saturation vertically and hue horizontally. The graph indicates the currently selected color with a small circle and the picker displays it as a color swatch.

Figure 11.25

The color graphs chart the colors' radio buttons that aren't selected (see color insert).

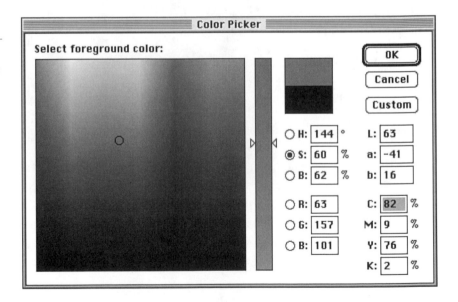

The HSB scale is sometimes referred to as the HSV scale for hue, saturation, and value. This can get confusing because Photoshop also uses HSL scale. The "L" in this case stands for lightness, rather than brightness. You can find

Photoshop measuring this way under Image: Adjust: Hue/Saturation and Image: adjust: Replace Color. In those cases, lightness is measured on a scale of -100 to 100 and can be thought of as light falling on the color. A medium amount, or a value of zero, is no change in light. A negative amount decreases brightness and darkens the color. A positive number does just the opposite. Be warned though that lightness can also affect the saturation value of a color. In general, the lightness command slider is not the greatest color correction tool Photoshop has going for itself.

HSB used to be its own color mode, rather than just a descriptive model in Photoshop. Today its use is principally referential. It can be a useful color correction tool, however, and shouldn't be discounted completely. HSB's power is its intuitive nature. Frequently we'll look at a color and think "that needs to be beefed up a little bit," rather than "that needs two percent more yellow and 1 percent less cyan." Nothing is wrong with this sort of thinking and HSB gives us a chance to correct with it.

The RGB and CMYK color models are actually instructions. They tell a device, be it a printer or a monitor, how to build up some color. They don't describe color; they describe how to make color. Because of this, they are thought to be device-dependent color models. Different machines can interpret the same instructions differently. All you have to do to see this is to look at the same file on two different monitors. The HSB model is a little better because it begins to describe color the way we think about it. It still doesn't completely accurately describe what color looks like.

Lab Color

Lab color in Photoshop describes color not as a series of instructions for creating color with a device, but instead as what color actually *looks* like. CIE stands for the Commission Internationale d'Eclairage. It's an international organization whose main concern is measuring color. The Commission has been around since the 1930s and has established several color models over the years. The most commonly used model in the printing industry is Lab color. Photoshop uses Lab color whenever it translates between color spaces. When you set all the Printing preferences, Photoshop uses Lab color to figure out what sorts of RGB and CMYK colors you're talking about and then builds a database called a Look Up Table. When you convert your color spaces, Photoshop refers to that look up table to make the switch.

Lab, like HSB, describes color on mathematical axes. The L in Lab stands for luminance, which is similar to HSB's brightness. The a and b in Lab color refer to color components. The "a" component ranges from green to magenta and the "b" component ranges from blue to yellow.

The model is a fine one for communicating color information between machines. Most device-independent color management systems and even some scanners use Lab in their reckoning of color. Even Kodak's YCC color space which it developed for its PhotoCD system is based on the Lab color space. Unfortunately, being abstract and mathematical, it does a horrible job describing color to human beings. Try telling a printer that you need to boost the a component in your file and see what they tell you. At some point, things need to become RGB or CMYK. Lab is available as not only a color description vehicle but also as a color mode. A Lab file can be saved as a Photoshop file, a TIFF, an EPS, or in the Raw format.

Although Lab color is currently the most popular and widespread device independent color description model around, it is not the only one. For that matter, Photoshop is not the only software that makes CMYK separations from RGB information. Other options are available to you for both of these things. For most purposes, though, both of these tools work as well as most people will ever need anything to. Before investing time and money into new software, make sure you've completely explored the ones you already have. Everything you need is probably already right there. If you really need to make the switch, you'll know. Don't do it just because you're temporarily frustrated with Photoshop. You'll likely have the same problems with the new product, plus you'll be facing a brand new learning curve.

OTHER COLOR MODES

With the exception of HSB, the three color models we've looked at are also color modes. That is to say, color can be thought of in those terms and the basic nature of the file can also be structured in those terms. A file that is converted to Lab color can be viewed as three channels, one for L, a, and b. Photoshop also has several other mode options that should be discussed as well.

FIGURE 11.2

Colors affect our perception of other colors around them.

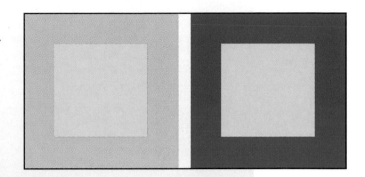

FIGURE 11.3

Very different colors can have the same tone.

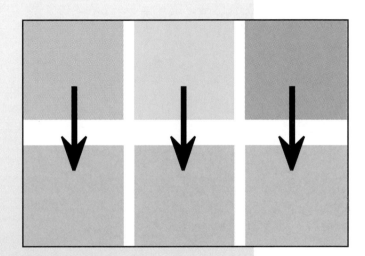

FIGURE 11.17

Printing test swatches isolates the correct combination of colors that produce a neutral.

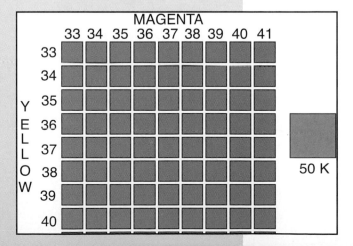

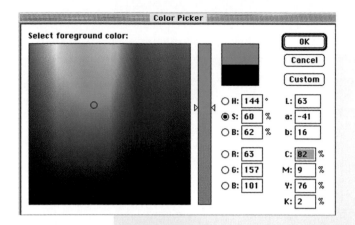

FIGURE 11.25

The color graphs chart the colors'
radio buttons that aren't selected.

FIGURE 12.6

Hue/Saturation is commonly used to
colorize black and white photos.

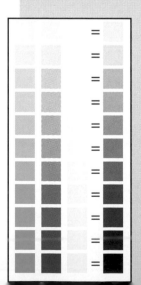

FIGURE 12.8

Gray Balance combinations.

FIGURE 12.10

Using the Eyedropper to target and adjust an endpoint.

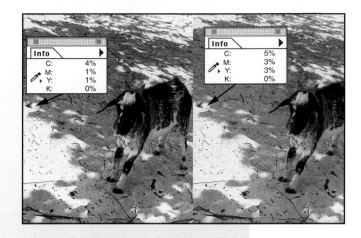

FIGURE 12.11

Neutralizing a yellow cast while compressing tones for printing.

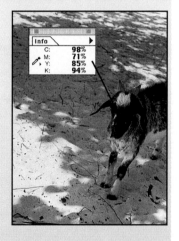

FIGURE 12.13

Half-cast removal corrects problems without large color shifts.

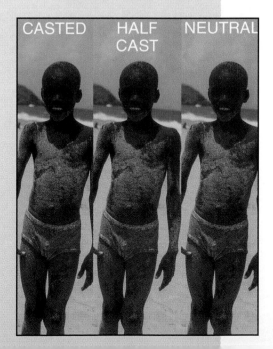

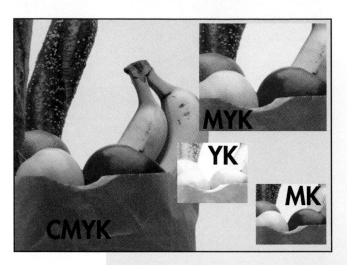

FIGURE 12.16

The tertiary color holds important detail.

FIGURE 12.17

Component flesh tone colors.

FIGURE 12.18

Correcting fleshtones.

FIGURE 12.19

Black deepens sky better than yellow.

FIGURE 12.27B

The final colorized quadtone.

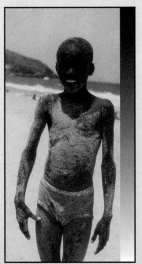

FIGURE 13.10

Desaturating the rainbow pattern out
of a reflective original.

FIGURES 16.1A AND 16.B

Trapping is only required when colors touch.

FIGURE 16.2

Four-color artwork with heavy black outlines usually doesn't require trapping.

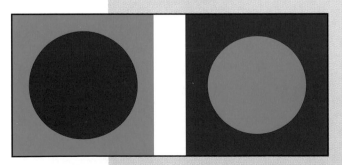

FIGURE 16.3

Lighter colors expand into darker colors.

FIGURE 16.4

An insufficient process bridge.

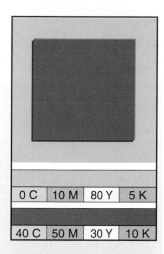

| 0 C | 10 M | 80 Y | 5 K |

| 40 C | 50 M | 30 Y | 10 K |

FIGURE 16.5

A sufficient process bridge.

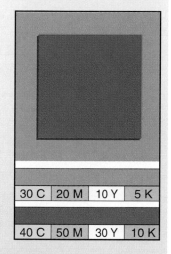

| 30 C | 20 M | 10 Y | 5 K |

| 40 C | 50 M | 30 Y | 10 K |

FIGURE 16.6

Knockout Black, Overprint Black, Rich Black, and Super Black.

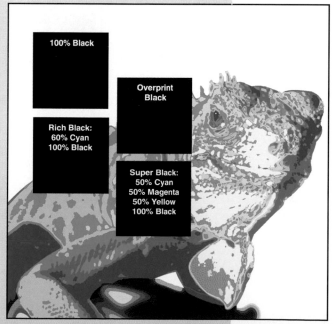

FIGURE 16.7

Exposed edges require rich black.

FIGURE 16.8

Black straddling an image and paper requires enriching.

FIGURE 16.9

Misregistered process inks causing fringe around black area.

The Bitmap and Grayscale modes were discussed earlier. The Duotone mode is essentially a special way to print richer halftones. The idea is that by printing the same color with different inks, you can increase the density of the image overall. The result is snappier highlights and richer shadows. A Duotone, as the name implies, is printed with two colors. You can also make tritones and quadtones from this mode. Collectively duotones, tritones, and quadtones are called multitone images. They'll all be discussed at greater length in Chapter 12.

Multichannel

Multichannel mode is similar to the other file modes that have channels, like RGB, Lab, and CMYK. The big difference is that it creates no association between them. In a CMYK file, each channel relates to the others in a manner that affects how they'll print. Multichannel files do have multiple channels, but the channels don't have an inherent connection. We'll talk more about the uses of multichannel files in Chapter 12.

Indexed Color

Another color mode available to you is Indexed Color. Indexing a file's color essentially takes whatever the bit depth of your file is and restricts it to an 8-bit depth. This means that no matter how many discrete colors your image started with, it is reduced to a scant 256. It literally writes down a list of 256 colors your image can have. As you might suspect, this is not a good thing if your file's final destination is printing. File size decreases dramatically, but image quality rapidly decreases also. Of course, you also can't print separations of it from QuarkXPress or PageMaker. What's more, indexing color also limits the tools and filters working in Photoshop. Anything that needs to average pixel values, like anti-aliasing, is going to have real trouble in this mode. The only real use for indexed color is presentation. If you are working in multimedia or for the Internet, indexing color may be useful to you. Making a CompuServe GIF, a file format used on the Internet, for example, needs to have indexed colors.

If you are going to index your colors and you care how they look, choose the following settings (see Figure 11.26).

Resolution 8 bits per pixel. If, for some reason, your image has less than 256 colors in it, Photoshop knows about it and will put that number into the Other: field. Otherwise, choose 8 bits.

Palette Adaptive. If your file has fewer than 256 colors, choose Exact so that every color in your image is written into the palette. Otherwise, if your goal is to keep the image looking remotely like its original state, choose Adaptive. This looks at the colors in the image and chooses colors for the palette based on what it sees. If you have already saved a palette from an earlier file, you can load it in from disk by choosing Custom. This offers the opportunity to create some continuity between files with special color palettes. Choosing Previous loads in the last indexed palette used.

Dither Diffusion. This really is the only option. Dithering affects how the indexed colors are distributed throughout the image. The Diffusion Dither distributes colors with some randomness to create a more natural looking effect. The other options, None and Pattern, create strikingly ugly things that aren't really good for anything. Try it, you'll see what we mean.

Figure 11.26

If you must index color, this way almost always produces the best results.

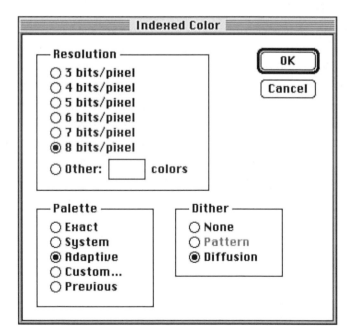

400

After you've indexed your color, you can edit the palette, or the colors to which you've limited your image. Even with the Adaptive palette, an errant pixel color can slip in. Just choose Color Table from the Mode menu and you get the Color Table dialog box. Editing the colors there is easy. Simply click the color you want to change and the Color Picker comes up. Change the values of the pixel to what you want and click OK. All the pixels that had that value get changed.

The not so easy part is finding the color that's the problem. You have to inspect pixels individually to find their RGB values and then do the same thing with your color palette. It can take a while.

Indexed color can be used to make a low resolution version of a file in order to be more easily Telneted to a client for approval. Even this isn't a wonderful idea. Other file size saving formats, like JPEG, aren't as damaging to image data as indexing color. In short, indexing your color is really only good for monitor display. Be that for the Internet, presentation software or multimedia, it really doesn't matter.

SUMMARY

The issues of color theory and conversion can seem labyrinthine and complex, but they really are within your reach. Keep in mind the color wheel we used to demonstrate the relationship between RGB and CMYK. Talk to your printer on a regular basis and keep notes about the choices you made and the results that you got. You'll find that, as with most projects, a little work up front will save a lot of grief down the road. You'll pick up your time investment on the margins. Understanding a little about color goes a long way towards producing better color on press and making everyone happier.

Chapter 12

WORKING IN COLOR

On one of Steve's first color correction jobs, he ran into a problem. He had spent the better part of the night fighting with a scan to make the colors match the original exactly, but it just wasn't good enough. The yellows were too saturated and the greens didn't look quite right. At long last, he resigned himself to the fact that he couldn't make it any better, so he'd call the client in the morning with the bad news that the file would be behind deadline.

The client was understandably upset but agreed to look at the proof, because he was going to be in the shop later that morning anyway. In the meantime, Steve poured more non-billable hours into the scan he still couldn't correct completely.

When the client finally arrived, Steve was apologetic. To set the stage for his tale of sorrow, he opened the original scan to show the client how far he had come and what a good job it turns out this really is, considering. He was about to open up the second, corrected, file when the client stopped him. "That one looks great!" he gushed, cutting off Steve's narration. "Do you have a proof?" Well, yes, Steve did. He showed the client and the client loved it and that was that. Steve never even opened up the corrected file that he worked so hard and fruitlessly on.

COLOR EXPECTATION

When you're working in color, you have a difficult task ahead of you. Not only do you need to understand the how-to of color, you also need to cope with the realities of working with a product it's very difficult to get people to agree on. Communicating and correctly setting expectations is more critical in the desktop world than any other industry, and nowhere is that in evidence more strongly than when you're working in color. The range of expectations and acceptable levels of quality varies from client to client. Some clients merely want colors to be bright and in the right places, while others drive you through rounds and rounds of proofing before ever signing off on a job. Even then, they may not sign off.

It's important to discuss with clients the level of color accuracy required for a job up front. If a job is color-critical, you'll often find out immediately. If that's not the case, you may try testing the client out by examining pieces they have produced in the past and seeing how satisfied they were with the results. Getting a gauge for where the client is at with their color needs prevents wasted time and saves unpleasant confrontations and rounds of proofing down the road.

This is not to imply that you should do an inferior job with some clients. Rather, the point is that living up to and exceeding a client's expectations is key to keeping them as clients. The world of color has some uncertain borders in it and whatever you can do to establish those is bound to help. Keep examples of your work on hand. If possible, include several complete examples of the process. The changes in media can confuse clients.

Having examples of the original, the digital file, the proof, and finally the printed piece can help them to understand that the same image can look very different in different states. It's not uncommon for proofing systems to oversell the image. The proofs look so clean and dynamite that the printed result on cheap stock looks shabby by comparison. The client may blame your film when it's really the paper that's at fault. Having printed examples up front establishes in the client's mind that this is a process with changes in it and helps establish realistic expectations of quality.

An artist brought several paintings into a prepress house wanting film separations made from them. If she liked the proofs, she'd be a big client. Sales told her that her artwork could be reproduced exactly to her satisfaction, or she wouldn't have to pay. Four rounds of correction, proofing, and rescanning later the client still wasn't satisfied. No one had discussed limits or expectations with her, and she was extremely critical of color. It was also her first experience with digital imaging, and she was completely unprepared for the realities of the process. She walked away from the prepress house thinking they had wasted her time. No sale. Beginning the process with concrete examples would have saved everyone involved hours, dollars, and raw materials. Not to mention the collective bad feelings, frustration, and negative word of mouth the entire escapade generated. Understand and help set your clients' expectations up front.

Digital Prepress In the Real World

Art Direction

Another key issue where client involvement goes a long way is art direction. Imaging is often a give and take process. You may have to sacrifice some element of your image to emphasize another. Any input the client can give you about what's important in the image can guide decisions from the moment the copy is scanned to the final rounds of color correction. Even very simple, seemingly ambiguous instructions like "the sweater needs to be really red" provide a starting place for you to build from. Without that information, you're guessing what the client wants.

Finding out what the client really wants is important because digital imaging opens up so many possibilities for color changes with the push of a button. The goal of CMYK correcting is matching an original, but that may not be the case. The intention may be to correct defects in the image, or to improve color. Unless you know that the client really wants the shadows in the image opened up and Mom's forehead to not be so shiny, you're chasing the wrong car and wasting everyone's time.

COLOR SCANNING AND CORRECTION

With these issues in mind, you can start to build a plan for the systematic correction of color files. It's important to build a plan for color correction and stick with it. A workflow plan builds an image checklist that directs your color correction activities. There are efficiency benefits, less image degradation, and better results all around if you have a plan. Working on color without a plan is akin to a trying to cut someone's hair with electric clippers and no comb. Fixing one section usually means you throw the whole thing out of whack so you have to go fix something else. Pretty soon you end up with a lousy haircut. Each time you make a move in Photoshop, you're clipping away some information. If you can establish a workflow, you'll enjoy speedier turnaround times and fewer mistakes.

Here is an overview of the color scanning and correction plan. You may find that varying it accommodates your working environment and style better. Except where noted, feel free. The important thing is to attend to the image in a systematic fashion that makes intuitive sense to you. When you're in a working system where things make sense, you'll produce much better files more rapidly.

Color Scanning Checklist

1. Assess the image, learn its purpose.

2. Preview, measure, and adjust your image.

3. Scan.

4. Assess your scan, rescan if necessary and save.

5. Fix any glaring problems.

6. Sharpen your image.

7. Retouch flaws.

8. Check/adjust endpoints for press.

9. Adjust tones.

10. Adjust colors.

11. Review, massage, and save (As).

The Conversion Question

Nowhere on the above list is Convert from RGB to CMYK. We touched on this earlier, but it seems appropriate to recap it now:

The reasons to work in RGB are: faster process times, special tools, and wider color gamut. The reasons to work in CMYK: no disappointing color shifts and it's easier to intuit color space.

Ideally, you should do the bulk of your correcting in RGB and fine tune your image in CMYK. This takes advantage of the RGB pluses and still addresses CMYK necessity. On the Plan list, this places conversion either as part of number 10, adjust colors, or number 11, massage file.

The entire question of when to convert presupposes you have an RGB file *to* convert and that you actually want to. High end scanners can convert to CMYK on the fly using settings similar to the Photoshop Preferences we discussed in Chapter 11. If you're getting your files from a service bureau, they probably have already been separated using general settings. You can request them be given to you in RGB format. If you're paying by the megabyte, this may even save you a few bucks. Given our druthers, we'd rather have the option of converting the file ourselves. This enables us to convert for several different output styles, fine tune the black printer, and repurpose for multimedia. In cases where we know how the file was pre-separated and its specific purpose, we seldom bother with rescanning to obtain RGB data. Using the CMYK data from a high end scanner is usually better that RGB data from a low end scanner.

Elements of Color Quality

It can be inferred from the steps above that several major elements of quality go into an image. Some of these are obvious, some aren't at first, but if any area is unattended to, poorly executed, or not correctly communicated, the proof is apt to be rejected. The elements of quality crucial to correct image reproduction are:

- Detail
- Tone
- Gray Balance
- (Memory) Color

Detail

Detail is often related to sharpness. We talked about the Unsharp Mask filter back in Chapter 10. The goal of sharpening is realism. Too much sharpening and things look unnatural—not enough and things look too soft. Detail is also a function of correct scanning and color correction. As we'll see, incorrect color balancing can wash out detail, and incorrect end point placement can destroy it outright. Correct image reproduction captures all the detail in the image and compensates for the damage done by scanning and printing.

Tone

Tone is the distribution of lights and darks in the image. Correct tones play a strong role in a realistic, three-dimensional appearance. Tone is often also associated with contrast. Tonal range is the difference between the lightest lights and the darkest darks. Differences in tones provide contrast. There is the contrast of the image overall and the tendency of abutting areas to contrast with each other. Each must be attended to for correct image reproduction.

It's sometimes difficult to see tones in a full color image, because color can be distracting. We perceive certain colors to be lighter than other colors although they may be tonally identical. A middle yellow dot may have the same tonal value as a much smaller cyan dot. The best way to understand tone is to work extensively with halftones. Failing that, set your Info palette to show gray values. This enables you to get a clearer idea of the relative tone of the color in question.

Gray Balance

Gray balance refers to a situation when colors combine on press to gray values. The combination of the inks is a special one and must be balanced carefully. If the proper balance is not maintained, grays acquire a color bias. Biased grays look wrong and have a tendency to throw other colors off as well. The proper relationship must be maintained to produce professional results.

In an RGB color space, equal amounts of color produce an unbiased gray. In CMYK, the combinations change. Until you develop an eye for neutrality, you'll need to rely on onscreen densitometers and a gray balance chart to assess neutrality.

Memory Colors

Memory colors are called memory colors because everyone knows what they look like from memory. White is a memory color. So are blue sky and green grass. No one needs a proof to tell them what color an orange is. They're important colors to nail on press.

Note

Equally important are corporate colors and ones that the client needs to reproduce exactly. This could take the form of matching a Pantone color from a logo or simply getting someone's hair color right. In any case, identifying and correcting important colors are a key issue over which jobs will be accepted or rejected.

Color Correction Tools

The first thing you need to start color correcting in Photoshop is an understanding of the tools you'll use. Of vital importance are Curves, the Info palette, the Rubber Stamp tool, and a solid understanding of selection techniques. Also useful to you are Levels, Histograms, Hue/Saturation, Replace Color, and Selective Color.

Curves Control

The best tool for color correction is the Curves control. This works the same way it does for grayscale images—all the same features and tricks that worked before still work in color. Now, however, you have the capability to affect any given color channel individually. This gives you the power to very specifically target the exact tones you need to change and make those changes with a high degree of precision. With this tool and the Info palette, you can do the bulk of your needed color correction work. We've even met people who rely on these two features almost to the exclusion of all other tools in Photoshop. This seems limiting, but it does underscore the point that the Curves feature and the Info palette are absolutely vital and cannot be overlooked.

The pop up menu at the top of the Curves dialog box lets you specify which channel you want to work on (see Figure 12.1). The key commands for the channels all work here as well. Changing the channel restricts the effects of the Curve to that channel. The delightful trick of being able to click a point in the image area and see the corresponding tone on the Curves graph no longer works in the CMYK composite channel. It does work on the individual C, M, Y, and K channels and it works on the RGB and RGB composite channels, but not on the CMYK composite channel.

Figure 12.1

Use Curves to adjust individual channels.

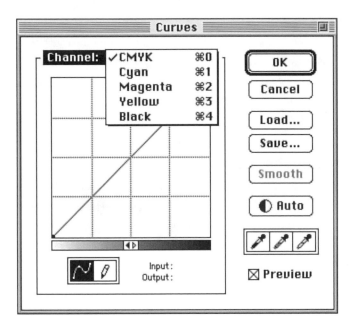

In addition to these features, Curves is the home of the black, white, and gray Eyedroppers, which you'll use to target your image for the printing press.

Info Palette

The Info palette also has little change to report. You have several things to be aware of, however. Although a file may be one color mode, you can set the Info palette to display the equivalent values of a different mode. So if you're working in RGB and want to keep an eye on the CMYK values you'd generate if you converted over to CMYK, set the palette to display them (see Figure 12.2). Likewise, setting the Info palette to display grayscale information gives you an indication of the relative light or dark of the pixels. It's also the pixel value you get if you discarded the color information in the pixels by changing to grayscale mode.

Figure 12.2

The Info palette uses your color preferences to calculate CMYK separation values.

The Info palette can also be set to display mouse positions. When Photoshop 4.0 comes out, it promises to feature placeable guides and a grid. In the meantime, these mouse position coordinates are the only real way to locate any given pixels repeatedly. If you want to know the exact effect your changes

411

are making, select the Show Mouse Coordinates checkbox in the Info palette options box. That way you can always return to the same position each time to take your measurements.

When you're working in CMYK, it's possible to exceed the total ink limit you imposed on the file. Back in Chapter 11 when the transition from RGB to CMYK was discussed, we delineated how and why to limit the total ink that goes down on press. Now that you've separated correctly, you don't want to undo it with an injudicious color correction. The Info palette can be set to display Total Ink for a given area (see Figure 12.3). This alerts you to times when you're putting too much ink down. This is usually a problem in the shadows only. The Total Ink setting adds up the percentages on the four printers and displays it for your perusal. In practice, we really only use this setting when we've got a file we're concerned about and want to keep an eye on ourselves.

Figure 12.3

Total ink coverage info from the Info palette.

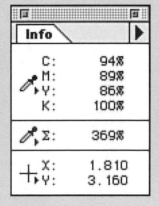

The Rubber Stamp Tool

Likewise, the Rubber Stamp functions exactly as it did in grayscale files. The thing to remember here is that its use exceeds straightforward cloning. By changing the Rubber Stamp Options, you can stamp from saved versions or snapshots of the file. The other options for the Rubber Stamp are less useful for us in the business of correcting scans.

The two pattern settings enable you to paint from, well, from a pattern. To do this, you need to establish a pattern first. Simply select an area with the rectangular Marquee tool and choose Define Pattern from the Edit menu. Your selection can't be feathered, smoothed, or in any way altered to be anything other than a rectangle. After you've defined a pattern, you can rubber stamp it on a selected area and Fill with the pattern. The nature of patterns make them nice for borders and other effects for graphics bound for multimedia or the Internet. In the world of color correcting, though, they don't play a strong role. Even less useful is the Impressionist option, which, if we're not mistaken, really doesn't do much of anything that you can use. It calls up the last saved version of the file and paints with a smeared version of that. Yes, we said "smeared." Try it yourself if you don't believe us.

The Levels Feature

The Levels feature works similarly to the Curves in color images. Each channel can be affected individually or as a group using the composite setting. Levels really don't provide the kind of accuracy that full color manipulation requires. For this reason, Levels are primarily an information-gathering tool in color work. They are handy for confirming what you should be teaching your eye to do automatically: figure out the distribution of tones in the image. The clipping display also works well for locating end points and saturated colors. To use this feature, turn preview off, Video LUT on, and Option (Mac) or Alt (IBM) click the end point sliders. You see which pixels are too hot. While we get behind this feature in principle and have used it on occasion, we still prefer to rely on a thorough inspection of the image prior to scanning and a quick once-over with the Info box to discern our endpoints. If you inspect the clipping pixels for individual channels using this method, you are treated to some psychedelic color displays. While entertaining as a trick to impress clients, this clipping display hurts your eyes and distracts you from the truth of the pixels.

Histogram

Choosing Image: Histogram also gives you a detailed chart of pixel values in the image by channels. It also provides useful information about the distribution and amount of pixels in the image. We say "useful" in the strictly-for-the curious sense of the word. In truth, we've almost never gotten much out of knowing exactly how many pixels of a given brightness value there are. What is useful, however, is the Histogram for the composite channel, which is labeled Gray. This histogram is showing you the overall tonal range for the image. From this, you can determine the strength of your lights and darks in the image.

This is different from the composite setting in Levels. In Levels, the composite histogram shows the maximum values for any given channel (see Figure 12.4a). The Histogram's Gray setting shows the tonal value of the pixels combined (see Figure 12.4b). A value of 255 in the Levels box means that at least one of the channels is maxed. Maybe all three, maybe only one—we just don't know. A value of 255 in the Histogram's gray channel means white. All three channels are maxed.

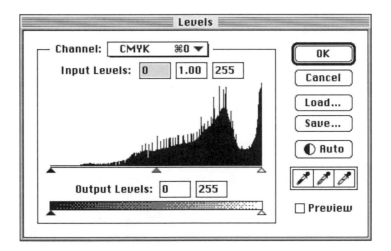

Figure 12.4a

The Levels composite histogram shows the maximum value for any channel.

Hue and Stauration

Hue and Saturation (Image: Adjust: Hue/Saturation) are nice tools to have in your back pocket. The command isn't a real workhorse for most files but can be handy for fine-tuning color. Video LUT doesn't work on this command, so to see the effects you need to turn on the preview option.

As you might expect from the name, it's mostly used for desaturating RGB files. It's also handy for adding pigment, color correcting, and pulling an image into a printable range. This command is often more efficient than using Curves when the intent is to pull some saturation out of an RGB color. For example, if you had a deep blue (0R 0G 255B) that needed to be pulled back, you could nudge back the blue with Curves and pull up the red and green, or just nudge back the saturation slider.

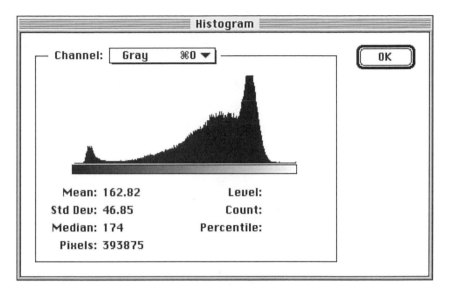

Figure 12.4b

The Histogram display shows how bright or dark the image really is.

Making color changes with Hue/Saturation is a dicier play. Adjusting the color, or hue of pixels, is a task better left to Curves. You also have cause for concern when making adjustments to anything other than the composite, or master image. The Hue/Saturation command enables you to make changes to any of the RGB or CMYK colors individually (see Figure 12.5). The results of this can be unpredictable, leaving you chasing results and wondering what really happened to what. When you're working in RGB, it's easy to slide your image out of the printable gamut. When you're working in CMYK, the results are even less predictable, but it's much harder to exceed your Total Ink limit with this tool. Hue/Saturation, as we stated earlier, is best used to tweak rather than the primary color correction tool in your kit.

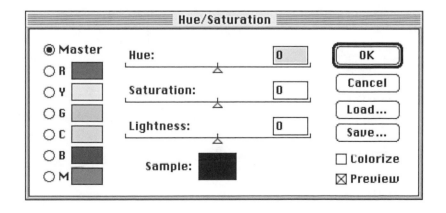

Figure 12.5

The Hue/Saturation commands.

A popular use for Hue/Saturation is to add color to grayscale images. The effect is similar to antique, hand-tinted photographs. To use this effect, convert your grayscale file to RGB or CMYK. Usually RGB works a little better. Open the Hue/Saturation command and click the Colorize button. Then adjust Hue and Saturation to produce the effect you want (see Figure 12.6).

For nice results, try selecting specific areas first and then colorizing them. Giving your selection a two pixel feather helps smooth the effect out. The rest of your image can be colored differently by inverting your selection and selecting Hue/Saturation again.

Figure 12.6

Hue/Saturation is commonly used to colorize black and white photos (see color insert).

Replace Color

Closely related to Hue/Saturation is the Replace Color feature (Image: Adjust: Replace Color). The command is essentially a combination of the Hue/Saturation controls and the Color Range selection method. We'll explain

Color Range selections in Chapter 13. For now, be aware that the Replace Color feature is a way to make the same Hue/Saturation adjustments to specific parts of an image. The challenge with these sorts of corrections, as opposed to the global ones we've been talking about so far, is to make the edge of the transformation as unnoticeable as possible.

For this reason, the Replace Color feature, like Hue/Saturation itself, is much better at making minor adjustments than at making large transitions. If you're looking for radical color shifts, you'll be better served by making selections and then using Hue/Saturation or Curves.

Selective Color

Last on the list is Selective Color. The idea is to pull a portion of a color out without affecting the other colors in the image. So, for example, if you wanted to add some magenta to the "red" pixels in your image, Photoshop determines which pixels are the red ones and increases the magenta content of those colors. Other pixels in the image would be unchanged. Which pixels are red? You have to take Photoshop's word for it.

Selective Color works in two modes, Relative and Absolute. The Relative mode looks at the color you're adjusting and tries to make it proportionally less or more of what you want. So if you wanted to make a red 25 percent more magenta, it would figure how red the red was and then try to make it 25 percent more magenta than that. It does this by adjusting all four colors. Not only do you not know which pixels are being affected, you don't know what's being done to them. The Absolute mode is confusing as well. The effect works by changing a percentage of the color content, not by changing by the amount you see. So if you've got a 75 percent magenta, and you remove 25 percent magenta with Selective Color you end up with 56 percent magenta, not 50 percent. $75 \times .25 = 18.75$. $75 - 18.75 = 56$. See how easy that was?

Adjusting Color

Now that you're more familiar with the tools, let's get down to the business of using them to adjust color. Just as the case with grayscale images, the first step of color correction needs to be a solid assessment of the original and the scan that was produced from it.

End Points and Detail

If you've lost detail in the scanning process due to incorrect endpoint selection, go back and rescan it. This will be easy to see in the highlights; it may be a little harder in the shadows. To find out if there is acceptable detail in the shadows, inspect the areas in question by running your cursor around them and checking for changes in the Info palette. You also may want to run through the channels to check for yourself. The keyboard shortcuts for the channels are as follows:

Shortcut Mac	Shortcut Windows	RGB	CMYK
⌘1	Ctrl 1	Red	Cyan
⌘2	Ctrl 2	Green	Magenta
⌘3	Ctrl 3	Blue	Yellow
⌘4	Ctrl 4...		Black
⌘0	Ctrl 0	Composite	Composite

If you selected Color Channels in Color from Photoshop's General Preferences, your channels also will be colored appropriately (if garishly) rather than the standard gray. It's really easier to see the image information in grayscale, and it runs faster, but some people prefer the visual clue the colors give them. In any case, it's important to confirm that the scan is one you can work with.

The next step is to make sure that the highlights are in the correct places. Inspect your original to find the diffuse highlight. You need to be sensitive to specifics of the image in this. The highlights may actually be much darker in the original than in the file your scanner produced. The result will be a scan with improper contrast (see Figure 12.7). You need to check to be sure that your endpoints are in the right geographical place, that they were selected correctly, and that they are the correct tone. If they're the wrong tone, you can correct that. If they're in the wrong place, you're probably facing a losing battle. Scan it again and manually select the endpoints.

We talked about sharpening and retouching image flaws back in Chapter 10. The issues are essentially the same in color. Refer to that chapter if you have questions about how to go about setting sharpness or retouching image flaws.

Figure 12.7

*Improperly lightening highlights
can lead to image problems.*

Gray Balance

At this point, we need to put a new wrinkle on a key idea. We've said that certain combinations of cyan, magenta, and yellow are the equivalent of gray. The idea is gray balance and we've used it before to limit the amount of ink we print with. Now we'll use it to color correct our files.

Because we know what combinations of colors add up to gray, if we see gray areas in our original, we've got a great tool for color correcting. You can measure the values that create the color in your scan. If it should read as a neutral and doesn't, you've got a color cast. What's even better is that because you know what colors add up to gray, you know how to correct the scan. If you can do this at the scan level, your color correction time will drop off greatly.

Identifying and Adjusting Neutrals

A fine place to look for a neutral is in your diffuse highlight. The highlight may not be neutral, but it's a good place to start looking. Run your cursor around the diffuse highlight and measure it. Remember that we're looking for two things now, neutrality and printability. If our highlight dot is too small, it will probably fall off the press. If the dot isn't the right color, the cast is probably also affecting the entire image. Fixing the neutrals often swings the rest of an image's color into line. Remember that as you inspect CMYK neutrals, let cyan be your guide. The cyan value will be greater than our other two colors, which will be about equal. The resulting gray will be roughly the same as the cyan value. So a highlight of 5C, 3M, and 3Y will be a five percent gray, the same value as the cyan. Refer to this chart:

TYPICAL GRAY BALANCE RELATIONSHIPS

Cyan +	Magenta +	Yellow =	Resulting Gray (K)
5	3	3	5
10	6	6	10
25	16	16	25
30	21	21	30
40	29	29	40
50	37	37	50
60	46	46	60
75	64	64	75
80	71	71	80
90	82	82	90
95	87	87	95

This chart should be thought of as a guide, not as gospel. The important thing is the relationship between the colors (see Figure 12.8). If a color is off by a point or two, it's pretty neutral. Cyan is greater than the other colors in differing amounts along the gray ramp. Typically, it works like this:

CYAN DIFFERENCE BY TONE

Tone	Extra Cyan
Highlights	2 - 3%
Quarter Tones	7 - 10%
Midtones	12 - 15%
Three Quarters	8 - 12%
Shadows	7 - 10%

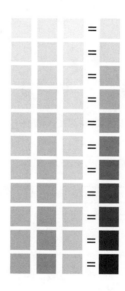

Figure 12.8

Gray Balance combinations (see color insert).

But back to our highlight dot. Let's say you have a neutral highlight in your original image and the highlight in your scan measures 5C, 5M, and 3Y, like in Figure 12.9a. The whites look slightly too warm and pinkish. They have too much magenta in them. This is where Curves come into play. A gamma correction like the one in Figure 12.9b pulls just a little magenta out of the highlights, and an even smaller amount out of the quarter tones. The rest of the image gets left alone. To make the curve, go into the Curves command and select the magenta channel. Place a point on the curve itself and then drag down to where five percent magenta became three percent magenta. You're working in percents of inks and not levels. Then check your work before and after by undoing and redoing the change.

Figure 12.9a

Improper color balance to produce a neutral.

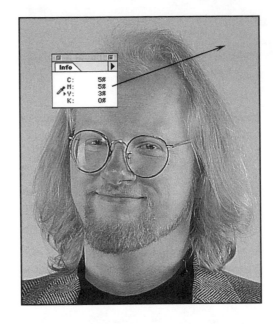

Figure 12.9b

A slight Curves adjustment neutralizes the cast.

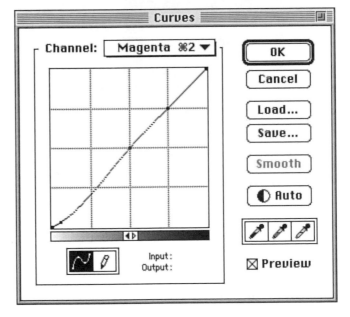

This is an essential methodology for neutralizing a cast specifically and color correcting in general. Identify problems, make slight changes to correct them, and review your work before proceeding. It's a good idea to take a snapshot here and there and periodically Save and Save As your work.

The Target Eyedroppers as a Color Correction Tool

Another powerful agent for color correction is in the Curves (and Levels) command. The highlight, shadow, and midtone Eyedroppers are all strong medicine for bad color problems. We talked about using them to target values for the press in Chapter 10; now we'll talk about their use as a color correction tool. Recall that you use them by double-clicking each tool to call up your target pickers. Enter target values into the highlight and/or shadow Eyedropper and then move out into your image and select a point you'd like to map to that value.

The Eyedroppers compare the value you plugged into the target picker with the value of the selected pixel. They then proportionally affect all the pixels in the image by that ratio. So all the pixels are affected, based on the two values you're working with. This makes the tool ideal for targeting our end points to meet press conditions. The pixel's values, if you pick shrewdly, keep their proportional distance. The result is smooth, clean transition of colors. The tonal range of your image constricts to a printable range without jumps. You need to be careful about the values that you dial in, though, and the pixels you map to them.

You'll carefully use the Eyedroppers to beat a color cast as well. By dialing in a neutral endpoint whose values are tonally similar to those in the original image, you can neutralize a cast and bring your image into printing range in one move. In the following example (see Figure 12.10), your diffuse high is an unprintably small 4C, 1M, 1Y, 0K. This is too small and not neutral.

Open the Curves box, double-click the highlight Eyedropper, and dial in a target value of 5C, 3M, 3Y, 0K, a reasonable neutral target for many coated stock printing situations. Armed with these values loaded into your Eyedropper, click the highlight point you identified. The point snaps to a printable size and the color correction is made.

Figure 12.10

Using the Eyedropper to target and adjust an endpoint (see color insert).

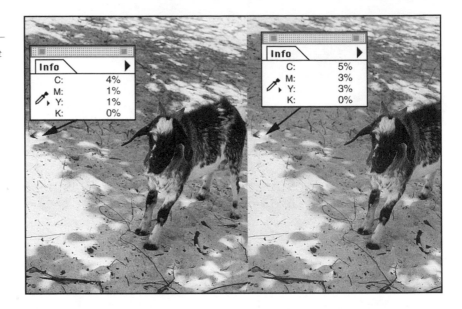

In the same file, your shadows are too dark to be printed correctly and too yellow (see Figure 12.11). By setting your shadow Eyedropper to a neutral you not only swing the tones back down to a printable value, but you also make the first big step towards neutralizing the yellow cast.

As you neutralize one end point, you also are affecting other colors in your image as well and you may also be affecting tone. Removing a color cast in the lightest areas affects all the light areas, just as neutralizing the shadows is apt to affect tones all the way down to your mids. This is especially important in the highlight to midtone dots. The human eye is designed to see these tones the most accurately. Correctly identifying color casts in this region is critical and delicate work. Thoughtful, systematic examination of both the original and the digital file are very important for this to be accomplished accurately.

Curves and Neutrals

Neutral endpoints take care of many color cast problems. In some cases, however, you may need to go further. Using the Curves control to add or subtract color from an image in specific tonal areas, just as you did with the end points, can remove unwanted casts. Let's look at it in action. In this scan, the gray jacket runs towards magenta. Our end points, however, are correctly neutral (see Figure 12.12). The cast can be corrected by writing a curve that pulls magenta out of the specific tones affected. If we had identified this cast at the time of the scan, or before we converted to CMYK, we could also push up the green tones in that area to bring magenta down because green and magenta are complementary colors.

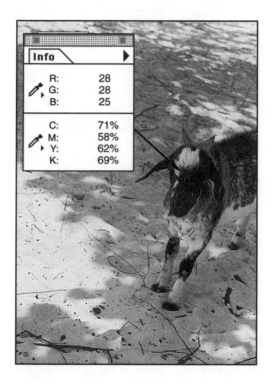

Figure 12.11

Neutralizing a yellow cast while compressing tones for printing (see color insert).

Half Cast Removals

In some cases, completely neutralizing an image may take it too far away from the original. Forcing a color to neutral may be too destructive and cause it to appear too clean and unnatural. In these cases, it is advisable to apply a half cast removal. This adjustment, as the name implies, determines how much change is required for a full cast correction, and then goes halfway. So if removing six percent yellow from a color would fully neutralize it, a half cast removal would subtract three percent. Figure out the difference between the two numbers and add half that number to the smaller figure. This method helps clear up unpleasant casts without dramatically changing colors (see Figure 12.13). This chart shows examples of the method in action.

Figure 12.12

Correcting a color cast with Curves.

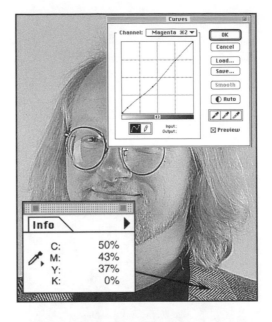

Figure 12.13

Half cast removal corrects problems without large color shifts (see color insert).

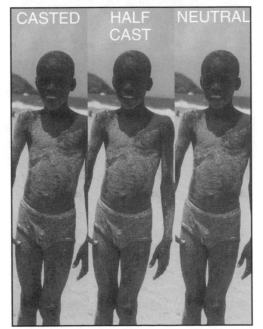

HALF CAST REMOVAL VALUES

Casted	Values	Neutral	Difference	Half Cast Correction
25C	25C	0	25C	
18M	16M	2	17M	(16 +1)
12Y	16Y	4	14Y	(12 + 2)
84C	80C	4	82C	(80 +2)
71M	71M	0	71M	
69Y	71Y	2	70Y	(69 +1)

These subtle corrections go a long way towards solving your color correction problems. Some further fine-tuning of the colors is still required, but you have a much clearer vision of the scan now. Fixing neutrals often clears up other color problems, which may have been much harder to identify.

Neutralization in Practice

As you do this, though, be sensitive to the image. In some cases, you have the choice of whether to neutralize by adding or subtracting ink. In these situations, concern yourself with matching the original and the amount of ink already in the image. In a heavy ink situation, you may want to pull ink, and in general, pulling ink out of a color is a safer move than adding color to it. In cases where color is washed out and weak looking, however, it may help naturalize an image by adding color.

Also be sensitive when identifying casts. Be sure to take several samples and set your Eyedropper tool to take 3x3 samples.

Images lit from different sources may also present a problem of multiple casts (see Figure 12.14). These can't be fixed with a global correction. You need to determine which cast is affecting the image the greatest. Then, select the affected areas, correct them, invert your selection, and correct again.

Figure 12.14

Two casts in one.

Be aware that although these tools are undeniably handy, neutralizing every-thing isn't the only answer. It's true that transmissive materials tend to be castier than reflective materials, but that's not always the case. Nor is every gray a neutral, and you should hesitate before forcing it to be. It's a common mistake to go into neutrality overload and neutralize everything. A better approach is to only neutralize what you really know to be neutral and be more circumspect about the rest. Keep in mind that neutrality is a proportional relationship. As you approach casted grays, let the neutral model be your guide, but keep your eye firmly on the original art.

Likewise, not every highlight should be set at the lightest printable value. Sometimes the lightest point in an image needs to stay at 20 percent for the image to appear correct. Let the image content and the client's art direction be your guide. If you push a quarter tone down to a highlight, you'll expand the tonal range of the image, but that's not always a good thing (see Figure 12.15). Increasing tonal range increases contrast. The differences between lights and darks becomes greater. The image appears to be less flat or have more contrast. This sounds great but may not help an image. Unnatural contrast can destroy the power of specular highlights and ruin a photographer's intention.

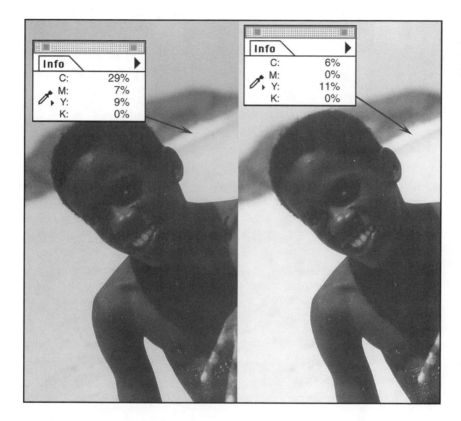

Figure 12.15

Unnatural appearances caused by incorrect adjusting.

CMYK Color Components

Getting a feel for color combinations is a major step towards correcting them. To do this, most people need to begin thinking primarily in the CMYK color space. The reason for this is simple visualization. Most everyone can visualize a color based on its CMYK components; few can visualize a color by its RGB values. For example, if you are interested in a color which is 50 percent magenta and 100 percent yellow, you can get a mental picture of what that might look like. When you ask for 255 red, 148 green, and 8 blue, few people think orange.

Color in CMYK can be thought of in terms of its components. The color component that dominates the color is thought of as the primary element or color component. In the last example, yellow would be the primary element of the color that was 100 percent yellow and 50 percent magenta. The primary element drives the hue and intensity of the color. It positions the color about the HSB wheel.

Adding a second color to the first changes the color and gives it depth. The more of the secondary element is added, the more the color will change. Adding 50 percent magenta to the 100 percent yellow gives it its orange hue and deepens the tone of the color.

Tertiary Colors

If you add a third, or tertiary, component to the color, you are graying, or dirtying, the color. If a color is described as being too dirty, there's probably too much of the third color. Remember that three colors can add up to a gray. It's the same principle that we've been using to swap colored inks for black on press. It can be useful to you here to take the comic book "pop" out of very pure colors.

This third color is also important in that it also gives detail and texture to the color. Without the third color, images look too saturated and detail falls off. When you reflect on it, it makes sense that the third color plays this role. The other two colors combine to make a color that is a compliment of the tertiary color. In our earlier example of the orange color, yellow and magenta combine to make an orange-red. Cyan and red are complementary colors. Although the third color is sometimes called the unwanted color, it's vital to image reproduction (see Figure 12.16).

Figure 12.16

The tertiary color holds important detail (see color insert).

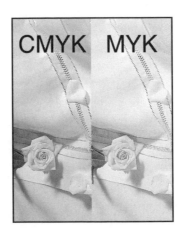

Black is added to help the tertiary color carry detail and shadow weight. You'll use it to replace ink on press and some printers also use it to replace the tertiary color. An example of this is red. How do you build a really strong red on press? Well, you'll need lots of magenta and then not as much, but still a lot, of yellow. Where do you go from there? The two colors put you in the ballpark but don't contain the required weight to solidify the red. You'll need either cyan, black, or a combination of the two. The way you go depends on your printer.

When starting to fine tune color in CMYK, you can think of the colors you're working on as having these component relationships. We'll look at some common colors and what elements comprise them. Knowing how these colors are built gives you a critical tool to correct colors that stray. This sort of color correction is best done on a selective basis. After the major tonal changes have been made, the end points have been established, and any color casts have been neutralized, you can zone in on specific areas and correct them.

Critical Color Components

You'll start making these changes with the important colors first. Corporate colors, for example, need to be corrected exactly. Large, solid background colors in photos should be corrected first. And of course, memory colors need to be accurate. People have expectations of what a Coke can looks like (a corporate color as well as a memory color) and things look wrong immediately if the color is incorrect.

Flesh Tones

Flesh tones are critical colors. Clients tend to squawk when they see scans of people, especially themselves, who are sunburned or jaundiced. When you're examining flesh tones, take a circumspect approach. Get several readings, trying to avoid any hot spots or shadows, but rather an overall assessment of the color.

The primary color element in CMYK flesh tones is usually yellow. Magenta also strongly comprises the color, typically flagging behind yellow by up to 10 percent. Cyan is the tertiary color in this combination, having values typically around 1/2 to 1/3 the value of the magenta dot. In Caucasian, flesh cyan usually never exceeds 30 percent, and then only in the shadows. If this relationship is tilted incorrectly, flesh starts to look odd (see Figure 12.17). If there is too much yellow, it has a sickly, jaundiced look. Too much magenta and it's sunburn city.

The relationship these colors have is the important thing. Typical value ranges are listed below.

Figure 12.17

*Component flesh tone colors
(see color insert).*

TYPICAL FLESH TONE COLOR VALUES

	African	Asian	Caucasian
Cyan	35	15	18
Magenta	45	43	45
Yellow	50	53	50
Black	up to 30	0	0

This chart should only be used as a reference as you learn to identify and correct colors. It is not intended as a standard to correct to. Its purpose is to illustrate different expressions of the same color relationship.

When adjusting these tones, use the Curves command again to swing printer values up or down accordingly. As with all color correcting, smaller steps are better than large ones where appropriate. That is, if you can make slight five percent adjustments and review them rather than sweeping shifts, you'll have much tighter control over the output process. With flesh tones, it's often also beneficial for you to make selective corrections rather than global ones. It's also much easier when first learning color corrections to make slight changes and then proof them. Taking notes on the values in the image, the corrections you made, and the resulting proof can greatly inform future decisions.

Let's look at a flesh tone correction in action to illustrate the point. In the following scan (Figure 12.18), the background colors and clothing look fine. The only real problem is the yellow cast in the skin tones. Measuring several points gives you a clearer idea of the problem. To fix this quickly, select the flesh tones and call up the Curves. You know that flesh should have cyan values between 1/2 and 1/3 of the magenta values, and this is fine in this case. The yellow, however, shouldn't be much more than 10 percent greater than the magenta. In this case, it is. Set your Curves to only affect the yellow values and pull the curve down in the requisite location. Check your work to the original for correctness and save your selection.

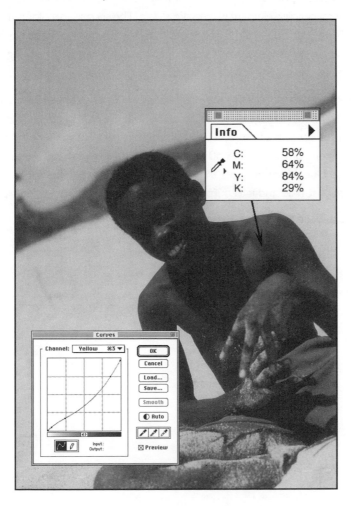

Figure 12.18

Correcting fleshtones (see color insert for another example).

Blue Sky

You might have heard about a newspaper out West somewhere where the skies are always blue and never cloudy. At least that's what the newspaper let its readers think. It established a standard color combination for blue sky. All outdoor photographs were to be corrected to this standard so that every photo in the paper always had beautiful blue skies. It's a good thing it never rained.

Now, this is certainly not an advocation for correcting all your skies to the same rigid, if happy, standard. But, just as with flesh tones, you can get an idea how to correct skies if you have an idea of what comprises it. As you might expect, the primary color element in blue sky is cyan. The secondary color is magenta. You'll want to keep yellow out of our blue skies as much as possible. Yellow tends to move blue towards teal. If our sky color needs deepening, you're better served adding black as a tertiary color than yellow (see Figure 12.19).

The relationship of cyan to magenta shapes the tone and hue of the blue you make. The more magenta you add, the warmer the blue becomes. Eventually, you'll end up with a purple. In cool blues, the magenta content is around 30 to 40 percent of the cyan. A 50 percent magenta to cyan ratio yields a more neutral blue. More magenta than that gives you a warm blue. At 75 percent, you're past blue and into purple. Here are some typical values for blue sky.

TYPICAL BLUE SKY COLOR VALUES

	Sky Blue	Warmer	Cooler
Cyan	60	60	60
Magenta	23	45	15
Yellow	0	0	0
Black	0	0	0

Figure 12.19

Black deepens sky better than yellow (see color insert).

As you begin to work with color, keep notes about the color you're seeing and what the CMYK values read. This gives you an idea about what to expect given your individual work station, proofing, and printing conditions. This forces you to apprise color numerically, rather than being seduced by the monitor's colors. After a while, you'll understand not only what colors will actually give you on press, but how they will need to be changed. When you first start color correcting, it's easy to tell that something "doesn't look right." It's much harder to translate that to "there is 10 percent too much yellow in this sky." Working on these combinations smooths out the process.

Typical Colors by Component

Target swatches are useful not only in calibration but in correction as well. Preparing a swatch page and proofing it out provides a solid reference point for color. Having a True Match book around is also a very good idea or beginners. The True Match book is a swatch book like the Pantone books except that it shows you what CMYK combinations look like when they're printed out. The book is available at art supply stores and through many mail order catalogs. As a starting place, we've listed some memory color combinations below.

TYPICAL MEMORY COLORS AND THEIR VALUES

	Cyan	Magenta	Yellow	Black
Silver	20	15	14	0
Gold	5	15	65	0
Beige	5	5	15	0
Highlight	5	3	3	0
25% Gray	25	16	16	0
50% Gray	50	37	37	0
Deep Violet	100	68	10	25
Deep Purple	85	95	10	0
Aqua	60	0	25	0
Green	100	0	100	0
Citrus Yellow	5	18	75	0
Dark Red	20	100	80	5

	Cyan	Magenta	Yellow	Black
Orange-Red	5	100	100	5
Orange	5	50	100	0
Chocolate	45	65	100	40
Pink	5	40	5	0

This list is clearly just a beginning. The values here are intended to convey an understanding of the combinations and proportions that build CMYK color. Its best use is as a reference guide.

Color Curves

The bulk of color correction work is often done with the Curves command. Curves satisfy both people who think visually and numerically. Another nice thing about them is that they can be saved and loaded. In cases where the curves are especially complicated or time consuming to perfect, you can take advantage of the ability to save and load them. We recall a client whose work consisted of product shots from industrial food shows. Bad florescent lighting left all the images with the same insane, greenish-yellow cast. After neutralizing the cast we saved the curve and recalled it every time his work came through again (see Figure 12.20).

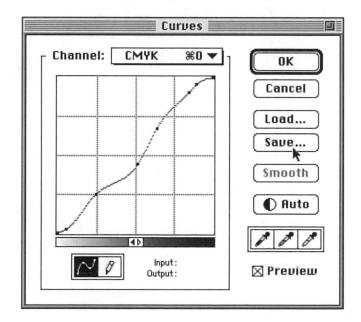

Figure 12.20

As a rule of thumb, if it took you longer than 30 seconds to create a curve, save it.

Photoshop is a handy thing in that it thinks of its curves the same no matter how you're using them. This means that you have some choices over when the affects of the curve take place. You can apply the curves normally, as we've been discussing, or you can have them take place when the file is printed. Photoshop 4.0, which is slated to be released around the same time as this book, also promises to include Adjustment Layers, which enable you to use write curves as separate layers that affect pixels in layers below them. The advantage is that the adjustment layer can be moved, removed, and changed without ever permanently affecting the core pixel information beneath them. This should be a major change in the average color correction workflow.

Photoshop 3.0 does enable you to make some color corrections that don't affect pixel information as well. The premise is you can write a Curve in just the manner you have been writing them so far and can load them in to be applied only when the file is printed. The major utility in this is its use in producing files that can be repurposed for more than one printing press. These adjustments are called transfer curves and this is how they're made.

Transfer Functions

Choose Page Setup from the File menu. Click the Transfer button (see Figure 12.21). The graph you see there should be a little familiar by now. The transfer curve also enables you to enter numerical settings for each value if you prefer. The default transfer function is a straight line curve: no change. You can also dial in curves for each printer if you have a notion to do so. When you print a file with a transfer function included, the RIP makes the changes the transfer function calls for.

Ideally, you'd like to be able to save and retrieve curves back and forth between transfer functions and the curves box. That way you can test out the results of the curve visually before you print it. Unfortunately, we've really only had any luck doing that with composite curves. Curves that affect specific channels are often misinterpreted as being meant for the entire image when they are loaded. This isn't very helpful.

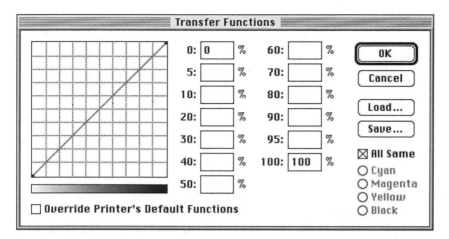

Figure 12.21

Transfer Functions.

If you are going to use a transfer function, pay attention to this important advice: communicate it somehow. If your file is moving out of house, you need to let the people receiving the file know that it includes a transfer function. It'll clear up confusion as to why the file is printing so differently than the pixel information shows. You should also talk to your service bureau before getting anywhere near the Override Printer's Default Functions. It may well throw out their calibration data, resulting in a file that is apt to print like who-did-it-and-ran. To include a transfer function in your file, save it as an EPS and select the Include Transfer Function checkbox.

Duotones and Multichannel Files

Another way curves are used to produce special printing effects is in the creation of duotones and other multichannel files. Duotones are a way to expand the tonal range of gray on press by printing with more than one color. Black is bolstered by a second printer in the case of a Duotone. Tritones and quadtones are created with three and four printers respectively. Duotones can be made out of process or spot colors. Typically, it's a spot color, often one is used as the second printer in a two color job. While the job of a duotone is usually to add depth and range to gray information, they can also be used to intentionally create tinted effects, similar to sepia tone photographs.

Duotones need to start from grayscale information. If you are working from a full color file, it needs to be converted before you can proceed. For some conversion tips, see the sidebar. The grayscale information that starts at its core always stays there unless you change it. The duotone setting tells printers to print it differently, much like how a transfer function works, but the core information stays the same.

Digital Prepress In the Real World

Discard Color Information?

Moving from color to grayscale can be a traumatic experience for a file. There are several ways to make the switch. One way is to simply pull down grayscale from the Mode menu. Doing this takes a weighted average of the color channels' brightness to produce an aggregate gray. This usually works okay but can destroy detail in some scans.

Another way would be to convert the file to Lab color. Then do the following:

1. Select the "a" channel and choose delete channel from the pop up channel's pop up menu.

2. Do the same thing for the "b" channel.

3. The file is now a multichannel document. It can only be saved in the Raw or Photoshop native formats. Change it over to grayscale to open up your saving options.

The resulting file takes its information from the relative brightness of the pixels and should be a better representation of the image.

Another option would be to inspect the channels for a suitable grayscale version of the file. Delete the other channels and correct the one left. You could also explore using the calculations features to pull detail out of the file. Whatever you choose, now you have more options than just taking what Photoshop tells you.

After you have your grayscale image, choose Duotone from the Mode menu. You'll invoke the Duotone options box. From here, you're given a pop up menu to select monotones, duotones, tritones, or quadtones. The type you choose determines how many inks will be used. Each ink setting has a curve, a swatch, and a name associated with it (see Figure 12.22). Each one is editable. Clicking the curve icon calls up the Duotone Curve box, which enables you to determine how that particular ink is printed along the tonal curve. Clicking the color swatch enables you to change the ink in question. From this box, you also have a gray ramp showing how your image may look with the current settings, and a button to change how things are displayed when they overprint.

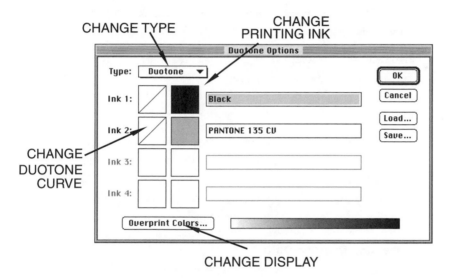

CHANGE TYPE

CHANGE PRINTING INK

CHANGE DUOTONE CURVE

CHANGE DISPLAY

Figure 12.22

The Duotone Options box.

The curves are important. If you just add even amounts of ink, everything darkens up into a muddy mess. Instead, you balance the inks by replacing gray with (at least) two inks. The curves let this happen intelligently. They need to also be applied intelligently. Otherwise, instead of expanding our tonal range and enhancing our image quality on press, we'll ruin a perfectly good black and white image. So in the place of a 50 percent gray dot, we can print a 29 percent black and a 30 percent cyan. If we printed two 50 percent dots, the image shifts. That's not our goal. Our goal is to reproduce the gradations accurately but to deepen the tones.

Photoshop's Duotone Presets

The fastest way to get decent duotone curves written is to start from the presets that ship with Photoshop. Check the Goodies folder in the Photoshop application folder. Choose Load from the Duotone Options box to call them up from memory. There are duotone, tritone, and quadtone curves available there, broken down into several categories.

The three general types of duotones (and when we say duotones we really mean tri- and quadtones too) are black and gray duotones, Pantone duotones, and process ink duotones. Each preset starts with a process black as ink # 1. The black and gray set uses a process black with a Pantone gray. The Pantone set builds with Pantone colors and the process set works with process black and some other process colors.

Inside each set is generally a series of four curves for each ink type combination. They're numbered one through four. The first two colorize the image. The third warms the image by mostly affecting the midtones. The fourth curve focuses its attention on the three-quarter tones.

These presets get the job done most of the time and with a little tinkering, they can get the job done even more frequently. If your Pantone color isn't on the preset list, it's easy work to swap it out with a different one. Just load the curve with the Pantone color that seems to have the closest brightness to yours and then click the color swatch to replace the color with your own.

Inspecting Duotone Data

Unlike other multiple color modes in Photoshop, duotones and their ilk all show up on the same channel. Without some trickery, you have no real way to tell what each printer looks like as you adjust the file. Your Info palette can give you the numbers, though. Set the Info palette to show Actual Color for the first color readout and grayscale for the second color readout (see Figure 12.23). This shows you how much of each ink is in each location and the aggregate gray value of the inks. Another option, if you have a question about what the inks are doing to different parts of your image, is to switch the image to multichannel mode. You'll get a document with a channel for each ink. You can slide through the channels and inspect where the inks are residing. If you undo the mode change, you're back where you started. Be careful not to do anything more than inspect the channels or you'll lose your chance to revert back to the duotone.

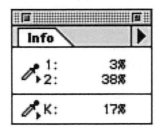

Figure 12.23

Info palette settings for a Duotone.

Another time-honored trick when color-correcting anything, duotones particularly, is to build a frame of reference.

1. Make a new grayscale Photoshop document that's as wide as your file and skinny, perhaps a quarter-inch high. It should also be the same resolution as your file.

2. Set your foreground and background colors in the new document to the defaults.

3. Drag the gradient tool across the file from one side to the other horizontally so that you get a gray ramp.

4. Choose Image: Map: Posterize. Set this for 20 steps. Each step should be at five percent increments.

5. Go back to your original document and increase the canvas size by a little more than the width of your gray ramp. Set the placement icon to add new space at the bottom of your file (see Figure 12.24).

6. Go back to the gray ramp file. Select everything and then drag your new selection into the duotone document. Let it sit at the bottom where you made space for it.

Having a reference point enables you to examine what's happening to each tone in your image as you adjust the duotone curves without hunting for the requisite pixels. You also have a reference point in the form of the original file. If your goal is to expand tonal range without obvious shifting, compare the ramp made from gray ink with the one in the duotone. They should stay similar as you work.

Figure 12.24

Building a static reference point
for Duotone adjusting.

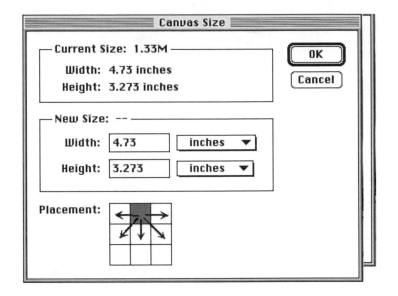

Onscreen Duotone Display

Another way to adjust duotones is to fine tune their onscreen display. If you have a Pantone color, you can open up the picker and fine tune its HSB, RGB, or Lab values. Don't touch the CMYK values here; you'll confuse Photoshop and nobody wants that. You can also control what colors Photoshop displays when two or more colors interact. Doing this doesn't affect how things print, just as changing how the Pantone color displayed doesn't affect how things print. They *do* affect how things print if you convert your duotone over to CMYK. Clicking the Overprint Colors button from the Duotone options box calls up the Overprint Colors box, which adjusts how Photoshop (see Figure 12.25). Each swatch corresponds to the color Photoshop expects will correspond to each color combination. It's usually a pretty good guess. If you think Photoshop is wrong about this, click the swatch to adjust it.

You can adjust your images with duotones in two ways. One, with the color of inks you choose, and two, by changing the curve of the ink to increase coverage or contrast in a given area. Usually, it makes sense in a duotone to pick a lighter ink as our second color if you're starting with black. Two dark colors aren't as flexible on press as a light one and a dark one. Because you have two inks to work with, you can increase detail in one area of our image with one ink and in another area with the other ink.

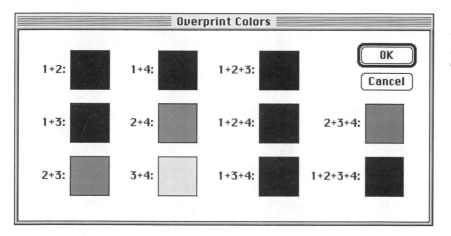

Figure 12.25

Fine-tuning how Photoshop displays duotone colors.

Here's an example of how that works in action. In Figure 12.26, you've got reasonably good image information throughout, but the image needs more punch in the highlights, stronger contrast throughout the quarter and midtones, and more depth in the shadows. You should work with a duotone in this case, adding a light gray to the black printer.

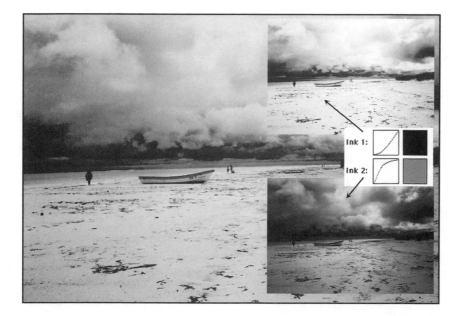

Figure 12.26

Duotone curves and their corresponding plates.

Notice that as we did this work, we paid attention to the press needs of your image. Remember that too-small highlights and too-dark shadows won't print correctly on press. You can compress the data before you move into duotone mode or use the curves themselves to compress the data.

Process Quadtones Versus CMYK Grayscale

If you've ever converted a grayscale file to RGB or CMYK, you know that Photoshop doesn't just take the gray information and write it to the black printer. Rather, it distributes the information across all the channels in a manner determined by the color preferences you have set. What you essentially have there is a quadtone, four colors printing together to produce gray values. You can make multitone images using the process colors.

Doing this has some ups and downs. File size is bigger for CMYK files than for quadtones, and the image is, in some ways, less flexible than the quadtone. It's not as easy, for example, to just swap colors at the last minute in a CMYK file. On the other hand, CMYK images give you the ability to easily create blends and areas of solid color that you can't do with quadtones. Be aware, also that if you're printing a CMYK quadtone to simulate other colors (that is, you're working in CMYK but you intend to print with spot colors) and you import the file into a layout program, it will separate as CMYK.

If your plan is to create CMYK quadtone from a grayscale image, you can simply convert and let the image info fall where it may. If you are going to do this, you'll need to be careful about how you separate and may consider increasing your UCA settings.

A more flexible method might be the following. Select All and Copy the grayscale image. Make a new file. Photoshop anticipates what you want to do and makes the file size and resolution the same as your grayscale image you just copied. Set the new file to be CMYK. Select each channel of the new file individually and paste the grayscale information into it. This is essentially the same as a quadtone with all 45° curves. From there, you need to adjust the gamma for each channel using the curves command. Keep the grayscale file open as a reference to ensure your tones are correct.

We'll build a quadtone with the process colors as an example of the process. In this photograph (Figure 12.27a), we want not only to deepen the tones of the original, but also to warm up the original and suggest the flesh tones that are the image's primary content. We'll start by making the image a quadtone. Next, we'll lay down the colors in the order we want them to print. We want the darkest color down first up through the lightest. The curves for each ink will perform different jobs. The black ink builds detail in the quarter and three-quarter tones. The cyan plate adds depth and detail to the shadows, while the magenta and yellow plates carry the highlight detail. The highlights are all flesh tones and we've suggested that by writing our duotone curves with proportions similar to the proportions used to create fleshtones (see Figure 12.27b).

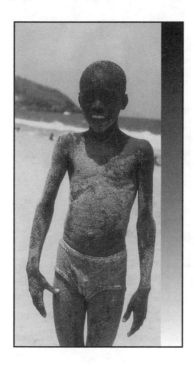

Figure 12.27a

A halftone image before being converted to a quadtone.

Saving and Printing Duotones

When saving our duotones, we need to make them EPS files. We also have the option when saving them of controlling the screen angles of each printing ink. The angle refers to the angle at which the array of halftone cells that comprise that plate will print. In traditional printing, each ink is at its own angle from the others. The 45° angle is the least visible to the human eye, so it's the best one to print at. The strongest color in the image goes there, usually black. The remaining angles are each spaced at least 45° away from each other. The exception is yellow, or whichever the lightest printing color is. Since it's less noticeable, it can be printed at 90° without worry. This leaves it a mere 15° from cyan.

Figure 12.27b

The final colorized quadtone (see color insert).

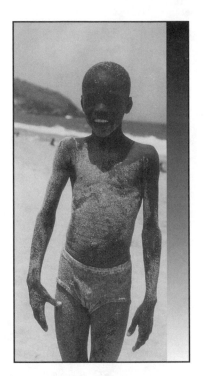

The core principle here to learn is that different inks should be printed at different angles. The strongest should rest at 45°, the weakest at 90°. If you're going to specify screen angles for your images you can do it by hitting the screens function from Page Setup under the File menu. When you start doing this, take a minute and call your printer. He or she can give you good advice about which inks are best served at which angles.

Printing Duotones

The only problems left now are proofing and printing. Proofing is a problem for custom inks. Your only real options are to spend the cash on a special system that will let you proof with spot colors or convert to process. Doing this gives you a ball park, but you're still in pretty far in the dark. If you have a Color Management System in place, converting the file and printing through the system may be your best bet. As far as printing the beast, make sure you're on press. You really ought to be on-hand for a press check on most jobs, but it's especially critical on duotones. There's really no way to know exactly what you'll see until the ink hits the paper. The decisions the press operators make are extremely important here. Plus, they usually don't have much by way of a proof to go by. Make sure by being there.

SUMMARY

Color is one of the most difficult problems in the world of publishing. Producing it correctly takes skill and requires specific information about the press that will print it. It is subject to possible change by all the devices it encounters along the production path. It's not always intuitive to know how to correct color and difficult because everyone sees it differently. Given all these problems, it would seem insurmountable to produce color cost-effectively day-in and day-out.

You can ease the process along by correctly framing client expectations clearly up front and then paying attention to the simple facts of color. Trust the things you know. Work from neutrals and memory colors and use the numbers. Get comfortable with several different correction tools. In no time, even complicated files like quadtones will be within your reach.

PRODUCTION TECHNIQUES

The production manager caught us as we were trying to sneak away for a meeting. She wanted to know if we weren't too busy, could we please do something for her? We *were* busy, but one of us was taking a phone call just then, so Steve thought he'd see what the matter was.

Steve asked the production manager what the problem was. She had a grayscale photograph of a house and she needed to place just the house and not the background of the photograph on top of another picture in Quark. And she needed it in the next 10 minutes. Whew! We thought this one would be hard. Fortunately, the house was against a solid sky with no power lines or other intruding details. Doing what needed to be done took about three minutes. The production chief was grateful and amazed.

And so were we. What we had done was extremely simple and exactly the kind of technique that gets used over and over again in a production house. How long had production gotten by without these tools? How long had this file been sitting there waiting for someone to fix it? How much money had delays like this caused us?

Most people who work in the digital graphic arts have no formal training in it. They've learned everything they know in the field and rarely have any time to try new things simply for the fun of learning. The fact of the matter is that sooner or later, you're going to need to know how to do a few things. This chapter will concentrate on several of those key points.

In this chapter, you'll learn how to:

- Tackle difficult scans

- Assign clipping paths

- Work with layers and channels

- Expand our selection tools

DIFFICULT SCANS

Regardless of how well you prepare your clients for the world of digital scanning, sooner or later someone will come to you with a really lousy original. "It's the only thing I have," they'll protest. "Can't you please make it wonderful for me?" Well, maybe. There's only so much you can do with a bad original. The only time you should agree to accept a lousy original is after you've spelled out in extremely clear terms that the level of acceptable quality has been lowered considerably and the onus for that is completely on them. We remember a client who produced a felt-tip original drawn on a cocktail napkin (no kidding) and then complained that the edges weren't sharp enough.

The other thing to pay attention to when accepting lousy originals is cost. Most of them take much longer to process and produce. In some cases, giving the client what they really want means extra hours redrawing a file in Illustrator. In any case, you'll have to either spend a certain amount of time on a scan and go no further, or go all the way and consider the additional work a bonus to your client. This wouldn't be such a terrible thing—just be sure to let your client know how much extra work they got free. Just be careful about establishing a pattern of behavior you can't maintain. If you scan a client's line art and then turn it into vectors when you have time, what will they think when you don't do that? Your bottom line is built by both good feelings and billable hours.

Prescreening and Moiré Patterns

Let's get down to some scanning difficulties. A common one is the ubiquitous prescreened art. Prescreened is jargon for "printed." Items printed in a traditional manner are really just a grid of halftone spots. This grid can interfere with the scanning process and cause unsightly visual interference. The interference is called a *moiré* (more-ay) *pattern* (see Figure 13.1). Prescreening isn't the only thing that can cause these patterns. They can be produced by the output process as well as the input process. In the output process, if screens are misaligned, moiré can result. What's more pernicious is that image content can cause moiré as well. It can come off fabrics and things with repeating patterns in them. In cases of moiré in output, the answer to beating the pattern is typically swapping the angles at which the color plates print. Try switching the magenta and cyan angles first.

In the case of scanning prescreened objects, you should be aware of a few techniques. We'll discuss them in the order of least damaging to most damaging in image quality.

Beating a Moiré Pattern by Rotation

The first series of tricks involves doing something akin to swapping the screen angles. Scanning the original at an angle and then setting it aright in Photoshop sometimes knocks out the pattern. This is happening essentially because of the averaging Photoshop does when it rotates pixels. If you're working with a flatbed scanner, propping an artist's triangle against the side of the bed and then laying the original against that lets you know exactly what angle the image is laying at. Having several different angles gives you a variety of choices. If one angle doesn't work, try another one.

Figure 13.1

*Scanning prescreened materials
can introduce a visual
interference pattern.*

To rotate the scan once you've scanned it, choose Image: Rotate: Arbitrary (see Figure 13.2). Dial in the angle of the triangle and you're off to the races. If you don't know the angle the image is turned to, you can also free rotate a selection or cropping marquee. To rotate a cropping marquee, hold down the Option (Mac) or Alt (IBM) key and click one of the corner points. The image swings freely.

Figure 13.2

*Dial in the precise angle you
need.*

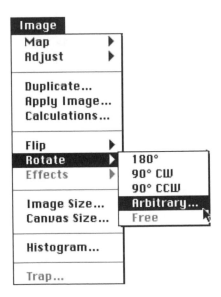

At the heart of that technique and the ones that follow is an amount of image blurring. How exactly it's done is a question of what works for the image and makes sense to you. The key is going to be in limiting the blurring so that you remove the pattern without substantially harming your image quality.

Beating a Moiré Pattern by Lifting

An image scanned on a flatbed scanner can be thrown out of focus slightly by raising it off the glass. The depth of field for even a midrange scanner is very limited, perhaps a quarter of an inch. The easiest way to lift an image off the bed is to build a framework of some sort. We had one made from some thin, corrugated cardboard cut into pairs of various lengths. It can slide together to make a square of different sizes depending on which set of ends you choose. That way you can accommodate originals of different sizes and flexibility without introducing a bow into the image. We've also seen people use pennies and dimes to lift an image off the glass. Once the out-of-focus scan is made, the image can be sharpened back into focus with an unsharp mask.

Beating a Moiré Pattern by Blurring

The most reliable, albeit damaging, method of beating a pattern is the one with the most flexibility. Flexibility here is defined as opportunity for user input. These are the basic steps of the plan; we'll add some finesse to it in a moment:

1. Scan the image at twice the resolution you need. This is often the same as four times the line screen.

2. Blur the image.

3. Cut the resolution in half.

4. Blur again as needed; touch up with other filters.

5. Sharpen, serve fresh, and enjoy.

Let's look at those steps in a little more detail. The first thing you do is double the amount of resolution you need. This serves two purposes. One, it builds more information into the image. Less damage is done by the forthcoming filters. Two, when half of the pixels are thrown away, the moiré pattern based on those pixels tends to be less visible.

Scanning at such high resolution can be time consuming and frustratingly slow, but it's required. Recall though, a quality factor of as low as one and a half is acceptable for many output types. This means that if you're printing to a 150 line screen device, a pixel resolution of as low as 225 produces acceptable results. Double this amount to 450 pixels in the scan. Compare that with 300 pixels doubled to 600. In a 4-by-5 inch CMYK scan, that's the difference between 27.5 MB and 15.5 MB.

We'll use two filters to beat the moiré pattern (see Figure 13.3): Despeckle (Filter: Noise: Despeckle) and Gaussian Blur (Filter: Blur: Gaussian Blur). We use the Gaussian Blur instead of other blurring filters (Blur and Blur More) for two reasons. One, an ellipsis is next to the words Gaussian Blur in the filter window. That ellipsis means that there is more to come, more things for you to fill in. You have to decide what happens, which means you *know* what happens. Other than a sneaking suspicion that Blur More blurs things more than Blur, we have no idea what those filters actually do to our pixels. It's the same reason that we use an Unsharp Mask instead of Sharpen, Sharpen Edges or Sharpen More. You don't know what they do. You can't control them. You don't use them.

Figure 13.3

The filters we'll use to beat a
moiré pattern.

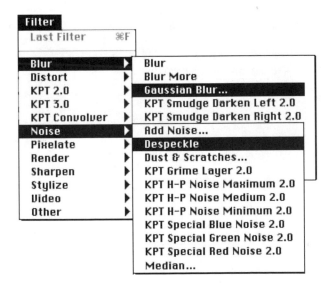

The other reason to use a Gaussian Blur is that you get a better blur. A Gaussian distribution, which you'll also see in other places in Photoshop, places the effects of the filter along a bell curve, which is stronger in the middle and weaker on the sides. This has the effect of mitigating, but not completely undermining, the filter's effect. Other blurs don't do this, resulting in a less subtle effect.

The Gaussian Blur can work in tenths of a pixel. The strength of the blur you select is driven by the intensity of the moiré pattern. We want to dial in a number that blurs the image enough to start to get rid of the pattern, but not so much that we loose detail irrevocably (see Figure 13.4). In our experience, we've never used a blur much past 1.8 pixels. Usually though, values closer to .7 work fine.

Dummy Buttons

We hear the little voice in the back of the class asking "If they aren't useful, then why did Adobe put them there?"

The reason these applications have features you shouldn't use is that Photoshop isn't just for geniuses like you and me. Strange as it may seem, non-professionals are using these products, too. They have different expectations about quality and different levels of interest in learning to do things right. For them, we have Sharpen More. It doesn't mean you're a dummy if you use it; it just means you aren't getting the best results.

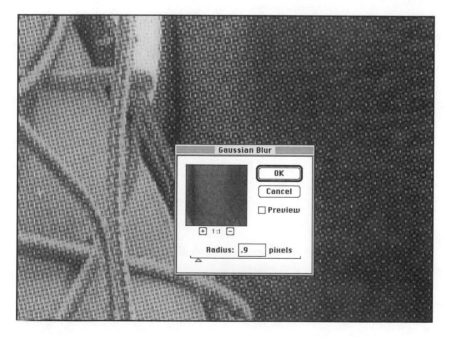

Figure 13.4

Some sort of blurring is usually involved in beating this pattern. The Gaussian one works best.

Before you go bananas blurring the image, you might want to take a quick run through your channels. Your goal in doing this is to find where the pattern lives. In many cases, a moiré pattern only affects one or two of the channels. The pattern is easy to detect in the channel (see Figure 13.5). If you blur only the channels the pattern lives in, your image quality won't degrade nearly so badly.

Figure 13.5

Moiré often lives in a specific channel or two.

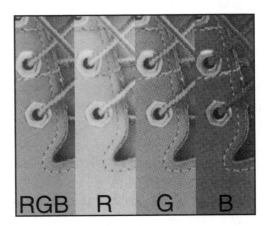

It's possible to go even a step further with moiré detection. Once you've found the channels with the patterns in them, run your cursor over the pattern and the surrounding areas. You should be able to determine a specific tonal range that the pattern occupies. Knowing that, the next step is to select that particular tonal range using Select: Color Range. Choose Selected colors and click the pattern itself. Dial up the fuzziness value until you've selected the moiré pattern and the neighboring pixels in that channel. Lay in your Gaussian Blur or perhaps even the Dust and Scratches filter. Then step back and examine your work. If you choose Select: Hide Edges (⌘ H), you'll get a better look without the selection marquee in your way. It's also a good idea to save that selection (this will be covered in more detail later in this chapter). Repeat these steps for any other channels with the pattern living in it. Remember that you still have some moiré-removing steps to make. It's better to err on the side of image integrity.

Next, cut the resolution in half. To do this, go to Image: File Size. Make sure the Constrain File Size check box is not selected (see Figure 13.6). Constraining the file size takes the same grid of pixels and makes them larger or smaller. Unchecking this check box enables Photoshop to add or, more commonly, subtract pixels. This is what you want. Cut the resolution to the size you want to print with and choose OK.

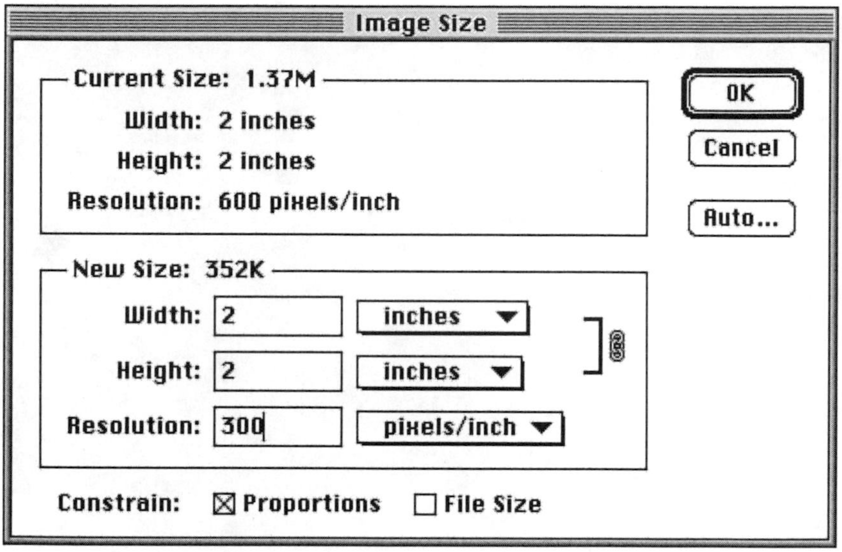

```
╔══════════════════ Image Size ══════════════════╗
║ ┌─ Current Size: 1.37M ──────────────┐  ┌──────────┐  ║
║ │    Width:  2 inches                │  │    OK    │  ║
║ │    Height: 2 inches                │  └──────────┘  ║
║ │    Resolution: 600 pixels/inch     │  ┌──────────┐  ║
║ └────────────────────────────────────┘  │  Cancel  │  ║
║                                          └──────────┘  ║
║ ┌─ New Size: 352K ───────────────────┐  ┌──────────┐  ║
║ │    Width:  [2      ] [inches  ▼]   │  │  Auto... │  ║
║ │    Height: [2      ] [inches  ▼]   │  └──────────┘  ║
║ │    Resolution: [300] [pixels/inch ▼]               ║
║ └────────────────────────────────────┘               ║
║                                                        ║
║  Constrain:  ☒ Proportions   ☐ File Size              ║
╚════════════════════════════════════════════════════════╝
```

Figure 13.6

Cutting the resolution in half

Image quality should improve when you throw out half the pixels. If the pattern persists, lay in another, smaller blur. You may also see rosettes (see Figure 13.7). which are a circular pattern of halftone dots. They're not inherently bad, unless they're visually distracting. We've found rosettes can be beaten back with the Despeckle filter (Filter: Noise: Despeckle). The filter searches for edges in the image and then gives everything but the edges a slight blur. Yeah, yeah, it doesn't have an ellipse after its name, so sue us.

Your image should be looking pretty good by now. The problem now is that sharpening the image tends to bring back the pattern you worked so hard to get rid of. If this happens, try loading the inverse of the selection you saved when you were working on blurring the pattern. Now you can sharpen everything but the pixels where the pattern lived. This usually isn't an overwhelming problem.

We've used this technique effectively when scanning clip art halftones. These ad slicks are typically screened with the coarsest of grids. Technically speaking, the problem here is usually not a moiré pattern, but rather a problem of visible screening. Scanning them as line art usually creates a mess and, on the rare occasions it does work, leaves you with files you can't do much with. Using the moiré removal method removes the conspicuous space between dots and reintroduces the illusion of continuous tones.

Figure 13.7

Another problem: rosettes.

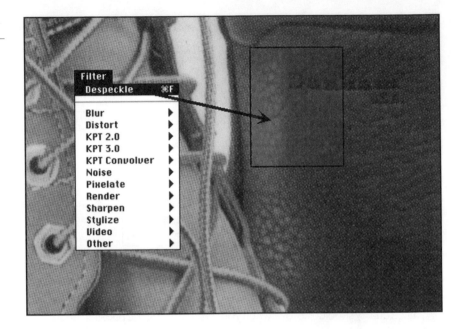

Now is as good a time as any to give you the lecture about not stealing people's copywritten or trademarked materials: Don't steal people's copywritten or trademarked materials. Scanning them and then using them in your pieces counts as stealing. So, although it might be really grand to have Garfield and Odie in your next brochure, you probably shouldn't.

Negatives

Film negatives provide another challenge source in scanning. Even if you're working on a mid- to high-end scanner, negatives can have you pulling out your hair. Part of the problem is caused by the nature of the negative itself. The substrate of a color negative is orange. The act of turning the image into a positive turns the orange cast of the negative into a complementary cast in the positive. This leaves you with a cyan cast in the positive. If you're working on a scanner with a negative setting, it probably works at least some of the time. When it doesn't, it's handy to know this trick: scan the negative as a positive. From there, neutralize the cast from the substrate and invert the image.

This is essentially taking the choices the scanner makes automatically away from it and putting it in your own hands. The first step is fairly self-explanatory. Scanning the image as a positive prevents the scanner from making any neutralization moves of its own.

The second step is a pretty big one. The cast in the positive is apt to be a pretty big one. You could neutralize it with Curves, which would be a matter of pulling a lot of red and some green out of the file. You could also attempt to neutralize with the eyedroppers, which is also difficult. This is one of the few cases where we may use a one-touch adjustment.

The Curves and Levels commands both feature an innocuous little button labeled Auto (see Figure 13.8). Normally, Auto *anything* gives us the heebie-jeebies, but this is a rare case. What the Auto levels and curves feature does is essentially the same thing that Image: Adjust: Auto Levels does. Photoshop looks through the image, finds the darkest and lightest pixels, and maps them to black and white. All the other pixel values get changed as well. They stretch to fill the spectrum. The nice thing about this feature is that unlike the Equalize command, which sees the image in toto, Auto levels looks at each channel individually.

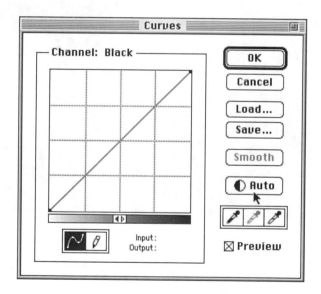

Figure 13.8

The Auto Curves feature

Are you starting to see the logic here? Equal values of RGB are neutral. So if you stretch out each color channel to its full spectrum, the effect is a force neutralization of the entire image. Several important caveats. If you use this on CMYK files, you will experience terrible color shifting and overall darkening. If you use this effect on images that already include full blacks and whites, you will have a partial effect or none at all. Unwanted effects and color jumps will result.

We're starting to feel like an old gypsy fortune teller here: *Your tonal range will expand beyond printable limits! Your colors will shift and sway like the wind! Your buddies in production will laugh at you for using the dummy buttons! You're DOOMED! DOOO-OO-OOOMED!*

Be aware that Auto levels or Curves isn't a panacea. In fact, this is really the only time you really use it. After you've gotten rid of the cast, you can invert the image normally (see Figure 13.9). You'll have to color correct, adjust, and target your image for the press, but now you're in the ballpark.

Figure 13.9

Beating the cast introduced by the substrate of a color negative.

If you're scanner doesn't offer a negative setting but does enable you to make tonal adjustments by channel, remember that inverting the gamma curve is the same as inverting the image. Identifying the start and end points for each RGB channel and writing gamma curves inverting them is the same as scanning an inverse image. If the corrections made to your image pushed it too far away from the original to be usable, try recording your Photoshop corrections and rescanning using those settings as your scanner settings. That is, if your scanner lets you save and load curves, it'll probably take Photoshop's curves, which can be saved as discrete files.

Correcting an image in Photoshop often serves as an instruction manual about how to rescan it. Most of Photoshop's basic tools are replicated somehow on scanners. Scanning correctly a second time, with the information you got from correcting the file, is often preferable to sticking with the heavily corrected Photoshop file. Consider this option on files that have caused you headaches. Rescan the file the way you corrected it and see if you don't get a better scan. Save the settings with a descriptive name and you'll be happier next time.

Sometimes it's a cost-effective necessity to scan three-dimensional objects. It's never an optimal condition and engenders specific problems. On the up side, though, scanning found objects can save quite a bit of do-re-mi in photo shoots.

The first problem is lack of lighting control and stability. The stability question usually resolves itself by mounting the objects on a board of some sort. A loop of tape does the job. Additional lighting may also have to be jury-rigged.

Scanning reflective objects presents another problem, but it's easy to fix. The problem is that scanners measure light absorbed by an original. Originals that reflect light, like metal objects, throw off scanners. The result is typically a rainbow pattern or blue halos. The first step to getting rid of the rainbow pattern once you've scanned the object is to select the area. Then call up the Hue/Saturation commands. Desaturating each channel pulls the color values out of it (see Figure 13.10). Touch up appropriately (found art usually needs a good bit of help) and you're done.

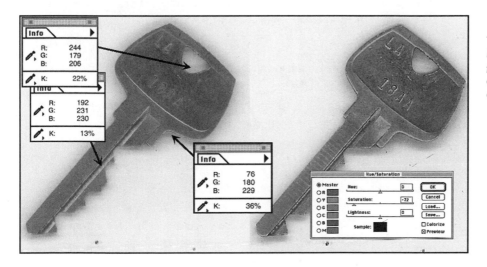

Figure 13.10

Desaturating the rainbow pattern out of a reflective original (see corresyponding example in color section)

SELECTIONS

Understanding selections and how they work is the key to really opening up Photoshop's power. In Chapter 10, we introduced the three basic selection tools. Now we'll expand on the subject and discuss how, and how not, to make silhouettes.

The first thing to think about is what selections really means. Selecting something is akin to masking, or protecting everything else. If you've spray-painted something through a stencil, you've worked with a mask. Back in ye olde traditional prepress days, this took the form of a rubylith overlay. With rubyliths, your work had two states: protected and unprotected. In the digital world, things are a little different. You can have many states and many levels of selected-ness. Pixels can be selected, unselected, or partially selected. When they're partially selected, whatever you do to them only partially affects them. This means that if you use the paintbrush on a partially selected pixel, only a portion of the paintbrush's value is applied to the pixel.

Look at how this selected-ness expresses itself when you save a selection. If you make a selection and then choose Save Selection from the Select menu, you're prompted as to where you want to save the selection (see Figure 13.11). The selection is saved to a channel; you should be familiar with channels. Each color channel in a full-color image expresses eight bits of the color information. The individual color channel is represented as a grayscale image, but there's another kind of channel and that's where we'll record our selections. They're sometimes referred to as *Alpha channels*, but they're commonly referred to as selection channels.

In a selection channel, the darker a pixel is, the less selected it is. Black pixels are unselected, white pixels are selected, and gray pixels are partially selected. When you add to this the notion that selection channels can be edited with all of Photoshop's regular production tools, you've got a whole new set of selection tools.

Let's look at this in action. In Figure 13.12, you start with a simple selection, even though parts of it are hard to get to. We'll save the selection, turn it into a channel, and edit it from there. Clicking the Selection icon in the Channels palette is the fastest way to do this (see Figure 13.13). This automatically generates a new channel, saving the selection. The selection is currently invisible, but notice what happens when you click the eye icon to display it. You get a rubylith display in which items under the rubylith are protected and items that aren't under the rubylith are selected.

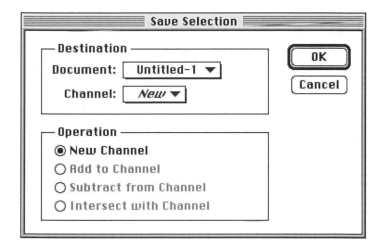

Figure 13.11

Selections are saved to channels.

Figure 13.12

This selection would be hard to isolate using the traditional tools.

Figure 13.13

The Channels palette

SHOW CHANNEL

SHORTCUTS

ACTIVE CHANNEL

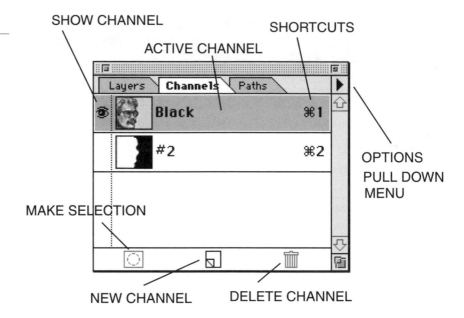

OPTIONS
PULL DOWN
MENU

MAKE SELECTION

NEW CHANNEL   DELETE CHANNEL

If you can't stand the color of rubylith, or perhaps were frightened by a rubylith as a child, you can change its color by selecting the channel and choosing the Channel Options from the pull-down menu. The swatch takes you to the color picker where you can select a new color. Be sure to select something distinct.

Working with channels can be a little confusing at first. Keeping straight what you're seeing, what prints, and what you're editing can be confusing. They're often nowhere near the same things. Rely on the channel keyboard shortcuts to navigate and activate channels, and keep your eye on the channel palette. You're editing the highlighted channels and looking at the ones with eyes next to them. With a little practice, it'll seem routine.

Select the new channel you've built, but keep the other channels visible. Choose None from the Selection menu to get rid of any confusing selections. If you set your foreground colors to white and start painting with the paintbrush, you'll erase parts of the mask (see Figure 13.14). To turn the channel back into a selection, drag the channel icon over the Selection icon or just Option-click the channel you want to turn into a selection. The new selection you get is based on the tones in your selection channel. White areas are completely selected. Note that all the other tools you use in Photoshop, like filters, are available to edit this channel as well.

Figure 13.14

Editing a selection channel.

Using Selection Channels to Fade Images

Making an image slowly fade out to a ghosted image is a snap with selection channels. Open up the file you want to ghost and make a new channel (click the new channel icon or, to bypass the dialog box, use a modifier key when you click: Option–click on the Mac, Alt–click on a Windows machine). Select your gradient tool and drag out a gradient blend from the point you want your image to start fading to where you want it to disappear. Viewing the composite channel as well may be helpful in placing the gradient. Remember the dark areas will be protected and the white areas will be totally selected.

Return to the Composite channel by clicking on its icon or hitting ⌘-0 on the Mac, Ctrl–0 on the IBM. Load the selection channel by Option-clicking it. Make sure the background color is set to white and hit delete. The pixels lose more value the more selected they are, creating a fade out, ghosting effect (see Figure 13.15). With a little creativity, you can use this technique to make images blend into each other.

467

Figure 13.15

*A gradient ghosting effect and
the selection channel that
created it.*

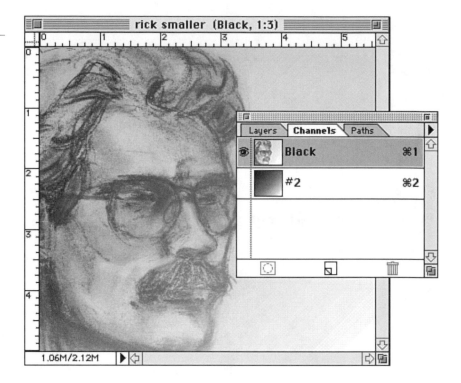

Selection Channels from Scans

A common source for a selection channel is existing scans. Let's say you've
scanned a leaf. You want the leaf's texture to be a mask for a picture of a
squirrel. Simply take the grayscale scan of the leaf, invert it, and copy it (Image:
Map: Invert and Edit: Copy). Then go to the file you want to put the selection
channel into, make a new channel, and copy the inverted leaf into the selection
channel. Load the selection. Go back to the scan of the squirrel, select an area
bigger than the leaf, copy it, and paste it into the selection in the other file (see
Figure 13.16). This works best when the mask file has plenty of dark areas, solid
shadows, and some funky edges.

Creating New Channels

You can make new channels in other ways as well. The simplest is to click the
New Channel icon at the bottom of the channel palette. You're prompted with
channel options. To bypass them, hold down the Option key as you click the
icon. You get a sequentially-numbered channel with the same color and opacity
as the one before it or the default.

Figure 13.16

A mask created from a scanned object

If you have more than one selection saved, you can load more than one selection at a time. The same keys that add to and subtract from a selection when you're working normally work here as well.

◆ To load a selection to replace to an existing selection, drag the channel onto the selection icon.

◆ To load a selection to add to an existing selection, hold down the Shift key as you drag the channel onto the selection icon.

◆ To load a selection to subtract from an existing selection, hold down the Command (Mac) or Ctrl (IBM) key as you drag the channel onto the selection icon.

◆ To load a selection to intersect an existing selection, hold down the Command (Mac) or Ctrl (IBM) and Shift key as you drag the channel onto the selection icon.

Remember that instead of dragging the channel onto the new selection icon, you can also hold down the Option (Mac) or Alt (IBM) key and click the channel. To replace an existing selection, Option (Mac) or Alt (IBM) click the channel you want to select. To add to a selection, Option (Mac) or Alt (IBM) and Shift (both platforms) click the channel to be added. You can also do this the hard way if you must. Choose Load Selection from the Select menu and the radio buttons for the above keyboard shortcuts are right there.

Saving Selection Channels

Saving selections is strongly recommended due to the possibility of repeating work. Because we hate to rework things so much, we are big believers in saving early and saving often. The same advice is true with channels. Any selection that took any effort at all to construct should be saved. This creates a slight file management problem in that a file with extra channels can't be saved in a file format you want to use for printing. It needs to be in Photoshop format or a Raw format. If you want to keep these selections (and I expect that you would—who knows what clients will want next?), you have a couple of options. One would be to simply Duplicate the file (Image: Duplicate), delete the additional channels, and save the file as you would normally. You end up with two files.

This is fine if you live the Land O' Infinite Disk Space. In the real world, it makes more sense to go one step further. After you've duplicated the file and deleted the offending channels, go back to the other file. This time, delete the color channels. When it comes time to load the selections from the pure selection channel file to the other color file, simply drag and drop the channel from one file to the other. You could also load the selection from the selection menu or pull it in using the Calculations feature. It's much easier to just drop it in. Remember that Photoshop's native file format features an automatic compression scheme that works especially well on these kind of files.

Quick Masks

Sometimes, you really don't need to keep your selections around, but you'll still want the option of using Photoshop's tools to see what's selected more intuitively. The marching ants used in the normal selection marquees enclose everything that's at least 50 percent selected. That makes no distinction between pixels that are 51 percent selected and 100 percent selected. Quick Masks to the rescue.

Quick Masking is a mode in Photoshop that gives you a better way to display selections. It displays selections with the same rubylith display used in normal visible selection channels. You get to Quick Mask mode by clicking the Quick Mask icon from the toolbox (see Figure 13.17) or by typing "Q." Quick Masks give you all the features of a selection channel without making it permanent. It shows up in the channels in italics to let you know that as soon as you leave Quick Mask mode, the channel disappears.

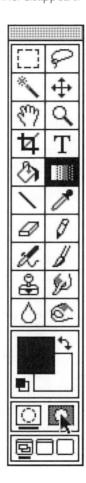

Figure 13.17

The Quick Mask mode button

When you move into Quick Mask mode with a selection made, the temporary Quick Mask channel is brought up and selected. The other channels remain visible and the selection marquee disappears to be replaced by the mask. The color picker, recognizing that you've moved into the eight-bit world of the Quick Mask, replaces any colors it may have had, showing their grayscale tonal equivalents. You're now ready to edit your selection. Use any of the tools you normally would. If your brush is set to white, you'll be essentially painting a selection.

If you switch back out of Quick Mask mode, the newly edited selection masks are replaced with the familiar marching ants. This can be very handy if you want to draw out a selection area quickly. Here's an example of Quick Masking in action.

1. With nothing selected, switch over to Quick Mask mode.

2. With the foreground color black, key in some text.

3. Deselect (Select:None).

4. Invert the channel (Image:Map:Invert) and switch out of Quick Mask mode.

5. You now have a selection area in the shape of the text you wanted. Switch to the gradient tool and drag it across your file to give the text a gradient.

What just happened? When we entered Quick Mask mode and laid down what would have been black, what we were really doing was painting a mask. In selection channels, the more black a pixel is, the less selected it is. Inverting the channel inverts the selection so that the text *is* selected. When we came back from quick mask mode, we ended with a selection in the shape of the (black) letters.

Value-Based Selections

So far all the selections we've talked about have been based on geographic space. Photoshop also offers you the capability to select areas based on pixel values. This can be especially useful when you're color correcting. Let's say you had an image like the one in Figure 13.18. Most of the image is okay, but you'll want to correct some tones. You could write a curve that locks out changes to certain tones. You also have the option of selecting only those tones you want to change, wherever they are in your image.

Grow and Similar

Several methods are available for us to do this. The first is the Similar command (Select: Similar). This is one of two commands linked to the Magic Wand. That is, both Similar and Grow use the Magic Wand's tolerance and anti-aliasing setting (see Figure 13.19). Grow looks at a selection and then does the same thing the Magic Wand does. It looks at the pixels around the selection, and if they fall within tolerance, they are selected. This is still a geographic selection, though. The pixels it selects need to be contiguous.

Figure 13.18

Often, we only want to correct a certain range of tones.

Not so with the Similar command. Similar looks at all the pixels throughout the image and selects the ones that are similar. Like Grow, it uses the Magic Wand's tolerance when it makes the decision about how similar is similar. This is fine, but, like the Magic Wand, Similar suffers from the incapability to partially select a pixel. Because of this, it can leave unduly harsh transitions when color corrections are being made. If you find that the corrections you're making are causing nasty tonal jumps, you might consider giving your selection a slight feather. A two pixel feather is usually plenty. Choose Select: Feather and dial in the number you want.

Color Range

A more robust way to select pixels based on their values is to use the Color Range commands (see Figure 13.20). Color Range lets you interactively select a range of pixel values and, unlike the Magic Wand and Similar, you get a good idea of what you're going to select.

Figure 13.19

The Similar and Grow commands are linked to the Magic Wand.

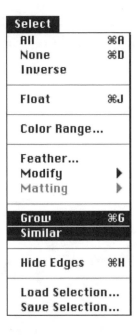

Figure 13.20

The Color Range commands

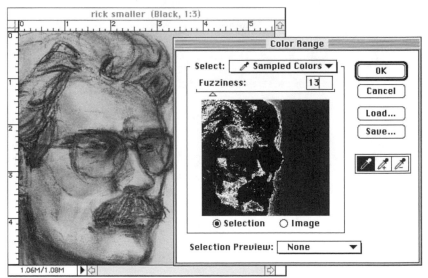

The first choice in color range is whether you want to pick the colors to select or you want Photoshop to select a range. The Select pull-down list features a list of preset colors, tonal values, and out-of-gamut colors. The preset ranges select all the pixels whose primary color is the color in question. Then it looks at the secondary and tertiary elements of the color in an attempt to find out how pure the color is. The purer the color, the more selected it becomes. The result of all this calculating and head scratching is a series of pull-down settings we don't use. It can produce unpredictable and unwanted results.

The tonal ranges are a little more useful, but still not a present from Santa Claus. These presets look at the L value, luminance, in the pixel's equivalent Lab color. Luminance describes the relative brightness of the pixel. Photoshop has a chart it consults as to what the highlights, mids, and shadows are, which works reasonably well. Sometimes we use these presets as an initial selection area and then move into Quick Mask mode to fine tune the selection with curves.

The color range really shines in its capability to let you pick the tones you want to go after. Choose Sampled Colors from the pull-down list. Once you do, the Eyedropper tool gets selected. If you move out into your image area and click a pixel, you begin to select those tones throughout your image. The preview window lets you toggle between the selection map and a preview of the image.

An additional pull-down menu lets you choose what, if any, selection preview you'd like the image to display. The grayscale preview shows you the same thing the thumbnail shows if you click the radio button selection. If you saved this selection as a new channel, it looks like a radio button. The two matte preview options show you what the selection would look like if every other pixel in the image were black (the black matte preview) or white (the white matte preview). In practice, when we want a preview (they slow things down a little bit), we often find ourselves sticking with the quick mask initially and then switching to one of the matte previews if we have a question about the selection (see Figure 13.21).

Figure 13.21

*Quick Mask versus White
Matte selection previews*

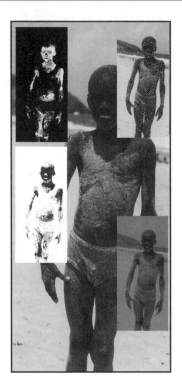

The next things to pay attention to are the additional eyedroppers and the Fuzziness slider. The two eyedroppers add and subtract from the selection area. The plus eyedropper, as you might expect, adds to an existing selection you've dialed up. The minus eyedropper takes away from one.

All three eyedroppers are driven by the cleverly named Fuzziness slider. Fuzziness is similar to the tolerance setting in the magic wand. Unlike the Magic Wand, though, color range can partially select pixels. The fuzziness setting not only decides which pixels will become selected, but also *how selected* they become. Figure 13.22 shows the same selection of a gray ramp with different fuzziness values selected. In our work, it's preferable to add to a selection before we increase fuzziness. Too high a fuzziness value tends to select errant or incorrect pixels, thwarting the good work of the color range command. Or maybe it's the fact that we can't stand the name. Now maybe if it had a more techie-sounding term for it like "relative deviation" or "chrominant viability" we wouldn't be so frustrated by it.

Figure 13.22

*Varying Fuzziness values and
their associated selections*

Another nice feature that keeps us coming back to the color range is its capability to limit its own behavior. If you make a selection before you call up the color range window, you'll only affect that selection. We've found this pretty tasty. Perhaps you've done some work selecting a figure from the background. Now you need to desaturate a specific color in the figure. Load the selection and choose color range to select just the colors you want to inside just the area you want to. Now you're cooking.

Modifying Selections

You can modify an existing selection in several other ways in addition to the ones we've discussed so far. A set of selection modification tools are in the Modify submenu of the Selection menu (see Figure 13.23). The Expand and Contract commands are handy for making slight alterations to your selection. These commands increase and decrease the size of your selection by a pixel value that you specify. Doing this comes in handy.

Figure 13.23

The Modify submenu.

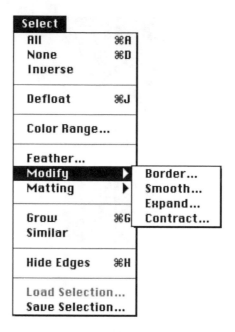

Border

The Border command operates like Illustrator's Outline Path filter. It takes the edge of a selection and straddles it on either side by half the pixel value you dial in. The result is a new selection that does not include the interior of the old selection (see Figure 13.24). This can be useful for smoothing the edge of selection into a background. The selection that results from the border command always has a soft edge. It also always moves in on the former selection area. If that's not what you're going for, consider saving the selection to a selection channel (click the selection icon in the channels box). Expand the existing selection by the amount of pixels you want. Without deselecting, load the saved channel by dragging it onto the selection icon with the command key held down. The resulting selection is an intersection of the two selections, has a hard edge, and doesn't intrude on the interior of the original selection.

Smooth

The final selection modification command, Smooth, softens the edge of an existing selection. It does this by comparing the state of a selected pixel with the state of those around it. If a preponderance of the surrounding pixels are deselected, the selected pixel gets deselected. We don't use this very much, preferring instead to soften a selection by jumping into Quick Mask mode and applying a slight Gaussian blur. At times when you want to smooth a jagged selection, the Smooth command would be a way to do that.

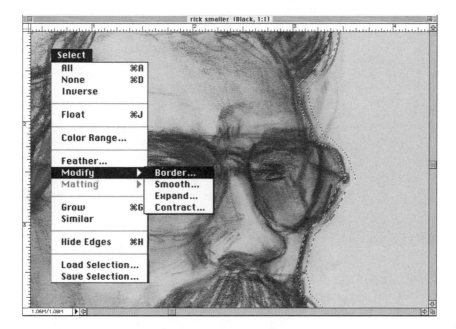

Figure 13.24

The Border command selects along the edge of a selection.

PATHS AND THE PEN TOOL

Another selection method you need to attain a level of comfort with is the Pen tool. The Pen tool and its buddies are kept in the Paths palette. The Paths palette defaults to being grouped with the channels and layers palettes. This is precisely where it belongs. The three palettes together make a powerful editing suite that complement each other nicely.

If you've ever done any serious work in Adobe Illustrator or Macromedia FreeHand, you already know how to use the Pen tool. If you haven't, it can be a little daunting at first. The idea is that Photoshop, although it's a pixel-based application, can understand the world of vectors. Just as many vector-based applications handle pixel-based data, so too can Photoshop understand vector-based data. And, just as vector-based programs don't do a fantastic job with pixels, Photoshop doesn't do a very good job with vectors. It really only shines in using vectors to describe areas. That is to say, as a selection tool. Paths do make fine selection tools, as long as you keep them simple.

479

Vectors are, as we've described, non-printing lines that delineate space. Vector shapes, unlike selections, have tangible points that define them. The points are editable, which makes them easier to correct. They are not selections in the traditional sense of the word. They are driven by abstract math and sit above our grubby pixels like Nero on the balcony. We take that back. Vectors are more like weird football coaches who you never do any of the hard work but get all the credit. Yeah! Vectors are Guy Lombardo! No, no, we meant Vince Lombardi, but that wasn't really what we meant, either. Well, never mind. Go back and read Chapter 8 if you really want to know.

Vectors build curvilinear shapes. The shapes are defined by a path. The paths are built up from anchor points that connect to form line segments. The angle of the segments is determined by the relative positions of the anchor points that define them. The shape, or curve, of the line segments are determined by curve handles. The curve handles live on the anchor points. There can be up to two curve handles for each anchor point. The curve of a line segment is a function of the curve handles on the anchor points on either side of it (see Figure 13.25).

Figure 13.25

Vector shapes and their components

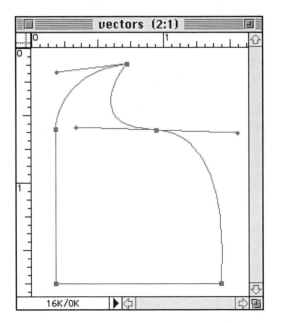

The Paths Palette

All of the tools for creating, saving, and editing paths are located in the Paths palette (Window: Palettes: Paths). Five tools and five buttons are in the Paths palette (see Figure 13.26).

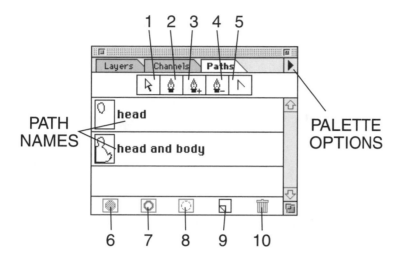

Figure 13.26

The Paths palette

Tools

The tools in the Paths palette behave similarly to the ones in Illustrator. It is easy to toggle between them with keyboard shortcuts.

1. **Arrow (Direct Selection).** Used to select and reposition anchor points, line segments, and curve handles. We refer to it as the direct selection arrow because it behaves and looks just like the tool of the same name in Adobe Illustrator.

2. **Pen.** Used to create anchor points, their curve handles, and the line segments that lie between anchor points.

3. **Insert Point.** Used to add anchor points to an existing line segment.

4. **Remove Point.** Used to remove anchor points from paths.

5. **Convert Point.** Used to edit weight bars.

Buttons

Buttons are shortcuts for the corresponding items in the Paths pull-down menu. To see the options for each button, Option-click it. To use the button, either drag and drop a path onto the icon, or simply click the button when the path is active (highlighted).

6. **Fill Path.** Works like Edit: Fill with the added feathering and anti-aliasing features.

7. **Stroke Path.** Paints along the edge of as path with the tool of your choice. Just as in Illustrator, the effect straddles the path.

8. **Make Selection.** Feathering and anti-aliasing are available here as well.

9. **New Path.** When you're creating on a path and you come back to the point you started from, the path closes up to become an object rather than a line. Unless you tell Photoshop you'd like to start working on a new, discrete path, it assumes you'd like to create another path under the same name.

10. **Delete Path.** To prevent accidental deleting, you need to drag your path onto the trash to remove it. It's a nice idea, but when a path is highlighted in the paths palette, the cut, copy, and paste functions all work on it. So does the Delete key. More paths get lost this way than by accidental trashing.

In Chapter 8, we discussed how vector shapes are created and they work the same in Photoshop. The only real difficulty in vectors is getting the hang of using the weight bars. They can cause confusion and despair. The thing to remember is to view them like magnets, pulling the line segment in their direction. Making them too long surely leads to grief just as making too many of them does.

Many people take advantage of Option (Mac) or Alt (IBM)-clicking an anchor point to release the line segment they're working on from the weight bar of the previous anchor point. Another wrinkle on the same philosophy is after you've clicked to establish an anchor point, drag out the curve of the line segment before it. Then Option-drag out the second weight bar (if you need one) for that point. The result is independent line segments. Although it's great to have the flexibility to do that, we often find that many curves are easy to draw if they aren't independent. Certainly, some anchor points need option clicking to cut a hard angle around, but often if you place your curve and weight bar with the next segment in mind, your line segment will practically draw itself. Remember that new paths are not automatically saved.

We mentioned the tools in the Paths palette could temporarily access each other for easier use. Here's the shortcuts:

MAC SHORTCUTS

Using the Pen Tool	Access this Tool
Command	Selection Arrow
Control	Remove or add point
Control–⌘	Convert Point tool
⌘–Option	Select all points on path

Using the Selection Arrow	Access this Tool
⌘–Option	Remove or add point
Control	Convert point

Shortcut	Effect
T key	Switch between selection arrow and Pen tool
⌘–Option Drag w/ pen	Drag copy of path

IBM SHORTCUTS

Using the Pen Tool	Access this Tool
Ctrl	Arrow
Ctrl–Shift	Selection Arrow, constrain to 45°
Ctrl–Alt drag	Drag copy of path

Using the Selection Arrow	Access this Tool
Shift	Constrain to 45°
Ctrl	Convert Point tool
Alt	Drag copy of path
Ctrl–Alt	Add/Subtract Anchor Point

Effective Silhouetting

This was a long way to get back to the production manager who wanted our help way back at the beginning of this chapter. Remember that can of worms? The issue is there are two methods of silhouetting in the world. One way is to select the object you want to silhouette, invert the selection so that the background is selected, and set your background color to white and delete.

This method is the wrong way. One, we've destroyed image data and if we want it back we have to do a Save As and rename our file. This means extra disk space and file management headaches. More importantly, perhaps, this method only works if the silhouetted object is going to be on white paper. Those white pixels are still there, waiting to knock out any object you put behind it. In QuarkXPress, you could set the background of your picture box to *none*, but that leaves behind a jagged white halo that's called a garbage mask (see Figure 13.27). Actually, it's usually called much worse things than that. It's roughly equivalent to a moiré pattern or type that's defaulted to Courier. Bad news for you, your client, and your career.

Figure 13.27

The Garbage Mask qualifies as a cry for help.

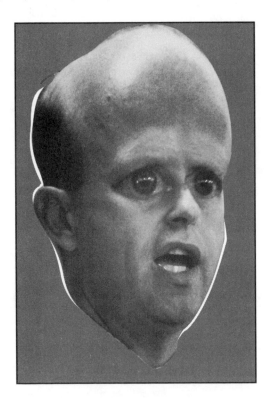

The preferred method of silhouetting a file is to draw a path defining the area you want silo'ed and define the path as a clipping path. When you define a path as a clipping path, the path instructs the printer to only concern itself with the pixels inside the path. The rest of the pixels are processed and ignored. This gives you a correct silo that you can place objects behind.

Clipping Paths

To create a clipping path, create and save the path. Then choose clipping path from the Paths palette pull-down menu. Choose the path you want for your silo from the pull-down menu (see Figure 13.28). The name of the file is outlined in the paths palette to indicate the path is a clipping path. When you save the file, you need to save it as an EPS. Otherwise the path, which is essentially a special set of PostScript instructions to the printer, won't get saved correctly.

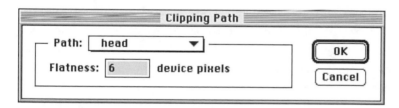

Figure 13.28

Specifying a clipping path

When you turn a path into a clipping path, you're prompted with a field asking you to dial in a Flatness value for the path. This needs a little explanation. The gist is this: although a path may by smooth and rounded, when it prints, it will actually be a series of flat line segments. The printer calculates straight lines much more quickly than it does a perfect curve. So you're trading accuracy for speed. What's more, PostScript lets you decide how much accuracy you're willing to trade. That trade is expressed as flatness. Flatness describes how inaccurate the curve is. The larger the number, the less accurate it is. The question, then, is how inaccurate can the curve be and still be acceptable for a given device. It's apt to vary a little bit from device to device and is worth testing out. For a starting point, though, consult the chart below.

Device Classification	DPI	Acceptable Flatness
High-resolution device	1200-2400	8-10
Low-resolution device	300-600	1-3

As you're considering the output of a clipping path, consider this. The thing that most frequently chokes or slows down a RIP is too much information. In files with clipping paths, this is also the case. Paths with too many points, over a hundred, can slow things down. Additionally, just because the RIP isn't printing all of the file doesn't mean it's ignoring it. Rather, just as when files are cropped in a layout application, the RIP processes the entire digital file and then only prints what's inside the path. If you don't need the extra space for some future use, crop it out in Photoshop. In clipping paths, as with most things, simpler is better.

We also should mention that although it's perfectly acceptable and routine behavior to make a path into a selection, it's generally not good to make a selection into a path. Doing so is easy. Just make a selection and then in the Path palette drag the selection icon onto the new path icon. You could also choose Make Path from the Paths pull-down menu. If you do, you'll be asked for a tolerance setting. This is a measure of how accurate the path will be. Any number higher than three is like calling up the mob to come mess with your files. Making paths this way is a bad scene anyway. Usually Photoshop does an inaccurate job anyway and uses too many anchor points. The paths usually need so much rework it would have been faster to just make a whole new path yourself. Staying away from this feature is usually, if not always, the best thing to do.

Drop Shadows

Another fundamental technique you'll need to know is how to create a quick drop shadow. Applications and plug-ins can do this for you automatically, but you're really better off knowing how to do it yourself. Often they produce full-color shadows that can cause misregistration problems during printing. The results you'll get doing it yourself are typically more predictable and satisfying.

1. The first thing you'll need to do is create a path around the object you want to shadow. Make it and then save it. Don't make it a clipping path.

2. Turn the path into a selection by clicking the Make Selection icon from the paths palette. Things will be easier if your background is white. We'll deal with colored backgrounds in a minute.

3. Check out your selection: it's going to form the basis for the drop shadow. Now consider one of the main descriptive features of a drop shadow: it's slightly offset. To do this, hold down the Option and ⌘ keys (Mac) or the Alt and Ctrl keys (IBM) and move the selection (not the background) until it's offset to where you want the shadow to fall (see Figure 13.29a).

Figure 13.29a

Move the selection to offset the shadow.

4. Save the selection by clicking the Make Selection button on the channels palette.

5. Click the new channel. Deselect everything (⌘-D). This is an important step.

6. To give the shadow its blurry edges, lay in a Gaussian Blur (Filter: Blur: Gaussian Blur). Experiment with the blur amount. It'll probably be

some value between 2 and 10, depending on the nature of your
selection (see Figure 13.29b).

Figure 13.29b

Shadows need to be fuzzy.

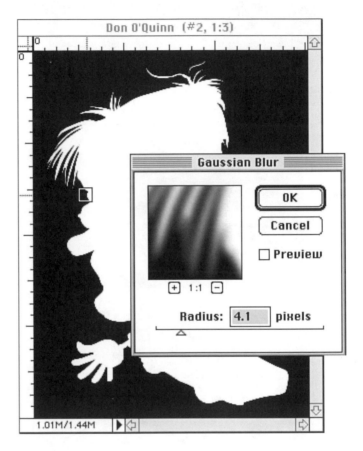

7. Now we need to knock out the part where the image will rest when
   we reload this selection. Go to the Paths Palette, select the path and
   click the Make Selection button.

8. Fill the new selection with black. This is masking out the area where
   the original object will sit (see Figure 13.29c). If you don't do this, the
   shadow will sit in front of the object.

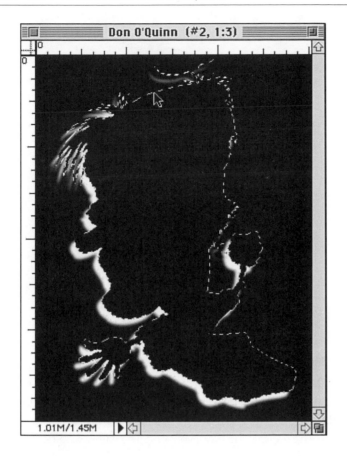

Figure 13.29c

The shadow minus the original object

9. Go to the channel that lets you see the whole image—the composite channel for color images, the black channel for grayscale.

10. Load the selection by Option-clicking the channel.

11. Fill the selection with black. You should get a drop shadow (see Figure 13.29d).

12. When you're satisfied with the results, either save the selection channel into a separate file or simply delete it.

Figure 13.29d

The finished drop shadow

Drop Shadows on Color Backgrounds

We've been asked a half dozen times recently what to do about images with drop shadows that are being placed on top of full color background files in a page layout program. The problem is that the diffuse edge created by the drop shadow isn't transparent. Not even a clipping path would help this problem.

The best solution is to take the background file into Photoshop and composite the two images there. Every time that's suggested, people grumble about unwieldy file sizes involved and the difficulty of positioning the object away from the layout. If they refuse, we offer them another solution. It could be done in other ways, but this one illustrates another use of selection channels.

The idea is to create a separate file in the shape of the shadow. The file will be the same size as the object file so they line up correctly but bitmapped so that its white spaces are transparent.

I. Go to the file of the object with the drop shadow. Select the object that gets the shadow.

2. With the Command and Option keys (Mac) or the Alt and Ctrl keys (IBM) down, drag the selection over to make the shadow offset (see Figure 13.30a).

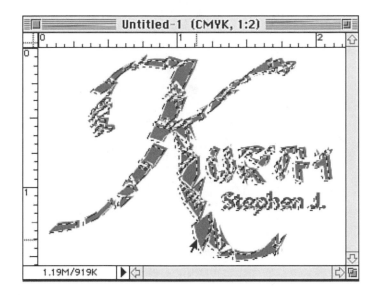

Figure 13.30a

Move the selection to where you want the shadow to fall

3. From the Select menu, choose Inverse. This selects everything but the shadow.

4. Click the Make Selection button from the Channels Palette. You get a new channel based on the inverted selection, but because black means deselected in the selection channel, the channel should be a silo of the shadow shape (see Figure 13.30b).

5. Click the new channel you've just made to select it. Select All and lay in a Gaussian blur to make the fuzzy shadow edges. Leave it all still selected and choose copy.

6. Make a new file. Photoshop plugs in the size of the object in the clipboard. Say OK to the settings it offers up. Then paste.

7. Now you need to convert the grayscale shadow file into a bitmap. We've had best luck choosing the Diffusion Dither setting under the bitmap mode dialog box (see Figure 13.30c).

Figure 13.30b

The shadow shape

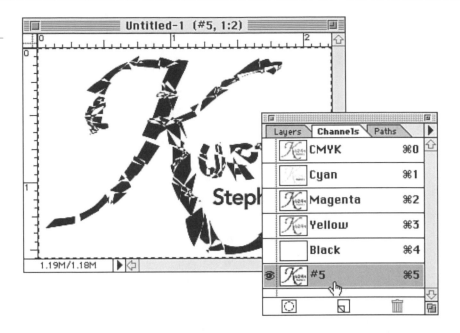

Figure 13.30c

Dither the shadow object

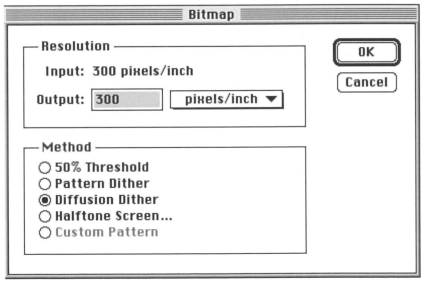

8. Save the shadow file as a TIFF. Composite the shadow and the object file in your layout program. Set the shadow file to overprint. The two files fit perfectly since they're the same size (see Figure 13.30d). Once you have them together, group them for easier selection and arrange them where you like.

Figure 13.30d

Group the files and place them on their background image.

You can experiment with lower resolution shadows and different methods of converting to bitmap, but you are better served composing the image in Photoshop, like we told you back in the beginning of this hint.

LAYERS

To use Photoshop effectively, you should also know a thing or two about layers. By now, everyone should be comfortable with the concept of what layers are.

The image of sheets of acetate stacked atop one another over a background image springs to mind. Each acetate layer has image information on it. The layers can be shuffled up and down, can mix with each other, and can react to the layers beneath them differently. All the features we discussed with respect to channels, such as hiding, showing, creating, and deleting are also applicable to layers (see Figure 13.31).

Figure 13.31

The Layers palette

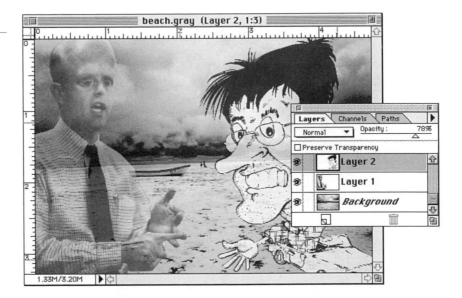

The acetate metaphor can be borne out a little further. The acetate is transparent in some places, opaque in others, and partially opaque in still other areas. Photoshop displays transparent areas with a checkerboard display (If you're feeling precocious, you can change the size and color of the checkerboard by choosing Preferences: Transparency). When an area is partially transparent, you can see part of the checkerboard showing through.

Moving images that sit on layers is easier than moving images that don't. Just select the layer you want to reposition, select all and drag. That way you're sure to include pixels that are partially transparent. What's more, as long as an image is still selected, Photoshop won't crop it if you drag it off the edges of your file. You can drag part of an image offscreen and still drag it back if you went too far.

Layers function the same as background areas with a few key differences. Those differences arise from the nature of their position as layers atop other things. The first one is that the layers follow a stacking order in regards to their relative positions, which matches their positions on the layers palette. The layer on the top of that list is the highest layer. You can change layers order by dragging them around in the list. When you do this, you'll see a black bar appear. It indicates the layer's new position (see Figure 13.32). Don't leggo that mouse until you see the bar come up.

Figure 13.32

Moving a layer

Deleting things, thankfully, works differently in layers. Instead of mapping the deleted pixels to the background color, deleting (cutting or clearing) turns the selected area transparent.

Each layer, including floating selections that are actually layers themselves, also has an opacity slider and an overlay mode. These control how the layers interact with the layers beneath them. It's for this reason that if you hide all the other layers, these controls get grayed out. The opacity slider is pretty straightforward. One hundred percent opaque is completely solid; 0 percent is invisible. You can slide the bar up and down or dial in the number you want from the keyboard. The keyboard trick works with the tool options, which have sliders as well, and these take precedence. The only time you can type in the opacity for a layer is when you have one of the following tools selected: Marquee, Lasso, Magic Wand, Move, Hand, Zoom, Crop, Type, Eyedropper, any tool in the Pen tool suite (and the Paths palette is visible). All the other tools have sliders of their own, usually an opacity slider!

Overlay Modes

Not so straightforward are the overlay modes. These functions are really more in the realm of design than production. On the other hand, they pop up all over the place, so knowing a little about them wouldn't hurt. In any case, we'll keep our discussion brief. These are what the modes do.

Behind. Available if you float a selection over a layer. Allows the floating selection to affect transparent or semi-transparent areas only.

Clear. Available if you float a selection over a layer. Essentially the same as an undoable, moveable delete. It's undoable because if you change your mind, you can just change overlay modes.

Normal. No screwy effects. With 100 percent opacity, it's the same as simply putting one image on top of another.

Dissolve. Really only any good with feathered edges. Randomizes them into background layers.

Multiply. Literally multiplies the pixel values together and then divides by 255. The effect is darkening the image. Can be useful for beefing up a shadow or pulling subtle detail out of a weak shadow.

Screen. The reverse of multiply. Lightens up an image.

Overlay/ Soft/ Hard light. All three use a combination of the preceding two modes. Of the three, overlay is really the only one subtle enough to be useful. It will mix the colors of the active layer with the composite image behind it without lousing up the detail in either one. This can be useful for knocking out color casts. See below.

Darken/ Lighten. These two apply the active layer only in cases where the they are darker or lighter, respectively, than the underlying composite. The results are much less predictable in color than they are in grayscale.

Hue/ Saturation/ Color and Luminosity. These modes look at the HSB color values for pixels (and have very little effect on grayscale images). The idea is to retain one value from the overlaying layer and mix them with the underlying composite image. The Color overlay mode combines hue and saturation.

We rarely use most of these modes in our work correcting files, only in montage images or when we're feeling artistic (okay, that's not true, but we can imagine that if *someone* felt artistic they might want to use them). We have used the overlay mode to make color correction changes, however. Usually this takes the form of beating a color cast (for more on color casts and neutrality, see Chapter 12, "Working in Color").

The overlay mode affects lights and darks differently. It ignores 50 percent gray. So to beat a color cast, we created a new layer in overlay mode and filled it with 50 percent gray. Then we wrote a gamma curve to neutralize the cast. So if the underlying layer had too much yellow, the gamma curve for the neutralizing layer would boost blue. Why bother taking the extra step? Flexibility. Photoshop 4.0's new adjustment layers should remove the need to take so many extra steps and simply let us write a curve to adjust the layers below it without the pain of filling with gray and setting to overlay.

There's a lot more to explore with layers, but it moves further away from the focus of this book. They are well worth the time required to explore them, however. Keep in mind several things as you do. One is that the price to pay for flexibility is, of course, RAM. Layers can buoy up an image considerably. Reflect on what you really want to do before rushing off to extra layers; often more effective solutions exist.

Secondly, recall that images with layers can't be saved in anything other than the native Photoshop format (3.0 or later), although layers can be merged before saving as a TIFF. The editability and flexibility of layers open up a whole new world. Be sure you need that flexibility before you sign up. We've seen client files with as many as twenty-eight layers all set to normal overlay modes. We asked them why they built such files and they replied it was to arrange objects atop each other. This is precisely one of the jobs of a page layout program. Working there produces the same results more quickly and just as flexibly.

Typically in the digital graphic arts, work with photos falls into one of two camps: production (scanning and color correcting) and design (manipulating and editing content). These two once-discrete camps are becoming more and more blurred. Designers need to know some scanning information and production people may be called on to produce clipping paths. Fortunately, neither package of information is terribly complicated. Whatever your job description, knowing a little bit about the nuts and bolts of the entire operation has tangible benefits. In most cases, the same five or six things come up again and again. You can own this information very quickly, making your company more productive and the amount of money you spend on aspirin each month smaller.

Chapter **14**

COLOR MANAGEMENT AND PROFILING

The voice on the phone was talking so fast we could barely keep up. The scanner seemed to be broken and a big job had to be done by four that afternoon. Everything looked great on the monitor, but the films that she generated were so dark and clogged, they were unusable. We drove over and sat down with her, explaining the variables that affect scan quality and showing her how to set up some simple, but very informative tests. Through it all she looked at us balefully. Finally she just blurted out what was on her mind: "Just tell me what's wrong with this thing!" She clearly wasn't prepared for any of this. As calmly as we could, we held the match print next to her monitor and twisted the brightness knob until the scan looked as dark as the proof.

Then we explained to her why it's important to do something about controlling your production environment. Next we explained that once you could compare apples to apples you could correctly assess and adjust each image accordingly. Silence. As the scope of the issue starting to sink in, she asked a question she desperately didn't want to know the answer to: "You mean I have to do things to *every* scan individually?"

QUALITY CONTROL AND DESKTOP COLOR

As the desktop publishing industry expands and technology becomes cheaper, responsibilities shift. Once upon a time, no one except highly trained crafts people had to worry about measuring and adjusting color. That's not the case anymore. Hand in hand with the ability to do it yourself comes the necessity to accept responsibility for the outcome.

In the case of color output, the inherent issues are complicated and require vigilance and attention to complex issues. People have dedicated years to understanding these issues and now you only have until four this afternoon to get that big job out. What will you do?

Several choices are available. Each one has its strengths and weaknesses. The one you should choose is a function of what your needs, workflow logistics, and expectations of quality are. The issue of maintaining consistent color in desktop publishing environment really gets down to variables and constants. In any given work flow model, a series of things can change. Changing the nature of something can positively (or negatively) impact the nature of your color output.

Constants and Variables

The knobs on your monitor constitute a variable and so do the settings you choose when you scan, the device you print to, the settings available for the printer itself, and the raster image processor (RIP) that controls it. Every step along the path a photograph takes from the scanner, through the computer to a proofing device, and then to a printing press introduces variables that affect how the image data is understood or re-expressed. Either the variables have to be adjusted to accommodate the data, or the data has to be changed to accommodate the device.

Let's look at how that might happen. Mechanical variables affect an imagesetter's ability to uniformly produce halftone spots. You would like it to function the same way all the time. That is, you want the 32-percent black box you created in PageMaker to look the same as the 32-percent black in your scan and the 32- percent black in the logo you built in Illustrator. Remember that the imagesetter is turning that 32-percent black into a halftone dot of a specific size. The imagesetter needs to make the same percent dot the same size all day, every day. Your friendly neighborhood service bureau probably tests and adjusts their imagesetter to do just that. The variable is changed to produce a constant, or to meet the needs of the data.

When you make an adjustment in the size of a midtone dot to anticipate dot gain on press, you're adjusting the image information to meet the needs of the device. When you color correct an image, you're adjusting the file to meet the needs of the original photograph. The data changes to meet the constant.

What you're driving toward is a model where you remove as many impediments to color reproduction as you can and then fine tune the remaining ones to compensate for things you can't change. All of this is done to remove the variable of color difference to satisfy the needs of the client. To do this, you need to be able to measure. Measuring color gives you a tool for understanding and controlling the variables your devices introduce into the color reproduction process. Not all steps in the process require mathematical expression, but being able to measure color gives you the ability to compare constants. The human eye is great at seeing color; it's lousy at measuring it.

COLOR CONTROL STRATEGIES

You can do several things to control color in your system. One is to manually test and assess each of the components. Another method is to rely on a machine or a piece of software to do that for you. It's also possible to create a model that involves both methods. For example, you could test and adjust your scanner by eye and still rely on a hardware calibration device to adjust your monitor.

Manual Color Control

The first option for calibration discussed here doesn't involve a full-blown color management system. Rather, it requires you to step in and take control yourself. This is a good thing for you to do anyway. If you don't invest in a color management system, and there are reasons not to, you have to do something about taking control of your color issues. This means rolling up your sleeves a little bit.

Manual Color Control Methods

Measuring and adjusting the devices in the input-output cycle has been the traditional system for color management in the digital graphic arts. Frequently in this model, color quality relies on the judgment and vigilance of trained professionals. The cycle of measuring and adjusting each element along the production chain requires continual attention due to the inherent instability of the devices involved. It's not a perfect system and it relies heavily on the competency of the human element. A fundamental discrepancy exists between light on the monitor and ink on the page. They will never look exactly the same. The problem is how to identify and eliminate all the impediments to that color to make it as accurate as possible.

Calibrating

It was mentioned earlier that you can adjust the image you're printing or adjust the device it's printing on. When you're adjusting the device, you can do one of two things. You can try to make the device match a known constant or you can change the constant to match what the device is doing now. Adjusting the device to match a constant is called *calibration*. When prepress techs adjust an imagesetter to make it function as it did yesterday, they're calibrating it. When you adjust a monitor to compensate for the instability of the device, you're calibrating it. It's also called *normalizing*. You are moving a parameter to match a constant norm.

Characterizing

Characterization is different from adjusting the standard to match the device. A flatbed scanner doesn't have knobs to adjust how it sees light. By testing it, you can arrive at a profile of how the device behaves. This becomes the norm. If you identify that the norm is flawed, adjust your images or your scanning software accordingly. If you check again and the profile has changed, you're required to change your response to the changing norm.

Establishing a Color Control Model

Both characterization and calibration are used as your color control model is established. Typically, devices are corrected back from the proof. The use of constants in this process is imperative. When you set up a system, you first prepare and run test files through your imagesetters and proofing system to test and achieve linear results. After you set this, prepare a test page with a wide range of color swatches and several different images (see Figure 14.1). Use images that emphasize different important aspects to test for, like sharpness and memory colors. Each file also is corrected twice with slight differences in ink density to show variance.

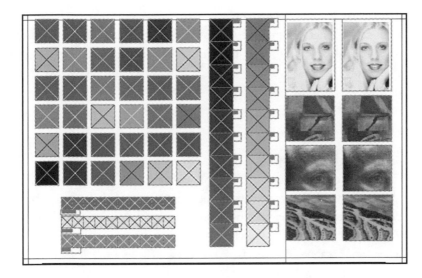

Figure 14.1

A typical calibration target.

After you prepare the file and have the proofing system and imagesetters functioning consistently, you can use the digital files from which the test page was developed to compare with the proof results. The monitors are adjusted to make the onscreen image match the proof. The scanners are tested against standards, and adjustment tables are written to compensate for the identifiable errors of the scanning system. The whole process repeats itself periodically to maintain consistent results over time.

Choosing a Monitor Calibration System

We've talked about your options for monitor calibration in Chapter 10. They basically break down into two paths: using a crude, stone age ax like the gamma control panel that ships with Photoshop, or investing in a more refined monitor calibration tool. The latter means paying for a hardware calibration utility. You can get one of these devices from companies such as Radius, RasterOps, and SuperMac. We like hardware calibrations because of the predictable results they give us.

Like most things, you get what you pay for with display calibration devices. Cheaper devices contain a light detector, or a photometer. More money gets you a colorimeter that measures the chroma of each red, green, and blue channel in addition to its brightness. The software that ships with the calibrator enables you to set the signal to a constant. The accompanying software lets you fine tune the results to achieve specific objectives. Once you calibrate this way you should do it again periodically to keep things constant.

Inexpensive Monitor Calibration

Most of these devices aren't terrifically cheap. Recently, though, Light Source released the Colortron. It's a reasonably full-featured color measurement utility. You can use it as a spectrophotometer, film densitometer, light meter, or monitor calibration device. All this for under $1,000. We've heard great things about it, but the one we got measured about three things and then simply refused to function.

Scanner Profiling Options

Controlling color in a scanner is a slightly different animal. You can't do much to a scanner, but it tends to be reasonably stable over time. Profiling a scanner typically involves scanning a color target and measuring the values it gives you. You can get a lot of information from a simple gray ramp. This tells you exactly where your scanner deviates from reality (see Figure 14.2). If your machine offers you a look up table, you simply update it for the necessary changes, then rescan and compare your results. If it doesn't offer you such a table, you may need to manually adjust the image data, or simply change the scanner's default curves to make the adjustment for you.

Figure 14.2

A gray wedge identifies specific scanner shortcomings.

You also can buy a calibration package to further measure your scanner's behavior and compare it to mathematical constants. Savitar makes a package called ScanMatch that ships with Pantone color targets. The scanned targets then get compared to the information the included software has about the color targets you just scanned. The software then makes adjustments as you scan in an attempt to better match the original.

OFOTO and Closed Loop Scanning

Another model for color control at the scanner level involves point-to-point calibration. OFOTO, a stand-alone scanning software package, uses this additive method. The idea is this: to heck with what the factory thinks your scanner can do, let's make the scan match the color your output device gives you. Let's scan back from the output, essentially, and generate a closed loop.

OFOTO generates targets based on its internal idea of color. A proof of the target it generated is made and then scanned again. OFOTO compares what the scanner saw with what was printed and then generates a table to adjust the scan to match the proof. The plan is to reduce repetitive time spent adjusting scans. In practice, though, our experience with OFOTO has been that it processed slowly. The colors it gave were nice, but we were so tired of waiting at that point that we didn't care.

Output Device Control

Imagesetters are still typically calibrated by professionals in service bureaus. The idea is to ensure that the imagesetter constantly and correctly interprets PostScript data to form dots correctly. The creation of halftone dots is crucial to correct output. Test pages are printed regularly and are evaluated with a densitometer. Most imagesetters have exposure tests built into them.

You should be aware that imagesetters typically adjust themselves with a set of PostScript commands called a transfer function (see Figure 14.3). A transfer function adjusts tones in an image as it's being printed without affecting the inherent image data. Photoshop enables you to override these by including a transfer function in an EPS file. You should be careful when you do this to communicate with the service bureau. If the imagesetter you're printing to is calibrated this way and you override it, it could produce unexpected results.

Frequently service bureaus use full-blown imagesetter calibration applications. These work in essentially the same fashion that we've described so far with some added functionality. For example, you may be able to test different spot shapes and line screens. As you discover variance, it's recorded and adjusted in a series of calibration tables that the imagesetter references at print time.

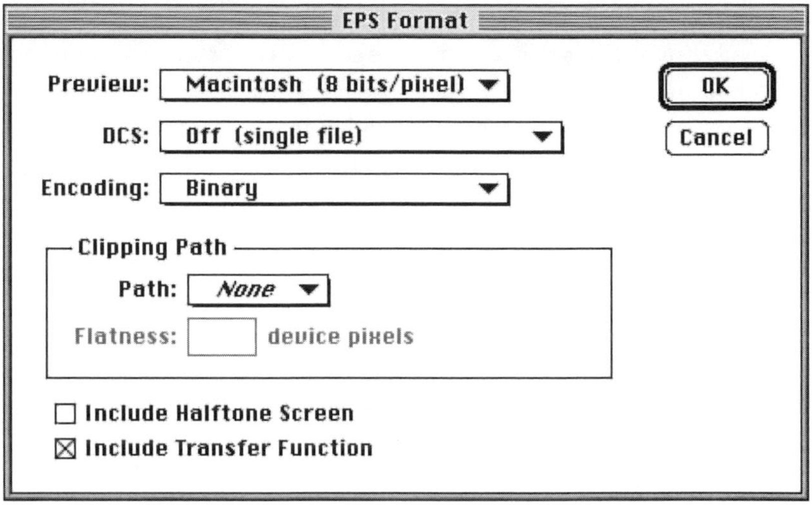

Figure 14.3

*Calibration adjustment curves
for an imagesetter.*

```
┌─────────────────────── EPS Format ───────────────────────┐

    Preview:  [ Macintosh (8 bits/pixel) ▼ ]      ( OK )

        DCS:  [ Off (single file)          ▼ ]    ( Cancel )

    Encoding: [ Binary                      ▼ ]

    ┌─ Clipping Path ─────────────────────────┐
    │   Path:  [ None  ▼ ]                     │
    │                                          │
    │   Flatness: [     ]  device pixels       │
    └──────────────────────────────────────────┘

    ☐ Include Halftone Screen
    ☒ Include Transfer Function
```

Color Management Systems

Combining hardware and software that can integrate, manage, and adjust color in a production system automatically has long been a goal in the industry. A model like that is called a color management system. The idea is to inform the color management system (CMS) what sort of devices and originals you're working with and let it adjust everything behind the scenes so that it all looks the same from monitor to proofing device to printing press. The user ends up mindlessly pushing a button like George Jetson, trusting the computer to make the right choices.

Color management systems sounds nice, if somewhat bloodless. If you know a couple things about computers, alarms should be sounding all over the place about now. The idea of trusting your color on press to a computer without being able to get your hands inside the works makes us dubious. Still, we try to keep an open mind. CMS technology has come a long way in the last three years. In fact, the industry is buzzing with new, smarter technology for color management. As this book is being written, we anticipate several major releases that could again change the face of color management.

For this reason, our comments on color management are pretty general. Rather, your options for color control will be discussed with the reasons behind them. If we went into much more detail, the information could be damagingly dated or just wrong by the time this hits print.

Don't get us wrong, though. Things are still very wrong with relying on a color management system at this stage. One problem is the inability of different color management systems to communicate with each other and the lack of unanimous hardware support. Colorsync 2.0 may be solving some of these problems.

The other problem is the systems don't always work correctly and require a lot of technical expertise. You have to know what to do when the system doesn't work. This defeats the purpose of having the system in the first place and adds an unnecessary level of complexity to an already complex problem.

Color management systems have traditionally fallen squarely into the realm of Dark Art, but that seems to be changing, which may make them more viable and downright useful.

Consistent Color

Color management systems have several objectives. One is to produce consistent color from device to device, make the Iris proof match the monitor and film proof, make the scan look like the original, and make the scan on your monitor look like it does when it's on someone else's. None of these are trivial issues. There are inherent variable differences between output devices. Toner is different than ink, so files printed on a toner machine, like a laser printer, look different from those printed with printing press inks. When you look at (laser) proofs, you have to imagine what the file will look like when it actually goes to print. What use is a proof if you have to imagine what it'll look like, though? You might as well not print anything at all and just ask the client to imagine it how they want it to look.

Accurate Color Space Conversion

The next goal is color space conversion. Color management systems take responsibility for the complicated process of transitioning between RGB and CMYK. If you didn't fall asleep back in Chapter 11, you know converting to CMYK is no small feat either. The variables of ink, paper, and press all collide to make correct color separation decisions of vital importance to handsome output. In a traditional model, it's up to the color separation tech to make the switch. How it's done varies from device to device. Until a few years ago, color scanning and separating was still the province of a craftsperson who ran a scanner that filled a room and looked like an airplane cockpit. Now we're asking machines to make the choices for us.

If you think about the problem of color accuracy between devices, you can see why the color management systems have to be able to address color space conversion. Monitors and scanners describe color in an RGB color space, printers use a CMYK space. The CMS needs to do both. When we're talking about RGB light and CMYK inks, we are talking about a set of instructions to build color. Use this much of this, a little of that, and there's your color. The problem with that is what one machine does with those instructions is different from what another machine does. In other words, there are more variables. The result is two different colors. Because of this, CMYK and RGB are thought to be *device dependent* color models. What one device does is different from what the other device does.

Device Independent Color Model

To combat this problem of color accuracy, color management systems make use of what is called a *device independent* color model. The idea is to use a color model that describes color, not how to make color. In most cases, that color model will be CIE L*a*b* color. What the color management system wants to do is keep track of what the color looks like in Lab color, and then send numbers to each device along the production chain to describe that color. What it tells each device differs depending on what it knows about each device's capability to express color. Each device receives color information depending on its capability to express color and the color the system wants to express (see Figure 14.4). So it's possible to tell one device to approximate the behavior of the other. Make the proof look like the monitor. This is why the color management system wants to be the one to make the separation into CMYK. It needs to alter that information to match the device that is printing the dots. It's easier to do this if the color isn't already CMYK.

CMS and Color Gamut

Separating from a color management system offers a strong advantage over separating in Photoshop. When Photoshop moves from RGB to CMYK, it clips colors that are out of gamut. That is to say, Photoshop gives colors outside of the CMYK color space (and therefore unprintable) the nearest printable CMYK values. So you may end up with different RGB colors translating to the same CMYK color. Not good.

Color management systems try to do the same sort of thing when we used Photoshop's eyedroppers to limit a tonal range for press. It constricts the entire RGB color gamut relative to itself into the smaller CMYK color space (see

Figure 14.5). As you might expect, this is not a simple procedure and every color management system does it a little differently. It can cause a loss of contrast and saturation in the image overall.

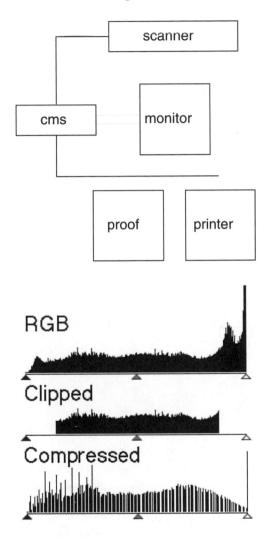

Figure 14.4

Information flow inside a color management system.

Figure 14.5

Photoshop's gamut clipping behavior versus gamut compression.

The final positive about a color management system, compared to Photoshop, is that although Photoshop knows about your monitor, the inks you want to print with, and how you want to separate color, it doesn't know a thing about how you scanned the original. A color management system that includes characterizing the scanner could potentially give you very accurate color.

CMS Components

Basically, color management systems have three main parts:

◆ A model. A device independent color space to reference color. (sometimes Lab color, but other models exist as well).

◆ An engine. Software that converts from the independent model above to the real-world values for printing or display.

◆ Tools. A set of device profiles that are referenced for different devices. Software may be included to let you generate and view the results of these tables.

Of the three components, the tools are the only ones that impact user workflow. Both the conversion engine and the color space model are invisible to the user in day-to-day work. You set them up and ignore them. The profiles work in a source/target relationship. You tell the color management system what you want to reference and what that should match. The color management system coordinates the activity. Here's RGB data from this monitor (source) moving to CMYK data for this machine (target). The color management system acts as a filter for the expression of the same (Lab) color in the two different color models. It does this by using information about the devices. This information set is called a *device profile*. The profile can come from either calibration or characterization.

CMS Profiles

It is the creation, editing, and use of these profiles that cause the problems in a color management system. The profiles themselves may be based on errant data. This risk is potentially the greatest in cases where preset, rather than custom generated profiles are being used. The nature of the mechanics in the machines can give rise to discernible differences between machines of the same make. Additionally, the profiles can't account for the specifics of your working environment or the inherent instability of some devices.

It is a point of interest that the color targets that ship with color management systems for characterizing your scanner themselves are measured before shipping. The measurements are then recorded as a reference file that the software refers to. When you replace scanning targets because of casts introduced by aging, you have to replace the reference file as well. Why aren't every target's values exactly the same? Because it's easier and more cost-effective for the manufacturer to measure than to make them all exactly the same. Their output isn't all exactly the same. This should illustrate, if anecdotally, that the process has limits.

CMS Profile Origins

Targets are used to characterize the behavior and to generate profiles for scanners. Profiles for monitors are best generated by a hardware calibration utility. Most of these utilities let you write off profiles for use in your color management system. If you don't have a hardware calibration system and are instead using the preset profile that came with your color management system for that monitor, good luck! Monitors are notorious for their instability. The profiles for presses and proofing systems attempt to account for the variables of press, paper, and ink.

Color Management Systems in Practice

Let's look at the color management system in action to see what happens when you push a file through. Start with your scanner. In this model, you need to rely on the color management system to make the initial color choices for you. At this point, the color management system asks you for a source and a target. The source is the scanner profile; the target can either be your monitor profile or your output device profile (see Figure 14.6). Of the two, the monitor profile offers you more opportunity to edit your image. You get a stronger idea of what the scan looks like and have a better opportunity to make color corrections. When it's time to print, the file gets run through the color management system again. This time the monitor profile is the source and the output device profile is the target.

This model has a downside and it bears a little exploration. The first is that one-touch scanning means you have to scan everything the same way. If you're working with a high bit scanner, you're not taking advantage of your extra scanning power. If you have a negative, you're also up the creek. No profile could capture the exposure latitude of a color negative.

You should also be aware that while setting the monitor profile as your target gives you more chances at correcting a not-so-good original, it also sends the image through the color management system twice. Although not as damaging to the image data as mode conversions in Photoshop, this process is nonetheless an information degrading one. A better approach might be to simply leave the color management system out of the scan acquisition phase altogether. Just adjust your image on the monitor and go. You work with less-degraded image data.

Figure 14.6

CMS scanning at work.

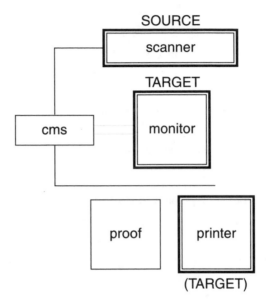

You also get to use your scanner to its full potential. This is good if you have a high bit scanner. All you're doing with the color management system is telling it more accurately what you're seeing on the monitor and asking it to reproduce that in print. This does, of course, rely heavily on an extremely accurate monitor profile. The one out of the box probably won't work very well. But keep in mind, that even in the tightest of calibration loops, what you see on your monitor is usually brighter and just plain different from what you see in print.

A big drawback about a color management system is that it only lets you see the separation it builds as a static preview. That is to say, you can't seamlessly open a rejected proof in Photoshop and correct the file based on the device profile you want to print to. Photoshop lets you do this with its CMYK Preview mode while working in RGB. You actually work on a preview of the separation you'd make if you used the current Monitor Setup, Printing Inks Setup, and Separation Setup to generate CMYK data. Some color management systems let you write off a device profile as a separation table. Using this table gives you a better approximation of the file as it will look when it's converted.

Commercial Color Management Systems

Several major color management systems are available with more being developed all the time. Here are the big ones:

Kodak CMS

Kodak has been a big name in the color industry for decades and continues to make excellent products. Their KCMS (Kodak Color Management System) group provides a variety of products for both users and systems developers. Part of the KCMS is included with Photoshop.

It's a small part, granted, but it gives you a strong flavor of what a color management system does. The only thing the free part of the system does for you is let you import Kodak Photo CD images correctly. Kodak stores its photo CD images in its own proprietary color space called YCC. They need to be imported into Photoshop in a manner that Photoshop understands. When you do this, you select a resolution for the image, source, and target profiles.

To set the source profile, you need to know what kind of film the file was made from: Kodachrome, Ektachrome, or negatives. If you don't know (and it does make a difference), click the info box and follow the dialog box. The target profiles included in Photoshop are pretty skimpy: Lab and RGB. Usually Lab works a little better. Kodak sells additional profiles that you can plug in to target specific RGB and CMYK outputs as well. The CMYK ProPack sells for about $100.

For one-touch scanning, the system component is the PICC (Precision Input Color Characterization) package. It comes with targets for generating custom scanner profiles and a plug-in that lets you make color adjustments on-the-fly into Photoshop. Also included are a linearization application for PostScript imagesetters (the Precision Imagesetter Linearization software) and a calibration utility for desktop color printers (the Precision Color Printer Calibration software).

The system works well overall and the technology is supported by other packages. The ColorMatch software component (formerly offered by DayStar) generates the onscreen soft proof. It also enables you to save the file with the CMYK profile information embedded so that wherever the file goes, if KCMS is active, it will know what the colors in the file represent.

EfiColor

Another three letter acronym. This time it's Efi, which stands for Electronics for Imaging. EfiColor got off to a great start. It was included with QuarkXPress, which gave it a wide field of users. The software comes in the form of a QuarkXTension, which lets you manage the color of incoming graphics placed inside a document. Since than initial push, however, there hasn't been much else released from Efi end users.

A full-service color management solution is available under the name EfiColor Works. It includes a variety of tools in the color management suite. The suite includes a color conversion processor, the XTension, a scanner characterization utility, and Photoshop compatibility. Works includes a profile editor that lets you customize the transfer functions for input and output devices, which is nice.

On the whole, though, EfiColor needs some work. The separations it generates tend to be too dark. Equally bad, the separation engine doesn't handle gamut compression very well. Rounding things out, the scanner profiling isn't nearly as accurate as Kodak's or Agfa's. Some fine tuning would help matters considerably, but that doesn't appear ready to happen too soon. What it comes down to is that a color management system is only as good as its profiles.

Agfa

At the core of Agfa's suite of FotoFlow color management tools is FotoTune. It has strong scanner support, a bunch of free profiles, and the ability to edit the separation and dot gain settings for output profiles.

The best thing about the system is that it integrates so well with Agfa scanners. Between the separations that FotoFlow builds and the Agfa scanning hardware, you've got a powerful color separation combination. We've had a fair amount of experience on the Agfa SelectScan and found it to be an excellent machine. While that doesn't really have anything to do with the subject of color management, we thought we'd mention it. The SelectScan got us out of a few tight jams and we still have a warm spot in our hearts for it. Plus, when it scans you get these shimmering red, green, and blue lights beaming out at you.

FotoTune also offers fine cross-referencing of colors. You specify the a source and target as always but add in a simulation profile. This way you can print to one device and ask it to simulate the output of another device. So you could print an Iris that looks like the proof.

FotoTune is not so marvelous when it comes to monitors. It doesn't offer a calibration utility and the profiles it ships with aren't the grooviest. Fortunately, you can edit them. That still doesn't solve the problem of monitor calibration, however.

ColorSync and the Near Future

Other color management systems are available and more are on the way. Things are changing very rapidly in the world of color management. Scanners are available that produce CIE Lab colors directly. The impact these developments make on the world of color management could change tomorrow. These synopses, then, should be taken for what they are: progress reports on a fast moving field.

One of the more promising developments for the color management world is the development of Apple's ColorSync 2.0. ColorSync is a management system, but that's not really the whole story. The fine thing about ColorSync isn't just that it's another system, but it allows the coordination and cooperation of parts of competing systems. It's essentially a system-level base architecture that allows other management systems to function as well. It's Apple's plug and play philosophy at its best.

ColorSync can do this because a group called the International Color Consortium (ICC) developed a device profile format that everyone is accepting. So the profiles my monitor calibration utility (bought from company X) creates can be understood by my color management system (bought from company Y). The reason it can do that is because ColorSync lives on the system. All the parts from all the different color management systems plug into it. Vendors can offer users whichever segments of their color management system the client needs or wants.

ColorSync has the capacity to apply color metric tags to TIFF and EPS files. This lets files identify what color space data they're using wherever they go. The system supports PostScript Level 2 and does a much better color matching job than ColorSync 1 did.

Between ColorSync, the ICC format, and the rise of inexpensive light measuring technology, is an exciting opportunity for custom output profiling. The principle involves printing a series of color swatches, measuring each one, and then feeding the information back into the software. Then you specify the ink limits and black generation your device can support and you're done. The software generates a profile specific to that printing system. You can create them for any separation settings and combinations of paper, ink, and press you can dream up.

It's clear that color management systems are moving towards an open interface, allowing greater cross communication. As new systems are developed and finer adjustments on the existing ones are made, CMS technology grows more and more viable. Prepress houses and printers have long avoided the systems, due in part to the swaggering claims vendors have made to solve everyone's color problems with the touch of a button. Often the color results the earlier generation of color management system provided were simply inadequate for the level of quality and flexibility today's service bureau needs. Often the people in the prepress houses and print shops simply regard CMS's as dangerous, ill-conceived, superstitious rituals that produce mediocre results for people too lazy or insecure to just learn how to correct the files themselves in the first place. This takes us back to the former stripper at the beginning of this chapter who was desperately searching for the Make It Right button. Perhaps by the time this book sees press, color management will have located that button for her.

PAGE LAYOUT ISSUES

The page layout program is the final destination of all text and graphics in a project.

At this point, you've already entered and edited our text in a more comfortable word processing program, you've created and modified your vector-based artwork in the appropriate program, and you've scanned and corrected your halftones in Photoshop. The page layout program is the "drawing board" where you combine all of these disparate elements, turning them from individual concepts into a cohesive product.

We focus only on the two industry standard applications—QuarkXPress and Adobe PageMaker—in this chapter. The reason we emphasize these two programs for the purposes of page layout is simple: *they were designed for high-resolution layout and color separation.*

Because these two programs are used by the vast majority of designers, today's prepress professional is expected to know both of them for the following reasons:

◆ **QuarkXPress and PageMaker have been around for years and are proven commodities.** Both applications define the expected capabilities of page layout software—their features are not just added to a pre-existing application.

◆ **QuarkXPress and PageMaker have the widest user base.** There will never be a question about whether or not a service bureau can accept your files.

◆ **Using industry standard software means less risk and lower costs.** Software becomes an industry standard for a reason. Design and prepress professionals owe it to themselves (and their clients) to seek the path of least resistance and proven success.

This isn't to say you can't do complex (multiple page) layouts in a program like FreeHand, Ready Set Go!, or Canvas and successfully create color separations. Sure, you can. Based on our experience, however, you're taking your chances. The further you deviate from the most widely proven and accepted software, the more you risk output problems, compatibility problems, troubleshooting problems, and a host of other hassles. The few hundred bucks you'll spend on a more expensive layout program will pay for itself with the first one or two large jobs that output successfully.

This chapter is not about all the minute details that comprise the immense power of QuarkXPress and PageMaker. It's about the most production-specific features and techniques involved in the science of page layout. It's a chapter designed to get you working as efficiently and quickly as possible, while ensuring that your documents will output properly. If there are elements of the page layout process that enrage and frustrate you, you may recognize some of the following:

◆ Preferences must be continually set and reset.

◆ You continually have to redefine commonly used type characteristics, colors, and images.

◆ Your PMS colors output as CMYK values, or vice-versa.

◆ Your scanned images take forever to output.

- Your images, when scaled, look jagged and pixelated, or fail to output at all.

- Elements appearing on more than one page in a document are inconsistently placed.

- Attempts to impose your pages for printing fail repeatedly.

- Uniform document-wide type changes are difficult, if not impossible.

Once again, we'll talk about a working system that helps you avoid traditionally problematic areas. In this chapter, we help make your work environment operate more smoothly and reliably by focusing on the following production-oriented QuarkXPress and PageMaker issues:

- Application and document preferences, to better tailor your programs to your specific work

- Setting up your initial document, ensuring that every step is geared toward efficiency and a quality press run

- Properly defining, applying, and outputting spot and process colors

- Priming your text for easiest importing, layout, and formatting

- Working with master pages

- Handling and outputting scanned and vector-based images

- Setting up style, color, and image libraries

As important as low costs and high production standards, it's long been our belief that people should spend *as little time as possible* in the software of each stage of the production process. Working in a page layout program should be like a Navy SEAL mission: draft a plan, pool your resources, then make your strike with surgical precision. A repetitive task or inefficient operation may only require 60 seconds to take care of—but if you have to do it 30 times a day (a very conservative estimate), that equals 125 squandered, non-billable hours every year. Five days! At $80 an hour, that's upwards of $10,000 that'll never see the light of your bank account. Now apply that figure to a staff of five. Or ten. Or twenty. At the very least, take the time you save and spend it with your loved ones.

BEFORE YOU BEGIN: SETTING PREFERENCES

When you think about it, hundreds of values can be entered into the tools and commands of a page layout program. These range from line thicknesses to color menus to default fonts. Every program ships with a set of default values, or starting points, for all the tools and commands contained within. These are flexible values, meaning we can change those defaults to best suit our work.

Once again, we ask that you keep a keen eye on your work. Keep a notebook at your workstation. Keep a record of any task you do over and over and over again. As we cover the most production-specific preference settings in QuarkXPress and PageMaker, you'll find that many of these tasks can be compensated for by adjusting the values accessible through the different Preferences menus.

Some people are fearful of changing these settings, thinking that they are tampering with the internal workings of the application, as if they were messing around with life-sensitive code with a program like ResEdit (they're not—that's what Preferences are for). Others are frustrated because no matter how many times they change those settings, they always revert back to the original numbers. The first thing to realize when you are re-establishing these settings is that there are two different types of Preference: Document and Application.

Document and Application Preferences

You have two different ways to set preferences. If you change any default setting when there is an document open, then all preferences will be specific to that document only. When the document is closed, the defaults will revert back to what they were before. Thus, when you open the document again, the settings shift to changes that were made earlier. These settings are always written into the document, whether or not you made any changes. If, however, you change any default settings when there are NO documents open, then those changes are permanent. So the trick here is to tailor those settings as closely as possible to your most common needs.

Open QuarkXPress or PageMaker without opening a document (or creating a new one). Examine the menus and the floating palettes. Commands and menu items not grayed out are most likely ones that can be reset. Since there can be hundreds of settings available in every program, we will only focus on the most production-intensive defaults.

Recommended Production-Oriented Preferences (QuarkXPress 3.32)

Of the two page layout programs we discuss, QuarkXPress has the more flexible and production-specific Preferences. This dovetails with QuarkXPress's long-held reputation of being the strongest production page layout program, although recent upgrades to PageMaker have made the program… well, more QuarkXPress-like.

Application Preferences

Actually, in partial contradiction to what we just said about preferences, you can change the settings of the Application preferences with or without documents open. Either way, the settings become defaults (see Figure 15.1).

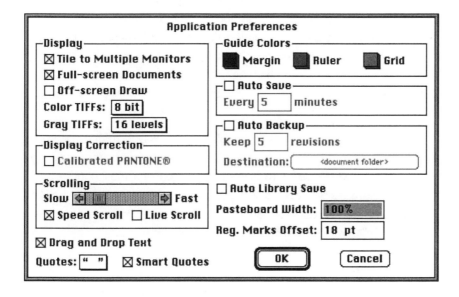

Figure 15.1

QuarkXPress's Application Preferences dialog.

◆ Under Display, in the upper left, turn on Full-Screen Documents. Since most of us are using 17-inch monitors, take advantage of every square inch of onscreen real estate.

◆ Set Color TIFFs and Gray TIFFs to the lowest values. This enables faster screen redraw, and it's safe to assume that color and tonality are not going to be adjusted in QuarkXPress. The page layout program is the wrong place to correct for color.

◆ Turn on Smart Quotes. Unless, of course, you're going to be using plenty of inch- and foot- symbols.

◆ Turn off Auto Save and Auto Backup. In our experience, we've found that these features can cause application crashes. Losing your work is hardly auto-saving.

◆ If you need to expand your Pasteboard Width (the work area around the onscreen page) to beyond 100 percent, you'll need an extra piece of software. Be careful, though. About a year ago, an XTension called Pasteboard XT began circulating throughout the industry. Early versions of this program caused problems. Although it did enable you to expand your pasteboard width, if you sent the file to a designer or service bureau who did not have the XTension, they couldn't open the file. Later versions of Pasteboard fixed this problem, but we recommend another XTension: Pasteboard XTerminator. This does not enlarge your pasteboard, but if your responsibility is working with client files, you don't need the larger pasteboard anyway. XTerminator just strips away all traces of of the original Pasteboard, should it exist in a file.

◆ Registration Marks Offset controls how far away from the page edges the registration marks will output. The default is 12 points, and every printer we've spoken to claims that's not enough. Most printers prefer their marks between 18 and 24 points away from the page edge. The best bet is to call your printer or speak to your pressmen. Otherwise, they'll simply be cutting and setting their own marks.

General Preferences

◆ Horizontal and Vertical Measures default to Inches. Change them to the more accurate (and printer's standard) Points or Picas (see Figure 15.2).

◆ Set Frames to Inside. This controls whether a frame applied to a text or picture box is placed on the inside or outside of the box (as opposed to illustration programs, which straddle a path with any stroke value). Placing frames on the inside ensures that your imported hi-res images trap properly into the frame. Also, since most frames are black, QuarkXPress's "keepaway" function will prevent any C, M, or Y inks from creating a multicolored halo around the frame.

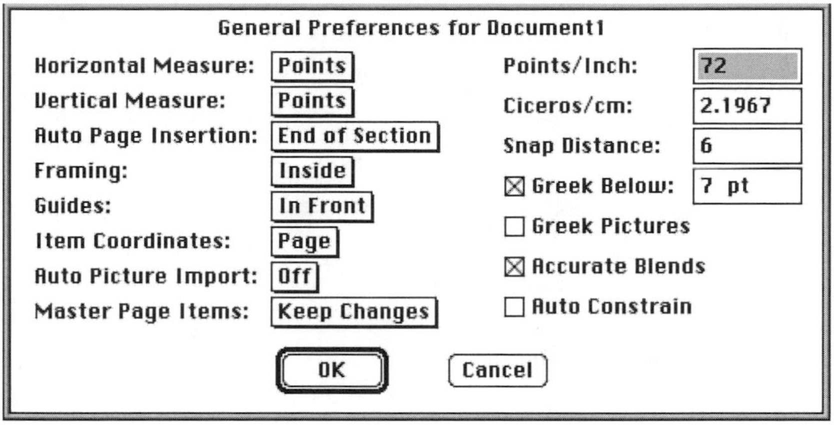

```
┌─────────────────────────────────────────────────────────┐
│              General Preferences for Document1            │
│ Horizontal Measure: [Points]      Points/Inch:   [72    ] │
│ Vertical Measure:   [Points]      Ciceros/cm:    [2.1967] │
│ Auto Page Insertion: [End of Section]  Snap Distance: [6] │
│ Framing:            [Inside]      ☒ Greek Below:  [7 pt]  │
│ Guides:             [In Front]    ☐ Greek Pictures        │
│ Item Coordinates:   [Page]        ☒ Accurate Blends       │
│ Auto Picture Import: [Off]        ☐ Auto Constrain        │
│ Master Page Items:  [Keep Changes]                        │
│              ( OK )        ( Cancel )                      │
└─────────────────────────────────────────────────────────┘
```

Figure 15.2

QuarkXPress's General Preferences dialog.

◆ Set Guides to In Front. It's painful to place a guide, only to have it obscured by everything on the page.

◆ Set Auto Picture Import to Off. Turning it on automatically updates any modified image in your document. Updating these manually ensures that you are aware of any modifications accepted into the file.

Trapping Preferences

These settings are covered in-depth in our chapter on Trapping.

Tools Preferences

Some of the infuriating factory defaults exist here. By selecting the tools one at a time, we can reset the available preferences for each one.

Line Tool Preferences

By selecting the Modify button, we can set our preferred thickness (see Figure 15.3). We like a nice, thin .5 pt thickness, but it's totally up to you. Beware, though. Do not, under any circumstances, select Hairline as a default for anything. It may look like a quarter-point line onscreen, or even when sent to a 600 dpi laser printer. Actually, it's a command to output the thinnest line possible on whatever device you print to. So, on that 600 dpi printer, it prints a line 1/600 of an inch thick. On a 2400 dpi imagesetter, you'll get a line 1/2400 of an inch thick. You can barely see this line, let alone reproduce or (heaven forbid) trap it. For best results, do not use any line thicknesses lower than .25 pts.

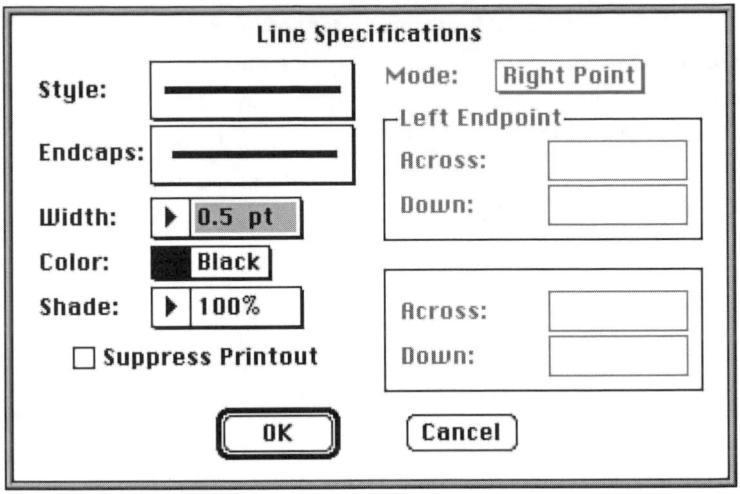

Figure 15.3

Setting Line Tool preferences.

Line Specifications

Style: ▬▬▬▬▬

Endcaps: ▬▬▬▬▬

Width: ▶ 0.5 pt

Color: ■ Black

Shade: ▶ 100%

☐ Suppress Printout

Mode: Right Point

┌Left Endpoint─
Across: [   ]

Down: [   ]

Across: [   ]

Down: [   ]

(OK)   (Cancel)

Picture Box Tools Preferences

The most problematic defaults are Runaround and Background Color (under Modify). Turn Runaround off by selecting None from the pop-up menu. Only apply a runaround value when you need one, and in our experience, we *don't* need one far more often than we *do*. The problem here is that you may not realize one of your picture boxes is touching one of your text boxes. This could cause your text to misposition or reflow.

The background color is less intuitive. It defaults to white, which is where it should be left. Many people change this value to None, which lets them "see through" the box to images lying underneath. The problem is QuarkXPress has a tendency to lose very light pixels in imported halftone images if the background is set to None. This is known as "garbage mask." The only images that can be successfully placed in a picture box with no background color are vector-based artwork, Photoshop line art, and images with a defined clipping path (see Figure 15.4). If your imported images fall almost exclusively into those categories, change the default background color to None. If you import many halftones, unclipped hi-res images, and standard silhouettes, leave the color at White and change it on a box-to-box basis.

Figure 15.4

Placing a bitmap silhouette in a picture box colored "None" results in a garbage mask.

Text Box Tool Preferences

Here, it is perfectly safe to set the background color to none, because all text is vector-based. The garbage mask will not occur. Set the Runaround to None, as well.

Later versions of QuarkXPress feature a Preference menu item called QuarkXPressPrint. This dialog enables you to control how your version of QuarkXPress is going to read the Preferences written into documents created using someone else's version of the program. Open a file created somewhere else, and you'll see a familiar dialog box. You have two choices: keep the document preferences or use the prefs of your own application (see Figure 15.5). Whenever you work with someone else's file, always keep the document preferences. This way, information such as trapping values, custom tracking, and kerning information is preserved. The only time you should override the document preferences is when you are certain you want to use the defaults of your own specific version of QuarkXPress. This often happens when a designer accepts a project halfway through completion, or when an output specialist knows for certain that erroneous preferences are built into the file.

Figure 15.5

QuarkXPress's Preferences request dialog.

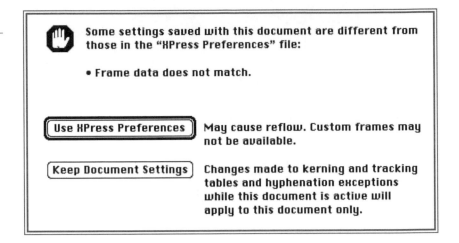

Although we prefer manually selecting "Keep Document Prefs" every time we open a file (we like to have a choice, just in case), you can reset the QuarkXPressPrint dialog to do it automatically (see Figure 15.6).

Figure 15.6

The QuarkXPressPrint dialog.

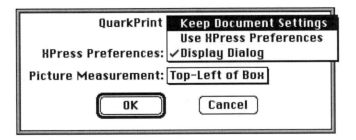

Default Colors

Examine your Colors palette. Chances are that Red, Blue, and Green all share space there. Also, you'll notice that Black and Registration look exactly the same. Let's change that.

Red, Blue, and Green have no place on a color menu. You will not, under any circumstances, apply these colors to any element on your page, so why leave them there? They actually pose a risk. If you were to define, say, Pantone Red, you'll find it residing right next to the factory default Red. If you're working in a hurry, as we all do, it's easy to apply the wrong color without realizing it. One will output. The other will not. Select Colors… from the Edit menu (with no documents open) and delete the offending colors (see Figure 15.7). Remove them permanently.

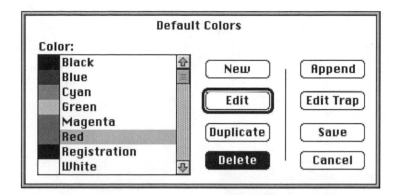

Figure 15.7

Removing Red, Green, and Blue permanently from the Color menu.

The same situation can occur with Black and Registration. Black is just that: 100 percent black. Registration is a command to apply 100 percent of all document colors (think of registration marks— solid on every plate). Again, when you're working quickly, it's easy to confuse colors. Swapping one of these for the other ultimately leads to unhappiness. Using the Registration command instead of Black will leave you with a black that is too dense (especially in a four-color job). If you ever define your own crop or registration marks, coloring them black will leave you with only one useable plate. In the same color dialog:

1. Choose Registration and select Edit.

2. Choose another color from the color wheel, preferably one you'll never use, like pink or bright purple. This changes the onscreen color and leaves the Registration command untouched (see Figure 15.8).

Also, if you find yourself using only a few different colors in your work— perhaps you only design with the corporate colors—add them as permanent items.

Default Fonts

The default font in QuarkXPress is defined as the Normal style sheet. To reset your default font:

1. Choose Style Sheets… from the Edit menu.

2. Select Normal, and make the appropriate changes.

Figure 15.8

Changing the onscreen color of Registration.

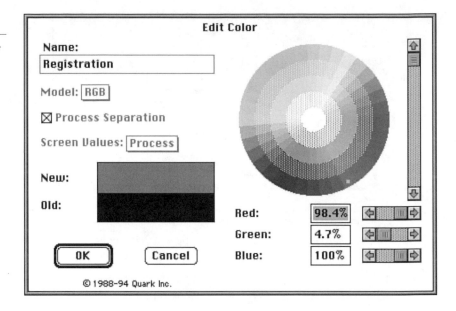

We recommend, however, that text in any document be defined as a separate style sheet. The safest bet is setting your default to one of the universal system fonts such as Chicago or Geneva. That way, your documents won't trigger any "missing font" messages at the service bureau.

Copying QuarkXPress Preferences

Whereas all document preferences are stored in the document proper, all Application prefs are kept in QuarkXPress's Preferences file, located in the application folder (QuarkXPress is one of the only major programs that keeps its preferences file here, instead of the Preferences Folder inside the System Folder). A quick way to unify all the preferences in a department (read: any place with more than one computer):

1. Make all your careful adjustments on one workstation.

2. Copy QuarkXPress's preferences file onto a diskette or access it over a network.

3. Replace all other QuarkXPress pref files with the new copy.

This way, we only need to set the preferences once. The next time the other versions of QuarkXPress are launched, they'll start up with the new settings.

Recommended Production-Oriented Preferences (Adobe PageMaker 6.5)

PageMaker's Preferences dialog is not as robust as QuarkXPress's, but you can still gain most of the control you need through other available menu items.

General Preferences

◆ Reset your measurements and ruler units to Points or Picas.

◆ Keep the graphics display on Standard. This gives a low-resolution display of imported graphics. High-Resolution will give 256-color displays, which are good for onscreen proofing by clients and the like, but slows down your redraw time considerably.

In the same dialog, click the More... button:

◆ Under Text, turn on Use Typographer's Quotes.

◆ Under Graphics, look for where it says "Alert when storing graphics over..." This setting dovetails with the Links Options setting (under the Element menu). As far as importing graphics goes, there are two ways to handle the information. You can import a low-resolution copy of the image and maintain a connection to the high-resolution information in the original graphic file. This is called *linking*. PageMaker's default is to import all high-res information into the document (this explains the sometimes enormous PageMaker file sizes). The alert setting defaults to 256K. This means graphics under that size are imported totally, without links. Graphics larger than that trigger a dialog offering a choice: create a link or import all the high-res information. Link *all* graphics files, regardless of their size. It's too tempting to send a file to the service bureau without the external graphics file. Theoretically, you don't need to, if all the information was imported into the file. But reality steps in if any of your graphics demand adjusting. Link all your graphics by doing the following:

1. With no documents open, select Link Options under the Elements menu.

2. Under Graphics, turn off "Store copy in publication" (see Figure 15.9).

Figure 15.9

Forcing PageMaker to link all placed graphics.

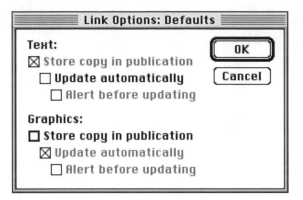

3. Ignore the Graphics alert in the preferences dialog.

4. Always supply all graphic files with your document.

Line and Fill Defaults

Because PageMaker doesn't use picture boxes, the demands here are more aesthetic than functional.

1. Determine your most commonly used line width, and select it from the Element menu, under Line. Again, do not use the Hairline width. If you prefer a thin line, use .5 or .25 pt as your default.

2. Leave your default fill at None. It's better to have to define a fill whenever you need one, than to accidentally leave a Paper fill where it doesn't belong.

Default Colors

Just as in QuarkXPress, delete Red, Green, and Blue from your color menu. PageMaker, however, will not let you change the onscreen color of Registration. You'll also find that you can delete cyan, magenta, and yellow from the default menu, but don't worry; four-color images will still separate.

Copying PageMaker Preferences

PageMaker prefs are stored in the Preferences folder, in the System Folder. Once your preferences have been set for one copy of PageMaker, copy this file into the Preferences folders of your remaining workstations.

DOCUMENT CONSTRUCTION

Now that your programs have a more production-oriented foundation, you can get through each phase of the document construction process more easily. Again, we'll concentrate on the most time-saving and print-specific aspects of each one.

When it's time to create your final page layout, we are assuming that your document has been appropriately planned (see Chapter 7, "Project Planning"). Once we enter this stage, we'll follow the same basic process every time:

1. Set up the document

2. Define the colors

3. Create the style sheets

4. Design the master pages

5. Design the individual pages

We'll loosely follow these steps as we talk about the most important production-oriented page layout issues.

Document Setup

Document setup creates the foundation for our entire project. It consists of:

◆ Setting the page dimensions

◆ Determining whether or not to use Facing Pages

◆ Adding the appropriate number of pages

These steps require that we understand:

◆ The setup dialogs of both PageMaker and QuarkXPress

◆ The difference between printer and reader spreads

◆ The basics of page imposition

◆ The conditions surrounding bleeds and crossovers

◆ What size press your document will be printed on

Page Dimensions

Determining your page size is one of the most fundamental elements of page layout. Some people design with nothing but 8.5 × 11 paper in mind, and if that's the only size you'll ever print to, fine. The moment you begin using custom sizes, however, things become more complex. Use these dimensions from the very start, and only change them if absolutely necessary.

◆ Page dimensions determine the placement of crop and registration marks. Using ruler guides, for example, to design a 9 × 6-inch booklet on letter-sized pages results in film that cannot be used by your printer (see Figure 15.10).

Figure 15.10

Always set the exact page dimensions.

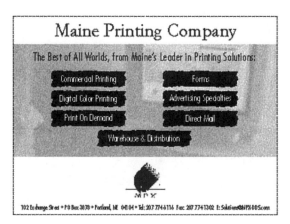

◆ Changing page dimensions halfway through a project means having to re-position your page elements. The more these elements are moved around manually, the higher the risk of human error.

◆ Don't forget to factor in elements such as perforated mailing cards or covers with the edges folded in. These must be added to the overall page size, but be careful. Depending on the size of your original document, the added inches may make your piece too large to print efficiently (or at all) on its intended press.

Page dimensions are set exactly the same way in QuarkXPress and PageMaker:

1. Launch the application and choose New from the File menu.

2. Enter the *exact* measurements for one single page of your document (for a 9 × 6 document, enter 9 inches and 6 inches). Don't try creating spreads on one single page (see Facing Pages). You'll only hate yourself later, and so will your printer.

3. If you need to change your page size, select Document Setup from the File menu.

4. Avoid creating multi-page documents in any program that lets you design with more than one page size at a time. In FreeHand, for example, you can apply different dimensions to all 8 (or 24, or 64) of your pages, if you wanted to. The logistics behind outputting and printing a file like this are nightmarish. We don't describe them here, but don't worry. Someday soon, some unfortunate output specialist will be pushed over the brink, take a hostage, and lead police on a murderous, cross-country rampage. Then you can read all about it in the supermarket tabloids. For now, if you need different page sizes within the same document, create new documents.

Facing Pages

A spread is a relationship between two pages in a document. As you work, you must design and produce with both printer and reader spreads in mind:

1. Pick up a coworker's magazine and flip through it. Page 2 is next to page 3, page 76 is next to page 77, and so on. This side-by-side arrangement of pages in the natural order that we read them is a Reader Spread.

2. Now pull the staples out of the binding and examine a single sheet of paper. You'll see that page 2 is printed on the same sheet as page 87, that page 33 is on the same sheet as 68. These are Printer Spreads, the result of imposing the individual pages so they'll appear in the proper order after printing and binding (see Figure 15.11).

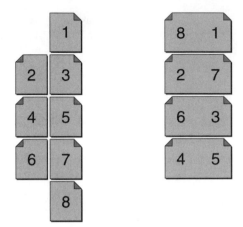

3. Put the magazine back. Deny everything when your coworker complains.

Both layout programs enable us to create documents using a feature called Facing Pages.

The upside: when designing a multi-page document, facing pages enable us to design using reader spreads. This is more intuitive and efficient, since we have a better idea how our printed piece will look and feel. They also give us the ability to output spreads—two individual pages outputting with one set of crop and registration marks.

The downside: we can create simple (and insufficient) page impositions by manually moving our pages into the proper order. Also, many people are compelled to use more complex page elements, including bleeds and cross-overs, not realizing how they impact final page imposition and printing.

Imposition refers to the arranging of pages on-press to ensure the correct order after the printed sheet is folded and trimmed. Unfortunately, imposing pages by computer is almost impossible. There are so many factors, conditions, and measurements involved that are unique to each press, there's no way to develop a standardized approach. In the time it takes to speak with the necessary people, get the right specs, run test sheets, calibrate the imposition software, and output final films, a job can be output as individual page films, stripped conventionally, and run on press. Eventually, digital presses will become so common, imposition will occur automatically, if desired. For now, the people most interested in electronic imposition are designers (many of whom do not understand how difficult it is) and service bureaus (many of which output films that are simply cut up and re-imposed on the stripper's table). The surest technique is to output individual page films and turn them over to the printer.

A technique we often employ takes place just before final output:

1. After designing a file using facing pages, turn the facing pages command off (under File: Document Setup).

2. Extend your bleeds—image information that runs off the page edge—to nine points beyond the page boundaries. This includes any information that occupies space on another page. These are called crossovers, and again, leave them to a stripper. Make sure the crossover image appears on both pages. Switching back to single pages will not make copies.

3. Output all pages as single pages (no spreads). The only exceptions are pages that naturally occur as spreads, like covers and centerspreads. Output these pages separately with the Spreads command turned on.

4. Group all films by page and turn them over to the printer.

Adding Pages

Add all the pages you need when you first create the document. Avoid simply adding them as you need them. Page count is based on two things: the amount of content and the budget. Since budget almost always wins, the page count in the approved job estimate should be adhered to as closely as possible. Adding another four pages to a job (remember the magazine—four pages to a sheet) adds considerable cost, especially when printing four colors to quality paper in high volumes.

PageMaker enables you to determine the number of pages as you create the new document. Add exactly the number of pages you need. In QuarkXPress, you must create the document first, then add the remaining pages using the Insert Page command. At this point, you'll already have one page, so add the number of pages you want in your document minus one. This is no big deal, but it helps keep things clean.

Even though you won't be numbering them, covers and inserts count as pages. Keep these items in separate files, and keep the guts of a publication in another. This allows for more efficient applications of special treatments, such as crossovers, spreads, and custom page sizes.

Multiple Page Spreads

QuarkXPress has the unique ability to create spreads based on three or more pages. Do this by dragging page icons next to each other in the Document Layout palette. As long as the width does not exceed 48 inches (QuarkXPress's page size limit), it doesn't matter how many pages you move together. This technique is particularly handy for such things as double-fold covers

Defining and Applying Color

Define your colors before you create or import anything. That way, you can apply color as elements are introduced into your layout. Color is also required in later steps of the layout process, such as style sheet and master page definitions.

There are three golden rules when working with color in a page layout program:

1. Choose colors properly.

2. Define colors accurately.

3. Apply colors wisely.

These have nothing to do with what colors you actually choose. If your brochure is purple and teal, or your skies are metallic bronze, or your oceans run red, we don't care— as long as they're the colors you want. Successfully pulling it off depends on your understanding of these issues:

◆ How to determine which colors to use

◆ The nature of spot and process color

◆ Naming the colors you define

◆ How colors defined in other programs impact your page layout

◆ Defining accurate tints for spot and process color

Spot and Process Color in your Page Layout Program

These two ink types live on opposite sides of the zoo. The most important difference is that spot inks are opaque, process inks are transparent. When you combine (or overprint) transparent inks, you get new colors. When you overprint opaque inks, the result is a sort of muddy pigment stew. So of course, process inks are the standard for what we have deemed photorealistic full-color print reproduction. If you find yourself defining spot colors in your document, it's for one of these reasons:

- **Budget:** your project consists of only one or two colors.

- **Color fidelity:** you add spot inks to your four-color job, compensating for the colors that cannot be accurately reproduced (only 10-15 percent of the Pantone library can be accurately printed using CMYK inks).

- **Style:** you intentionally create a job consisting of multiple spot colors.

Because we have these two disparate families of color, our methods for selecting, defining, and applying them determines our ultimate success. One mistake, and we have colors that don't separate or reproduce with any accuracy.

Choosing Colors Properly

The only time we don't define which colors we use in a document is when we scan full-color images. Sure, we have great control over the percentages that ultimately output, but here we rely as much on hardware, software, proofing, and luck as we do on defining exactly what the output percentages will be. Everything else in our document—boxes, bars, backgrounds, type, rules, colored line art and halftones—is based on color values we specifically enter.

The only accurate way to choose these colors is by referring to a swatchbook. For $50–100, you can purchase:

- True printed samples of spot ink libraries. These are made from the very same custom inks that will be used when printing your job. Pantone is the American standard.

- Process ink combinations that dovetail with the predefined libraries accessed in the color menus of your graphics software. Trumatch and Pantone Process are two widely used process swatchbooks.

There are other ways to choose colors, of course, but they range from mildly inaccurate to downright folly. Devices such as Light Source's Colortron II, provide a decent starting point for color by calculating the RGB values of preprinted or pre-existing objects. These values are never absolute, but it beats starting from scratch, especially if you don't have a vast history of color science. The worst thing you can do is choose your colors based on the what appears onscreen in your color menus. Your software can't even display *cyan* consistently, let alone custom inks or subtle process combinations. It's worth buying a swatchbook just to hold samples up to your monitor to see the difference between onscreen and printed colors. Cracks *us* up every time.

Follow these basic steps:

1. Determine the type of color to be printed: spot or process.

2. As you plan your document, determine which elements will be colored.

3. Refer to an appropriate swatchbook to select the colors that will be used. Don't use a spot color guide to define process colors (or vice versa), even though your program will let you do so.

4. Define the colors. It's easy to change color definitions down the road, if needed.

Defining Colors Accurately

Defining a color means adding it to the color menu of your document. But we're not really defining *colors*—we're defining *output commands*. These commands control which information is printed to which plates when a file is separated. This is obviously important: if you reproduce a logo or line of type using Pantone 287 ink, it means you want that information printing to a film plate titled "Pantone 287." If you're creating bright red headline type in a four-color file, you want the letters to print appropriately to the magenta and yellow plates. If information appears on the wrong plate (or plates), you can't expect the piece to print accurately on press.

Two issues cause the most problems when defining colors:

◆ Naming your colors

◆ Determining whether or not they will be process or spot separations

The Importance of Color Names

Naming requirements are totally different for spot and process colors. For spot colors, naming is everything. You may have noticed that the name of your spot colors are exactly the same as the name printed at the top of your page films. That's right: whatever you name a custom color is the name of the plate that ultimately separates.

Applications use different standards for naming spot colors. Let's use PMS 506 as an example:

◆ QuarkXPress, Illustrator, and Photoshop name this color Pantone CV 506.

◆ PageMaker and FreeHand name this color either Pantone CVC 506 (presumably for coated paper) or Pantone CVU 506 (for uncoated). Don't be fooled—the only difference between the two is a slightly different onscreen appearance, a half-hearted attempt to show the different results when printing to coated or uncoated stock. Your Pantone swatchbook illustrates that a hundred times better by giving you real-life printed samples.

> ### What's in a Name?
>
> A designer we know created a two-color logo in Illustrator 6. When she output separations to her in-house imagesetter, she wound up with four plates for each page: Pantone CVC 484, Pantone CV 484, Pantone CVC 310, and Pantone CV 310 (see Figure 15.12). Since this was no way to print a two-color job (can you imagine having a press operator run a two-color job on a four-color press with only two different inks?), she had to go back and make her color names consistent to get the proper separations.

You'd think all those software programmers would have a meeting and straighten this all out over coffee and donuts. As it is, we have to double-check every spot color name to ensure it's the same in every application involved in our project. We prefer the "CV" designation, so if we use PageMaker or FreeHand, we just shorten the color name by the one letter.

Many people recommend defining colors by importing a graphic containing the same colors. After all, importing color information into a document with no defined colors automatically adds the items to the Color menu, right? We can just use those imported colors throughout the rest of our document, right? Theoretically, sure. Our designer friend could have placed her logo and the imported color names for the rest of the project. The reason we *do not* recommend this is the fact that we no longer design in a vacuum. What happens if she were to import a graphic made in Illustrator? Or a duotone from Photoshop? A veritable Babel of color names.

Figure 15.12

*Multiple versions of the same
spot colors.*

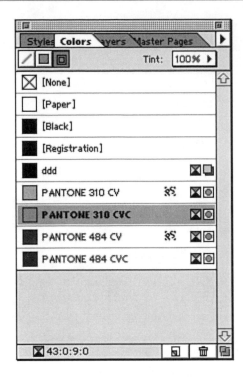

Naming process colors is a much less rigid affair. It doesn't matter what we name these colors, because the components are always the same: cyan, magenta, yellow, black. Even if you access colors from the Trumatch library, you can ignore the numerical color titles and change them to something more descriptive and useful, like "Rich Black," "Brown Headline Type," or "The Azure of My True Love's Eyes." Because you can create thousands more colors using process inks than by using a couple of spot inks, its easy to define dozens of different colors. Name them as concisely as you please, with no worries of creating new separation plates (see Figure 15.13).

How Will Your Colors Separate?

The type of separation—spot or process—is another command we build into a color definition. Unless a color is told to separate into its four-color components, it outputs just like a spot color— onto its own plate, even if the plate is titled Trumatch 36-a7 (a color from a process library). Likewise, if we tell a spot color to separate as a process color, that's just what we'll get, whether we want it or not.

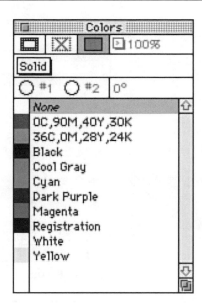

Figure 15.13

Naming process colors with descriptive abandon.

Choosing Separation Types in QuarkXPress

The ultimate success of your color separations rests on one little button. As you define a color, take special note of the Process Separation button in the Edit Color dialog:

◆ If you are defining a spot color, make sure the button is clicked Off.

◆ If you are defining a process color (including colors from process libraries like Trumatch and Pantone ProSim), make sure the button is clicked On. Even if you switch to CMYK mode and manually define your own percentages, you need to choose Process Separation (see Figure 15.14).

Always check this button! You'd think that the right setting would be built into the color library selection, but it's not. The only information we tap into when choosing a color from an electronic library is the color name and its process components. This separation command, like many commands in today's software, lingers. Rather than reverting to a default setting after we close the program, it clings to the most recently applied choice. This is most evident when we move from a four-color to a two-color job.

Figure 15.14

Making sure Process Separation is clicked On.

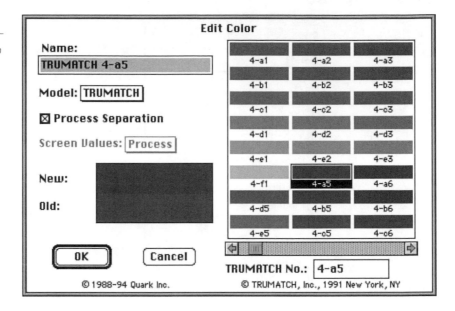

Choosing Separation Types in PageMaker

When defining a color in Pagemaker, pay attention to the Type pop up menu in the Define Color dialog:

- ◆ If you are defining a spot color, make sure Spot is chosen from this menu.

- ◆ If you are defining a process color, make sure Process is chosen from the Type menu, as well as CMYK from the Model menu just below. PageMaker has an edge here. It should automatically set these two menus when you choose a color from a built-in library.

Applying Color Wisely

Again, this has little to do with the actual colors you choose. Rather, it has to do with what colors you apply to which objects. It also concerns many trapping issues, but that issue is covered in depth in the next chapter. As we'll see, there will always be some restrictions on what we can color, the colors we can apply, and how accurate our printed result will be.

There are six elements we can apply color to in a layout document:

- ◆ Type

- ◆ Rules

- Frames and Background color (Line and Fill in PageMaker)

- Imported line art (1-bit TIFF)

- Imported halftones (grayscale TIFF)

There are two different ways we can color them:

- Apply a solid color (100 percent)

- Apply a tint of a color (1-99 percent)

And there are two elements which cannot be colored:

- Full-color images (24-bit TIFF)

- Any Encapsulated PostScript File (EPS)

Let's cover the issues involved in each of these items.

Type

When colors are improperly applied to small type sizes (14 points and under), the result can be unreadable. When very thin areas—especially serif type—are colored, three things can happen.

- Invariably, areas colored with process inks are comprised of overlapping screen values. If the linescreen is too low, the individual dots of the halftone screen will be larger than the thinner parts of the type characters. This renders the otherwise crisp lines of the characters indistinct and difficult to read. Solution: Color body text 100 percent black whenever possible. Only color text over 14 points with process combinations.

- If the slightest misregistration occurs on press, the effects will be grossly exaggerated by the fine details of the type. Solution: again, color body text 100 percent black whenever possible.

- If you place body text of one spot color on a background of a second spot color, trapping is next to impossible. You'll either fatten or thin the character shapes by attempting to trap them, or the type will misregister anyway. Solution: Use either drop-out (white) type on a colored background, or use colored type on a white background. Trapping small type using spot colors is always next to impossible.

Rules

The same guidelines for small type apply here as well:

◆ If a rule is too thin and colored with either a tint or process combination, then low linescreens and misregistration could well be the kiss of death. Solution: Color rules 100 percent black if want a nice, thin line. If you want colored rules, use at least a one-point width.

◆ When using at least two spot colors, don't place thin rules of one color on top of another. If you spec .5-point lines and then apply a standard trap value of .3-point, you'll have rules that are either spread to over a point in width or choked to non-existence. Solution: When using rules in a two-color job, keep the colors separate.

Frames and Background Color (Line and Fill)

When using thin frames or borders, the same guidelines discussed in the items above apply. For best results when trapping a full-color image, use black frames in QuarkXPress or black line values in PageMaker.

Imported Line Art (1-bit TIFF)

These images can be re-colored in both QuarkXPress and PageMaker with spot or process colors. The original image file isn't touched. Rather, the image that resides in the page layout is told to output to different plates.

Some people re-color line art by creating monotones in Photoshop and saving the files as EPS. This is not recommended because of your inability to change the color in the layout file (you'd have to go back into Photoshop and re-spec the monotone). Also bear in mind that standard line art, which outputs at 100 percent black, automatically overprints. As soon as the line art is reduced to a tint or re-colored, it knocks out, and neither program's trapping functions will apply to the re-colored image. Solution: line art that sits untouched by any other color never has to be trapped. Or, if using process colors, be sure to create a process bridge (see Chapter 16, "Trapping").

Imported Halftones (grayscale TIFF)

The techniques and issues here are essentially the same as imported line art files, except that halftones do not automatically overprint when you first place them.

◆ Again, color these images in your layout program instead of Photoshop. This gives you the flexibility to change colors at the drop of a hat.

◆ Do not confuse coloring a halftone with creating a duotone or quadtone. If accurately and deeply reproducing the tonal range of your halftones is paramount, by all means define a multitone image in Photoshop.

Defining Tints

Unless you have a printed sample to work from, then defining a tint is based on guesswork. Fortunately, help and resources are right nearby:

◆ Pantone has released a swatchbook based not only on their custom inks, but different printed tint values. Referring to this guide is a great help in choosing the right percentage. Beyond that, choosing a tint is as easy as entering a percentage in the color palettes of QuarkXPress or PageMaker.

◆ Process tints require greater care. Applying a 50 percent tint of a Pantone Process color, for example, results in an unsatisfying tint. This is because each process component is scaled back by 50 percent, regardless of their values, and they just don't act proportionately like single spot colors do. You can either settle on inaccurate (but easier to define) tints or use a swatchbook like Trumatch, which is based on initial colors and subsequent tint values.

Full-Color Images (24-bit TIFF)

These images cannot be re-colored in your layout program, and that's good. Presumably, the color information was already adjusted in Photoshop.

Encapsulated PostScript Files (EPS)

These can be vector-based images from Illustrator, duotones from Photoshop, five-part DCS files, or even a page from QuarkXPress. Theoretically, these images cannot be touched by a page layout program. PageMaker, however, enables you to apply a color to an EPS file. Why it does, we don't know: it replaces all colors in the image with only the one, and the change doesn't appear onscreen, so you can only tell if you've made the change by referring to the color menu. If you need to make any changes to an EPS file, open it up in the original application and do it there. This way, you can also readjust any trapping information, if necessary.

Working with Text, Type, and Style Sheets

The life-cycle of the formatted word is a lot like the cycle of a butterfly's life: first there's a disgusting, fuzzy crawling monster, then a less-repulsive but still-curious cocoon, and finally a pretty flying bug.

The first text we bring into our document, whether we import it or enter it by hand, is creepy beast. It's ugly, unformatted, and as far away from the finished product as it can be. Soon, the text is transformed into type as we slowly but surely determine the characteristics we want to apply. When this transition is complete, we not only have formatted type, but a quick and fluid way of applying, re-applying, and changing those formats: style sheets.

Entering and working with text, whether you create it yourself or receive a file from someone else, involves the following issues:

◆ Whether or not your layout program can recognize the text files you want to import

◆ The difference between local and global formatting

◆ When and how to define style sheets

The Fuzzy Monster: Text

If there is any text at all in your layout document, chances are it was either entered by hand or imported from a word processing file. The vast majority of documents involve both of these techniques. Typically, shorter items such as headlines, captions, copyright tags, and other brief lengths of text are entered by hand. Longer stretches of text—stories, columns, book chapters, articles—are more efficiently created and edited in a word processing program, such as Microsoft Word. In fact, Word is the program we recommend that everyone use, even though we've found version 6 to be the clumsy, slow, and homely bastard cousin of the sleeker and more productive version 5.1. The reasons for using Word to enter large amounts of text are clear:

◆ The only focus is on typing and editing. In a layout program, the focus is on formatting and positioning.

♦ Entering text in a word processing program is easier on the eyes and head, since it was specifically designed to perform this function most efficiently.

♦ Your end-user options are much more flexible. After creating the text file, it can go to someone using QuarkXPress, PageMaker, or any other program that accepts that type of file. In fact, Microsoft Word (as you might expect) is the most universally accepted text file format.

♦ Word's editing tools —spell check, grammar check, thesauruses, and dictionaries—are more powerful.

♦ Word can open many text files that simply leave QuarkXPress and PageMaker confused. Once, someone gave us an old Atari document from, like, 1981. When we finally cracked it open in Word, it was chock-full of crazy symbols and textual garbage, but it only took a few minutes of editing to clean up. We saved the document as a Word file and immediately imported it into PageMaker.

♦ Word is indispensable if you need to save your text into a different text file format, such as RTF, ASCII, or WordPerfect. Word can save into 21 different formats, QuarkXPress 13, and Pagemaker only nine.

Don't be put off just because you're using yet another application in your production process. Word is easy to learn (since we're only using it for rudimentary tasks and some built-in features), and the time and frustration saved by not performing this work in a page layout more than pays for the extra cost. Be aware of these issues, however:

♦ Avoid formatting type in a word processing program, if possible. Only enter the textual information. Like many other apps, more and more word processing programs are including incongruous features like vector-based illustration and page layout. These are fine if it's the only application you have, and if you're printing to the office laserprinter. Otherwise, ignore them.

♦ Your page layout program must have a filter (a small piece of soft-ware) that allows it to recognize your text file. QuarkXPress's filters reside in the Xtensions folder, inside the QuarkXPress application folder. PageMaker's Filters folder is located in the application folder, in the RSRC folder. If you've just upgraded to Word 6, you may have noticed that QuarkXPress no longer notices your text files. Since Word 6 was not released before your version of QuarkXPress, you need to download the Word 6 filter from QuarkXPress's Web site. Install it in the Xtensions folder, re-launch QuarkXPress, and you're golden.

The Curious Cocoon: Text Becomes Type

After you've imported text into your document, you stand at a crossroads. Should you format the text locally or globally? You'll almost always do a little of both, but we'll get to that point in a couple of pages.

When you started using a page layout program, one of the first things you learned was how to format type. You remember: highlight the text, choose a font, set a point size, change the line spacing, set the alignment, and so on. This is the essence of localized formatting—any change you make is specific only to the text you've highlighted. It seems a very intuitive way to set type. After all, you know exactly what text is being changed, when it's changed, and you walk step-by-step through every attribute. There's a catch, of course. All it takes is handling one multi-page document this way to find out that localized formatting is difficult and time-consuming, and creates a minefield of potential errors and miscalculation:

◆ You'll quickly discover that your simple, eight-page document may have dozens of text fields. These would all have to be formatted individually.

◆ If we apply an average of seven text attributes to an area of formatted text (for example, font, size, leading, alignment, color, track, space after), and we average ten areas that need formatting per page (headlines, subheads, captions, text columns, headers, footers, page numbers, etc.). That's 70 formatting commands per page. Eight pages require 560 commands. Forty-eight pages: 3360. A 300-page book? Forget it. Unless we're all Dustin Hoffman starring in *Rain Man*, something's gonna get missed.

◆ There's no way to make any quick, universal changes to your text formatting. If you change your mind about any attribute, you have to make that same change by hand throughout the document.

- Unless all of your text—even spaces—is selected when you change fonts, the layout program will "remember" the old font and possibly call for it when the job is opened at the service bureau. This wastes valuable time at the precise moment you cannot afford to.

There are only two occasions when you can safely and efficiently format text locally:

- **When you're working on a simple one-page document**, like a poster or business card. If you just don't have that much text, it's easy enough to get away with lightning-strike formatting.

- **When you locally format text that already has a style sheet applied to it.** This is unavoidable if you want to italicize, boldface, color, or otherwise format individual words. If a style sheet has been applied to text and you've formatted parts of it locally, then those words will retain the "extra" formatting whenever you edit the style. Just remember to supply entire font families with your document (as discussed in Chapter 4, "Font Management").

Beyond these two examples, always work on the assumption that you'll be using style sheets as the basis for all of your type attributes.

The Butterfly: Style Sheets

Those of you who have worked with conventional typography systems already realize the term "Style Sheets" is a bit of a misnomer. Actually, the formatting applied to a single paragraph is called a style, and when all the styles in a document are made into a list, it's called a style sheet. QuarkXPress and PageMaker refer to their paragraph formatting tags as style sheets, presumably to avoid confusion with type styles and other uses of the word.

The premise of style sheets is simple. Rather than format all of our text by hand, we set the attributes for each style ahead of time, store a list of these attributes in a readily available floating palette, and apply them at will at the click of a button. There are three fundamental but oh-so-important reasons for doing this:

- Styles are applied easily and efficiently, unlike localized formatting.

- Once style sheets have been used, you only have to go back to the original style definition to make changes that automatically apply through the document.

◆ If a style needs to be changed after a document has left your control (or after it has fallen into your hands), the change can be made intuitively and at lower risk.

If you're new to using style sheets, pick up a publication and scan a couple of pages. Note how the formatting generally remains consistent from page to page. Body text remains the same. Figure callouts, too. Headers and page numbers, pull-quotes and captions, any style that appears *more than once* is best formatted with a style sheet. The process for defining and applying a series of styles is easy, and we'll go step-by-step through making basic style sheets in QuarkXPress and PageMaker.

Before we do that, let's cover a few aspects of style sheets that are the same in QuarkXPress and PageMaker:

◆ **These styles apply only to paragraphs** (that's why they're sometimes called "paragraph styles"). A paragraph is anything that exists between two carriage returns, whether it's a single letter, a fourteen-page Faulknerian sentence, or a 30,000-word novella. Any attempt to apply a style sheet to a smaller part of a paragraph such as a letter or word changes the style of the entire paragraph. This is where localized formatting ultimately comes in.

◆ **Type does not have to be highlighted when applying a style.** Inserting the flashing text cursor anywhere in a paragraph is enough.

◆ **Avoid empty returns.** Entering extra returns to provide space between paragraphs throws a couple obstacles in your path. First, the spaces are only one size, usually the point size of the leading value. Changing the size would either involve local formatting or extra spaces. Second, those extra spaces misalign your text if one of them spills over to the next column. Always use a Space Before or Space After value to provide the necessary breathing room between paragraphs.

◆ **Each program lists "No Style" in their Style Sheets palette,** and it means exactly that—text with no style sheets applied. You'll see this tag in two situations: imported text and type you've manually stripped the style information from. It's not a style sheet. It's the absence of a style sheet. It cannot be edited, so don't work under the assumption that you can somehow apply attributes to text by changing the No Style tag.

◆ **Each program lets you create a new style based on a current selection.** This is a pretty intuitive way to create a style. Enter some sample text, format it locally, and highlight it. Then, when you define a style sheet, all of the characteristics are automatically plugged in. Name the style sheet, double-check everything, and you're ready to go.

◆ **Use style sheets when placing tab spaces.** This is especially important when similarly-styled type requires different tab spaces, such as body text needing hanging indents on page three and a table on page six. Use the "Based On…" option to create variations on a style, and name the new style sheets appropriately: "Body Text," "Body Text/Hang Indents," "Body Text/Table."

Defining Style Sheets in QuarkXPress

I. Access the style sheet dialog by selecting "Style Sheets…" from the Edit menu, or by Command-(Alt) clicking a style tag in the Style Sheets palette (see Figure 15.15).

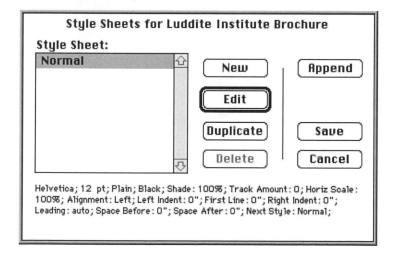

Figure 15.15

Select Edit: Style Sheets to define styles.

2. Click New to create a new style.

3. Name the style sheet and apply a Keyboard Equivalent, if desired (see Figure 15.16).

Figure 15.16

Naming styles accurately.

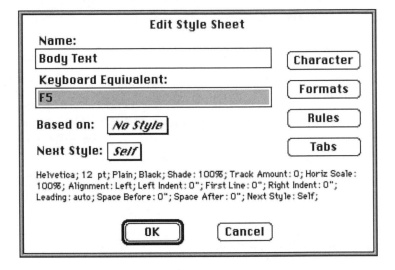

Edit Style Sheet

Name:

Body Text

Keyboard Equivalent:

F5

Based on: *No Style*

Next Style: *Self*

Helvetica; 12 pt; Plain; Black; Shade: 100%; Track Amount: 0; Horiz Scale: 100%; Alignment: Left; Left Indent: 0"; First Line: 0"; Right Indent: 0"; Leading: auto; Space Before: 0"; Space After: 0"; Next Style: Self;

Character

Formats

Rules

Tabs

OK   Cancel

4. One by one, enter the values for the Character, Format, Rule, and Tab settings. PageMaker users will find Hyphenation as a separate item under the Edit menu. These settings can be accessed under Formats when defining style sheets (see Figure 15.17).

5. Click OK to switch back to the original dialog.

6. If you need to define another style, click New and repeat the process. If you need to make any changes, select a style from the window and choose Edit. If you're finished, click Save. The styles will appear in the floating Style Sheets palette (see Figure 15.18).

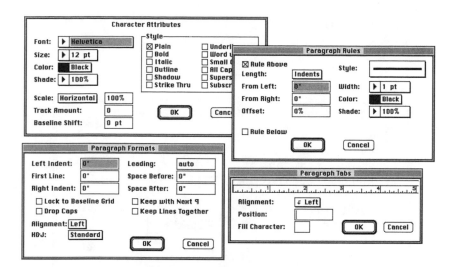

Figure 15.17

QuarkXPress's four style sheet definition dialogs

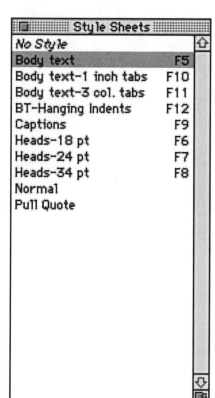

Figure 15.18

The Style Sheet palette.

Using "Based On"

1. Define a basic style, as mentioned above.

2. In the Style Sheet dialog, duplicate the basic style (see Figure 15.19).

Figure 15.19

Duplicating a style.

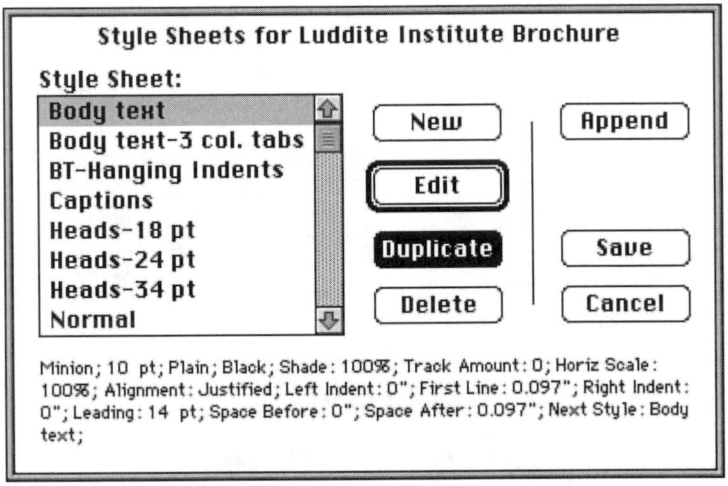

Style Sheets for Luddite Institute Brochure

Style Sheet:

- Body text
- Body text-3 col. tabs
- BT-Hanging Indents
- Captions
- Heads-18 pt
- Heads-24 pt
- Heads-34 pt
- Normal

New · Append · Edit · Duplicate · Save · Delete · Cancel

Minion; 10 pt; Plain; Black; Shade: 100%; Track Amount: 0; Horiz Scale: 100%; Alignment: Justified; Left Indent: 0"; First Line: 0.097"; Right Indent: 0"; Leading: 14 pt; Space Before: 0"; Space After: 0.097"; Next Style: Body text;

3. With the duplicate selected, click Edit. You'll notice all the values and settings are the same as the original.

4. Make the necessary changes. The example we used earlier had subtle differences in Tab spaces.

5. Under the Based On pop up menu, choose the original style sheet. This creates a connection between the two style sheets. Not only are the settings largely the same, but any changes we make down the road to the original style sheet (such as font, point size, leading, and so on.) will automatically apply to the styles based on it (see Figure 15.20).

6. Click OK and save the styles.

Importing Style Sheets in QuarkXPress

If you've already defined a set of style sheets once, why do it again? If a set of styles that you need already exists in another document, there's no need to define them all over again.

1. Select Style Sheets… from the Edit menu.

2. Instead of choosing New, click Append (see Figure 15.21).

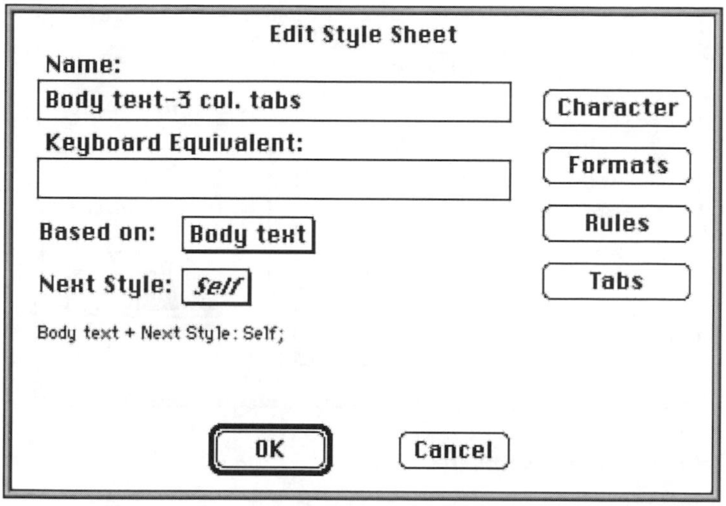

Figure 15.20

Basing one style sheet on another.

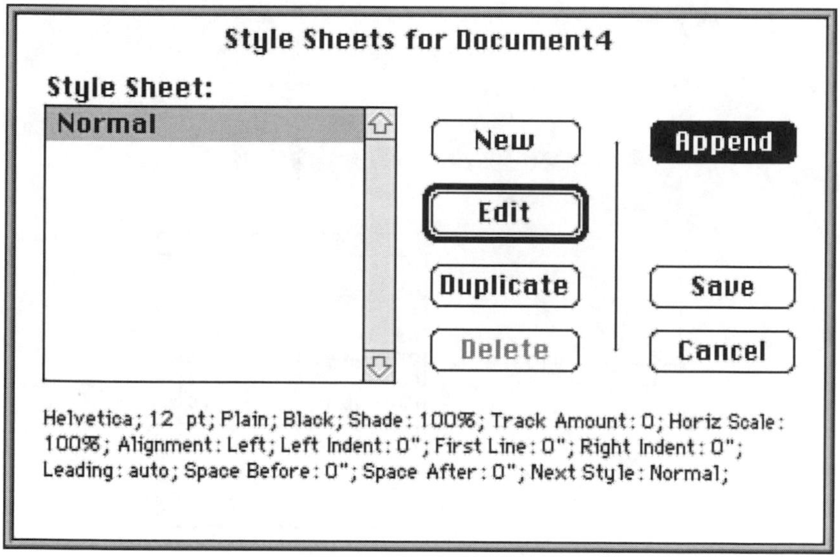

Figure 15.21

Appending style sheets.

3. In the navigational dialog that appears, find and open the document that contains the styles you want. You don't really open the document—you just import the style sheets (see Figure 15.22).

4. Click Save.

Figure 15.22

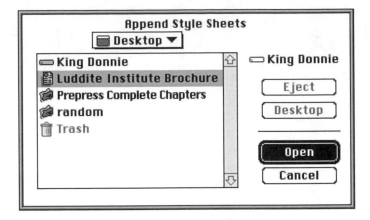

Applying Styles in QuarkXPress

There are two ways to apply styles in QuarkXPress:

◆ Highlight the desired text (or insert the cursor in a paragraph) and click the appropriate style tag in the Style Sheet palette (see Figure 15.23).

Figure 15.23

*Applying styles from the Style
Sheet palette.*

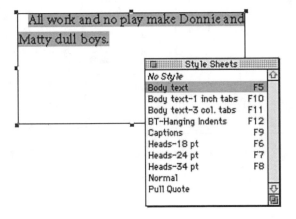

◆ Use a Keyboard Equivalent. KE's are fine things. They enable you to assign a style at the punch of a key instead of always having to refer to a floating palette. Use the F-keys on the top of your extended keyboard (we use F5–F12). Never use the numeric keypad for KE's! We don't care if QuarkXPress allows you to or not! Doing so prevents you from using the keypad to type numbers when entering text. What you'll get instead is a spastic, rapid dance of styles, depending on what keys get hit. This also prevents anyone else—a service bureau, perhaps, making some last-minute edits—from using the pad.

Note

Special note: QuarkXPress always has a style sheet named Normal. If you'll remember, this is actually the default font. Don't use it in a publication. Define your own styles and use specific and accurate names instead. Normal? Oh, please.

Defining Style Sheets in PageMaker

PageMaker 6.5 has wisely incorporated Photoshop's palette system for its style sheets, layers, colors, and master pages. We love these palettes. They're not, however, as thorough as we would have liked. To edit styles and permanently delete the default settings, go to the Define Styles dialog, under the Type menu.

Creating Basic Styles

1. Choose New Style from the Styles palette submenu (see Figure 15.24).

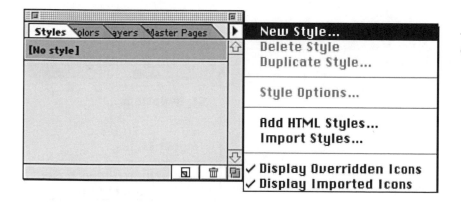

Figure 15.24

Creating a new style.

2. Name the style appropriately.

3. One by one, enter the values for Character, Paragraph, Tabs, and Hyphenation. QuarkXPress users will find Rules as an option under Paragraph (see Figure 15.25).

Figure 15.25

PageMaker's four style sheet definition dialogs.

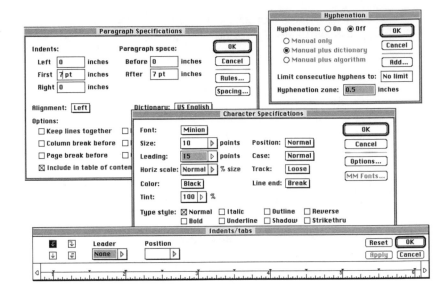

4. Click OK to add the style to the palette.

Using "Based On"

1. Select the original style in the Styles palette.

2. Select "Duplicate" in the styles palette submenu (see Figure 15.26).

Figure 15.26

Duplicating a style.

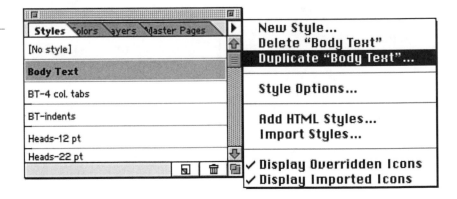

3. Name the new style accurately.

4. Make the necessary changes.

5. Under the Based On pop up menu, select the name of the original style (see Figure 15.27).

6. Click OK.

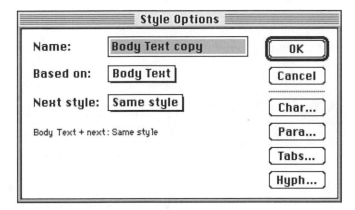

Figure 15.27

Basing one style on another.

Importing Style Sheets in PageMaker

PageMaker is a teensy bit confused about this command, but it works just fine. There are two different commands for importing styles from another PageMaker document:

1. Open the Define Styles dialog.

2. Click Copy (see Figure 15.28).

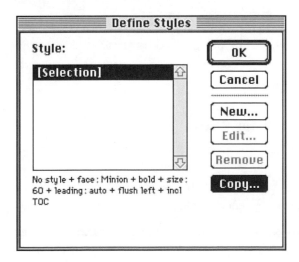

Figure 15.28

Copying styles from another document using the Define Styles dialog.

3. In the navigational dialog that appears, find and open the document containing the styles you want.

4. Click OK.

Or,

1. In the styles palette submenu, choose Import Styles (see Figure 15.29).

Figure 15.29

Copying styles using the Styles palette.

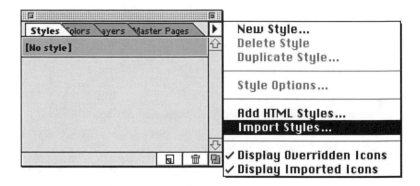

2. In the navigational dialog that appears, find and open the document containing the styles you want.

3. Click OK.

Applying Styles in PageMaker

PageMaker has no Keyboard Equivalent function. You can only apply a style by highlighting text (or inserting the cursor in a paragraph) and clicking the desired tag in the Styles palette.

Designing Master Pages

Only after you've defined our document setup, colors, and style sheets should you start laying out your project. Before you lay out your individual pages, however, there's one more thing you need to take care of. You need to import and position any repeating page elements that appear in your layout:

◆ Headers (information at the top of pages, usually in the margin area, which includes publication titles, chapter numbers, page numbers, and rules)

◆ Footers (the same as headers, only at the bottom of a page)

◆ Siders (typically found on the outside edge of pages, to avoid being obscured by binding)

◆ Page numbers

◆ Borders

◆ Any logo or graphic appearing on all (or many) pages

Of course, you can do this in two ways:

◆ You place each repeating element by hand on every page, carefully measuring and positioning them all, eyeing and nudging everything into place. If you change your mind about something, you repeat the entire process. You place page numbers manually, hoping you don't have to add, subtract, or rearrange any pages. And when the piece comes off press, you obsess madly over the one or two items that escaped your lunatic eye.

◆ Or, you define master pages. These are actually page templates that reside inside your document, and work with page designs in much the same way that style sheets work with your type. This way, you only have to import and position these repeating elements once. Later on, if you have to make any changes, you change the templates.

In the last couple of years, master page tools in QuarkXPress and PageMaker have improved considerably. Except for some minor differences, they may as well be the same. Regardless of which application you use, the rules and restrictions of setting up master pages are almost the same as laying out regular pages. There are some slight differences though, so follow these guidelines:

◆ Not every document requires the use of master pages. If you're not designing with any repeating items, you don't even have to think about them. Few things become more cumbersome than attempting to use features you do not need. A nice rule of thumb is looking for any item that appears in the same place on different pages three or more times.

◆ Master pages are *templates*, so only place elements on them that can be used on the pages they're ultimately applied to. Elements that belong only on one page or another are placed on the actual pages, never the master pages.

◆ The most popular master page item is page numbering. QuarkXPress and Pagemaker use the same keystroke, Command-3, to create the auto-numbering symbol. It looks like <#>, but don't try typing that in as three different characters. Only Command-3 makes the symbol, and it'll only appear on a master page (see Figure 15.30).

Figure 15.30

The automatic page number symbol, entered on a master page.

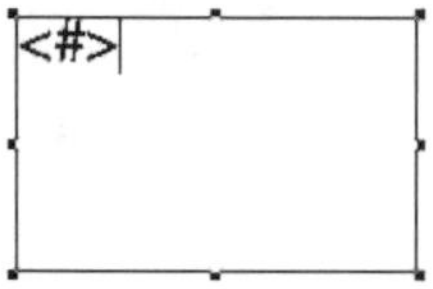

◆ Both programs enable you to define multiple master pages. You can also apply no master at all, depending on your need. You have two choices when applying master pages. You can apply them at the time you insert the new pages, or you can apply them individually, after all your pages have been created. We prefer applying our master pages one at a time, after we've defined the number of pages we'll use. It takes only a couple minutes longer, and it gives us more exacting control over our pages.

◆ Avoid using crossovers, or items that extend across two pages. In neither program will the image automatically impose on output, and in most cases, the image will appear on only one page. In either case, the crossover image will not output with the appropriate bleed.

Issues Specific to QuarkXPress

◆ Automatic page numbering applies to your pages in the order they appear in your document, so your world will temporarily crumble if you relocate your pages using the Document Layout palette. So, if you're imposing a simple job and want to move page 8 so it's next to page 1, you'll quickly find it renumbered page 2—thereby causing your pages to be misnumberd after folding and trimming. In this case, the numbers have to be replaced with *hard* page numbers, which involves highlighting the existing page number and typing in the right digit.

◆ QuarkXPress's master page items are actually copied onto each page they're applied to. This means you can edit any of these elements when you're working on the regular pages. Warning: as soon as you edit *any* master page item, that page no longer adheres to the master page! It may look like it for the most part, but editing the items placed there by the master page severs the connection. This means that if you edit the original master page, you must re-apply it to the individual page. And if you do that, double-check it for duplicate items. If all this stresses you out, lock all of the elements in your master pages. This will keep you from accidentally editing the wrong stuff, and you can simply unlock anything that you do want to change.

◆ QuarkXPress's Automatic Text Box is really an internally linked master page text box. Although the Auto Text Box is great for importing long stretches of text (like books), it too often gets in the way when we use multiple master pages. We prefer to eschew the Auto Text Box in favor of placing unlinked text box on our master pages, then taking a moment or two to manually create our links. This sounds like it takes a long time, until you zoom out to 20 or 30 percent, Option-select the Link tool, and proceed to link like mad.

Issues Specific to PageMaker

PageMaker's master pages act like more of an overlay. All the items appear on the regular pages they're applied to, but they cannot be edited.

Designing Individual Pages

All digital prepress professionals share a common fantasy. In the innocent moments just before sleep carries them away, visions of this elusive dream-world steal through their minds:

In this world, all the animals are really friendly and speak fluent English. Fat, fruity gumdrops hang heavy in the trees, ripe for easy picking. Output specialists spend their days whistling while they work, printing the King's Publications with ease and aplomb. When the day is done they go home to the Love Boat, where they dine at the Captain's table, crack jokes with Gopher, and fall in love with Charo.

You see, years before, the benevolent King banished all designers from the kingdom. Now, all publications are the same: no bleeds, no crossovers, no angled graphics. Gone are fifth and sixth colors, spot varnishes, custom folds and die cuts. All pictures are the same size, the same resolution, the same colors, and they output flawlessly every time. "Sure, it's boring to look at," the King's Minions think, drifting off to sleep, "but compared to the mind-bending, hair-pulling, stomach-clenching tedium of hunting down an elusive PostScript error, I'll deal with it!"

Of course, in the real world design and production go hand in hand. We shudder to think of a world of print and no design. Why, it'd look like…like…1988! Unfortunately, the single most common cause of problem files is—you guessed it—design. The more "challenging" a file is to create, the higher the potential is for problem output and printing. In these modern times, designers must create *responsible* as well as attractive and effective products. This means not succumbing to the myth that if you can see it on a computer screen, you can make it happen in real life.

Successful output invariably depends on how well we place and handle our graphics files, which depends on our knowledge:

◆ Importing different graphic styles

◆ Scaling graphics

◆ Rotating graphics

◆ Cropping graphics

◆ Layering graphics

We'll also discuss some time-saving techniques for those of you who use the same information in many different documents:

◆ Image libraries

◆ Color libraries

◆ Style sheet libraries

Importing Graphics

If anything is going to cause your file to misprint, chances are it's a graphic. That's no big surprise, when you think about it. A document is only a combination of words and pictures, and those pictures come from at least three different programs (Illustrator, FreeHand, and Photoshop), two different forms (pixels and vectors), and two file formats (TIFF and EPS). How these files are handled is just as important as how they are created. The following sections cover the most common output-related problems that occur when importing graphics into a page layout document.

The first and most important rule concerning the use of graphics in a page layout program is this: create and adjust your graphics in the appropriate programs. Don't create graphs in QuarkXPress or PageMaker; Illustrator has a Graph Tool, and any vector-based drawing program is more adept at fine linework. Don't use a layout program's so-called image editing tools to adjust a halftone; that's what Photoshop is for. Both major layout programs ship with simple graphics tools—circles, rules, boxes, and so forth—but these are only for minor page flourishes and supplimentary graphics. As soon as you require something more complex than that, go to another program. There, you can create the graphic with infinitely more precision. Then, once you import it, your only concerns will be working with the single element.

Scaling Graphics

Although the question of scaling graphics has been asked and answered countless times, there still remains an air of mystery about it. The degree to which graphics can be scaled in a page layout program depends almost entirely on whether it's a vector- or pixel-based image.

Vector-based images can be scaled with wanton abandon, because the lines and shapes comprising the image have no resolution until they are sent to an output device. Beyond that, there are still a few guidelines to follow:

◆ Although PageMaker lets you scale almost infinitely, QuarkXPress only scales graphics up to 1000 percent. If you need to enlarge a vector-based image more than that, scale it first in its original program, then import it for fine-tuning.

◆ If your Illustrator or FreeHand artwork contains an embedded pixel-based image, you can't scale to the same extremes. You're essentially limited to pixel-based scaling restrictions. The best solutions are to avoid embedding graphics, trace any pixel-based images, or avoid scaling too much by creating the original graphic closer to the intended size (see Figure 15.31).

Figure 15.31

Vector-based graphic containing imported pixel-based artwork.

◆ Nothing points out flaws in an auto-traced image like massive scaling. In the original program, make sure you zoom in close to double-check the smoothness and shape of your lines.

It's pixel-based images, though, which are most shrouded in confusion. The scale window on these graphics is considerably smaller because of the relationship that must exist between file resolution and linescreen value. Simply put, there must be enough pixel information to satisfy the needs of the halftone cells. Conventional wisdom states that a resolution-to-linescreen ratio of 2:1 accomplishes that (that's why service bureaus ask a client for the target linescreen when they have images scanned—they double that number and scan at that resolution). In all actuality, we can have a 1:1 ratio between resolution and linescreen, but as soon as we scale up the tiniest bit, our images begin to pixellate. The 2:1 ratio was developed to give designers a little elbow room once they received their scans. This does not give you free reign to scale, however.

◆ The more you scale up or down, the more likely the possibility of misprinting occurs. Remember the basic rule: increasing scale decreases resolution, decreasing scale increases resolution. Too little resolution, and your image becomes jagged. Too much, and you could have a PostScript error. It's a lot like vitamin C; too much or too little inevitably causes problems. We prefer keeping the scale window between 75–125 percent.

◆ Scaled pixel-based graphics take longer to output. Between establishing a scale percentage at the time of the scan and using Photoshop's
tools to set image size, you can nail the intended image size and
reduce your output times.

Rotating Graphics

Rotating a graphic, like scaling, is considered image editing, and should be done
whenever possible in the original graphics program. This is not a problem with
most vector-based illustrations, but it can be with medium to large scans. Again,
processing a rotated graphic increases output time and can sometimes lead to
PostScript errors. We recommend using the page layout program to determine what degree of rotation needs to be applied (by rotating the imported
graphic), the applying that value to the original image in Photoshop. Re-import
the image, and you'll immediately see faster re-draw and output times.

Cropping Graphics

Cropping images in a page layout program is much the same as cropping
conventionally. Only instead of marking a photo with crop lines for the stripper
to handle, we crop by literally hiding the portions of the image that we do not
want. Unfortunately, cropping in a layout program is not the same as cropping
in Photoshop, Illustrator, or FreeHand. In Photoshop, for example, the
information cropped away is discarded, gone forever. In QuarkXPress or
PageMaker, the information is still there; it's just not showing. This means that
even if you import a full-page image and crop it down to the size of a postage
stamp, the rest of the image has to process (see Figure 15.32). Whenever
possible, crop in the original program.

The most common cropping problems:

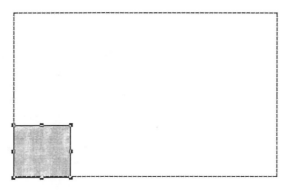

Figure 15.32

*Cropping in a page layout
program does not delete any
information.*

◆ When creating vector-based illustrations, many people create different versions of an image, leave them all on the same page for easy reference, and crop away the unwanted ones after they import the file into their layout. This causes untold problems, because the person processing the file has no idea what could have been done to the invisible items. Maybe they contain an imported RGB TIFF. Maybe one item is comprised of six billion points. Maybe another was tagged with one of those awful, non-reproducable, error-generating custom patterns. Solution: One file. One graphic. Make a special copy, if necessary.

◆ If you need to crop a scanned image, there are two places to do so before importing it into a page layout. First, crop as closely as you can at the time of the scan (if you're the one making the scan). Second, use Photoshop's tools to crop more closely. Cropping in the page layout should be minimal.

◆ Whenever cropping an image, make sure you leave enough image area for bleeds.

Layering Graphics

By layering graphics in your page layout program, we mean the process of placing one on top of another. Each graphic type you work with is subject to a different set of requirements.

Line Art

Line art simply overprints black, wherever you place it. As long as the file is saved as a 1-bit TIFF, the whites remain transparent, allowing the background information to show through. If, for whatever reason, you save the file as an EPS (the earlier version of Illustrator, for example, would not import TIFFs), remember to click Transparent Whites. Otherwise, the file will behave as a grayscale file—the whites inside and around the image will import as white (see Figure 15.33).

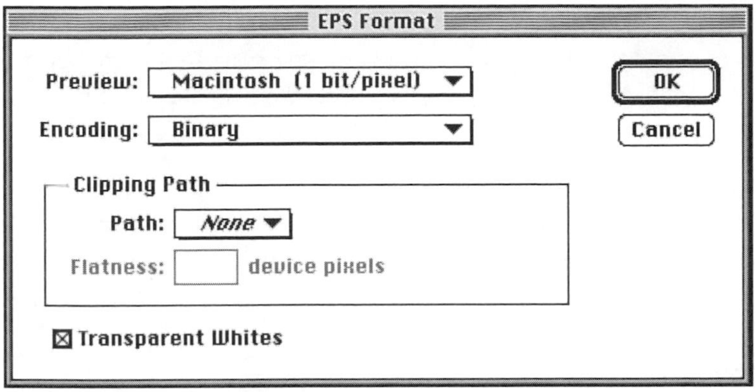

Figure 15.33

Imported Photoshop line art, saved as both TIFF and EPS.

Silhouettes and Clipping Paths

A basic silo is created by deleting all of the pixels around an image in Photoshop. Trouble is, we don't really delete these pixels. We turn them white, and that information is imported right into our page layout. If we don't place the silo on top of anything, even a colored background, we'll be just fine. As soon as we do, we'll see those white pixels getting in the way. We'll also see the primary reason for defining a clipping path.

Whenever you want to place a silhouetted Photoshop image on top of other page elements in your final document, you have to define a clipping path. This technique is based on the use of vector-based paths made with Photoshop's Pen Tool. A clipping path works as a mask on the image, allowing only the part of the image you want to be visible to show. See Chapter 13, "Production Techniques" for more on silhouettes and clipping paths.

Vector-Based Artwork

When you import vector-based artwork, you import only the objects that were created or placed in that file. Some of the the differences between imported illustrations and scans include:

◆   The color white has to be intentionally applied. Although white isn't really a color—it's a "print no ink here" command—it appears as an item in the color menus of all applications. Also, no white "box" is around the image, like a silhouette from Photoshop.

◆ Before you save the final form of the graphic, make sure that all stray points and guides are removed from the image. Although they may not be seen on your page, they affect the placement of the image when it's imported.

◆ One of the most common uses for these programs is creating customized type. Whenever working with type in an illustration file, always convert that type to paths (or outlines). This removes the font information, so we avoid having to deal with missing fonts on output.

Saving Time with Libraries

Find yourself importing the same graphics again and again? Wish you could save a combination of page elements for easy use down the road? The purpose of a library is to hold commonly accessed information. QuarkXPress and PageMaker both have image libraries, which give you tremendously convenient control over graphics, small layouts, and even entire page geometries. Since both programs enable you to import style sheet and color information, you can use that to set up your own "libraries" for those as well.

Image Libraries

Both layout programs feature separate floating palettes that work like little orbiting warehouses. Depending on how you choose to title and organize these libraries, you can simply add copies of your desired page elements and give each one a label. Accessing that information in the future is as easy as dragging from the library to the page—the information already exists in a form that the layout program recognizes!

We'll be talking about three different uses of image libraries:

◆ Storing and placing individual graphics

◆ Storing and placing complex page elements (more than one item working together)

◆ Storing and placing entire page layouts

Before you begin creating libraries, though, have a reason for doing so. Why are you saving these graphics together? What cataloging function will the library serve? How can you best use this library in the future? It doesn't make any sense to create a library that you cannot use efficiently. We'll include some of our favorite and most useful examples.

Adding Individual Graphics

In both programs, these involve adding a single imported graphic to the library. The entire graphic is not added; rather, the low-res FPO and the linking information is added. Later, when you add a graphic from the library to another layout, all that information carries over. Bear in mind that moving or deleting the original graphics destroys the link, and the library graphics will have to be re-linked, like any other graphic. Some of our favorite graphic libraries include:

- **Vector-based credit card logos**, in color and black-and-white.

- **Screenshots of all dialog boxes from all major graphics programs.** You wouldn't believe how much easier it is to create training materials with this information right at hand.

- **All our client logos.** Actually, we have a specific library for black-and-white, 2-color, and four-color versions.

- **Our most commonly needed pricing codes.**

- **All of our corporate identity images.** Because you never know which one you need next.

Complex Page Elements

Here, you can add text and rules to a graphic before adding the entire thing to a library. Information like type formatting, line thickness, and color carry right into the library with the page items. Our favorite use of this function is employed by a regional magazine we've worked with in the past. All of their imported graphics have the same overall treatment: a 2-point rule above, photographer's credit on the side, and caption below. The picture's size may vary, but the values and placement of these extra elements remain constant.

Each month, one of the designers opens a template containing these items, plus grids for the placement of the picture. One by one, they import the image, enter in the necessary text, group all the items, and drag them onto that month's graphics library. Then, rather than do all that work in the final page layout, they drag the preformatted elements onto the page, treating the entire thing as one item instead of four. Variations on this type of library include:

- **Custom headers and footers.** This is especially useful if some information changes from page to page, section to section, chapter to chapter, or what have you.

- **Publication mastheads.** Keeping them all in one place is not only useful for quick access to one in particular, but it lets you access all at once for any of your own collateral pieces.

- **Formatted figure callouts,** or any other recurrent graphical treatment text.

- **Sidebar designs,** for those brief, by-the-way digressions.

Entire Page Layouts

These are treated exactly the same way as the items of the previous section, except that these are complete page geometries. Some of the more useful reasons for doing this include:

- **Ads for a publication.** Design them in their individual files, drag them all into the same library, make sure the necessary fonts are turned on, and place them in the final document.

- **Rough-n-ready page templates.** If you'll need quick access to page designs from another document, creating a library gives you a quick solution without the inconvenience of separate file templates, and without the enforced immediacy of cutting-and-pasting.

Creating a Library in QuarkXPress

1. Under File: New, select Library (see Figure 15.34).

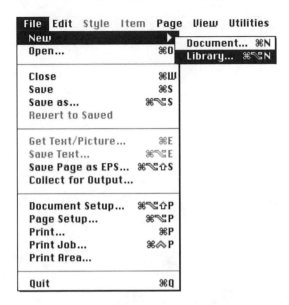

Figure 15.34

Creating a new image library.

2. Name the library. This creates a separate file that contains the library information. A small palette appears (see Figure 15.35).

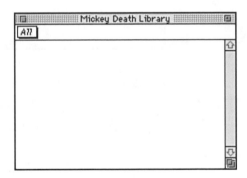

Figure 15.35

The Library palette.

3. On your QuarkXPress page, create a picture box and import a graphic. If desired, add additional formatting such as text and rules.

4. Select all the page elements you want to add to the library.

5. Using the Item Tool, drag the selected items so the cursor is over the Library palette the cursor icon will change to a pair of eyeglasses. Go figure. (See Figure 15.36).

Figure 15.36

Placing images in the library.

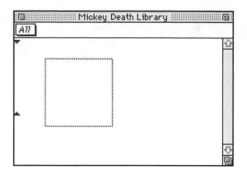

6. Release the graphic. It appears as a thumbnail in the palette (see Figure 15.37).

Figure 15.37

Images in the library.

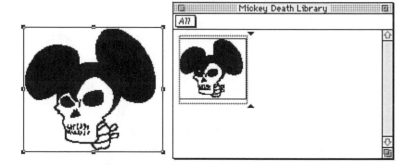

7. Double-click the thumbnail and give the item a label. This helps keep the items organized (see Figure 15.38).

Figure 15.38

Labelling images in the library.

8. At this point, keep adding graphics (labeling each one), or close the library.

Accessing these graphics is the easiest part:

1. Open your target document.

2. Open the library by choosing File: Open.

3. Locate the image or images you need.

4. Drag each item from the library palette onto your page (see Figure 15.39).

Figure 15.39

Placing images from a library.

5. Position each item appropriately.

Creating a Library in PageMaker

1. Under the Windows menu, choose Show Library from Plug-in Palettes (see Figure 15.40).

2. From the palette sub-menu, choose New Library (see Figure 15.41).

Figure 15.40
_____

PageMaker's Library palette.

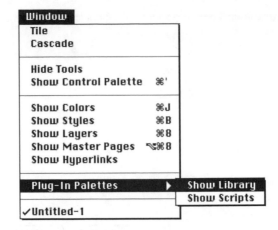

Figure 15.41
_____

Creating a new library.

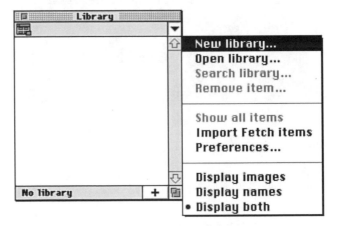

3. On your PageMaker page, import a graphic. If desired, add additional formatting such as text and rules.

4. Select all the page elements you want to add to the library.

5. Click the small plus sign in the lower-right corner of the library palette. This adds the item to the library (dragging does not work) (see Figure 15.42).

6. Double-click the thumbnail that appears and give it a name (see Figure 15.43).

Figure 15.42

Adding items to the library.

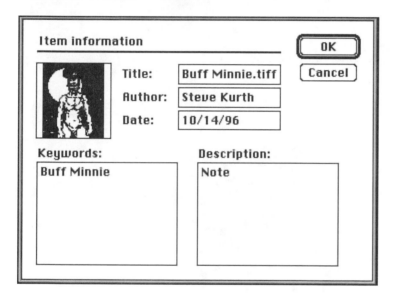

Figure 15.43

Naming a library image.

7. At this point, keep adding graphics (naming each one), or close the library.

Accessing the graphics is the same as in QuarkXPress:

1. Open your target document.

2. Open the library by choosing Open Library from the library palette sub-menu (see Figure 15.44).

Figure 15.44

Opening a library.

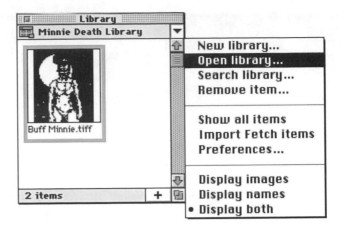

3. Locate the image or images you need.

4. Drag each item from the library palette onto your page (see Figure 15.45).

Figure 15.45

Placing images from a library.

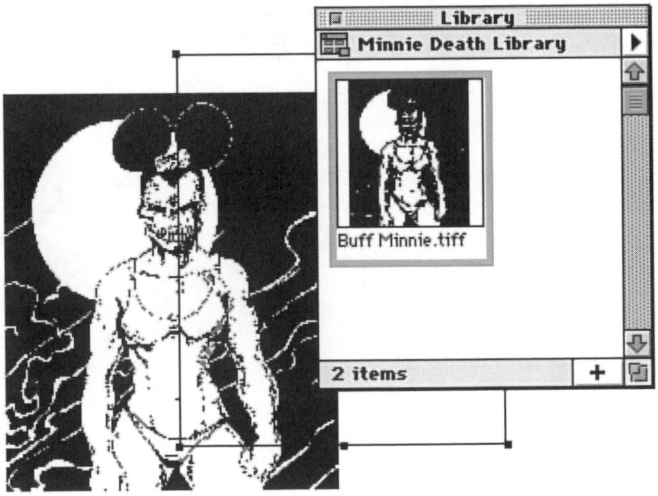

5. Position each item appropriately.

Style Sheet and Color Libraries

These aren't libraries in the literal sense (they do not require the Library palette in either program), but the premise is just the same. Many people have style sheet and color information they need to define over and over again. Maybe it's corporate work that routinely requires this information, maybe it's a series of pieces for one project. Whatever the reason, you have a choice: do you define all of this information manually every time you need it? Of course not. As you already know, you can append style sheet and color information from one document into another. The catch is, you need to have a document on hand that contains the desired information. For these libraries, you create just that—documents which contain nothing but the color or style sheet information you'll import in the future:

1. In QuarkXPress or PageMaker, create a new document.

2. Define the colors or style sheets (keep styles and colors in separate files). If another document is on hand to copy this information from, Append or Copy the information.

3. Save the file into the appropriate Library folder. You don't have to create or import any more information.

When you need to access the information, it's still similar to our image libraries:

1. Open the Define Colors or Define Style Sheets dialog.

2. Choose Append (or Copy) instead of defining the information manually.

3. Locate the right library file and open it. The information appears in your new document.

Storing Library Files

Regardless of which program you use, libraries actually exist as separate files. While they're not exchangeable between programs, they do need to kept in an easy-to-access location on your hard drive. We suggest keeping a Libraries folder on your main volume. By doing this, we'll not only keep our image libraries, but the systems we set up for color and style sheets:

1. Create a folder called Libraries.

2. Create two folders inside: QuarkXPress Libraries and PageMaker Libraries.

3. In each of those folders, create three more: Image Libraries, Style Sheet Libraries, and Color Libraries.

4. Now, as soon as libraries are created, place them directly into the right folder.

To further organize your libraries, you may want to make client folders in the Style Sheet and Color Library folders. The easier it is to find the right library, the happier everyone is.

And that's just the way we want you—happy enough to burst wide open.

We cannot overemphasize the importance of the page layout stage. Ignoring these issues is much like spending lots of time and money on building materials for a house, only to pour a substandard foundation.

Often, laying out your pages takes place at the very end of a project, after you've planned, delegated, scanned, corrected, illustrated, and otherwise generated the content for a project. As this material is generated, it's your responsibility to prepare the page layout document to receive this information as easily as possible:

◆ Set your default preferences, making sure they dovetail with our output and press requirements.

◆ Properly set your page dimensions, making sure that they fall within the reproducable range of the target press.

◆ Define the colors to be used in your documents, making sure that the names are consistent throughout all of our graphic files.

◆ Use style sheets whenever possible, making sure you have a way to format your type quickly and consistently.

◆ Apply colors thoughtfully throughout your page layouts, making sure that no fine details are going to be lost through difficult trapping.

◆ Define master pages, making sure you have an easy, consistent method of applying images on multiple pages.

◆ Import and position your imported graphics, making sure you scale, crop, rotate, and layer them in a way that does not hinder successful output.

Not so long ago, there were some very compelling reasons to choose one layout program over another, similar to the arguments heard when defending the Boston Red Sox over the New York Yankees. Nowadays, the industry-leading layout programs are so close to each other in terms of capabilities and ease-of-use, it becomes almost pointless to recommend one in particular.

As a result, both programs will be in widespread use for many years to come. The smartest thing any graphics professional can do is become familiar with QuarkXPress and PageMaker. Use one primarily for the projects you create, but be secure in the knowledge that you can step up and win one for the Gipper using the other. At the very least, you will simply increase your market value. At best, you will improve the efficiency of your production environment, saving untold hours and dollars every day.

Chapter

TRAPPING

After agonizing over color selections, staging two photo shoots, and squeezing more accurate color from her production department than they ever thought possible, she expected her project to be flawless. She knew her concepts were top-notch, her attention to detail unsurpassed. She handed her job over to the printer, confidently proclaiming the films ready to be used as-is.

When the piece came off press, she wrinkled her face in disgust. Misregistered plates left razor-thin gaps between colors. Overprinting blacks didn't conceal the underlying inks. Color shifts occurred on the abutting edges of colored shapes. Like many modern-day designers, she was never trained in the techniques of trapping, an age-old conventional process. Considered by many to be the responsibility of the lithographer (and considered by many others not at all), she found out too late that it's just another prepress task that more and more designers are expected to handle themselves.

THE TRAPPING TRAP

A printing press is not the perfect reproduction tool we'd all like it to be. Rollers and plates spin wildly, sucking paper through the works at speeds of up to 2200 feet per minute, applying ink faster than the human eye can track. Even on a multi-million dollar press, the paper or ink-applying plates may shift ever so slightly. When this happens, overprinting colors fall out of *register*. That is, they are no longer perfectly aligned, which is required for picture-perfect printing.

Humans have tried for centuries to create a press that consistently holds its register. We've come close, but we still have to compensate for some basic laws of physics. Whenever inks are printed out of register, gaps and color shifts appear between the different objects on the page.

One strategy can combat this phenomenon: trapping. We compensate for misregistration by slightly expanding one color into its adjacent color. This way, even though a shift may take place, the overlapping inks conceal any resulting flaws without distorting the shapes of the objects.

Until recently, trapping was a mysterious process best left to conventional prepress professionals. Even though this often is still the best option, desktop trapping tools and techniques are more powerful than ever. With a little time, experience, and forethought, you can easily assume the responsibility of trapping your files digitally.

Be cautious, though: desktop tools have not simplified the issues of trapping. Your colors are subject to the same laws of physics they've always been. Trapping is not the result of a single mouse-click applied in a page layout program. No miracle-cure software packages can step in and save the day while we extend our coffee break into lunch. Effective trapping requires a knowledge of process and spot color, thoughtful design, and an awareness of each object in your layout.

Often, your work will not require any special attention to trapping: For example:

◆ Publications containing elements of isolated, solid colors don't need to be trapped. There are no adjacent colors, so no gaps would show if misregistration occurs (see Figure 16.1).

Figure 16.1

Trapping is only required when colors touch (see color insert).

◆ Overprinting black information, such as small text or thin lines, compensates for misregistration because of the underlying inks.

◆ Images using an abundance of thicker black outlines, such as cartoon drawings, may not need to be trapped (see Figure 16.2).

Figure 16.2

Four-color artwork with heavy black outlines usually doesn't require trapping (see color insert).

◆ A publication comprised of process colors does not need trapping if adjacent colors share high enough percentages of process components (see "Building a Process Bridge," later this chapter).

One of the best ways to deal with trapping is to avoid it. Designing your work so that trapping is kept to a minimum should always be an option. When your needs for trapping become more complex, your entire job becomes more complex. For example:

♦ **The document takes longer to prepare.** Even though QuarkXPress and PageMaker both have "Automatic" trapping features, neither one is thorough enough to stand alone, untouched by the user. Also, imported vector-based files are not affected by these commands, so nearly every job will need some sort of manual trapping.

♦ **The file takes longer to process.** The trapping commands in a page layout program add to the time a file takes to output. If a program like Adobe TrapWise is used, there's no telling *how* long the file will take to process.

♦ **The file can cost more money to produce.** Many designers hand over trapping responsibilities to the service provider, who can charge upwards of $80 an hour.

♦ **The margin for error increases.** Incorrect values are applied, images are left untrapped, lack of communication results in strippers misreading your film. The more variables you add to your work, the more likely it is that one of them could explode.

Does that mean you shouldn't attempt to control these values on your own? Of course not! As long as you understand the need for trapping, how much you are able to do, and which applications will give you the best result, you can trap with the best of the big dogs.

Trapping commands are applied in the following different places:

♦ **In your page layout program.** These commands affect anything created within the programs, such as type, rules, and boxes.

♦ **In your illustration program.** Neither QuarkXPress nor PageMaker can trap EPS files. You can't edit the color information in one of these files. Editing trap, however, means editing color information and any imported EPS file prevents that. So, you'll have to establish your traps in Illustrator or FreeHand.

- **In a dedicated trapping application.** Adobe TrapWise, the most popular example, does nothing but trap, trap, trap. This sounds like a wonderful solution and sometimes it is. Typically, this is the best option for difficult traps (such as gradients-on-gradients) or establishing very precise trapping values. Otherwise, TrapWise falls short of a panacea, being very expensive and requiring a dedicated high-speed workstation to process most efficiently.

This chapter focuses on the issues involved in manually trapping images in your page layout and illustration programs, such as the following:

- Compensating for deficiencies inherent in the color black

- Maintaining a process bridge in four-color work, eliminating the need for trapping

- Manually trapping artwork in Illustrator or FreeHand

- Properly establishing trapping Preferences in QuarkXPress and PageMaker

Each section also will offer advice on how to best avoid the need for trapping altogether.

TRAPPING ESSENTIALS

Before you begin, let's cover some of the basic terminology.

Chokes and Spreads

Chokes and spreads are almost the same thing. Because trapping involves expanding the printed area of one color into another, choking and spreading describes which direction that expansion takes.

The direction a color expands depends on which color is lighter and which is darker. One simple rule applies to chokes and spreads: Lighter colors expand into darker colors.

You trap this way to maintain the integrity of your shapes as best you can. By expanding the lighter colors into darker colors, the overlap is less apparent to the eye. If you move the darker colors, the change of shape becomes more obvious.

Picture a foreground and a background object, such as a circle within a circle. The background circle is PMS 287 (a dark blue), and the foreground circle is PMS 185 (a light red). Because the red is the lighter color, it will expand, or spread, into the blue.

Now switch the colors. This time, the lighter background expands, or chokes, into the darker foreground shape. By trapping the lighter colors into the darker, the change is much less apparent to the eye after printing (see Figure 16.3).

Figure 16.3

Lighter colors expand into darker colors (see color insert).

Building a Process Bridge

When working with spot colors, the need for trapping is ever-present. Do the colors touch? If so, you have to trap.

When applying process colors to adjacent objects, plan to use colors that share percentages of component inks sufficient to create a process bridge. A process bridge occurs when two objects share at least 20 percent of one component color (cyan, magenta, yellow, or black). Generally, this eliminates the possibility of white gaps appearing as a result of misregistration, because the most that can be revealed are colors common to both objects. Depending on the adjacent colors in question, however, additional trapping may be necessary. When adjoining colors contain significantly higher percentages of one component ink, trapping may be needed. Misregistration may reveal a visible third color (see Figure 16.4).

Figure 16.4

An insufficient process bridge (see color insert).

If two objects share high enough percentages of more than one component color, extra trapping isn't required. The third color revealed during misregistration isn't visually distracting (see Figure 16.5).

Figure 16.5

A sufficient process bridge (see color insert).

Typically, if all the ink values of one color are higher than the percentages of another, a trap is not needed.

THE BLACK HOLE: LIMITATIONS OF BLACK INK

When someone mentions the color red, or the color blue, there are thousands of possible shades that person could be talking about. Light blue, dark green, medium red with cool purple undertones, *all* the colors you work with can only be described accurately by precise mathematical numbers. Except, we have come to believe, black. Black means…well, *black*. Darkness. The absence of all light. The combination of all inks on paper. There is only one black and when you apply black in your documents, you expect it to behave that way.

Unfortunately, it doesn't. In process printing, black, like all process inks, is a transparent ink. Because of this, it can't cover ink or paper as thoroughly as we want it to. Take a close look at a four-color publication and check for the following traits:

◆ **Unimpressive knockout blacks.** You can see paper grain through process black and you don't need a microscope to see that it looks a little on the thin side. Ink transparency prevents robust coverage, which becomes even more noticeable compared to denser blacks (see Figure 16.6).

Figure 16.6

Knockout Black, Overprint Black, Rich Black, and Super Black (see color insert).

◆ **Unimpressive overprinting blacks.** Theoretically, overprinting black negates the need for trapping. Yet if you overprint too large an area—a big, black box placed over a high-res scan, for example—you can see the underlying inks through the black.

Because you can't use opaque black ink in four-color printing, you must improvise. You're going to add new and improved blacks to your color menus. How you define them will depend on how and where the black is applied.

Rich Black

This black is really a combination of black and one other process ink. You define and apply it in either your illustration or page layout software or wherever you need it. Adding the second ink increases the density of the black, making it appear fuller and darker. In short, blacker.

Applying a rich black is appropriate on the following two occasions:

◆ When the edges of an object—a box, for example—are exposed (see Figure 16.7).

◆ When a black box straddles other image information (see Figure 16.8).

Figure 16.7

Exposed edges require rich black (see color insert).

Figure 16.8

Black straddling an image and paper requires enriching (see color insert).

Traditionally, you create a rich black by defining a new color comprised of 60 percent cyan (the *undercolor*) and 100 percent black. If all the edges of a black item are exposed and there are no adjoining colors, this is perfectly fine.

If there are adjacent colors, then cyan may not be the best option. Choose an undercolor that creates a sufficient process bridge with the surrounding image area. Magenta, or even yellow, may be the best choice.

The reason you only add one undercolor is because of those exposed edges. If you added more than one color to a black area with exposed edges, then misregistration may result in *fringe,* or one or more of the undercolors peeking out the sides of the object like a multicolored halo (see Figure 16.9). Both page layout programs have a built-in function called *keepaway,* where the undercolor is made slightly smaller than the black area. If misregistration should occur, the undercolor is still covered by the black area. The bridge and the keepaway function take care of any trapping needs and any extra colors would just increase the likelihood of fringe.

Figure 16.9

Misregistered process inks causing fringe around a black area (see color insert).

Defining a Rich Black in Quark

To define a rich black in Quark, follow these steps:

1. Choose Colors from the Edit menu.

2. Click New.

3. Choose CMYK from the Model pop up menu.

4. Type in 100% black and 60% cyan (or your desired undercolor) (see Figure 16.10).

Figure 16.10

Creating rich black in Quark.

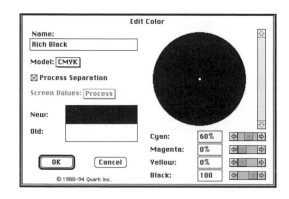

5. Make sure Process Separation is clicked On.

6. Name the color clearly. "Rich black" is a fine name, but on occasion we have renamed the color "60C, 100K" to be absolutely certain about the colors we're applying.

7. Click OK and save the color.

Defining a Rich Black in PageMaker

To define a rich black in PageMaker, follow these steps:

1. Choose Define Colors from the Utilities menu.

2. Click New.

3. Under the Type pop up menu, choose Process.

4. Under the Model pop up menu, choose CMYK (see Figure 16.11).

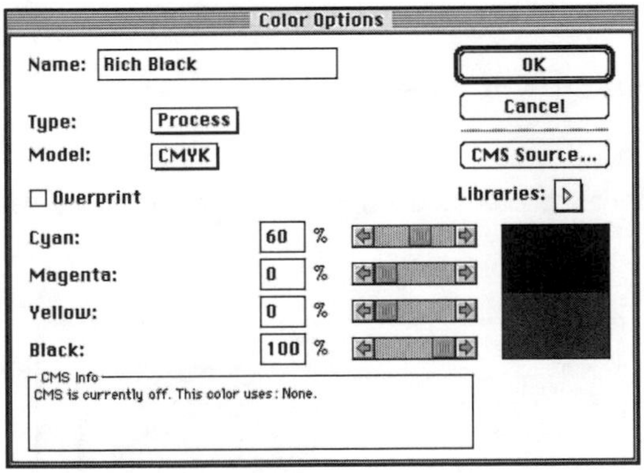

Figure 16.11

Creating rich black in PageMaker.

5. Type in 100% black and 60% cyan (or your desired undercolor).

6. Name the color clearly.

7. Click OK and save the color.

Super Black

A super black is black defined with three undercolors instead of one: 50 percent cyan, 50 percent magenta, 50 percent yellow, and 100 percent black. This provides the deepest, most satisfying process black you can reproduce on-press.

Super blacks are not for all occasions. Consider the following:

◆ Apply super blacks when all sides of an object are found within other colors or they bleed off the edge of the page. This removes the possibility of fringe, as no edges will be hanging over that vast, white, vulnerable landscape.

◆ If you're considering using a super black in your document, consult your printer first. The ink density of a super black may be too much for either the paper stock or printing press utilized for your project. Waiting forever for a job to dry, only to find that the ink soaked through the newsprint is a drag.

Defining a Super Black in Quark

To define a super black in Quark, follow these steps:

1. Choose Colors from the Edit menu.

2. Click New.

3. Choose CMYK from the Model pop-up menu.

4. Type in 100% black and 50% of cyan, magenta, and yellow, or if your printer has recommended lower undercolor values, use them (see Figure 16.12).

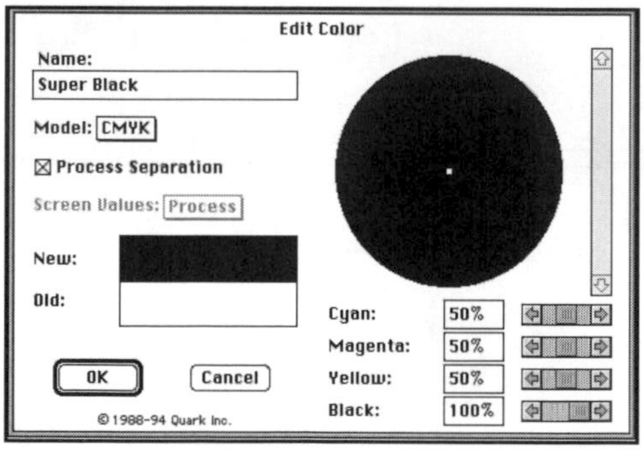

Figure 16.12

Creating super black in Quark.

5. Make sure Process Separation is clicked On.

6. Name the color clearly.

7. Click OK and save the color.

Defining a Super Black in PageMaker

To define a super black in PageMaker, follow these steps:

1. Choose Define Colors from the Utilities menu.

2. Click New.

3. Choose Process from the Type pop up menu.

4. Choose CMYK from the Model pop up menu (see Figure 16.13).

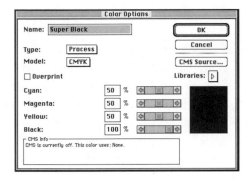

Figure 16.13

Creating super black in PageMaker.

5. Type in 100% black and 50% of cyan, magenta, and yellow.

6. Name the color clearly.

7. Click OK and save the color.

Overprints and Knockouts

Usually, when you define and apply a color, you allow that color to *knock out*. This means the colors you spec do not mix with any underlying ink combinations. The knockout command is automatically applied to every color you define (with some exceptions for black). So if you place a red circle on top of a blue square, for example, no blue ink will print anywhere within the boundary of the circle.

When you *overprint* a color, that color combines with the inks of all underlying shapes. This always results in color shifts.

One hundred percent black is the only color that successfully overprints. By that, we mean that when black is printed on top of other inks, it remains black. The result is always a different color when overprinting any other color ink, spot, or process.

Overprinting black removes the need for trapping, which is essential for certain page elements. The only problem is, some black elements in some programs automatically overprint; others will not. You may need to build in overprint behavior.

Black Type

In QuarkXPress and PageMaker, black text automatically overprints. This is one of the primary reasons that black text, particularly at small sizes, is preferable to any other. Color trapping 12-point body text is impossible. Black text in Illustrator or FreeHand, however, automatically knocks out. The overprint command has to be applied in the original program and saved as part of the graphic file.

Black Line Art

Line art files from Photoshop (1-bit TIFFs) automatically overprint when placed in a page layout program. Applying any other color to those files, even 99 percent black, forces the image to knock out.

Line art from a vector-based program always automatically knocks out. Just as with type, the overprint command for the black shapes has to be turned on and saved into the file if the image is going to overprint when output from the page layout document.

A process bridge can be easily applied to either form of line art. For an imported 1-bit TIFF, simply define and apply one of the enriched blacks discussed earlier. For line art in Illustrator or FreeHand, define an enriched black, apply it to the image, save, and import. In this case, it does not matter if the image is told to overprint or not because the bridge assimilates the line art into the adjacent colors.

VECTOR-BASED TRAPPING TOOLS

We cannot repeat often enough that color information in an imported EPS file is uneditable. As far as we're concerned, the image is locked in a transparent room with no windows, no door, no way in. We can only gaze upon the image from our distant vantage point.

Therefore, all trapping commands must be built into the graphic file in the original program *before* the image is placed and the document output.

Illustrator and FreeHand use the same technique to create simple traps. If the image is constructed of process colors, we encourage designers to choose colors that form a process bridge. For both spot colors and bridgeless process colors, we apply extremely thin overprinting strokes to objects filled with colors that knockout. This provides the necessary trapping information.

A Simple Trap, Manually Done

The color of a vector-based shape is defined by its fill and its stroke. Fill refers to the color of all the area within a path, whereas stroke pertains to the color of the path itself. Unless told otherwise, and you will rarely have a reason to do so, strokes always straddle the path. This means that half the stroke-width lies inside the path, half lies outside. Understanding this concept is most important in establishing traps.

1. Create a foreground and background object. In this example, continue to use blue (PMS 287) and red (PMS 185).

2. Determine if the foreground color is lighter or darker than the background. In this example, the red is lighter than the blue, so we know we are going to spread the red into the surrounding blue.

3. Apply an overprinting stroke to the foreground object. Because we're spreading, make the stroke the same color as the foreground. Click the overprint command. (Note that in both illustration and page layout programs, only foreground objects receive trapping commands.)

4. Set the stroke to *double* your intended trap width. Only half of the stroke will be printing into the adjoining color, so double the width to achieve the proper value. We recommend a default trap value of .3 points for most printing presses. In this case, the stroke should be .6 points (see Figure 16.14).

5. Save your file and import the graphic. The file now is trapped and ready for output.

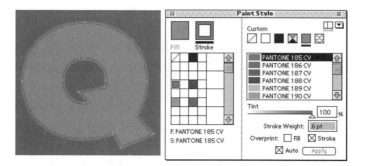

Figure 16.14

The overprinting stroke creates the trap.

If the foreground object is going to be choked instead of spread, apply the background color to the stroke. This way, the half of the stroke-width *inside* the shape overprints, in effect expanding the background color into the foreground shape (see Figure 16.15).

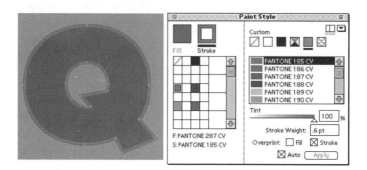

Figure 16.15

Reversing the stroke color reverses the direction of the trap.

A Simple Trap, Automatically Done

Both FreeHand and Illustrator can trap objects automatically with surprisingly similar plug-ins. Illustrator uses a filter called Trap, found under the Pathfinder submenu and FreeHand uses an Xtra called Trap, found under the Create submenu.

The method of trapping is different from the manual trap we just discussed. Instead of establishing overprinting strokes, the trap is made of narrow shapes that hug the contours of the foreground objects with their colored *fill* set to overprint (see Figure 16.16). Trapping this way has benefits and drawbacks.

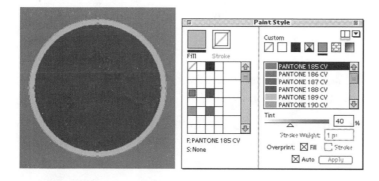

Figure 16.16

The automatic trapping filters use overprinting shapes instead of strokes.

The Good News

More complex traps, such as multiple shapes of different colors, are much more easily trapped. The tools available are pretty smart when it comes to determining what needs to be trapped and what doesn't. If two process colors share enough of a common component ink, for example, no trapping will be applied.

The Bad News

Only flat, solid fills can be trapped. Gradations, strokes, patterns, imported artwork, and other attributes cannot be trapped with these tools. All the new objects that are placed to create the traps make it more difficult to edit the graphic later. Each new, thin shape will have to be deleted before you can move on.

After you've decided to use the trapping filters, you only have to understand the values before selecting objects and applying your traps (see Figure 16.17). Consider the following values:

- ◆ **Thickness** (Illustrator/FreeHand). The most important value in the dialog, this controls the width of the overprinting path made by the filter. The default is set to .25 points, which is a little on the thin side, but much better than QuarkXPress' .144 point default. Increase the value to between .3 points and .5 points, depending on the registration of your target printing press.

◆ **Tint Reduction** (Illustrator/FreeHand). If you're trapping spot colors, these filters fill the traps with the lighter color. This value determines the tint of the overprinting fill. Although these tinted shapes look a little funny onscreen, the fact that they overprint means they will not affect the lighter-colored object and will only darken the other color slightly upon printing, like any good trap should.

◆ **Reverse Traps** (Illustrator/FreeHand). This changes the direction of the traps, forcing the program to fill traps with the darker color instead of the lighter. Select this option if you do not agree with Illustrator's decision over which color is darker.

◆ **Convert Custom Colors to Process** (Illustrator). This automatically fills the trap with process color, regardless of the colors used in the original objects. Usually, this option is turned off. If you're trapping spot colors, you want a spot trap. This option is most useful when trapping a spot color into a process color and the screen angle of the spot color might interfere with the underlying process tints.

Figure 16.17

The trap dialogs of Illustrator and FreeHand.

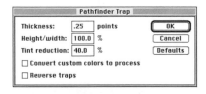

These tools only trap objects that are selected. After you've plugged in the necessary information and clicked OK, you'll immediately notice the new shapes appearing on your image. Because further editing gets a little harder from this point on, leave trapping until the very end.

Complex Vector-Based Traps

Some objects just can't be effectively trapped in either page layout or illustration programs. The demands of gradients on gradients, custom colors, patterns, and complex arrangements of objects all exceed the meager range of manual and automatic trapping tools. In these cases, you have three choices:

◆ Ignore trapping and take your chances. Not a pretty option, but still an option.

◆ Avoid these situations altogether. Designing around the need for trapping saves you from more headaches than the folks at Tylenol and Advil combined can handle.

◆ Use a dedicated trapping program such as Adobe TrapWise. For the most complex traps, this is often the only solution.

PAGE LAYOUT TRAPPING TOOLS

QuarkXPress and PageMaker both have built-in trapping schemes. QuarkXPress' are the best known primarily because they have been around the longest. It's true that QuarkXPress has the most extensive capabilities, but neither program is the trapping Robocop you wish it were. Neither program, for example, will touch imported EPS graphics. Trapping to a gradient still is done primitively by spreading the foreground color, and the default trapping preferences in both programs desperately need to be changed.

Page layout programs only trap the following information:

◆ Multiple items created in the layout program, such as abutting text, rules, and boxes.

◆ Objects created in the layout program overlapping imported bitmap TIFF images. Neither program traps the imported image itself, only the objects placed on top of it.

Note

Any imported item must have the necessary trapping commands built into the graphic and this can only be done in the original application.

Trapping in QuarkXPress

Trapping in QuarkXPress can be controlled three different ways:

♦ **Automatic trapping.** This means you simply let QuarkXPress trap the way it will during output, based on the settings in the Trapping Preferences dialog.

♦ **Trapping color-to-color.** Here, you build trapping behavior directly into a color's definition. These values override the automatic settings.

♦ **Trapping object-to-object.** We use the floating Trap Info palette to change or re-apply trap values to individual objects in our layout. These settings override both automatic and color-definition trap values.

Each method of trapping has its own appropriate time and place, and it's rare that all three are applied in a single document.

Often, QuarkXPress' automatic settings will suffice, with maybe a little double-checking or tweaking from the Trap Info palette. If you trap color-to-color, you're ignoring automatic settings. Again, you'll use the Trap Info palette for any exceptions to your self-imposed trapping rules. Never rely solely on trapping object-to-object. Think about the hundreds or thousands of colored objects in a single project. We understand how trapping every object individually becomes prohibitively time-consuming.

Automatic Trapping

Automatic trapping refers to the trapping values that QuarkXPress applies when left to its own devices. You may have noticed that trapping values are never visible in your page layout like they are in Illustrator or FreeHand. All trapping values in QuarkXPress, automatic or otherwise, do not officially exist until the file is output. Just because you can't see something doesn't mean it's not there.

Automatic trapping is always turned on. Unless you tell it to do something else, the default trapping values are always applied to page layouts. Examine the automatic settings (see Figure 16.18).

◆ **Auto Amount.** This is the trap width QuarkXPress applies, which is too narrow. We haven't found a press on the planet that can consistently hold this thin a registration. Based on conversations we've had with innumerable printers, we emphatically proclaim, "Set the auto amount value to .3 points!" Of course, always consult with your printer before you assume control of your own trapping. If your job is an expensive, high-quality piece run on a well-maintained press by quality-conscious professionals, then you can get away with setting the auto amount to .25 points. Depending on what you are printing and the type of press used, this value could increase to 3 or 4 points.

◆ **Auto Method.** If Absolute is chosen, the auto amount width is applied to every object that's trapped. Choosing Proportional means that fractions of the auto amount value will be applied, depending on the lightness or darkness of the colors. Unless recommended to do otherwise by your printer, leave the default on Absolute.

◆ **Indeterminate.** If you place an object over a blend, a high-res scan, or more than one different color, QuarkXPress simply refers to the underlying information as if it were one color. It calls this color Indeterminate and the value here should set the same as the auto amount.

◆ **Overprint Limit.** This controls the percentage at or above that a color will overprint, according to the setting in the Trap Specifications dialog. The value is set to 95 percent to accommodate the shadow-dot settings of many imported images. If you really want to overprint a lower-tinted spot color, lower this value. Otherwise, don't worry about it.

◆ **Ignore White.** When this box is checked, any white areas that an object crosses as part of a multiple colored background are ignored when trapping occurs. This may result in more noticeable trap lines, depending on the colors in question and the direction of the trap. Bear this in mind and examine any colored object that overlays white information.

◆ **Process Trap.** With this checked, objects colored with process inks are trapped on a plate-by-plate basis. If you routinely compensate for trapping by choosing colors that form a process bridge, leave this function off.

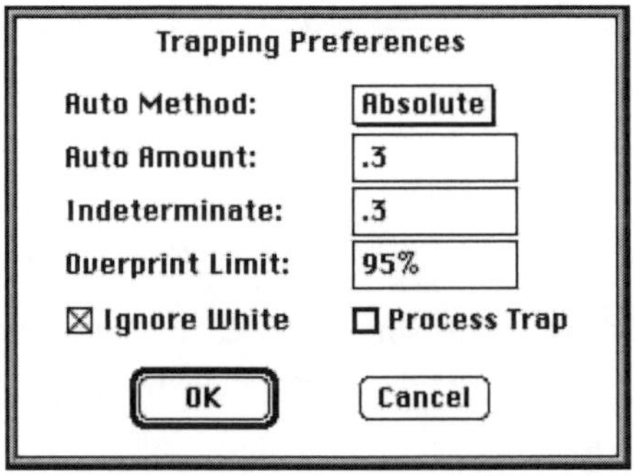

Figure 16.18

QuarkXPress' trapping preferences.

```
┌─────────────────────────────────────────┐
│          Trapping Preferences             │
│                                           │
│   Auto Method:      [Absolute]            │
│   Auto Amount:      [.3        ]          │
│   Indeterminate:    [.3        ]          │
│   Overprint Limit:  [95%       ]          │
│   ⊠ Ignore White    ☐ Process Trap        │
│      ( OK )           ( Cancel )          │
└─────────────────────────────────────────┘
```

Theoretically, if you've planned your use of color well, considered the presence of a process bridge, and have taken care of your blacks and vector-based trapping, your automatic trapping settings should be enough to trap any of the remaining layout-file elements. Still, automatic trapping doesn't address the following situations adequately:

◆ **Small type.** If you have to place small type on a colored background, color it black. At least it will overprint and be easiest to read. If we attempt to trap, say, spot-colored type under 24 points on another spot-colored background, the result will always be heartache and misery. Whenever possible, if you need to color type, place it on a white background.

◆ **Thin rules.** Fine details are always distorted by trapping.

Trapping Color to Color

Don't like the idea of letting a program trap your file automatically? Want more control over the trapping values that are sent to your output device? You can build in predetermined trapping relationships between two or more colors under the Trap Specifications dialog found in the Define Colors window. This, however, is the method of trapping *least* used by designers. You don't have to expect to manipulate these controls every time you want to take control of your own trapping. Many people use the automatic trapping tools, which often do the trick if combined with good color planning.

You edit trap information this way for three reasons:

◆ To change the automatic trap relationship between two colors, as specifically instructed by your printer

◆ To expand or shrink the automatic trap value of only one color, while letting the other color be subject to the automatic settings

◆ To build automatic overprint or knockout (no trap) commands into a color

Changing Trap Specifications

Before you can reset the trap specifications for individual colors, you have to define your colors first. This is not necessary if your job is going be based on process color.

To define the specs, do the following:

1. In the Define Color dialog, select the color you want to edit.

2. Click Edit Trap (see Figure 16.19).

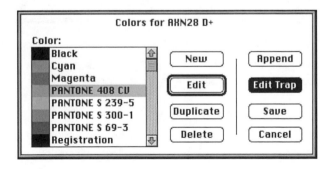

Figure 16.19

Accessing the trap specifica-tions.

3. Select the second color involved in the new trapping relationship (see Figure 16.20). The colors in the document that could potentially underlay the selected color are listed in the dialog. Selecting one and changing the settings means that new trap values will be applied every time the first color you select overlays the second color.

4. Make your change (see Figure 16.21). Clicking Overprint forces the first color to overprint the second. Entering numerical values—such as .5 pt, 2.5 pt, or 4 pt and clicking the Trap button establishes a new trap width. Entering a trap value of 0 pt forces the color to completely knockout, or print with no trap at all.

5. Click Save.

6. Repeat this process for the remaining colors.

Trapping Object-to-Object

Trapping object-to-object refers to editing the trap information of just one object or another. You do this through the floating Trap Info palette found under the View menu.

You can reset the trap values for any object created in QuarkXPress by selecting an object and referring to the pop up menu in the Trap Info palette. In the Trap Info palette, you will find the following six options (see Figure 16.22):

◆ **Default.** This means no changes have been made from the Trap Info palette. If an object is receiving the Auto Amount value in the Automatic Trapping Preferences dialog, then Auto Amount appears in the palette. If changes were made in the Trap Specifications dialog, the numerical value used appears. Clicking the question mark reveals a brief summary of the existing trap information (see Figure 16.23).

◆ **Overprint.** Applying this option forces the one selected object to overprint the underlying inks. One good use: if you insist on placing small colored type on a different colored background in a two-color job, force the type to overprint. The color will shift a bit (how much will depend on the two colors used), but it remains legible. Colored type that's been trapped or told to knockout often doesn't.

◆ **Knockout.** Applying this forces the selected object to knockout, or receive overprinting or trapping information.

◆ **Auto Amount (+).** This applies the Auto Amount width defined in Trapping preferences to the selected object. Because the number is positive, it forces the color to spread into the underlying inks.

◆ **Auto Amount (-).** This applies the Auto Amount width to the selected object, but the negative value means the object is choked by the underlying ink.

◆ **Custom.** This enables you to enter your own trap widths, positive or negative, for the objects in your document.

If either more than one or no objects is selected, you can't change any of the settings. This tool only works on one item at a time.

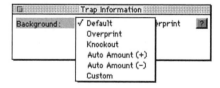

Figure 16.22

QuarkXPress' Trap Info palette.

Figure 16.23

Checking the trap summary.

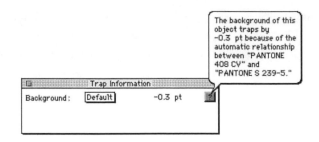

Trapping in PageMaker

PageMaker's trapping information is controlled in the Trapping Preferences dialog, found under the File menu (see Figure 16.24). Contrary to QuarkXPress' tools, this is the only area where you can define trapping values and your chances for successful trapping ultimately suffer because of this. You can't build new trap values into your color definitions, nor can you edit your object one-by-one, adding new settings as you go.

Figure 16.24

PageMaker's Trapping Options.

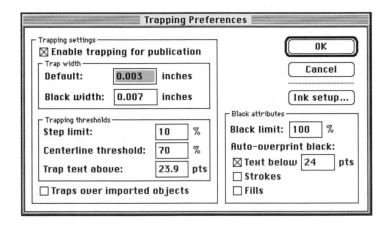

One advantage PageMaker has is the capability to turn on and off document trapping. To prevent PageMaker from applying any trap, unclick the Enable Trapping for Publication button in the Trapping Preferences dialog.

Trap Width

Trap width has the following two settings:

◆   Default specifies the trap width for trapping all colors except those involving solid black.

◆ Black Width specifies the trap width for trapping colors next to or under solid blacks. The Black Width generally is set to 1.5 to 2 times the value of the default trap width.

Trapping Thresholds

Some jobs need only their extreme color changes trapped, and others require traps for even the slightest color changes. The Step Limit value determines the point that PageMaker considers trapping necessary. Increasing or decreasing the value determines how much the component inks must differ before PageMaker traps. The lower the percentage, the more often PageMaker traps between colors.

Centerline traps use the highest ink components from both of the abutting colors. If colors have similar neutral densities, neither color defines the edge. To trap these colors, PageMaker adjusts the trap position from spreading the lighter color into the darker one to straddling the centerline between them. We can set the threshold anywhere from zero percent to 100 percent. At zero percent, all traps default to centerline. At 100 percent, centerline trapping is turned off, resulting in a full spread or choke. At the risk of sounding like Dear Abby talking about psychiatric help, consult your printer on this issue.

Trap Text Above determines how large type has to be before PageMaker applies trapping values.

Black Attributes

The setting for Black Limit determines what PageMaker considers a solid black or enriched black. The default, 100 percent, states that only colors containing 100 percent black will be treated as solid or rich blacks. When PageMaker encounters a color whose black percentage is the same or higher than the percentage for Black Limit, PageMaker applies the Black Width trap size to all solid and enriched blacks, and uses a keepaway value for the enriched blacks.

Auto Overprint Black lets us determine if our black lines and fills will trap or overprint.

At the bottom of the dialog, you'll find an option for trapping PageMaker items into imported graphics. This is similar to QuarkXPress' Indeterminate color, which is used to apply one flat trap setting into the underlying image, regardless of the inks.

DEDICATED TRAPPING SOFTWARE

Dedicated digital trapping systems have been available to publishers for years. Until recently, such systems were enormously expensive and complex, and therefore out of the reach of most professionals.

In the last couple of years, trapping software packages such as Adobe TrapWise have been garnering favor in the industry, with the promise of flawless, effortless traps.

TrapWise is an ingenious program. Generally, it processes PostScript files on its own dedicated workstation. It rasterizes the information in the file (converts it to pixels and dots, just like an imagesetter's RIP), then makes trapping determinations based on all the adjacent colored bitmaps. Using this technique, it can trap information that programs like QuarkXPress and PageMaker cannot, like adjacent gradients and imported EPS graphics. The controls of TrapWise give the user control over the finest details, allowing us to tailor the values of each output job to the most unique on-press demands.

Note

Service bureaus and print shops who use a program like TrapWise often charge trapping fees of up to an extra 25 percent per four-color page.

Unfortunately, there is a downside to this software that makes it less appealing to many designers and service providers: time and money.

First of all, the software is expensive. Complete packages can run as high as $5000 (and they're hardware-protected, so don't get any ideas). Plus, the program requires its own dedicated Windows or Macintosh workstation to run most efficiently, which adds thousands of dollars to the initial cost.

The software is also notorious for its wildly unpredictable processing times. A 24-page publication may take 30 minutes; a tabloid-sized poster might take all day. It all depends on the types of graphics used in the publications, the trap settings for this particular job, and the output settings when the file is sent for process. In other words, we usually don't know how long it will take until we download the information and start checking our watches.

Many professionals will benefit greatly from the proper use of dedicated trapping software. Many service bureaus use TrapWise as a potent weapon in the fight against complex documents. Service bureaus also benefit from a high demand for trapping services. As more and more print shops become proficient in digital technologies, they desire to gain more control over the files that they output for reproduction on their own presses. Trapping software, if the demand for the service is high enough, gives them much more flexibility.

But a design firm, for example, would not want to invest in the equipment and training in such a system if they just send the files to be output off-site. Many small print shops that are either new to digital prepress or don't have the intense need for exacting control can afford to pass on dedicated software.

Trapping Options	Illustration Software	Page Layout Software	Dedicated Trapping Software
Trapping Consider-ations	Use to create simple traps manually or automatically.	Use to trap elements created in layout program.	Typically traps rasterized PostScript files.
Item does not overlap any colored objects	n/a	n/a	n/a
Item overlaps one other colored object (2 spot colors)	Create simple manual trap.	Auto trap in PageMaker; auto trap or set trap specifications in Quark.	Auto traps where necessary.
Item overlaps multiple objects.	Trap with built-in tools: Trap filter in Illustrator Trap Xtra in FreeHand.	Auto trap in PageMaker; auto trap or set trap specifications in Quark (mult. colors referred to as Indeter-minate).	Auto traps where necessary.

continues

Trapping Options	Illustration Software	Page Layout Software	Dedicated Trapping Software
Item overlaps imported image	Use overprinting strokes on image edge to create trap.	Turn "Traps Over Imported Objects" on in PageMaker; Define Indeterminate traps specs in Quark.	Allows user more control when items trap to underlying image.
Item overlaps gradient fill	Use overprinting strokes on image edge to create trap.	Cannot trap in PageMaker; use Indeterminate settings in Quark.	Auto traps, adjusting edge color and position.
Enriched Black item	Add overprinting 100% black stroke to build in trap.	Quark and PageMaker both keep undercolor from the black edge ("keepaway").	Applies adjustable keepaway value.
Imported EPS graphics	Cannot trap.	Cannot trap.	Automatically traps, but with wildly varying processing times.

You can escape the need for trapping in only two ways:

- Never letting your colors touch
- Printing with just one color ink

Effective trapping, however, cannot be accomplished without the following:

- **An understanding of spot and process color.** These two color types have different trapping considerations. Whenever two spot color touch, trapping is required. If two process-based colors touch, they may or may not need to be trapped. If you choose your colors wisely and if your adjacent process colors share enough CMYK components to form a process bridge, you do not have to worry about trapping.

- **Thoughtful design.** The need for trapping should rest at the center of all our design decisions. Whenever possible, design to avoid trapping. If you can't, then apply your colors wisely, making sure that the ultimate trapping values will not degrade any fine details or obscure any type.

- **An awareness of every object in your layout.** Be prepared to double-check each page, each object, and each color in your layout to ensure that all trapping guidelines are being met.

Your best resource for trapping assistance will always be your printer. Either he will be able to tell you the values that best suit your job and the press it's run on, or he will be able to trap your films conventionally. Don't feel obliged to assume control of your trapping if you are not prepared.

Chapter

17

PREFLIGHT AND FILE PREP

If you're anything like us, your deadlines leave no room for wasted time. The idea of extra expenses or wasted resources conjures images of roomfuls of green-visored accountants, who click their tongues while dashing off memos to your boss. At the end of a project, the mere thought of surprise problems is enough to make you take a disgruntled postal worker hostage. Unfortunately, everyone involved in the digital graphic arts can relate to some of the following situations:

- You stand by the door, holding a stack of unusable page films.

- You miss print dates in order to output a job again.

- You absorb the cost of repairing files and re-outputting films for your clients.

- You find out too late that your traps are wrong, your fonts defaulted to Courier, your text reflowed, and your colors output incorrectly.

- You find out too late that your file can't be output at all.

Preflight is more than just a cool-sounding term ripped off from NASA. At the core of preflight is a quality-control process that helps to avoid problems. For the designer, it ensures successful document output and reduces extra "file fix" charges by his printer or service bureau. For the production house, it means shorter processing times, conservation of resources, and a more satisfied client base. For both parties, it's quite possibly the most important stage of the workflow process. After all, if a document can't be output, it's worthless and all the time and money spent creating it will have been squandered.

Preflight is also more than simply handing over fonts and graphics with an output job. For designers and service bureaus alike, it's a tangible system to incorporate into your work environment. From organizing project files, to properly transporting them to the service bureau, to outputting test separations and checking traps and bleeds, preflight and everything it means should be on your mind during every stage of handling a document and its component files. In this chapter, we discuss:

- The three stages of successfully preflighting a digital file: gathering information, reviewing the file, and outputting paper proofs.

- The issues involved in establishing a preflight system.

- The client and vendor issues that arise when instituting these new output requirements.

- The hardware and software required of a successful preflight department.

Back in the Dark Ages of digital prepress, production specialists were held prisoner by an undefined industry, an uneducated designer base, and the desire to please their clients no matter what the cost. Viable color PostScript publishing was still relatively new, and most people responsible for creating electronic documents didn't realize how complex a science it really was. Everyone had to behave as if all client files could be output easily and properly, but the vast majority of them simply could not. One service bureau which conducted a study in 1993, randomly pulled and examined 100 jobs, only to find that 96 of them needed some sort of extra work or adjustment to output successfully.

So if we assume that service bureaus everywhere were experiencing the same phenomenon, that 96 percent of the output jobs received needed "massaging," who was responsible for doing the work? In the vast majority of cases, the service bureau did the work. Most clients, they found, got upset if a job was refused, or if they got billed for time spent making a file output-ready. Because there was no existing basis for demanding this of their clients, service bureaus would either have to put in the time free of charge or risk losing the client to another company that was willing to satisfy these demands.

For a while, most service bureaus were willing to "take that extra step," thinking they were maintaining their customer base. In reality, they were getting reamed by the costs hidden in that endless stream of poorly constructed files (see Figure 17.1). Eventually, an industry hung in the balance.

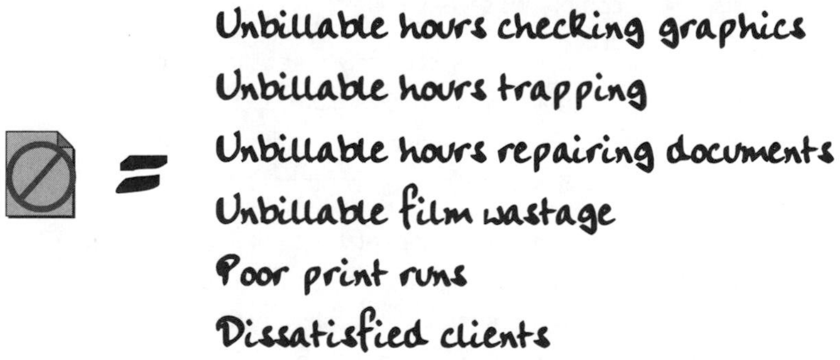

Unbillable hours checking graphics
Unbillable hours trapping
Unbillable hours repairing documents
Unbillable film wastage
Poor print runs
Dissatisfied clients

Figure 17.1

The hidden costs of a poorly constructed file.

On one side were designers and most of them were already stretched to the limit by being forced to learn the new digital tools required to continue their craft. Their job, it was widely believed, was simply to design the file, and the finer points of getting film separations were best left up to the output specialists. "Besides," they said, "my service bureau bends over backwards for me. Why would I possibly want to change *that?*" On the other side were the service bureaus, who had to choose between losing customers (by refusing to process inadequate files) or losing profits (by accepting responsibility for those files).

Partial relief came from Scitex, who had released their CREF (Computer Ready Electronic Files) standards, creating a platform for designers and output specialists alike to follow when constructing their documents. Trouble was, it's one thing for a file to be *computer* ready, it's quite another for a file to be *print* ready. *Any* file can be displayed on a computer monitor. Not every file can be output successfully.

A method was needed to ensure a document's printability *before* the information was downloaded to an imagesetter. To the eternal thanks of digital graphics professionals everywhere, preflighting has become that method.

The goal of preflighting is producing composite and separated versions of a file on a PostScript laser printer. Composites (or "comps") are document printouts with no color separations, which give the viewer a feel for the overall page layouts. Separations (or "seps") are document printouts divided into their component color plates. This is performed by both designer and output specialists. This accomplishes several things:

◆ It proves that a file can be successfully output to a PostScript imaging device. The vast majority of printers, from laser printers to imagesetters, are PostScript-based. Separating a file on one is the surest indication it will separate on another.

◆ It places responsibility for an unprintable file back in the hands of the file's creator where it belongs. If a file cannot be output to a designer's PostScript printer, we can safely assume it will not output to an imagesetter. Troubleshooting can begin before the file is handed over.

◆ It proves that all graphic files and fonts were in place and linked at least once before being handed over to a service bureau.

◆ It lets output specialists ensure that all graphic files and fonts have been provided by the client.

◆ It allows a final, last-minute proof of bleeds, text flow, font use, and trap.

A trend has begun over the last three years. Service bureaus now can firmly request all output jobs be handed over with accompanying laser comps and separations. If they receive them, they accept responsibility for outputting separations. If they do not, then the client accepts responsibility for all cost overruns, hours spent repairing bad files, and wasted film. To provide a transition into this requirement, many companies outputting film for clients offer a small discount—from 5 percent to 10 percent—for a short period of time to encourage their clients to put that extra attention into their work.

The benefits of preflight go beyond the savings of time, money, resources, and customer relations. It's made us all smarter. As the digital graphic arts evolve, becoming more complex and thorough, so do we. We've all gained a better understanding of the issues and techniques required of successful file construction. We flex our minds, become more open to new ideas, and continually strive to improve ourselves and our work. We hand these traits down to our children, who ultimately cure cancer and grow bigger heads to hold all those brains.

Before we begin describing the elements of what preflight is, let's first consider what it's not:

◆ It's not the time for last-minute changes and tweaks at the request of the client.

◆ It's not the place for graphic design or production.

◆ It's not the forum for quick, well-intentioned freebies by an output staff. Remember our two benefits: we encourage designers to learn more about output-specific issues, and we stop giving away our production time.

STAGE ONE: GATHERING INFORMATION

Think about all the components of your average four-color project. A 48-page color catalog can easily contain 100 color images. An annual report may use several dozen vector-based graphs. Even a simple newsletter can involve a lengthy series of logos, halftones, fonts, and supplementary graphics. Unless you have a way of accounting for all, and we mean *all*, of a file's vital information, you can't really expect your file to output successfully, either in-house or at the service bureau.

For the Designer

Those of us who create electronic files are responsible for keeping track of the same information as the service provider, but in a slightly different way. This process begins as you first plan your document and continues until you hand over the project files to a service provider. Throughout the entire project, we keep a detailed report of all the settings, parameters, and special instructions pertaining to your document and the ultimate print run. As you generate your supplemental files, we develop a system of collecting them into a form most easily transported to a service provider and used by an output specialist.

Maintain a Project Report

On the surface, creating a project report sounds like just another time-consuming activity that distracts designers from their *real* jobs. Actually, maintaining this kind of document serves two immensely helpful purposes:

◆ **It forces you to see your project from your vendors' perspective.** Good design is an equal blend of visual acuity and realistic production demands. By extending your mind's eye beyond the computer screen and into the realm of what can and cannot be printed, you add untold value to your work.

◆ **It gives your output specialist and printer a better understanding of your expectations.** The more accurately you can communicate your desires, the closer to your vision the final product will be.

For small projects, you may want to output thumbnails and write your information in the margin of the single page (see Figure 17.2).

Fonts: Simoncini Gar., Futura Condensed

Page 1
   Background graphic: Press/ghost.tiff (PMS 266)
   Duotone: Roller.eps (PMS 875, Black)
   Header: Charcoal Bar.eps (Black)

Page 2
   BG Graphic: Circuit board/ghost.tiff (PMS 875)
   Duotone: Circuit.eps (PMS 266, Black)
   Header: Charcoal Bar.eps

Ink order: Black, 875, 266

Figure 17.2

A project report based on thumbnails.

When working with multipage documents, print lasers of every page, number them, and write down the pertinent info on each one. Include any blank pages that'll be included in the final print run.

Avoid planting any surprises in the report that may be missed by the reader. There should be no new instructions. Keep it to a short series of notes for each page of your document.

Include the following topics in your reports:

◆ **Output Settings.** Assuming that you have already consulted with your commercial printer and service provider, include such information as linescreen value, output resolution, UCR/GCR settings, and trap tolerance. Indicate whether your film will be positive or negative, and list the emulsion reading. If necessary, list any color management system or color profiles used.

- **Detailed Page Information.** List all the pages in the document, including blank pages and page numbers. Use the page numbers to reference any special needs on the pages. In longer documents, list sections, chapters, and any other breaks.

- **Graphic Files and Folder Names.** This includes the name of the page layout document and its location on the transport media (if more than one layout document is handed over, be sure to list the name of every one). List the name and location of every graphic file used in the project, as well as the file format and original application. If you've organized your work adequately, print the window of the folder containing the graphics for your project and staple it to your report.

- **Colors and Separation.** For each page, list the colors used, whether they're spot or process, and the specific number of seps to be output for each page. Also list any spot varnishes that have been defined.

- **Fonts.** List all the font families used in the document, as well as any that might have been embedded in imported EPS artwork.

- **Special Notes.** Use these to list any special needs on each page, including bleeds, crossovers, and any images to be manually stripped. Also describe items that have been trapped, as well as those that still need to be by the service provider.

This report doesn't take the place of the output request form—it augments it. As you create this report, notice the information often changes as your project evolves. Keep the report up-to-date by outputting fresh pages and noting the most recent changes. This report should always be close by, allowing you immediate access to all the nuances of your printed project. You never know—printers call, contractors call, service bureaus call, and you'll need to be able to talk succinctly about your project and note new conditions.

In essence, this report is your little bible, to be read, believed, interpreted, fought over, and revised. Around it, wars will be waged, your spirit will be nurtured, and your faith will be tested. Ultimately, if you follow the teachings, guidelines, and laws, you will find salvation, which lasts until the *next* project.

Assemble the Elements

Before your project can be handed over to a service provider, we need to make sure all of the necessary information is organized, easy to find, and ready to use.

In a perfect world, collecting the project files would be a snap. Just imagine this scenario:

1. Just before you begin the project, you create a folder with the job number included in the title.

2. When you create the page layout document, save it directly into this folder.

3. As graphics, scans, and FPOs are generated by the designers and service bureaus, you place them into the project folder *before* importing them into your page layouts.

4. When the layout is completed, output and check your laser proofs.

5. Before you copy the job folder to your transport media, place copies of the same fonts in the project into a folder called "Project Fonts." Move that folder into the job folder.

6. Copy the single job folder containing all the necessary project information onto a universally omnipresent media cartridge, such as an Iomega Zip or SyQuest.

7. Hand over the entire bundle—cartridge, proofs, and your own report—to your service provider.

Unfortunately, our imperfect world is rarely that straightforward. We import images stored on different parts of our hard disk. We download FPOs from file servers. We use images and fonts stored on SyQuests and DAT. We feel we don't have enough time to output preflight comps and seps of the most recently saved version of a document. We forget to hand over an image or font.

If you haven't contained all of your graphics in a single job folder, you are faced with a choice. Either hunt down every single graphic by hand, or utilize a more automated process. Both Quark and PageMaker offer features that enable you to collect document graphics into a single folder. Both programs generate small reports that tell the original location of any graphic imported from an external source. This report also lists such information as style sheet definitions, fonts used, and built-in trap values, but it should not be considered a replacement for the report we discussed earlier. It won't include conversations that you have with your printer, customized page settings, bleed and crossover instructions, and so forth.

In Quark, this function is called Collect for Output. This copies all linked images into a single folder, adds a copy of the layout document, and includes a written summary of the file components. In PageMaker, the Save As dialog contains the options for copying the document and graphics, and the summary is created via a PageMaker plug-in.

Collecting for Output in QuarkXPress

To collect the document and graphics, follow these steps:

1. Open your completed document.

2. Choose Collect for Output from the File menu (see Figure 17.3). If any of your graphic links have been broken, you are prompted to re-establish them, if you can. If you have made any changes to the document, you are prompted to save.

3. If you have not already created a job folder, choose New Folder from the Collect for Output dialog, name it, and click Create (see Figure 17.4). This is the folder the document and graphic files are copied into, so keep track of its location.

4. Click Collect.

5. Examine the folder. Copies of the document and all currently linked graphics have been placed there, as well as a single text file containing the document summary. If any of your imported graphics came from beyond your hard drive, this summary contains their original locations (see Figure 17.5).

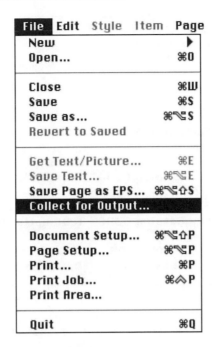

Figure 17.3

Collect for Output.

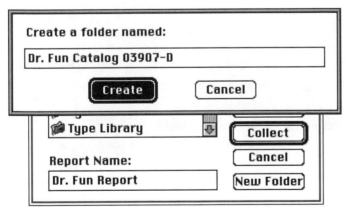

Figure 17.4

Creating a new project folder.

Figure 17.5

The document summary.

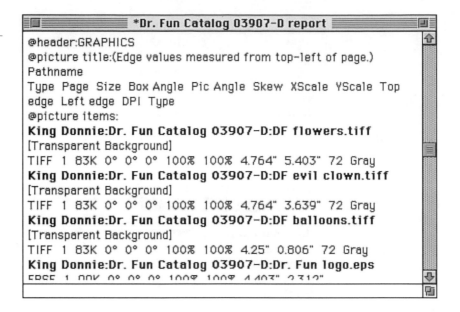

```
*Dr. Fun Catalog 03907-D report
@header:GRAPHICS
@picture title:(Edge values measured from top-left of page.)
Pathname
Type Page Size Box Angle Pic Angle Skew XScale YScale Top
edge Left edge DPI Type
@picture items:
King Donnie:Dr. Fun Catalog 03907-D:DF flowers.tiff
[Transparent Background]
TIFF 1 83K 0° 0° 0° 100% 100% 4.764" 5.403" 72 Gray
King Donnie:Dr. Fun Catalog 03907-D:DF evil clown.tiff
[Transparent Background]
TIFF 1 83K 0° 0° 0° 100% 100% 4.764" 3.639" 72 Gray
King Donnie:Dr. Fun Catalog 03907-D:DF balloons.tiff
[Transparent Background]
TIFF 1 83K 0° 0° 0° 100% 100% 4.25" 0.806" 72 Gray
King Donnie:Dr. Fun Catalog 03907-D:Dr. Fun logo.eps
EPSF 1 00K 0° 0° 0° 100% 100% 4.403" 2.312"
```

6. Place copies of the external graphics files into the job folder.

7. Notice that no fonts copy into the Collect for Output folder. Fonts are never touched by this function, so they need to be copied into the folder by hand. Make sure you don't simply move the fonts from your type library into the folder. Option-dragging the font files ensures copies are made (see Figure 17.6).

Collecting for Output in PageMaker

To collect the document and graphics follow these steps:

1. Create a job folder on your desktop (see Figure 17.7).

2. Open your completed document.

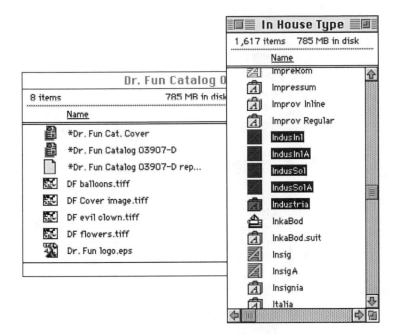

Figure 17.6

Option-dragging fonts to place copies into the project folder.

Figure 17.7

A job folder must be present.

3. Choose Save As from the File menu (see Figure 17.8).

Figure 17.8

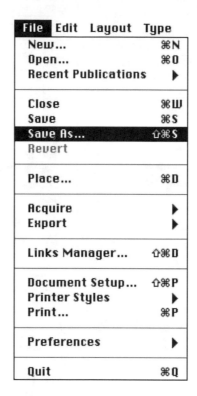

4. Under the Save As option, select Publication.

5. Under the Copy option, choose All Linked Files.

6. Click Save.

7. Examine the folder. Just like Quark, the document along with all currently linked graphics is copied into the folder. The fonts have to be copied manually, and unlike Quark, without a written summary (see Figure 17.9).

To create the summary follow these steps:

I. Under the Utilities menu, choose Pub Info from the PageMaker Plugins submenu (see Figure 17.10).

2. Under Display, choose the information you want included in the summary: fonts, links, and/or styles.

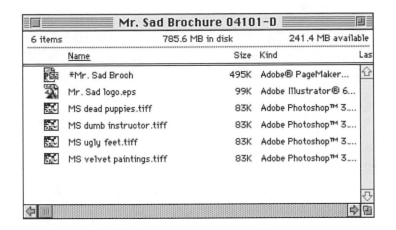

Figure 17.9

PageMaker does not automatically create a project report.

3. Click Save.

4. Through the navigational dialog, place the summary into your job folder.

5. Click Done.

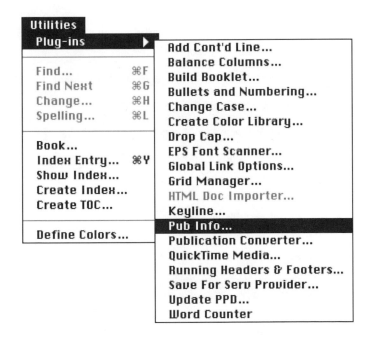

Figure 17.10

Choosing Pub Info...

Although these features are convenient and usually helpful, double-check your work every time you use them. We prefer to greet any so-called "automated" process with a certain degree of doubt and scorn. Following these guidelines will result in the most accurate transport of project documents and support files:

◆ Any files not linked while collecting for output must be gathered manually.

◆ Fonts must be gathered manually.

◆ The document summaries are never adequate replacements for your detailed reports.

◆ Always open the document that was copied into the new job folder and check the links before copying the information to your transport media.

Handing Over the Project to the Service Provider

This is the simplest task of the process, as long as you've lined up your ducks in their proverbial row. You can hand your project over to the service provider when the following have been accomplished:

◆ Your graphics and document have been created, copied, and tested.

◆ All reports and summaries have been completed.

◆ All laser comps and seps have been produced.

◆ You've acquired a removable media device accepted by your service provider.

Warning

The only issue you have to worry about here is whether to use file compression. Our recommendation is simple: you don't need to compress, so don't bother. These days, removable media is so cheap and abundant, we don't have to be nearly as uptight about space considerations as we used to be. File compression also can lead to unnecessary delays:

◆ *Compressing and decompressing information takes time. Not much, perhaps, but if space is not a huge consideration, save yourself and your output specialists those few precious minutes.*

◆ *Let's say you send compressed files, but you don't save them as self-expanding archives. If your service provider does not have the same compression program (or the same version or higher), all progress stops.*

Service Provider: Use Your Output Request Form

The output request form is the most important organizational tool a service provider has. All too often, it's the most under-utilized. This form is the only written source of all the parameters of an output job, which makes it an invaluable source of document information.

Unless it is completely and accurately filled out, it is of little use. Every job that crosses the desk of an output specialist should be accompanied by a completed job ticket, with no exceptions. Without this form, the record of client output demands is lost as well as the individual file components.

The output request form is typically filled out by one of the following people (in descending order of preference):

◆ **A trained customer service representative.** Not long ago, we dropped off a simple job at a service bureau across town. We were met at the door with a smile, and we weren't even allowed to touch the output request form. We were led through the process item-by-item, and it was probably the most complete form we'd ever seen. Even well-trained designers can forget or misunderstand items on these forms (after all, they're invariably filled out at the very end of a long project). Not only does having a customer service rep fill out the forms ensure that each item gets the attention it deserves, it provides blessed relief for any clients with too much on their mind.

◆ **The client.** This person is probably most intimate with the components of the file, the profiles of the intended printed piece, and any special instructions. However, the form they fill out is only as good as their knowledge of the issues covered. If necessary, offer to train your clients on the meaning and importance of each item on the form.

◆ **A sales representative.** Often, sales reps pick up jobs from their accounts and fill out the output request form for them, as a service. Unless your sales reps are well-trained in the issues of digital prepress, the forms will be of little use.

The job ticket requests all information pertaining to the type of output and necessary print values (see Figure 17.11) as the following:

Figure 17.11

A sample job ticket.

◆ **Platform.** Includes choices between Mac System 6 (some people still use it), Mac System 7, and DOS/Windows.

◆ **Application.** The program (and version) used to create the final document.

- **Pages to Print.** The page range and number of copies to print.

- **Fonts.** All fonts used in the project and supplied by the client, listed by name. Also lists whether the fonts are PostScript or TrueType.

- **Graphics.** Lists whether client supplies graphics or FPOs.

- **File Saved As.** Lists whether a working document or PostScript file has been supplied.

- **Colors.** Offers choice between Spot, Process, or Both. Also includes space to list any custom color names.

- **Trapping.** Lists whether the client has trapped the file or wants the service bureau to trap for them. Usually, space is provided for special trapping instructions.

- **Proofing.** Lists the type of proof desired by the client, if any.

- **Output Type.** This typically lists choices between imagesetters, color printers, and film recorders.

- **Media.** For imagesetting, this lists the choices between media type (RC paper or film), exposure (positive or negative), and emulsion (up or down). For color printing, this lists choices between printers and output stock. For film recording, this lists slide and transparency sizes.

- **Resolution.** Lists various imagesetter resolutions, usually 1200, 2400, and 3600 dpi.

- **Page Size.** Lists standard and custom page sizes.

- **Separations.** Lists choices between None, Process, and Spot. Space is typically provided for special instructions concerning overprint and knockout commands.

- **Options.** For imagesetting, this includes information on crop and registration marks, reduction or enlargement percentages, and linescreen values. For color printing, it includes options for crop/registration marks, reduction/enlargement, and lamination.

- **Preflight Requirements.** States whether the client has supplied laser composite and separations or if the service bureau is to do so.

Also lists the option of running blind, which means processing the file without any laser proofs. This option effectively releases the service provider from any responsibility for unusable film.

This form is the primary source of information specific to an output job. It works closely with all other written forms and reports provided by the client, but it is essential all the facts most important to outputting are kept in one easy-to-read location.

STAGE TWO: REVIEWING THE FILE

This stage takes place just before laser comps and separations are printed. This same process should be followed by both the designer and the output specialist on the same job.

◆ The designer reviews the file contents and outputs preflight pages just before copying the job folder to their transport media. This ensures that the most recently saved version of the document is used during preflighting.

◆ The output specialist reviews the file and outputs preflight pages immediately upon receiving the job. This ensures that all the information is in place before attempting to print to film.

Optimum Preflight Conditions

When a service provider opens a client job on an output or preflighting workstation, he must do his best to duplicate the conditions that were in effect when the file was created. The service provider mimics the designer's workstation by doing the following:

1. The project folder is copied to the hard drive of the output station.

2. All fonts on the output station are turned off, using the installed font management utility.

3. Only the fonts supplied by the client are turned on, using the same utility. This does two things. First, it makes sure that exactly the same font information is being used when outputting the document. Second, if any fonts have not been supplied, there's no way incorrect fonts will be used instead.

4. Now, when the service provider opens the document, he is flagged if any graphics or fonts are missing, eliminating the need to rely on paper proofs for this particular information.

Opening and Examining the Document

This is where the service provider reviews the contents of the transport media supplied by the client. The simplest way to do this is by opening the document. The service provider will check preferences and linking information in documents opened into both Quark and PageMaker.

Reviewing a Quark Document

Preferences

The first thing an output specialist should see upon opening a client Quark document is the preferences dialog (see Figure 17.12). This indicates the document was created on a different copy of Quark and the prefs built into the document are different from the prefs built into the active version of Quark. So, do you click Use XPress Preferences or Keep Document Settings? Don't even play around! Always select Keep Document Settings!

Some settings saved with this document are different from those in the "XPress Preferences" file:

• Frame data does not match.

Use XPress Preferences May cause reflow. Custom frames may not be available.

Keep Document Settings Changes made to kerning and tracking tables and hyphenation exceptions while this document is active will apply to this document only.

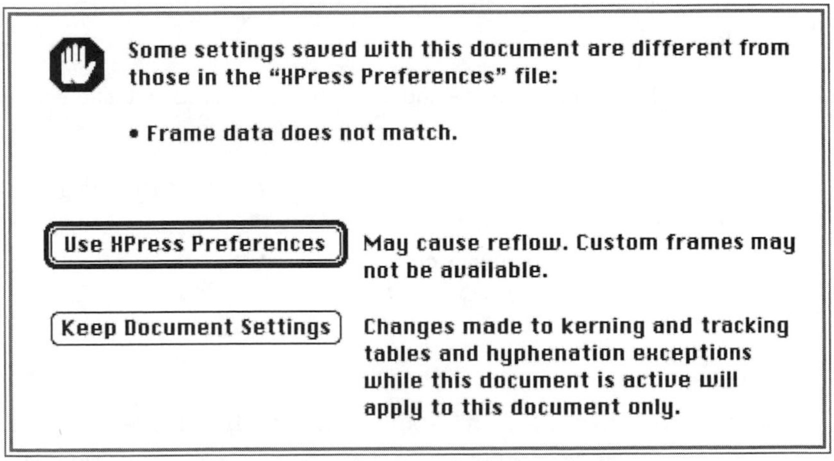

Figure 17.12

Quark's Preferences Request dialog.

Clicking Keep Document Settings maintains all the prefs that were in place while the file was created. Choosing Use XPress Preferences overrides the document prefs, replacing the original settings with different values from a different copy of the program. This puts values such as automatic trapping, custom tracking, and kern tables at risk. Ignore the fact that Use XPress Preferences has the "maybe-I-should-click-here" heavy border. It's a dirty trick.

Fonts

After you elect to keep the document settings, you are notified if any fonts are missing (see Figure 17.13). If this dialog appears, do the following:

Figure 17.13

Quark's Missing Fonts dialog.

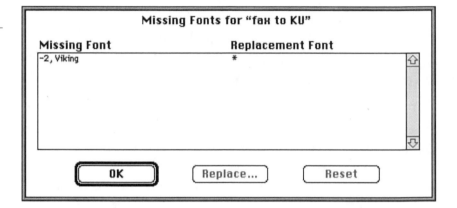

1. Write down the missing font titles, Most often, this occurs because a client did not supply entire font families, opting to send individual fonts.

2. Check the transport media and see if they are stored in a different location.

3. If the font is not present, contact the client and have them bring (or transfer via modem) the entire font family of each missing font. Do not replace fonts with your own versions or other typefaces without written consent of the client.

Graphics

Quark will not automatically notify you if any links have been broken, unless you are printing or collecting for output. To check them upon opening a file, do the following:

1. Under the Utilities menu, select Picture Usage (see Figure 17.14).

Figure 17.14

Selecting Picture Usage.

2. Scroll down the window, checking the status column (see Figure 17.15). Hopefully, everything reads "OK," indicating that all graphics are present and linked. Other messages include "Modified" (graphic was updated somehow since the last time the document was open), "Wrong Type" (the graphic's file format was changed since the last time the document was opened), and "Missing" (meaning no link is established).

Picture Usage

Name	Page	Type	Status	Print
MPX Bro/Mail backup :...:horizontal bars.aif	1	EPS	OK	✓
MPX Bro/Mail backup :...:Forms GHOST.bknd	1	TIFF	OK	✓
MPX Bro/Mail backup :...:MPX Images :Forms.duo.eps	1	EPS	OK	✓
MPX Bro/Mail backup :...:finishing icon.eps	1	EPS	OK	✓
MPX Bro/Mail backup :...:distribution icon.eps	1	EPS	OK	✓
MPX Bro/Mail backup :...:platemaking icon.eps	1	EPS	OK	✓
MPX Bro/Mail backup :...:stripping icon.eps	1	EPS	OK	✓
MPX Bro/Mail backup :...:corner image.tiff	1	TIFF	OK	✓
MPX Bro/Mail backup :...:connection GHOST.bknd	1	TIFF	OK	✓

[Update]   [Show Me]

Figure 17.15

Check the status of every graphic.

3. If any graphics are read as Modified or Wrong Type, they can be updated by selecting the graphic and clicking Update (see Figure 17.16). Be sure to check the graphics' positions in the main document.

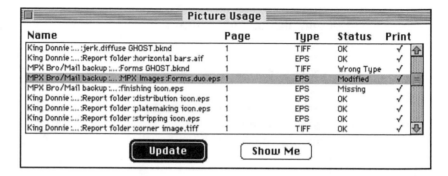

4. If any graphic is listed as Missing, check the transport media to see if any files were moved out of the project folder.

5. If a graphic has not been supplied, contact the client immediately and arrange to have the file transferred, dropped off, or shipped.

Reviewing a PageMaker Document

Because PageMaker's preferences are not as intensive as Quark's, you won't be dealing with the same type of dialog, asking you to choose between document or application preferences. The document preferences are maintained when the file is opened into PageMaker.

Fonts

When you open the document, you are notified if any fonts are missing by the Font Matching Results dialog (see Figure 17.17). If this appears, do not accept the changes it is attempting to apply. Do the following instead:

1. Write down the missing font titles. Most often, this occurs because a client did not supply entire font families, opting to send individual fonts.

2. Check the transport media and see if they are stored in a different location.

3. If the font is not present, contact the client and have them bring (or transfer via modem) the entire font family of each missing font. Do not replace fonts with your own versions or other typefaces without written consent of the client.

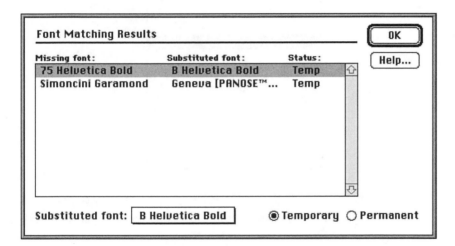

Figure 17.17

PageMaker's Font Matching results dialog.

Graphics

PageMaker will not automatically notify you if any links have been broken, unless you are printing. To check links upon opening a file, do the following:

1. Under the File menu, select Links Manager (see Figure 17.18).

Figure 17.18

PageMaker's Links dialog.

File	Edit	Layout	Type
New...			⌘N
Open...			⌘O
Recent Publications			▶
Close			⌘W
Save			⌘S
Save As...			⇧⌘S
Revert			
Place...			⌘D
Acquire			▶
Export			▶
Links Manager...			**⇧⌘D**
Document Setup...			⇧⌘P
Printer Styles			▶
Print...			⌘P
Preferences			▶
Quit			⌘Q

2. Scroll down the window, checking the graphic titles. Any graphic starting with a question mark is an unlinked file. Selecting an individual graphic reveals its "Status" down below.

3. If any graphics are unlinked, they can be updated by selecting the graphic and clicking Info and directing PageMaker to the proper file (see Figure 17.19). Be sure to check the graphics' positions in the main document.

4. If any graphic is missing, check the transport media to see if any files were moved out of the project folder.

5. If a graphic has not been supplied, contact the client immediately and arrange to have the file transferred, dropped off, or shipped.

Only after you have proven that the client documents can be opened, all fonts and graphics were supplied, and all the preferences were maintained (if appropriate) are you able to output paper proofs. It's only after you output these paper proofs that you can output to film.

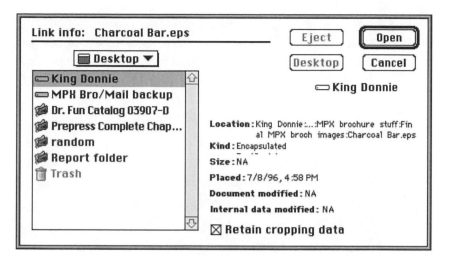

Figure 17.19

*Directing PageMaker to
unlinked graphics.*

STAGE THREE: OUTPUTTING PAPER PROOFS

Printing laser proofs is the last and most important stage of the preflight process. Always print two sets of proofs: composite and separated. The composite proof is a non-color separated printout and is used to examine your overall page geometry, bleeds, crossovers, and text. The separations are used to check that colors are printing to the appropriate plates. Both printouts prove as much as possible that the document can be successfully output to a film plotting device.

Outputting these proofs is the responsibility of both the designer and the output specialist. When designers hand these proofs over to their service provider, they're saying, "I've done all I possibly can to make a file that will print right the first time." When output specialists output the file again to laser proofs, they're saying, "I have duplicated your paper proofs. We will now accept responsibility for outputting this file to film."

Necessary Hardware

Before any paper proofs can be printed, you must have the appropriate tools. Substandard equipment inhibits the success of any preflight department.

The Laser Printer

This is the most important component of preflighting. Many people bypass preflighting because printing color separations to their laser printer takes too long and they feel their own productivity being compromised. Usually, this happens because their laser printer is the technological equivalent of an old dog. It's ancient, it hardly works, it makes messes more often than it should, and you know deep down you should do the right thing and put it out of its misery. But because you've had it so long and you've been through so much together, of course you've developed a sentimental bond with it.

If your laser printer is more than three or four years old—or, heaven forbid, you're still using that archaic LaserWriter II—it's time to upgrade. Newer laser printers are faster, cheaper, and more capable than ever, and the accompanying rise in productivity will pay for a new printer in weeks or months. Look for the following features:

♦ **PostScript Level 2** (or Level 3, coming soon). This is the recent upgrade to Adobe's page description language and the platform that drives this very industry. Compared to PS Level 1 laser printers, Level 2 is the Six Million Dollar Man: better, stronger, faster. They had the technology, they built it, and we all benefit. On these printers, there is virtually no ceiling on the number of points in a vector-based path (including clipping paths), separations output at more than twice the speed, and composite printing screams. Plus, you can buy a Level 2 laser printer for under $1000 nowadays (compare *that* to the $7000 Apple's first LaserWriter cost). Most printers produced today are either Level 2 or Level 2 compatible.

♦ **600 dots per inch.** These days, 300 dpi simply isn't enough. 600 dpi enables you to check traps and fine type, causing your overall page printouts to look crisper and more accurate. For preflight and proofing purposes, 600 dpi is just fine. Any amount more than that— LaserMaster and NewGen, for example, produce models capable of 1200 dpi—is superfluous, unless you're looking for camera-ready artwork.

♦ **RAM.** Upgrading the amount of RAM in your printer (not to be confused with the RAM in your computer) can radically expedite the printing process. Some lower-end models only have room for two to four MB of printer RAM. Consider this the barest minimum. Your best bet, especially if much of your work consists of process separation, is to have between eight and 16 MB of RAM installed. Many printers, depending on your workload, can be upgraded to 32 MB and beyond. When purchasing your printer, check the amount of on-board RAM, how high it can be upgraded, and factor in the amount and type of work you will be printing to it.

◆ **Paper Size.** As far as preflighting goes, a letter-sized printer will suffice. Our comps and seps can be tiled or scaled, depending on the document's overall size. Larger laser printers, usually 11×17 or 12×18 (for tabloid-sized printouts with registration and crop marks), are much more expensive and should be purchased only with a tangible need beyond simple preflighting. Service providers typically have both letter- and tabloid-sized printers to generate the most accurate paper proofs as a service to their clients. Designers usually get by with a letter-sized printer, unless their needs include full-sized mock-ups or two-page camera-ready art.

◆ **Ethernet.** Purchase a printer with built-in Ethernet, if possible. Using this type of networking to transfer the information to your printer gets the job done ten times faster than using LocalTalk.

The CPU and Storage

An output workstation must have enough speed and storage space to deal with large volumes of client traffic.

At the very least, PowerMac 601/80 MHz machines (such as the 7100 or 8100) or basic Pentium-driven PC's have enough raw horsepower to efficiently work with this amount of information. The goal of these workstations is to open, review, preflight, and output files as quickly as possible.

Have at least 2 GB of storage space on every output station. This gives you the capability to copy large files onto your own drive, as well as hang onto a few jobs that might need to be re-output in the near future.

Software

The rule here is simple. Decide what software will be supported, purchase copies of that software, install them on each workstation, train your operators, and stick to your guns. If a client insists on handing over a document created in unsupported software, CorelDRAW! or MacDraw perhaps, only accept the file if:

◆ The client enables you to temporarily install their software on your workstation for the express purpose of outputting their file.

◆ The client understands you cannot guarantee final output if the software used is not a supported industry standard.

In most situations, the supported software is the same that we have covered in this book: QuarkXPress, Adobe PageMaker, Adobe Illustrator, Macromedia FreeHand, and Adobe Photoshop. This software has the widest user base, the highest number of trained operators, and the highest rate of proven output success. Often, service providers expand their range of supported software to include such packages as Adobe FrameMaker or Deneba Canvas, software that has an established user base, but not necessarily as large or as proven as the other programs.

If you do add new software packages to your list of supported programs, make sure you have at least one trained and knowledgeable output specialist in-house and you purchase legal copies of the software.

As you promote your supported software, promote the supported versions of the programs as well. Typically, service providers accept files for the most recent and formerly most recent version of a software package (for example, Quark 3.32 and 3.31, PageMaker 6.5 and 6, Illustrator 6.0 and 5.5, FreeHand 7 and 5.5, Photoshop 4.0 and 3.0.5).

Encourage your client base to upgrade as soon as a new version becomes supported and viable. Handing over files created in obsolete program versions easily results in page information getting skewed by conversions.

Output Laser Proofs

Now you begin the process of ensuring the integrity of the final film output. As you prepare to output our comps and seps, follow these guidelines:

◆ Your proofs should exactly match the file going to film. Any changes made to the file after these proofs are made will require new re-proofing.

◆ Scale your pages no less than 75 percent of the final output size. If necessary, leave the scale value at 100 percent and tile the pages to your laser printer, rather than scale the pages so small that it makes proofing impossible.

◆ Be clear about which images are FPOs, which are live scans, and which images are the low-res PICTs of a series of DCS files.

◆ Delete all unnecessary pages from your multi-page documents.

Outputting Laser Comps from Quark

1. Open the file to be output.

2. Select Page Setup from the File menu (see Figure 17.20).

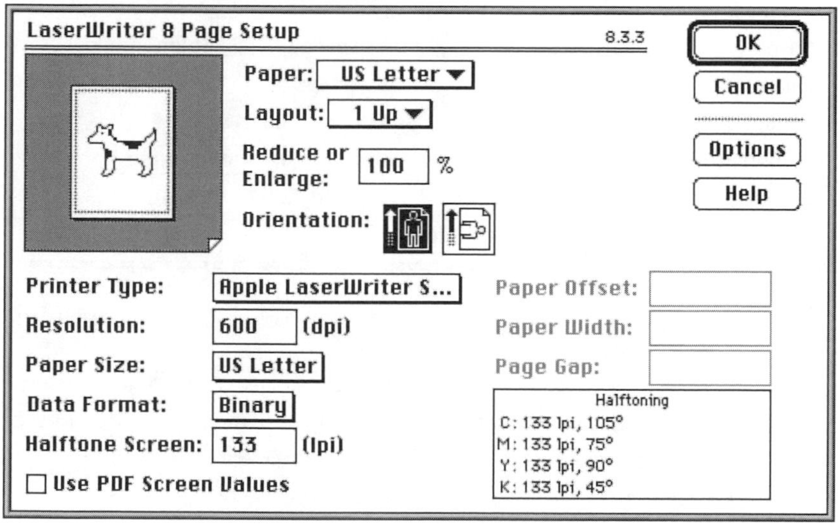

Figure **17.20**

Quark's Page Setup dialog.

3. Select the appropriate PPD file from the Printer Type pop-up menu. These files contain information for a specific PostScript output device. Using the right PPD for your printer ensures the best possible results when printing comps or separations.

4. Set your target halftone screen value. It doesn't matter at this stage whether your laser printer can accurately reproduce higher linescreens. You need to make sure that they can be output by a PostScript device in general.

5. If you need to scale your output for preflight, enter the value here. Otherwise, use the Tile function in the Print dialog.

6. Select Print from the File menu (see Figure 17.21).

Figure 17.21

Quark's Print dialog, set for comps.

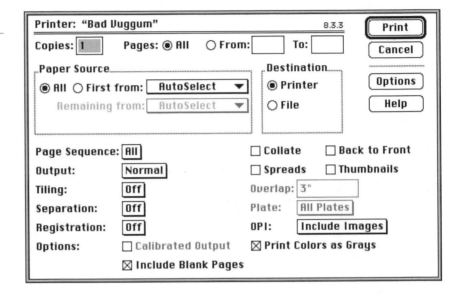

7. Select Off in the Separation pop-up menu.

8. Turn on Print Colors as Grays. This option outputs black tints based on overall brightness values, rather than flat percentages. The printed result is easier to read, since 100 percent magenta, for example, outputs as a lighter tint instead of 100 percent cyan.

9. Turn on Include Blank Pages.

10. Click Print.

Outputting Laser Comps From PageMaker

To open laser comps, follow these steps:

1. Open the file to be output.

2. Select Print from the File menu.

3. After clicking the Document button, select the appropriate PPD from the Type pop-up menu (see Figure 17.22).

4. Turn on Blank Pages.

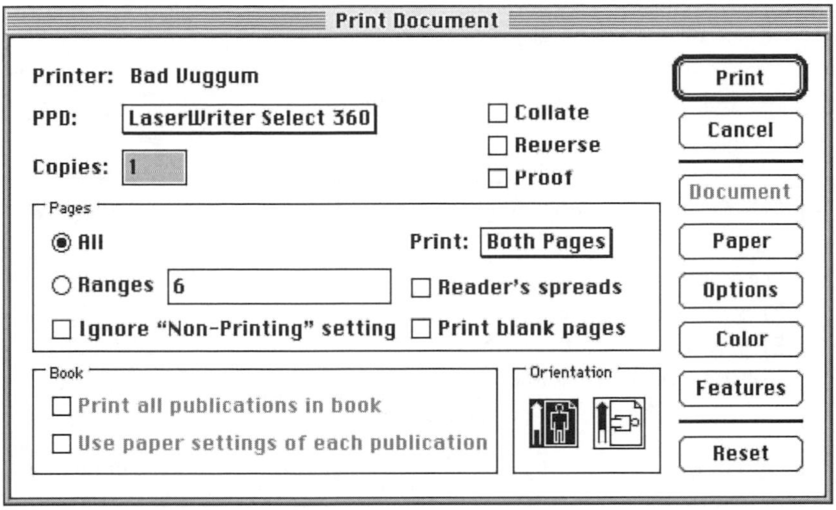

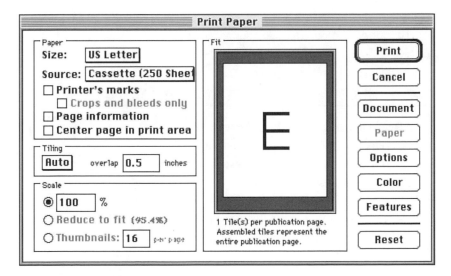

Figure 17.22

PageMaker's Print: Document dialog.

5. After clicking the Paper button, set the scale value, if necessary. Otherwise, turn tiling On and set the Auto:overlap to .5 inches (see Figure 17.23).

Figure 17.23

Pagemaker's Print: Paper dialog.

6. Under Paper, turn off Printer's Marks and Page Information.

7. Click the Options button. Under PostScript, turn off Include PostScript Error Handler.

8. Under Tiff/Images, select Optimized (see Figure 17.24).

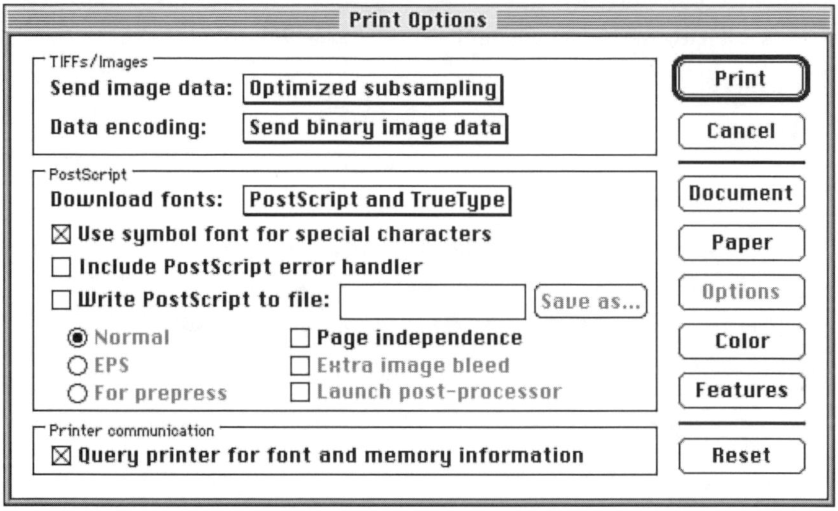

Figure 17.24

Figure 17.24

PageMaker's Print: Options dialog.

9. After clicking the Color button, set the halftone screen in the Ruling field (see Figure 17.25).

10. Under Composite, select Grayscale.

11. Click Print.

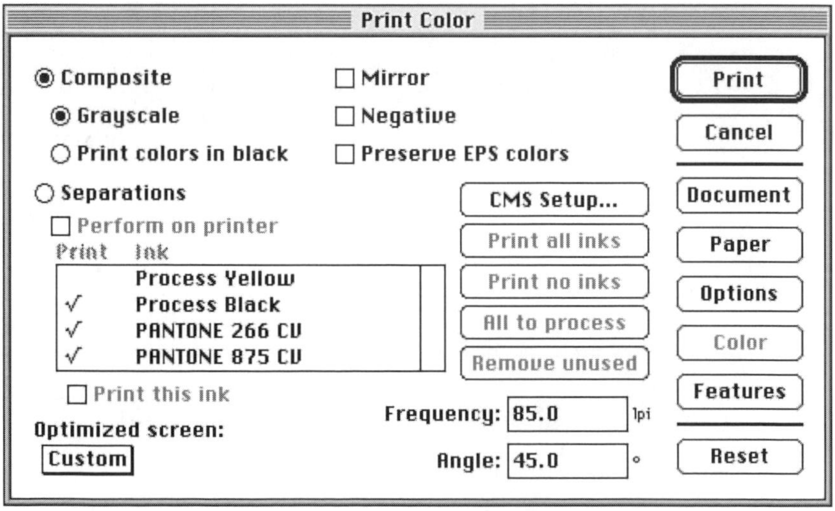

Figure 17.25

PageMaker's Print: Color dialog, set for comps.

Outputting Laser Seps From Quark

To open laser seps, follow these steps:

1. Open the file to be output.

2. Select Page Setup from the File menu.

3. Select the appropriate PPD file from the Printer Type pop-up menu.

4. Set your target halftone screen value.

5. If you need to scale your output for preflight, enter the value here. Otherwise, use the Tile function in the Print dialog.

6. Select Print from the File menu (see Figure 17.26).

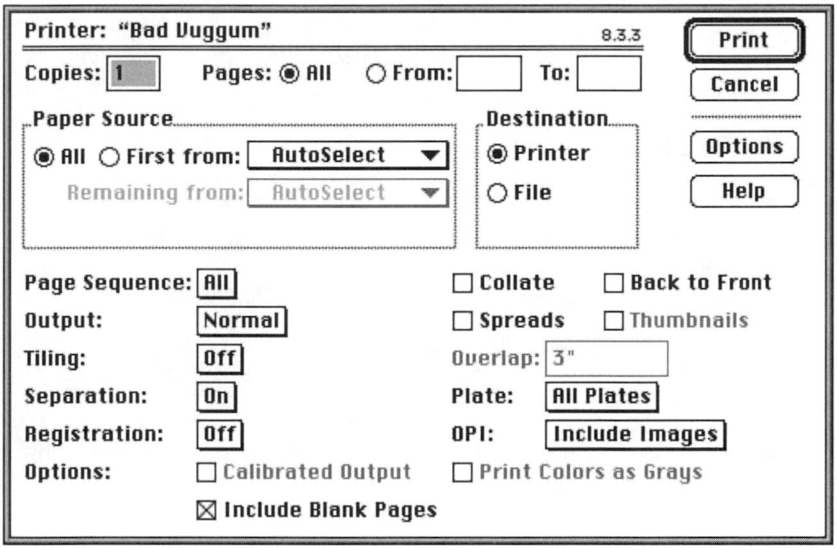

Figure 17.26

Quark's Print dialog, set for separations.

7. Select On in the Separation pop-up menu.

8. Choose an option from the Registration pop-up menu. This outputs plate names as well as placing crop and registration marks (remember to account for the larger print area required when placing these marks).

9. Notice that Quark only enables you to print one plate at a time or all plates at once. Quark also has an annoying tendency to print plates where there are none. When separating a file consisting of two PMS colors, for example, Quark also outputs an empty Black plate. This

only wastes a few sheets of paper when preflighting the file, but the extra pages become quite annoying and costly when output to film down the road. Many output specialists print one color at a time for spot-colored documents and print All Plates only for process files.

10. Turn on Include Blank Pages.

11. Click Print.

Outputting Laser Separations From PageMaker

To output laser separations, follow these steps:

1. Open the file to be output.

2. Select Print from the File menu.

3. After clicking the Document button, select the appropriate PPD from the Type pop-up menu.

4. Turn Blank Pages on.

5. After clicking the Paper button, set the scale value, if necessary. Otherwise, turn on tiling and set the Auto:overlap to .5 inches.

6. Under TIFF/Images, turn on Printer's Marks and Page Information.

7. Click the Option button. Under Graphics, select Optimized.

8. Under PostScript, turn Include PostScript Error Handler off.

9. After clicking the Color button, set the halftone screen in the Ruling field (see Figure 17.27).

10. Choose Separations.

11. Examine the inks printed in the scrolling field. Make sure only the colors of the document are checked.

12. Click print.

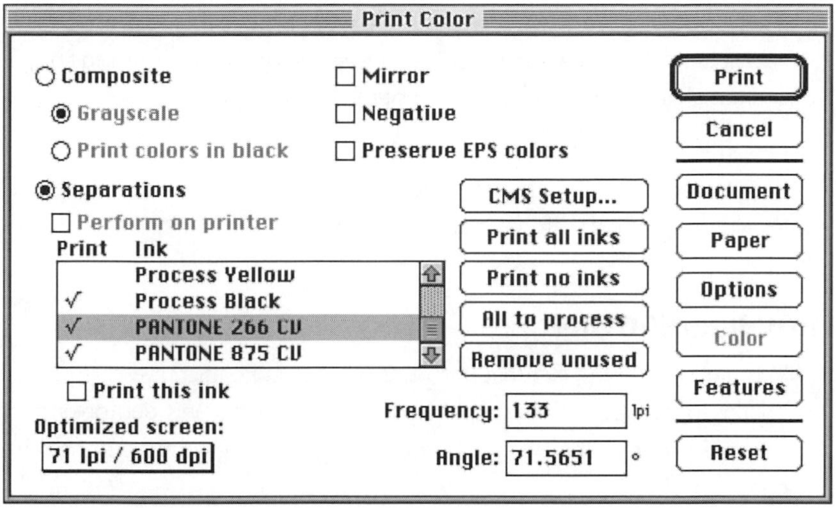

Figure 17.27

PageMaker's Print: Color dialog, set for separations.

Items to Check in Your Laser Seps

Check your separation proofs for the following:

◆ Unnecessary pages have been deleted from the file.

◆ Colors are defined and named correctly. Check for extra plates, spot colors printing as process (and vice versa), and duplicate colors.

◆ The proper number of plates are printed for each page.

◆ Bleed allowances are satisfactory, about an eighth of an inch.

◆ Crossover images appear in the appropriate places on the right pages.

◆ Traps specifications are accurate. This may require placing your proofs on a light table, registering them, and checking through a loupe.

◆ Every graphic output is at the appropriate resolution, with no jagged edges or pixelated images.

◆ Text did not reflow or default to Courier.

◆ Clipping paths clipped and that no standard silhouettes were placed on top of colored backgrounds.

◆ Pages are appropriately numbered.

If any changes have to be made based on the proofs, the best option is to output at least the new pages again. At the very least, if you're pressed for time and the changes are not extensive, note them on the latest proof.

Designers must hand these comps and seps over to the service provider with their transport media. The preflight proofs created by the output specialist should be included with the material sent back to the client.

TROUBLESHOOTING

We can't ignore the fact that problems will occur. PostScript errors halt the printing process; graphics output badly; clipping paths and duotones don't separate properly; the file appears to print, but nothing comes out the other end.

When you think about it, thousands of variables can cause a file to misprint. Never fear, though. A friend of ours once confided in us the Secret of PostScript Troubleshooting, and we share it with you now: "Learn everything there is to know," he said. "Then go fix the problem." Yeah, sure, we're a couple of wiseacres, telling you something like that. But there's more than a grain of truth here. There are two approaches to troubleshooting:

◆ Acquire a resource, like this book, that describes the most common prepress techniques, skill-set requirements, problems, and solutions. Use this as a basis for learning to fix (or better yet, *avoiding*) output-related problems.

◆ Work in the industry for years, make lots of costly mistakes, talk to hundreds of professionals, output thousands of files, and work hands-on with millions of problems. Keep detailed journals and strive to improve your knowledge base. Share what you know with others, never hoard your secrets, and always be ready to learn something new.

Your work will always consist of a combination of these approaches.

Documentation

Earlier, we suggested keeping detailed journals. We mean that in two different ways:

- Keep a personal record of problems you encounter. Describe all the variables, what was supposed to happen and didn't, and the ultimate solution. If you think you can remember all the myriad output problems you'll encounter in your head, you're wrong. There are too many.

- Keep a record of problems recurring in a client's work. Clients who continually commit the same file construction errors can be trained in those issues, making everyone's lives more pleasant.

Billing Practices

Fixing problems in a file that won't print takes time. For all intents and purposes, this is billable time and the industry standard hourly wage for this service runs between $70 and $125. Of course, no one likes a surprise charge appearing on their invoice, regardless of how life-saving the service might have been.

The only recourse a service provider has in successfully charging for file repair is the following:

- Announce your preflight requirements to all clients. Do this when they drop off jobs, have the sales staff explain it expressly to their accounts, send out mailers with all invoices, and announce it in your newsletter. Explain what the requirements are and why they need to be followed.

- Establish a firm date when the requirements go into effect.

- Offer all clients the option of supplying laser proofs or not, but make it expressly clear you are not responsible for wasted or unusable film.

- If any repairs need to be made to a file, contact the client immediately and explain the situation. Include a detailed description of the problem, how long it will take to repair, and how much it will cost. The client should either bring in a fresh file (with fresh preflight proofs) or agree to the charges.

♦ Because it's unlikely that every client will actually be asked to pay for these services, be careful over which charges get dropped and which will be billed. Be consistent. Do you drop only certain charges for certain people? Do you just offer a discount? Is only one person responsible for these decisions, or do the output specialists have autonomy? Should your sales staff handle the issue instead?

File repair services are every bit as tangible as graphic design or image acquisition. If we continue to do it for free, we may as well forget the entire preflight process and the tens of thousands of dollars in potential savings every year.

Another Preflight Option: Software

Many software packages are available that automate much of the preflight process.

The one we like is FlightCheck, from Markzware ($399). It's a stand-alone application that scans Quark, PageMaker, and FreeHand files for over 140 potential output problems. Just by dragging and dropping your document, FlightCheck examines and verifies colors, fonts, and images. If there are any problems such as missing fonts, dupe colors, or inappropriate graphic file formats, it creates its own report detailing the problems.

This program also checks for unused spot colors, fonts affected by typestyle menus, picture boxes with no background color, and a bunch of other potential nightmares. After you've checked the file, FlightCheck collects all of the document elements into a job folder for you (including the screen and printer fonts, which we like a lot).

A panacea? No, not really. Your files still need to be examined manually for design and press-specific issues and you still need to pore over your individual pages before giving the final OK. As far as automating the more mundane aspects of checking file construction, it's a useful tool to add to your collection.

Until recently, we thought of design, production, and output as the only three stages an electronic document journeys through before printing. A couple of years ago, the concept of preflighting arose to gel those three areas into one cohesive, predictable, and profitable industry: digital prepress.

Even though the preflight process seems to be most intensive in the moments just before outputting to film, the responsibility for proper output rests with everyone who ever lays their mitts on a file, regardless of the task they perform. Successful file output and printing is only possible if care is taken during every stage of a project to ensure that the appropriate decisions, values, and commands are applied to our work.

Outputting and checking our laser prints should be the easiest and most painless stage of a job. But if we do make an error somewhere along the line (and believe us, there are literally thousands that can be made) the guidelines in this chapter offer us hope of a safe oasis in a sea of risk and chaos. Only by placing our files to the ultimate test—printing, even if only to a laser printer—can we determine if the file will make it through the rest of the process.

C h a p t e r 18

PROOFING

A large client of a graphic design company ordered ten thousand brochures to launch a major marketing campaign. The client submitted the text for the brochure and transposed two of the digits in the phone number. The mistake passed five separate proofing stages used by the design firm because the client failed to read the copy carefully. No one noticed the mistake until the job, complete, sat in boxes at the mailing house. All ten thousand pieces went into the trash.

A retail clothing company prepared a new catalog to mark the coming change in season. Several articles of clothing were photographed, scanned, and saved to disk. The images went into the catalog. The scanning and color separation vendor urged the company to use scatter-proofs from actual films. In an attempt to save money, the client used direct-from digital proofs off an Iris Ink jet printer, which wasn't calibrated to the press. Because of the difference between the catalog colors and the actual clothing, the company lost several thousand dollars in returned clothing.

RESPONSIBILITY

Proofing a project is the responsibility of the designer. This person created the document and should know it better than anyone else. If proofing does not occur, the entire project suffers.

THE PURPOSE OF THE PROOF

The proof is designed to give you the opportunity to catch and correct mistakes in the project before expensive output and printing steps are taken. Since several things can go wrong, you need to use a variety of proofing techniques.

The project items we'll proof are:

◆ **Text.** Read the copy carefully to make sure it says what you want it to.

◆ **Composition and Layout.** Check for obvious omissions, changes, or additions to the document.

◆ **PostScript Code.** This essentially means preflighting the document.

◆ **Color Accuracy.** If the color of the images in your project are remotely critical, use color proofs to check.

◆ **Press Sheets.** After the press operator gets the color to come up, you want to be on hand to check for any problems with the final pieces on-press.

Each of these proofs require slightly different methods, and the wrong proofing method can be worse than none at all. If you get work back from the press expecting it to be flawless because of an inappropriate proof, you could be in for some nasty surprises.

Proofing Text

Long before committing yourself to a job by outputting it to film, make sure the text says what you want it to.

Spelling, Grammar, and Readability

Proofing text hasn't really changed all that much since the first days of printing. Many of the same methods are employed to ensure the absence of typos, spelling mistakes, and poor grammar.

Here are some ways to prevent such problems:

1. **Spell check.** Most word processors have one and it will take you a good bit the way there, but don't treat it like the only editing necessary. It *will* catch incorrectly spelled words, but it *can't* prevent usage problems.

2. **Print it out.** Seeing the ink (or toner) on paper enables you to look at the words differently. Plus, any mistakes can be written as edits for you or others to correct.

3. **Sleep on it.** If you reread the text right after you finish composing it, you'll have real difficulty spotting anything wrong, much less subtle mistakes like an "e.g." in place of an "i.e."

4. **Read it aloud.** Force yourself to read each word you see as it is written. It's too easy to read in skim mode, which enables your brain to edit the text on the fly. Since you know what the text should say, your brain paraphrases as you read. Don't let it.

5. **Have someone else read it.** If you wrote it, you know what it is, and what it's supposed to be. It is very difficult for you to spot differences between what *is* and what *should be*.

A single mistake is enough to discredit the piece for the reader. No matter how well the document is designed, spelling and grammatical errors, once spotted, become the focus of piece. At worst they can cost money, customers, and clients.

Revisions

After each revision, make sure that your changes are applied to all aspects of the project. Make sure that changes to a text file make it to the page layout. The blessing and bane of working on a computer is the capability to create many versions of the same thing. Develop a system for incorporating revisions and keeping track of changes. It may be useful to save earlier versions of a document, but make sure these are stored in an area where they don't make it back into the production flow. Unrevised versions make it to the printer all too often.

Never use the word "final" in a title. This guarantees you will be have to redo the file and your only option will be to title the file "final final" and then "REALLY final final." It is much more useful to include the date and time which the file was last saved.

PROOFING COMPOSITION AND LAYOUT

Graphic design is an extremely subjective business. The only way to know if your client is happy with a project is to show it them. The composition/layout proof is your way to communicate with the people paying for the job.

The proof itself is a mock-up of the project that enables the client to see the job before committing to the design. The closer you can come to making the proof look like the final output, the better the client is able to visualize what it will look like. This will avoid confusion and disappointment.

- ◆ **Color.** If the document uses color, use a color printer to create the mock-up.

- ◆ **Duplexing.** If it's a double-sided project and you can't print on both sides of the paper, tape the two pieces together to create a double-sided proof.

- ◆ **Folding.** Fold the mock-up to match the folds in the real job.

- ◆ **Binding.** If the project will be bound, use staples to simulate the binding.

- ◆ **Printer's spreads.** To simulate the pages in a book, re-order the pages using the pages using the document layout (for QuarkXPress, see Figure 18.1) or the Build Booklet addition (for PageMaker, see Figure 18.2). Then print the document out so that when it's folded and bound together, the correct pages lay side by side.

Show it to the client and get approval in the form of a signature before you commit the job to print. If the client doesn't accept the project as is, make the requested changes.

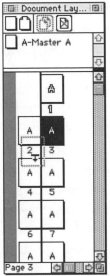

Figure 18.1

Quark's document layout enables you to move pages around.

Document Lay...

A-Master A

Page 3

Figure 18.2

PageMaker's Build Booklet command sorts your pages for you (refer to the PageMaker manual for instructions on its use).

Utilities   Layout   Type   Element   Arrange   Window

PageMaker Plug-ins ▶   Build Booklet...
                        Create Color Library...
Find...   ⌘F   Drop Cap...
Find Next   ⌘G   Keyline...
Change...   Pub Info...
Spelling...   ⌘L

Book...
Index Entry...   ⌘;
Sho
Cre
Cre

Tra

Build Booklet   OK

Publication: King Donnie:Desktop Folder:The book   Cancel
Spread size: 8.500 x 11.000 inches   Reset

 ▶ ☐ Page 1   Blank page   Layout: None ▼
   ☐ Page 2   Invert pages Pages per group: 4 ▼
   ☐ Page 3   Delete
   ☐ Page 4   Revert   ☐ Use creep
   ☐ Page 5   Total creep: 0.000 inches
   ☐ Page 6   Gutter space: 0.000 inches
 ┌ Messages ─────────────
 │ Page count: 30   ☒ Place guides in gutter
 │   ☒ Preserve page numbering
 └   ☐ Impose entire booklist

PROOFING THE POSTSCRIPT CODE

After you have decided the project is complete, you need to create a set of proofs to test the PostScript code. It is possible to create files from all five of the major publishing applications that aren't intended for output to a PostScript printing device. This means that the software has features that will cause problems if you try to print them to one. Files can also contain incorrect PostScript as a result of corruption or mistakes by the software.

Problems with PostScript waste time, output material, and, as a result, money. The whole idea behind proofing is to catch such problems long before film is burned, plates are made, or a press operator commits your work to ink on paper. In fact, you're trying to prevent the waste of expensive output material. These proofs use inexpensive paper instead of costly film.

If the PostScript code is so bad that it crashes the computer and printer, you'll be glad you proofed. The crash may not occur until you are several pages into the job, using time and output material. At very least, you'll know sooner when a problem needs correction.

Using a laser printer that "speaks" true PostScript gives you the ability to proof your files. Printing the document to paper, at less than a penny a page, is a good insurance policy against service bureau or print-house surcharges because of wasted materials.

If you are setting up a proofing printer, consider the following items:

- ◆ Use a true PostScript Level 2 printer, not one that emulates PostScript.

- ◆ If you create documents larger than letter-size, buy a tabloid (11×17) size printer. You'll tile fewer documents, get a more accurate representation of the printed file, and save yourself a lot of time.

- ◆ Use an Ethernet connection to the printer, rather than LocalTalk. If you create documents of any size or complexity, a significant bottleneck is removed with Ethernet. It will cost more now, but time is money. You'll save both with Ethernet.

- ◆ Use cheap, recycled paper for proofing. You're not going to give these to clients as finished products, so don't throw money into the recycling bin.

Composition Proofs

The first type of proof makes sure that nothing in the document is out of place or printing incorrectly.

Print the document:

◆ With separations off (for QuarkXPress, see Figure 18.3) or Composite on (for PageMaker, see Figure 18.4).

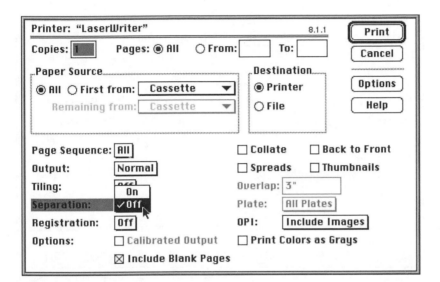

Figure 18.3

Quark's print dialog box with Separations off.

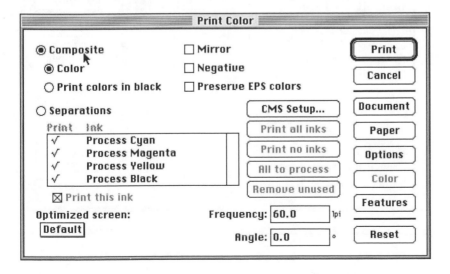

Figure 18.4

PageMaker's print dialog box with Composite on.

◆ Using gray to represent colors.

◆ Turn registration marks off (for Quark and PageMaker, see Figures 18.5 and 18.6) and printer's marks off (for PageMaker, see Figure 18.7).

Figure 18.5

Quark's print dialog box enables you to turn registration marks off.

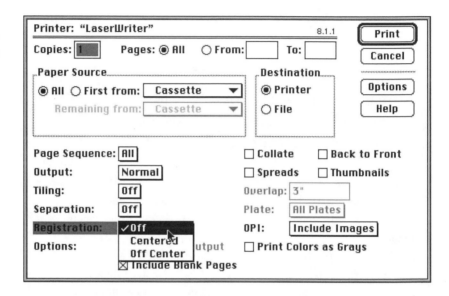

Figure 18.6

In PageMaker, the registration marks can be turned off in the print dialog box.

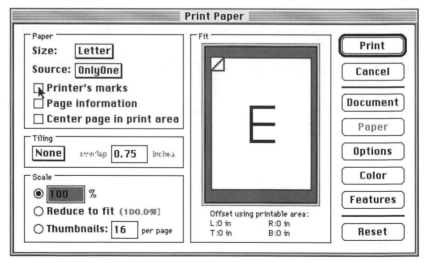

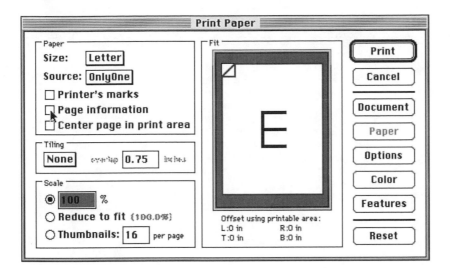

Figure 18.7

The print dialog box in Pagemaker enables you to turn printer's marks on.

After printing, check for:

◆ Lines and rules dropping out or appearing with jagged edges.

◆ Graphic elements dropping out, appearing at low resolution, or printing incorrectly.

◆ Text defaulting to Courier because of missing or corrupted fonts.

◆ Text requiring more or less space than onscreen. Pay close attention to this one. Check each story's end very closely to make sure some of the text hasn't flowed out of the text box (for Quark, see Figure 18.8) or block (for PageMaker, see Figure 18.9).

Color Separation Proofs

The second set of proofs is used to check that the colors are separating to the correct plates.

Print the document:

◆ With Separations on (for QuarkXPress, see Figure 18.10; for PageMaker, see Figure 18.11).

Figure 18.8

Quark's text box warns you if text has flowed beyond the box.

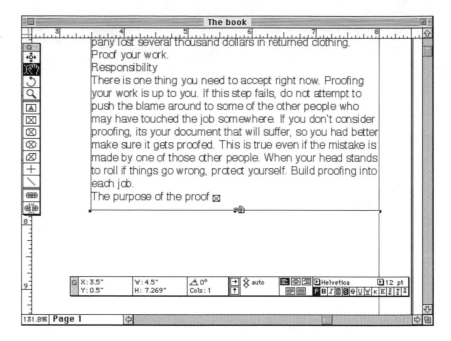

Figure 18.9

PageMaker's text block also warns you when text flows beyond the block.

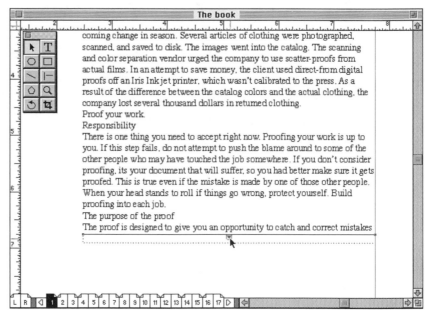

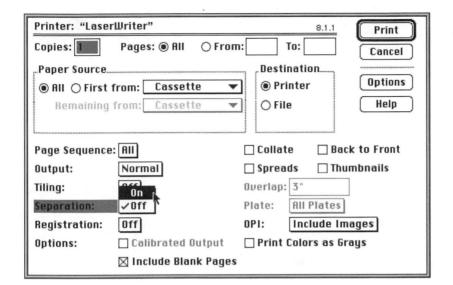

Figure 18.10

Quark's print dialog box with Separations on.

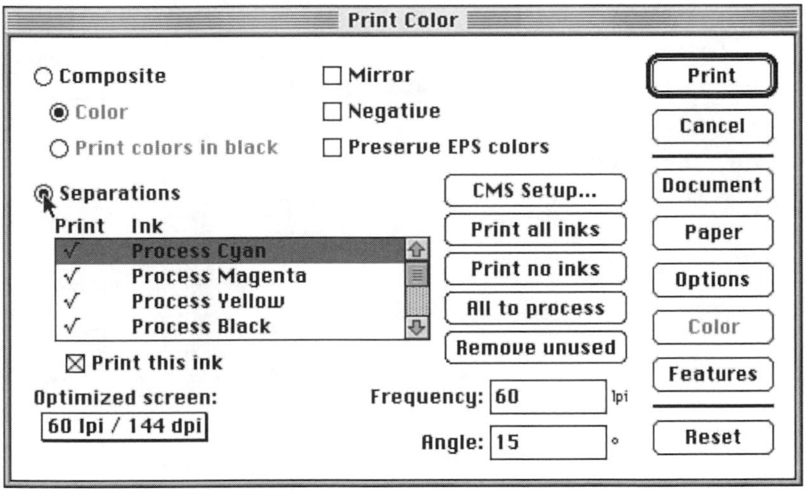

Figure 18.11

PageMaker's print dialog box with Separations on.

- ◆ Using gray to represent colors.
- ◆ Turn registration marks (for Quark and PageMaker, see Figure 18.12) and printer's marks on (for PageMaker, see Figure 18.13).

Figure 18.12

Quark's print dialog box enables you to turn registration marks on (use either Centered or Off Center).

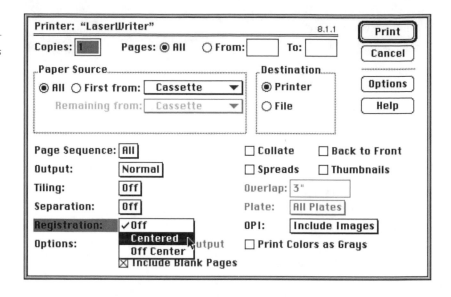

Figure 18.13

PageMaker's print dialog box enables you to turn registration and printer's marks on.

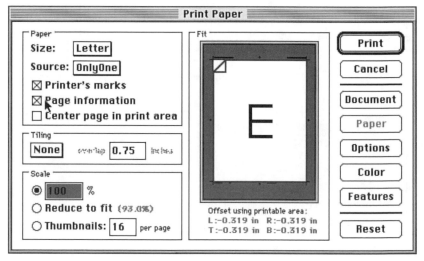

How to Use These Proofs

The first purpose of the proofs is to make sure what you have onscreen is what will end up on paper.

Mistakes to Check For Before Sending Files to the Vendor

◆ **Extra plate names.** If you have accidentally used a spot color somewhere in the document, you end up with extra plate color names—and extra pieces of paper, film, or plate material (see Figures 18.14 and 18.15).

◆ **Missing plate color names.** On the other hand, if you *want* colors, make sure they are listed and that they print.

◆ **Objects separating to the wrong plate.** If an object is colored incorrectly, it will be on the wrong plate. Keep a swatch book handy when you first begin proofing this way. Note an object's color and its CMYK makeup. For example, if an object is green, it should be on the cyan and yellow plates.

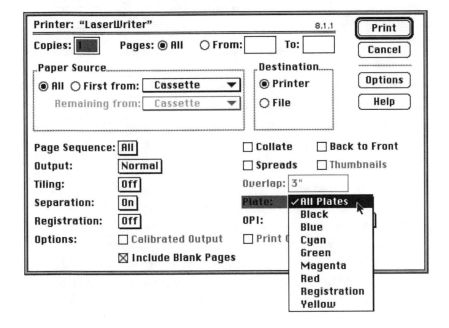

Figure 18.14

Quark's plate name pop up menu.

◆ **Spot colors separating.** Spot colors don't separate to different plates. If they do, you have accidentally replaced the spot color with a process simulation.

◆ **Colored objects on the black plate only.** Any object that uses color should separate to at least two plates (unless it's a spot color). If you failed to convert RGB images to CMYK, they only appear on the black plate.

Figure 18.15

PageMaker's plate name window.

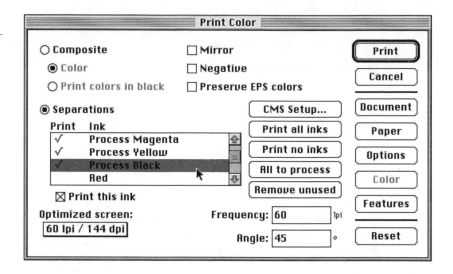

Submit the Proofs to the Output Vendor

If you're submitting the file for output, the proof is your way of proving the document to the output vendor. By printing the document to a PostScript device successfully, you are proving that it *can* print to a PostScript device. Sending the proofs along with the job is your way of communicating that fact.

With such complex technology, mistakes can happen that are hard to trace. Proofs can help you assign the responsibility for an error. If, for example, you send files to be output at a service bureau and they are output wrong, it is either because the file was prepared wrong or because the service personnel made errors while outputting the file. If it is the former, then you have to pay for the bad output. If it is the latter, then they will have to correct things at their cost. Without proofs, it is your word against the service bureau's, and this can cause hassle and cost money.

If you are in the business of outputting files, you need to collect proofs from clients. When you receive the files, print your own set of paper proofs and compare them page for page to the client-supplied proofs. If they match the client's, then you have proof that the file was output properly. This can save so much time and hassle that it may be cost-effective for you to offer a discount to clients who provide proofs with their digital files.

Either way, make sure all sets are created from the final revision of the document. If any changes are made, reprint the proofs. Any changes can have unexpected effects on the document, causing it not to print correctly. If you submit proofs, submit proofs of the final document. If you accept them, accept only final proofs.

PROOFING THE FILM

The paper proofs are a way to test the PostScript before committing the job to a more expensive output device. It works because PostScript is PostScript, whether it's used on paper, film, plate material, or whatever. In theory, no differences exist between the film and the paper proofs. Theories usually fall. To keep this one from falling on you, have contact proofs made. A contact proof—also called a blue-line proof—is a positive representation of your film negatives, designed to make the information on the film easier to read.

These are made by exposing the film to photo-sensitive paper and then developing the paper. Often this means running it through the same machine that developed the film. Compare the contacts to the paper (or the file onscreen) to make sure the output device hasn't.

If the project is a four-color job and you don't want to pay for the contact proofs, at least examine the films on a light table.

What To Check For

If you are responsible for creating the films used to burn plates, you need make sure that the film you create doesn't introduce problems into the work. For the most part, keeping the imagesetter calibrated and clean ensures the film's usefulness, but some things to check regularly are as follows:

> ### What Good Are Contacts?
>
> First, the films need to be proofed directly. You never know how the difference between the paper printer and a film output device will affect your job. Seeing the films as contacts enable you to check.
>
> There is another use for contacts, though. If you don't get much call for positive output onto paper, you can provide this service without keeping extra paper output material on hand. Print negative film, create contacts, and sell them as positives.

- ◆ **Exposure.** If the imagesetter overexposes film, it darkens halftones, thickens lines, and fattens type. If it underexposes, it lightens halftones, thins lines and type, and softens edges.

- ◆ **Developing.** Poorly developed film also affects the quality the images.

- ◆ **Scratches.** Poorly handled films can get scratched.

- ◆ **Smudges or blurs.** as a result of poorly developed areas of the film.

- ◆ **Alignment.** Don't check to see if the contacts were made with the films in register, but to see if the films *can be* registered.

- ◆ **Font problems.** You can never check this enough. Look for Courier, odd spacing between characters in a line, and lines in a paragraph.

- ◆ **Missing or added elements.** Make sure nothing has been dropped or added to the pages on film.

- ◆ **Anything unusual.** Occasionally, the difference in the RIP between the laser printer and the imagesetter leads to PostScript problems. Look for any oddities. Remember that the contact is exactly how the piece will be printed, only in one color. This is your chance to find the mistakes before it gets printed.

Checking for these problems requires knowledge about your imagesetter, developing system, and the film used. You also need a film densitometer to measure the results you get from your imagesetter. For more information regarding the care and feeding of film, see Chapter 19, "Output."

Non-film Output

Increasingly, the final output is something other than lithographic film for use in burning press plates. For a complete discussion of output options, see Chapter 19.

For non-film output, you either need to trust the laser proof or use the first piece of actual output as the proof. In either case, the final output device should be tested against a paper printer to make sure that the results match.

PROOFING FOR COLOR

Cyan, magenta, yellow, and black are the only four colors of ink used to represent all colors in a four color process printing job. Theoretically, all the colors in the visible spectrum can be created using cyan, magenta, and yellow. The inks used in four color presses, however, are so impure that it is necessary to add black to the mix to print anything with any semblance of realism. Even with the addition of black, CMYK printing can only capture 3,000 to 4,000 different colors. An additional challenge is that process printing needs to create the illusion of continuous tone using varying sized spots of CMYK inks.

Compare the small range of colors in CMYK process printing to a color monitor that can display 16.7 million different colors. Colors on a color monitor are also restricted by the fact that they are being created by pixels, squares of a fixed size, shape, and quantity.

Photographic film, on the other hand, uses chemicals that, when exposed to light, become colored. Photographs have the ability to represent more color variety than ink-on-paper printing. The unit size of color for photographs is at the molecular level, while for CMYK it is measured in hundredths of an inch, and for monitors it is measured in seventy-seconds of an inch.

Finally, monitors are transmissive, that is, the images are generated by light, while photographs and printed pieces are reflective. We see them by light reflecting off the paper.

Simply put, print, photographs, and monitors are physically different and therefore it is physically impossible for them ever to match each other precisely. The final printed piece may look dramatically different from the original photograph (or item) that it is representing. If the color of the printed document has to match the original very closely, you need to know before you see the press sheets that the CMYK representation of your images is accurate enough for your needs. You need to proof the color images.

Color Proofing Methods

Proofing an image for color can be done in several ways. Some are more accurate than others, but they are all only attempts to emulate the printing process. They may never match exactly, so don't expect them to. Also, expect more accuracy to cost more money. Your particular needs may make the cost worth it, and if so, spend the money.

The methods are:

◆ **A calibrated workstation.** The least accurate over the long run, it isn't necessarily the least expensive either.

◆ **A color printer.** These run the gamut from $200 ink jet printers all the way up to $100,000 composite color printers. The accuracy of the device depends on the ability of the device and the willingness of the operator to keep it calibrated.

◆ **Laminate proofing.** Produced from actual films, this type of proofing is usually very accurate. It's also expensive.

◆ **Wet proofing.** Essentially, wet proofing uses a little, slow printing press to create an actual press sheet. It's very accurate, very expensive, and not very common any more.

◆ **The press sheet.** This is the only completely accurate proofing tool. In fact, the press sheet is what we are trying to proof to. However, its cost makes it an unpopular proofing method at best.

A Calibrated Workstation

One purpose for using proofing is related to the problem with your workstation. The monitor uses a Red, Green, and Blue (RGB) transmitted light to show your graphic image onscreen. The RGB color space is inherently different from the CMYK reflective color space used for printing. It is physically impossible to represent the CMYK color space accurately on an RGB monitor. Through proper color calibration, however, it is possible to come close.

The Need for a Calibrated Workstation

You can set up your system to more accurately represent the files you use. Should you set up your system this way? It depends on what you do.

You should if:

◆ You offer scanning services of any kind. Your clients will demand color accuracy, which will require you to correct the color of the scans. It is impossible to do so without a calibrated system.

◆ You are offering final output from color printers. The system saves you money by enabling you to calibrate to your output devices.

◆ You have only medium-accurate color needs and want to skip some of the following proofing methods in favor of speed and cost savings.

♦ You produce files that are difficult or impossible to proof using other methods, as screen printers and people do who print with inks other than CMYK.

♦ Completely closed-loop shops. If your files go from start to finish entirely in-house, you can and should calibrate your system from the output device back to the workstation.

Creating a Calibrated Workstation

Setting a calibrated workstation requires five basic things:

♦ **A monitor, monitor cup, and monitor card combination.** These work together to read color information from a file, interpret it, convert it to RGB, and represent it onscreen. The cup reads a target image and feeds back to the card the values it sees. If they are not correct for the target image, adjustments are made.

♦ **Software.** The card and monitor also need to be adjusted to match a given output device. Since each type of output device prints colors a little differently, a calibrated system must be set up to represent the RGB colors to more accurately emulate the various types of output you use. At very least, it must be set to match S.W.O.P. standards.

♦ **A regular routine for maintaining the calibration.** Monitors wear out, the temperature shifts, and any number of other conditions change to affect the way the monitor shows you color. This requires you to re-calibrate. The calibration system directs you in this effort.

♦ **A color balanced room.** The color of the light and objects in the room affects how colors are perceived. Walls should be a neutral gray and nothing should be nothing on them. The lighting should also be from color balanced lights, available from photography stores.

♦ **A constant light source.** A 5000K light box is a must for a calibrated system. The light that shines on an original affects how you perceive it. If you make corrections to it while viewing it under non-constant conditions, you'll have a difficult time proofing your file to match the original. Most professional photographic supply stores can get one for you.

Using Onscreen Proofing

After you set up such a system, how do you put it to use? Providing you keep things calibrated as instructed by the software/hardware combination, you can use the monitor as a way to pre-approve files that will be printed. Keep in mind you'll discover slight differences between what you see and what ends up on paper. If the difference is small enough for to live with, your system will work.

The longer you use such a system, the better you'll be able to use it. At very least, the system will keep your monitor consistent, so you'll be able to predict how a file will look when printed—even if it isn't exactly like the image onscreen.

A Color Printer

Using a color printer is an attractive option for proofing because it can be far more accurate than onscreen proofing, yet less expensive than laminate proofing. For those who use printing presses that need no film, color printer proofing is a must. However, not all color printers serve the purpose, so using a color printer as a proofing device requires some consideration.

Choosing a Printer

The strategy behind a color printer as a proofing device is simple. Set the printer up to match the final output device. This means that the printer must:

♦ Use CMYK inks.

♦ Be able to be calibrated.

♦ Give consistent color output.

♦ Handle paper sizes large enough to represent your work.

♦ Have the capability to emulate the characteristics of the final output device.

The variety of color printers on the market is wide. Choosing one to meet your needs means weighing the cost of the device against its features. Aside from the required features of such a printer, some features make the device more desirable:

♦ **Ease of calibration.** The easier the device is to calibrate, the smoother your workflow is.

◆ **Flexible calibration.** If the device will be proofing to more than one single output instance, say, three different printing presses, it must be able to calibrate to each of those options. More importantly, though it must be able to print to each output option quickly.

◆ **Paper type.** Many printers use special paper. This increases costs and decreases the similarity of the printer's output to the final output. If the proofing paper is glossy, for example, it won't accurately portray glossy paper.

◆ **Speed.** The faster the printer can print, the faster you'll get your proofs made.

◆ **Ease of use.** Ideally, the proofing printer should be accessed as easily as a regular paper printer.

Setting Up a Proofing Printer

After you decide on a printer to use, you'll need to set it up for your needs. Before you begin, you'll want some tools on hand:

◆ **An understanding of color.** Calibrating the system requires an understanding of the complexities of adjusting color in CMYK color space.

◆ **A target image.** When you calibrate your printer, you'll need an image to help you. The target image must be photographic (printed images will not work for this purpose). Ideally, it should use a variety of colors representing the spectrum available from CMYK inks, areas of detail, and objects that are familiar enough that you know what color they should be (fruit, grass, and skies are all good candidates).

Note: Kodak makes a color photographic target, called a Q-60, that is an excellent target image. You can get one through most professional photography supply stores.

◆ **A scan of the target image.** If you have scanning and correcting capabilities, scan an image, correct it, and save it. If not, pay to have this done. It will become the image file you use for proofing calibration.

- **A Densitometer.** This a color measurement device that can read CYMK percentages from a colored object on paper. They are fairly expensive yet necessary when evaluating the output from a color printer's results.

- **A printing press.** Since you are targeting to an output device, you'll need to make arrangements to run the target file on press.

Calibrating the Printer

With tools in hand, here's what to do:

1. Obtain or make a scan of the target image.

2. Correct it or have it corrected for accurate color.

3. Have the file printed on the printing press or presses you typically use.

4. Print the image from your proofing printer.

5. Use your eyes to note any glaring color differences.

6. Use the densitometer to check the color areas to see how closely they match and how much they differ.

7. Based on comparisons between the two, make adjustments to the device so its output matches the final output's results. This is usually accomplished by applying software adjustment to the computer controller of the device.

8. Save the calibration settings as a profile for the particular press you used in the comparison.

9. If you are calibrating to different output devices, complete the previous steps for each.

Although quick to describe, this process may take some time. If you set up a proofing printer, build in enough time to do it right.

Using the Proofs

These proofs enable you to pre-approve the color of an image. If you did the scanning, use the proof to assess the need for more color correction. After you are comfortable with the image, show the client. They will either sign off on it or return it for more correction.

After the file has been accepted, the proof goes to the press for the press operator to use while making the print run ready. The proof becomes the standard by which the color off the printing press is judged. Once the proof is accepted as the correct color for the image, the press can target to it.

Drawbacks

A color printer proofing system is not for everyone. Some of the drawbacks to the system are:

◆ They can't proof for trapping well if at all.

◆ Keeping them calibrated to match true press conditions is often time-consuming.

◆ You may still need to proof films directly to check for film-specific problems (see "Proofing the Film" earlier in this section).

◆ Typically, speed and accuracy oppose each other. The IRIS inkjet, which is considered good enough to use for contract proofs in situations where there is no film output, is very slow. The Tektronics Phaser, a relatively fast machine, has trouble maintaining constant, accurate color.

◆ Color printers capable of giving the kind of output needed for this job are very expensive. The prices start in the tens of thousands of dollars.

◆ The materials for accurate-color printers are not cheap either. After adding up ink or toner costs, special paper costs, and monthly lease payments, the cost per proof becomes quite high.

When you sit down to decide whether a color proofing printer is worthwhile, be sure to factor in all associated costs. Don't rely on a sales representative to give you an accurate picture of those costs either. Find out who else is using the device you are examining and ask them about unexpected costs, accuracy, and down-time. With the costs in hand, find out what it would cost to outsource those proofs to someone who already owns a proofing system. If it would take more than three or four years to pay for itself, you may be better off using a vendor.

Overlays

Overlay proofs use acetate sheets to represent the four ink colors. Separations are printed onto the sheets in their color (cyan, magenta, yellow, and black) and are laid onto a white board.

The acetate is created by either printing directly to the acetate from a color printer or by exposing a colored acetate sheet to the film. The light hardens the color to the acetate and the remainder is washed off.

Overlays are not as accurate as the laminate proof and more cumbersome than the color printer output.

Using Overlays

If you decide to use overlays, they are the same as any other proofs. Compare the components of the document and the color. Keep in mind that the color is not very accurate so if your color needs are critical, don't rely on this kind of proof.

Laminate Proofs from Film

With all of the output options available, there is still a preference for acetate film negatives. These are used to create plates for printing (see Chapter 19 for more information about film output). Once these films are created the *laminate proofing method*—also called pressmatches, AGFA proofs, and Enco proofs—is an excellent method for examining the color of an image.

How It Works

The proofing system works by emulating the actual printing process:

1. **Select a Substrate.** The substrate is the paper backing used to build the proof. The paper can be glossy or matte, depending on the paper used for the printed piece. Coated stock papers are best emulated by glossy proofs and uncoated papers.

2. **Lamination.** To simulate the printing of CMYK inks, gel lamination is used. The ink color is a thin layer of translucent gel fused to the substrate with a heat press. Once fused, it is ready for the next step.

3. **Exposure.** The gel laminate, when exposed to ultraviolet (UV) light, hardens and binds to the substrate. The films are negatives (in most

cases), so the film is laid over the laminate/substrate combination and the whole thing is exposed to UV light. The exposed film allows the light to pass through the image areas in the film onto the laminate, hardening it.

4. **Rinse and Repeat.** By running the exposed laminate/substrate through a chemical bath, the unexposed laminate gel is washed off. This process is repeated for each of the four colors used in four-color process printing. The laminate proof is built up one color at a time until all four are down.

Setting Up a System

This is not a simple system to create. You're not going to go down to a hardware store, pick up the pieces you need, and set this system up. Most laminate proofing systems are integrated, in that you purchase the components together, and you spend a good deal of money to do so.

Most people don't do this. This type of proofing system, because of its complexity and cost, is the domain of the color separation house, film output service bureau, or print shop. If your needs for color proofing are very high, it might be cost-effective to bring such a system in-house. An analysis of all the costs, not just of the machine and materials, but of having a dedicated staff to use, calibrate and maintain such a system.

If you use the services of a vendor, for print, film output, or color scanning anyway, laminate proofs are usually a part of the package. At very least, you should have the option of buying them.

Using Laminate Proofs

Laminate proofs have two basic uses:

◆ **Color correction.** The laminate proofs are a quick, easy, and inexpensive way to see how the digital data looks as "ink" on paper. The proofs allow the correction staff to match the file to the original.

◆ **Targeting the press.** The press operator uses the laminate proofs to match color. The operator needs something to determine the accuracy of the colors in the press sheets. The laminate proofs are that something.

For more about using these proofs, see the upcoming section, "Checking a Proof."

Wet Proofing

Wet proofing, or machine proofing, is the closest thing to printing. It uses film, plates, and a printing machine that emulates a press, complete with ink and paper. The operator uses your actual films to burn a set of plates and hangs them on the machine. The sheets are hand-fed to printer and the result is a press sheet that very closely resembles the sheets that will come from the real press.

The advantage to the wet proof is its accuracy. Using the paper and ink that you will use for the real press run, you get to see what the press sheet will look like. The disadvantage is the cost and time involved. However, if your needs are for super accuracy before committing to a very high-volume run, you may want to consider this option.

CHECKING A PROOF

You're going to use the color proofs in two situations. First, they are a way of knowing what the colors in the digital file will look like as ink on paper. This proofing uses the scatter or random proof. Second, the press operator is going to use the final proofs to match the color on press. He or she can usually adjust the press to affect the colors in the printed piece. Each uses a different type of printed proof. For this, you'll want to use page proofs.

Scatter Proofs

Scatters are pages with nothing but color images on them. They enable you to proof images without wasting time and energy by removing text and other elements that needn't be printed until the final proofs.

Scatters are used first to correct the file after its initial creation. For example, scanners often do a less than adequate job of capturing the color of a photograph. This requires a color correction specialist to adjust the colors in Photoshop. Once this has been done, the file is proofed along with others in the project. The proofs may reveal the need for further correction or show that the file is acceptable.

You should have scatter proofs made of the following:

- **Scans.** You want to see how the scanner and color corrector have captured the original photograph.

- **Pixel-based computer art.** Since this artwork uses continuous-tone color, you can't really rely on the monitor to know how this will look on paper.

- **Blends, vignettes, or degradés.** Stair stepping is impossible to proof onscreen, so proof these.

- **Type on a screened background.** The screening does more than you might expect to hide type or make it difficult to read.

In short, you should have scatter proofs made any time you have multiple images in a document where getting the right color is critical. Anything you are unsure of should be examined to see how it will look as ink on paper.

It is important to pay particular attention to the scatters because this is your chance to affect the outcome before the press deadline looms too near. If you wait until the next set of proofs, the page proofs, are made you'll be too late. Some of the changes you'll want to make can be very time consuming, especially if you need to have an original rescanned or even re-photographed. Consider the scatters very thoroughly.

Look for:

- **Colors** in the image that don't match the original photograph. Pay particular attention to skin tones, memory color objects (grass, skies, tomatoes), and anything that is the focus of the image because of its color.

- **Contrast** or a tonal range that is either flat or exaggerated.

- **Burned out (totally white) highlights** that contain too little or no detail.

- **Plugged up (totally black) shadows** causing a loss of discernible detail in dark areas.

- **Poor detail** or blurriness, either from the initial scan or as a result of the color and tone adjustments.

- **Alignment problems** seen when an object has fringes, yet the registration marks do not.

- **Artifacts** from manipulations, such as fringes around composites, montages, or retouching work.

- **Moiré** or unwanted patterns in images such as screen doors, striped shirts, and grids of dots. Moiré can also be the result of scanning a printed image instead of a photographic image or the use of incorrect screen angles when printing films.

- **Stair stepping** (non-continuous color variations) in blends, vignettes, or degradés.

- **Reversed images** resulting from an upside down or backwards scan.

- **Unwanted elements** in the image that detract from the focus of the scan.

When the images have been corrected and accepted, they'll go back into the production cycle for placement and layout. Once the document is complete and ready for printing, a final set of proofs are required, the page proofs.

Page Proofs

Page proofs are designed to give you one last opportunity to check your project for costly mistakes before the job goes to press. They also serve as the target for the press operator, so make sure they are correct.

The page proofs contain all of the elements on a given page as they appear on the printed piece. Text, graphics, page numbers, and anything else in your document are included there. In fact, if you were to trim these proofs, staple the pages together, and view it beside the finished piece, you should see no appreciable differences.

Most of the time, these come from the actual films that are used to burn plates. As such, these proofs should not come from a color printer because the color printer can't show you some of the problems you'll need to check.

If the final output is plate material, you need to check the actual press sheets as if they were page proofs. This introduces two dangerous aspects to the world of direct from digital printing (See Chapter 19 for more information on digital printing). The first is that you must build extra time into the press check to look at the sheet carefully enough. The second aspect is the responsibility involved with setting up a file correctly in the first place. If you keep making the same mistakes that require reworking, you'll be out of a job quickly. The reworking costs for digital printing are enormous if you don't find the mistakes until the press check.

In addition to the things you looked for in the scatter proof, (which you'll want to double check on the page proofs), you need to look for:

- **Trim lines** or cut lines that tell the printer where to cut the press sheet.

- **Tints** that are mottled or uneven.

- **Colors** that shift from page to page. Make sure they indicate the correct cut location.

- **Bleeds** which are a necessity when an image buts up to the edge of the page. The image actually needs to bleed beyond the cut lines, usually by about 1/8 of an inch.

- **Trapping** (or the lack thereof) seen by white fringes of blank paper between two supposedly touching objects.

- **Pagination** to be correct and in the correct order.

- **Crossover** elements need to line up when the pages are aligned.

After you are comfortable with the page proofs, pack them up and send them to the press with the films.

Marking a Proof

Examining a proof is half of the battle. The next step is to tell someone what to fix and how.

Describe the Faults

When you examine a proof and find a problem, you need to feed that information to someone so that the appropriate changes can be made in as few a set of steps as possible. This means that you need to be descriptive in your markings. Leave nothing up to chance.

- Use clear, concise instructions.

- Circle the particular element in question.

- Use cyan, magenta, yellow, and black when describing color. When something is "too green," ask for the removal of yellow or cyan.

- Be specific. Instead of using terms like warm or cool, describe the problem with the color.

- Define the difference between what you see and what you want to see, instead of referring to the original (for example, "The detail is missing in the mountains" versus "See the transparency").

- Avoid words like improve, brighten, and correct unless you provide the specifics about the improvement, brightening, and correction.

- Use plus (+) and minus (-) signs to indicate the increase or decrease of the CMYK inks.

SPOT COLORS

The previous color proofing information focused heavily on process inks. This is because CMYK is a limited color space trying to represent the entire world of color. You have to be careful and persistent to get the colors of your images to look real when using such a limited system.

Spot colors are a bit different. Because they are a constant color, you won't really need to scrutinize them to see if they are correct. It is highly recommended that you always check the press sheet to make sure the color looks the way you expect it to. If not, the printer may have used the wrong ink or have old, expired ink. You'll need, however, to proof some things ahead of time:

- **Color mixes.** When you use two spot colors together, you may want to see them interact. This doesn't require extensive or expensive proofing. A smear of each ink side by side might do the trick.

- **Duotones, Tritones, and Quadtones.** These can be very difficult to get right. You definitely want to proof these to a very accurate system.

◆ **Trapping.** Spot colors, unlike process colors, never have a bridge between objects of different colors. This increases, significantly, the need to proof for traps.

Color printers rarely offer true spot color proofing. They usually create a process simulation of the spot color using the CMYK inks they use for process proofing. Because the difference between a process simulation and a spot color varies wildly, color printers are poor proofing systems for spot color.

Most laminate proofing systems have spot laminates, but they are costly. Finding a vendor for the proofs may be also be difficult. If you need to visualize the file in its true colors, however, the effort and cost may be worth it.

Wet proofing, especially for Doutones, Tritones, and Quadtones is an attractive option if you want to really see the effect of the colors on your job.

THE PRESS PROOF

After the images have been approved, it's time to create a set of proofs for the press operator to use. Without some sense of the project's look, the press operator is in the dark about it. He or she can only guess what you expect to see during the press check. If your job uses accurate color, create a set of complete proofs, that is a laminate or color printer proof of each page as it should look. When the operator prepares the press for the run, these become the target.

THE PRESS CHECK

We've spent a lot of time getting files ready to go to this place called a press. The paper that comes off the press is expected to look a certain way, and you are ultimately responsible for that look. The only way to fulfill that responsibility is to go to the press and check the results. This is a given for process color work. One, two, or three color jobs should be checked unless the quality of the output is not an issue.

Color

This is your last opportunity to affect the color of your document. The hard copy proofs you made, whether from films or from a color printer, are your guide to what the images should look like on the final output. The press operator can affect the color of images by reducing or increasing the amount of ink given to a specific area of your printed page. Therefore, subtle color corrections are a part of this last, crucial step.

After the press operator gets the color to "come up," he or she adjusts the ink flow to the plates to match the proofs. Color is such a subjective thing, however, that you won't want to leave that step up to someone else, especially if accurate color is important to you.

Your part of the press check begins after the operator makes his or her adjustments. You now step in and examine the proofs and the press sheet. Approach the check with the following questions in mind:

◆ Ask yourself, what is it about the image on the proof that appeals to me?

◆ How does the image on the proof differ on the press sheet?

◆ Pay attention to the direction in which the sheet (or paper roll) is fed through the press.

◆ Examine the rest of the sheet to determine the effect changing one image might have on another. If you deplete cyan to "warm an image up," you might deplete it for a photograph of trees, causing them to look too yellow.

Specifically look for:

◆ **Contrast.** Poor tonal range because of too much or too little ink causes either flat or exaggerated contrast.

◆ **Tints.** These should be even, not uneven or mottled.

◆ **Colors.** Consistency from page to page is crucial.

◆ **Crossover elements.** These need to line up when the pages are aligned. If the element uses color, the color should be consistent.

◆ **Slurring.** This results from insufficient tack in the ink, causing unevenly shaped dots in the halftones or colors. This gives the images a soft or blurry look overall.

◆ **Picking.** If the ink is too tacky for the paper stock being used, it may pull up little pieces of the paper as the roller squashes it down. (You should have been warned in advance of this kind of problem.)

◆ **Smearing.** If the sheet or roll moves from side to side on its way through the printing press, it causes the image to smear. The results are blurry images and type.

◆ **More smearing.** Some inks dry very slowly and never quite set up correctly. These smear in the end user's hands. The cure for this is a clear coat of sealer, called a varnish. The salesperson should have warned you about this up front, but sometimes you won't know until the press check.

◆ **Hickeys.** If a speck of dust, a blob of ink, or a hunk of paper gets on the plate, it leaves a small spot on the press sheet.

◆ **Ghosting.** If the ink on a plate gets depleted because of heavy coverage in one area of the sheet, the result is a ghosted area on the press sheet.

◆ **Bleedthrough.** Some papers are too thin for heavy coverage on both sides. Look for the image on one side to show through to the other.

◆ **Misregistration.** Since more than one plate is used in jobs of more than one color, multiple plates need to deliver ink to the same relative location on the page. Look at the registration marks on the sides of the sheet.

◆ **Trapping.** If you produced the file, trapping was your responsibility. The print shop, however, might be able to help you out of a jam. Be prepared to pay for it.

After examining the press sheet, you either sign off on it or ask for adjustments. If you ask for adjustments, the operator will make them and run a few more sheets (usually around 25). The process continues until you are satisfied with the results. Once you sign off, the press runs at full speed cranking out the pages of your project. Some businesses have a person doing the press check for the entire length of the print job. This might seem excessive, but many factors can change print quality over time, such as temperature and humidity.

No matter how much time you invest on the press check, you need to have a working relationship with the printer. Don't be afraid to take your business elsewhere if the printer isn't willing to work with you.

Super Critical Color

If your color needs to stretch beyond the world of accuracy, you may need another approach. In the fashion industry, slight differences in the color of a catalog image and the real object results in tens of thousands of dollars lost in returned merchandise. In these cases, the actual items are often brought to the press, instead of relying on just a proof.

SUMMARY

As the world of digital publishing puts the power of the printed piece into your hands, your ability to communicate is improved. Along with that improvement comes the responsibility of getting it right. Everything from the text to the color of the images needs to be examined carefully to make sure you are saying what you want to.

To be sure you are, you need to proof the work you do long before you commit several hundred or thousand dollars to ink on paper. This isn't really a new concept, nor is it a smaller issue for those working in digital prepress. In fact, digital prepress, by offering a variety of proofing methods and strategies, moves the issue of proofing closer to the desktop. If you are producing digital files as a way to save money, you'll need to know which proofing method is best for you.

All along the way of proofing your work, you gather information. The why's and how's of the problems you are proofing become valuable information you must keep and use for future projects. The importance of a good logbook can't be stressed enough. Without one, you'll lose forever the information provided by the many experts involved with your work. Considering they can charge up to a thousand dollars an hour for this information as consultants, it is economically poor form to allow this information to vanish into the recesses of your memory. Write it down, save any proofs you can, and the whole proofing step will become quicker and more effective.

Finally, as you gather data, experience, and final pieces, you'll gain a better understanding of the things that stand between you and the perfectly printed piece.

Chapter

After you have spent the time it takes preparing a document, collecting the many pieces it uses, and have successfully proofed it, it's time to commit it to the world of many, many copies.

The world of output options is a big one. You no longer need to depend on the kindness of strangers to see your long hours of work result in a finished product. You can do it yourself. The question is, "should you?"

Yes and no. If you are a print shop, the answer is yes. If you are anything but a printer, the answer is…maybe. It depends on the quantity and quality of the pieces you need produced.

The following factors shape your decisions about an output choice. Each of these play a role in your decision about your work, who should produce it, and how:

- Number of pieces

- Quality

- Number of colors

- Types of images used

- Speed of delivery

- Finishing/binding needed

- Method of delivery (mail, hand, point of sale)

DO YOUR HOMEWORK

Before you can make these decisions, you need some information about your work. You must consider these well in advance of the output stage. If not, you will need to redo a lot of work to match the specs for your job. Plan for the output when you start. Know how you will have the work done, so you can prepare the files for that purpose the first time.

CHOOSING OUTPUT

If your work is going to be reproduced in any quantity, however, it must pass through an imagesetter to become lithographic film. There are many other options for the kind of output you can choose for your work. We discuss them at the end of this chapter. The majority of all printing, however, is done using lithographic film.

You no longer need to be a printer, a service bureau, or a millionaire to purchase a film output device. As they get faster and more accurate, imagesetters are also getting cheaper. More and more people are creating film themselves and sending it directly to the printer, where it gets processed for printing.

The more you can do to prepare the work for press electronically, the more saving you see from an in-house imagesetter. This includes stripping, imposition, trapping, and any other traditional prepress technique normally applied at the press.

Whether you output the film yourself, or if you leave the film output to others, a working knowledge about the film for the job, and what needs to happen to it for printing, gives you more control over the quality of the output. It can also save you money. Some of the work typically left to the people outputting the films can be brought in-house, as well as some of the money you spend having them do the work. You must weigh the cost of in-house production against farming the work out.

IMAGESETTERS

Imagesetter is a term used to describe an entire suite of tools and processes that output electronic data directly to lithographic film. This film is used in the printing process to expose the press plates that deliver the ink to the paper for printed documents. An imagesetter and its component parts used to be well out of reach to all but very large companies, but that is changing.

The reduction in the prices of imagesetters has lead more people to consider owning one. For a print shop, an imagesetter is a must. The costs associated with having someone else produce the film needed for plate making quickly justify the cost of a lease payment for an imagesetter and all the tools that go along with it.

More people are buying them, however, who aren't involved with the actual ink-on-paper printing phase. By producing films in-house, they hope to save prepress costs the same way they save stripping costs by doing the work electronically in the first place. The further along the job is in the production cycle when it goes to the printer, the lower the printing costs are.

To Buy Or Not To Buy?

Should you own an imagesetter? It depends on the quantity of output you do. You have no litmus test for making that decision, although there are certainly extremes. If you produce less than a file a week for printing, it is not cost-effective for you to own an imagesetter. You would spend more money on purchasing and maintaining the imagesetter, and training someone to operate it than you would spend if you bought the output from a service bureau. If you publish several magazines or catalogs a month, you should weigh the cost of the output from the service bureau against the cost of owning and operating an image setter. If you own a printing press, a film output device is a must.

The Necessary Components

The imagesetter alone is useless. All it can do is roll film through itself at a constant speed while shining very small dots of light on it as it rolls by. It can neither read nor interpret your electronic file without the help of a very powerful computer between itself and your workstation. After it has been told how to expose the film correctly, the film needs to be developed and fixed. The last step is to proof it. All of these steps require an investment in equipment or personnel.

The Imagesetting Device

For the imagesetter to work successfully, it has to do four things really well:

1. Keep Light Out

Stray light leaking into the exposure area causes the clear areas of the film to turn hazy, greatly affecting the quality of the plates created from them. Because many imagesetters aren't kept in dark rooms, the outside light needs to be kept out.

2. Move the Film at a Constant Speed

The size of the dot created by the laser is affected by the speed of the film moving through the device. The film doesn't actually stop for the laser to burn each row. The stopping and starting are too difficult to manage. Instead, the film moves slowly and constantly, while the laser scrolls across the width of the film. If the speed isn't accurate and constant, the image becomes distorted on the film.

3. Move the Laser at a Constant Rate

The laser mechanism moves across the width of the film and must do so at an accurate, constant rate. The laser blinks on and off to expose the film, and if the blinks are too far apart because the laser moved too quickly, or they overlap because the laser moved too slowly, the image on film is unusable.

4. Shine the Laser at a Constant Brightness

When the laser exposes film, it must do so just enough to make each dot appear at the correct size. To do so, the laser must shine just the right amount of light. Too much and each dot fattens, causing them to encroach on clear, image areas (see Figure 19.1). Too little and the image areas grow fatter, because the dots don't define them well enough.

Frankly, you shouldn't see any of these problems with a new imagesetter. An older device may start to show signs of age by exhibiting the symptoms of these things failing. All but the last problem requires the assistance of a trained technician. The level of the lasers brightness can usually be controlled by adjusting it in the RIP or on the imagesetter's control panel.

Figure 19.1

If the laser doesn't expose the film well enough, objects fatten.

A Raster Image Processor (RIP)

Your images need to be represented by the imagesetter's dots on film. This is the RIP's job. The RIP can either be a dedicated computer, with proprietary software built into it, or a software package loaded onto a regular production type PC. Either way, it receives a long series of instructions in PostScript that it must interpret. It then creates a page area in its mind that is broken into a grid of dots (see Figure 19.2). Images on your page are built up, dot by dot, from top to bottom and left to right, as a series of these small dots create the page, called a *raster*. This raster uses two basic methods for representing the many elements of your work.

Figure 19.2

Part of a page as an imagesetter thinks about it.

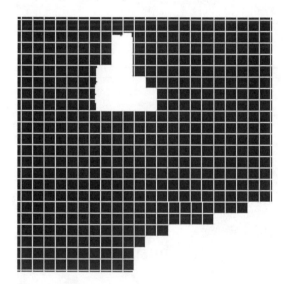

Lines, Text, and Other Solids

Solid objects are easy for the RIP to make. It simply collects dots together into a mass that looks like a letter, line, circle, or whatever solid object it is representing. As solid collections of dots (see Figure 19.3), the objects look smooth only when those dots are very small. Because the naked eye can't really tell the difference between two dots smaller than 1/1000 of an inch squared, dots going into solids need to be that small. As long as the imagesetter has a laser that can make a dot that small, solids look crisp and tight on film (see Figure 19.4).

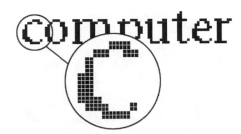

Figure 19.3

A solid object as an imagesetter thinks about it.

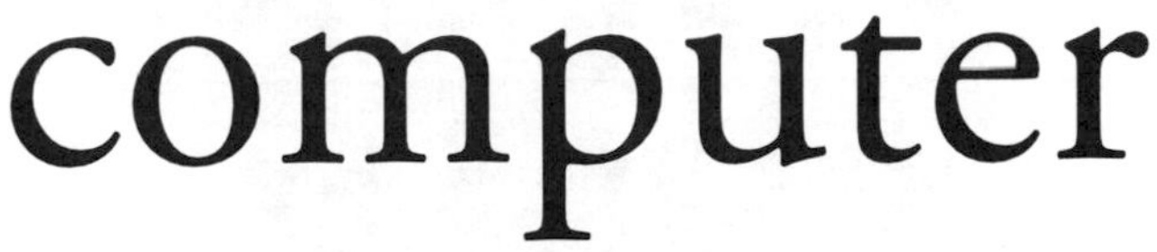

computer

Figure 19.4

When printed, the dots are small enough not to be seen.

Halftones and Screens

If it weren't for halftoning, imagesetters would be very inexpensive. Some paper laser printers get close to 1000 dpi. For lines, solids, and text, 1000 dpi is all you need for smooth edges on solids. Halftones are a different issue, and the problem with halftoning is the laser. In an imagesetter, the laser cannot readily change its size to make the variably sized spots needed for the process of halftoning or screening. Most imagesetters have a fixed dot size. The dot created by the imagesetter is called a machine dot and is determined by optics and the quality of the laser in the device.

To create the variably sized spots in a halftone, it has to create them as collections of the very small machine dots. An imagesetter's dots must be very small to be able to create spots of varying size within halftone cells at extremely high line screen rulings (see Figure 19.5). This requires an imagesetter to have very small machine dots indeed.

Figure 19.5

The halftone spot is created from a collection of very small machine dots.

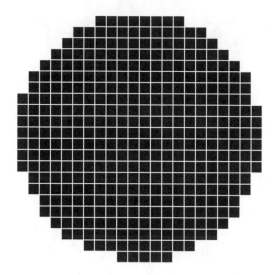

Consider this: an imagesetter capable of achieving 3600 dots per inch of resolution must be willing to burn 1,112,760,000 little dots to image an 8 ¹/₂×11 sized page. The RIP has to create this raster and store it, so it can tell the imagesetter which of those dots gets burned and which gets ignored. One billion dots are a lot of dots for anything to be responsible for counting, much less making a decisions about, so the RIP can make or break an imagesetter.

PostScript

The way your software describes its images to a RIP is with PostScript. Therefore, it is crucial the RIP understands it completely. The data you send to an imagesetter is extremely complex and you want to be sure it can understand it thoroughly and interpret it quickly. The reason PostScript has become the standard for printing is because it is a very stable and efficient way to describe a page to the printer.

PostScript, the language, actually exists as software on the RIP that converts the code from your files into the dots of the raster. This means that the software, like any other, can be upgraded. Adobe is about to release its third, major revision of this language that both increases the speed of printing and enhances the abilities of PostScript compatible application software. To be able to take advantage of these upgrades, you need to be using PostScript to begin with.

True PostScript costs money. Other options emulate or mimic PostScript, but they are dubious at best. The savings usually end up costing money in the long run because the RIP's that use them take longer to work, misinterpret more files, and crash more often. The down time and wasted materials quickly eat up any savings you might be offered up front. Pay now or pay more later.

A Hardware RIP

A typical RIP is a software/hardware combination that interprets the PostScript code you send. It comes in the form of a dedicated computer connected to the imagesetter via a SCSI cable. It connects to the output workstation usually via Ethernet or some other, fast networking solution. This allows the imagesetter to appear as a normal printer on the network. As a dedicated machine, it does one thing and does it well.

The advantage of a hardware RIP is its speed and stability. The computer that runs the Postscript interpreter for the rasterizing process has nothing else to do. Therefore, it is unlikely to crash and become corrupted. Since the RIP computer is also a bit more beefy than the average desktop workstation, the dedicated RIP can do its work more quickly.

The disadvantage is cost. Dedicated RIP's can be quite expensive to buy. Plus, you aren't buying a computer that is useful for anything else. The money you spend is spent solely on the ability to process data for use by your imagesetter.

Hardware RIP's are also difficult to fix when a problem occurs. For the most part, you'll have two tools to use when trying to fix one problem. The first is the on/off switch. It's used in hopes that a re-boot will clear garbage data from the computer's memory buffers. The second is the telephone, which is used to contact a professional RIP fix-it person. You shouldn't be tinkering with the software or hardware to try and fix it yourself.

A Software RIP

For those who only print occasional films, a "software" RIP can save money. This is actually a software/hardware combination that rides in a desktop computer system. The hardware is in the form of a card that uses NuBus or PCI to access the computer's CPU. The software sits on the computer's hard drive. In most cases, the system also requires a dedicated, external hard drive to hold the raster of the page or pages before sending them to the imagesetter. The whole setup comes as an integrated package that you can install (or have installed) in its entirety. It is possible to buy these as stand alone products designed to work with a variety of imagesetters, but most imagesetter manufacturers make one specifically for their devices.

The advantages of a software RIP are mostly related to cost. Because it rides in a desktop system, you can use that system for other tasks—as long as you aren't using the RIP at the same time. Most enable you to quickly readjust the operating system software so you can use the computer for production with the RIP turned off. When it's time to print, reconfigure the system, turn the RIP on, and print the file or files.

Furthermore, the RIP package costs less (much less in some cases) than buying a dedicated hardware RIP. First and foremost, they are cheaper to purchase. Plus, as a product that you can install and maintain, they often require less outside support. Many of the problems you encounter can be fixed using troubleshooting techniques that are used for a regular production station.

The money you save up front may end up costing more in the long run and this is the major disadvantage of a software RIP. They take longer to create the raster, they're slower to communicate it to the imagesetter, and less stable while doing either one compared to a hardware RIP. The speed is an issue, but at least it's a predictable one. The stability problem can be significant. If you are trying to get some film out on a deadline and the RIP crashes, corrupting the software in the process, you'll need to reinstall it before you can continue. The extra time spent waiting for the RIP to process needs to be a part of the equation.

Choosing a RIP

So which should you choose? Dedicated RIPs are faster and more reliable. They are also far more expensive. You need to pay tens of thousands of dollars more for a dedicated RIP than a software-based RIP.

The more work you need to do, the more quickly you need to do it. If you are printing files daily, choose the dedicated system. Set up a test. The salesperson can let you see the RIP in action, enabling you to run a simple test.

For the test, choose a document that is fairly representative of the work you do or hope to do. Then do the following:

◆ Take the file to the salesperson who wants your business.

◆ Make sure to include a variety of elements such as colored photographs, complex illustration files, text, and anything else you normally use in your documents.

◆ Have them run it on both systems and time it. Make sure the software RIP is configured to a desktop computer similar to the one you would be using if you bought one.

◆ Note the time difference. Be sure to keep track of all of the differences, not just the amount of time it takes to watch the print dialog clear.

◆ Pay attention to any extra steps required for imaging through either system.

◆ Multiply that number by the number of jobs you will print over a set time period.

◆ Calculate the hourly worth of the person doing the work on the device.

◆ Compare that cost to the difference in cost between the two systems.

◆ Obtain a list of others using each solution and call them.

◆ Ask them to describe the system to you.

◆ Note crash frequency, reinstallation or reconfiguration ease and flexibility, and customer service and support from the manufacturer and the sales vendor.

◆ If you can, visit the site where the RIP is being used to see the system in action.

If the cost of using the software RIP is more than the cost of owning (or leasing) a dedicated system, buy a dedicated system.

No matter what RIP system you choose, keep in mind that it is responsible for the speed and quality of the imagesetter's ability to output your files. It is not a place to skimp.

A Stable Surface

Vibrations are the bane of the imagesetter's existence. The laser needs to accurately shine light on areas of film as small as 1/3600 of an inch. It takes very little shaking to get the laser to burn the wrong place on the film.

Great lengths are taken to make sure the imagesetter doesn't move in the face of vibrations from the outside world. Most have weights of some sort that help to stabilize it. The weights won't work, however, if it sits on a rickety floor. Other sources of vibration need to be avoided as well. Roads, other machines with moving parts, and heavy foot traffic all contribute to background vibrations.

A Technician

Good help may be hard to find. Finding some is not an optional component to an imagesetter. Imagesetters are not simple, easy devices to keep up and running, so they require a champion to stand by them. Although the people who work on them don't need to be rocket scientists, they need to be able to grapple with complexity and solve problems.

Running an imagesetter is more than grabbing the take-up roll, feeding it to a developer, and refilling the supply roll. There are cleaning schedules, PostScript problems, and who knows what all to be managed. Whoever does it should be someone who can be trusted to take the initiative of coddling this very expensive setup.

Training

Even the smartest among us need to be trained to run an imagesetter correctly. Although an intelligent person could eventually figure out the workings of an imagesetter, a RIP, a densitometer, and a developing system, he or she could waste a lot of time and money doing it. Imagesetter and developer manufacturers offer training for their devices. It may be a cost added item, but the dollars are an investment and they are a good one.

A Service Contract

When we go into a department store, buy a TV, and suffer through the pitch for a service agreement, we hate it. These agreements make no sense so we ignore them. Our livelihood doesn't depend on the TV to stay running. Plus, they are actually pretty simple devices that tend to stay working for a long time—if they work in the first place. Don't make this mistake with an imagesetter.

A service contract is an absolute must. When the RIP crashes, the laser burns out, the rollers quit rolling, or anything at all goes wrong, the costs of fixing one can be more than the cost of purchasing a new one. A service contract is essentially insurance that the imagesetter will be able to continually turn a profit. Such a contract contains some essential elements:

◆ **Immediate attention.** When things don't work, the contract must get them back to work quickly.

◆ **Total coverage.** Parts, labor, and travel should all be covered, even it costs extra in the premium.

◆ **Phone support.** The telephone can shave hours off a service call if the problem can be fixed by an in-house technician.

◆ **Coverage beyond the Warranty.** Paying for something already purchased is poor economic strategy.

The Care and Feeding of an Imagesetter

There is more to the story than the pieces needed for a film output system. They require regular maintenance.

Calibration

Two factors affect the imagesetter's capability to give predictable, reproducible results. The strength of the laser and its ability to expose the film combine to be the first factor. The second is the size of the halftone spot it builds for a given screen tint. If a 40 percent spot is requested, the spot needs to be 40 percent.

Exposure

If the light from the laser is too weak or too strong, the imagesetter does not expose the film correctly. This shows up in the solids as lines that are too thin or fat, text that loses serifs or fills in counters, or blurring around edges. It also appears as halftone spots that are too small or large for the tint they are representing. Remember, a color is the result of a spot of ink in a halftone cell. The size of the spot determines the color you see when you look at a halftone. If that spot is too large or small, you'll see a different color. See Chapters 10 and 11 for more about halftoning and color reproduction.

Imagesetters have an exposure test built in, which enables a technician to set the correct exposure. The test is a series of squares printed to film that are supposed to be a 50 percent screen. If the exposure is too low, the dots it burns will be too small. This increases the size of halftone spots and the tint percentage of a halftone. During the test, the imagesetter varies the exposure for each one. After developing the film, the technician uses a densitometer to read the swatches. One of them gives the correct reading. Telling the imagesetter, either directly or through the RIP, which one was correct sets the exposure.

Linearization/calibration

The second test determines if the imagesetter knows how big to make the spots for different tints. The test is a series of rectangles ranging from zero percent up to solid coverage in five percent increments. After developing the film, the technician uses a densitometer to read the swatches. After comparing the target value with the actual value, the technician enters the differences to the imagesetter directly or feeds them to the RIP. The imagesetter adjusts its spot sizes in response to the feedback. The adjustment to spot size in either case is done by adding to or removing dots from the spot machine.

When Should the Tests Be Run?

The first step every morning is to make sure the imagesetter is working properly. Running the test is a good way to check.

FILM

The film, similar to the kind used for black and white photography, is exposed by a very fine beam of light from a laser. As the film rolls through the imagesetter, the laser burns row after row of tiny dots. The areas of film that were exposed to the laser become black after the film is developed. The film must be of a very high quality and sensitivity to respond correctly to the exposure process. The areas where the laser shines its light need to become completely opaque after developing. Areas that didn't get exposed need to be perfectly clear. Otherwise, the images have blurry edges.

There is more to film than the exposure, though. Since it is going to be laid against a piece of plate making material to expose the plate to light, the film must be very smooth and of a constant thickness. Any variations result in distortions of the sizes of the elements that get transferred to the plate.

The chemistry of the film is also important. When light hits the film, it causes a chemical reaction that darkens the film. The reactive chemical is a *silver-halide* molecule, which the light changes slightly. When mixed with the developer chemicals, the exposed molecules turn black and the unexposed ones do not. The development process washes away the unexposed silver-halides and leaves the exposed ones in place. All of these chemical reactions depend on the quality of the film to give opaque exposed and clear unexposed areas.

The Film Developer

After film is exposed, it needs to be treated to become the film used for plate-making. The silver halide molecules that were exposed need to be turned black, and the non-exposed molecules need to be washed from the picture. A developer is a machine that does this.

Without one, what you get out of the take-up cassette is essentially useless plastic. The developer uses a series of chemical baths to react the exposed halides and turns them black. To process the film, the developer pulls the

Imposition is the process of converting page films into flats for plate making. For more on Imposition, see the section later in this chapter, "Imposition."

Plate making converts the flats of film into plates for printing. Plates are pieces of sheet-aluminum with silicon on them. Exposing light to them hardens the silicon. The film determines what on the plate is exposed, by allowing light to shine through.

The plate's silicon covered areas hold the ink and deliver it to the paper during the printing process.

exposed film directly from the take-up cassette into its light-proof interior. Once inside, the film is washed in a series of chemicals that develop, harden, and clean it. After all is said and done, the film rolls out the other side and is ready for imposition and plate-making.

Speed

If the film is dragged through the processor too quickly, it won't get its fair share of development time. All chemical reactions need time to complete and these are no exception. The processor needs to run the film through the baths as fast as it can without going too fast for the reaction. The processor has a speed control that allows it to be adjusted to develop a particular kind of film.

Temperature

Warm chemical reactions are faster chemical reactions. The temperature of the developer baths needs to be kept constant so it develops the film thoroughly yet not too much. A good developer has a control that can adjust the temperature and a thermostat to keep it in line. It will need to be adjusted, however, for the particular film used and the environment the developer is in.

Clean Water

The chemistry of the development process is not fond of contamination. As the film is processed, it generates plenty of waste that needs to be kept from building up in the works. The water that comes into the system, by a dedicated water line, must also be clean. For most, this means the addition of a filter system. Lime deposits, bacteria, and algae all need to be kept out of the development process.

Fresh Chemistry

As the developer turns exposed film into a finished product, the chemicals get used up. Exhausted chemistry is less able to either develop the film or fix it so that further exposure to light has no effect on it. The particular chemistry of the developer has a life span as recommended by the manufacturer. Do *not* cheat on this and try to sneak extra time out of the deal. You'll be producing lower quality film as a result.

Oxygen also shortens the usable life of the chemistry, so the less of it you allow near your chemicals the better. The machine itself doesn't hold the liquids until it is washing them over the film. They usually sit in a jug under the machine with a feeder tube that sucks up what it needs and spits it out when it's done. Keeping this jug covered protects the chemicals inside. Agitating the chemicals also should be avoided, as it aerates the solution adding oxygen.

Dust and Grit

As the rollers in the developer roll the film on by, any grit can scratch the film, thus ruining the film. The best way to prevent this is to keep the area that the developer occupies clean. The dusty corner of the storage closet will not do. In fact, a room that is sealed from outside foot traffic and kept swept or vacuumed is the best option. Anytime the developer sits idle, it's a good idea to keep it covered with a lint-free cover.

Regular cleaning improves matters dramatically. If it gets used very often (at least once a day), it stays cleaner because it stays active. The liquids keep moving through it, so they don't sit and deteriorate as much. However, even the most consistent usage won't supplant the need for regular cleaning.

Chemical Storage and Disposal

Exhausted chemistry used to be dumped down the sink, until someone realized it was poisonous. That became illegal pretty quickly, so the chemicals need to be processed. Most areas have companies that come get the stuff and deal with it. However, the Occupational Safety Hazard Organization (OSHA) has whole volumes of requirements when it comes to storing the chemicals on site for any amount of time. Since most disposal contractors pick up every other week or so, storage facilities need to be set up and approved. OSHA is usually all too happy to inspect them for compliance and should be contacted before any chemicals are brought on site.

As one of the main components of the chemical process for creating film, silver can drive costs way up. In the early eighties, when silver prices soared, film prices shot right up behind them. Although the price of silver has come back down since those days, it still isn't cheap. The unexposed silver halide that is washed off the film can be processed to remove the silver. This is done with a silver recovery device. All it does is filter the waste chemicals from the developer and remove the silver from the wash. It makes no sense not to own such a device, because it pays for itself by extracting a valuable metal that would otherwise be hauled off with the rest of the waste.

A Warm-up

In the morning, the developer needs to warm up before it can be used. The daily film test also helps to check the developer. If the temperature is too low or the chemicals are exhausted, the film won't develop well.

A Transmissive Densitometer

The imagesetter does its work by exposing the film with light. The film, after being developed, has clear areas surrounded by opaque areas. The line between the two must be clear and sharp. Under- or overexposure results in film that does not accurately represent the image you sent to the imagesetter. A densitometer is your tool for testing the film.

How It Works

A densitometer shines light at a fixed brightness to a photo-sensitive collector. The collector reads the light and determines how much of the brightness is absorbed by whatever you might place between the light source and the collector. It can test two things. The first is the density of the opaque areas of the film. They must be black enough to block all light shined on them. If not, the light that gets through causes problems with the plates made with the film. It exposes the plate material in areas that should not be exposed.

A densitometer also can read the tonal percentage of a halftone. When the light passes through an area of screening on film, it diffuses to give the effect of less light. This is essentially the same effect that the halftone on paper creates. The densitometer reads the amount of light that penetrates through the dots and reports the percentage of the tone. This is a crucial tool for testing the film to see if your imagesetter is creating halftones with the correctly sized halftone spots.

Good densitometers cost in the thousands of dollars, but they are absolutely necessary to assess the output of an imagesetter.

A Proofing System

The film that you produce can suffer a number of defects. You must always check it before you send it off to the press.

Contacts/Blue-lines

Print shops undoubtedly have proofing systems in place to check the films, but service bureaus and design shops that purchase imagesetters have a way to check the film for scratches, PostScript errors, or other problems. If a contact proofing system is too expensive, a light table goes a long way towards solving the problem of proofing for composition or blemishes. Whatever method makes the most sense, something must be used to check for problems.

Color

The densitometer tells you if the black areas of film are truly opaque, and if a 43 percent gray results in a 43 percent screen. That says nothing about the similarity between the electronic file that is printed and the original it's attempting to represent. This requires a proofing system.

If color is an issue, you have three basic options:

◆ Create films and use a laminate proof to match color.

◆ Create films and use a wet-proofing system to match color.

◆ Create direct from digital output from a digital printing device that has been calibrated to match a printing press.

For more about these kinds of proofing, along with other options, see Chapter 18, "Proofing."

Given the options for proofing mentioned in the previous chapter, it's up the individual to decide which will best represent the files that are headed to press. Whatever choice is made, it is crucial to proof the files to something before committing them to film. Plus, the press operator needs to have something to use as a press match. Submitting films alone to be printed is dangerous unless color is of absolutely no consequence.

PRINTING

Printing to an imagesetter is not that much different than printing to a paper laser printer.

The imagesetter is a more capable device, which is communicated to the output workstation by the PostScript Printer Description (PPD) file. When you choose an imagesetter's PPD, the page setup (QuarkXPress) or print dialog box (PageMaker) changes to reflect the capabilities of the device. This information determines how the RIP prepares the information for the imagesetter.

Choose a PPD

Before you print to any device, you need to tell the application software how to set the information up for that device. The easiest way is to choose the correct PostScript Printer Description (PPD) in the Page Setup dialog box (for QuarkXPress see Figure 19.6, for PageMaker see Figure 19.7).

Figure 19.6

QuarkXPress' Page Setup enables you to choose a Printer Type.

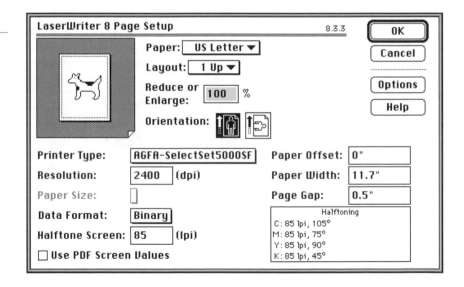

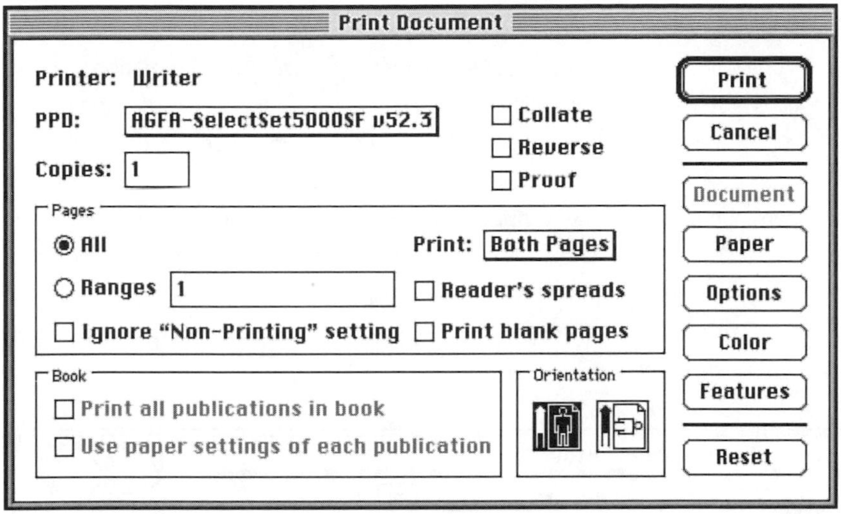

Figure 19.7

PageMaker enables you to choose a PPD.

The PPD is a group of settings that describe the printer in detail to the application. The information includes:

◆ Available paper sizes

◆ Optimized screen sizes and angles

◆ Available resolution settings (machine dot sizes)

◆ Availability of Postscript

◆ Any choices that are specific to the printing device, such as tabloid page sizes, or color

When you select a PPD, the print dialog box changes to reflect the options available from the PPD. It is extremely important to select the correct PPD before you send the file to print. If not, the results are potentially useless.

The PPD choice and any print dialog settings become a default for the file anytime you choose them and OK the print dialog box. Because you are proofing the document to a paper printer before sending to film, make sure to reset the PPD before you print it to film.

After you set the PPD, you need to set some of the other options to match the specs for the job.

Screening

When an output device uses halftoning to represent tonal variation, it must convert the pixel data to halftone spots on a grid determined by the line screen ruling. The Page setup or Print dialog box enables you to set a screen value for the document before you print it (see Figures 19.8 and 19.9). This value is communicated to the output device, so it can create halftones to your specifications. The choice for the screen ruling is made prior to the job's composition phase as a function of the paper stock the job will be printed on, the quality desired of the printed piece, and any special requirements such as special ink usage.

Figure 19.8

In QuarkXPress, use the Page Setup to set the Halftone Screen.

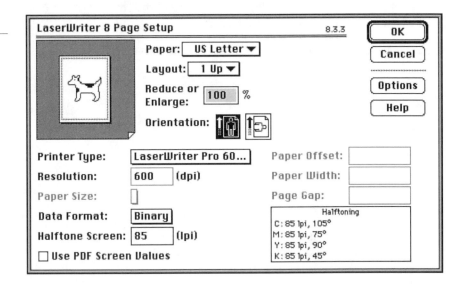

Remember though, that a halftone spot is created from a group of machine dots by the laser. The RIP has to figure out the best way to create the spot given this and the fact that the machine dots are actually square.

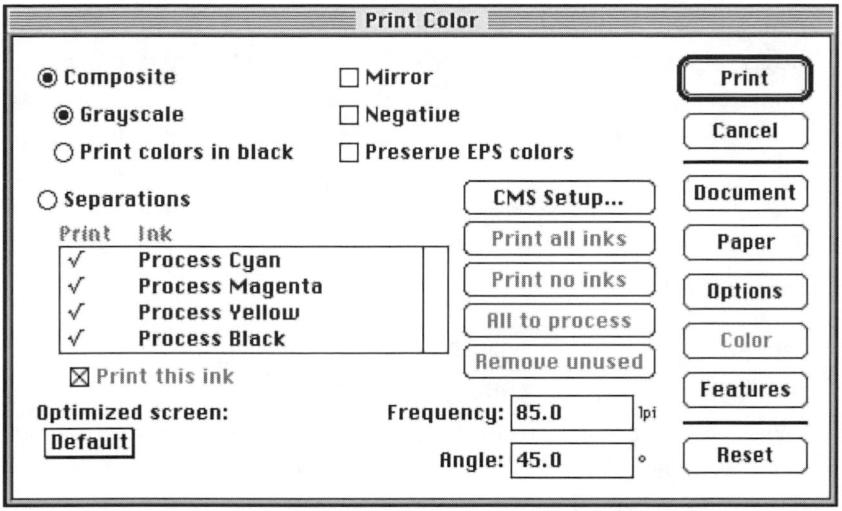

```
╔════════════════════════════════════════════════╗
║                  Print Color                     ║
╠════════════════════════════════════════════════╣
║  ⦿ Composite        ☐ Mirror           ( Print )║
║   ⦿ Grayscale       ☐ Negative                  ║
║   ○ Print colors in black  ☐ Preserve EPS colors ( Cancel )║
║                                                  ║
║  ○ Separations      ( CMS Setup... )  ( Document )║
║   Print  Ink                                     ║
║    √    Process Cyan      ( Print all inks )  ( Paper )║
║    √    Process Magenta   ( Print no inks )   ( Options )║
║    √    Process Yellow                           ║
║    √    Process Black     ( All to process )  ( Color )║
║                           ( Remove unused )      ║
║   ☒ Print this ink                            ( Features )║
║  Optimized screen:   Frequency: 85.0  lpi        ║
║   [Default]          Angle: 45.0   °    ( Reset )║
╚════════════════════════════════════════════════╝
```

Figure 19.9

In PageMaker, use the Print Dialog Box to set the Halftone Screen.

Angles

In the traditional printing world (the world before electronic prepress), the halftone grids are set to specific angles. This keeps the grids from creating moiré patterns when cyan, magenta, yellow, and black plates arc laid on top of each other. Those angles have been established and used for years. They are:

Black   45 degrees

Magenta   75 degrees

Yellow   90 degrees

Cyan   105 degrees

These angles enable the four overlapping grid patterns to give the impression of color rather than interference pattern. The problem with the patterns, however, crops back up when imagesetters try to use square machine dots to build up halftone spots. At the angles used by traditional printing, a slight moiré pattern appears. Plus, the rosettes—the little circular patterns created by the overlapping spots—become more pronounced and easier to see with the naked eye. All of this requires some trickery by the RIP.

The screening technology achieves that trickery by calculating very precise screen angles that are very close, but slightly askew from the traditional screen angles. Plus, it uses a screen that is also different from a normal screen ruling value. In fact, it may even use a different screen value for the different inks. The strategy behind all of this is to mix things up a bit and vary the grids enough that they don't interfere with each other. It all depends on a very powerful RIP and the math it can accomplish. The results are excellent color images with a minimum of patterning.

RIP Screens

The PPD for a given imagesetter tells the output program what the angles are. When you choose a particular line screen from the list of choices for your imagesetter (PageMaker) or enter a screen ruling (QuarkXPress), you are telling the imagesetter what target value to use (see Figure 19.10 and Figure 19.11). It adjusts that value for optimum output. The screening is calculated in the RIP of most imagesetters and ignores attempts to override it by the application software. This is the RIP's way of assuring the quality of the work coming off the imagesetter. Plus, by keeping the angles calculated and handy, the RIP avoids the need to recalculate them each time you enter some strange screen settings.

Figure 19.10

Setting a line screen in QuarkXPress sets a target. The PDF screen value gets as close to the target as it can.

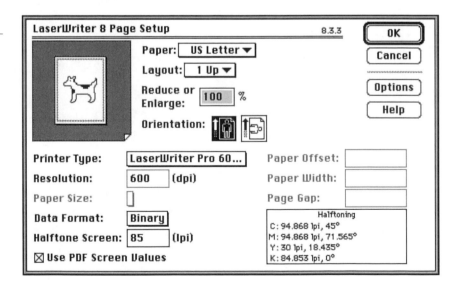

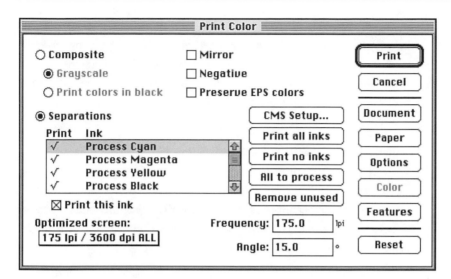

Figure 19.11

PageMaker enables you to choose a target from a list of possibilities.

Sometimes, however, the screening of the device is too limiting and needs to be overridden. Screen printing is a good example. The halftoning uses larger spots at differing angles because of the different inks used in printing. For these occasions, the RIP can be ordered to ignore the screens it holds so dear. Dropping the screens is accomplished through utility software that comes with the imagesetter.

When the screens are out, they are completely out. This means they need to be put back before any films are made for normal printing. Otherwise, the films either use some default value, traditional angles from the layout/output software, or the screens from the specialty screening that require the dropping of the original screens. In any of these cases, you'll waste a lot of film.

Stochastic (FM) Screening

Halftones reproduce tones by varying the size of a spot within a halftone cell. The darker the color, the larger the spot. This method of screening is known as *AM* or *Amplitude Modulation* screening. Amplitude refers to the size of the spots, and modulation means that it changes to represent different levels of gray. This method of halftoning has been around for hundreds of years. Of course, digital reproduction technology has produced a more effective halftoning method—in theory, at least.

That method is *stochastic*, or *Frequency Modulated* screening. Instead of varying the size of a spot within a set halftone cell size, stochastic screening varies the number of tiny spots within a given area of the page. By varying the number of dots in an area and randomizing their placement, the whole problem of screen angles and moiré patterns is eliminated: no patterns or angles are involved.

Limitations of Stochastic Screening

FM screening is supposed to eliminate the need for traditional screening, because it gives higher quality while allowing more tolerance for misregistration, less concern for screen angles, and the removal of printed rosettes. Although it does an impressive job in capturing fine details, it doesn't entirely shatter the halftoning paradigm.

◆ FM screening results in an image that appears softer. The differences may be minor, but people have come to expect those rosettes, and their absence gives people the impression of a slightly diffuse, less-sharp image.

◆ The dots need to be very small. If they are too big—at 1200 or 2400 dpi, for example—the image appears grainy. Although 3600 dpi imagesetters can easily burn the small dots needed for stochastic screening, not all presses can handle the dot size. Even if they can burn onto the plates, there might be difficulty in getting the ink to lay down accurately on the paper. Because of the tiny dot sizes, reproduction is only feasible on newer, more expensive presses controlled by experienced personnel.

◆ The film output is more expensive. It costs more to purchase software that gives your RIP the capability to calculate and place the randomly placed dots. Those costs are often passed off to the customer as a premium for the advantage of stochastically screened output. Because most people needing high quality output can live with 200 lines per inch of AM screening, they won't pay extra for something that doesn't give much benefit.

◆ Wide areas of flat tints, such as a solid-colored cover or box, tend to appear blotchy.

Advantages of Stochastic Screening

This is not to imply that stochastic screening does not have its place. It excels in images that traditional screening methods have difficulty reproducing. Patterns, clothing, ultra-fine details are all excellent candidates. The clothing industry often uses difficult images. A garment that has a pattern in the fabric, such as a tweed coat, is difficult to print without some sort of moiré showing up. The problem of interference patterns is made worse by the scanning process, because a scanned image is broken into a grid of pixels before it goes to film. Defeating the moiré is hard enough at this stage of the game—anything that can eliminate it down the road in the process is a welcome tool.

Setting the Screen to Stochastic

RIPs that enable the use of stochastic screening usually are triggered by a specific, atypical value being entered into the screen value field, such as "104" or "127." When the RIP sees the trigger value, it shifts into stochastic mode. Also, we can embed stochastic images within a standard-screened image by building the stochastic trigger value into a Photoshop EPS file.

Spot Shape

Theoretically, the shape of a halftone spot is round. (Of course, the spots are really made up of square machine dots, so it isn't a *perfect* circle.) Some imagesetters use a rounded-corner square spot instead, because it is easier to create with square machine dots. The effect of this type of spot is that it appears fairly round on paper.

These are not your only options for dots, though. Screens can use lines, triangles, ellipses, little pictures of Elvis, or any other shape that can be varied in size and frequency. Photoshop gives you a host of options, or you can create your own spot shape and build it into the file by saving it as an EPS format.

The trick is getting the RIP to use it. For the RIP to be able to calculate the accurate angles and sizes it uses to create a halftone screen, it needs to control dot shape. You may need to drop the angles before you send such a file to film. The RIP's manual describes the requirements for special screening and should be consulted before attempting to output film with such a screen.

Special Screening

You may encounter other instances of special screening along the way. They affect either the angles of the screens or the shape of the spot that is varied to create a different effect. In any of those cases, check the RIP software manual to see if it requires any special setup to use it.

Color

When color data makes its way to the imagesetter, it is sent as a solid or screen to a particular plate. In process color printing, there are four plates, one for Cyan , Magenta, Yellow, and Black. For spot colors, the color data goes to the plate that carries the spot ink. When you select a PPD that supports separations, be sure to turn them on before you send the pages to print.

Process color

Scans or other process color files have to be in a CMYK form before they are printed. Some RIPs are able to create CMYK data automatically from RGB, but it is unwise to let them. The RGB color space, when converted directly to CMYK ink, in theory results in no black ink. Managing the conversion to CMYK from RGB is best left to a color specialist using a program like Photoshop. For more about this process, refer to our chapters on scanning and color.

If you use a color management system, you can provide the data to the RIP in an RGB format. Be certain that you understand your specific RIP's requirements and capability to recognize the profiling setup. For more about color management, see Chapter 13, "Production Techniques."

Calibration/Linearization Revisited

The whole process of setting the correct exposure and ensuring the correct spot sizes in screens is directed towards two basic goals:

♦ **Outputting clean, crisp lines and edges on film.** This results in similarly crisp images on press.

♦ **Color.** Your final output device must be able to generate spots that are exactly the right size for the screen being printed. This is important because spot size variations ultimately account for the different tones of color reproduction. Eliminating the RIP and imagesetter as variables in this process is a must, and doing so requires things to be clean, tested, and calibrated.

Page Orientation

The positioning of our pages on the output material is an important consideration. The correct orientation saves wasted materials by reducing the amount of unexposed, unused film.

Film Size

We can take steps during the output process to reduce costs. It requires a slightly different mentality than printing to a paper printer because of the difference in the output material. Film is loaded into the supply cassette in a roll, making the length a variable. Depending on the capacity of the cassette, you can print to any number of lengths. The width of the roll, however, is more fixed.

This means that you can save a lot of film by rotating the page to make use of as much of the film area as possible. If a negative is narrow and tall, rotate it so it lays on its side, so it doesn't force a longer piece of film with wasted space on either side (see Figures 19.12 and 19.13). A document laying on its side is laying *transverse* to the imagesetter's laser.

Figure **19.12**

A tall, thin negative wastes film on either side if printed.

Figure 19.13

Figure 19.13

A tall, thin negative should lay on its side to prevent film waste.

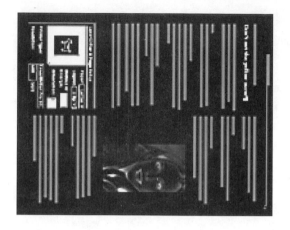

Both QuarkXPress and PageMaker enable you to set the film for transverse printing directly, so you won't need to manually move the file after you compose it to lay over on its side (see Figures 19.14 and 19.15).

Figure 19.14

The orientation of the page in QuarkXPress determines how it lies on the film.

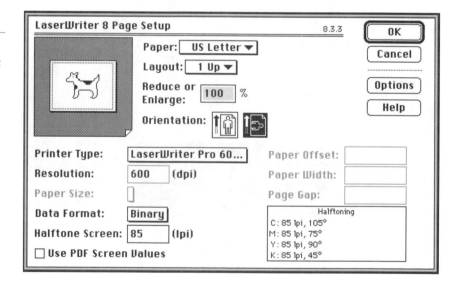

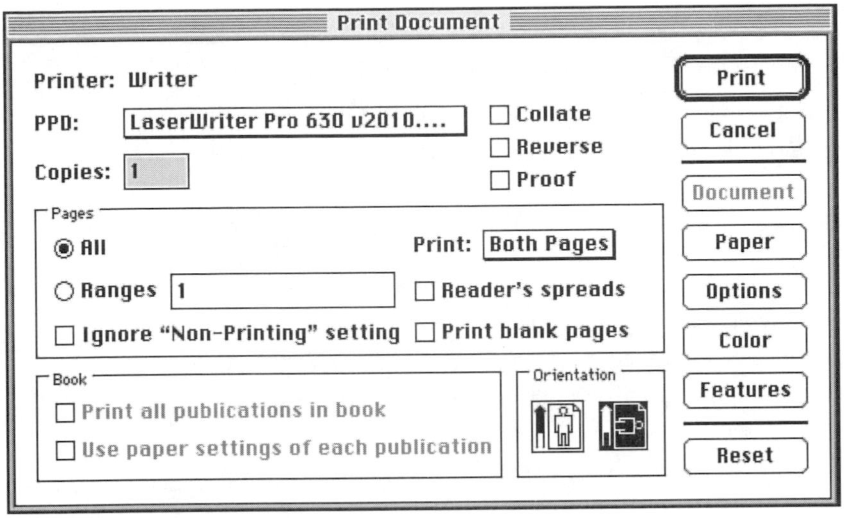

```
┌─────────────────────────────────────────────────────────┐
│▨▨▨▨▨▨▨▨▨▨▨▨▨▨ Print Document ▨▨▨▨▨▨▨▨▨▨▨▨▨│
├─────────────────────────────────────────────────────────┤
│                                                           │
│ Printer: Writer                            ┌──────────┐   │
│                                            │  Print   │   │
│ PPD:   │LaserWriter Pro 630 v2010....│  ☐ Collate    └──────────┘   │
│                                            ┌──────────┐   │
│ Copies: │1     │        ☐ Reverse          │  Cancel  │   │
│                         ☐ Proof            └──────────┘   │
│ ┌─Pages────────────────────────────────┐  ┌──────────┐   │
│ │ ⦿ All          Print: │Both Pages│    │  │ Document │   │
│ │                                       │  └──────────┘   │
│ │ ○ Ranges │1          │ ☐ Reader's spreads │ ┌──────────┐│
│ │                                       │  │  Paper   │   │
│ │ ☐ Ignore "Non-Printing" setting ☐ Print blank pages │ ┌──────────┐│
│ └───────────────────────────────────────┘  │ Options  │   │
│ ┌─Book──────────────────────┐ ┌Orientation┐ └──────────┘ │
│ │ ☐ Print all publications in book │ │      │ ┌──────────┐│
│ │                           │ │      │      │ │  Color   ││
│ │ ☐ Use paper settings of each publication │ └──────────┘│
│ └───────────────────────────┘ └──────┘     ┌──────────┐   │
│                                            │ Features │   │
│                                            └──────────┘   │
│                                            ┌──────────┐   │
│                                            │  Reset   │   │
│                                            └──────────┘   │
└─────────────────────────────────────────────────────────┘
```

Figure 19.15

The orientation of the page in PageMaker determines how it lies on the film.

Setting Film Size in QuarkXPress and PageMaker

◆ From the Page Setup dialog box, choose the landscape orientation icon.

◆ If the document is wider than it is tall, then choose the portrait orientation.

PageMaker is a little more tricky because you can set the page orientation in two different places. This enables you to cancel out appropriate orientation. The first place you can set the orientation is the Print dialog box with the Document button selected. The landscape and portrait options are found there and are the same in Quark. With the Paper button selected, however, you see a list of possible paper sizes derived

Printer Styles in PageMaker

PageMaker has a useful feature for anyone who deals with multiple output devices and settings. Printer Styles enable you to save and name a group of settings. For example, if you have a set of preferred values for sending a file to a laser printer for proofing or to your imagesetter, these values can be set once and automatically applied just before you send the file to print. We prefer to create styles for comps and seps for our letter and tabloid laser printers, plus any color proofing device and most common imagesetter requirements. Make as many as you need—just make sure that the titles are descriptive and easy to read.

from the PPD. Some PPDs offer a transverse paper size option. Setting the file to landscape *and* transverse cancels out the transverse feature.

Negative or Positive

Reproductive film is very similar to photographic film. It's composed primarily of a plastic base layered with a light-sensitive silver-halide coating.

Most printing processes require negative film. Letterpresses, for example, always require negatives. The clear areas on the film enable light to hit the plate material, which cures the coating. The plates become positive after they are processed. Some methods of printing, such as gravure or screen printing, require positive film. If this is the case, tell your RIP to reverse the image.

Your laser printer defaults to positive. When you print to paper, the image needs to be positive to be seen correctly. Since most printing demands negative film, imagesetters typically default to negative film exposure.

Emulsion Reading

The emulsion side of the film needs to be placed against the plate material when the plates are imaged. This reduces the amount of distortion caused by the diffusion of light as it passes through the film. The film must image so the information reads correctly when ink ultimately hits the paper. To make the films deliver the image to the plate correctly, the films are usually burned as right-reading when you are looking at the films, emulsion side down. Depending on the printing method—and your discussions with your printer—this value can be changed to right-reading emulsion up.

Imposition

Outputting from a page layout program with no additional page-positioning commands results in page films, or color separations for each individual page. These page films are imposed, or laid out in a multipage signature before the printing plate is burned (see Figure 19.16). If the pages are properly imposed, the different pages on the press sheet appear in the right order and position when the sheet is folded and trimmed.

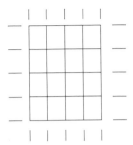

Figure 19.16

A multi-page signature.

Stripping: Traditional Imposition

Traditionally, imposition is done by taping the page films together during a process called *stripping*. The stripping results in imposed flats of film that are then exposed to the plates as a unit. The size and position of pages in a signature depend on the size of the sheets used on the particular press used for the job. Special marks are included in the flats to help the press operator and the bindery complete the job. These marks include:

◆ **Registration marks** enable the press operator to register the colors.

◆ **Color bars** help the press operator adjust the inks on press for coverage, test for trappings, and register the colors.

◆ **Cut lines** tell the bindery where to cut the sheets to make the pages.

◆ **Plate names** tell the press operator which ink to use on which plate.

These are all exposed to the plate material, and are printed onto the paper with the rest of the palet information. These marks and their location on the sheet are determined by the stripper and the press operator for a particular press.

Page Film Marks

When the page films are made, printers marks for registration, trimming, and plate colors need to be burned into the page films so the stripper can properly compile the press sheets.

> Stripping is a cost item usually built into the price of a job. The skill and experience needed to strip for imposition makes the job a non-trivial one. The costs of stripping manually can be quite high leading the industry towards another method.

To turn on the marks:

- ◆ In Quark, turn on the registration mark. This also turns plate names on.

- ◆ In PageMaker, this is a two step process. In the Print dialog box, choose the Options button. There are check boxes for both Printer's marks and Plate names.

Electronic Imposition

Electronic imposition has a variety of cost advantages to a printer. First, it saves time—traditional stripping is a very labor-intensive process.

Electronic imposition can also save money on film. The more of the film's image area you use when you print, the less waste you have. Imposing the films gives you a larger "page" size to print. Electronic imposition can do this for you.

You have a few options for electronically imposing a document so that the films are completely plate-ready when they come out of the imagesetter. This starts in the layout software.

QuarkXPress: Outputting Spreads

QuarkXPress' print dialog box enables you to output two pages as a single, large page rather than two single-page films. Normally, a stripper needs to tape the two pages together, aligning them exactly (see Figure 19.17).

This is not complete imposition, however. It adds no color bars and doesn't set up signatures of more than two pages. A Web press capable of 32 page signatures wastes a lot material if it prints only two pages at a time.

This tool is useful when printing page films, though. It saves you money on stripping costs to provide crossovers as a single film.

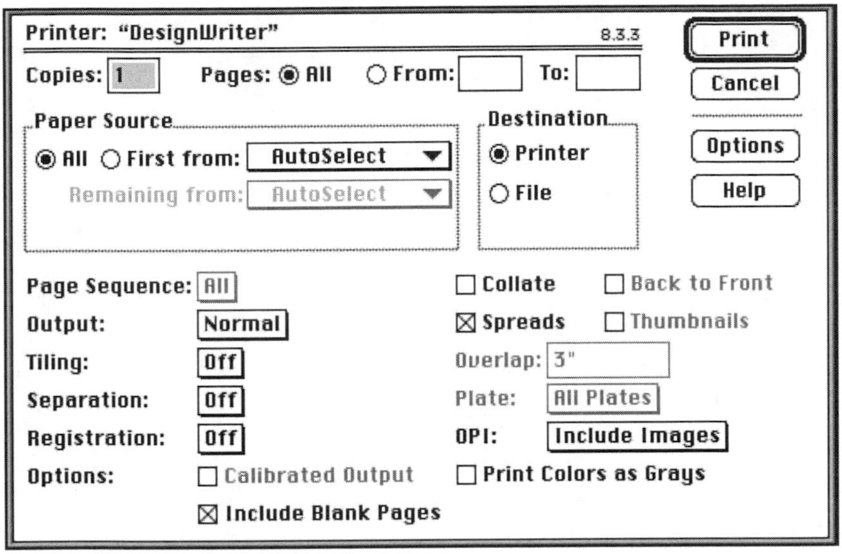

```
┌─────────────────────────────────────────────────────────────┐
│  Printer: "DesignWriter"                    8.3.3   ╭────────╮ │
│                                                     │  Print  │ │
│  Copies: 1      Pages: ◉ All    ○ From:     To:     ╰────────╯ │
│                                                     ╭────────╮ │
│  ┌Paper Source─────────────────────┐ ┌Destination┐ │ Cancel  │ │
│  │                                  │ │           │ ╰────────╯ │
│  │ ◉ All ○ First from: │ AutoSelect ▼│ │ ◉ Printer │ ╭────────╮ │
│  │                                  │ │           │ │ Options │ │
│  │   Remaining from: │ AutoSelect ▼│ │ ○ File    │ ╰────────╯ │
│  │                                  │ │           │ ╭────────╮ │
│  └──────────────────────────────────┘ └───────────┘ │  Help   │ │
│                                                     ╰────────╯ │
│  Page Sequence: │All│         ☐ Collate    ☐ Back to Front     │
│  Output:    │ Normal │        ☒ Spreads    ☐ Thumbnails         │
│  Tiling:    │ Off │           Overlap: │ 3" │                   │
│  Separation: │ Off │          Plate:   │ All Plates │           │
│  Registration: │ Off │        OPI:     │ Include Images │       │
│  Options:   ☐ Calibrated Output   ☐ Print Colors as Grays       │
│             ☒ Include Blank Pages                               │
└─────────────────────────────────────────────────────────────┘
```

Figure 19.17

QuarkXPress' spreads feature.

QuarkXPress: Document Layout Palette

The document layout palette enables you to move pages around. As an example, you can create two page signatures from a facing pages document by doing the following:

1. Convert the facing pages to non-facing pages.

2. Move the last page to sit next to the first page.

3. Move the next to last page to sit next to the second page, and so on until the pages have been reordered.

4. Print the document with spreads on and the films will be 2-page signatures.

This only forms very basic impositions. The best use we have found for this feature is imposing simple files containing eight pages or less.

PageMaker's Build Booklet Feature

Applying the Build Booklet command reorganizes your document pages into multiple page signatures. Although it isn't a professional imposition tool, it can be useful for printing small booklets to your paper laser printer.

Dedicated Imposition Software

The problem with attempting to impose your pages by making spreads in QuarkXPress or building a booklet in PageMaker is that these do not result in thorough, usable press sheets. They still require work from a traditional stripper to complete a flat for plating.

To truly impose pages electronically, color bars, multiple pages, and specific flat shapes need to be a part of the flat. True imposition can offer this. Anything from varying signature sizes to custom cut lines can be established and saved into a template. Most print shops have specific requirements for the flats used with their printing presses. When you add a document to the template, the work of adding the marks is already done.

Imposing files electronically does have some limitations. First, the flats may be quite large. Thirty-two pages on a single flat makes for a very large piece of film indeed. Most imagesetters don't produce films large enough to image an entire flat. Imagesetters that do are quite expensive.

Second, the software may not give enough options for every situation. A good stripper will still be needed to provide them, although a cost savings is available for those willing to redesign around imposition requirements. Better yet, if your imposition requirements can be made to match the software's capabiltity, you'll reap the cost savings each time.

Handling of Printed Film

After the films come out of the imagesetter and developer, they must be handled carefully; scratching or creasing the emulsion creates marks that may appear on the final printed piece. Here are some tools that can help protect your film:

- ◆ **A pair of lint-free cotton gloves** to keep you from leaving fingerprints, scratches, or smudges behind.

- ◆ **Plastic bags** to store the films before they go to press, eliminating dust and other grit.

- ◆ **Hard cardboard mailing envelopes** to keep the film from getting wrinkled or creased.

A Final Note About Printing to Film

The step from printing to paper to printing to film is a big one that should not be taken lightly. It requires time, money, and effort to get it right. It also requires energy spent setting up templates, making decisions about output orientation, and establishing a workflow. Spend it. The more you invest in porting elements of the workflow over to digital, the less time you'll waste re-inventing the wheel.

OTHER OUTPUT OPTIONS

It's true film is the most common output vehicle. Knowing how to work with it is important, but new options are slowly but surely establishing themselves in the marketplace. This bodes well for the consumer, because it means the bar of expectation is raising, both for color quality and cost-effectiveness. In other words, people think it should be better and cheaper simultaneously. With the entrance of new technologies, this is exactly what is happening. No longer is a printing press the only option for excellence in color fidelity. Depending on your needs, you may want to consider the following possibilities.

Direct to Plate

As technology moves forward, film will begin to be replaced by direct-to-plate solutions. This means that the imagesetter will burn the plate directly instead of exposing film.

Platesetters

The technology used in an imagesetter to burn film can be used directly on material used for plating a press. In fact, you can buy plate material for many film imagesetters, which turns them into platesetters. The laser burns the plate the same as film, except that the laser burns the image areas instead of the non-image areas. The laser cures a polymer coating on the plate material. When the plate is developed, the non-cured coating is washed away, creating the difference between ink carrying and water carrying areas.

The advantage of burning plates directly is that we bypass the film-output stage of production. The time needed to make the films, develop them, ship them, impose them, and create plates from them is saved. Furthermore, you won't need to purchase and use all of the film-making materials. Skipping the film part of the process can be very cost-effective.

This technology is excellent for creating work with tight budgets and deadlines, but is not necessarily complex in terms of page geometries or color demands.

The Disadvantages of Platesetters

Direct-to-plate is not for everyone. Since the technology is still defining itself, it may be a couple more years before we can expect the same quality from our direct-to-plate technology as from our conventional plating systems and presses.

Number of Impressions

The plate material is not the high-grade aluminum used for traditional plates. The plates are made of a flexible polyester, which is a softer, less sturdy material. The number of impressions possible per plate is limited to between 10,000–30,000. This means the plates are less useful for longer runs, because they wear out more quickly than aluminum. Although burning new plates is easier and more accurate with direct from digital, the cost of re-plating in the middle of a job can be prohibitive, because of the make-ready process This limits the direct to plate technology to shorter-run jobs.

Line Screen Limits

The material's softness also creates another problem. Extremely high line screens require very small dots, which are often too small for the plates to hold accurately. This limits the plates to lower line screens. Stochastic screening is difficult to achieve because it uses very small dots as well. Several companies are working on more durable direct from digital plate materials, and they will be on the market soon. Check with your local film vendor and platesetting service provider.

Imposition

Imposition can't be done after the plates are burned. There isn't any way to strip these things together, so the results from the platesetter have to go onto the press. This also means that the plates are limited in size by the size of the imagesetter. Extra-wide devices can be prohibitively expensive, so their larger signatures may not be cost-effective.

Trapping

Plates can't be trapped after they burned. This forces us to use either trapping software or a dedicated trapping workstation. Both enter some costs and complexity to the process. Software trapping is slow and not always accurate. Although it is getting better, it still means potentially long waiting periods for the trapping software to work.

Dedicated systems are expensive and have a learning curve to them. Although they are fast and effective, they may be out of reach for smaller shops. For more about digital trapping, see Chapter 16.

Proofing

Proofing these plates is more difficult. For blemishes and postscript errors, you may actually need to hang the plates on-press and make some impressions to examine the accuracy of the plates. Wet proofing machines are also ideal for this, so if you have one, it may have a new task in the digital age.

Color proofing is also a problem. Plating a press, making it ready, and running a few sheets is an inefficient way to check the color results from a digital file. Without films, a pressmatch isn't possible, so digital proofing becomes a more attractive option. An ink jet system, such as a 3M Rainbow or Iris Smart Jet that can be calibrated to match press condition closely, reduces the amount time and money lost wet proofing or press proofing.

Digital Presses

A digital press is the combination of a printing press and an imagesetter. The plates are burned *after* they are hung on the roller. The RIP is a dedicated and very powerful computer that can do its work very quickly and with many options for the press operator. After the job is rasterized, it is saved as a huge raster file and fed to the lasers on each of the color plate rollers simultaneously.

After the lasers burn the plates, they are developed by wiping them with a solution of some sort, usually alcohol-based. When dried, they are inked and the press operator can begin quickly afterwards.

Registration is easy because the system's lasers all know where they are in relation to one another, because they burn in register. The operator has little responsibility to get the registration on.

Advantages of Digital Presses

The advantages to such a system are clear. If you need a product printed in a hurry but don't want it to look like it was, a digital press is the way to go. They are very expensive to set up, however, so the costs are high because they are sold more for their speed with medium-high quality color. As more presses are installed, the competition will drive costs down. It lowers margins for the producer, but lowers costs to consumers.

Disadvantages

The problems with this kind of printing are essentially the same with direct-to-plate printing from an imagesetter. However, a digital press operator must be computer-savvy in addition to his/her knowledge of press operation. Such a person is worth a great deal of money and should be treated as such. Keeping a qualified person on staff who can run complicated computer equipment and sensitive press equipment requires an investment in salary and training. This adds to the cost of using a digital press, but it isn't really an option, so it needs to be factored into pricing from the start.

Large-Format Output

Posters used to be found exclusively in the domain of the screen printer. Printing large items was expensive because it required expensive, big equipment to image expensive, big film to make expensive, big screens to run on expensive, big presses. Plus, they were slow.

Posters from the desktop had to jump through all sorts of weird hoops to get onto the screens. Many screen printers use a CAD plotter to cut rubylith masks for screen making. These plotters don't really like PostScript much, so they require a lot of inventiveness and ingenuity to get them to work correctly. Now comes the really big color printers.

Ink Jet

These range from $250 StyleWriters to $60,000 Smart Jets. They can be true PostScript printers with powerful RIP's or non-PostScript printers with no RIP at all. Some use plain copier paper and others use very expensive paper design specifically for them. It boils down to the fact that extra money buys two things: color accuracy and color consistency.

Large format ink-jet printers use very high quality inks and have an accurate RIP, so the color can be linearized and calibrated.

Unfortunately, they are slow and fairly expensive to run. The cost per square foot is high. It isn't, however, as slow and expensive as using screen printing for a short run. Larger run printing still uses screen printing over large ink jet formats because of the economy of scale.

Electrostatic Output

By all rights, the electrostatic machines will soon rule the large format world. They use a process very similar to a photocopier's to deliver the image to paper. Instead of using a plastic toner, like a photocopier, they use a liquid ink. Electrostatic machines print to regular paper on a roll. To create color, the device uses a random dot screen to avoid any resolution-oriented problems. Such a dot, when viewed from a "poster distance" of several feet or more, makes for a very smooth image without requiring a huge, high resolution file.

Advantages of Electrostatic Output

The speed allows one-time posters to be reasonable to produce from a cost and time perspective. The paper type keeps the costs down and the paper size opens the device to many possible uses. Plus, the devices can accept different types of media, allowing for a variety of uses.

Disadvantages of Electrostatic Output

The printing inks are CMYK. Spot colors can be used but often cost much more. Unless process simulations are acceptable, it may be better to have a screen printer do the job. As an electrostatic device, climate control is a big issue, as temperature and humidity affect the device's ability to print inks evenly.

Electrostatic devices also have a problem when it comes to solid coverage. Striations and banding are often visible in even-colored areas of heavy ink coverage. Even with these disadvantages, however, these are an excellent choice for large format output from the desktop.

Color Printers

Color printers have begun to provide enough quality for use in short-run and throwaway color work. There are a variety of color printing options ranging from inexpensive desktop ink jets to high-end electrostatic devices. Depending on your needs, they might be a cost-effective solution for you.

Color Laser Output

If you add C, M, and Y toner to the black toner, you can print CMYK files to paper with a laser printer. Of course, you need to have a printer that can do this. Some are a part of a color photocopier and some are stand-alone, but all work similarly.

In essence, they receive information from the output printer in CMYK and print each page four times, once for each color. For accurate color, they require a RIP with calibration capabilities. For color consistency, they require regular maintenance. Canon's color copier (driven by a Fiery RIP) is a popular example.

Advantages of Color Lasers

They are excellent choices for short-run (under 500) color pages up to tabloid size paper (without a full bleed). Plus, they can run transparency, transfer material, and specialty papers.

Disadvantages of Color Lasers

These have lower resolution than is needed for many jobs. Printing on both sides of a page drives costs up and extends schedules because the printers often gum themselves up trying to print on the back side of a page with toner on it. Calibration and consistency are also difficult to create with the machines, so it limits the use of them for accurate color.

Black and White Laser Output

Don't forget our friend, the black and white laser printer. If you are producing documents that don't use color, you might be able to create the output from one.

A 600 DPI laser writer is a good device for printing small, very short run flyers or booklets. For reproduction, use a photocopy service. Especially when printing back to back, the printer itself is a poor choice for creating multiple copies, but the combination of a printer and a copy service provides very good results.

If you are going to go this route, keep two things in mind. Elegant design is essential. Since you have only blacks and grays to deliver your message, do it carefully and with simplicity. Also, use an appropriate line screen. Seventy lpi is the maximum a 600 DPI printer can give you. Slightly lower rulings, down to about 50 lpi, improve the tonal range, but you'll need to keep an eye on the coarseness of the halftone.

Solid screens tend to photocopy poorly. A simple texture looks better. Otherwise, paper output may be a very cost-efficient way to produce your work.

Others

A variety of other color printers are available to those who want to print very short-run color. If you are considering purchasing such a device, consider the following factors before you make a purchase:

- **Speed.** How fast does it print the first page and each successive page?

- **Sharpness.** How readable is text, how sharp are lines and frames, and how is detail in halftones captured?

- **Color.** How accurate and consistent are the colors from the device?

- **Cost.** How much does paper and ink cost?

- **PostScript.** Does it use true PostScript? If not, how well does it do with difficult PostScript documents?

SUMMARY

The world of output is ever-expanding. Today, your choices range from printing to an inexpensive laser printer to sending data directly to a digital printing press. Just as you need to make sure that your electronic files can be output and printed, you need to make sure that the final output device selected fits your needs.

When you start your project, determine your final output method, allowing you to create the project with optimized specs. The better able you are to make the appropriate output choice, the better service you can give clients. This applies to the designer all the way through to the pressman.

It is the rare designer, even today, who does not output work to film. Whether you output to an in-house imagesetter or use a vendor, you must familiarize yourself with outputting, handling, and using film. If you are going to print your own film, you need to know how to produce films correctly and how your films are going to be used. Rework, imposition, and proofing are all steps that add unnecessary costs.

Whatever your choice of output method, keep an open mind about the next run. As technology rockets forward, the options will grow. Digital presses will begin to rival traditional ones, film will begin to lose serious ground to plate material, and short-run color will continue to improve. Keeping all these changes in mind, you can be more successful by knowing the best way to output your work.

Index

. . . .